REFORM AND REACTION IN TWENTIETH CENTURY AMERICAN POLITICS

Recent Titles in
Contributions in American History

The Fragmentation of New England: Comparative Perspectives on Economic,
Political, and Social Divisions in the Eighteenth Century
Bruce C. Daniels

The Southern Frontiers, 1607-1860: The Agricultural Evolution of the Colonial and
Antebellum South
John Solomon Otto

Progressivism at Risk: Electing a President in 1912
Francis L. Broderick

The New Deal and Its Legacy: Critique and Reappraisal
Robert Eden

Campaigning in America: A History of Election Practices
Robert J. Dinkin

Looking South: Chapters in the Story of an American Region
Winfred B. Moore, Jr., and Joseph F. Tripp, editors

News in the Mail: The Press, Post Office, and Public Information, 1700-1860s
Richard B. Kielbowicz

North from Mexico: The Spanish-Speaking People of the United States. New
Edition, Updated by Matt S. Meier
Carey McWilliams

Reagan and the World
David E. Kyvig, editor

The American Consul: A History of the United States Consular Service, 1776-1914
Charles Stuart Kennedy

REFORM AND REACTION IN TWENTIETH CENTURY AMERICAN POLITICS

JOHN J. BROESAMLE

Contributions in American History, Number 137
JON L. WAKELYN, Series Editor

GREENWOOD PRESS
New York • Westport, Connecticut • London

Library of Congress Cataloging-in-Publication Data

Broesamle, John J.
   Reform and reaction in twentieth century American politics / John
J. Broesamle.
      p.   cm.—(Contributions in American history, ISSN 0084-9219
; no. 137)
   Bibliography: p.
   Includes index.
   ISBN 0-313-26799-5 (lib. bdg. : alk. paper)
   1. United States—Politics and government—20th century.
   2. United States—Politics and government—20th century—Philosophy.
   I. Title.   II. Title: Reform and reaction in 20th century American
politics.   III. Series.
   E743.B764   1990
   320.973—dc20   89-11751

British Library Cataloguing in Publication Data is available.

Copyright © 1990 by John J. Broesamle

Library of Congress Catalog Card Number: 89-11751
ISBN: 0-313-26799-5
ISSN: 0084-9219

First published in 1990

Greenwood Press, 88 Post Road West, Westport, CT 06881
An imprint of Greenwood Publishing Group, Inc.

Printed in the United States of America

The paper used in this book complies with the
Permanent Paper Standard issued by the National
Information Standards Organization (Z39.48-1984).

10 9 8 7 6 5 4 3 2 1

Copyright Acknowledgments

For Carolyn and Bob,

who grew up with it.

CONTENTS

ACKNOWLEDGMENTS   xiii

A NOTE ON TERMINOLOGY   xv

INTRODUCTION   1

1.   Liberalism and Reform   7

     PART I: REFORM   27

2.   The Look of Reform   29

     The Odd Legacy of the Gilded Age   33

     Populism and the Politics of Self-Interest   36

     Progressivism and the Problem of Focus   39

     The New Deal: Selling the Welfare State   55

     Reform Engorged: Kennedy, Johnson, and the Sixties   65

3.   Does Reform Run in Cycles?   81

4.   The Far Left   99

5.   Democrats and Republicans   115

6. The Fortuitous Presidency   139

7. The Nature of the Reform Regime   147

    PART II: RESISTANCE   173

8. Blurred Vision   175

9. Government, Liberals, and the Business Culture   179

    Antitrust and Regulation   192

    The Conundrum of Labor   199

10. Mass Inertia   207

    PART III: REACTION   249

11. Distant Distractions   251

    The Foreign Policy Escape Hatch   251

    War   256

    The Liberal Hubris   268

    Afterword: The Cold War   274

12. The Welfare State as Police State   281

13. Fortunes of War   289

14. Moods Change   297

15. Demythologizing the Beneficiaries   309

16. The Demise and Departure of the Intellectuals   317

17. The Disaffection and Departure of the Young   339

18. Backlash   361

    Liberalism and Libertinism   361

Suspicion, Disgust, and the Social Issue   370

The Opportunism of the Conservatives   383

19. The President and the State under Suspicion   393

A Diversion on Scandal   400

20. From Disorientation to Apathy   411

Disorientation   411

The Liberal Cannibalism   423

Defensiveness, Exhaustion, and Apathy   427

Guilt Revisited: Some Final Speculations   438

Conclusion: What Does It All Mean?   447

BIBLIOGRAPHIC ESSAY   465

INDEX   469

ACKNOWLEDGMENTS

Over the fifteen years I have worked on this book, I have requested help from many friends and colleagues. Two, busily writing their own books, were asked to provide such extensive criticism that I worried for the future of our friendship. To Paul Koistinen and Ronald Schaffer I gladly express my profound appreciation.

Many others have read particular portions of the manuscript, given advice, clarified points, and patiently endured my soliloquies on the reform tradition. Prominent among them are Anthony Arthur, Charles A. Bearchell, Elizabeth Berry, Richard and Norma Camp, Robert Cleve, Jeff Craig, Ronald L. F. Davis, Michael Dunnicliffe, Veronica Diehl Elias, Erika A. Endrijonas, Mary Finley, Robert Greenspan, Gail Said Johnson, Paul Kirk, Joseph Morris, Gerald Prescott, Eugene Price, Kelly Sciortino, the late Rena Vassar, Edmund and Nevo Warne, and Janet Zielinski. Reading the manuscript for Greenwood Press, John M. Allswang made many valuable suggestions.

No author could ask for finer cooperation than I have received from Greenwood. I wish to thank the three superb editors with whom I worked, Cynthia Harris, Margaret Brezicki Maybury, and William Neenan. Barbara Goodhouse provided precise and creative copyediting.

My two principal typists deserve special thanks because they possess quite special talents. Marcia Dunnicliffe and Mary Lou Priest have keen eyes for the flat phrase and the sentence with pieces missing. At a particularly crucial time, after breaking her arm, Mrs. Priest astonished me by continuing to type week after week with one hand.

Through financial support and released time from teaching, research and writing were sustained at several important points by California State University, Northridge.

Kathy, my wife, has devoted uncountable hours to this book while carrying on her own demanding professional life. Her work has benefited vastly less from my insights than mine has from hers.

Never have I been denied a request for help by those named above. Their contributions are reflected throughout the book. I can take sole credit only for the errors.

A NOTE ON
TERMINOLOGY

While this volume stops at the mid-1980s and does not carry through to the 1988 election, that election confirmed many of the key points in the pages which follow. One point is that a good deal of the meaning attached in past eras to such words as "liberal" or "conservative" has been drained from them. Nineteen eighty-eight was the year when the GOP twisted "liberal" into the dreaded "L word"——a political scarlet letter like "commie" or "pinko" a generation ago. With this in mind, it seems especially important to establish a preliminary, skeletal lexicon of terms, leaving it to the chapters which follow to flesh them out.

First, while the word "reform" appears in the title, I find myself uneasy with it and with its counterpart, "reformer." Each has an archaic ring. Yet no terms in our political vocabulary serve quite the same function. I have employed them reluctantly, preferring them to such recent atrocities as "change agent." "Reform" is an umbrella word for broad-scale center-left movements in this country which have tried throughout the twentieth century to use government to create significant social and political change within the framework of a capitalist system.

The word "liberal" has taken on any number of meanings. This variability of hues reflects the ideological looseness of American politics. I use the term in a more restricted sense than the very broadest, which suggests that virtually every American is a liberal. I attach the word instead to the mainstream of American reform in this century, which has directed itself most fundamentally toward the welfare state. This implies, among many other things, an active government which seeks as a matter of public policy to produce change by continuously intervening in the nation's social and economic life. At its best, such a government broadens the number of people who participate in making society's choices. All too often it recruits elites to make the choices. The welfare state endeavors, in one way or another, to underwrite the well-being of all (or most) citizens, and of numerous interest groups.

I employ the word "movement" in a conventional way, to describe a political drive (often with social and cultural appendages) involving large numbers of people, with identifiable leadership, and directed broadly toward particular political (social, cultural) goals. Movements vary in breadth, embracing anything from one to a panoply of causes. As we will see, movements continually interweave with various fads and fashions.

During the first two decades of the century the great prevailing umbrella movement was called "progressivism." Since then the term "liberalism" has replaced it, although recent years have seen an impulse to return to "progressivism." For all the differences between the original progressivism on one hand, and more recent liberalism on the other, each has represented a broad drive toward the use of government —toward governmentalism—in order to serve major social and political ends. Such also typifies many narrower movements focused toward single goals—feminism, the elimination of poverty, civil rights, and so on.

Finally, unless otherwise implied the terms "left" and "right" are used with exceptional breadth to include not just extreme fringes on either side, but aspects of progressivism/liberalism and conservatism as well.

INTRODUCTION

> So we beat on, boats against the current, borne back
> ceaselessly into the past.
>
> F. Scott Fitzgerald, *The Great Gatsby*

This is a work of interpretation——an extended, speculative essay on
American reform in the twentieth century. As an historian, I have
written the book for historians, but also for a wider audience in the hope
that people with a variety of interests and backgrounds will find it useful.

In order to comprehend the plan of the book, imagine yourself
traversing the pitched roof of a house. You begin at the bottom of one
side and work your way up. You pass row after row of shingles. You
reach the peak, then edge down the other side.

As we ascend, the structure of this book emphasizes the ways in
which a reform movement arises and develops. Pausing at the peak, I
then lead the reader down the other side, showing how a reform
movement declines and eventually ends. The shingles represent chapters,
each overlapping the one below it, yet each also self-contained. There
are twenty chapters in the book.

Let me present some of the fundamental arguments here. For
generations many scholars have described the workings of American
politics as a cycle. What is meant by this term varies from writer to
writer, even from discipline to discipline. Political scientists, for instance,
have stressed alternating electoral coalitions: eras of domination by one
party are punctuated from time to time by great events that traumatize
the voting public and usher in a phase of domination by the other party.
Some political scientists have seen an "equilibrium cycle" operating: the

minute a party takes power its majority begins to erode, so that power shifts automatically to the opposing party.

A number of historians have been intrigued by a somewhat different phenomenon. Roughly every generation, they find, an age of reaction gives way to an age of reform, or vice versa. Stated crudely in terms of this century: the reformist progressive movement emerged, then gave way to reaction in the 1920s; the New Deal appeared, but fell in time to Eisenhower Republicanism; and reform enjoyed a third revival in the 1960s, only to yield to a reaction which culminated with the Reagan era. Some historians would argue that this adds up to a true cycle——that the alternations are roughly constant in duration, and that similar patterns can be more or less predicted for the future.

This book takes a different tack. I argue that the forces leading toward reform or reaction are more complex than previously thought. Some of these forces originate in places not conventionally associated with politics at all. And so it is misleading to speak of a purely political cycle independent of dozens of other variables.

Indeed, if we think of true cycles as being fairly precise in their timing and duration——as coming along once per generation, for example——then the surges of reform and reaction do not literally resemble cycles at all. Reform eras will emerge at variable times in response to very different causes. Prosperity may help stimulate reform in one era, for instance, but suppress it in the next. What links eras of reform together in a common pattern is not so much their origin or duration as the forces that have consistently destroyed them. Here are a few of these forces: foreign policy distractions; war; the disillusionment of youth and intellectuals; weariness of reformers and the mass public with causes, politics, and politicians; and a turn to preoccupation with the self.

To say that the greatest commonality among reform eras lies in the way in which they have declined rather than in what has precipitated them in the first place is not to argue that no common purpose has existed at all. Reform as I employ the term has taken a great many ideological shapes and embraced many causes. Yet the one overriding thrust of American reform in the twentieth century has led it in the general direction of the welfare state. This was true even before the welfare state had dawned on Americans as a comprehensive idea. It remained true as the early New Deal welfare state took form. It held true yet again as the New Deal state was fleshed out by the Kennedy-Johnson reforms of the 1960s.[1]

I will argue that surges of reform and reaction follow the dynamics of fads——to state it baldly, that working in behalf of beneficiaries such as the poor tends to pass in and out of fashion just as styles do in music or clothing. Seizing advantage of this faddism, reform administrations in

Washington proceed opportunistically. Often they co-opt ideas from the radical left and drive these through as liberal legislation. Liberal regimes respond to their own internal dynamics, showing a consistent tendency to turn leftward after an initial flurry of measures passes. In time, though, the leaden forces of inertia wear down reform's energy. Much of the resistance comes from business, and more broadly, from the restrictions imposed by a capitalist economic system. Resistance originates, too, deep within the American mind.

This book pursues an approach to reform and reaction that has not been followed before. The approach embraces elements of theory developed by such political scientists as V. O. Key, Jr., Angus Campbell, and Walter Dean Burnham. It also embraces elements of the cycle theory propounded most notably by Arthur M. Schlesinger, Sr., decades ago, and recently restated and elaborated upon by Arthur M. Schlesinger, Jr., in a book suggestively titled *The Cycles of American History*.[2] While I deeply respect all of these scholars, I fully agree with none.

If this book does take a lead from earlier writings, however, it takes it from the Schlesingers. Although some scholars have seemed to accept elements of their theory, strikingly little has been written using their argument as a point of departure——perhaps because historians have not displayed much comfort with cycle theory generally. Whatever the reason, the literature on the subject remains confined to articles and brief, often hesitant, passages of books.

This volume will not take shape as a comprehensive history or a critique of liberal reform, but instead will examine the conditions under which it emerges, flourishes, and declines——its life cycle, as it were. I have pursued those aspects of reform which interest me the most, or about which I feel the most needs to be said. Seen another way, the study represents an intellectual foray, a kind of raid. A broad-front strategy would have entailed the writing of numerous monographs and articles involving a great deal of survey research and other techniques. On much of what the book treats we can now only speculate; we will repeatedly venture toward the unknowable or the unverifiable. The work does focus mainly on similarities between eras of reform on one hand, and between reactionary phases on the other. But another volume could certainly have been written on the dissimilarities.

I have written rather elliptically about two particular themes which took a quite central place in earlier studies of American reform: the economic and social origins of the reform impulse itself, and the specific techniques which reform leadership has employed to advance its aims. The reason I have said so little about these matters is, in fact, that the literature of both subjects has simply grown huge.

As to origins, the question is, What has generated the passion, even outrage, in reformers and radicals? Answers vary to some degree by era;

they will appear implicitly in what I say about each period. Since I focus repeatedly upon the internal, personal motivations of reformers, I run the risk of implying (as some earlier historians have done) that to become a reformer one must be socially maladjusted or suffer some other abnormality. Not so. While each reform era has raised its own set of issues, some of the problems that have animated reformers have existed perennially throughout this century——to name just a few, oligarchy or the threat of it; business misbehavior; poverty; racism and sexism; political corruption; and farm crisis. Plenty of cause exists, in other words, for the best-adjusted, least-neurotic citizen to become upset.

As to the techniques of reform leadership, the enormous literature that has emerged focuses in particular upon the presidency. My approach has been to look at the reform presidency in a different way ——to portray it as a sort of accident, a product of the fortuitous.

One can no longer discuss the liberal reform tradition with the breezy sense of assurance which characterized a number of the finest studies in the forties and fifties. We have become newly aware of the perennial gap between the size of the problems reformers have confronted and the limited solutions they have advanced. We have learned a good deal about corporatism and "corporate liberalism." We have also heard much of organizations, bureaucracy, professionalization, efficiency, and order——some of these perspectives projected through the lens of modernization theory, and integrated most particularly into interpretations of very early twentieth century American reform. Differences between the private and public sectors, or between various interest groups, which once were seen as profound and ideologically loaded, have been smoothed over. New interpretations emphasize similarities among the motivations that propel all of them. The reasons for conflict have become blurred, conflict itself, downplayed. The breathlessness of earlier studies of reform and reaction has been superseded by a rather bloodless line of argument which obscures the differences between the two. Speaking of battles over liberal or conservative ideals has fallen out of fashion; now we talk about drives for stabilization, social cohesion, predictability. "The liberal-conservative dialogue," Theodore J. Lowi argues, "made no sense after the establishment of the principle of positive government."[3] Little but the ritual remained.

This book is, unapologetically, a throwback. I have taken into account a great deal of value in the newer interpretations of American political history. They have permanently altered the way we see things. Yet they often also reflect the disillusionment and conservatism of recent years, revealing a tendency to blur differences that once brought people into the streets.

My argument is this: If we jettison the reform-reaction dichotomy completely, or play it down excessively, a good deal of American history becomes unintelligible. The continuity so many scholars find pervading the past becomes a false similarity. Perhaps in a way it reflects the state in which liberalism finds itself now, administering institutions it has created, a liberalism-turned-establishmentarian. In much of the recent historical literature, the liberalism of 1915 or 1935 seems almost as dull as the liberalism of today. Yet there was fire and anger then. Theodore Roosevelt and Woodrow Wilson divided people, grated on nerves. So, most of all, did FDR. And later Harry Truman. And, despite their best efforts, John Kennedy and Lyndon Johnson.

We know altogether too little about the way in which reform movements have interrelated with one another over the decades. This book will look at relationships and probabilities: it will examine what has been called "the mechanics of historical reform movements"[4] and the manner in which one such movement may or may not give rise to another. Again, we really do not know much about all this. Nor can I do more than toss a few words in the direction of some of the issues raised. Once more, this book is a foray.

Here I lay out at considerable length a theory of American politics in the twentieth century which seeks to explain some of the fundamental dynamics of the system. The book leads the reader into unexpected byways for clues, as well as down the main thoroughfares of mass behavior. The volume will not proceed strictly chronologically. It is essentially analytical in nature, employing historical examples and surveying chronology afresh chapter by chapter. Following an examination of the relationship between liberalism and reform, each of the three parts of the book will be introduced by a short statement establishing its fundamental direction.

NOTES

F. Scott Fitzgerald, *The Great Gatsby* (New York: Charles Scribner's Sons, 1953), p. 182.

[1]This insistent connection between reform and welfare statism may seem restrictive and New Dealish; it may seem old-fashioned. Certainly much else called "liberal" has passed under the name of reform. Yet in this book I have tried to follow one of my own dicta for reformers, which is to keep their eyes on the ball. Liberal reform may mean many things, but primarily it means the welfare state (or "welfare liberalism"), together with the role of government which has gone with it. The term "welfare liberalism" comes from Robert N. Bellah et al., *Habits of the Heart: Individualism and Commitment in American Life* (Berkeley:

University of California Press, 1985), p. 262. Initial letters capitalized in the original.

[2](Boston: Houghton Mifflin Co., 1986). Hereafter I refer to the elder as Schlesinger, and to the younger as Schlesinger, Jr.

[3]*The End of Liberalism: Ideology, Policy, and the Crisis of Public Authority* (New York: W. W. Norton & Co., 1969), p. 60. "The most important difference between liberals and conservatives, Republicans and Democrats," Lowi argues, "is to be found in the interest groups they identify with." Ibid., p. 72. Italics deleted. See also Robert Paul Wolff, *The Poverty of Liberalism* (Boston: Beacon Press, 1968), ch. 4.

[4]Howard W. Allen and Jerome Clubb, "Progressive Reform and the Political System," *Pacific Northwest Quarterly* 65 (July 1974): 130.

1

LIBERALISM
AND REFORM

A Liberal is a man too broadminded to take his own side in
an argument.

Robert Frost

A reformer is a guy who rides through a sewer in a glass-
bottomed boat.

New York Mayor Jimmy Walker

During the 1976 primaries, Representative Morris K. Udall of Arizona,
acknowledging that he still regarded himself as a liberal, proceeded to
erase the word "liberal" from his presidential campaign. The term, he
observed, "is associated with abortion, drugs, busing and big-spending,
wasteful government." As a substitute, Udall opted for "progressive."[1]

By 1976 it was getting hard to find a liberal candidate for President
willing to march under the banner of liberalism. The word had become
something of an embarrassment. Thus former Senator Fred Harris,
perhaps reflecting his Oklahoma roots, declared, "I am a populist."
Jimmy Carter refused both liberal and conservative labels, was accused
of evasiveness, and won the nomination. Only Senator Henry Jackson
of Washington seemed content with the liberal tag, but Jackson's
campaign evoked mainly boredom. Udall joked about his preference for
"progressive." "Liberal," he observed, had become a "worry word."[2]

These politicians feared connotations, and the connotations had
altered the political lexicon of the seventies. In literature, the media,
and ordinary conversation, the term "liberal" became associated with a
soft and forgiving position on crime. For every offense from prostitution
to rape to child molesting, "liberal" suggested a preoccupation with the

rights of defendants.[3] A liberal, ran one line, was someone who tried to understand the other person's point of view while being mugged. In the twenties, the *New York Times* had referred to a "liberal" position on (that is, against) strict prohibition enforcement;[4] in the sixties, liberals found themselves suspected of looseness on drug-law enforcement. Always they remained identified with the "effete," "degenerate," "crime-plagued" Northeast.

Liberalism got tied in with "deviant" attitudes toward religion, too, including atheism. "Liberals, not all, tend to be agnostic," pronounced Los Angeles Chief of Police Edward M. Davis in 1977. "Conservatives tend to be religious"; or, at least, there was "greater religiosity in conservatism than in liberalism."[5]

Liberals seemed to be muddleheaded internationalists, soft on national defense and even self-defense. Liberalism became associated with arms control and gun control: with not building new generations of bombers, aircraft carriers, submarines, and missiles, and with not keeping a pistol in the bureau drawer.

"A swing of the pendulum is in motion against excesses identified with the liberal era," noted Robert J. Donovan in 1975, "including campus riots, pornography, racial disturbances, swelling welfare rolls and the drug culture."[6]   What did liberalism add up to?   Chief Davis provided a refreshing note of clarity in the observation that liberals "tend to fly together, like geese; conservatives fly alone, like eagles."[7]   A liberal, ran one assessment, was someone whose interests were not presently at stake.

All this suggested a bleak situation indeed. But much of the picture was semantic, a point which Udall's comments imply. Liberals had allowed the term "liberalism"——*their* word——to get bandied about in the sloppiest and most pejorative ways, with scarcely a challenge. They had even done some of the bandying themselves.

In order to understand the travail of liberalism, we must first examine liberalism's past.[8] This examination will confirm the point that the term bears an inherent semantic burden. But it will also establish that some of the difficulties in present-day *reform* are fundamentally an outgrowth of present-day *liberalism*. The two, reform and liberalism, cannot be precisely equated.

One of the difficulties in using the word "liberal" lies in its varying denotations: wholly apart from the negative connotations, the term has various primary meanings.   And the meanings alter with changing times——the term moves and shifts continually, resistant to being glued here or there. We can pinpoint variants called economic liberalism, or cultural liberalism, or philosophic liberalism, and others. We think of liberal education; we identify a liberal temperament or style.[9] But *political* liberalism is the form which will most occupy our attention here.

We will find that it represents as much a temper or mood as any settled political philosophy.

Liberalism originally carried a far different meaning than it does today. As Louis Hartz has shown, this nation's whole political background can be described as liberal.[10] Conceived in this sense, liberalism has to do with the evolution in the seventeenth and eighteenth centuries of the middle classes, and their confrontation with the classical conservatism of the old aristocracy. Although liberal thought has never closed itself off into a set of inflexible dogmas, in the American context the liberal tradition, rooted in the colonial past, has presupposed certain rights and values, among them a democratic political system, with government by consent of the governed; equality, but also the widest possible liberty and freedom for the individual; substantial laissez-faire and private property; equal justice; a suspicion of privilege and power; resistance to potent and oppressive hereditary monarchies, aristocracies, armies, and churches; and relegation of the state to a minimal role— decentralized, weak government. The point of early liberalism was to release the individual from the constraints and oppression of government or class or guild, in short, to set the individual free.

The liberal temperament thrives on freedom. Absolute authority of any kind arouses its resistance. This implies (though it does not always guarantee) a high tolerance for, indeed an encouragement of, diversity and even idiosyncrasy among groups and individuals. Instead of authority, liberalism has based itself on the idea of the individual's dignity and value. Opposed to the restrictions governments have placed on the person, liberals have defined the place of government in such a way that its primary role involves sustaining individuals' equality, liberty, and security, and respecting their privacy. One offshoot of this is the emphasis on equality of opportunity; another, on freedom of association; yet another, on freedom of thought and expression, based on the idea that human beings are essentially reasonable and rational, if not with perfect consistency. Liberals, in consequence, have tended to oppose censorship as a restriction on the free flow of ideas and an embarrassment to human reason. Faith in reason, in progress, and in reason as the handmaiden of progress remains central to the liberal perspective.

Related to this, liberals have tended to lean toward the concept of objective truth, and the idea that human reason can seek out and identify it. Though at times reformers have deviated from it, notably in the nineteenth century, the basic tradition of rationalism has set all questions, including religious ones, under the microscope of free inquiry and personal scrutiny. Just as reason is the arbiter of truth, science provides the principal tool of reason. Within this rationalist framework, religion becomes an individual option. The liberal's secular outlook has conceived of religious institutions, taken collectively, as one more kind of private endeavor to be tolerated along with other institutions. This sort of benign tolerance, this freedom of religion or atheism or agnosticism or whatever, has meant that the public order must be secular, and so liberalism has undertaken the separation of church and state.

Optimistic by nature, liberalism has traditionally envisioned time as a machine which generates progress. The idea of progress——of life as dynamic, the past suspect, and the belief that civilization and the human prospect improve——lies at the core of liberalism. People themselves provide the instrument of advance. From this derives the abiding liberal faith in reform. Its direction set by high ideals, reform must proceed consistently, but also cautiously. Gradualism inheres in the liberal perspective.

Since liberalism has placed such heavy emphasis on happy evolution, it is not surprising that liberalism itself has evolved. In its classical phase, it worked very heavily in the interest of its espousers, the bourgeoisie. The classical economists, notably David Ricardo and Thomas Malthus, grounding their ideas on the bedrock of natural law, sanctified even more rigidly than had Adam Smith the then-revolutionary concept of laissez-faire. But at length liberalism passed through a transition which grew out of the industrial revolution. "The prophets of democracy," wrote Carl Becker, "could not foresee that the industrial revolution, superimposed on a regime of free competition, would give to the possessors of machines and the instruments of production powers and privileges which would have reduced dead and gone kings and nobles, could they have imagined them, to envious admiration."[11]

In power, precisely, lay the great dilemma. The outcome of competition was winners, but also losers——a new world of concentrated wealth and gnawing poverty. Mass migration from the American hinterland to the cities, as well as from abroad, poured workers into urban factories like coal into a furnace. The industrial revolution ushered in a new age of exorbitant hours, inadequate pay, child labor, and numbing misery. Here, as in Europe, the proletariat organized. Even in America (with its record of labor conservatism), laissez-faire liberals found themselves confronting Marxian socialists and others who demanded an end to the competitive system, a regulated economy, and restraint on the profit-maximizing greed (which is to say, the liberty) of individuals.

"It has been the function of the liberal tradition in American politics, from the time of Jeffersonian and Jacksonian democracy down through Populism, Progressivism, and the New Deal, at first to broaden the numbers of those who could benefit from the great American bonanza and then to humanize its workings and help heal its casualties," wrote Richard Hofstadter.[12] As the nature of the economy changed, as a massive working class and a corps of dispossessed farmers emerged, the nature of this broadening process and the demands of humanization and healing underwent a great transformation. Classical liberalism, notably the economics that underpinned it, came under a barrage of criticism. In the words of John Dewey, the liberalism of limited government and laissez-faire was denounced as "in effect simply a justification of the brutalities and inequities of the existing order."[13] Industrialization had transformed some of the biggest pillars of classical liberalism into props beneath an oppressive status quo.

Dewey was writing in 1935. By then the thrust of liberalism had dramatically changed, a shift measurable in the remarks of the newer liberalism's critics. Joseph Schumpeter observed with heavy irony that "as a supreme, if unintended, compliment, the enemies of the system of private enterprise have thought it wise to appropriate its label."[14] "Beginning in the late nineteenth century, and especially after 1930 in the United States, the term liberalism came to be associated with a very different emphasis, particularly in economic policy," notes Milton Friedman.

> It came to be associated with a readiness to rely primarily on the state rather than on private voluntary arrangements to achieve objectives regarded as desirable. The catchwords became welfare and equality rather than freedom. The nineteenth-century liberal regarded an extension of freedom as the most effective way to promote welfare and equality; the twentieth-century liberal regards welfare and equality as either prerequisites of or alternatives to freedom. In the name of welfare and equality, the twentieth-century liberal has come to favor a revival of the very policies of state intervention and paternalism against which classical liberalism fought. In the very act of turning the clock back to seventeenth-century mercantilism, he is fond of castigating true liberals as reactionary![15]

Exponents of the change as well as critics agree on what happened as this transformation took place. They differ, of course, over the implications. Traditional liberalism had consisted of three main dimensions: the free economy, free opinion, and free behavior. Reform liberalism[16] speaks of implementing the old liberal values, but at the same time it reshuffles the importance of these values. The big twentieth century change has affected primarily the first dimension. Traditional liberalism and reform liberalism both concern themselves with individuals, individualism, and freedom, but modern liberalism tends to see the human experience in a broader way than primarily as the fulfillment of homo economicus. Here again, a fundamental alteration of perspective has occurred. Attempting to come to terms with the urban-industrial age, and in the name of democracy, the liberalism of the New Deal ambivalently embraced centralized, powerful government. Liberals came to see public life in terms of problems, for which they must identify solutions. (Conservatives, by contrast, have typically responded by trying to show that these problems do not exist, have already been solved, or cannot be solved at all.)

If we look past these changes and return to underlying liberal values, we find that they remained remarkably consistent: the faith in reason; the sense of personal dignity and worth; the belief in the powers of the human mind to shape a better future; the stress on democracy, individual freedom, civil rights and civil liberties, and equal opportunity and justice; the tension between property and equality; the suspicion of privilege as well as of power itself; and a measure of egalitarianism. The original reliance on negative action to ensure these values——notably the anti-statism that had formerly been a liberal credo——became redefined as a faith which held that in the face of industrialization and its consequences, the ancient negativism would undercut cherished values. Positive state action might save them. In the modern environment, their rationalism led liberals to classify issues as "problems," and then to search out largely governmental "solutions." The state would take over, or at least share, the formerly private role of steering society. It would serve business, but would also discipline it.

The new egalitarianism of the liberal welfare state went beyond older measures toward democratization, such as suffrage expansion, by attempting a more equitable distribution of income (higher wages, social programs) and the limitation or eradication of poverty. Yet there was no pretense toward complete leveling. To a degree, government would now protect the individual against private interests, much as the old liberalism had perceived private interests as protection from government. Through government, new sorts of rights became partially or fully established: the right to opportunity regardless of race, sex, or religion, the right to a living wage, to work-free time, and to be educated to one's fullest potential. But as a practical matter, "equality" still meant political and civil equality, not literal economic equality.

Americans believe in equality and liberty, as they insist they do. Yet the two exist in ambiguous tension. What does equality mean? To some, equal opportunity; to others, equal condition. Likewise liberty: it might mean protection from government, or it might mean liberty achieved through government.[17] More than fifty years ago Carl Becker pointed to "the predicament in which all liberals find themselves," to wit:

Our predicament arises from the fact that, having been long enamored of both liberty and equality, we are now ever more insistently urged (by the gods that be, those wooden-faced *croupiers* at life's gaming table) to choose between them and the truth is we cannot with a clear conscience or a light heart choose either without the other. So we stand irresolute, pulled one way by our humane sympathies, another by our traditional ideals.[18]

Liberty versus equality: the classic dilemma. In traditional liberalism, equality meant equality before the law. It has been a growing characteristic of American liberalism in this century to take an active role in creating equality of opportunity, to compensate groups for past or present injustices which handicap them before the race. In its bias against government interventionism, classical liberalism stressed the rule of law as opposed to the rule of persons. It accepted unequal rewards from individual to individual. Contemporary liberalism shows rather less willingness to tolerate these wide differentials unquestioningly.

A phrase such as contemporary liberalism suggests that classical liberalism has now yielded to some new unitary form; yet the definition of liberalism today is very much in flux, and public perceptions of what the word means, or ought to mean, have changed. Over the past few decades the Gallup poll has asked people whether they regard themselves as liberals or conservatives. Conservative respondents have increased, the liberal proportion decreased. But as the implications of the term "liberal" have changed, so have the implications of both question and answer. During the fifties the word retained much of its New Deal grounding on economic-welfare state questions; it was also acquiring a civil rights tinge. By the late sixties the term had taken further coloration from precisely those connotations that Udall bewailed: liberalism now suggested permissive deviance. The implications of other words altered as well: during the thirties, "welfare" meant relief for unemployed heads of families, widows, orphans, or young people out of work, the able but temporarily dispossessed; by the sixties welfare suggested unwed minority mothers. "Big government" once meant the politics of domestic rescue; by the late sixties it implied failed promises and Vietnam.[19] Hence the flight of so many politicians from "mere" words.

This last, Vietnam, brings up yet another problem we face in defining terms. Just as a liberal approach to domestic affairs has emerged (which, if inconsistent as to strategy, has at least more or less shown continuity in fundamental goals), so it is widely supposed that there exists such a thing as a bona fide liberal foreign policy. Most contemporary political dialogue takes it as a given fact that liberalism is, at least loosely, a worldview. But national and international issues that have no particularly logical association with one another at all often get wrapped together in public discourse.

True enough, such matters as defense, immigration, and trade function broadly as intersections between domestic and foreign policy.[20] And certainly in the foreign sphere, American liberalism exhibits a pattern of tendencies. Liberals invest themselves in U.S. foreign policy in part because they must. By nature, they are critics. Their criticisms do not stop at the shoreline. The liberal biases toward centralization and peaceful, ordered change have manifested themselves in the United Nations, and before it in the League. More broadly, one can identify in liberalism an inherent inclination toward internationalism, up to and (in the desires of some) including world democracy and world government. Wilsonian internationalism, its missionary approach to diplomacy, and its anticolonialism have remained important themes in the Democratic party.[21]   Relative to conservatives, liberals have commonly tended to think less nationalistically, talk less about patriotism and defense, and see the United States as morally responsible for the well-being of other, especially poorer, countries in a world with which America has become closely intertwined.

In fact, if we allow for plenty of exceptions, we could develop a paradigm of the relationship between liberal theory and temperament on one hand, and the conduct of foreign affairs on the other. The liberal faith in human rationality and dignity, and liberal humanitarianism, we might argue, impel liberals to conceptualize in terms of humankind as a whole rather than in terms of more restricted institutions like the nation state or even the family. These same values incline many (though by no means all) liberals away from militant patriotism and toward antimilitarism or even pacifism and disarmament. Liberals have tended openly to despise war. Many have perceived defense outlays as wastefully sidetracking funds that could feed social programs.   Perhaps a characteristic impulse toward reconciliation and forgiveness helps account for liberals' willingness to push for disarmament and negotiate with the Soviets. Modern liberalism's penchant for active, interventionist reform leads liberals to conceive even of reforming the world; impelled by conscience and a sense of mission, they naturally want to advance their humanitarian values both at home and abroad. At least in recent years, they have shown more inclination than conservatives to push for international human rights, and perhaps less inclination to support reactionary anticommunist regimes.[22]   Finally, the ancient liberal predisposition toward free trade carries over into the modern world.[23] Free trade acts as a solvent on barriers of nationhood and race. (It also opens doors to U.S. economic penetration of other countries.) We might argue that their passion for democracy and sympathy for the downtrodden and oppressed lead liberals off into crusades for aid and democracy everywhere; and that the liberal tendencies toward activism, government centralization, executive power, and organization create the indispensable groundwork for maximum involvement abroad, even for war.[24]

Yet "liberal" foreign policy has not taken shape any more out of preexisting liberal notions or biases toward this or that posture, than from perspectives shared between the parties, and from what reformist Presidents have actually worked out as policy in the process of governing. To most of these Presidents, foreign policy initially had second priority to domestic. Down to World War II, indeed, the international sphere *normally* took second place no matter which party held power. It was Wilson, of all people, who remarked that "it would be the irony of fate if my administration had to deal chiefly with foreign affairs."[25] By and large, international questions got used as levers in domestic political or economic policy: hence Wilson preached foreign markets in 1912 in order to bolster the domestic economy,[26] and Franklin Roosevelt opted for economic nationalism in 1933 for the same reason. Both liberal and conservative regimes intervened abroad in the interest of American business. Both parties indulged in the partial isolationism of the thirties. In fact, liberalism has long held foreign involvement suspect, and running through it one finds a strong, if intermittent, strain of isolationism. To one degree or another, Wilson, FDR, and Johnson, domestically our most productive twentieth century Presidents, each pushed foreign affairs to the rear.

Reformers have not stayed put on foreign policy. No overriding consistencies link their actions. Before World War II, many were isolationists, most afterward, internationalists. The Cold War, foreign aid, and the UN became good liberal causes. But degrees of agreement on all this varied, and a weaker isolationism ("neo-isolationism") recurred in the wake of Vietnam. This looseness accords with the rather disjointed attitudes of the mass public: from at least the late 1930s to the 1960s, linkages between views toward domestic and foreign affairs remained weak. Only in the sixties did the correlation strengthen.[27]

All this runs against the grain of conventional political wisdom, which has generally portrayed liberal domestic and foreign policies as closely bound together (typically without specifying precisely how). Much of what I have said will be unfashionable, too, among revisionist historians whose research focuses on the supposedly intimate relationship between the domestic and foreign spheres. Particularly in the 1960s, many historians began to identify ties between a purportedly imperialistic foreign policy running through this country's history, and the exploitation of the great masses of Americans at home. To generalize excessively about these historians' work would do violence to the shadings of difference in their views. Most of their writings were implicitly or explicitly suspicious of capitalism. They had a good deal to say about the ways in which American reformers had been duped by or had intentionally acted in the interest of an Establishment which was essentially oligarchic. A new term appeared in the historian's lexicon: "corporate liberalism."

In fact, the revisionist critique does contain a good deal of validity. This book will explore the profound constraints which capitalism has placed on reform. It will acknowledge the fascination with which reform administrations have sometimes entertained the idea of expanding foreign markets as a means of alleviating class tensions at home. It will have much to say about liberal anticommunism. What it will not do, however, is confirm the underlying assumption that domestic and foreign policies are Siamese twins.

Those linkages that have existed do not derive from any necessary relationship between *reform* and foreign policy; rather, the correlation has existed between the *liberal* predispositions we have already described and certain tendencies toward action both at home and abroad. While liberals have often displayed these tendencies, the impulses themselves do not fit into any proper definition of American reform. The great animating theme of domestic liberalism and of reform in general has centered on the development of the welfare state. No comparable single motif has emerged in foreign policy over which conservatives and liberals have divided. Indeed, the biggest aims of United States foreign policy——winning world wars, expanding markets, keeping the Soviet Union in check——have, every one of them, been fundamentally bipartisan, especially since World War II.

At one juncture, though, domestic reform and foreign policy do intersect, with some of the worst consequences for reform. This is the point at which war or other foreign policy involvements drag the nation's attention away from domestic policymaking. Every time this has occurred during the present century——and it has taken place massively on three occasions——foreign policy has distracted from or finished off reform. We will examine the phenomenon as we look at the down side of a reform era. The point to note here is that the very same liberal values that may, conceivably, help to propel liberal regimes into foreign involvements can erode reform at home once they do. In other words, *liberalism in foreign policy may undermine reform.*

Often this becomes partly masked, as with trade programs and battles over the defense budget. Those occasions when liberals have pushed foreign trade in order to expand prosperity and alleviate class tension may all seem benign enough. But the trade icon has also served as a means of avoiding hard domestic decisions——in particular, on the distribution and redistribution of wealth. Foreign/defense policies and domestic reform have gotten aligned against one another in battles over defense spending, where some liberals seek cuts specifically to provide added funding for their programs at home, and conservatives attempt the opposite. (Both Nixon and Reagan aligned domestic against military expenditures, claiming to stand for the interests of taxpayers while doing so.) Domestic and defense spending do conflict. Still, an examination of military budgets pays higher tribute to the legacy of foreign/defense policy bipartisanship and the basic agreement between liberals and conservatives than it does to any profound rift over these priorities. Defense policy has served as a great red herring for liberals, precisely because their differences with conservatives here are minimal and distract from other questions which ought to have gotten debated, but have not.

We return to the main point, that while foreign and defense policies have come and gone, domestic policy has fundamentally animated the long-term debate between liberals and conservatives in America. More than that, domestic policy evolution has taken a far more nearly linear direction over time. The foreign policies of the Wilson Administration ultimately varied more widely than its domestic ones; the same holds true of the other primary reform regimes, those of FDR and Lyndon Johnson. And domestic policy provided the main link between them. I would not for a moment deny the close identity at times between reform and nationalism, as in the mind of Theodore Roosevelt, for example, or Herbert Croly, or Willard Straight. As TR wrote an English friend: "I am a genuine radical. I believe in what you would call an 'imperialist democracy.'" British "Democratic Imperialism" was identical to Roosevelt's "Democratic Nationalism."[28] Latent, at least, in this kind of thinking, one could find every danger that scholars have identified with it.

Yet the basic point still remains. Before the Cold War provided a permanent excuse for setting foreign priorities ahead of domestic, these latter constituted the nation's primary political agenda. To the extent that liberal values have drawn their holders into foreign involvements, reform at home has generally been subverted. Finally, because of this, if for no other reason, we must draw a distinction between liberalism on one hand, and reform on the other.

Our differentiation between liberalism and reform, and between foreign policy and reform, carries us to still another kind of distinction. In examining the history of American reform, many intellectuals——the historians, political scientists, and others who have done most of the recounting——have shown a marked fondness for analyzing the ideological undulations of previous generations of intellectuals. Hence our fascination, for example, with the transformations in the social sciences late in the nineteenth century and early in the twentieth, or with the

Brain Trust episode of the New Deal. Many fine studies exist of liberal ideas.

Because so much has been said about the role of intellectuals in reform, one might almost conclude that shifts in ideas mean shifts in national behavior and policy: that the idea is nearly equivalent to the act. I would not for a minute minimize the role that intellectuals have played in guiding reform during this century. But American politics has not operated as a politics of ideas, in the sense that European politics has or that many of our own intellectuals would like it to. And when the ideas of intellectuals have intruded directly into the political landscape, they have often done so erratically or uncertainly (Theodore Roosevelt and Herbert Croly, for instance), or somewhat accidentally or incongruously (Daniel P. Moynihan and Richard Nixon). The history of American reform is not primarily a history of the intellectuals.

Yet in saying this we risk underrepresenting their role. Intellectuals often exemplify, epitomize, or herald political and social change. And intellectuals have played a growing role in government, to the point that it has become impossible to conceive of the modern state without their prominent involvement. Part of the problem in arriving at a proper assessment of the intellectuals' place in reform derives from their own tendency to combine (or confuse) political questions with broader cultural ones.[29] Another is the difficulty in assessing interaction between intellectuals and important politicians. While the history of American reform does not simply amount to one variant of the life of the mind, the liberal mind has been far better chronicled——by intellectuals, of course——than has the story of, say, the working class.

One final, difficult liberal theme requires our attention. It is religion. During the nineteenth century, the relationship between religion (notably evangelical Protestantism) and reform seemed so obvious that it scarcely required mention, and this relationship has continued on through the twentieth. But since the Puritans, the ties between reform and religion have remained perennially ambiguous. The ambiguity has deepened in modern times. Less anti-religious than irreligious, Martin K. Doudna observes, "with his belief in reason, science, and progress, the [contemporary] liberal tends to be skeptical about religion and about tradition in general."[30] Liberalism, after all, disestablished entrenched religions and preached the doctrine of progress. Even so, as Arthur M. Schlesinger, Jr., remarks, "the Puritan conscience and the Enlightenment sensibility" have joined to promote a complementary spirit of reform.[31]

Talking about religion today requires qualifications and yet more qualifications. Compared to other Western nations, the United States retains a strong religious bent. Yet the potency of religion behind whatever cause, good or ill, amounts to less now than early in this century simply because——despite all the revivalism of the 1980s ——organized religion plays a less important role than it did then. It is impossible to imagine the social gospel, for example, having the impact on Americans today that it exerted in 1900. Only one generation into the century, New Deal thought forged itself in decidedly secular shapes.

Then too, what clerics and their flocks define as "reform" (for instance, *liberal* interpretations of scripture) often falls well outside the mainstream of change which we will treat here. Through all of its incarnations and permutations, liberalism has shown a strong streak of perfectionism, especially when it has spoken with a Yankee-Protestant accent. Because of their religiosity, many, especially among the less cosmopolitan congregations, are apt to go chasing off after prohibition or Sunday-closing laws or anti-gay ordinances, and label these "reforms." The notion of using reform to purge sin made its deepest bow of the century in the 1920s, but the impulse still survives like postmortem jerks and twitches. And the sometime appeal of a William Jennings Bryan or a Jimmy Carter reminds us that behind an often maudlin mask of fundamentalism one may also discover a framework of positive social ideals.

References to conscience do not necessarily presuppose that conscience belongs exclusively to the religious. But the role of the specifically clerical conscience in progressivism, for instance, gave the movement greater force than it would otherwise have had, together with an added measure of naïveté.[32] With the general decline of religion, the clerical conscience has played less of a role since; yet I would still argue that where it has had significance, the nature of its idealism has retained this same naïveté. Nor should we take surprise that since World War II, reform religiosity has most closely associated itself with the rise of racial-ethnic subgroups (blacks, Chicanos) where religion retains a stronger hold than it does on the population as a whole——that is, where modernization has had less of a corrosive effect upon religion than on the public at large. Today, the specifically religious conscience still provides sustenance for positive social change. Martin Luther King, Jr., helped found a great movement around it. Activist pastors revived the social gospel in the sixties. Catholic priests helped lead the antiwar movement.

Partly (though only partly) because of the breadth of clerical concerns, liberalism has tended to shoot off in all directions, trying to change many institutions at once. In this way the classic liberal perspective, that life is dynamic and that broad-scale change is the way of the world, ironically undercuts reform by rendering it too eclectic for its own good. Some individuals, conservative by temperament, will always balk at change; and beyond those afflicted by torpor, change always threatens certain interests. Reform, in consequence, creates its own opposition simply by existing. When too many things get tried at once, when efforts scatter, opposition multiplies precisely as resistant interests multiply, and so the braking phenomenon becomes generalized. Now reform itself falls into question, and not merely individual reforms.

Classical liberalism sought to protect the individual from government. Today, liberal government tries to provide some protection to the individual against private interests. But it does so in a society where capitalism remains enduringly popular, which in itself limits government's effectiveness in the role. This helps to explain why public disenchantment toward government has been endemic and often intense. Disenchantment is a misnomer; the public never really showed enchantment to begin with.

In recent years, the philosophical underpinnings of liberalism have been allowed to rot through neglect. This does not mean that liberals have undertaken no articulate or searching intellectual forays in the past decade or two; only that by contrast with the early part of the century, relatively little has been said or proposed. Theorists have sunk a few new pilings into the sand. They have not, to all appearances, lessened the public's hesitancy about liberalism.

So, in the public imagery of the late 1960s through the early 1980s, the old liberal quest for equal opportunity came down among other things to swollen welfare rolls, racial disturbances, busing, and often an easy identification of welfare statism with totalitarianism. How ironic this last is. Classical liberalism placed great faith in the people, their individual dignity and value. The masses might not be consistently rational, but they were at least fundamentally rational. In the face of majoritarian reactions in the twentieth century (McCarthyism, for example), the liberals have responded with bewilderment. Liberal philosophy, and the liberal temperament, thrive on freedom and free expression; unfortunately, freedom of expression has mattered less consistently than it should to the great majority of the public. The recent unliberal uses of the initiative process would have appalled the optimistic progressives who pushed it through in state after state at the turn of the century.

Part of the trouble reform faces today, as we have noted, stems from liberals' allowing the term "liberal" to be employed too loosely and in unfriendly ways, so that it seems synonymous with permissiveness —teaching, as Charles Frankel summarized the very old and classic critique, "a bottomless relativism," "anomic," even "permissive to the point of being suicidal."[33] Liberal leaders who have retreated to the less loaded word "progressive" have helped to confirm the misimpressions.

Yet in truth, since the Enlightenment latitudinarianism *has* inhered in the liberal scheme of things. Liberalism stresses science and the scientific, rationalistic approach to life. Faith in progress produces a welcome for change, whether it represents real progress or not. Implicit in this one finds the suspicion or outright rejection of custom and tradition. Liberalism is tolerant, secular, and sponsors a secular public order. The freedom to be unreligious which a liberal-capitalist society lists among its other freedoms does provide a fertile environment for (in the current jargon of right-wing religious dread) secular humanism. We cannot trace this to welfare state liberalism; it has inhered in liberalism from its classic beginnings. From the freedom to think emerge free thinkers, insisting as they should on the right to deny anything. The hazard of this lies not in open-mindedness, nor certainly in resistance to thought control, but in a genuinely corrosive relativism. Too, all of these values contain a tremendous potential for arousing opposition.

In the specifically modern American social context, liberalism implies a tolerance for outright libertinism. As a general matter, liberal reform approves of and utilizes the existing political system toward dealing with social, economic, and political problems, meanwhile modifying but not for the most part jettisoning established values. It sees government as the steward of the popular will. Yet a well-ingrained liberal perspective will tend not to stop where politics leaves off. It will extend into the realms of morals, religion, fashion, and so forth, and in each of these domains it will lean toward the new.[34] Broadly speaking, support or at least tolerance for untraditional lifestyles has become a part of the identity of modern liberalism.[35] An association exists today, for example, between liberalism and freer mores, abortion, and gay rights.

The liberals' sense of conscience inspires them to back often-unpopular underdogs and causes. In the name of toleration and civil liberties, they continually get stuck defending things which many of them oppose. ("I am not a communist, indeed I am an anticommunist, but I will stand up for your right to be a communist even if it makes me look like one for doing so.") This has become a point of pride for many liberals. Rightly so; but it carries costs. Opposition to censorship, for example—which liberals tend broadly to regard as an affront to reason—leads them to sanction, if often reluctantly, the free flow of pornography. This may imply a sense of priority in principles (toleration taking precedence over one's personal repugnance at pornography). Or it may suggest a sense of moral relativism (morality seeming a matter of individual judgment anyway, pornography gets treated as a question of individual discretion and taste).[36] Either way, the political costs remain.

The powerful belief of modern liberalism that people go wrong because of a bad upbringing or deprivation leads liberals to appear softer on crime than conservatives. On one hand, this manifests itself in a preoccupation with the rights of defendants; on the other, in a tendency to deny that some "victimless crimes" really amount to crimes at all —including, for example, prostitution. Compared to many conservatives, liberals are soft, and appear even softer, on such issues as gun control or the death penalty. Wholly apart from the often-unfair connotations of the term liberal, its denotations once more suffice to undermine it.

Again, cultural liberalism suggests a cosmopolitanism which by its very definition is hostile to the parochial, even if the majority of Americans remain parochial. Philosophical liberalism suggests rationalism, which remains unpopular with great masses of people at any time. Liberal education, grounded like liberalism generally on a faith in human beings, too easily becomes discredited as non-education when numerous sociopathic teenagers infest high school classrooms. Finally, nearly all of the liberal values we have described are associated in the public mind and in actual fact chiefly with the Northeast, doubtless the most unpopular region of the United States. All of these values continually generate tremendous latent or active opposition. No matter that liberalism has taken life as well from idealism and the Judeo-Christian tradition, or that its appeals for human compassion and social justice derive significantly from them.

Liberalism, then, reveals itself both as an indispensable asset and as a massive burden for reform to bear. On the one hand, liberal values create the climate reform requires. On the other, these values are so diffuse that by scattering liberals' attention in all directions they militate against the development of a coherent approach to change. Liberal causes often conflict with each other. Since the thirties, reform in the United States has meant primarily the welfare state, bread-and-butter issues, and social programs. More recently it has meant civil and equal rights. Everything else fits onto the periphery. But liberalism implies each of these things plus so many more that, except in times of extreme economic crisis, genuine reform proposals must be negotiated through a veritable sea filled with red herrings which lure liberals this way and that and make them highly vulnerable to their enemies.

NOTES

George H. Nash, *The Conservative Intellectual Movement in America: Since 1945* (New York: Basic Books, 1976), p. 271 (Frost quote); Richard Shenkman and Kurt Reiger, *One-Night Stands with American History: Odd, Amusing, and Little-Known Incidents* (New York: Quill, 1982), p. 215 (Walker quote).

[1]*Los Angeles Times*, 16 March 1976.

[2]Ibid., 27 March 1976.

[3]See, for instance, Susan Brownmiller, *Against Our Will: Men, Women and Rape* (New York: Simon & Schuster, 1975), pp. 272, 390, 393.

[4]17 November 1923.

[5]*Los Angeles Times*, 25 September 1977.

[6]Ibid., 26 December 1975.

[7]Ibid., 25 September 1977.

[8]Eric F. Goldman, *Rendezvous with Destiny: A History of Modern American Reform* (New York: Alfred A. Knopf, 1958), pp. 317-18, contains a useful discussion of the emergence of the term "liberal" as well as a provocative analysis of the hazards of the relativistic strain in American reform (passim). See also Ronald D. Rotunda, *The Politics of Language: Liberalism as Word and Symbol* (Iowa City: University of Iowa Press, 1986). To some degree, the way in which liberal ideas have become part of the national consensus regardless of social class has been measured in polls. See, e.g., Kay Lehman Schlozman and Sidney Verba, *Injury to Insult: Unemployment, Class, and Political Response* (Cambridge, Mass.: Harvard University Press, 1979), pp. 220ff.

[9]Terms and thrust of discussion are from William Theodore deBary, speech delivered at California State University, Northridge, 6 May 1977; and Charles Frankel, "Does Liberalism Have a Future?" in *The Relevance of Liberalism*, ed. Research Institute on International Change (Boulder, Colo.: Westview Press, 1978), pp. 97ff. A distinction has also been drawn between "economic liberalism" on one hand, and "noneconomic liberalism (issues concerned with civil liberties, race relations and foreign affairs)" on the other. See Seymour Martin Lipset, *Political Man: The Social Bases of Politics* (Garden City, N.Y.: Anchor Books, 1963), p. 318. A useful recent overview of liberalism is Anthony Arblaster, *The Rise and Decline of Western Liberalism* (Oxford, England: Basil Blackwell, 1984).

[10]*The Liberal Tradition in America: An Interpretation of American Political Thought since the Revolution* (New York: Harvest/Harcourt Brace Jovanovich, 1955); John Patrick Diggins, *The Lost Soul of American Politics: Virtue, Self-Interest, and the Foundations of Liberalism* (New York: Basic Books, 1984), especially pp. 4-6.

[11]Carl L. Becker, *Everyman His Own Historian: Essays on History and Politics* (New York: Appleton-Century-Crofts, 1935), p. 94.

[12]*The Age of Reform: From Bryan to F.D.R.* (New York: Alfred A. Knopf, 1956), p. 18.

[13]*Liberalism and Social Action* (New York: G. P. Putnam's Sons, 1935), p. 27.

[14]Joseph A. Schumpeter, *History of Economic Analysis*, ed. Elizabeth Boody Schumpeter (New York: Oxford University Press, 1954), p. 394.

[15]*Capitalism and Freedom* (Chicago: University of Chicago Press, 1962), pp. 5-6.

[16]The term is coined in Kenneth M. Dolbeare and Patricia Dolbeare, *American Ideologies: The Competing Political Beliefs of the 1970s* (Chicago: Markham Publishing Co., 1971), p. 80.

[17]James MacGregor Burns, *Leadership* (New York: Harper & Row, 1978), pp. 389-90.

[18]*Everyman*, p. 97.

[19]This assessment draws heavily upon Norman H. Nie, Sidney Verba, and John R. Petrocik, *The Changing American Voter* (Cambridge, Mass.: Harvard University Press, 1976), p. 11. As a cautionary note, see W. Russell Neuman, *The Paradox of Mass Politics: Knowledge and Opinion in the American Electorate* (Cambridge, Mass.: Harvard University Press, 1986), especially pp. 40, 44.

[20]See Charles A. Beard and G.H.E. Smith, *The Idea of National Interest: An Analytical Study in American Foreign Policy* (New York: Macmillan Co., 1934), pp. 315ff.; and David P. Calleo, *The Imperious Economy* (Cambridge, Mass.: Harvard University Press, 1982), passim.

[21]Robert Kelley, "Ideology and Political Culture from Jefferson to Nixon," *American Historical Review* 82 (June 1977): 559. See also Schlesinger, Jr., *Cycles*, pp. 43-45.

[22]On this point, see Marshall Cohen, "Toward a Liberal Foreign Policy," in *Liberalism Reconsidered*, ed. Douglas MacLean and Claudia Mills, Maryland Studies in Public Philosophy (Totowa, N.J.: Rowman & Allanheld, 1983), p. 79. See also Michael H. Hunt, *Ideology and U.S. Foreign Policy* (New Haven: Yale University Press, 1987); and Charles S. Maier, "Idealism and Intervention," review of *Safe for Democracy: The Anglo-American Response to Revolution, 1913-1923*, by Lloyd C. Gardner, in *New Republic*, 24 June 1985, p. 39.

[23]Nor would I deny the salience of traditional Democratic tariff policy as an aid to domestic consumers. Tariff policy has been a matter of liberal concern both in the classic phase and in the more recent welfare state phase, for individuals as diverse as Cleveland, Wilson, and Kennedy. Even tariffs have produced inconsistencies within liberal regimes, though, and policies have undulated.

[24]Robert J. Bresler, "The Ideology of the Executive State: Legacy of Liberal Internationalism," in *Watershed of Empire: Essays on New Deal Foreign Policy*, ed. Leonard P. Liggio and James J. Martin (Colorado Springs: Ralph Myles, 1976), pp. 13-14. Certainly the Democrats have acquired an unenviable reputation as the party of war. James L. Sundquist has observed that "if activism and conservatism are matters of temperament, then one would expect a party leadership that is activist at home to be activist——or interventionist——abroad. It may therefore be no accident that it has been the Democratic party that has been in power when the country has become most deeply involved in world affairs, including military involvement." *Politics and Policy: The Eisenhower, Kennedy, and Johnson Years* (Washington, D.C.: Brookings Institution,

1968), p. 502. See also David C. McClelland, Power: *The Inner Experience* (New York: John Wiley & Sons, Irvington Publishers, 1975), ch. 9.

[25]Arthur S. Link, *Wilson: The New Freedom* (Princeton: Princeton University Press, 1956), p. 277. See also Eric F. Goldman, *Rendezvous with Destiny: A History of Modern American Reform*, abridged ed. (New York: Vintage Books, 1977), p. ix.

[26]This export emphasis went back a long way in the Democratic party, notably in the South.

[27]Nie, *Changing American Voter*, pp. 180-81.

[28]Charles Forcey, *The Crossroads of Liberalism: Croly, Weyl, Lippmann, and the Progressive Era, 1900-1925* (New York: Oxford University Press, 1961), p. 136.

[29]This problem of politics and culture, and of distinguishing between political and cultural change, is indeed a tangled one. The two cannot be fully separated, of course; and the literature is diverse. See, e.g., Christopher Lasch, *The New Radicalism in America [1889-1963]: The Intellectual as a Social Type* (New York: Alfred A. Knopf, 1965); and T. J. Jackson Lears, *No Place of Grace: Antimodernism and the Transformation of American Culture, 1880-1920* (New York: Pantheon Books, 1981).

[30]*Concerned About the Planet: "The Reporter" Magazine and American Liberalism, 1949-1968* (Westport, Conn.: Greenwood Press, 1977), p. 16.

[31]Preface to Arthur M. Schlesinger, *The American as Reformer* (New York: Atheneum, 1968), p. v.

[32]Hofstadter, *Age of Reform*, p. 152.

[33]"Does Liberalism Have a Future?" p. 102. The confusion of liberalism with bohemianism goes back a long way. See, for example, Robert E. Humphrey, *Children of Fantasy: The First Rebels of Greenwich Village* (New York: John Wiley & Sons, Ronald Press, 1978), p. 23.

[34]Hadley Cantril, *The Psychology of Social Movements* (New York: John Wiley & Sons, Science Editions, 1963), pp. 72-73.

[35]Everett Carll Ladd, Jr., "Liberalism Upside Down: The Inversion of the New Deal Order," *Political Science Quarterly* 91 (Winter 1976-77): 592.

[36]Michael J. Sandel, "Morality and the Liberal Ideal," *New Republic*, 7 May 1984, p. 15.

I

REFORM

In Part I, we encounter reform movements as they confidently surge forward. Chapter 2, "The Look of Reform," explores these movements since the 1890s: Populism, progressivism, the New Deal, and the Kennedy-Johnson 1960s. In focusing on a particular period of reform, each section of this chapter raises, too, a particular theme central to reform movements. Thus, in the discussion of Populism, I stress self-interest as a motivating force in reform by looking at agrarian demands during the late nineteenth century. The segment on progressivism emphasizes the problem reformers have had in focusing on coherent aims and proposals. (Complex and protean, the progressive movement receives especially close scrutiny.) An examination of the New Deal points out that "selling" reform resembles other forms of marketing. Finally, the discussion of the sixties suggests the importance of maintaining balance and proportion in enacting a reform agenda. Chapter 2, then, provides brief interpretive histories of the reform epochs to which we will refer throughout the book.

In chapter 3, we explore theories of cycles in American politics, asking whether politics in this century has really followed cyclic patterns and offering a preliminary answer to that question. Having summarized the history of recent reform movements, then examining cycle theory as it relates to them, we move on to discuss the carriers of the reform tradition throughout this century. Central to that tradition has been a radical fringe which has emerged during each era of reform and has established an agenda which more moderate reformers have often raided for ideas and priorities (chapter 4).

The actual implementation of policy, the form it will assume, takes shape through friction between the two major political parties, examined in chapter 5. For the most part this chapter explores broad patterns and trends in relations between the parties. But detailed attention is devoted to the Bryan-to-Wilson era among the Democrats, a time when (despite a good deal of backing and filling) the Democratic party began to assume its modern role as the main party of reform in this country.

In chapter 6, I stress that a great deal of the reform tradition has depended upon key Presidents——but that their appearance has to a disarming degree been a matter of fortuitous circumstances. These circumstances range all the way from unforeseeably securing the presidency to surviving attempted assassination.

Chapter 7, "The Nature of the Reform Regime," serves as a capstone to Part I. Here I explore the way in which a reform regime actually initiates policy, stressing that however carefully an agenda for change has been defined, reform occurs in a milieu of opportunism. Reform administrations are experimental. Yet limits always circumscribe what they will prove willing or able to do. As a case study, the chapter probes the one domestic issue which has most tortured reformers in this century: race. The chapter concludes with discussions of the poverty problem, feminism, and the courts.

2

THE LOOK OF REFORM

> Only he is able to follow the course of events intelligently
> who comprehends the structural alignment which underlies
> and makes possible a given historical situation and event.
> Those, however, who never transcend the immediate course
> of historical events, as well as those who so completely lose
> themselves in abstract generalities that they never find the
> way back to practical life, will never be able to follow the
> changing meaning of the historical process.
>
> Karl Mannheim

Reform in the United States has resembled a series of crash diets. At
first there is a tendency to ignore one's own blowsiness——to assume the
prior generation's changes went just far enough, that they are legitimate,
adequate, and ultimate. Then we step on the scales and wince. We
discover that everything that went before seems "reactionary" or
"puritanical" or "outmoded." As Walter Dean Burnham and his
colleagues observe:

> Normally the political and governmental systems react slowly
> and imperfectly to social, economic and technological change.
> As a consequence, unmet human needs increase without
> adequate governmental response, tensions mount, and social
> and economic dysfunctions remain unreconciled until crisis
> conditions are reached.[1]

The great reform eras also resemble fault lines, occasionally
bisecting an otherwise orderly historical landscape. These periods have

been brief. If we remember to prefix each date with *circa*, we may remind ourselves that progressivism lasted from 1900 to 1917;[2] the New Deal from 1933 to 1939; and the high point of Kennedy-Johnson reform from 1964 to 1966. Significantly, reform periods have become shorter and shorter, for reasons which I shall endeavor to explain. For the moment it will do to remark that phases of high reform activity are brief and have become briefer. They do not, though, include every reform passed in this century. The New Deal, for example, substantially ended in 1939. Important gains not keyed to the New Deal came for blacks and veterans between then and Roosevelt's death in 1945.

In saying all this I wish to emphasize once again the risk of suggesting a process of change which looks more linear, more consistent, than it really has been. Along with many other fine examinations of reform, three classic studies have brilliantly called attention to the disjunctions in the reform tradition. Before proceeding to examine the consistencies, we will pause for a moment to dwell on the inconsistencies.

"One's generation," wrote Jean-Paul Sartre, "forms part of one's given situation, like one's social class or nationality."[3] In the case of the progressive and New Deal generations, Edgar Kemler certainly thought so. In *The Deflation of American Ideals* (1941), Kemler emphasized that the New Deal had concentrated on putting the economy back together again, practically to the exclusion of anything else. The New Deal was institutional in approach, realistic, worldly, and "hard-boiled." The preceding generation of progressives had contrasted in every respect: their aims had mainly been moral, ethical, and religious, even millennial; their designs, optimistic, perfectionist; and their values, rooted in individualism, personal regeneration, and self-righteousness. "And here is the paradox," Kemler wrote, "that while we have increased our devices and moved on from individualist to collectivist solutions, we have done so only at the cost of deflating our ideals."[4]

Kemler made his share of mistakes, including overstatement and underqualification. But as Otis L. Graham, Jr., has written, Kemler

> described with admirable clarity and timeliness an important turning point in the history of reform in America——the transition from progressivism to liberalism. He saw that the New Dealer was in important ways a new type, and he described the characteristics of the New Deal collective mind in a fashion that historians have subsequently ratified.[5]

The most important ratification came from Graham's own study of the progressive mind, *An Encore for Reform*, which appeared in 1967.[6] In it, Graham examined the reaction of a sample of surviving progressive leaders to the New Deal. "Kemler," he wrote, "saw the apparently inexplicable opposition of old progressives to the New Deal for what it was—consistency."[7] "Of 168 surviving progressives," Graham summarized, "reliable information regarding political attitude in the 1930's exists for 105. Of these, 60 opposed the New Deal, 40 supported it, and 5 were aligned consistently to the left of it."[8]

Why this high level of opposition? Graham offered as complex and subtle a response as the idea of sampling survivors' reactions was simple and direct. The New Deal's "coercive collectivism as a general operating principle, with the attendant atrophy of private strengths," seemed to many of them the New Deal's main lapse. And other problems existed: the expansion of the federal government and of federal power; setting class against class; legislating in behalf of special interests (in progressive rhetoric, "class legislation"), then taking political advantage of all the divisiveness which ensued; the decline of politics as a moral crucible; the new materialism of politics; economic planning; and the patently urban nature and focus of the New Deal, including its close relationship to the political machines and the ethnics. Graham did not deny that links existed between progressivism and the New Deal. Still,

> for the majority of surviving reformers, there was no way to reconcile progressivism and the New Deal, and, as they had never ceased to believe in the long-run wisdom of the former, there was nothing for it but to fight the Democratic Roosevelt as they had once fought corruption and the trusts. Most of them chose to do so in the language . . . of the principles of true progressive reform.[9]

Richard Hofstadter's *The Age of Reform* forms the third leg of our inconsistency triad. Hofstadter's study is, quite simply, the most brilliant book ever written on twentieth century American reform. Once again acknowledging the relationship between Populism, progressivism, and the New Deal, Hofstadter also noted "essential differences."

> Granting that absolute discontinuities do not occur in history, and viewing the history of the New Deal as a whole, what seems outstanding about it is the drastic new departure that it marks in the history of American reformism. The New Deal was different from anything that had yet happened in the United States: different because its central problem was unlike the problems of Progressivism; different in its ideas and its spirit and its techniques.

The "central problem" was economic collapse. "The earlier American tradition of political protest had been a response to the needs of entrepreneurial classes or of those who were on the verge of entrepreneurship." The New Deal geared itself to social legislation; dispensed favors throughout society; developed new fiscal approaches; philosophized relatively little; and jilted issues dear to the progressive generation——moralism, uplift, bossism, political reform, and, to some extent, business size and monopoly.[10]

Acknowledging the power of these scholars' works and others, which emphasize the disjunctions between reform eras, it remains true that historians have generally overstressed the discontinuities. One reason for this, I suspect, is that most studies of reform focus exclusively upon one era rather than on two or three together. The nature of historical writing biases its practitioners toward telling well-rounded stories with an introduction, body, and conclusion. This creates an overemphasis on periodization (the Progressive Era had a beginning, proceeded, and then ended), but an underemphasis on linkage (progressivism tied in to the New Deal). In cutting, so to speak, longitudinally, we run the risk of doing the opposite. While the nature of our study inherently stresses similarities, we must not forget that the dissimilarities are there, are important, and occasionally, are profound.

Fortunately, historians have amassed a very rich storehouse of information on reform movements, so that we may trace them rather as if we were tracing the descent of Homo sapiens. Now and then some group branches off or disappears; occasionally the line of evolution remains stubbornly obscure; but the direction is clear enough. To examine all of it, even to present a fully rounded brief history, would fill a book in itself. We will not try to do that. Instead, we will concern ourselves with understanding the main episodes and their implications.

"Any political system which attempted to exploit all of the tensions in the community would be blown to bits," E. E. Schattschneider has written.

> On the other hand, every combination involves the dominance of some conflicts and the subordination of others. Politics deals with the effort to *use* conflict. Every political party consists of discordant elements which are restrained by the fact that unity is the price of victory. The question always is: *Which battle do we want most to win?*[11]

Want *most* to win——a critical consideration because the agenda of issues, the terrain of the battle, has remained surprisingly unchanged since the urban-industrial age began. The first problem for reformers involves setting priorities.

A master agenda of twentieth century reform would include these issues: the distribution of power and income; the nature (and decline) of the political system; the place and power of business in American life; business regulation; attendant questions having to do with banking and tariffs; labor and unionization; agriculture and its problems; poverty, unemployment, and old age; immigration and "Americanization"; taxation; the rights of racial minorities and women; the environment; and—with major restrictions and qualifications—foreign policy. This is the agenda of an urban-industrial era. Most of its elements had already become key issues by roughly 1900.

"Liberalism," it has been said, "has lost confidence in its past."[12] We now turn to an examination of that past. We will focus our attention on certain themes and constants which make up the legacy of twentieth century American reform, and we will emphasize the pivotal eras.

The Odd Legacy of the Gilded Age

A drunkard in the gutter is just where he ought to be, according to the fitness and tendency of things. Nature has set up on him the process of decline and dissolution by which she removes things which have survived their usefulness.

William Graham Sumner, 1883

The roots of many of the questions which twentieth century reformers have faced inhere in democratic politics and go back to the beginnings of the Republic: liberty versus equality, statism versus antistatism, laissez-faire versus planned and ordered change, the role of Washington versus that of the states. Well before the present century began, the industrial revolution had given these issues new twists and a new urgency. By 1890 the United States had the greatest industrial economy in the world, its manufacturing production nearly totalling the combined output of Britain, France, and Germany. This generated a staggering bill of social costs. Industrialization and mechanization displaced vast agricultural populations and produced an urban proletariat. In 1900 the United States Industrial Commission reported that from 60 to 88 percent of the nation's population ranged from poor to very poor.[1]

In Gilded Age America, business enjoyed a reputation as the country's most prestigious group; politics, by contrast, was widely viewed as something less than a legitimate vocation—a place for people who had failed at business, even as a base, mean enterprise. Given popular attitudes toward politicians, together with the low respect in which many held government itself, it comes as no surprise that the reflex answer to government's shortcomings was to prune it further yet.   Laissez-faire liberals denigrated it as inefficient by its very nature.   Pure government equalled frugal government.   Rising corporate power did produce widespread anxiety, but so did the idea of a government strong enough actually to confront it.   A great deal of the nineteenth century reform tradition had been cast in negatives, focusing on the disestablishment of power structures: the Jacksonians and the Bank, or the abolition of slaveocracy.   And behind these lay the greatest of disestablishing "reforms," the Revolution itself.   Yet for all the negativism toward power, and for all the ambivalence that surrounded government, wheels began slowly turning in the late nineteenth century that have never stopped revolving since.   Much of what transpired developed around two groups: workers and farmers.[2]

Both labor and agriculture experienced a highly spiritual phase, broadly transforming and uplifting in intent, before ultimately settling down to interest-group bargaining and pressure politics.   For workers, this phase was epitomized by the Knights of Labor (founded 1871).   Like gold miners chasing down a big vein, late nineteenth century reformers had a tendency to search for single cure-alls for the nation's ills.   Some were utopias of various kinds.[3]

After the 1880s labor generally lowered its sights from ownership of the means of production, more or less accommodating itself to the wage system——and thus to its status as a permanent proletariat in confrontation with management.[4]   Under Samuel Gompers, labor focused on pure and simple unionism, economic benefits——as Gompers put it, "more."[5]   Labor stood to gain, among other things, from "the [even then] widespread acceptance of the view that the state bore some minimal responsibility for the safety and well-being of its citizens," as Morton Keller writes.[6]   Workers did benefit somewhat from measures that made their appearance on state statute books, including employers' liability laws, which provided a kind of primitive, de facto, albeit inadequate system of accident insurance compensation.   But other laws and judicial decisions worked directly against unionization and other labor interests. Modern unionization, born in the Gilded Age, was still stumbling through its first, awkward steps around the turn of the century, uncertain indeed where it wanted to go, and with whose help.

As labor hesitated over the possibilities of the state, the Gilded Age produced some tantalizing beginnings——hints, really——of governmental things to come; for example: the Interstate Commerce Act (1887), the Sherman Antitrust Act (1890), the Dependent Pension Act of that same year, and an income tax law (1894) promptly struck down by the Supreme Court.   "Not the jealous limitation of the power of the state, but the release of individual creative energy was the dominant value," writes James Willard Hurst (a brilliant student of the relationship between law and the broader society). "Where legal regulation or compulsion might promote the greater release of individual or group energies, we had no hesitancy in making affirmative use of law."[7] Between 1878 and 1908 federal spending went up 400 percent, more than four times the rise in population. One should not make too much of this, though. During the late nineteenth century, it reflected the ironic need to dispose of revenue surpluses rather than spelling any revolution in attitudes toward the proper role of government.

Of all this legislation, perhaps the most interesting—particularly for one who savors incongruities—was the Dependent Pension Act of 1890. The law provided pensions to disabled Union veterans, as well as to various of their kin. Somewhat more than a hundred thousand veterans received pensions just after the Civil War; by the mid-1890s, nearly a million people got government benefits.[8] As David Hackett Fischer has remarked, "ironically, at the same time that compulsory old age pensions were condemned as un-American, the United States maintained much the largest public pension system in the world." Meantime, the former Confederate states paid out pensions to their own veterans. "From the 1880's to nearly World War I," Fischer writes, "veterans' pensions were by far the biggest single item in the federal budget. In some years they accounted for more than 40 percent of the whole." As the veterans aged, the pension system became a de facto program of income supplements to the elderly. The 1890 law carried extremely broad eligibility and affected possibly two-thirds of the aged. "Americans studied the pension question as if it were a branch of theology. Military pensions were defended as necessary to maintain the honor of the Republic, but old age pensions were condemned as an unholy amalgam of sin and socialism."[9] Sin or not, the pension program came complete with its own bureaucracy; Morton Keller has called it the nation's "first large-scale federal welfare system."[10]

Late in the nineteenth century, laissez-faire began to come under concerted attack, partly because in practice it was a sham—it never applied to business; partly because growing numbers of people who remained outside or who had come to feel outside the purview of government wanted in, even arguing they had a moral right of admission; and partly because of a growing fear that if these people were not let in the nation would run the risk of open class warfare. For the working class, laissez-faire meant the sweatshop, child labor, wretched pay and living conditions, and, in times of unemployment, the freedom to starve. Many among the nation's farm population sought shelter from the economic forces which pressed in on them: overproduction, falling commodity prices, and debt. In the late nineteenth century, the search began for ways to protect these two key groups—workers and farmers——as well as others, by finding some middle ground between laissez-faire on one hand, and socialism on the other.

Populism and the Politics of Self-Interest

There is a vast difference between the generation which made the heroic struggle for Self-government in colonial days, and the third generation which is now engaged in a mad rush for wealth. The first took its stand upon the inalienable rights of man and made a fight which shook the world. But the leading spirits of the latter are entrenched behind class laws and revel in special privileges. It will require another revolution to overthrow them. That revolution is upon us even now.

James B. Weaver, 1892

At the turn of the century, two-fifths of the American population lived on farms. In the United States today, less than 3 percent of the people produce food for all the rest, and more food yet for shipment abroad. There were 6.7 million farm families as recently as 1936; in 1969, just 2.7 million.[1] For a nation whose identity and values had substantially taken shape in a rural-frontier environment, this shriveling became a long, drawn-out trauma. Richard Hofstadter labeled Americans' emotional-sentimental attachment to rural life (at least as they imagine it) the agrarian myth, "a kind of homage that Americans have paid to the fancied innocence of their origins."[2] Last stands against oblivion were staged by rural America in the 1890s, then again in the 1920s and 1930s. Even as farmers' sons and daughters moved to towns and cities, one of the primary aims of the nation's reform agenda became the preservation of the small family farm.

When "progress" came to the late nineteenth century farm, it arrived in the form of commercial agriculture, mechanization, the cultivation of fresh lands beyond potential demand for output, and excess production. This has been typical of progress in the United States; it generally damages or destroys the life patterns and values associated with old status quos.

In the 1890s, rural America reacted with Populism. And "Populism," as Hofstadter remarked, "was the first modern political movement of practical importance in the United States to insist that the federal government has some responsibility for the common weal; indeed, it was the first such movement to attack seriously the problems created by industrialism."[3] Historians have viewed Populism in various ways, from a "radical" impulse of frustrated country entrepreneurs to a great democratic, cooperative movement crusading against besieging banks and corporations.[4]

We can best examine Populism against the backdrop of the general economic crisis which fell like a gray curtain in 1893. This intensified long-term difficulties which had already plagued agriculture, especially southern and western agriculture, for years. The decade of the nineties brought on the first great crisis in the politics of the industrial era. This was not the only depression in living memory; in the past, repeated declines had produced waves of mortgage foreclosures. Depressions forced surviving farmers to borrow; so did purchases of land and the new equipment which mechanized American agriculture. Meantime real farm prices dropped steadily——but the value of the dollar rose. This deflation marked up debts by hiking the value of the money used to pay them back. And the dollars became more difficult to come by because crop prices kept slipping. Loans were scarce in the South and West anyway, and when a farmer got credit it usually came at high interest. Ultimately most loan money came out of the northeastern money market, so that Wall Street became an easy villain in the story. Another villain, the railroads, levied charges on freight which could not entirely be passed on to consumers.

If we cut through the billowing agrarian rhetoric and a good deal of agrarian political philosophy to examine rural demands in light of the concrete economic constraints which farmers faced, then we can understand Populism at its most elemental level in terms of what most of its supporters really wanted. Without focusing on what they were after, the movement remains literally unintelligible.

In the presidential election of 1892, the Populist candidate, James B. Weaver of Iowa, polled more than a million votes running on a platform written for the new party's first national convention, at Omaha. "We believe," the platform read, "that the powers of government——in other words, of the people——should be expanded . . . as rapidly and as far as the good sense of an intelligent people and the teachings of experience shall justify, to the end that oppression, injustice, and poverty shall eventually cease in the land." The platform had a good deal to say about the conditions of urban workers, and averred that "the interests of rural and civic labor are the same; their enemies are identical." It called for railroad nationalization, together with nationalization of the telephone and telegraph systems. ("We believe that the time has come when the railroad corporations will either own the people or the people must own the railroads"; "the government should own and operate the railroads in the interest of the people.") The platform demanded an expanded, governmental, flexible currency system, including inflation through the "free and unlimited coinage of silver and gold at the present legal ratio of sixteen to one." It included a subtreasury plan envisioning farmers' depositing nonperishable commodities in government warehouses, then borrowing against them. The platform called for the limitation of governmental revenues, a graduated income tax, a postal savings system, and the prohibition of land ownership by aliens. In addition to the platform, but not actually part of it, certain "resolutions expressive of the sentiment of this convention" were adopted. These called for shorter hours for workers and other labor measures, tax reduction, liberal veterans' pensions, immigration restriction, the Australian (secret) ballot, the initiative and referendum, limitation of the President and Vice-President to a single term, and the direct election of U.S. senators, and opposed "any subsidy or national aid to any private corporation for any purpose."[5] The Populists had very concrete political reasons for reaching out to labor—urban workers if not farm labor! They needed the votes.

The most notable characteristic of the Omaha platform, indeed, is not its democracy or its humanitarianism but its self-interestedness. Over the past century, a great deal of American reform has originated in the flight of different groups (capitalists, workers, farmers) from a free market economy.[6] Economic by its very nature, grass roots in its origin, Populism represents a primitive instance of a phenomenon which would become common in the twentieth century: business interests seeking to use government to rationalize their operations. True enough, Populism placed a heavy emphasis on redistributing power and wealth[7]—in demanding inflation, farmers called for nothing less than their own form of subsidy. They wanted to benefit from the hidden tax which inflation imposes on consumers. Previously, they had enjoyed the subsidy of cheap land, which, yielding an agricultural bounty and financial disaster, ironically helped bring on the demand for inflation, the new subsidy. The fresh dimension in Populism in contrast to prior reform drives lay in its cry for federal help. Thorstein Veblen observed at the time that "the classic phrase is no longer to read 'life, liberty and the pursuit of happiness'; what is to be insured to every free born American citizen under the new dispensation, is 'life, liberty and the *means* of happiness.'"[8] Behind Populist rhetoric lay the hardest sort of economic reality, specifically, who would take money from whom.

Superficially, Populism failed. Most farmers ultimately did not go along with the movement. Many who did "were committed to the reform cause in no greater depth than the mortgage that hung over their heads," as O. Gene Clanton puts it.[9] Workers and farmers might jointly identify as "producers," but workers had no interest in inflation or higher food prices. In this case, their self-interest clashed with the Populists'.[10] Samuel Gompers grumbled that the party was comprised "mainly of *employing* farmers without any regard to the interest of the *employed* farmers of the country districts or the mechanics and laborers of the industrial centres."[11] Strictly speaking, Gompers was unfair, but he had no doubt where the lines of interest ran.

Populism had a mixed upshot in the end. Eventually, much of what the Populists wanted saw enactment, including, in effect, the subtreasury scheme. The Farmers Alliance movement from which Populism sprang produced the world's first big cooperatives.[12] Yet along with its cry for government aid, Populism harbored a deep and traditional agrarian suspicion of power, and its ambivalence toward government produced odd results. In Nebraska, for example, Populist lawmakers reduced outlays for prisons, homes for the aged, industrial schools, and asylums.[13]

From 1897 into the early 1920s, agriculture enjoyed one of its most prosperous eras. The agrarian political vision shrank, from broadly transforming national crusades led by farmers toward more circumscribed campaigns specifically in the farmers' own behalf.[14] The voice of those who remained on the land would be heard less on the soap box now, and more in whispers in legislative corridors.

Progressivism and the Problem of Focus

> Millions of people in the United States find it hard to think that anything is seriously the matter in so prosperous and comfortable a country. . . . [But] a large minority of the American people, which is likely soon to be a majority, feels dissatisfied and resentful and is bound to make things different. Unless that movement is checked, within sixteen years there will be a Socialist President of the United States.
>
> Albert Bushnell Hart, 1912

Among the many factors which can work to circumscribe the influence of a reform movement, ambivalence has proved one of the most important. Ambivalence has undermined the nation's policies toward big business and antitrust. The woman movement has been forever plagued by it. So too in the case of blacks: ambivalence has affected a huge group of people who might have moved one way or might have gone another, but wound up at times heading in two or more directions at once——for example, toward integration on one hand and black nationalism on the other.

One of the cardinal features of the progressive movement was its ambivalence. From this derived a perennial struggle for focus.

After a fashion, progressivism emerged out of the depression of the 1890s. The confrontation between two patterns of thought, Robert H. Walker has written——"one centering on individualism and laissez-faire, the other on collective welfare and social controls——has never again been so stark as it was in the 1890s."[1] Earlier political battles over culture (race, ethnicity, religion, mores, education) were substantially displaced by the economic struggles which swept through in mid-decade, climaxing in the Bryan campaign.

While the slump drew some people to the right, it radicalized others. The middle class took fright at the depression, coupled with the agrarian unrest, class antagonism, labor troubles, and violence it bred. Yet the depression's effects were not entirely divisive. David P. Thelen has argued that it "drove Americans to make common cause across the social barriers of age, nativity, occupation, and religion."[2] And ultimately large elements of the middle class became reformist.

In response to the depression, new precedents emerged. As a reaction to political prodding and interest-group pressure, Washington awkwardly attempted to stir the economy back to health. In this sense, 1893 foreshadowed 1929. Public demand for Washington to stimulate a recovery was something new, and likewise, government's response. Its actions were mostly fumbling; but the precedents remained.[3]

After the depression of the nineties came prosperity, including farm prosperity. Progressivism——at least the middle-class variety——could take some degree of economic well-being and social stability as given. This freed the progressives to experiment, while the pressures of their time led them to experiment. Among these pressures was inflation. Many blamed it on corporate consolidation, which boomed at precisely the same time. Both phenomena gave a spur to social-activist consumerism. "We hear a great deal about the class-consciousness of labor," noted Walter Lippmann. "My own observation is that in America today consumers' consciousness is growing very much faster."[4]

It would be easy to overemphasize the changes that came after 1900. The old ambivalences and reservations remained strong, as did laissez-faire, localism, and individualism. Yet now reform ideas became less monistic, more subtle and complex. Currency and tariff questions receded in importance. Americans began to learn that business had massively corrupted the political system. "Those who now discovered corruption," Richard L. McCormick has written, "grasped that private interest could conflict with the public interest and that government benefits for some groups often hurt others."[5]

While government had become tainted, fresh hope developed that it could help to redeem society. This paradox takes us back to one of the more ironic legacies of the Gilded Age. The civil service movement, with its manifest function of cleaning up government, had produced the latent effect of legitimating the state *because* government had at least to some degree become purified.   Historians have often shown amusement over the energy poured by elitist Gilded Age reformers into civil service reform.   But the spoils system reinforced decentralization and a provincial, localized, disreputable politics.   In order to create a societal willingness to vest increased authority in government, politics had to be cleaned up.   Progressivism carried a strongly bureaucratic thrust which became safe only after reform of the civil service.[6]   Paul P. Van Riper argues that

> the economic reforms considered so essential by others would not have been possible except for civil service reform.   A relatively stable and effective civil service is indispensable for the functioning of the modern state.   The civil service reformers diagnosed better than they knew or than others have usually given them credit.   They did put first things first.[7]

The civil service mugwump had no intention of building a big state.   But political centralization and bureaucracy do go with modernization.[8] Nationalization demanded a modern civil service, and the spoils system seemed an enormous blot on the credibility of government.

This pattern of vesting fresh credibility in government just prior to reform waves which expand the functions of the state would repeat itself in the new century.   If the manifest function of the civil service movement's successor, good government progressivism, involved cleaning up the state, the latent function, once again, legitimated it.   In the Progressive Era, the old drive for a pure civil service gave birth to new demands for bureaucratic expertise and efficiency.   During a reform period, people of competence, notably young people, enter politics, at least for a time.   Their emergence brings additional credibility to the system.   Civil service and progressive good government reform helped to make their entry "safe."

As the twentieth century dawned its first and longest great reform wave swept in.   In 1915 a classic study of contemporary trends appeared: Benjamin Parke De Witt's *The Progressive Movement*.   What was progressivism?   We will let De Witt provide the initial answer.

> In this widespread political agitation that at first sight seems so incoherent and chaotic, there may be distinguished upon examination and analysis three tendencies.   The first of these tendencies is found in the insistence by the best men in all political parties that special, minority, and corrupt influence in government—national, state, and city—be removed; the second tendency is found in the demand that the structure or

machinery of government, which has hitherto been admirably adapted to control by the few, be so changed and modified that it will be more difficult for the few, and easier for the many, to control; and, finally, the third tendency is found in the rapidly growing conviction that the functions of government at present are too restricted and that they must be increased and extended to relieve social and economic distress. These three tendencies with varying emphasis are seen to-day in the platform and program of every political party; they are manifested in the political changes and reforms that are advocated and made in the nation, the states, and the cities; and, because of their universality and definiteness, they may be said to constitute the real progressive movement.[9]

Our examination of progressivism will focus in particular upon the last of De Witt's three themes, the governmental theme.

The country which Americans inhabited in 1915, when De Witt published his book, was rapidly changing. Penrod had already begun to fade, but Studs Lonigan had yet to appear. A sense of confidence, a spirit of "practical idealism"——the term came up frequently——mingled with the anxious feeling that urbanism and industrialism were brushing aside things of value. "Most Americans in the Progressive Era," Henry F. May has written, "believed that institutions and methods needed to be changed but that ultimate values and goals could be taken for granted."[10]

A very great deal has been said about the limitations of progressivism and the progressive system of values. Historians at one time thought that the New Deal descended directly from Populism and progressivism, but many studies have disabused us of too-easy correlations. By and large, the progressives looked at government intervention and authority with ambivalence. Although they often conceded the demands of different interest groups, a ready response to group pressures had not yet achieved legitimacy in American society. Such legitimacy did not emerge until the New Deal.[11] On the subject of democracy, progressivism seemed almost schizophrenic. Woman suffrage and the direct election of United States senators, for instance, dramatically opened up the political process. Yet at the same time a powerful drive erupted to take issues out of the normal political channels and turn them over to supposedly more "efficient" experts and bureaucrats. Dark strands of nativism and racism wound their way through the fabric of progressive egalitarianism. Humanitarian impulses coexisted with a desire to control behavior as part of a politics of Uplift. Progressivism embodied an abundance of religiosity, sermonizing, and utopianism, as well as a heavy dose of moral Victorianism. Its impulse to regulate private behavior——drinking, drugs, prostitution, and the like——made it one of the ancestors of modern conservatism. Progressives devoted great attention to the realm of values and ideas, discussing means and identifying ends. But the implementation of goals which seemed laudable and concrete sometimes broke down in confusion or indecision.

As one of their legacies, the progressives left a large body of ideas; *"ideas,"* writes Otis L. Graham, Jr.,

> were their chief product. They . . . had unbounded faith in exhortation and revelation. A basic progressive belief was in the possibility of a conscious re-ordering and subsequent control of society and its direction, a re-ordering accomplished by a public awakened by ideas, a control guided by trained intelligence and backed by right values.[12]

Many progressives devoted themselves to thought and to prescription: writing, educating, analyzing, philosophizing, theorizing. Like other Americans, they tended to boil complicated problems down into issues of morality or of personal responsibility. This at least had the virtue of making the questions seem more understandable. Progressives shared a deep belief in the efficacy of exposure and publicity. Some progressive faiths——for example, in the possibilities for constructive change if only the public could be educated, or in the potentialities of supposedly detached bureaucratized expertise, or even in leadership itself——appear terribly naive to the jaded mind of the late twentieth century. But of these ideas collectively, we can only say that at one time or another they had to be explored.

They competed with other faiths. Some writers have thought of the progressive period as an era of innocence. One wonders just how innocent any age could be which featured, for example, such labor-management violence or outbreaks of terrorism. (William McKinley fell victim, after all, to an anarchist. That mad act opened the door to the twentieth century reform presidency.) "We think Russia is on the verge of a tremendous social upheaval," wrote business theorist Arthur Jerome Eddy in 1913; "we may be quite as near one ourselves."[13]

Progressivism, though fundamentally political, had to do with far more than politics. A remarkably broad and complex phenomenon, it endeavored at once to preserve the value system of a fading America and to come to terms with the organizational transformations of the future. This helps to explain some of the progressive ambivalences and dualisms, for example, the tension between individualism and governmentalism. This tension went unresolved; it remains unresolved today. Clearly, though, individualism was a far stronger strain in progressivism than it would be in the New Deal. Middle-class progressives liked to frame their thinking around the idea of the national, or the general, interest, which did not necessarily mesh with the demands of special interests. A major progressive theme called for smoothing over class differences and avoiding anything which smacked of "class legislation."

Another strong theme in progressivism was opposition to the political machine (even though some reformist machines did emerge). The New Deal, pivoting on class strife and special favors to groups, became the political machine writ large, on a national scale. It did far less moralizing than the progressives, preoccupying itself less with the spiritual and selfless and more with the concrete and material. In part, I think, anti-machine progressivism stemmed from the progressives' deep concern about the nation's moral state. We might expect an anxiety of this sort to produce ambiguous responses, which it did. In contrast, the very nature of the economic collapse the New Deal inherited dictated an unambiguous reaction. As Graham has pointed out, progressivism de-emphasized material issues as the coin of American politics. Instead, progressives favored more abstruse

> moral—that is, general—concerns. . . . Note that the moral and the general were synonymous, and that which was unworthy turned out to be the private, the partial, interest. This, if a great number of old reformers may be believed, was an essential part of the progressive concern.[14]

The perspective Graham describes reflected, I suspect, at least two things: a desire to elevate political thought and discourse above the level of the Gilded Age, and the fear of a dangerous clash of interests which the "wrong" actions by government might unleash.

A good deal of scholarship has conclusively proved that we should never make the mistake of equating progressivism with the New Deal. This is particularly so if we focus upon the realm of values and ideas, at least among those who recorded theirs. Its values, indeed its very concern with them, make progressivism distinct among twentieth century reform movements.

What does interlock progressivism with later movements, what makes it at one with them, is its *results*. We have focused too much, I think, on what the progressives said, insufficiently on what they actually did. And if we do turn to the realm of practice, we find progressivism far closer than we might otherwise imagine to the New Deal. Often, as we shall see, these similarities resulted from the inclination of progressives to talk one way but to behave another—from an extraordinary gap between rhetoric and reality. The issue did arise, quite centrally, of who would manage the nation, of the fundamental relationship between the public and private sectors. And the rhetoric-reality gap developed inevitably; it took a huge storm of protest to produce any change at all. Reform as practiced by a Wilson or Theodore Roosevelt involved a great deal of moralizing alongside a good deal of horse trading and compromise. In other words, the progressives, although moralistic, behaved *politically*. Appeals to higher values had a real political resonance in that era and served to clothe naked decisions on power in appealing style.

Some progressives concluded that the task of coming to terms with the new century would require making the society less democratic; others sought to meet the future in the opposite way, by mobilizing new groups into the political process. Many progressives believed in direct democracy because they had faith in the wisdom and good sense of the public. This lay behind numerous political reforms of the era, to give power to the people. One reason for espousing "direct democracy" —primaries, the initiative, referendum, and recall, direct election of U.S. senators, or any other technique of mass participation—was to employ the electorate as a lever against entrenched power. The progressives did not merely take an interest in "the people" as an abstract ideal; they wanted to *use* votes to drive their enemies from power.[15]

The growing impulse toward "collective action to control one's surrounding environment," as Samuel P. Hays puts it, influenced economic and professional groups—industry, commerce, workers, farmers, and many others.

> In almost every field . . . the possibility of common action to exercise control over the conditions that affected particular occupational situations arose spontaneously. In almost every case it involved a marked shift in the tactics of control from individual and generalized outburst and protest, to a focused, often highly limited and highly technical approach to specific problems in the economic system. Control was meaningless if action was diffuse and general; but organized influence could be brought to bear on specific points in the larger system with some degree of effectiveness.

Among farmers, for example, a scattershot ideological blast (e.g., "nationalize the railroads") gave way to regulating certain practices which threatened agricultural shippers.[16] The "organizational revolution"[17] meant that reform would increasingly amount to brokerage between powerful pressure groups.

Progressivism undulated constantly, with coalitions appearing and dissolving around issues and candidates. It exhibited a complex, baffling diversity of causes, people, and scenes of action (federal, state, local, regional). And it changed. Different types of progressives behaved in different sorts of ways. In any period, a politician may convey more than one image to a constituency, and I suspect that during the Progressive Era, a good many politicians carried unusual multiplicities of images. The free-floating nature of progressivism, the fact that so many issues appeared and disappeared, increased its possibilities of success by remarkably multiplying opportunities. Yet it also sustained a set of bobbing targets, often very difficult to hit. So many subtypes of progressives and substyles of progressivism appeared that one scholar has argued that "'the progressive movement' never existed." "A diffuse progressive 'era' may have occurred," writes Peter G. Filene, "but a progressive 'movement' did not."[18]

Filene overstates. We would do well to conceive of the progressive movement as a sort of laboratory in which scientists from different fields experimented on different sorts of problems, their work sometimes running parallel but oftentimes not. Seen this way, progressivism (or *progressivisms*) becomes the exploratory phase of twentieth century American reform. A large number of problems needed addressing (or else no experimentation would have been taking place); but people were more relaxed about them than in the thirties because they had no general economic collapse to confront. Therefore, behind all the moralizing, the experiments could proceed with a certain dispassionateness, with the freedom to speculate and philosophize. The progressives—the middle-class cohort of progressives, anyway—had a passion for ideas logically and clearly thought through, for a dialogue, in effect, between the citizenry and its leaders, and for careful consideration prior to action.

Some partisans of the New Deal have found this approach slow and ponderous, and surely the New Deal could not have proceeded this way. But the New Deal was constructed in substantial measure upon the progressive body of thought and on the concrete precedents it had produced. The fact that the New Deal often plunged ahead now and contemplated later reflected its times and FDR himself; but it also reflected the existence of a body of ideas already worked out. The recent concern, shared by a number of students of our reform tradition, with the results of operating the way the New Deal did, echoes the reservations John Dewey expressed in 1935: "Experimental method is not just messing around nor doing a little of this and a little of that in the hope that things will improve. Just as in the physical sciences, it implies a coherent body of ideas, a theory, that gives direction to effort."[19]   To this and to its recent echoes we might rejoin, "How progressive!"

Progressivism, then, became a kaleidoscope of causes in which conditions continuously changed. It varied from state to state and from section to section. Like Populism, it was provincial and agrarian—but unlike Populism, also national, urban, middle-class, and working-class. However uncertainly, it tended to conjoin the two fundamental pro-reform interest groups, farmers and workers, in an uneasy but, during the Wilson era, fruitful political relationship. It involved both major parties. It had a claim to legitimacy which Populism never shared. That process of legitimation had begun as early as 1896, when Bryan had co-opted Populism; after 1901, Theodore Roosevelt simply co-opted Bryan.

Characteristic progressive ambivalences and disagreements revolved around the role of the state and the corporation in American life, the place of the city and of the new immigrants, and the organization of labor. Progressivism cut a broader swath than Populism had, but with a duller blade. A key explanation for this, no doubt, lies in the nature and immediacy of the problems the two movements confronted. Populism arose out of economic chaos and collapse. Apart from slips in 1907 and 1913, the Progressive Era was prosperous.

Yet progressivism did not fail to address the basic questions of economic reality. Issues summoned by the rapid growth of a corporate economy, which appeared to threaten the country's treasured individualism and to promise oligopoly and monopoly in exchange, took center stage. Organized labor wanted a place at government's table alongside business. So did farmers. The cities were mushrooming, filling rapidly with immigrants from new, disparate ethnic strains. Considerable fear existed among middle-class progressives of both a burgeoning plutocracy and a burgeoning, restive, "foreign" proletariat. We can view progressivism in very considerable measure as a movement to preserve and adjust a value system which seemed (and to a great extent was) threatened by all this. Progressives did tend to reduce these difficulties to a battle between "the people" and "the interests." Big business got blamed for a whole gamut of problems——inflation, restricting opportunity, urban troubles, controversial sources of immigration. For reformers the challenge was to go beyond blaming the corporations, and beyond the vague demand that government do something to control big business, and to agree on precisely what ought to be done. Here lay the problem: goals varied, and frequently conflicted.

If progressivism represented the idealistic phase of American reform, we must set this idealism, too, in perspective. First, it provided a necessary means of mobilizing a still-sentimental public: idealism was politically vital. It helped to legitimate politics, to distinguish it from the blandness and corruption of the Gilded Age and from the discord of the nineties. In this way, idealism provided a high but relatively safe tone. It served to lubricate the searching and questioning of the period. And their idealism once again reflected the progressives' inflated but no doubt politically popular expectations of the mass public.

Any movement designed to bring change will best serve its own purposes by beginning, at least, on a note of idealism and of moral rectitude.[20]   The time for elbows-on-the-table bargaining will always arrive; it is generally better to mobilize first idealistically, and get down to green eyeshades later. Raw, bitter, unending confrontations tend to produce a sense of dirtiness and disillusionment in the public mind. If possible, reformers should reserve these for late in the game. Idealism asks, "What do we want?" Realism responds, "Here is what you can get." Better to begin with the first, then move on to the second. Progressive idealism may seem old-fashioned or sentimental today, but it provided an excellent way of opening the door to twentieth century reform. And although the ideological justifications for much of later nineteenth and early twentieth century reform bear a quaint Victorian obsolescence, many of the platforms, policies, and measures these ideas spawned have remained resilient.[21]

The searching, probing, and questioning of the era identified a great many issues, provided a few answers, and produced an enormous body of literature. It was a literature of muckraking journalism, for one thing. As Robert H. Wiebe has pointed out, "attributing omnipotence to abstractions——the Trust and Wall Street, the Political Machine and the System of Influence——had become a national habit by the end of the nineteenth century."[22] Highly significant books appeared as well, among them Henry Demarest Lloyd's *Wealth Against Commonwealth*, J. Allen Smith's *The Spirit of American Government*, Charles A. Beard's *An Economic Interpretation of the Constitution of the United States*, Thorstein Veblen's *The Theory of the Leisure Class*, Walter Weyl's *The New Democracy*, Walter Lippmann's *Drift and Mastery*, and especially Herbert Croly's *The Promise of American Life*. People tested out ideas as they tested the new airplane or the new automobile. And if some of their ideas seem as antiquated now as the Model T, one envies their sense of possibility.

Monistic, utopian, panacean proposals belonged to a certain phase of American reform, the late nineteenth century phase of Henry George and Edward Bellamy.[23] Too pat, too simple, these panaceas failed to come to terms with the new complexities that gave them their tone of anguish. But other writers who followed, such as Croly and Lippmann, moved well beyond. Certainly a gap continued to exist between rhetoric and reality. The literature of the progressive period was very heavily a literature of exposure, of diagnosis as distinct from prescription. But those searching for solutions to problems today might well examine, for example, Charlotte Perkins Gilman's *Women and Economics* (1898),[24] an often profound exploration of relations between the sexes. And those who question too easily the seriousness of progressive intent might read *Philip Dru: Administrator; A Story of Tomorrow, 1920-1935*.[25] The book was published anonymously in 1912. On reading a passage or two one can instantly perceive that no Dickens wrote it. In fact, Edward M. House wrote it a short time after he met Woodrow Wilson. House's fanciful novel has a benevolent dictator taking over the United States government, suspending the Constitution——and pushing through wide-ranging reforms. House became Wilson's confidant and chief adviser.

Regarding the much-derided progressive notion of the "people" versus the "interests": save for the New Deal, which revived it, no subsequent reform generation has put things in a simpler, more politically advantageous way. This was a reductionism which won votes. How many present-day *radicals* would label it a false dichotomy? Here again we should hesitate to condescend. A shift toward reform will be signalled by increased concern for the broad needs of the masses as opposed to the rights of a handful——a change in emphasis from property to more general human well-being.[26] Today we should find it easy, too, to appreciate progressive anxieties about monopoly capitalism. Much of the confusion of goals and methods which appeared, for example, in the 1912 campaign speeches of Woodrow Wilson represented the kind of sorting out inevitable in a transitional period. And one wonders how many Chief Executives in the late twentieth century might have said this, as Theodore Roosevelt did in addressing the Progressive party convention that year:

> The first charge on the industrial statesmanship of the day is to prevent human waste. The dead weight of orphanage and depleted craftsmanship, of crippled workers and workers suffering from trade diseases, of casual labor, of insecure old age, and of household depletion due to industrial conditions are, like our depleted soils, our gashed mountainsides and flooded river-bottoms, so many strains upon the national structure, draining the reserve strength of all industries and showing beyond all peradventure the public element and public concern in industrial health.
>
> Ultimately we desire to use the government to aid, as far as can safely be done, in helping the industrial tool-users to become in part tool-owners, just as our farmers now are. Ultimately the government may have to join more efficiently than at present in strengthening the hands of the working men who already stand at a high level, industrially and socially, and who are able by joint action to serve themselves. But the most pressing and immediate need is to deal with the cases of those . . . who are not only in need themselves, but because of their need tend to jeopardize the welfare of those who are better off.[27]

A good deal of hybrid Bismarckianism ran through Teddy Roosevelt, a good deal of emphasis on class accommodation and efficiency and nationalism. But in the New Nationalism Roosevelt evoked the welfare state and, with whatever opacity, pointed toward Social Security, occupational safety and health, the minimum wage, and many other government operations now taken for granted. Roosevelt's social justice advocacy in 1912 was doubtless more advanced than middle-class progressivism as a whole. Still, as a body of inquiry, the literature and the rhetoric of progressivism to which he contributed comprise the most important corpus of reform thought in the twentieth century. And they bring us to the pivot of our inquiry into the meaning of the Progressive Era.

The generation of Populism and progressivism became the first to define the urban-industrial agenda for what it was and to confront it (if often obliquely). The progressives responded to it in an essentially governmentalist way (if sometimes hesitantly). They reconsidered the whole subject of government aid to business. They made a preliminary decision as to which other groups would receive aid. Progressives talked a good deal of averting class legislation, but passed it anyway (however much they denied it). What class legislation actually amounted to was ultimately a matter of definition. All a progressive had to do in order to deny that a bill for labor or for agriculture amounted to class legislation was simply deny. Ipso facto the measure became a method of serving the general interest without recognizing any specific class. In ignoring their own strictures about class legislation, the progressives responded to the pressures of specific interest groups, though they often camouflaged this in words.

The confrontation with these issues ultimately boiled down to a question of the fear and uses of power. Predominantly middle-class, the progressive impetus carried with it that class's anxiety about the state. But the fear of power concentrated in private hands drove middle-class progressives to government. At first, at least, it was expected that the state which emerged would be powerful but neutral, operating where the middle class saw itself, between or above the clash of interests, and meting out balanced justice.[28] In retrospect, the concept of the neutral government provided a transition between the deeper anti-statism of the Gilded Age and the New Deal broker state. It represented an accommodation to middle-class biases and values.

More than anyone else, Theodore Roosevelt made reform respectable, gave it the probity and propriety of a middle-class *image*. He both publicized the century's new agenda for reform and responded to it; he transformed Washington, and the presidency, into the principal locus of power for dealing with it; and he made the federal government appear a responsible vehicle for advancing the general welfare. He vested reform with legitimacy. Power: again, this lay at the heart of reform. Roosevelt had to demonstrate——ceremonially, at least——that the federal government had more power than Wall Street or the trusts. The question stood at issue when he inherited the presidency. Power constantly hemmed him in, not just the power of the "interests," which he chose quite variably to accommodate or confront, but also power within the Washington establishment. The centralization of reform implied a growing role for the federal government as distinct from the states, and for the President as against Congress. But Roosevelt had to operate within the constraints of the Republican party——*his* party——and of a Republican Congress. TR was the most powerful individual in government and, theoretically, in America; but the second most powerful man in government was the legendary mossback Speaker of the House, Joseph Cannon.

The fadeout of the progressive impulse began before World War I, perhaps as early as 1912, yet around this time progressivism was passing through a significant transition. The change involved economics, class, and interest. Economic issues and the concerns of specific interest groups organized around types of work became more important; agriculture and labor maneuvered for fulfillment of their demands.[29] No single, convenient date or event signalled this shift. We can see signs of it occurring as early as the Roosevelt Administration. Roosevelt's 1912 campaign symbolized it, and the administration of Woodrow Wilson proved pivotal to it. "At this point in the history of American progressivism," Edgar Kemler wrote, "we cross the Great Divide. The progressives outgrew their efforts to reform wicked individuals, bosses and robber barons, and acquired a much broader vision."[30] Kemler overstated things, but his words point clearly to a major transition. The New Nationalism presaged the welfare state. The *New Republic* intellectuals were raising ideas for rebuilding society. Besides Roosevelt, Wilson, and Taft, a fourth candidate ran in 1912, Eugene V. Debs, and that year his Socialist party polled its greatest vote in history. Yet amid all this flux, the man who won the election——the man who ultimately presided over the shift in American reform——at first seemed hesitant, uncertain.

On encountering the 1912 speeches which aired his New Freedom,[31] one might simply conclude that Wilson knew he would win no matter what, and could afford to release a rhetorical fog. Second and third readings fail to clarify things very much; objects appear murkily, then disappear in the mist of words. Wilson had very broad concerns, among them the distribution of power, class conflict, alienation, dehumanization, oligarchy, democracy, the eclipse of freedom, corporatism and trustification, and the national character. For all his tentativeness, vagueness, and lack of coherence or consistency, he presented an extraordinarily wide-ranging critique of the country's social and economic problems. But the solutions were as narrow as the critique was broad. Ambivalent toward accepting large industry as a permanent fact of American economic life, Wilson became trapped between Roosevelt's view, which the two men shared, that big business had simply become inevitable, and a pining for the creative individualism of the previous century. Unwilling to risk class strife with an explicit program of class legislation, Wilson tried to ignore a permanent working class whose existence Roosevelt already knew had made the welfare state a necessity.

Wilson consistently denounced paternalistic, "big-brother government" and seemed to set his face squarely against granting special privileges to any group under any circumstances, whether labor, farmers, or business. Speaking above all in behalf of the middle class, he talked of reconciling and unifying classes but not of recognizing them. He tried as much as possible to avoid the subject of labor and social welfare legislation altogether. On the other hand, he left the back door open to such measures through heroic feats of rhetorical ambiguity. Many of the problems he identified stemmed from the existence of a permanent working class, and to deal with those problems he would have to head in the direction Roosevelt pointed. Yet Wilson remained substantially noncommittal on government centralization and intervention in the economy. He had not worked out a final, comprehensive series of approaches to the larger problems he identified. Nor did he fully comprehend the inadequacy of strictly economic solutions to them. His prescriptions, in fact, utterly failed to match his diagnosis. Yet for all its incoherence, the New Freedom harbored two vital qualities—flexibility and a focus on economic trends and their implications. Like FDR's campaign rhetoric twenty years later, Wilson's left open many possibilities.

The progressives had a way of seeing the future, then recoiling from it into platitudes. Yet the future had already become clear enough. As Robert H. Wiebe observes of Wilson:

> The nature of the program . . . fell largely beyond the President's control. By 1913, as the new Congress met in special session, years of struggle had already defined the issues it would debate. A full complement of private groups stood at hand to demand their due, and their firmness betokened scant leeway for the politicians, legislative or executive. The challenge before Wilson, therefore, lay in balancing, in imaginative compromise, rather than in evoking or initiating.[32]

"We are just upon the threshold of a time," Wilson observed, "when the systematic life of this country will be sustained, or at least supplemented, at every point by governmental activity."[33]

Ultimately, in the realm of antitrust and banking reform, ambivalence and ambiguity prevailed. Wilson compromised the Federal Reserve Act through poor appointments to the Federal Reserve Board. The Federal Trade Commission Act and the Clayton Antitrust Act, crippled in the drafting, were crippled again through weak, procorporate appointments to the new FTC. But if these measures reflect (as one student of the subject has put it) "the failure of nerve that characterized so much of progressive reform,"[34] one can only respond that the failure of nerve continues on today. We shall encounter it again.

It is true of the New Freedom——just as of the New Deal——that some of the most impressive changes it ushered in affected workers and farmers. In 1912 Wilson had employed rhetorical loopholes which left him free to opt for class legislation if he wished. In time, he so wished. Its original agenda largely behind it, the Wilson Administration took wing in 1915-16, guided by its opportunities more than by a well-conceived philosophy.[35] Various reasons account for all this. The Democratic party consisted of sharply urban and sharply rural constituencies, precisely the interests that would inevitably apply the greatest pressure on a Democratic President. Wilson was a politician, after all, indeed, a political scientist. As the nature of progressivism changed, his response had to change too. He needed votes. Other considerations probably concerned him as well: the matter of social justice pure and simple; pressure from business; a need to avert strikes; and——very important as well as tied to the strike issue——mobilization for war. In order to dampen the class conflict Wilson feared, he had to bargain with classes and interests, and ultimately to expand the state.

Organized labor as a whole stood to benefit from this. Among other things, Wilson's administration became the first to provide continuing support for workers' rights to collective bargaining and union recognition, and the administration took a stab at ending child labor. The Wilsonians, complained William Howard Taft, had begun "surrendering everything to Gompers."[36]

Agriculture benefited too. Practically from the day he arrived in Washington, William Gibbs McAdoo——Wilson's Secretary of the Treasury and a full-time promoter——manipulated the money market and employed a host of other methods to support farmers, especially the Democratic party's demanding rural constituency in the South. Specific legislative concessions went far toward meeting desires which rural America had nourished for years.

Something else had begun to emerge as well, signs of a distinctly urban brand of liberalism.[37] This represented a very different approach from progressive styles which tried to solve urban problems by reforming morals (anti-vice ordinances, Sunday blue laws, prohibition) or by unhinging political institutions ("clean" government, restrictions on democratic practices, expertise, limited outlays, efficiency). "In the main," John D. Buenker has written, "'urban liberalism' included a desire for government intervention in the economy to protect the less fortunate, the welfare state, a tax policy based primarily upon the ability to pay, a 'one man, one vote' political philosophy, and a determined opposition to legislated morality." The principal vehicle for this sort of approach was the Democratic party. The impetus arose from the values and needs of urban, new-stock, working-class constituencies, as well as from the politicians representing them, politicians who in a number of industrial states became progressivism's driving wedge.[38] Urban liberalism crested in the New Deal, but despite lawmakers' willingness to go only so far, it was also very much a phenomenon of the late Progressive Era. Through the progressive years, a politics of class assumed increasing political importance.[39] Some middle-class reformers were shrewd enough to run clean administrations which provided urban services. Even the "last hurrah" political machines of legend began to change. Most became constructively reformist, and a new brand of urban politician moved into ascendancy, symbolized by Tammany's Al Smith and Robert Wagner.

"The inauguration of the national welfare state during the New Deal Era was not a sudden departure from the nation's past history," Buenker observes.

> The programs it embodied were essentially a broadening of those that had been developed in most of the major industrial states during the Progressive Era. Then, for the first time, serious efforts were launched to cope with such effects of industrial urban living as child and female labor, inadequate housing, low wages, excessive hours, dangerous working conditions, industrial accidents, and lack of retirement benefits. Although no state provided solutions for these problems in this period, the attempts at least established precedents for more comprehensive measures in future years.[40]

In pressing their programs, urban new-stock lawmakers relied on a good deal of old-stock, Protestant, humanitarian support, even as they resisted the Yankee-Protestant impulse toward Uplift. They got backing as well from elements of organized labor, social workers, and intellectuals. Coalition politics proved vital. The symbiosis of issues led new-stock lawmakers to support labor unions, tax reform, expansion of the franchise, and the regulation of business. Above all, urban liberalism stood for welfare measures.

Although urban liberalism flourished primarily at the state and city levels, it also surfaced in Washington, notably during the Wilson era.

One way or another, Wilsonian reform touched virtually all the important issues of the period. As John Milton Cooper, Jr., has written, "Wilson stopped short of openly approving competition of interests or frankly celebrating governmental favor to the less fortunate, but he came close to those positions."[41] No solidly organized group failed to gain something, yet neither did any achieve a thoroughgoing ascendancy over the others.[42]

The war, in turn, set new precedents for massive federal intervention in the economy. It brought business into the open arms of government, their collaboration permanently heightened.[43] The war also produced a boom in agriculture and led to unprecedented (if mixed) gains for labor. Old Populists doubtless smiled when the administration nationalized the railroads. And the war produced great victories for feminism and prohibitionism. Yet the ambivalence and internal division of the Wilsonian mind remained unresolved. Anyone who thought that all these experiments would survive the conflict was mistaken: the administration dropped most of them as if it had suddenly grasped hold of a rose stem[44] (though precedents remained for the New Deal). Ultimately, like progressivism more generally, Wilsonianism remained an amalgam of old-style antimonopolism and anti-special privilege rhetoric living uneasily with new-style social welfarism and the encouragement of organization, consolidation, and bureaucracy.

Placing a tremendous emphasis on the concept of fulfilling the "general" or "public" interest, rather than "special," "selfish" interests, progressivism took that concept about as far as it could go. The intensification of interest-group politics in the era clearly showed where the future lay. The whole of the progressive experience legitimized further expansion of the state by cleaning up government, turning it into a more effective instrument, and offering something gratifying (if often maidenly tea and crumpets) to nearly everyone. World War I speeded up the process. The next step, as some reformers saw, would involve interest-group politics straight-out. The progressive concept of the public interest came to seem antique until the 1970s or so, and devil take the unorganized hindmost.[45]

The New Deal:
Selling the Welfare State

In a fundamental sense, the major goal of early-twentieth-century liberalism was to make all white Americans at least middle-class.

Eric F. Goldman

Looking back over the span of this century, we can see that the Progressive Era was primal in nurturing ideas for reform, and the 1930s the great decade when ideas became programs. A remarkable range of programs was, in effect, sold to the country by the foremost political marketing expert of the modern presidency, Franklin D. Roosevelt. It all happened in a brief period of time, during years convulsed by individual desperation and class confrontation.

E. E. Schattschneider has written that "the crucial problem in politics is the management of conflict."   "Every major conflict overwhelms, subordinates and blots out a multitude of lesser ones," and "the unequal intensity of conflicts determines the shape of the political system." "The definition of the alternatives is the supreme instrument of power. . . . He who determines what politics is about runs the country, because the definition of the alternatives is the choice of conflicts, and the choice of conflicts allocates power." "The substitution of conflicts is the most devastating kind of political strategy. . . . In politics the most catastrophic force in the world is the power of irrelevance which transmutes one conflict into another and turns all existing alignments inside out." And finally, "the party which is able to make its definition of the issues prevail is likely to take over the government."[1]

The Great Depression, together with the response of Hoover and his party to it, turned the political system left over from the 1890s inside out. It swept largely cultural questions of the twenties from the stage by overwhelming them in importance. It substituted a new set of conflicts that dissolved the Republican majority. What the massive dislocations and unemployment did was to focus attention on the economy——to provide a very convincing demonstration that it, and not just individuals, as the Horatio Algerists would have it, suffered from mighty flaws. Only government provided a recourse, an out. The Depression gave Roosevelt Democrats an opportunity to make their definition of the issues prevail. Any President who wanted to keep power after 1929 had to respond *successfully* to the demands of labor and farm interests. There was simply no choice.

Since the New Deal was very substantially an exercise in buying and selling, the process by which this occurred commands our attention. We will call it *marketing* reform. The precondition for a marketing situation is that someone needs something, and that someone else wants to sell it. If the sale goes well, then both the buyer and seller feel satisfied, and the seller can expect repeat business.

The thirties saw the emergence of all sorts of groups and organizations which provided shifting but remarkably dynamic vehicles for reform. The institutions pushing for change put pressure on government. Government responded in varying ways and degrees. If we envision the system as a dynamic marketing operation, then we can easily visualize interest groups "selling" causes to government, and government "selling" solutions back to the original proponents in order to win at the polls. Hence, for example: agricultural organizations worked to market programs for federal intervention to the Hoover Administration, and the Hoover Administration tried to countersell its programs to the farmers. The process began all over again when Roosevelt took office.

Marketing reform also involves selling proposals and candidates to individual voters as "consumers."[2] The two big parties comprise the major sellers in this particular marketplace; like other large industries, this one enjoys limited competition. The ascendant party will dominate the political discussion. The voter shops and buys, and the buying (multiplied manyfold) yields a profit to the successful party——victory and the perquisites which accompany it. As in the private marketplace, consumers sometimes show bizarre patterns of product loyalty. Today the marketing of causes and candidates involves all sorts of Madison Avenue techniques and types, as well as predictable strategies ——supposedly new and better products/politics, together with advertising and sales approaches designed to put them over.[3] The presence of advertising specialists and PR experts simply underlines the fact that politics heavily amounts to an exercise in mutual buying and selling.

A variety of "intermediate targets" fall between reformers and their "ultimate targets." One intermediate target may be the public; another, business or the professions; still another, government (as in a battle, for example, between Ralph Nader and General Motors). The reformer may try to alter the target's behavior through "education," "persuasion," or "coercion," and through various substrategies of these (as in the distinction within persuasion between appeals to logic and appeals to the emotions).[4] The reformer may use the personal approach, or operate through the media or political workers. And, of course, all these strategies may be combined in almost infinite variations.

When selling, one constantly has to take account of one's own constituency. "The candidate must develop a marketing strategy not only calculated to win the support of voters but also of the party, contributors, and interest groups."[5] People involve themselves in political causes for a variety of reasons: to achieve tangible ends, but also, perhaps, to feed their own egos through power or status, or to garner favors and rewards. There exists a "phase pattern" which Philip Kotler has described:

> Each individual will pass through several stages marked by growing or abating devotion. The psychological phase pattern in the typical case goes from *enthusiasm* to *frustration* to *reduced expectations* to *adjusted participation*, with occasional returns to earlier emotions with the ups and downs of the

cause's successes.   Some of the participants will drop out, usually those who joined the cause with unrealistic expectations or more personal motives.[6]

And reformers, in particular, quickly encounter the cardinal temptation to oversell their proposals by making extravagant claims about them, claims the changes cannot possibly live up to. Reformers tend especially to concentrate excessively on single proposals, advertising them as panaceas. The very slogans New Freedom, New Frontier, and Great Society hint at overblown promises.

In order to produce the potential for such a big transaction as the New Deal, the nation had to go through a more than three-year wringer under Herbert Hoover. Hoover's battle against the Depression lasted just about as long as U.S. involvement in World War II. In fact, both Hooverites and New Dealers, as William E. Leuchtenburg has brilliantly shown, had a way of drawing a parallel between their antidepression struggle and fighting a war.[7] Under Hoover's generalship, the country had lost one battle after another. By 1932 it was desperate for a success.

Hoover did more than any of his presidential predecessors to stem a depression.[8] In this sense he was a vital transitional figure in the history of American government. But he did not do enough. His program initially relied on voluntarism, with Washington serving largely as cheerleader. This did not work. His second approach involved the government more directly, but not as deeply as Congress demanded. Ultimately he fell back on voluntarism again. Hoover got part way to the finish line but failed to complete the course. As Ellis W. Hawley has put it:

> The shift was not from laissez-faire to a managed economy, but rather from one attempt at management, that through informal private-public cooperation, to other more formal and coercive yet also limited attempts, efforts that still made numerous concessions to individualistic and village ideals.

Hawley describes

> the Hoover years . . . as a distinctive yet integral stage in the continuing process whereby twentieth-century policy-makers have tried to reconcile conflicting visions of a new order with the dreams that they inherited from nineteenth-century liberalism and agrarianism.[9]

Because of the horrendous mess in the private sector which 1929 exposed and complicated, the public sector seemed "clean" by comparison. This, ironically, resulted also from the fact that Hoover had set such a cautious course; voluntarism had not worked. The governmental alternative appeared relatively sane.

For a moment, things simply stalled here. From 1929 to 1932, GNP and industrial output in the United States plunged by nearly half. World unemployment hit an estimated 30 million in 1933. Some 13 million ——nearly one out of two!——were Americans. Now many members of the middle class·could identify, and identify their interests, with the working class and the poor, in part because with 25 percent unemployment, so many middle-class Americans had recently joined them or felt threatened.[10] A veritable passion for security pervaded the decade. FDR announced in his First Inaugural Address that the greatest undertaking of 1933 was "to put people to work."[11]

Roosevelt inherited the ambiguous legacy of progressivism. That movement had arisen from the fears, tensions, and anxieties of an industrializing society, yet it had flowered in a prosperous era. It had summoned an increase in the role of government, but the degree of reliance on government, and at what level, remained in debate. It was heavily made up of the urban and rural middle classes, but also of elements of business and, particularly toward the end, representatives of the working class. Its constituency and concerns were broader than Populism but its prescriptions generally less drastic. It was on the main line of twentieth century American reform in its revolt against some of the formalism and rigidities of earlier patterns of thought, its quest for a middle ground between laissez-faire and socialism, and its reliance on a more active state. In the heat of the greatest depression in history, the New Deal forged this perplexing legacy, together with the experiments of World War I and an admixture of new approaches, into a reform tradition that would dominate American politics for much of the rest of this century.

The term "progressive" had connoted, at least, a faith in progress; in 1929 progress suddenly lurched to a halt. Now reform and recovery became synonymous, and if recovery failed to materialize there must at least be relief. Everything turned visceral and immediate when people could not eat. Unlike earlier reform drives, the New Deal did not endeavor to improve or perfect human beings, but tried instead to improve their conditions of life. "When capitalism was in its ascendency, the progressives could afford the luxury of a Platonic dream," wrote Kemler. "Now with capitalism *in extremis*, all they can ask is that the system keep working and providing a minimum of life's necessities. We have reduced a rich heritage of hopes and dreams to the bare endeavor to make the system work." Kemler, for one, celebrated the new earthiness, feeling that in the past "moral and spiritual objectives have obscured material objectives."[12] True enough, the New Deal represented a certain casting away of Uplift, a "deflation of American ideals," a turning toward concrete social and economic objectives which the federal government could engineer with concrete results through the politics of the broker state. The urban side of progressivism came into its own in the thirties, and with it workers and ethnics. Roosevelt talked consensus but grounded his politics on conflict. Along with the heightened interest-group orientation of the New Deal, it differed from progressivism, too, in its tolerance for and collusion with political machines. And it proved expensive. Reformers as recently as the twenties had had no massive federal spending programs to propose; the thirties took care of that.

More generally, depressions seem to have had a common impact on this society. First, they make conspicuous displays of wealth exceedingly unfashionable. Second, they undercut the Algerist notion that one holds exclusive responsibility for one's own economic fate. And third, they bring large numbers of people together. To a unique degree since Lincoln, at least, New Deal reform tied itself to just one man. Another piece of luck arose from the very smallness of government. When he took office, Roosevelt could in substantial measure mold it into what he wanted, but big government could only be constructed once. No succeeding President enjoyed the same advantage. Lucky in other ways, Roosevelt became the first reform President with the good fortune to confront business in such an extreme state of collapse. The bulk of the twentieth century reform agenda awaited him like a feast on a table. The New Deal simply skimmed off the big issues around which any sort of consensus had developed. As Harold Laski put it in 1940, Roosevelt "has gone for the big things; he has dramatized the issues upon which men know that their lives depend. He has communicated his own eagerness to those upon whose interest he has to rely."[13]

The New Deal was a unique time, more basically, because of where it fell in the history of modern American liberalism. Previously, liberalism had more often than not been an out-movement—a critique. For any movement, out-status affords the luxury of criticism without power. This today's liberals can appreciate, with the encrustations of more than a half century of reform on them. But when the old order collapsed in 1929, the liberals of the thirties stepped into a vacuum. Within it they found extraordinary focus: a narrow slot of time, not a half generation like progressivism; one very primary level of government; and one political party. The New Deal had a distinctly political thrust with one clear leader.

Yet huge obstacles remained. As James L. Sundquist has observed, "the United States is unique among the world's democracies in the extent to which the institutional system is weighted on the side of restraint regardless of the mandate of the people."[14] The New Deal had to operate within the legendary balance of powers, as well as with state and local resistance. It had to coexist with the two-party system. The major parties, as Arthur M. Schlesinger put it, "strive for the common denominator, to please as many as possible and offend as few as possible, with the result that compromise and evasion become the rule."[15] And there were other barriers, not least among them enduring caution in the public mind despite the desperateness of the times.

So, in marketing terms, the proponents of change still had to sell the New Deal to the vast political center over which both parties fought, and to market programs to the Democrats' own coalition of interests and regions, conservatives as well as liberals. A great many of the millions of unemployed were temporarily declassed members of the middle class. Their tolerance for social experimentation never even approached mass approval of a socialist economic system, and their tolerance for the comparatively modest gyrations of the New Deal existed substantially because they had fallen out of class and craved security. Give these people middle-class incomes again and they would become more conservative. Quick movement became crucial.

The New Deal slashed through much of reform's old ambivalence toward government. In Richard Hofstadter's classic epigram: "If the state was believed neutral in the days of T.R. because its leaders claimed to sanction favors for no one, the state under F.D.R. could be called neutral only in the sense that it offered favors to everyone."[16] The urban-labor-ethnic complex, which had started to bubble toward the top as the progressive pot began to cool, reappeared. One of its prime spokesmen, Robert Wagner, now in the Senate, numbered among his other legislative monuments the Social Security Act and the National Labor Relations (Wagner) Act. Antitrust as a war against bigness per se, and ideas about restoring the old competitive order, largely dropped out of the reform lexicon. The New Deal showed a primary interest in distributing goods based upon an acceptance of the corporate system. This also signified a desire to reestablish the new consumer culture that had briefly appeared in the twenties.

American reform has persistently experimented, even when it has sanctimoniously dressed itself as Uplift. But when FDR called for "bold, persistent experimentation" in May 1932, economics came first.[17] His program had a profoundly domestic focus, riveted on the problems of the United States and economically nationalist.[18]

The demands of the thirties allowed the New Deal to enjoy this combination of freedom and focus. Narrowly political, it did little intellectualizing and generated little original thought. Save perhaps for the writings of Thurman Arnold, the New Deal produced nothing approaching the political criticism which had undergirded progressivism. Even the New Deal's friends have criticized its failure to consider, as had the progressives, broader questions, meanings, and values. But it was, after all, a narrow and desperate time. "Private experience," William E. Leuchtenburg has written, "seemed self-indulgent compared to the demands of public life."[19] The emphasis, not just in Washington but throughout the country, on economics, public matters, and the state proved crucial in providing an environment so uniquely accommodating to rapid reform. The moral absolutism[20] which had yielded up the likes of prohibition substantially drained out of reform. The twenties were repudiated. "Escapist" became the most damning term of the 1930s, and a great deal in the twenties had been escapist.[21] Yet reform's new emphasis on systems and institutions, on engineering and administration, symbolized at least some degree of dehumanization. Not just individual morals and behavior, but individuals themselves, counted less. This left liberalism vulnerable to charges of absolute relativism (or, in a favorite liberal self-descriptive term, absolute "pragmatism"). Finally, all the military analogies of the Depression era remind us of the ultimate dangers of the powerful state. The Roosevelt government itself provided some examples——in the incarceration of the Japanese Americans, or the behavior of the FBI.

The New Deal produced a great deal more organization in American life, while powerful, well-drilled interest groups became more important than ever before.   Given central direction——a reform atmosphere, an ideology, *Roosevelt*——all this had a sweep and coherence about it. But once the direction and coordination and leadership faded, a danger existed that all that would remain would be an agglomeration of powerful interest groups raising a clamor in Washington, each of them thoroughly educated to look for concessions from the federal government——and each with a stake in a government powerful enough to provide it with services. To secure benefits, groups *had* to organize. The fact that business had begun the process decades before virtually dictated that others do the same. But the changeover from a cross of gold in 1896 to parity prices forty years later implied a letdown, as if the construction of a church steeple had been suspended in order to install plumbing in the basement. The new democracy would see the Congress of Industrial Organizations (CIO) and its army pitted against the National Association of Manufacturers (NAM) and its army. Middle-class progressives had feared just this; the workings of political machines had presupposed it. These progressives extolled participatory democracy; the machine embraced a professional politics of organized loyalty and reward. The New Deal embodied the second tradition, not just because this perspective inhered in one whole wing of the party, but because disciplined organizational politics is far better suited to times of crisis.

It worked. But once the economy turned up again, and in particular once a new generation came along which could not remember the old struggles, much that had gone before would fall into question.

These after-the-fact reflections should not obscure the essence of the matter, that modern liberalism came of age in the New Deal. During the twenties, conservatives and especially business took pride as the special repositories of "reality," the appointed guardians of revealed truth. The year 1929 called the conventional wisdom into question. During the thirties liberals expropriated reality.

Of late it has become fashionable to criticize them. Yet the critics often fail to consider the New Deal in its fullest sense. The New Deal became in great measure a story of outs getting in——into, or at least part way into, the structure of power. Among the Roosevelt coalition were first-generation Americans, Catholics, Jews, organized labor, southerners, city dwellers, and, to a lesser degree, blacks. In the few years it held sway——it began in 1933 and had burned out by 1939——the New Deal went a long way toward restoring the national nerve, educated the public in the uses of government, and set a great many healthy precedents for the future. The New Deal's more recent critics have often ignored the restraints which prevailed against reform even in the bottom of the Depression, and the paucity of economic knowledge on which the New Deal could base itself. Economics, regrettably, remained a crude science then——as it still does. The great surprise of the New Deal is the number and importance of the things it did accomplish.

I suspect that one reason the New Deal no longer seems so innovative as it once did arises from the nature of the groups which it helped most. Organized labor and agriculture are not as fashionable or popular today as they were. Once, not too long ago, they were the most important groups fighting for social change. During the New Deal, they finally managed to get a foot lodged in government's door (not one wearing as large a shoe as big business, but firmly lodged anyway). Now ins, they lost their appeal as outs.

Take the case of agriculture. Theodore Roosevelt had argued in 1912 that "the farmers must own and work their own land; steps must be taken at once to put a stop to the tendency toward absentee landlordism and tenant-farming; this is one of the most imperative duties confronting the nation." He had talked of "bring[ing] people back to the soil" and had spoken of methods to undergird farming "and to make country life more interesting as well as more profitable." He had embraced the little operator: "the man in whose interests we are working is the small farmer and settler, the man who works with his own hands."[22] Following the collapse of Populism, as we have seen, agriculture had substantially abandoned third parties and pursued the interest-group pressure politics made familiar by business. The values of agrarian America had taken a tremendous drubbing in the cultural struggles of the twenties, but what Hofstadter labelled the "'hard' side" of the agricultural movement[23]—the business side—had earlier attracted favors from the Wilson Administration.

As its numbers diminished, the influence of agriculture actually grew. The New Deal basically regarded farming as a business and encouraged agriculture to organize and control production along business lines.[24] An intricate system of controls and subsidies appeared. Over the span of FDR's first term gross farm income jumped 50 percent. Efforts were made to help small farmers, farm tenants, and migrant workers—those for whom the first Roosevelt had spoken back in 1912—but with mixed results.

As the number of farmers continued to dwindle, agriculture became a bigger and more consolidated enterprise, increasingly turning into agribusiness. Even though it enjoyed more prosperity as a result of New Deal innovations, much of the charm wore off as the benefits dispensed by Washington increasingly took the form of business subsidies worked out through lobbying and bureaucratic politics. Ironies abounded. The government continued to pour out price supports to tobacco growers after it began requiring cigarette companies to warn smokers on the authority of the Surgeon General that their habit endangered their health. A good many of the nation's vaunted yeomen were raising a crop that could kill. Other "farmers" began cultivating marijuana. Perhaps all this, and not prohibition, was rural America's final revenge on the city.

Looking at urban as well as farm policy, some historians have faulted the reformers who preceded the New Deal for failing to become New Dealers in their own time. And in assessing the New Deal, a number of historians fault it for failing to go farther. This reflects in part a refusal to appreciate the New Deal fully for what it was. More important, it reveals a tendency to denigrate the New Deal because it did not solve the problems of future decades along with those of the 1930s. The issues of later years get read back into the New Deal, and it comes up short—of course. Roosevelt did not end our troubles, and the New Deal produced difficulties of its own which endure today.

Basic, comprehensive central economic planning, truly fundamental challenges to the power of big business, and public ownership were all excluded from the main line of New Deal thought. As with Wilson, a big gap emerged between theory—that income redistribution had become critical—and practice.[25] But another consideration also excluded such ideas from the New Deal: plain political reality.

The New Deal had "deflated" the moral lyricism of progressivism, substituting, first, the imperatives of dealing with the Depression, and second, Roosevelt. Take these two away, and lyricism would once again be missed. During the Truman era the reform impulse survived, but with neither the excitement nor the sense of urgency of the New Deal.

Harry Truman resembled a bantam rooster strutting along behind a lion in a circus parade. Most of the Roosevelt circle Truman dismissed as "crackpots and the lunatic fringe." "I don't want any experiments; the American people have been through a lot of experiments and they want a rest from experiments."[26] Reform's momentum had dropped off before the forties dawned, and Truman's most advanced, freshest proposals—for civil rights, aid to education, national health—got practically nowhere. Peacetime inflation produced fresh difficulties, as did prosperity; these, too, help account for the change of tack and style from the New Deal. The growth economy, rather than continued structural change, caught the fancy of midcentury liberals like Leon Keyserling, who called for government-business cooperation to stimulate expansion. So, in matters of image, and in some matters of substance, the New Deal and Truman's Fair Deal are distinct. Yet, along with pressing matters of foreign policy, the classic New Deal bread-and-butter interclass divisions continued to dominate public political concerns.

And some gains occurred. The Employment Act of 1946, though watered down, has been seen as a kind of climax to one side of the New Deal. The Truman era—the 1948 campaign in particular—witnessed the turning toward a more or less consistently pro-black policy in the Democratic party. Overall, Truman protected and helped to entrench the New Deal and built on New Deal economic policy. He made a few legislative gains. And he established a noteworthy record for the time in civil rights.

Reform Engorged: Kennedy, Johnson, and the Sixties

The aim of the Great Society was not a large-scale redistribution of income, but rather the opening of opportunities for those at the end of the line so that they could gradually pull themselves up. Meanwhile it attempted to provide minimal income, goods, and services for all citizens.

Sar A. Levitan and Robert Taggart

During the 1960s, government's domain expanded extraordinarily in education, civil rights, regulation, the provision of services, and science and technology. Sometimes in response to pressures from below, often in reaction to impulses in Washington itself, government's role as promoter reached its post-New Deal apogee. Reform drew much of its élan and many of its ideas from the New Deal tradition; indeed, reform in the sixties devoted itself to tying together the loose ends that remained from the Roosevelt and Truman eras. There were striking successes. There were also bitter failures which have haunted American reform ever since.

All this began in the Kennedy presidency. It began slowly. In domestic policy, particularly at first, Kennedy was cautious, remarkably so in retrospect. As New Deal projects gathered rust, they got repainted, but proposals scarcely abounded for constructing new ones. Structural solutions seemed out of place in a prosperous era, free (or so it seemed) of ideology, and with problems abroad. Kennedy preoccupied himself with foreign affairs. He tended to see remaining difficulties at home as fundamentally technical, not ideological. Yet his own charisma inspired reform, however reluctantly he pursued it himself. Kennedy glamorized politics and in time began to shift his own agenda toward such issues as race and poverty.

Following the death of Kennedy, Lyndon Johnson's Great Society projected a truly massive expansion of the welfare state. In a fascinating revival of the New Deal's war analogy, Johnson insisted on "total victory" in his own "war on poverty."[1] "This Administration," he proclaimed in his 1964 State of the Union Message,

> today, here and now, declares unconditional war on poverty in America. . . . It will not be a short or easy struggle, no single weapon or strategy will suffice, but we shall not rest until that war is won.[2]

Grounded on the assumption that continuous government-stimulated economic growth would provide an ongoing surplus, so to speak——a "fiscal dividend" for social spending——the Johnson Administration attempted to tie the country to future expansions in social programs.[3] These were very much federal programs, involving a high degree of centralization. They also entailed experimentation. "We have the power to shape the civilization that we want," the President insisted.[4] This shaping implied the possibility of creative trial and error. It also implied that waste would occur. The fiscal years 1964 to 1969 saw a two-thirds jump in public cash transfers, most of them going to people with incomes lower than the average. Service and in-kind programs mushroomed, becoming hallmarks of the Great Society.[5]

Like FDR, Johnson tried to produce a program which would give something to practically everybody. In 1965-66 he fed 200 domestic proposals to Congress and got 181 of them through. Legislate now, the reasoning ran; worry about administering all this later.[6] In an era of rising expectations, confidence, effervescent expansiveness, and relative generosity, the Johnson approach seemed to suit the national mood. By the end of the sixties, practically everything the Democrats had been proposing had seen enactment in one form or another. Only some of the most recent ideas remained in the air.[7]

Johnson pursued his party's highest goal since it had turned toward modern liberalism, aiding people who needed government help. The New Deal's commitment to society's bottom third had come fairly late. Johnson opened with that commitment. Yet the fact that the Great Society focused so heavily on the very worst off made it vulnerable. Its rate of success would, in the nature of things, often come in low, making it appear ineffectual.

Unfortunately, less than any other twentieth century reform wave did the Great Society specifically meet the needs of the ordinary, white, blue-collar worker. This held true in spite of the adoption, for example, of Medicare, pure food legislation, or aid to education, which benefited broad segments of the population. TR, Wilson, and FDR had moved during their administrations toward greater concern with the problems of industrial labor. But Johnson made a classic mistake: he pushed through programs intended mainly for the poor and the black (all too often the same); then he asked people just a notch or two up the social scale to pay heavily for them. The problem of poverty was substantially presented and perceived through the prism of race. No wonder LBJ's programs engendered, in the argot of the decade, backlash. Economically marginal people will show less inclination to slur "giveaway" programs if some of the giving gets to them. Progressivism and the New Deal had appealed to the self-interest of a majority of Americans. To many among this same majority, the Great Society, for all its fine aims, looked like one huge transfer payment. A burgeoning bureaucracy replete with procedures and forms, together with large dollops of fraud, reinforced public antipathies.

Tax policy provides one of the prime indicators of any era's ideological tinge. Many of the great progressive causes early in the century had not cost anything and in fact promised pocketbook savings (municipal reform, antitrust, lower tariffs). The income tax inaugurated under Woodrow Wilson was sufficiently light and progressive that at first an overwhelming majority of Americans remained completely untouched by it. But in the Kennedy-Johnson period, tax policy cut politically the other way. People saw their taxes going into programs from which they either derived no benefit or from which they *perceived* themselves as gaining nothing. Johnson held the view that a rising GNP could muffle intergroup conflict. His political perceptions and eagerness to sustain a national consensus precluded either huge new public expenditures on one hand, or tax reform on the other.[8] In practice, between 1965 and 1969, while the proportion of the budget allocated to defense declined, the proportion going into domestic social spending went up markedly. The administration cut taxes *and* launched social programs.

The war on poverty kept on expanding, so that by 1978 its cost ran at nearly $12 billion a year, twelve times the level of 1965. Between 1960 and 1979, public outlays for social welfare rose from 10.5 percent of the gross national product to 18.5 percent (1940-60: 9 to 10 percent). Between 1964 and 1974, the percentage of poor people in the population fell from 19.0 to 11.6.[9]   Yet the poor and the blacks still felt shortchanged.[10] They had reason to. Benefits became so diffused——for all the public grumbling that only the dirt poor and undeserving got help——that a great deal of Johnsonian social spending wound up benefiting the emphatically unpoor, from middle-class college students on subsidized loans to middle-class communities undergoing urban "renewal."

Had the economic growth of the early sixties prevailed, Johnson's political momentum, which depended on it, might have continued far longer. Wealthy people could support antipoverty because it came cheap and they had tax loopholes. But just as the Great Society programs for minorities and the poor got under way, the real incomes of blue-collar workers began to stagnate.[11] Once real income flattened out, masses of middle-income taxpayers (for whom taxes helped produce the treadmill effect) grew angry that they did not see the benefits coming back to them. As one economist put it, perhaps with intentional irony, "the higher taxes aren't going for improved government services. They are going to support other people."[12]

No wonder so many concluded that government was simply wasting money. While they provided many benefits in employment and growth, as implemented the Keynesian policies of the Kennedy-Johnson era actually made the tax system less fair and gave away an important part of the revenue base. This might have been used against poverty or for other purposes. When inflation hit, the game came to a halt. The proponents of the social programs of the sixties had dramatically oversold them. The margin between realistic expectation and sheer exaggeration offered a soft flank for conservatives to attack.

The chief public philosophy that guided the Great Society was that more meant better——essentially Gompers's philosophy. But it amounted to no public philosophy at all. Programs got passed and benefits piled up without even the concern for the general interest still evident in the New Deal. A good part of the Great Society fit Neil Gilbert's term, "unbridled incrementalism," an improbable label for an improbable process.[13] "Men of good will," writes Allen J. Matusow, "Johnsonian liberals were constrained to act within a political culture that imposed severe limits on the extent of permissible change. To accomplish social reform, they had to buy off vested interests and call it consensus."[14] The

New Deal had become the great portent of interest-group liberalism. Its Johnsonian reincarnation brought the style to near-bankruptcy, stretching and bending the tradition, and worse, making it look more than a bit foolish. It may be argued that the Great Society "attacked more problems and affected the lives of more people" than even the New Deal had.[15] But the Great Society certainly did not convey that impression. Often its specific results seemed difficult if not impossible to ascertain at all.

In a cruelly ironic way, Johnson even did liberalism a disservice by his success in tying up the loose ends from the New Deal. Enacting the post-World War II liberal agenda practically in toto, he left liberals groping for a new one. Writes Alonzo L. Hamby: "The Johnson revolution, by allowing the liberal impulse to search for its limits, may well have carried it beyond the range of practical accomplishment."[16] In the familiar way of reform administrations, the reform impulse had overrun itself. And certainly Hamby is right if liberalism is taken to mean, as it did in the sixties, the consensus, interest-group approach. The ensuing quest for a liberal agenda which convincingly addresses the issues of the late twentieth century has continued ever since.

NOTES

Karl Mannheim, *Ideology and Utopia: An Introduction to the Sociology of Knowledge* (New York: Harcourt, Brace and Co., 1946), p. 157.

[1]Walter Dean Burnham, Jerome M. Clubb, and William H. Flanigan, "Partisan Realignment: A Systemic Perspective," in *The History of American Electoral Behavior*, ed. Joel H. Silbey, Allan G. Bogue, and William H. Flanigan (Princeton: Princeton University Press, 1978), p. 74.

[2]For a periodization which departs from historians' normal progressivism-war-reaction account of this era, see John F. McClymer, *War and Welfare: Social Engineering in America, 1890-1925* (Westport, Conn.: Greenwood Press, 1980).

[3]Simone de Beauvoir, *The Prime of Life* (Cleveland: World Publishing Co., 1962), p. 342.

[4]*The Deflation of American Ideals: An Ethical Guide for New Dealers* (1941; reprint, Seattle: University of Washington Press, 1967), pp. xi, 32-33, 44. Otis L. Graham, Jr., has written an enlightening introduction to the 1967 edition, pp. ix-xix.

[5]Ibid., pp. xvi-xvii.

[6]*An Encore for Reform: The Old Progressives and the New Deal* (New York: Oxford University Press, 1967). See in conjunction with Graham Ronald L. Feinman, *Twilight of Progressivism: The Western*

Republican Senators and the New Deal, Johns Hopkins University Studies in Historical and Political Science, 99th series (1981), no. 1 (Baltimore: Johns Hopkins University Press, 1981); John Chamberlain, *Farewell to Reform: The Rise, Life and Decay of the Progressive Mind in America* (New York: John Day Co., 1932; reprint, Chicago: Quadrangle Paperbacks, 1965); Larry G. Gerber, *The Limits of Liberalism: Josephus Daniels, Henry Stimson, Bernard Baruch, Donald Richberg, Felix Frankfurter and the Development of the Modern American Political Economy* (New York: New York University Press, 1983); and Ronald A. Mulder, *The Insurgent Progressives in the United States Senate and the New Deal, 1933-1939*, Modern American History series (New York: Garland Publishing, 1979).

[7]Kemler, *Deflation*, p. xvii.

[8]*Encore*, p. 24.

[9]Ibid., pp. 4-5, 38-40, 66, 68-73.

[10]Pp. 4, 18, 301-3, 305-14, 317, 323.

[11]*The Semisovereign People: A Realist's View of Democracy in America* (Hinsdale, Ill.: Dryden Press, 1960), pp. 66-67.

[12]David Burner and Thomas R. West, *The Torch Is Passed: The Kennedy Brothers and American Liberalism* (New York: Atheneum, 1984), p. 268.

The Odd Legacy of the Gilded Age

William Graham Sumner, *What Social Classes Owe to Each Other* (New York: Harper & Bros., 1883; reprint [?], New Haven: Yale University Press, 1925), p. 131.

[1]Morton Keller, *Affairs of State: Public Life in Late Nineteenth Century America* (Cambridge, Mass.: Harvard University Press, Belknap Press, 1977), p. 373.

[2]Ellis W. Hawley has aptly termed the upshot of their efforts "counterorganization." *The New Deal and the Problem of Monopoly: A Study in Economic Ambivalence* (Princeton: Princeton University Press, 1966), p. 483.

[3]A tradition which has, of course, carried on. See Robert H. Walker, *Reform in America: The Continuing Frontier* (Lexington: University Press of Kentucky, 1985), pp. 117ff.

[4]Samuel P. Hays, *The Response to Industrialism: 1885-1914*, Chicago History of American Civilization (Chicago: University of Chicago Press, 1957), pp. 63-65.

[5]Jack London, *War of the Classes* (Oakland: Star Rover House, 1982), p. 14.

[6]*Affairs of State*, p. 398.

[7]*Law and the Conditions of Freedom in the Nineteenth-Century United States* (Madison: University of Wisconsin Press, 1964), p. 7.

[8]Harold U. Faulkner, *Politics, Reform and Expansion, 1890-1900*, New American Nation Series (New York: Harper & Bros., 1959), p. 97; David Hackett Fischer, *Growing Old in America: The Bland-Lee Lectures Delivered at Clark University*, expanded ed. (New York: Oxford University Press, 1978), p. 169.

[9]Fischer, *Growing Old*, pp. 169-71.

[10]*Affairs of State*, p. 311. As late as 1920, 96 percent of federal social welfare outlays still went to veterans. Edward Berkowitz and Kim McQuaid, *Creating the Welfare State: The Political Economy of Twentieth-Century Reform* (New York: Praeger, 1980), p. 65. In a number of respects, the private sector remained ahead of government in innovating new social welfare policies from the late nineteenth century on through the beginning years of the twentieth. See Michael B. Katz, *Poverty and Policy in American History* (New York: Harcourt Brace Jovanovich, Academic Press, 1983), pp. 8-9. For a broader treatment of themes taken up here, see William R. Brock, *Investigation and Responsibility: Public Responsibility in the United States, 1865-1900* (Cambridge, England: Cambridge University Press, 1984).

Populism and the Politics of Self-Interest

James B. Weaver, *Call to Action: An Interpretation of the Great Uprising. Its Source and Causes* (Des Moines: Iowa Printing Co., 1892), p. 362.

[1]Gilbert C. Fite, *American Farmers: The New Minority*, Minorities in Modern America (Bloomington: Indiana University Press, 1981), p. 234; Jonathan R. T. Hughes, *The Governmental Habit: Economic Controls from Colonial Times to the Present* (New York: Basic Books, 1977), p. 188; U.S., Department of Commerce, Bureau of the Census, *Historical Statistics of the United States: Colonial Times to 1970* (Washington, D.C., 1975), pt. 1, p. 449.

[2]*Age of Reform*, p. 24.

[3]Ibid., p. 61.

[4]On this latter, see Lawrence Goodwyn, *Democratic Promise: The Populist Moment in America* (New York: Oxford University Press, 1976); and Norman Pollack, *The Just Polity: Populism, Law, and Human Welfare* (Urbana: University of Illinois Press, 1987).

[5]The platform is reproduced as an appendix in John D. Hicks, *The Populist Revolt: A History of the Farmers' Alliance and the People's Party*

(N.p.: University of Nebraska Press, Bison, 1961), pp. 439-44. The quotations come from pp. 441-44.

[6]On this, see especially Hughes, *Governmental Habit*, pp. 96ff.

[7]Robert W. Cherny, *Populism, Progressivism, and the Transformation of Nebraska Politics, 1885-1915* (Lincoln: University of Nebraska Press, 1981), p. 160. Populism did have a radical dimension which I do not wish to obscure, and which is especially emphasized in Goodwyn, *Democratic Promise*.

[8]Faulkner, *Politics, Reform and Expansion*, p. 169.

[9]In Kansas, at all events. *Kansas Populism: Ideas and Men* (Lawrence: University Press of Kansas, 1969), pp. 31-32.

[10]But see also John H. M. Laslett, *Labor and the Left: A Study of Socialist and Radical Influences in the American Labor Movement, 1881-1924* (New York: Basic Books, 1970), pp. 244, 299. Here the nature of that labor support for Populism which did emerge, and the common interests that bound elements of labor and agriculture together for a time, are made clear.

[11]Keller, *Affairs of State*, p. 579.

[12]Goodwyn, *Democratic Promise*, pp. 546-47.

[13]For a sunnier account focusing on Congress, see Gene Clanton, "Hayseed Socialism' on the Hill: Congressional Populism, 1891-1895," *Western Historical Quarterly* 15 (April 1984): 139-62.

[14]See Grant McConnell, *The Decline of Agrarian Democracy* (Berkeley: University of California Press, 1953), pp. 42-43.

Progressivism and the Problem of Focus

James Weinstein, *The Corporate Ideal in the Liberal State: 1900-1918* (Boston: Beacon, 1969), pp. 169-70 (Hart quote).

[1]*Reform in America*, p. 168.

[2]*Robert M. La Follette and the Insurgent Spirit*, Library of American Biography (Boston: Little, Brown & Co., 1976), p. 23. Thelen excepts the corporate elite from this broad coalescence. See also his *The New Citizenship: Origins of Progressivism in Wisconsin, 1885-1900* (Columbia: University of Missouri Press, 1972).

[3]Gerald T. White, *The United States and the Problem of Recovery after 1893* (University, Ala.: University of Alabama Press, 1982), pp. ix, 81, 101, 115-16.

[4]Thelen, *La Follette*, p. 71. On the wider implications of consumerism in twentieth century American politics, see Russell L. Hanson, *The Democratic Imagination in America: Conversations with Our Past* (Princeton: Princeton University Press, 1985), pp. 392-93.

[5]"The Discovery that Business Corrupts Politics: A Reappraisal of the Origins of Progressivism," *American Historical Review* 86 (April 1981): 265-66. See also his chronological breakdown of the movement, p. 257.

[6]The bureaucratic theme has been examined by a number of scholars. In a crucial treatment of the subject, Robert H. Wiebe argues that "the heart of progressivism was the ambition of the new middle class to fulfill its destiny through bureaucratic means." *The Search for Order: 1877-1920*, Making of America/American Century Series (New York: Hill & Wang, 1968), p. 166. See also, e.g., Stephen Skowronek, *Building a New American State: The Expansion of National Administrative Capacities, 1877-1920* (Cambridge, England: Cambridge University Press, 1982).

[7]*History of the United States Civil Service* (Evanston, Ill.: Row, Peterson & Co., 1958), pp. 83-84. "As the civil service improves," wrote Walter E. Weyl at the time, "the government is enabled to conduct business both honestly and efficiently. As the state becomes increasingly democratized, the people accept it as their natural representative, as opposed to an entrenched industrial oligarchy in a monopolized business." *The New Democracy: An Essay on Certain Political and Economic Tendencies in the United States* (New York: Macmillan Co., 1912; reprint, New York: Harper Torchbooks, 1964), p. 283.

[8]Geoffrey Blodgett, "A New Look at the Gilded Age: Politics in a Cultural Context," in *Victorian America*, ed. Daniel Walker Howe (N.p.: University of Pennsylvania Press, 1976), pp. 104-5.

[9]*The Progressive Movement: A Non-partisan, Comprehensive Discussion of Current Tendencies in American Politics*, Citizen's Library of Economics, Politics and Sociology——New Series (New York: Macmillan Co., 1915), pp. 4-5.

[10]*The End of American Innocence: A Study of the First Years of Our Own Time, 1912-1917* (New York: Alfred A. Knopf, 1959), pp. 14, 21, 28.

[11]See Richard M. Abrams, *The Burdens of Progress: 1900-1929* (Glenview, Ill.: Scott, Foresman & Co., 1978), p. 82.

[12]*Encore*, p. 11. Italics in the original.

[13]*The New Competition: An Examination of the Conditions Underlying the Radical Change that Is Taking Place in the Commercial and Industrial World—The Change from a Competitive to a Cooperative Basis* (Chicago: A. C. McClurg & Co., 1913), p. 306.

[14]*Encore*, pp. 69-70.

[15]It may be that, given the sharp pattern of one-party sections after 1896, the drive toward nonpartisan politics made more sense than we have commonly assumed. As a means of inducing some measure of political competition, the nonpartisan approach provided a surrogate of sorts for a two-party system that did not in fact exist either in the South or in large areas of the North.

[16]Introduction to Jerry Israel, ed., *Building the Organizational Society: Essays on Associational Activities in Modern America* (New York: Free Press, 1972), pp. 6-7.

[17]Samuel P. Hays, *The Response to Industrialism: 1885-1914*, Chicago History of American Civilization (Chicago: University of Chicago Press, 1957), p. 48.

[18]"An Obituary for 'The Progressive Movement,'" *American Quarterly* 22 (Spring 1970): 20, 33.

[19]Graham, *Encore*, p. 149.

[20]The moral emphasis which accompanies reform imposes two heavy responsibilities. Reformers must pursue their ends ethically, since they have claimed the high moral ground. And it becomes imperative that they succeed. Burns, *Leadership*, p. 170.

[21]Richard Hofstadter made this latter point specifically in regard to Populism. *Age of Reform*, p. 61.

[22]*Search*, p. 164.

[23]Steven Kesselman, *The Modernization of American Reform: Structures and Perceptions*, Modern American History series (New York: Garland Publishing, 1979), pp. 120, 188, 194. See also John L. Thomas, *Alternative America: Henry George, Edward Bellamy, Henry Demarest Lloyd and the Adversary Tradition* (Cambridge, Mass.: Harvard University Press, Belknap Press, 1983), passim.

[24]*Women and Economics: A Study of the Economic Relation Between Men and Women as a Factor in Social Evolution* (Boston: Small, Maynard & Co., 1898; reprint, New York: Harper Torchbooks, 1966).

[25](New York: B. W. Huebsch, 1912).

[26]See Arthur M. Schlesinger, "The Tides of National Politics," in Schlesinger, *Paths to the Present* (New York: Macmillan Co., 1949), p. 81. For a harsh critique of the idea that all this represented "progress," see Frank Tariello, Jr., *The Reconstruction of American Political Ideology: 1865-1917* (Charlottesville: University Press of Virginia, 1982).

[27]"A Confession of Faith," in *The Progressive Years: The Spirit and Achievement of American Reform*, ed. Otis Pease (New York: George Braziller, 1962), p. 319. A fascinating examination of the humanitarian strain in progressivism is LeRoy Ashby, *Saving the Waifs: Reformers and Dependent Children, 1890-1917*, American Civilization series (Philadelphia: Temple University Press, 1984).

[28]Hofstadter, *Age of Reform*, p. 232.

[29]This is not to imply, though, that progressivism evoked any gigantic surge of mass support, or that it left any profound, permanent imprint on national voting behavior.

[30]*Deflation*, p. 62.

[31]The following discussion of the New Freedom is taken from John J. Broesamle, *William Gibbs McAdoo: A Passion for Change, 1863-1917*,

National University Publications, Series in American Studies (Port Washington, N.Y.: Kennikat Press, 1973), pp. 65-67.

[32]*Search*, p. 129.

[33]Abrams, *Burdens of Progress*, p. 81.

[34]Ibid., p. 85.

[35]Writes Robert H. Wiebe:

> With the completion of that agenda and the outbreak of war in Europe, Wilson allowed his grip on Congress to relax. The reforms of the next two years came piecemeal, bearing the mark of the jerry-builder. This was the time when the late arrivals to national progressivism claimed their measure. . . .
>
> These were also the years when traditionally powerful businessmen regained a fair portion of their lost influence. The magnates of Wall Street, who had had little direct effect on the laws concerning the tariff, finance, and the corporations, returned in strength with the European war. Like Roosevelt, Wilson and his Cabinet depended upon these wizards of popular myth to stabilize finance in the face of a sudden disturbance, and once welcomed back the magnates remained to modify a variety of economic policies——railroad rates and the application of the antitrust laws among others.

Search, p. 220.

[36]John J. Broesamle, "The Democrats from Bryan to Wilson," in *The Progressive Era*, ed. Lewis L. Gould (Syracuse, N.Y.: Syracuse University Press, 1974), p. 107.

[37]On this change in progressivism, see especially J. Joseph Huthmacher, "Urban Liberalism and the Age of Reform," *Mississippi Valley Historical Review* 49 (September 1962): 231-41; John D. Buenker, *Urban Liberalism and Progressive Reform* (New York: Charles Scribner's Sons, 1973); and Michael Paul Rogin and John L. Shover, *Political Change in California: Critical Elections and Social Movements, 1890-1966* (Westport, Conn.: Greenwood Press, 1970), pp. 46-51, 62-89, and passim.

[38]*Urban Liberalism*, pp. viii, 1.

[39]Useful on this point is Roger E. Wyman, "Middle-Class Voters and Progressive Reform: The Conflict of Class and Culture," *American*

Political Science Review 68 (June 1974): 488-504.

[40]*Urban Liberalism*, p. 42.

[41]*The Warrior and the Priest: Woodrow Wilson and Theodore Roosevelt* (Cambridge, Mass.: Harvard University Press, Belknap Press, 1983), p. 255.

[42]Wiebe, *Search*, p. 221.

[43]Paul A. C. Koistinen, *The Military-Industrial Complex: A Historical Perspective* (New York: Praeger, 1980), ch. 2; David M. Kennedy, *Over Here: The First World War and American Society* (New York: Oxford University Press, 1982), p. 141.

[44]Following the war, the rail lines went back to their owners, the planning and coordinating structure was dismantled, and the collective bargaining system lost administration sanction.

[45]On this point, see Kennedy, *Over Here*, p. 142.

The New Deal: Selling the Welfare State

Goldman, *Rendezvous* (1977), p. vii.

[1]*Semisovereign People*, pp. 68, 71. Italics in portions of the original have been deleted.

[2]Translated into pure marketese: "The office seeker must put himself on a market, the voters' market. He has to go through many of the steps that occur in product marketing: develop a personality (brand image), get the approval of an organization (company image), enter a primary election (market test), carry out a vigorous campaign (advertising and distribution), get elected (market share), and stay in office (repeat sales)." And again: "A product concept is the major orienting theme around which buyer interest will be built. It is the 'unique selling proposition,' the 'promised benefit' of the product. The political candidate must choose a product concept on which to market his candidacy. . . . Choosing the product concept is the most important single decision made by the candidate." Philip Kotler, *Marketing for Nonprofit Organizations* (Englewood Cliffs, N.J.: Prentice-Hall, 1975), pp. 373, 379. Italics in portions of the original have been deleted.

Seen in this light, a 1932 Hoover or a 1964 Goldwater becomes the political equivalent of a 1958 Edsel.

Nelson W. Polsby's *Political Innovation in America: The Politics of Policy Initiation* (New Haven: Yale University Press, 1984) contains a useful discussion of the role of what Polsby terms "the policy entrepreneur" (especially pp. 168, 171-72).

[3]Described, for instance, in Joe McGinniss, *The Selling of the President 1968* (New York: Trident Press, 1969). See also Kotler, *Marketing for Nonprofit Organizations*, especially p. 369.

[4]Philip Kotler, "The Elements of Social Action," in *Creating Social Change*, ed. Gerald Zaltman, Philip Kotler, and Ira Kaufman (New York: Holt, Rinehart & Winston, 1972), pp. 179, 183-84. Italics deleted in all quoted words.

[5]Kotler, *Marketing for Nonprofit Organizations*, p. 370.

[6]"Elements of Social Action," p. 178. Italics in the original. I have depended heavily on Kotler's scheme for both concepts and terminology.

[7]"The New Deal and the Analogue of War," in *Change and Continuity in Twentieth-Century America*, ed. John Braeman, Robert H. Bremner, and Everett Walters (New York: Harper & Row, Colophon Books, 1966), pp. 81-143.

[8]Though Hoover's assumption of federal responsibility for stabilizing the economy did have precedents in past administrations. On this point, see p. 40, and Albert U. Romasco, "Herbert Hoover's Policies for Dealing with the Great Depression: The End of the Old Order or the Beginning of the New?" in *The Hoover Presidency: A Reappraisal*, ed. Martin L. Fausold and George T. Mazuzan (Albany: State University of New York Press, 1974), p. 84.

[9]"Herbert Hoover and American Corporatism, 1929-1933," in Fausold, *Hoover Presidency*, p. 119. A number of observers have tried, too hard, to make out Hoover as a proto-New Dealer. Some of Hoover's actions did presage the New Deal, but only in a very limited way. True enough, Hoover had been a progressive. True enough, Hoover served as a transitional President. Hoover was an important theorist of business self-"regulation" and cooperation. But when the Crash hit, he resembled a man who walks into a superb Parisian restaurant and orders the plainest dishes for fear of the bill. In time, on principle, he balked at any additional extension of direct involvement by Washington.

[10]Robert S. McElvaine, *The Great Depression: America, 1929-1941* (New York: Times Books, 1984), pp. xiv, 202, 342; James T. Patterson, *America's Struggle Against Poverty: 1900-1980* (Cambridge, Mass.: Harvard University Press, 1981), p. 42; John A. Garraty, "Radicalism in the Great Depression," in *Essays on Radicalism in Contemporary America*, Walter Prescott Webb Memorial Lectures VI, ed. Leon Borden Blair (Austin: University of Texas Press, 1972), p. 83.

[11]Franklin D. Roosevelt, *The Public Papers and Addresses of Franklin D. Roosevelt; With a Special Introduction and Explanatory Notes by President Roosevelt*, 13 vols., ed. Samuel I. Rosenman, vol. 2: *The Year of Crisis: 1933* (New York: Random House, 1938), p. 13.

[12]*Deflation*, p. 71.

[13]Harold J. Laski, *The American Presidency: An Interpretation* (New York: Harper & Bros., 1940), p. 267.

[14]*Politics and Policy*, p. 510.

[15]*American as Reformer*, p. 53.

[16]*Age of Reform*, p. 305.

[17]Roosevelt, *Public Papers*, vol. 1: *The Genesis of the New Deal: 1928-1932* (New York: Random House, 1938), p. 646.

[18]Albert U. Romasco, *The Politics of Recovery: Roosevelt's New Deal* (New York: Oxford University Press, 1983), pp. 242-43.

[19]*Franklin D. Roosevelt and the New Deal, 1932-1940*, New American Nation Series (New York: Harper Torchbooks, 1963), p. 342.

[20]Hofstadter's term, *Age of Reform*, p. 16.

[21]Leuchtenburg, *Roosevelt and the New Deal*, p. 343.

[22]"Confession of Faith," pp. 323, 335, 338.

[23]*Age of Reform*, p. 95.

[24]"The New Deal and Agriculture," in *The New Deal*, ed. John Braeman, Robert H. Bremner, and David Brody, vol. 1: *The National Level* (Columbus: Ohio State University Press, 1975), pp. 86-87, 105. See also Theodore Saloutos, *The American Farmer and the New Deal*, Henry A. Wallace Series on Agricultural History and Rural Studies (Ames: Iowa State University Press, 1982).

[25]Theodore Rosenof, *Dogma, Depression, and the New Deal: The Debate of Political Leaders over Economic Recovery* (Port Washington, N.Y.: Kennikat Press, 1975), p. 17 and passim.

[26]Alonzo L. Hamby, *Beyond the New Deal: Harry S. Truman and American Liberalism* (New York: Columbia University Press, 1973), p. 83.

Reform Engorged: Kennedy, Johnson, and the Sixties

Sar A. Levitan and Robert Taggart, *The Promise of Greatness* (Cambridge, Mass.: Harvard University Press, 1976), p. 269.

[1]Doris Kearns, *Lyndon Johnson and the American Dream* (New York: Harper & Row, 1976), p. 219.

[2]Eric F. Goldman, *The Tragedy of Lyndon Johnson* (New York: Alfred A. Knopf, 1969), p. 46.

[3]Levitan, *Promise*, p. 29.   "Public social welfare spending," the authors point out, jumped from 11.6 to 17.7 percent of GNP between fiscal 1965 and 1974. Ibid., pp. 283-84.

[4]Ibid., p. 30.

[5]Ibid., pp. 30, 33, 191, 195.

[6]Michael Foley, *The New Senate: Liberal Influence on a Conservative Institution, 1959-1972* (New Haven: Yale University Press, 1980), pp. 52, 56.

[7]Sundquist, *Politics and Policy*, p. 506.

[8]Kearns, *Lyndon Johnson*, p. 189.

[9]Data from *Los Angeles Times*, 19 November 1978; Neil Gilbert, *Capitalism and the Welfare State: Dilemmas of Social Benevolence* (New Haven: Yale University Press, 1983), p. 157; and Levitan, *Promise*, p. 196.

[10]Jim F. Heath, *Decade of Disillusionment: The Kennedy-Johnson Years*, America since World War II series (Bloomington: Indiana University Press, 1975), p. 301.

[11]Godfrey Hodgson, *America in Our Time* (New York: Random House, Vintage Books, 1978), pp. 254, 482.

[12]"The Tax Mess," *Newsweek*, 10 April 1978, p. 71.

[13]*Welfare State*, p. 159.

[14]*The Unraveling of America: A History of Liberalism in the 1960s*, New American Nation Series (New York: Harper & Row, 1984), p. 270.

[15]Heath, *Disillusionment*, p. 292.

[16]*Liberalism and Its Challengers: FDR to Reagan* (New York: Oxford University Press, 1985), p. 344. For a more cheerful view of the past generation of governmental policymaking and its results than I have presented here, see John E. Schwarz, *America's Hidden Success: A Reassessment of Twenty Years of Public Policy* (New York: W. W. Norton & Co., 1983).

3

DOES REFORM
RUN IN CYCLES?

There is a mysterious cycle in human events. To some generations much is given. Of other generations much is expected. This generation of Americans has a rendezvous with destiny.

Franklin D. Roosevelt, 1936

He who would help himself and others should not be a subject of irregular and interrupted impulses of virtue, but a continent, persisting, immovable person. . . . It is better that joy should be spread over all the day in the form of strength, than that it should be concentrated into ecstasies, full of danger and followed by reactions.

Emerson

Political reform in the United States has often been described as a cyclic phenomenon. Reform movements emerge, decline, emerge once more, and again decline. For a while, an ascendant movement and its party (or parties) and groups will tend to set the terms for and to dominate public discussion. Then their influence wanes. Why should this pattern have been so consistent——or has it? Our task for the moment will be to examine the phenomenon and offer some tentative conclusions about it. We will leave a good many incisions unsutured for further exploration in the following chapters.

We must start with some caveats. In the first place, no period is purely liberal or entirely conservative, an Age of Reform or an Age of Reaction. Reform eras are periods when sweeping change occurs in response to public and other demands. Non-reform periods may see specific pressures from individual interest groups, or at times from the public at large, usher in narrow interest-oriented reforms or even reforms of wider significance. We may draw a distinction here between two general types of reform, rapid and broad-based in the one era as against more incremental and particularistic in the other.[1] Again, no reform period is wholly without reaction, and no reactionary period completely without reform. Sometimes change arrives in response to events, regardless of ideology or widely held social values. For example, World War II propelled millions of married women into the labor force in the face of simple necessity. Before the war, they would not have found themselves there. After all, they had husbands; many had children. Yet, having arrived, many married women stayed, and the beachhead became consolidated.

When we talk about reform we must not make the mistake of assuming that the same things occur at the same pace from New York to Atlanta to Chicago to Los Angeles. Pace, timing, and intent vary from one section of the country to another. As Arthur M. Schlesinger pointed out, the East and West have acted together to a considerable degree. The South has lagged, in part, perhaps, because its dissenters left, and certainly because of slack resources to undertake programs calling for government funding and because of the conundrum of race. Sectionally, reform has emerged significantly as a response to regional need: the crises of urbanization and industrialization in the Northeast, the demands of agriculture in the West and South. Some questions, of course, have cut across sectional lines. The problem of corporatism provides a prime example in this century.[2] In discussing reform periods, then, we must be aware of varying responses from section to section. We must also resist the temptation to assume that everything gets handed down from Washington; this is not the case even today, still less in the early part of the century.

Mindful of these caveats, we move to the matter of cycles.

In a famous essay, "The Tides of National Politics" (1949),[3] Arthur M. Schlesinger advanced what doubtless remains the most famous cyclic theory of American political change developed by an historian:

> Any scrutiny of American history discloses the alternation of . . . [conservative and liberal] attitudes. A period of concern for the rights of the few has been followed by one of concern for the wrongs of the many. Emphasis on the welfare of property has given way to emphasis on human welfare in the belief, as Theodore Roosevelt put it, that "every man holds his property subject to the general right of the community to regulate its use to whatever degree the public welfare may

require it." An era of quietude has been succeeded by one of rapid movement. Mere motion, however, is no proof of liberalism: it may be forward or backward or even in circles. The test is whether the object is to increase or lessen democracy, and the achievement is evidenced not by words but by the resulting legislative and executive accomplishment. Such oscillations of sentiment, moreover, express themselves through changes of direction within a party as well as by displacement of one party by the other.

These shifts of mood can be plotted with reasonable precision. In some instances historians might quarrel as to the exact terminal dates, but such differences would involve only trifling alterations. The analysis cannot be pushed back of 1765 because before then nothing resembling national political movements existed in America. Thereafter the periods run:

*	(1) 1765-1787	*	(7) 1861-1869
	(2) 1787-1801		(8) 1869-1901
*	(3) 1801-1816	*	(9) 1901-1919
	(4) 1816-1829		(10) 1919-1931
*	(5) 1829-1841	*	(11) 1931-1947
	(6) 1841-1861		

The asterisks indicate the liberal dispensations.[4]

While acknowledging that political "alternation" comprised "no mere automatic process," and allowing for some "major deviations" from 1861 to 1901, Schlesinger went on to ask:

Are these trends in American politics cyclical? Do they obey a rhythm which may afford a clue to the future as well as to the past? The average length of the eleven periods is 16.55 years; the actual duration has seldom varied far from the norm.

Rejecting the analogy of the pendulum, Schlesinger noted that the terminal points for shifts in one direction or the other never remained in place——the contexts and meanings of conservatism and liberalism changed as times changed. And he predicted that

we may expect the recession from liberalism which began in 1947 to last till 1962, with a possible margin of a year or two in one direction or the other. The next conservative epoch will then be due around 1978.[5]

What factors produced the "tides" which Schlesinger described? Not, in his view, the business cycle. An economic slump apparently had political repercussions, but it took more than this to generate major change. Likewise, Schlesinger discounted, among other considerations, foreign wars; an expanded electorate; and an aggressive Chief Executive (though he acknowledged that "a strong-willed President has inaugurated every liberal dispensation under the Constitution"). What, then, did account for the alternations?

> It is reasonable to believe that American politics has undergone a[n] ... interplay of subjective influences——influences springing from something basic in human nature. Apparently the electorate embarks upon conservative policies till it is disappointed or vexed or bored and then attaches itself to liberal policies till a like course is run.

Conservatives or liberals gained power with a driving spirit. But in time they flagged, grew stale. After a while, the electorate ejected them. By and large, though, the public inclination has taken a liberal bent. So, ultimately:

> The alternating process of conservatism and liberalism casts a significant light on the workings of American democracy. Not preconceived theory but empiricism has been the guiding star. The ship of state has moved forward by fits and starts, choosing its course in obedience to the prevailing winds of opinion.[6]

Some of Schlesinger's discrete insights remain more useful today than does his theory as a whole.[7] We will occasionally return to them.

Like Schlesinger, Charles Forcey has observed that "the rise and fall of reform sentiment in the United States has followed a recurring pattern. Each wave of reform has run its course at intervals of twenty years or so since the founding of the republic." Jeffersonianism was followed by Jacksonianism, and thereafter by the Republicans, the Liberal Republicans, and "the tariff-civil service-trust reformers around 1890," bringing us down to our own century. Forcey continues:

> The pattern has had a certain momentum of its own in terms of the shifting moods of the populace. Each reform movement has usually begun with a prolonged period of agitation and protest at the state and local levels; then the new issues have been dramatized nationally by some dominant political figure; then, seemingly inevitably, there comes a slackening of public

interest followed by a period of reaction and the undoing, usually by indirection, of most of the reforms.[8]

Perceived in twenty-year intervals, reform becomes in effect a phenomenon of generations.[9] An especially prominent hallmark of all this has been the generational re-emergence of a prominent left: the left before World War I, the Depression-era Old Left, and the New Left, which appeared in the sixties.

As this suggests, ideology itself has moved in alternations. Lewis S. Feuer has examined the phenomenon in his important books, *Ideology and the Ideologists* and *The Conflict of Generations*.[10] Any brief summary does injustice to the complexity of Feuer's ideas. He makes an oedipal argument with which I only partially agree.[11] Still, some of his insights carry keen importance for us here, and we must sketch them out. Feuer associates ideological propensities with the younger intelligentsia, and observes that equilibrium is foreign to ideology. To each oncoming generation the ideas of the preceding one seem repressive. "That repressed emotional need, which by virtue of social circumstances in the life of the emerging generation, has been most dramatically ignited in its unconscious, will tend to become the prime determinant in the choice among successive contrary tenets." The new, reactive ideology will be carried along by a new "generational wave" animated by "generational consciousness"; for each generation of young intellectuals must bear an ideology. Though older individuals may lay out the basics of such an ideology, youth are the ones who kindle it. Generation after generation, the young burst out against formalism, against seemingly repressive received doctrine.[12]

Thus every new generation attempts to find a definition for itself which will set it against the preceding one. "Since each generation of intellectuals tends to reject its predecessors' doctrines," Feuer argues, "a law of intellectual fashion arises,——the alternation of philosophical tenets."

A generation which imbibes a determinist, analytic creed from its fathers will in its revolt tend to attach to its political ideology voluntarist, anti-intellectual tenets. And that portion of the public which wishes to partake of the experience of initiation is characteristically composed of the intellectuals of the younger generation.

There results "an alternating wave pattern" of perspectives: "The history of ideologies is thus a continuous document of a periodic, wave movement." "Each intellectual wave" has had "a period of roughly thirty years." Meantime, approximately each decade over the past half-century, an ideological revolt has erupted among a younger generation.[13] (Even the politically vapid fifties youth got themselves labeled rebels, though rebels without a cause.)

In what he calls "the principle of wings," Feuer argues that "every philosophic unit-idea in the course of its career makes the passage through the whole spectrum of ideological affiliations." A doctrine emerging on the left will work its way rightward, and vice versa. Once the received wisdom has gone from left to right in its identity, the time arrives for a fresh generational ideology. Between waves, there is "de-ideologization." The young grow older; their emotions no longer demand ideology. Arriving in middle age, onetime ideologists have become "post-ideological." This fits with the cliché that as young radicals age they grow more conservative. Having moved from youthful insurrection to defensiveness while passing across the generational spectrum, the former left-radical man or woman may proceed to become an ideologue of the right.[14]

Beyond the question of generations, a pendulum motion seems to some scholars to inhere in the political system itself. James L. Sundquist, for example, has theorized that

> because the governing party stands either left or right of center, it finds itself in a state of permanent disequilibrium with the electorate. It is either moving too fast and doing too much—the pitfall of the Democrats—or moving too slowly and doing too little, the bane of the Republicans. At the point of party change, the electorate is correcting the current disequilibrium by the only means available to it—by transferring power to the other party. During the "honeymoon" period of a new administration, the electorate enjoys the satisfaction of feeling the old tensions removed—as when the country began "moving again" under Kennedy. But gradually the voters become aware of the new disequilibrium. The party out of power drums away at the new tensions; the party in power can only call up memories of the tensions of the past. . . .
>
> Thus the pendulum swings. The particular issues, and personalities, of each election determine the speed of the pendulum movement—may slow or even halt it for a time, as in 1956, or accelerate it, as in 1958. It is a pendulum of fits and starts, but the direction of its movement is constant. Once a party firmly establishes its power, it is already on its way to losing that power. It is only a matter of time.[15]

Robert S. McElvaine has described in U.S. history a pattern of "pendulum swings in public attitudes between self-centered individualism and concern with social problems" (though ultimately McElvaine finds himself less than comfortable with the pendulum analogy). McElvaine summons the "wave" metaphor to describe these "periodic swings of mood, opinion, and values," "with each wave of reform and each trough of reaction usually lasting between ten and twenty years." Every swing or wave, McElvaine believes, shifts between spots representing some 40 and 60 percent of the voting public, "which seem to be the lower and upper limits of support for one viewpoint or the other."[16] Albert O. Hirschman has argued that popular moods alternate from time to time between "public action" and "private interest," a view which we will take up further along.[17] Herbert McClosky and John Zaller see shifts between eras stressing democracy and equal opportunity, as against other eras emphasizing a conservative capitalism.[18] Arthur M. Schlesinger, Jr., has described twentieth century cycles running some thirty years "from one period of centralization of energy to the next," and "between public purpose and private interest."[19]

Theories of a cycle in American politics do go back a long way, but they raise certain problems. Describing any political phenomenon as a wave, pendulum, or cycle tends to presuppose a certain periodicity and a regular, self-generated return to equilibrium. All this has a mechanistic cast to it, together with more than a whiff of the primordial theorizing which used to characterize some of the social sciences. Claims to true periodicity in alternation between equilibrium and disequilibrium offend most contemporary historians' understanding of most human behavior.[20] There is also the problem of duration. McElvaine's waves and troughs, for example, run in length anywhere from ten to twenty years. This falls pretty short of genuine periodicity. Over cycle, I favor Pitirim A. Sorokin's somewhat looser concept of rhythm, which may or may not be periodic.[21] Yet even this tends to suggest a predictive dimension which I would consider tenuous if it were argued that the "rhythm" of reform and reaction will continue in the future just as it has in the past. What each of these thinkers has identified, however, is a fundamental pattern of action and reaction, more precisely, of reform and reaction.

Keeping in mind all the insights we have gathered together and examined, we may start to generalize about this pattern. Ideology, to begin with, is heavily though by no means exclusively a generational phenomenon. To the degree that it is generational, rhythms, as Feuer suggests, become part of it. Similarly, fluctuations occur in public perspectives more broadly.

Fairly subtle factors beyond those we have already examined help to explain much of this behavior. One involves fad. There is a good deal of faddism in American reform.[22]

I do not especially like to use the word fad. Other terms might do, for example, fashion, mood, vogue, mode, rage, style, craze, or trend. But we will stick with fad. In itself, the term hints at an important relationship between the mass public and a reform movement.

In considerable measure, a reform fad arises out of tensions which demand resolution. The fad need not sweep up everyone. It may affect only limited classes or groups. To them, action is required, indecision repellant; an itch has to be scratched.[23]   During conservative eras, arguments from the heart and the gut get turned into abstract debates, but the converse becomes true in liberal periods. In a liberal phase, an H. L. Mencken goes out of style in favor of agitating proletarian literature.

This leads us to the concept of what Hadley Cantril called the critical situation: "A critical situation may be said to arise when an individual is confronted by a chaotic external environment which he cannot interpret and which he wants to interpret." More broadly, the culture at large may fall into "a critical condition. The whole social environment, current affairs, and attempted solutions of difficulties may be relatively meaningless and directionless to the masses." People may become "suggestible."   A combustible environment appears for demagogues or dictators.[24]

Certain other factors produce the will-to-change which typifies a reform era. The fad phenomenon may partly arise from the fact that liberalism and conservatism appeal to different, even alternating impulses that most people share internally, whether they identify themselves as liberals or conservatives. Each person responds favorably to certain aspects of each perspective, but unfavorably to others. This may underlie the suggestibility which in turn underlies fad: initially most people react positively to a reform surge because it arouses at least one set of sympathies in them. Stated another way, almost all find something in reform that they can approve of, at least at first, and masses of people feel enormously enthusiastic. The country leans left for a while. There is also the American passion for the new, which helps to offset the equally American suspicion of government. This particular passion explains the terms we use to describe reform drives: New Nationalism, New Freedom, New Deal, New Frontier.

A case study of what I have called the fad phenomenon emerges from Theodore P. Greene's fascinating *America's Heroes: The Changing Models of Success in American Magazines.*[25]   Greene finds dramatic changes over time in "hero-image[s]."   "Each era has admired some particular character type, some form of career, some standard of success more than others." Based on biographical articles in general magazines,

Greene's study does not give us what a Gallup poll might supply, but it does at least suggest important things about transitions in the national mind and mood. From 1894 through 1903, Greene argues, the hero was a Napoleonic, individualistic type, commonly engaged in business. But the progressive period, from 1904 to 1913, downplayed business prestige. While formerly business had served as the most important litmus test of character, now the captains of industry found themselves on the defensive, their wealth-as-virtue discounted. The business-hero gave way to the politician-hero——still a forceful individualist, but one devoted to other people's welfare. Then, during the war years 1914-18, the progressive "idols of justice" fell behind "the idols of organization." Business prestige experienced a renaissance; the new managerial types in business and government, the organization men, emerged as the role models. What went into eclipse this time was individualism, both of the 1890s sort (personal success) and of the progressive variety (social benefaction).[26]

Fad alone, all this? Of course not. The man in the pinstripe suit both then and later more importantly betokened a shifting national character and the changing ways in which Americans thought and lived——the emergence of Babbittry, the consumer society, organization, bureaucratization, and white-collar America. But each of these transitions also bears two conspicuous characteristics of a fad: deep attachment and evanescence.

Reform movements, then, are not only movements. They are also fads. Unlike other sorts of fads, these lead to permanent change. In reform eras, one's attributes and contributions as a member of the broader society take on increased importance. What, people ask, has he or she——the politician, the business person, the minister, whoever ——recently done for other human beings?

As Greene makes clear, the reputations of the private and public sectors fluctuate over time.[27] Early in this century the private side fell under fire, the Rockefellers and Morgans on the defensive against muckraking journalists and politicians. By the early twenties, dissatisfaction with the public sector had become massive because of the war and because of disenchantment with progressivism and progressive politicians; the business person returned as heroic type. The year 1929 brought business into disrepute again, and because it had been relatively inert in the twenties, government appeared the "clean" alternative. From World War II on, business has ridden relatively high. Government received fresh confidence and prestige in the early and mid-1960s, until Vietnam and Watergate left it discredited and the public again suspicious. Ironically, the relatively torpid Washington of the post-Harding twenties and the Eisenhower era probably helped to create a level of trust in government as an institution which would not have been possible had activist administrations held office. The widespread unease which Hoover and even Eisenhower produced emerged because they did too little, not too much. This, in turn, spurred the demand for more government. Roosevelt and Kennedy both took advantage of a relative absence of hostility toward government per se, together with the feeling that Washington ought to do more.

The cleaner and more inert a conservative administration, then, the better things may go for the reformers who follow. On the other hand, when reform administrations move in to fill demands which conservatives have allowed to develop, conservative resistance automatically builds. Shrill opposition from the right goads reformers into going overboard. The excesses of the reformers, in turn, reinforce the right by encouraging backlash. The rhythmic nature of reform and reaction becomes a predictable pattern.

Other factors also ensure that alternations will occur. In purely personal terms, the shift from private to public concerns will likely seem "liberating," a release from the grubbing and boredom of the private sector, a way of addressing "higher" things.[28] In time, though, the attractiveness of the public sphere declines, and the private side rebounds. We will look at this more closely in later chapters.

Another factor involves the tie-in between political reform on one hand and broader social change on the other. "In the history of the world the doctrine of Reform had never such scope as at the present hour," said Emerson in 1841. All institutions, he believed, had come into question: "Christianity, the laws, commerce, schools, the farm, the laboratory," so that every "kingdom, town, statute, rite, calling, man, or woman . . . is threatened by the new spirit."[29] The same thing occurred in the 1960s. Not only does social change tend to run parallel with political reform; social change also tends to undermine political reform. But why?

As Emerson suggested, the questioning process which ultimately leads to political reform does not stop with purely political issues. *All* the major pieties fall under scrutiny. Pejoratives like "the System" or "the Establishment" get bandied about. People start to laugh at conventional taste and morality. Not only do the current weaknesses of liberal democracy get questioned; liberal democracy itself gets questioned. This kind of outburst has occurred twice in this century, in the twenties and again in the sixties and seventies. At first glance, the appearances of political protest and cultural protest seem to run inversely. Political reform was a creature of the period before World War I, and most of the new social raucousness followed. The same in the sixties—the counterculture peaked well after the apogee of reform.

As we examine the phenomenon in a later chapter, we will find that this observation oversimplifies and misleads. The questioning process, initially limited to politics and to matters subject to political amelioration, broadens into every other realm like ripples over a pond. This makes centrist politicians uneasy: the questioning exceeds the realm of their power, even threatens to dissolve that realm. The story of the 1910s and 1920s, like the sixties and seventies, resembles fireworks burning from color to color, reform and radicalism passing through to hedonism, then both giving way to disillusioned, exhausted apathy.

In this view of things, the decade of the thirties, of which we have tended to think as the incarnation of American reform, becomes aberrant for two reasons: its narrow focus on political and economic questions, and the unique significance of the New Deal's legislative achievements. These accomplishments resulted in large measure from its very narrowness of focus. "In an ideological age," as Feuer writes, "the impulse toward rejection embraces all the values, culture, mores and folkways of society."[30] During the thirties, though, exotic Eastern cults, astrology, and new sexual fads were neither called for nor welcome. The Depression did steep the era in ideologies, but precisely because of the depth of the economic disaster, an order of priorities imposed itself on politicians and ideologues alike: economic recovery, antipoverty, justice for workers and farmers. What seems aberrant in a more typical full-blown "ideological age" is precisely this sense of priority. The two most enduring legacies of the New Deal, the welfare state and a new political balance, sprang from its sense of focus——from the priorities imposed on it by the Depression. In the modern era, only depressions (1893, 1929) have fundamentally changed the political order.

If by contrast we cluster the 1910s and 1920s and the sixties and seventies as periods of political *and* social reform, we are struck by the degree to which their legacies arise out of their social divagations. For the first era, the blow to Victorianism proved more important in the end than the initiative, referendum, and recall. For the second, women's rights and the sexual revolution have proved more enduring than, say, the war on poverty. Unlike the depressions of 1893 and 1929, which fundamentally changed political attitudes, the teens-twenties and the sixties more basically altered social behavior.

All this said, the reason why dramatic social change undercuts politically generated reform becomes clear. Rapid social transformations ——which political questioning helps originate——subvert reform, first, by distraction. We can clarify this by way of analogy. At the beginning, reform resembles an automobile moving upgrade. The car stops now and again to pick up passengers and their luggage. Then a trailer is hitched on the back. (The passengers squabble. One is a union chief, another a radical feminist, a third a gay rights advocate, a fourth a Porsche populist from the suburbs. They cannot even agree on which road the car should take, or who should do the driving. Each grabs at the steering wheel.)   More passengers get on.   Pretty soon the overloaded automobile begins to bog down. It overheats. It lurches to a stop. The passengers get out, collect their luggage (squabbling all the while), and walk off their separate ways.

Social change undermines political reform, too, by generating backlash against change in general. The social issue——to borrow a term from the late 1960s——has arisen spectacularly twice in this century, in the twenties and the sixties, and each time it subverted reform by contesting and greatly expanding original priorities, thus immensely broadening the front against which resistance could form. Rather than ending cleanly with a well-defined set of political changes on the books, progressivism and Kennedy-Johnsonism terminated with massive moral uncertainty, the sanctity of the family and the home seemingly threatened, and charges of anti-Americanism ringing in reformers' ears.

And terminated with something else: a resurgence of individualism. The ingrained social "radicalism" of the twenties and the seventies——the institutionalized counterculture of the flapper and the hip flask, the pot party and living together——produced an ideal environment for pursuing unalloyed self-interest.   Here more than anywhere else, political radicalism and social radicalism clash.   Political radicalism (and, to a lesser degree, political liberalism) has traditionally sought collective solutions to social problems. Social radicalism only asks more for "me": freer sex, freer alcohol, freer drugs, a fair field and no favor in singles bars.   The counterculture of the sixties unleashed a renewed individualism in this society which was exceedingly hostile to the cooperative collectivization of New Deal liberalism, mild though it may have been. In short, the seventies' emphasis on social libertarianism——on doing one's own thing——de-emphasized collective endeavor. This always happens in an era of reaction. These periods favor the self-made person, individualism, and individual responsibility or irresponsibility.

"Our political history," Arthur M. Schlesinger, Jr., commented at the end of that decade,

> demonstrates an inherent cyclical rhythm in our public affairs.
> We customarily go through sessions of action, passion, reform
> and affirmative government, until the country is worn out. We
> long for respite and so we enter into sessions of quietism,
> apathy, cynicism and negative government. We are for the
> moment in the depressive phase of the cycle. But we will not
> be in that phase forever.[31]

Schlesinger certainly listed some classic symptoms of reform and reaction; we will examine each of them further along. I wish I could find enough order in it all to describe the process as cyclic, but I cannot.

While American politics may contain certain inherent pendulum impulses, the reform-reaction pattern is more specifically a response to broad, complex social and political events, many of them occurring at the fringe of politics. These do not respond to any particular cycle at all, and they appear at different times, precipitated by different things: a national concern over corporations in one era, a great depression in another, a civil rights revolution in a third. I do believe, though, that when reform does emerge it can be expected to assume certain common forms, certain shared patterns of growth and decay. For cyclic, we might better substitute the term "episodic."

Before the capitalist and the Puritan can get trotted out for another whipping, certain changes must occur. "Two things," Schlesinger argues, "always happen during . . . periods of quiescence and stagnation. The national batteries begin to recharge; and the problems we neglect in the years of indifference become acute and threaten to become unmanageable."[32] Stress does build during the intervening eras. In a balance-of-powers system, every institution from the presidency to Congress to the courts to the implementing and regulatory agencies (and on to the states and cities, oftentimes) must be lined up like stars in order for massive change to occur. Because the U.S. political system does not usually deflate mounting pressure for change by making incremental alterations, reform takes responsibility for relieving crisis by relieving the stress. But the new arrangements it brings deteriorate in time, producing fresh tensions. Stanley M. Elkins has pointed out that one "element that a typical American reform situation appears to require is some sort of disruption of expectations, not necessarily connected with the actual objects of reform." But "there must be *some* maneuvering space, an absence of *total* crisis conditions. A total involvement of energies in a crisis would leave none for a reform movement."[33]

Rather than likening reform to a pendulum, which must always return to the same point, I prefer to compare it to a ratchet.[34] Every political action of any consequence may produce a reaction, but not a reaction which is precisely equal and opposite. Instead, a political drive typically carries change to a certain point; counter-pressure forces change back *part way*; and a new status quo settles in some distance from the original starting place. The ratchet analogy applies not only to eras or movements, but to ideas and individuals. After the progressive theorists, American political thought never returned to where it had been before, nor did it after FDR or Martin Luther King, Jr. But what makes the ratchet work? What gets change going? We will begin to address that question in the next chapter.

NOTES

Roosevelt, *Public Papers*, vol. 5: *The People Approve: 1936* (New York: Random House, 1938), p. 235; "Man the Reformer," in *The Portable Emerson*, ed. Mark Van Doren (N.p.: Viking Press, 1946), pp. 87-88.

[1]In an article on social security programs in the United States and Canada, Christopher Leman coins the felicitous terms "big bang" for change in America, and "steady state" for Canada's "more frequent instances of nonincremental change." "Patterns of Policy Development: Social Security in the United States and Canada," *Public Policy* 25 (Spring 1977): 261-62.

[2]*American as Reformer*, pp. 19-21.

[3] In Schlesinger, *Paths to the Present* (New York: Macmillan Co., 1949), pp. 72-92. An earlier version appeared as "Tides of American Politics," *Yale Review* 29 (December 1939): 217-30. The 1949 essay is cited throughout this book.

[4]"Tides," p. 81.

[5]Ibid., pp. 84-87.

[6]Ibid., pp. 87-88, 90-91.

[7]While certainly provocative, Schlesinger's theory has significant weaknesses. Resting heavily on a set of perceptions about the character of different eras which scholars have since revised or rejected, even on its own terms the essay often becomes conceptually quite opaque. It focuses heavily on the federal government and the presidency, giving inadequate attention to lesser layers of government. Schlesinger confusingly intermingles foreign with domestic policies and events. He tends to discount the impact of foreign wars on domestic politics, a misreading, I think, of the twentieth century experience even as of 1949. The Schlesinger framework is pegged excessively to specific dates and year-spans, and claims a rather dubious predictive value. Yet "Tides" remains a pioneering essay which deserves to have evoked more work by other scholars.

[8]*Crossroads*, pp. xv-xvii.

[9]Reflecting these reform surges in a ragged way, third parties have broken loose from a major party. The Liberal Republicans, Gold Democrats and Silver Republicans appeared late in the nineteenth century, and, in this century, Progressive parties of various stripes in 1912, 1924, and 1948, the Dixiecrats in the latter year, and in the sixties the American Independent party. See Schlesinger, *American as Reformer*, p. 57.

[10]*Ideology and the Ideologists* (New York: Harper & Row, 1975); *The Conflict of Generations: The Character and Significance of Student Movements* (New York: Basic Books, 1969).

[11]See Eileen Eagan, *Class, Culture, and the Classroom: The Student Peace Movement of the 1930s* (Philadelphia: Temple University Press, 1981), pp. 253-54.

[12]*Ideology*, pp. 58, 70, 160. The term "generational consciousness" is drawn from *Conflict of Generations*, p. 31.

[13]*Ideology*, Preface, pp. 23, 41, 56-57, 60-61, 70-71.

[14]Ibid., pp. 56-57, 82, 90. On generations, see also Schlesinger, Jr., *Cycles*, pp. 29-31.

[15]*Politics and Policy*, pp. 501-2; but see also his important qualifications, p. 502. "The period 1953-65 may be seen as one swing of the political pendulum," Sundquist writes, "from a peak of Republican strength to a peak of Democratic strength. But the pendulum denotes more than just the ebb and flow of party fortunes. It describes the cyclical nature of the policy-making process itself." He finds "the policy-making cycle just completed [as of 1968] . . . impressive not only in its rhythm but in the aura of inevitability about the outcome." Ibid., pp. 506-7. Sundquist has portrayed the liberal-conservative "pendulum" as swinging about every thirty years. "Has America Lost Its Social Conscience—And How Will It Get It Back?" *Political Science Quarterly* 101 (1986): 529. I find this description perhaps a bit too tidy. For more on equilibrium and equilibrium theory, see V. 0. Key, Jr., *Politics, Parties, and Pressure Groups*, 5th ed. (New York: Thomas Y. Crowell Co., 1964), p. 542; and the citations in n. 20, below.

[16]*Great Depression*, pp. xiv, 4-5. See also McElvaine's more recent *The End of the Conservative Era: Liberalism after Reagan* (New York: Arbor House, 1987), pp. ix-x, 4-6.

[17]*Shifting Involvements: Private Interest and Public Action* (Princeton: Princeton University Press, 1982).

[18]*The American Ethos: Public Attitudes Toward Capitalism and Democracy* (Cambridge, Mass.: Harvard University Press, 1984), especially, p. 292.

[19]"The Election and After," *New York Review of Books*, 16 August 1984, p. 36; *Cycles*, pp. 27, 31; "The New Conservatism: Will It Last?" *Family Weekly*, 10 January 1982, pp. 4-5. The Schlesinger, Jr., theory has twentieth century "activism" running two decades (except for the sixties) within each complete cycle. Ibid., p. 5.

[20]My thinking about this subject has been influenced by Harold D. Lasswell and Abraham Kaplan, *Power and Society: A Framework for Political Inquiry*, Yale Law School Studies, vol. 8 (New Haven: Yale University Press, 1950), pp. 240-50; and by Pitirim A. Sorokin, *Social and Cultural Dynamics*, vol. 4: *Basic Problems, Principles, and Methods* (1941; reprint, New York: Bedminster Press, 1962), especially ch. 8. Robert H. Walker has perceived cycles operating within a long-term reform movement. See *Reform in America*, especially ch. 4. See also Samuel P.

Huntington's examination of what he terms major eras of "creedal passion," running at sixty- to seventy-year intervals with a notable degree of regularity. Huntington claims that "at about the midpoint of these intervals, other significant changes have occurred in political power among major economic interests. The instances are limited but the suggestion of periodicity is strong, and the pattern may well antedate the American Revolution." Huntington further speculates as to the possibility of "a moralism-cynicism-complacency-hypocrisy cycle in American public consciousness." *American Politics: The Promise of Disharmony* (Cambridge, Mass.: Harvard University Press, Belknap Press, 1981), especially pp. 147-49.

   For a variety of reflections concerning political equilibrium, action/reaction, and cycles, in addition to those cited elsewhere, see: Henry Adams, *History of the United States of America During the First Administration of James Madison*, 9 vols. (New York: Charles Scribner's Sons, 1921), 2:123; Theodore J. Lowi, *At the Pleasure of the Mayor* (Glencoe, Ill.: Free Press, 1964), ch. 8; James David Barber, *The Pulse of Politics: Electing Presidents in the Media Age* (New York: W. W. Norton & Co., 1980); William J. Crotty, *Political Reform and the American Experiment* (New York: Thomas Y. Crowell Co., 1977), ch. 9; McClelland, *Power*, ch. 9; Key, *Politics*, pp. 304-5, 541-42; Donald E. Stokes and Gudmund R. Iversen, "On the Existence of Forces Restoring Party Competition," *Public Opinion Quarterly* 26 (Summer 1962): 159-71; Pitirim A. Sorokin, *Society, Culture, and Personality: Their Structure and Dynamics* (New York: Harper & Bros., 1947), especially pp. 681-90; Benjamin I. Page, *Choices and Echoes in Presidential Elections: Rational Man and Electoral Democracy* (Chicago: University of Chicago Press, 1978), pp. 246-50; Arthur M. Schlesinger, Jr., *The Age of Roosevelt: The Coming of the New Deal* (Boston: Houghton Mifflin Co., 1959), pp. 529-30; Nathan Glazer, "Towards an Imperial Judiciary?" in *The American Commonwealth-1976-*, ed. Nathan Glazer and Irving Kristol (New York: Basic Books, 1976), especially pp. 104-6; Charles Sellers, "The Equilibrium Cycle in Two-Party Politics," *Public Opinion Quarterly* 24 (Spring 1965): 16-38; Frank L. Klingberg, "The Historical Alternation of Moods in American Foreign Policy," *World Politics* 4 (January 1952): 239-73; Frank L. Klingberg, *Cyclical Trends in American Foreign Policy Moods: The Unfolding of America's World Role* (Lanham, Md.: University Press of America, 1983); William Nisbet Chambers, "Party Development and the American Mainstream," in *The American Party Systems: Stages of Political Development*, 2d ed., ed. William Nisbet Chambers and Walter Dean Burnham (New York: Oxford University Press, 1975), pp. 29-30; Kenneth E. Boulding, *A Primer on Social Dynamics: History as Dialectics and Development* (New York: Free Press, 1970), pp. 38-40; Louis H. Bean, *How to Predict Elections* (New York:

Alfred A. Knopf, 1948), chs. 2, 14; William H. Riker, *The Theory of Political Coalitions* (New Haven: Yale University Press, 1962); J. Zvi Namenwirth, "Wheels of Time and the Interdependence of Value Change in America," *Journal of Interdisciplinary History* 3 (Spring 1973): 649-83; William L. Shade, *Social Change and the Electoral Process* (Gainesville: University of Florida Press, 1973); Walter Dean Burnham, *Critical Elections and the Mainsprings of American Politics* (New York: W. W. Norton & Co., 1970); James T. Patterson, "American Politics: The Bursts of Reform, 1930s-1970s," in *Paths to the Present: Interpretive Essays on American History since 1930*, ed. James T. Patterson (Minneapolis: Burgess Publishing Co., 1975), pp. 57-101; and, for some rough analogies to the present work, along with many dissimilarities, Crane Brinton, *The Anatomy of Revolution*, rev. ed. (New York: Random House, Vintage Books, 1965).

[21] *Social and Cultural Dynamics*, 4:389ff., 421. See also Schlesinger, Jr., *Cycles*, pp. 30-31, where he qualifies his own concept of cycles.

[22] To my term "fad," compare Schlesinger's "basic pulsations of opinion," "mass [or "fundamental"] drifts of sentiment," and "irresistible sweeps of sentiment" ("Tides," pp. 85, 87-88). For a discussion of specific meanings assigned to such words as "fad" and "fashion," see Neil J. Smelser, *Theory of Collective Behavior* (New York: Free Press, 1962), pp. 170ff. The term "fad" does not suggest chiseled goals or honed organization. "Fad" does hint at material things (wide ties/narrow ties, flared pants/straight pants). Fads have been identified as a modern phenomenon, and particularly a youth phenomenon. Regrettably, "fad" may connote more shallowness than I really mean here.

[23] Though my thrust differs somewhat from his, much of this has been suggested by Hadley Cantril, *Psychology of Social Movements*, especially pp. 61-62.

[24] Ibid., pp. 63-66. Italics deleted.

[25] (New York: Oxford University Press, 1970).

[26] Ibid., pp. 8-9, 164, 278-83, 286-87, 308-10, 333. Caps reduced to lower case.

[27] On this score, see also, for example, Sigmund Diamond, *The Reputation of the American Businessman*, Studies in Entrepreneurial History (Cambridge, Mass.: Harvard University Press, 1955); and Louis Galambos and Barbara Barrow Spence, *The Public Image of Big Business in America, 1880-1940: A Quantitative Study in Social Change* (Baltimore: Johns Hopkins University Press, 1975).

[28] Hirschman, *Shifting Involvements*, pp. 126, 129.

[29] "Man the Reformer," p. 70.

[30] *Ideology*, p. 88.

[31] "Who Needs Grover Cleveland?" *New Republic*, 7 & 14 July 1979, pp. 15-16. Schlesinger, Jr.'s rather guarded views on the future of the

"cycle" may be found in *Cycles*, pp. 45-48.

[32]Ibid., p. 16. "We can be confident," he adds, "that sometime in the 1980s the dam will break, as it broke at the turn of the century, in the 1930s and in the 1960s." Ibid.

[33]*Slavery: A Problem in American Institutional and Intellectual Life* (New York: Grosset & Dunlap, Universal Library, 1963), p. 159. Italics in original.

[34]After coming onto this metaphor I discovered that other scholars have employed it as well, and recently one used it in much the same sense that I have here. See Robert Higgs, *Crisis and Leviathan: Critical Episodes in the Growth of American Government* (New York: Oxford University Press, 1987), especially pp. 30ff. Instead of a pendulum, the Schlesingers, Sr. and Jr., have preferred to compare change to a spiral, which, like the ratchet metaphor, takes into account cumulative forward movement. "Tides," pp. 86-87; *Cycles*, pp. 30-31.

4

THE FAR LEFT

The various admirable movements in which I have been engaged, have always developed among their members a large lunatic fringe; and I have had plenty of opportunity of seeing individuals who in their revolt against sordid baseness go into utterly wild folly.

Few things hurt a good cause more than the excesses of its nominal friends.

Theodore Roosevelt

Reform in America has often shown a linear pattern in which a cause originates on the far left, in time attracts broad popular support, and winds up as a statute presided over by a bureaucracy. The first phase is frequently led by outcasts or misfits, at least by the standards of their own era—people who seem eccentric or weird. Only later do the respectables move in and some of the aims more or less get carried out.

In this century these outcasts have often been young: a radical generation. F. Scott Fitzgerald coined the expression "real generation" to describe "that reaction against the fathers which seems to occur about three times in a century. It is distinguished," he added, "by a set of ideas inherited in modified form from the madmen and the outlaws of the generation before; if it is a real generation it has its own leaders and spokesmen, and it draws into its orbit those born just before it and just after, whose ideas are less clear-cut and defiant."[1]

In 1863 Lincoln told abolitionist Wendell Phillips that "it looks as if the first reformer of a thing has to meet such a hard opposition and gets so battered and bespattered that afterwards, when people find they have to accept this reform, they will accept it more easily from any other man." Nearly a century later Arthur M. Schlesinger added that

> many are turned against proposed social cures by distrust or disapproval of the self-appointed doctors and surgeons. The reformer is apt to be self-righteous, untidy in dress, truculent, humorless, with a single-track mind and an almost ostentatious liking for the hair shirt and martyrdom: he makes virtue repulsive. Besides, he is frequently so indiscriminate in his choice of causes, taking on all comers, that the underdog appears to have him on a leash. In addition, he is often a failure at his own business, and though a strident lover of mankind, may neglect his family and shirk his neighborhood obligations.[2]

Adds William L. O'Neill, "radicals often more correctly analyze a given situation than their adversaries, but . . . the very traits responsible for their insight prevent them from exploiting it successfully."[3]

The left serves like a magnifying glass which focuses the rays of the sun and makes things burn. Radicals create the sense of common grievance and desire and zeal that bind together the people who comprise a movement.[4] They function as publicists, "dramatiz[ing]," as William Allen White put it, "the injustices of the present situation."[5] The broad themes which have characterized the twentieth century lefts include their advocacy of the underdog (at least some underdogs); their cultural deviance; and their hostility to the bourgeoisie, philistinism, two-party politics, established government, conventional liberalism and conservatism, and corporate capitalism. The radical always assumes the burden of identifying and publicizing an alternative future, a counter-future, a future with things as they should be rather than as they are. Schlesinger called the radicals "the shock troops of reform."[6] They expand a society's range of conscious concerns and the breadth of political debate. The passage of time confers on reforms such respectability that it seems impossible they could ever have aroused resistance, still less that the initial proponents could have seemed such headstrong and unpleasant people. To follow Schlesinger's military analogy, the afterglow of the victory obscures the carnage which came before. The function of these particular "troops" is precisely to shock, but shock troops, so often the first wave in a military operation, are often prodigiously slaughtered. Alone or small in numbers, the radicals attract the maximum possible ridicule and hostility. This can sour them, driving them to extremes even if they do not begin as extremists. Vilification spawns counter-vilification, usually verbally or in print, because the radicals lack institutional weapons. In the opening phase of the battle both sides trade volleys of words.

Individuals who shock the public with new ideas wind up getting labelled heretics, subversives, or worse; the crime of the radicals is glimpsing the future too soon. But after a while, an idea's time has arrived. It becomes assimilable. The lag between the heretical stage and acceptance may be relatively brief, or it may drag out over a long time.

William Jennings Bryan, for example, remained stuck between the two stages for years. It was said of Bryan that he was historically unique in his ability to produce terror without actually killing anyone. Throughout his public career he alternated between the roles of prophet and fool. Again and again Bryan martyred himself (a term he would probably have liked) because he came onto issues just before their time. Truly a tragic figure, Bryan nearly always seemed mawkish or dangerous or both. In the end it became convenient to remember him as a fossilized country bumpkin, partly because the rustic side—fundamentalism, prohibition, man-versus-ape—ascended in the years before he died, and partly because even the most prescient reformer seemed slightly silly in 1925, when Bryan went to his grave. He died at the wrong time, fair tribute to a life lived through with bad timing. But just as the working out of modern liberalism required experimentation, it required experimental types such as Bryan. And for him the monkey trial at Dayton was martyrdom just as surely as war and peace martyred Wilson.

A distinction exists between the pure radical who never holds power, and a person like Bryan who worked at both agitation and practical politics. The very nature of the role virtually dictates that the pure radicals will have difficulty relating to the power structure. Should they move too close to established power, even for the purpose of bargaining, fellow radicals may grow suspicious, restive. Once a reform movement gets started, the true extremists outside the power structure must sooner or later be politically quarantined by reformers on the inside. Otherwise, the right will focus on them and claim that they personify reform. Up to a point, radicals spur change; past this point they encourage reaction. So the shock troops are slaughtered, often in a crossfire between their enemies and their politically smart friends.

The twentieth century has produced three major eruptions on the far left, during the Progressive Era, the thirties, and the sixties. Each of these eruptions, John P. Diggins has reminded us,

> had different social origins and evolved from different historical contexts; and each projected different self-images, political objectives, ideologies, and life styles. Lacking historical continuity, each Left is best approached as a unique generational rebellion, for each tended to deny paternity to its

predecessor and enduring legacy to its successor. Revolutions may devour their children; in the rites of political passage that characterize generational revolts it is the children who slay their fathers.[7]

In a way, the difference between the relative innocence of progressivism and the more hard-boiled New Deal exaggerated itself in the gap between what Diggins aptly calls the Lyrical Left of the 1910s, and the Old Left of the 1930s. Lyricals, in Diggins's term, were mostly "'tender' radicals," products (like so many progressives) of small towns, inclined more toward rebellion than revolution, "festive" and "vague."[8] Max Eastman called one of his autobiographical volumes *Love and Revolution*.[9] The book dealt with both, but the title, and the order of juxtaposition, struck a symbolic ring. The Lyricals had a fascination with the intuitive, the spontaneous, the erotic, and the new, everything new. Robert E. Humphrey observes that Greenwich Villagers

hoped to build a sanctuary for rebels and to revolutionize society; they wanted to live freely and to influence public policies. Village rebels thought that they could isolate themselves from society and yet have an impact on it. They assumed that there was a positive relationship between self-development and social reform, and they infused personal gestures with political meaning. Their first priority was an unstructured existence in Greenwich Village. They wanted to establish an open community based on social and sexual equality that could serve as a model for the rest of society. But expectations exceeded opportunities and capabilities.

Villagers acclaimed private acts of rebellion as significant attacks on conventional values.

. . . .

Their goals, however, were never integrated into a coherent program, and little thought was given to the problems of implementation. Although they assumed that self-expression contributed to social reform, the history of the Village illustrates the conflict between living uproariously and working for political objectives.[10]

The world of the Old Left was far more unpleasant, the world of fascism and Stalinism and economic collapse. The Old Left had more of a new immigrant-urban-ghetto cast. It was less informed by native radicals like Thoreau, and more by Marx.[11]   Since the turn of the century, left-wing radicalism had taken on a foreign hue, rather unlike its earlier coloration, making it seem unindigenous, un-American. The Lyricals' bohemianism and other forms of revolt, largely limited to the individual, had no place in the disciplined left of the thirties.

Yet despite their revolutionary self-image, not many of the thirties radicals were genuine revolutionaries. A remark by Socialist great Norman Thomas epitomized the shallowness of the left's roots: "What cut the ground out pretty completely from under us was this. It was Roosevelt in a word. You don't need anything more."[12] *You don't need anything more.* In 1932, three years after the Crash, the Socialist party could boast a factionalized membership of around 15,000. That year Thomas took just under 882,000 votes for President, and Communist William Z. Foster, 103,000. Five years into the Depression, Communist party membership stood at only a little over 30,000.[13] In 1936 Thomas got 187,000 votes, Communist Earl Browder, 80,000. The radicals split (as usual), and the New Deal co-opted some of their most attractive and feasible proposals.[14]

The gap between the Old Left and the New spanned a generation, but when the New Left appeared it yielded nothing in marginality to the Old. In fact, it provides the best case study of marginality, and so we will give it special emphasis in this chapter. The 1960s produced a tremendous, perhaps an unprecedented, convergence in lines of dissent, what William Lee Miller has called "the simultaneous return of the cultural protest of the twenties and the political-economic protest of the thirties."[15] Abundance spawned the Lyrical and New lefts, not poverty. If the left of the thirties had emphasized what we might call the "classical" themes——science, technology, reason——the left of the sixties leaned, like the Lyricals, as much or more toward the "romantic" emphases on sensation and emotion. A form of revolt emerged which I have chosen to label pop radicalism. Less absorbed——and less disciplined——by hard-edged dogmas, theories, or determinisms, at least at first, it was middle-class in origin and distinctly young in contrast to earlier movements. Morris Dickstein has put it this way: "The spirit of the fifties was neo-classical, formal; the sixties were expressive, romantic, free-form."[16] This echoed the 1910s far more than the thirties. To many of the young, New Deal liberalism seemed amusingly passé. The counterculture offered things a suburban upbringing had not: some sense of purpose, personal value, broader community, and an element of risk. Unlike Levittown, it stirred the senses. Finally, the sixties left reflected feelings of guilt——over being affluent, over being middle-class, over being draft-deferred. Economically unthreatened, middle-class young often found themselves haunted, as Irwin Unger writes, "by guilt and self-disgust over their own good luck."[17]

Only a small segment of the public, even of youth, aligned themselves with the New Left. The dissidents found themselves a minority even on college campuses. Among their age-contemporaries in the white working class, the counter*culture* swayed some, but leftist *politics* did not. (Arguably, middle-class young were merely catching up with the patterns of indulgence which many in the lower strata had always enjoyed.) Despite its limited numbers, the counterculture differed from anything earlier in part because of its sheer size. Revolt had become democratized, to some degree because of television, which radiated the new values around the country and gave them a quick, visceral impact.

The middle-classness of the New Left offers, I think, the most important clue to its eventual demise. Easy affluence, here as in other favored countries, had spawned a generation gap between the Old Left and the New. The Old had been materialist and believed in discipline and organization; by and large, the New allowed the individual more sway, indeed often revelled in individuality. In varying degrees and at different times the New Left combined elements of the counterculture of the 1910s with the hard materialism of the thirties. What Kenneth Keniston calls "two poles of dissent" pervaded the Movement——"political radicalism and cultural alienation"——with the latter oriented toward human interiors and inclined to ignore the international, social, and other issues which animated the former.[18] The New Left went hunting for older, pre-New Deal radical-to-progressive philosophies, values, and traditions of idealism, individual participation, even utopianism.[19] It reinvigorated old suspicions of expertise and decisions made "dispassionately" at the top.

As much of this suggests, though, the New Left was politically spongy. Students born in the forties had not experienced a depression or a world war. Prosperity in the sixties, similar in some ways to the comfortable era in which the Lyricals had thrived, yielded a similarly soft rebellion, unlike the hard surge of the thirties. No economic prod pushed radicals toward taut ideologies or organizations. The Old Left, like the New Deal, had focus, almost to the point of narrowness and dullness. The New Left by and large ignored economics. Young rebels spoke of the People, but not typically of the Proletariat. They had multifold aims, but no great, underlying theoretical goal.[20]

The New Left and hippiedom, cultural and political criticism and insurgency, shared the same pool but swam together uneasily. Some of their humanistic goals were similar. But the hippies——in their anomie, their unease over conformism, bureaucracy, and mass society——carried out their revolt mainly in the head and through interpersonal relations. A head trip would do nothing for a hungry child in Mississippi. The student left could not shake the contradiction: society-versus-self acted on the Movement like opposing magnetic fields.

Like liberalism, American radicalism has shown an enduring ambivalence toward change. To a very considerable degree, the rebels of the sixties reacted against what they perceived to be a plastic society but answered it with plastic rebellion, pop radicalism. They reacted against "a felt sense of injustice and a sense of meaninglessness" and against personal oppression——but of a subtle sort.[21]   In the words of one commentator early in the decade, "the problems of income distribution, full employment and the rights of labor unions are not the major crises faced by modern America." The essence of the thing, it seemed, was "the style and quality of our lives." Writing off the hard economic issues which remained, and talking about "the reality of life in Los Angeles, Syracuse, and Sacramento, with their bowling alleys and shopping centers, and those vast stretches of America which are a blight upon the idea that man is sensitive, searching, poetic, and capable of love,"[22] the critic oddly echoed much of the shallow *liberalism* of the 1950s. Inchoate and hard to get hold of, all of this proved harder yet to organize a movement around. Young people might suffer anomie, but the causes tended to resist detection or cures. What the young complained about flowed in substantial degree from the very prosperity their elders had struggled to attain. Young students could live off the fat while rebelling. Meanwhile, economic abundance freed them to think about the style of life in Syracuse or Sacramento.

Much of their rebellion scarcely departed from the realm of ideas. This we might expect of an insurgent, budding intelligentsia, but it made the left more formless and diffuse than it might have been. When youth initially rebelled in the sixties, they set out very considerably in behalf of others: blacks or the poor. Admirable as this selflessness was, it did not carry the sting of selfishness. In this way, the revolution of the sixties originated as a revolution at second hand, analogous to the limousine liberalism which the students decried.

One issue, however, did produce plenty of personal sting——the draft. It threatened students' lives. With the escalation of the Vietnam War, thousands of young men fled the country.

But the draft aside, to a great extent the New Left reflected the soft dynamics of a fad. A good many members of Students for a Democratic Society (SDS) "were merely curious and rebellious and given to easy enthusiasms as well as easy discouragement."[23] Much of the involvement in the Movement stemmed from a desire simply for experience, not the serious pursuit of a cause. The innocent, the unstable joiner, the hanger-on, and the fair-weather ideologue will always find it tempting to come in from the cold, especially when society can be rejoined at the cost of a suit and a shave. None of this questions the devotion or the effectiveness of some of the Movement's membership, still less their goals, or that thousands of adults involved themselves as well. Yet for some of these adults, too, radicalism was a fad, embodied in the term "radical chic." Radical chic hardly provided a hardcore cadre to rebuild society or uplift the downtrodden. It could as easily veer off into peripheral matters or, since it had as much to do with self-development as with social causes, into yoga or herb tea.

The intellectualizing and vaporousness of so much of the New Left became epitomized in the proximate target of the young radicals, the universities. Half-sympathetic to the radical students' positions to begin with, the campuses provided soft targets, perhaps the softest ones available. Yet much of the energy even of the students' more radical academic elders got dissipated in intramural confrontations within their disciplines and in scholarship, an arm's length enterprise at best.[24] The university symbolized a good deal that the left found wrong with America, and accordingly, much of the campus protest of the sixties took form symbolically. "Beneath the political demands," Dickstein writes of the Columbia crisis, "the students were playing out a psychodrama of self-validation, which involved above all the demystification of authority."[25]

Along with the perennial vulnerability of the left has run a strand of elitism which unquestionably helps to account for the vulnerability. (We encounter elitism early in the century in Emma Goldman, for example, or Max Eastman; and in the sixties among those who admired blacks or Indians but lashed out at the white ethnic working class.) When radicalism moves prominently through the cultural realm, as it did before World War I or in the sixties, it will spurn mass tastes, deriding and threatening them. An outspoken sense of cultural superiority hardly eases the way for a mass movement.

But elitism sometimes occurs more subtly. In the mid-sixties, with Vietnam heating up, the left made its split with more conventional reformers. In opposing the war, it altered its emphasis from the domestic realm to the foreign. It also switched its focus from the blacks and the poor to the students and the campuses——that is, it moved up a notch in class perspective and from blacks to whites in racial perspective.[26] Insofar as the left shifted emphasis to foreign policy and war, it became extremely vulnerable to events at the furthest distance from its control. Then, in 1972, Nixon went to China. Vietnam slowly cooled down. All of this undermined the left. Other things beckoned it toward collapse as well.

Perhaps the legendary factionalism of American radicals has produced the greatest obstacle to the construction of a permanent, influential left. It certainly did in the 1960s. As we survey the landscape of twentieth century radicalism we encounter one ruined structure after another. Some show signs of slow decay, while others have been torn down or blown apart. The wreckage appears so confusing that amid the rubble and the weeds it takes us time even to determine where the buildings once stood. What were they used for? Was this a single structure or several?

From its founding, political democracy has existed in this country (save for women, slaves, Indians, and other huge groups); radicals have sought to produce an economic democracy to match. The Socialist party, noted De Witt in the Progressive Era, limited "its demands to a single proposition; i.e., that the community should own the means of production and distribution."[27] This single, focused, *positive* demand helps to explain the party's early, phenomenal success. But in general the left has failed to organize itself nationally as an effective, focused political movement. It has tended to hold politics itself in suspicion. The Lyricals stressed culture and poetry; the Old Left, Marxist dialectics; the New Left, the expedients we have just examined. Over time, the grist of the left has been "*negation.*"[28] This persistent negativism has diminished its potential appeal.

Leftist movements seem unable to transcend generational lines. One of the few ties between the Old Left and the New was their mutual hostility. Each left has reacted against different things in different times; and while broad common themes do tie the various lefts together, notably the socialist theme, the specific events leading to outburst have been diffuse. As each left dissolves into a sense of apathy or defeatism or despair or ambiguity, an emergent left must react against this along with everything else. An older left holds up a mirror to a new, and in the mirror the younger generation sees age-lines of submission. The young must affirm their own exemption from the rule that lefts die out.

Another source of fragmentation lies in the gulf between culture and politics. Left intellectuals have shown truly remarkable determination to make politics poetry and poetry politics. This may stem from a greater interest in poetry than in politics (I suspect that it often does). Yet the two are at least as antithetical as compatible. The New Left was not the first whose adherents often called culture and politics the same thing; nor the first to see welling up within it a fascination with intuition and the deeper recesses of the mind, with spontaneous expression, astrology, mysticism, magic, and the various permutations of religion and the occult. A good deal of this "romanticism" wafted through Greenwich Village before the Great War. The Lyrical Left and the sixties counterculture, if not close blood relatives, at least shared this distant kinship.

Combining a cultural movement with a political one raises dual problems. On one hand is focus—the cultural side will pull against the political, diverting political direction and energy. The other problem involves credibility. Political and cultural insurgency naturally enough run together, but cultural deviance serves as a warning flag against its accompanying political ideology. Simply put, the best way to sell left politics in this country is in a suit and tie.

Fragmentation of ideology has troubled the left throughout this century. Sectarian battles of various sorts have gone on endlessly. During the thirties, truly legendary cleavages developed between Communists and Socialists, Stalinists and Trotskyites. In the Sixties the broad white-black civil rights movement saw black power, black nationalist, and black separatist groups sheer off, nonviolence giving way to violence, interracial coalition to separatism. The New Left turned increasingly doctrinaire, a good part of it eventually becoming a sect-squabbling echo of the thirties. "Lyricalism" (of a sort) yielded to Leninism or Maoism. Radicalism destroyed itself in extremism and factional mitosis. As New Left ideology grew harder and extremists took over key organizations, the Movement spun followers away like a berserk merry-go-round. Some elements became violent, terroristic, but this brought down the law, proving suicidal. The Black Panthers split. SDS split. (SDS membership kept changing. So did SDS ideology. And the members did not get along.) What the New left turned into was symbolized by the rise of the Beijing-oriented Progressive Labor party, the Yippies, and the bombing-prone Weathermen. Even the crucial antiwar crusade rattled apart.

More and more isolated, the left shed followers like rain. While Progressive Labor planned for an uprising of the working class, in the best tradition of the Old Left, some of the "soft" leftists whose countercultural affinities they (rightly) held in suspicion had taken to tooling leather and milking cows in places like Vermont, in the best tradition of the eighteenth century. The ideological menu of the sixties far left went on and on, contained no specialties of the house——though daily specials came and went——and while perfectly tantalizing in all its variety, produced numerous dishes which got served half-cooked. The *agenda* of the sixties in effect co-opted the left by drawing it from issue to issue, cause to cause. Government goaded the left in this direction by repeatedly enacting un-radical but co-opting "solutions," and the left in fact co-opted itself. Unable to focus on a handful of problems with priority, responding to the fad dynamics that helped keep students aroused, radicalism moved reactively. By 1970 the entire left was drifting and crumbling like some expiring iceberg. At least the liberals had power; the far left influenced power but did not control it. And we are tempted to say, "Of course. Inevitably. The radical left never holds power in America."

Walter Lippmann pinpointed a profound problem with the left when he remarked: "The rebel feels his rebellion not as a plea for this or that reform but as an unbearable tension in his viscera. He must break down the cause of his frustration or jump out of his own skin."[29] The perennial role of the left is to agitate, not hold power. Wendell Phillips, who refused even to vote, insisted that "the agitator must stand outside of organizations, with no bread to earn, no candidate to elect, no party to save, no object but truth—to tear a question open and riddle it with light."[30]

The visceral nature of rebellion, when multiplied by the number of protestors in a group, can generate tremendous instability. Dissent is only partly a matter of causes and beneficiaries. It also amounts to experience as experience, revolt for the exhilaration of revolt. This helps to account for the factionalism of the sixties and for the fad dimension in sixties radicalism. The Old Left at least knew who it wanted to help; its differences arose over means. But the New Left resembled a ragtag army moving across the landscape from battle to battle, with people joining and deserting all the time.

Whenever a new radical movement emerges, it has to start afresh organizationally and ideologically, debating first principles all over again. This discontinuity provides one explanation for the wide differences between left movements, as well as for the upheavals within them after they emerge. Without established structural channels for an initial radical surge, it pours out all over the place, losing force and velocity until little of either remains.[31]

Invariably, or nearly so, the radicals give way to the implementors, who usually arrive in the agitators' ideological vicinity by a roundabout and (what usually amounts to the same thing) a political route. Thus, Lincoln: "If I could save the Union without freeing *any* slave, I would do it; and if I could save it by freeing *all* the slaves, I would do it; and if I could do it by freeing some and leaving others alone, I would also do that."[32] The radical makes progress by influencing others to do the implementing. Partly this results from the fact, as James Q. Wilson points out, that "the militant displays an unwillingness to perform those administrative tasks which are necessary to operate an organization. Probably the skills of the agitator and the skills of the administrator . . . are not incompatible, but few men can do both well."[33] The two sets of skills surely produce clashes of roles.

Even when radicals have held power, the results have generally turned out disappointing in terms of declared ideology. The Socialist party, for example, might be able to take power in Milwaukee, Schenectady, or other cities early in the twentieth century, but the city Socialists generally proved far better at implementing progressive goals than Socialist ones. The New Left was fond neither of bureaucracy nor of other institutions: SDS had trouble even governing itself. Part of the difficulty arose from fission, part of it from ideology, and part of it from a shortage of discipline. After the leftist impulse surged off into communal living, the communes folded in droves. The problem of organizing has always plagued the far left. The general negativism of much of indigenous American radicalism has led it not to build systems of authority, but to undo them and to keep government at a distance.[34] Such organizations as radicals do fashion typically shatter. Organization per se flew in the face of the spirit of much of the Lyrical and New lefts, but not of the Old Left. Hence, this irony: the Communist party, so central to the Old, still chugs along decade after decade, fueled by discipline, while other radicals have come and gone.

The liberals, on the other hand, live to govern. Tension, often creative tension, has always divided the far left from political reformers. When the two groups come too close, the liberals can get burned, as in the 1972 McGovern campaign. The purpose of radicalism is to polarize; of liberalism, to fashion coalitions. Zeroing in on liberalism as the main antagonist, the far left has traditionally opposed its faith in pluralistic, interest politics. Liberalism has sought to balance classes off rather than (as the left would wish) undo the class system; has held to competition and achievement as ideals where the left would substitute cooperation; has taken a more guarded view of human potential than the left; and has participated in the system of power as a given, trying to alter some things but not to undo fundamental arrangements. The left's critique of liberalism arises from the ultimate truth that liberals will not break through the capitalist barrier and institute some sort of socialism. This means that virtually any liberal proposal, and literally any liberal government, will fail to measure up. It also explains why, as a general proposition throughout this century, the liberals govern and the radicals do not. Anyone and any group intending to deal in the realities of power so as to implement change (as opposed to just agitating for it) must ultimately deal with the liberals because now and again the liberals hold power.

What role, then, has twentieth century American radicalism filled? First let us take up some of its direct achievements. The far left has represented a generational phenomenon, a surge of energy by an ideologized younger generation with a fresh consciousness and a new or revivified set of ideas for transforming society. Of no generation was this more true than the New Left. It did not hold power in the way that the early twentieth century Socialists did; but ironically, it had far more influence than they or any other left of this century could claim, by affecting the way in which those who did hold power in Washington and elsewhere actually used it. The sixties left helped bring an end to Vietnam, its most important single accomplishment. It raised the nation's awareness of poverty, racism, and eventually, sexism. It threw a searchlight on the distribution of wealth and power, U.S. foreign policy, the nature of work, the success-consumption syndrome, competitiveness, family, education, sexual hypocrisies, the environmental costs of growth, bureaucracy, corporatism and corporate liberalism, advertising, and many other things. It left dissent behind as a style.

The New Left did alter some of the nation's patterns of thinking. In the social realm it worked like acid on outdated beliefs and conventional mores. Yet the Movement did not amount entirely, or perhaps even principally, to helping other people. "The quest for personal fulfillment," as Peter Clecak calls it, always underlay it.[35] The changes were primarily social in nature, far less, political. And while the social innovations brought new personal freedoms into the nation's life, they did not alter the basic power structure in fundamental ways, the civil rights movement and feminism notwithstanding. In this sense, the New Left produced change precisely where one might have expected it to. All this makes it clear that in the 1960s, the far left served in the role which the left in America perennially fulfills, as a gadfly and publicist, a visionary of how things ought to be.[36] The left has always functioned as a kind of ad hoc, transitory lobby. It has greatly feared and generally suffered from co-optation. Ironically, though, its biggest victories have ultimately been accomplished through co-optation. The way out of Vietnam lay precisely there.

Co-optation can occur in part because the left has made it safe for centrist politicians to assume the initiative. The radicals give liberals room to maneuver by pulling the median of dialogue and debate further left and then beckoning or dragging a certain number of respectables in that general direction. (During the sixties, the effect was also reciprocal: the rising expectations of the Kennedy era helped summon the New Left into existence in the first place.)[37] Not only does the left introduce issues into the mainstream of debate, or accentuate them. It also serves as a kind of stalking-horse for the liberals by doing the publicizing and taking the pressure early on. Once the public becomes aroused or at least aware, the liberals look respectable, even conservative, when they do something about a problem. And their doing something about it——even if on no more than a symbolic level——relieves the tensions originally stirred in the public mind by the left. Sometimes radicals themselves ultimately find ameliorative reform sufficient. Regardless, by forcing the liberals to act, the left invariably assists in its own co-optation.

"Mr. Roosevelt did not carry out the Socialist platform," Norman Thomas remarked, "unless he carried it out on a stretcher."[38] The real radicals will cry for something dramatic, for a social transformation; but they will see their most marketable proposals co-opted, while they get left with assorted un-negotiable demands. The political system tends to respond to focused aims rather than to cries for sweeping change. This is the meaning of Upton Sinclair's famous remark after his socialist novel, *The Jungle*, led to meat packing legislation instead of something bigger: "I aimed at the public's heart, and by accident I hit it in the stomach."[39]   I suspect this sort of thing is one reason why radical movements sometimes become hysterical late in a reform era. What they wind up with, their most elevated hopes and dreams, amounts to little but the political dregs. When they move still further left, they whirl off old backers and narrow their range of support.   Yet they keep on grinding out new demands—ideas which may find favor eventually, but which for the time being appear farfetched, even insane.

NOTES

Cooper, *The Warrior and the Priest*, p. 249 (first Roosevelt quote); Theodore Roosevelt, "Latitude and Longitude among Reformers," in Roosevelt, *The Strenuous Life: Essays and Addresses* (New York: Century Co., 1902; reprint, St. Clair Shores, Mich.: Scholarly Press, 1970), p. 52 (second Roosevelt quote). See also *Theodore Roosevelt: An Autobiography* (New York: Charles Scribner's Sons, 1920), p. 206.

[1]Quoted in Malcolm Cowley, "The '60s," *New Republic*, 20 & 27 August 1977, p. 37.

[2]*American as Reformer*, pp. 40 (Lincoln quote), 67.

[3]*Everyone Was Brave: The Rise and Fall of Feminism in America* (Chicago: Quadrangle Books, 1969), p. 291.

[4]Key, *Politics*, pp. 41-42.

[5]Quoted in "Where Are the Pre-war Radicals?" *Survey*, 1 February 1926, p. 556.

[6]*American as Reformer*, p. 67.

[7]*The American Left in the Twentieth Century*, Harbrace History of the United States (New York: Harcourt Brace Jovanovich, 1973), p. vi.

[8]Ibid., p. 118.

[9]*Love and Revolution: My Journey Through an Epoch* (New York: Random House, 1964).

[10]*Children of Fantasy: The First Rebels of Greenwich Village* (New York: John Wiley & Sons, Ronald Press, 1978), pp. 237, 252.

[11]There was also an upwelling of movements—notably those of Huey Long, Father Coughlin, and Francis Townsend—which defy easy ideological categorization.

[12]David A. Shannon, *The Socialist Party of America: A History* (Chicago: Quadrangle Paperbacks, 1967), p. 235.

[13]Arthur M. Schlesinger, Jr., *The Age of Roosevelt: The Politics of Upheaval* (Boston: Houghton Mifflin Co., 1960), pp. 177, 197.

[14]See Shannon, *Socialist Party*, p. 235.

[15]"The New Anti-Americanism," *The Center Magazine* (Center for the Study of Democratic Institutions), September 1969, p. 39.

[16]*Gates of Eden: American Culture in the Sixties* (New York: Basic Books, 1977), p. 185.

[17]*The Movement: A History of the American New Left, 1959-1972* (New York: Dodd, Mead & Co., 1975), pp. 150-51. For a far broader discussion of the origins of countercultural outbursts than is offered in the present volume, see J. Milton Yinger, *Countercultures: The Promise and the Peril of a World Turned Upside Down* (New York: Free Press, Macmillan Publishing Co., 1982).

[18]*Youth and Dissent: The Rise of a New Opposition* (New York: Harcourt Brace Jovanovich, 1971), p. 143. Italics deleted. For a far different interpretation of cultural versus political radicalism than will follow here, see Richard Flacks, *Making History: The Radical Tradition in American Life* (New York: Columbia University Press, 1988), especially pp. 187-91.

[19]See Kesselman, *Modernization*, p. 505.

[20]Cowley, "The '60s," p. 38; Peter Clecak, *America's Quest for the Ideal Self: Dissent and Fulfillment in the 60s and 70s* (New York: Oxford University Press, 1983), p. 118.

[21]Ibid., p. 120.

[22]Robert Scheer, quoted in Unger, *The Movement*, pp. 28-29.

[23]Ibid., p. 152.

[24]Apart, at least, from the possibility of altering the nature of the university itself, or using it as a point of departure for changing the middle class.

[25]*Gates of Eden*, p. 268.

[26]See Unger, *The Movement*, p. 93, and Diggins, *American Left*, p. 177. Todd Gitlin identifies a shift in the student movement from being *"for others"* (blacks, Vietnamese, Cubans) to being *"for itself"* (young whites). See *The Sixties: Years of Hope; Days of Rage* (New York: Bantam Books, 1987), p. 353. Italics in the original.

[27]*Progressive Movement*, pp. 106-7.

[28]Diggins, *American Left*, p. 16. Italics added.

[29]*Men of Destiny* (New York: Macmillan Co., 1927), p. 106.

[30]Schlesinger, *American as Reformer*, p. 35.

[31]The remarks in this paragraph draw very heavily upon Elkins, *Slavery*, p. 160.

[32]Letter to Horace Greeley, 22 August 1862, in Henry Steele Commager, ed., *Documents of American History*, 7th ed. (New York: Appleton-Century-Crofts, 1963), pp. 417-18. Italics in original.

[33]*Negro Politics: The Search for Leadership* (New York: Free Press, 1960), p. 225.

[34]See C. Vann Woodward, "Home-Grown Radicals," *New York Review of Books*, 5 April 1979, p. 3.

[35]*Ideal Self*, p. 123. On the changes of the sixties, see also pp. 222-23.

[36]Diggins, *American Left*, p. 18.

[37]Christopher Lasch, *The World of Nations: Reflections on American History, Politics, and Culture* (New York: Alfred A. Knopf, 1973), p. 125.

[38]George Wolfskill and John A. Hudson, *All but the People: Franklin D. Roosevelt and His Critics, 1933-39* (N.p.: Macmillan Co., 1969), p. 121. Italics deleted. As another example, on the co-opting of black leadership in the sixties and seventies see James W. Button, *Black Violence: Political Impact of the 1960s Riots* (Princeton: Princeton University Press, 1978), p. 169.

[39]Upton Sinclair, *The Autobiography of Upton Sinclair* (New York: Harcourt, Brace & World, 1962), p. 126.

5

DEMOCRATS
AND REPUBLICANS

> Roosevelt, we progressives never beat the conservatives because they, wanting to disturb nothing, and maintaining a purely defensive position, have the cohesiveness and resistance of a closed fist; but we, being determined to make progress and each knowing best how it should be done and being therefore utterly unable, any of us, to support any others of us, have about as much striking power as you'd expect from the fingers of an open hand, each pointing in a slightly different direction.
>
> Woodrow Wilson to Franklin D. Roosevelt

> The ironic flaw in American liberalism lies in the fact that we have never had a real conservative tradition.
>
> Louis Hartz

The main direction of reform in the twentieth century has pointed toward the welfare state; and the ultimate bargaining over its policies takes place between the two major parties. The relationship of such a state to the party system is clear: a party determines to intervene in the private sector of the economy in order to benefit a certain interest group or groups. Typically it does so in response to pressure from these groups. The party may act in order to lure new client groups into its coalition, or it may wish to reaffirm the adherence of the ones which already belong. This intervention comprises the now-familiar process by which, in favorable conditions, reform movements develop. A dilemma or a crisis which for some time may have fed radical agitation arrives at length on the liberals' table. The crisis is fully politicized.

In dealing with parties, historians and political scientists have often talked past one another, and this chapter may seem to do so too. I do not address party systems, partisan realignments, the theory of critical elections or realigning eras, or the frequently perceived cyclic pattern in American voting behavior and party systems in the way a political scientist might.[1] But I have certainly been influenced by the insights of political science, and by the debate which continues over these issues. Let me say briefly that a reform movement as I define it may or may not appear specifically in connection with a major realignment of voters. Whether it does or not, new issues boil up in such an era. Often the political system has trouble coming to terms with them. A reform movement may ride along on one party or it may straddle both. Either way, it will ultimately take partisan, political form, and will work toward its aims through the political process.

It would be easy to overemphasize the role and importance of party in American politics, both historically and especially today. Parties have always operated under severe handicaps and constraints. For example, the Democrats and the Republicans have only occasionally advanced carefully honed programs in opposition to one another, and the sharp edges have soon dulled again. But the points of clarity mark the points of rapid change. Strong ideological confrontations between the parties also reveal the temporary supremacy of a faction within one or each of the parties. So a change of political direction is suggested not just by a switch in which party governs, but in who governs the party.[2]

Liberals and conservatives have never fundamentally disagreed over the desirability of a capitalist economic system. They have disagreed over how, and how much, to leaven it by applying governmental power. At times, for instance, each party has tried more or less to regulate big business. But these efforts have often resulted in business regulating its regulators, the agencies set up to oversee it. Sometimes this has been the idea behind regulation in the first place——actually, to stimulate business stability with no serious expectation that this will operate in the broad public interest. The regulative system is not per se anti-business, nor does it propose an alternative to capitalism. And it very often takes the form of a business-government partnership.

In order to make some sense of these ambiguities and others, I want to draw a fundamental distinction between two subtypes of welfare statism. One supports business through subsidies, collaborative regulation, inflated contracts, and partnership with government; but we never call these things "welfare" at all. The other provides support to certain downtrodden, oppressed, or threatened groups——for example, the poor or the unemployed. This is *social* welfare statism. Each variety of welfare statism intertwines with the other. The primary question always is (to paraphrase Harold D. Lasswell),[3] Who will get what from government, when, and how? The two major parties have faced that question in one form or another since long before the welfare state began.

As we look back to the Civil War era and its aftermath, the relationships which have prevailed between the two major parties can sometimes startle us. Originally, the GOP was the party that fought the war and liberated the slaves. Ironically, it was the GOP——that temple to property rights——which presided over the biggest liquidation of private property this country has ever experienced. It also backed public education and free homesteads. True enough, as time passed and its ideological founders departed, party leadership passed to organizational types. But the GOP started out as a great instrument of American reform.

And what of the Democrats? If we test party ideology against the standard I mentioned earlier——movement in the direction of the welfare state——then the Democrats as late as the Grover Cleveland era of the mid-1880s through the mid-1890s look even more conservative than the Republicans. Typically, at any given time one of the two major parties has had an agenda for change, while the other has looked backward.[4] Late in the nineteenth century, the Democratic party played the nostalgic role. During this great age of supposed laissez-faire, the Republicans at least demonstrated a willingness to bring one group under the wing of government; it was just that this group happened to be business. The Democratic leadership, on the other hand, clung obstinately to literal laissez-faire, or something close to it, and wanted interest groups kept away from government altogether. Ironically, the earliest and biggest threat to these good conservative values of diffused power and decentralization was the corporation itself. But during the Gilded Age, as great corporations emerged, the Democratic party operated by the philosophy of states' rights, limited government, and decentralization. As one Clevelandite put it, the administration had as its main job to resist "'reforms' which mean that the Government is to rock the cradle and drive the hearse, weep over the grave and sit up with the widow, and pay every man for cracking his own lice."[5] Or, as Cleveland himself pronounced, "while the people should patriotically and cheerfully support their Government its functions do not include the support of the people."[6] Meanwhile, as the answer to giant business, the old Jacksonian antimonopolism still prevailed in the party. Bryan would open the new century for the Democrats by running on it.

Grover Cleveland was the avatar of the Bourbon Democrats ("they have learned nothing, and forgotten nothing"). The Bourbons spoke much of small government, individual freedom, sound money, and free trade.   But while these Jeffersonisms and Jacksonisms had seemed appealingly "liberal" early in the century, they sounded an increasingly tinny ring toward its end.   For one thing, Bourbonism conveyed a tone of respectability——of comfort and probity, the conventional wisdom, the prevailing virtues and pieties——quite foreign to the Democratic party at most times in its history, and positively embarrassing during some.   As in other eras when the party has felt in a conservative mood, under Cleveland it resided to an unusual degree in the laps of the well-off.   Yet we might also note that Cleveland suited an age of scarce, blurred political issues.   "Neither party," observed James Bryce, "has any clean-cut principles, any distinctive tenets.   Both have traditions.   Both claim to have tendencies. . . . All has been lost, except office or the hope of it."[7]   Cleveland was a political, though not altogether a personal, prude in a Victorian era.   Far more honest and moralistic than imaginative, he became one of history's great vetoers.

Unfortunately for Cleveland, he belonged to the wrong party.   He wanted to appear respectable, but the party he led kept betraying him.   The Democracy (a term then in use) had acquired a reputation as the party of rum, Romanism, and rebellion.   By no means was it exclusively comprised of the great unwashed, but to a disproportionate degree this was so.   From time to time——the Cleveland era, the Al Smith era, the Stevenson era, the Carter era——the Democratic party, typically frayed from a previous reform binge, has tried to polish its shoes, put on a vest, and reacquaint itself with respectability.   But it can never outpoint the GOP on that, and it looks foolish trying.   This has become part of the general pattern of mounting conformity which typifies our inter-reform eras.

And what of the GOP in the Gilded Age?   The two parties were remarkably even in strength, but the Republicans managed to control the presidency most of the time.   The GOP billed itself as the "party of prosperity," of forward movement and national stability.   From its origins as an organization of ideology and high purpose in the era of Lincoln and Seward and Sumner and Stevens, the party moved increasingly toward organizational politics and the status quo.   This conservatism ran the gamut from backing high tariffs to supporting prohibition or opposing polygamy.   But neither the Republicans nor the Democrats totally ignored the interests of workers or farmers; and apart from the usual platform grandstanding this reflected the fact that both parties represented a wide coalition of interests and attitudes ranging from place and type of work, to section and ethnicity, to religion (then a very important source of political identification).   And in each party, the well-heeled had a large say.

The widening search for a middle ground between laissez-faire and socialism threatened both parties.   It threatened to consolidate the amorphous politics of the Gilded Age into a politics of class, interest groups, and ideology. It threatened a return to the principled polarities of the Civil War era, but over new issues. The problems of the industrial age also offered each party a great opportunity. No inevitabilities exist in history; but looking back from the perspective of a century it does seem clear that history played a cruel trick on the Republicans when, early on, it rendered the GOP disproportionately the favored child of the comfortable, the propertied, and the WASPs. The party that emerged in this role was almost bound to reflect, and to be perceived as representing, the desires of this favored group——a minority clothed in the attractive raiment of respectability, prosperity, and piety. The GOP's handicap remained concealed for many years. Nor would any suitor likely find the dull Bourbons more alluring. But the Democrats held the potential of supremacy because they were disproportionately the party of the rapidly growing new ethnics, the cities, and a large (southern) share of the farmers. Properly organized, these constituencies could produce a majority. The names of the third parties which passed across the political horizon reflected the possibilities: the Greenback party, the Labor Reform party, the Anti-Monopoly party, the Union Labor party, and others. The most important of all was the Populist party. These served as reminders that issues had emerged which the major parties wanted to play down or ignore.

Any party with a President in office when a depression strikes finds itself in a dangerous position;[8] in 1893 the Democrats had their turn to be victimized. Cleveland made himself deeply unpopular in the way he handled the depression. Americans were treated to the spectacle of an administration truckling to J. P. Morgan in order to salvage the government's gold reserve. The Democrats went through a political depression in the 1894 elections. The party of rum, Romanism, and rebellion had become the party of economic collapse. The onus stuck for a generation.

In 1896 the Democrats repudiated Cleveland, their own sitting President, and the party of depression became the party of Bryanism. The Populists nominated Bryan as well, and a whoop went up for inflation. Bryan attempted to put together a coalition of the troubled: farmers, middle-class small business people, and urban workers. With inflation the coalition's primary cement, this would have created an odd company indeed had it worked. Instead, Bryan lost the industrial Northeast, the cities, labor, immigrants, and Democratic conservatives. By 1896 the GOP had clearly emerged as the nation's majority party, and the politics of stalemate had come to an end. The political system which emerged from the 1890s was the least competitive since the early nineteenth century. It was exceedingly sectional. In the South, what remained of the GOP was practically obliterated. In large areas of the

North, the Democrats suffered a similar fate. For the most part, the country divided into "the big Republican monopoly in the North and the little Democratic monopoly in the South."[9] The 1896 system also had remarkable stability. The GOP found itself controlling the most industrialized, urbanized, and heavily populated regions of the country. Excluding the election of 1912, from 1896 to 1928 Democratic candidates for President garnered 84.5 percent of their electoral votes in the South and the border states. Democrats lost a good deal of their backing among big business and the press, and considerable financial support. The GOP spoke for and was sustained by the urban and rural middle strata. The Democracy largely became a rural party in appeal and leadership, with outposts in the North organized around urban political machines.

When a party gets shattered as thoroughly as the Democrats did in the Cleveland-Bryan era, it tends to lose some of its cosmopolitanism and to become more localistic. The same thing can happen on any level of politics. Part of the game is to drive one's opponents into isolation, shut them out of the places where decisions involving real power are made, and leave them grumbling to themselves.

The Bryan campaign did not represent the coming-of-age of modern liberalism; far from it. The 1896 Democratic platform extolled the fact that the party "has resisted the tendency of selfish interests to the centralization of governmental power," and condemned "the profligate waste of the money wrung from the people by oppressive taxation and the lavish appropriations of recent Republican Congresses."[10] Ever the spokesman, or would-be spokesman, for the rural, the small town, and the middle-class, Bryan could not lead a national coalition because his suspicion of the cities and what they represented equalled his abiding love of the West and the South. Although he would lead his divided, struggling party into the twentieth century, he never really became a twentieth century man.[11]

But for all of his provincialism and Bible-thumping, Bryan had caught on to something: *if* a coalition of workers, farmers, and petty capitalists could be forged, he or someone else could win the presidency. To later generations that view inflation as a menace, the money issue of 1896 may seem frivolous or worse. Yet modern reform has emerged through a series of experiments. In 1896 the great experiment was money. Eventually (though not until after the New Deal), its time passed. So did the age of biblical campaigns. (Bryan, whose Cross of Gold address electrified the Democratic convention, got attacked in turn as a political apostate.) The heart of Bryan's campaign, the part which endured, was neither the cause nor the style, but the idea of the coalition. Denounced as the fomenter of class hatred, Bryan basically knew what Woodrow Wilson and Franklin D. Roosevelt understood about putting coalitions together; he differed from them only in that he failed to carry it off. Bringing to an end a very long dry spell for great causes and principles, the silver campaign came as a shock. Bryan committed his party to a defined stand on economic issues—and split it.

In 1896 GOP candidate William McKinley, together with businessman Mark Hanna, waged what might be considered the great original model of the corporation-fueled political campaign. McKinley's administration in turn represented the nineteenth century epitome of business-oriented GOP regimes, committed to economic modernization, growth, and prosperity. After the 1890s, the Republican party, in the words of Robert Kelley, was more than ever "a broad coalition of white, Anglo-Saxon Protestant peoples."[12] Broad, yes, and internally diverse; yet the coalition contained great potential for political ossification unless it could become even more diverse, embracing groups stepping off ships every day from southern and eastern Europe. The GOP, then, ran the long-term demographic risks we have already identified in being the party of the Establishment. Equally important, the solidity of the GOP among the well-off and the native stock would imperil the party's future unless it could somehow overcome the conservative drag which these groups produced.

Over the short run, though, over the span of a generation, the Democrats were the ones who suffered. From Cleveland's departure in 1897 down to FDR's election in 1932, the Democracy seated just one President. Cleveland had become a living skeleton in the party's closet, the Herbert Hoover of the late nineteenth century. Yet a good number of Democrats continued to extol Cleveland well into the Progressive Era precisely because they agreed with him.

Actually, the Democracy had two skeletons, not just one. The other was Bryan. The party had taken on a schizoid appearance of vest-and-watch-chain conservatism on one hand, and crackpot clodhopper radicalism on the other. A party with multiple identities had multiplied its identities: Clevelandism, Bryanism, far left, far right, Catholic, Confederate, personal freedom, economic depression. Among those who remained in the party, a deepening hostility divided WASP farmers and small townspeople on one hand, and on the other new immigrants, many of them Catholics and Jews from southern and eastern Europe.

The first presidential hero of the progressive movement was Republican Theodore Roosevelt. Indeed, looking at the GOP in 1865 under Lincoln and again in 1905 under Roosevelt, one might almost conclude that, new issues aside, not much had altered. By the time the GOP entered the age of its real hegemony in the nineties, though, this onetime party of radical change had severely declined as an engine for innovation. True, the GOP had become the handmaiden of one client group, business, which at least set a precedent for other groups, most importantly labor and farmers. And some elements of the party did help spearhead middle-class and business progressivism. Yet Roosevelt was a man so out of tune with his own party that he could never have secured its nomination for President except through incumbency. In Roosevelt the GOP provided the country with its only first-rate twentieth century Republican Chief Executive. Yet in 1900, the GOP leadership had put TR in the vice-presidency precisely to shelve him. Labeled "His Accidency," Roosevelt became Chief Executive through assassination. His reform policies and proposals went far enough that they had split the GOP long before he left office in 1909. And when he made his next try for the presidency in 1912, this erstwhile rock-ribbed Republican had to do it as the leader of a third party. Roosevelt was an aberration. Apart from the "accident," he would in all likelihood have suffered the same dreary fate his fellow New Yorker Nelson Rockefeller experienced decades later.

So Roosevelt stepped into the presidency one year out of the nineteenth century as head of a basically conservative party. Wholly apart from his own ambivalence toward reform, he had to carry on a juggling performance. He was cautious enough, yet found himself labeled an encourager of socialism, a leveler, a lawless autocrat, a demagogue. Actually, Roosevelt viewed moderate reform as a conservative calling. "I have always believed," he wrote, "that wise progressivism and wise conservatism go hand in hand, and that the wise conservative must be a progressive because otherwise he works only for that species of reaction which inevitably in the end produces an explosion."[13]

Roosevelt's New Nationalism of 1912 gave reform a model, a coherent design for how to proceed in the twentieth century. This design pointed toward the welfare state. Yet because his party would not follow Roosevelt's agenda, the GOP left it to the Democrats to usher in the welfare state in America and to inherit the political rewards. The turning point in this direction was the administration of Woodrow Wilson.

In order to comprehend what happened under Wilson, we must first follow the Democrats as they wandered through their political wilderness from 1896 to 1912. This span of years might be called the party's Bryan era. The Democrats nominated Bryan three times and he lost three times. Any party willing to put up a loser again and again either has no serious expectation of winning or else suffers an extreme shortage of talent. In fact, the Democratic party was a wreck, and Roosevelt skimmed off much of Bryan's appeal. But during this long hibernation, the party started to experience some significant metabolic changes.

Throughout this century, as a period of torpor has worn on within the Democratic party, the initiative and power of its reformers has grown. That started to happen after the turn of the century. For one thing, the Democracy began to assume the dual association with workers and farmers at which Bryan had aimed in 1896. And it started to revive. Measured by success in seating members of Congress, the party began to emerge from its somnolence in 1906. This could have involved a number of factors——one of them, perhaps, that after 1906 organized labor leaned toward the Democrats more than toward the Republicans, the origins of an alliance between the party and the American Federation of Labor. This was not the joint big parade of the thirties, by any means. But it provided a faint beginning; and in 1908 it produced the first AFL endorsement of a party in a presidential election——the candidate, none other than William Jennings Bryan. In 1912 and 1916, the AFL endorsed Woodrow Wilson. The emerging relationship between labor and the Democracy was symbiotic. The Democrats' disorganization allowed new groups such as workers to fit in. Emergent groups and ambitious individuals found space precisely because the party had grown so weak and barren of leadership. The party's urban-machine strongholds were of course heavily blue-collar. Democratic anemia in the urban-industrial East and the Middle West led it to respond to union demands. And the AFL needed the Democratic party for the sake of its own political influence. Meanwhile, the rupture which had separated urban from rural Democrats had begun to heal. The party developed a new focus on reforming state and local government. In 1910 Democrats won a congressional landslide. In 1912 they nominated Wilson for President.

The possibility existed to forge a national coalition by inviting the party's two great actual and potential constituencies——farmers, particularly southern farmers, and the cities, especially urban workers——to join big business under government's wing. This would be a drastic step, and the Wilson of 1912 felt uncertain himself whether to take it. In his campaign rhetoric that year, as we have seen, he hedged by remaining substantially noncommittal on the questions of governmental centralization and legislation for labor and farmers. But the party did make special appeals to the cities, workers, immigrants, Catholics, and Jews, in a drive to forge a truly national coalition. Democrats also worked to show that they were competent to govern, something which demanded proof.

Then as now, any reform proposal which Democrats put forth would have to confront a hurdle of conservative opposition from within the party. The Clevelandites had acted out their antipaternalistic rhetoric and immolated themselves in a politics of anti-politics, yet the Wilsonians used much of the same sort of rhetoric. A good deal of nineteenth century genteel liberalism endured in Wilson; but the man who took office in 1913 was an exceedingly shrewd politician, not a diehard. Once in office it did not take long for the new administration to find its direction. Wilson was a southerner. Under him, the South took power.

And the South wanted things. Southern agrarians in Congress comprised the party's most active lobby for interest-group legislation, specifically, for farm measures, which they got. Meanwhile the administration shelved Wilson's early anti-bossism and arrived at understandings with practically all of the Democratic machines. The President twice vetoed a literacy test for immigrants.[14]   Wilson oriented his party toward labor; his measure of cooperation with organized labor had no precedent. The turn toward social welfare, urban-oriented progressivism became Wilson's most inspired act as the leader of his party.

By 1916-17 the administration and the party were edging up toward welfare statism like a group of soldiers unsteadily approaching some enemy bunker in the woods. No overall conceptual Democratic planning existed for a welfare state; no presidential intent existed to create one whole.   Instead, not quite knowing what it was encountering, the administration infiltrated the area by degrees.   When progressivism reached its apogee throughout a large part of the industrial Northeast, Democratic regimes led the way. The roots of the politics of the thirties had already begun to spread,[15] though lacking the rich nourishment which Franklin D. Roosevelt would later provide them. In some ways Wilson personified the party's identity crisis.   Even so, through him a sense of purpose and direction had been found.

In the 1914 elections the Democracy slipped badly; faced with this, two years later Wilson would have to succeed in putting together the coalition Bryan had tried to construct twenty years before.   The 1916 Democratic campaign went after interest-group support more than the party had ever done before.   In this, and in playing up class consciousness, it again anticipated the New Deal.[16]   The labor vote, though not thoroughly marshaled, largely went to Wilson.   Possibly this marked a turning point, the beginning of labor's significant integration into the Democratic coalition.   If Wilson did bring this off, he did so in different degrees and at varying places.   The Socialist vote dropped from 902,000 in 1912 to 585,000 in 1916, most of the defectors apparently switching to Wilson.

An examination of 1916 produces the picture of a reform party making gains among constituencies which it had benefited.   Howard W. Allen and Jerome Clubb have written that congressional "Democrats tended to support progressive reform legislation most consistently, and most Republicans opposed these same reform measures" in the Progressive Era.   We also get a glimpse of the problems Roosevelt and his Republican successor Taft had confronted.   With the GOP in control of both houses of Congress, each President had backed specific progressive proposals.   "The great majority of Republicans, however, voted against reform measures when these measures were not made an issue of loyalty to the President.   Almost all Democrats, by contrast, voted consistently in support of progressive reform measures." Indeed, "progressive strength in Congress increased as the number of Democrats increased."[17]

Wilson's 1916 victory had its shortcomings, which in turn suggest dissimilarities between progressive and later reform movements. The Wilson coalition generated its greatest electoral strength in the rural South and West; he took a mere handful of industrial states, and he nearly lost the election. Bryan symptomatically called the outcome a victory of "the West and South without the aid or consent of the East."[18] The administration had nudged up to the welfare state; but on urban questions the party's rural-oriented Bryan wing differed little from the midwestern and western congressional Republican insurgent reformers of the era, feeling more or less indifferent to them.[19] Most of the Democrats in Congress came precisely from the rural West and South. As Allen and Clubb observe,

> congressional supporters of progressive reforms . . . tended to represent constituencies in the South and West, and the reform measures which received the greatest attention——including railroad regulation, political and tariff reform, banking legis- lation, and business regulation——tended to reflect the needs and interests of these regions.[20]

This also helps us to understand why the later, more urban phase of Wilsonian reform was rather disorganized and haphazard. The nation, the Democratic party, reform Republicans in Congress, and hence the pressure, were all more rural than in later eras.

The Wilson coalition of 1916 brought together traditional Demo- cratic constituencies in addition to perhaps 20 percent of the Bull Moosers; social justice advocates; independent progressives, along with independent periodicals and newspapers; many farmers; business people, perhaps more of them than usually opted for the party; most enfranchised women; radicals; isolationists and pacifists; and, as we have seen, a good number of workers.[21] Wilson had given the Democrats power, direction, the prototype of a coalition of outs, a national outlook, heightened unity, and respectability. The 1916 election did not mean that the Democrats had achieved a coherent identity, or that they had completely transformed their party into the mainspring of the big broker state. Yet, in a foretaste of the thirties, 1916 did demonstrate the political potential of moving in that direction, and those who supported the idea of the Democracy as the party of bigger government held the intellectual edge in the party during the twenties and thereafter.[22] Wilson co-opted the Socialists in 1916, as did FDR in 1936; and turnout shot up in both elections. "The battle lines of the New Deal," writes Lewis L. Gould, "were drawn in Wilson's race for a second term."[23]

What Wilson failed to do——what no individual could have done——was to throw out the political constellation inherited from the nineties. His party still suffered illnesses. Nineteen-sixteen was a deviating election. Wilson's fragile coalition soon collapsed, many farmers, immigrants, and progressives defecting, the party splitting. Voters surged toward the GOP from 1918 on. German Americans, roughly dealt with during the conflict, added their hostility to other immigrants' unhappiness over the war and the peace. Resentment had erupted over the policies of war agencies; over agricultural price ceilings; over rationing; over prohibition. And all these led back to one name: Woodrow Wilson.[24] The Democrats fell to quarrelling again. And they fell to losing again.

Over the longer haul, though, the Republican party was in for even greater trouble than the Democrats. The twenties demonstrated that the GOP had returned to its older manner, almost as if no Roosevelt interregnum had occurred. Roosevelt's apostasy in 1912 had prefigured this. "With all his faults," Gould has written, "he represented the best parts of the GOP's future. He spoke for an inclusive party, receptive to new groups of voters, young men with creative ideas, and a measured program of innovation."[25] In effect, the Republicans handed the industrial era over to the Democrats, together with the workers, the blacks and new ethnics, and the cities where so many of them lived. The GOP's role as the main party of dynamism and change, to the degree that the title still appropriately belonged to it, ended in the progressive period.[26] Large-scale social reform, together with the federal power and movement that accompanied it, was unwelcome, something to oppose.

By the time Wilson's successor, Warren Harding, died in 1923, the GOP had once more set to entertaining business in a warm and comfy parlor while other interests banged on the door and shivered in the cold outside. "The business of America," Calvin Coolidge pronounced grandly, "is business."[27] And of government and business: "Each ought to be sovereign in its own sphere."[28] While Hoover, as Secretary of Commerce, labored to rationalize the corporate-capitalist system, Coolidge gave the country the absolute archetype of a business administration. He left office just in time to miss the Great Depression. The Coolidge-era policies were intended to satisfy big business as the peak interest in the national hierarchy; the benefits of all this would supposedly trickle down. But if a sudden failure interrupted the flow, single-interest government, big business, and the GOP would find themselves in a position of terrible exposure.

During the twenties, the Democrats produced two men of national stature who might have made effective Presidents, Al Smith and William

G. McAdoo. The party's state revealed itself when, in 1924, these two canceled one another out in a 103-ballot national convention. The country was in a conservative mood, and, as it had under Cleveland, the Democratic party reflected this mood. A McAdoo presidency would probably have shown something of a business cast, but a more complex, healthier business coloration than what finally emerged. McAdoo never won the nomination. When Smith did in 1928 he tried the conservative approach——the Cleveland era again, with variations. John Raskob, a director of General Motors, headed Smith's campaign. Under Raskob, the Democratic party took up headquarters in the General Motors Building in New York. The Democratic platform sounded like the Republicans'.

But if Smith intended to outpoint Herbert Hoover in respectability, he had tremendous catching up to do. British Ambassador Lord Halifax met Al Smith during World War II, then confided to his diary: "He was exactly like a rather elderly and demoralized bookie."[29] Smith had graduated, as he described himself, from the Fulton Street Fish Market.[30] Like Bryan he was in some ways a tragic figure, the one too Protestant, the other, being Catholic, too Catholic. Smith arrived too early on the national scene for the presidency. But his nomination in 1928 evidenced the demographic, religious, and urban shifts taking place in the party, which would later make it possible for a man like John F. Kennedy to go to the White House. The Smith candidacy split Catholics and Protestants more than any other election of the century.[31]

The axes of political conflict in the twenties pitted Protestant against Catholic, city against country, dry against wet, old stock against new stock, and pro-KKK against anti-KKK.[32] In effect, the Democratic party became a sort of stage on which these passions raucously played. Trapped by its disjointed constituencies, "village democracy" against "urban democracy,"[33] the party pursued a zigzag course back and forth and sideways, struggling over all the ethnocultural issues which brought a measure of excitement and bitterness to an otherwise politically placid era. The Democratic identity crisis went on and, for the moment, ethnicity and its correlates became more important to the party than economics. Feuding Democrats reinforced the image of incompetence which Wilson had half-concealed, in contrast to the GOP's image of sanity, sanctity, and stability. As the party of the vast middle strata, and as the majority party, the GOP glided smoothly almost completely through the twenties. Being more distinctly Protestant and middle-class and reflecting the attendant moralities, it experienced less bitterness precisely because of its greater homogeneousness. The conservative Protestant pieties——prohibition, immigration restriction, and the like——have always tended to make their way more easily in the GOP. Under no national obligation to govern, the Democrats had maximum

freedom to maneuver in the twenties, even to behave irresponsibly, and
they had correspondingly less stake than the GOP in the status quo. As
late as 1932 the Democratic party could still produce planks calling for
cutting federal outlays and balancing the budget, states' rights, and other
old totems. But when 1929 shattered the status quo, the Democrats got
their fresh opportunity.

"The election of 1932," writes E. E. Schattschneider, "was much
more than the defeat of a political party; it was something very much
like the overthrow of a ruling class."[34]   Republican hegemony
evaporated.   In 1932 Hoover took six states.   Four years later Alf
Landon got two. The 1936 election left the GOP with sixteen seats in
the Senate and eighty-nine in the House. Roosevelt's coalition stood
at its height, a combination of the cities and the South, organized labor,
blacks, ethnic minorities, Catholics, Jews, many farmers, the poor, and
some in business.   The lower birthrates of Republican constituencies
meant that the Democratic advantage would increase.[35]   And under
Roosevelt, outside the South, the deep sectionalism of the 1896 system
broke up.

No more than in 1912 had the Democratic party of 1932 been
ideally prepared to take office. The New Deal, and Roosevelt's political
genius, made up for that.   He became the prime example of a
progressive who smoothly adapted to the thirties. During the Progressive
Era, the Democracy had divided along conservative-liberal lines, and
between machine politicians and good government types. In the twenties
it split primarily along urban-rural axes. The thirties saw a return to the
liberal-conservative schism.   Under FDR as under Wilson, the act of
holding power with a strong Executive tended to obscure the ideological
rifts in the party. A dominant party can substantially set the direction
of the nation's political dialogue, and the Democrats did that.   They
became what the GOP had been earlier, the party which controlled
debate and direction. They also became more distinctly than ever before
or since a party of the working class. As Richard Jensen has written:

> In the four presidential contests after 1936, the Democrats
> lost their wealthiest voters to the GOP and gained few poor
> switchers in return. Such a pattern may seem paradoxical, but
> the evidence is consistent. By 1948 the Democrats had
> ridiculously little support among the top one-fourth of the
> socioeconomic   structure,   whether   measured   by   wealth,
> occupation, or education. The party's overall support slid
> steadily, as the Democrats lost one percent of the electorate
> every year. That is, the *net* loss was one percent, comprised of
> offsetting trends. Defections were high but the Democrats
> gained among young voters entering the system, while old

voters who died were heavily Republican. The polarization along class lines increased after 1936 (possibly after 1934, but we lack poll data), reaching a climax in 1948, when European-style divisions between the working class and the middle class almost became paramount in American politics.[36]

Following 1933 the GOP faced its turn to scramble, now me-tooing, now digging in its heels, generally attempting to freeze the changing status quo. The party passed through an identity crisis similar to the one the Democrats had begun in the nineties. The GOP's politically adept acceptance of the New Deal legacy moderated partisan polarization.[37] Eisenhower offered the GOP some of the same things Wilson had given Democrats long before, but in the end he left his party with the same impotence and bewilderment in which he had found it. The fact that his legatee was Richard Nixon, who stood essentially for nothing, provides the most convincing evidence of this. During the twenties, the party had represented something, at least——namely, capitalism, aided but supposedly unencumbered by government. The Crash had cracked this, yet the party had failed to produce any convincing new perspective. Instead, it lived half in and half out of its old one, like some damaged sea creature trying to survive in a battered shell.

While throughout this century the GOP has represented a more uniform segment of the public than have the Democrats, in recent decades it has grown even more homogeneous. "The Democratic party" note Norman H. Nie and his colleagues, "has become more black, less southern, and has developed a larger 'silk-stocking' component. The Republican party, in contrast, has become more southern, less black, less Catholic, and relatively less of a silk-stocking and Protestant party compared to the fifties." In the seventies nearly a fifth of Democratic support came from blacks, who had become critical to the party. (Blacks furnished the GOP with under 3 percent of its clientele.) The Democrats had lost a considerable measure of their old constituency in the white South, which had transferred some conservative clout away from the party and toward the GOP. In effect, the Democrats had traded white southerners for blacks. Meantime, the GOP had moved to the right, exchanging for white southerners liberal as well as lower status northern white Protestants, and blacks.[38]

The Democratic party took in a large proportion of the upper-middle-class educated and "hip"——an important acquisition, since the percentage of Americans with high school and college degrees had risen enormously over the past few decades. Intellectuals and the young, with their often-"offensive" latitude of ideas, found a more secure niche, when they located a niche at all, among Democrats than among Republicans.

The GOP raised more cultural banners at which the young and the bright tended to sneer. The process of absorption ran a pattern similar to the earlier Democratic assimilation of fast-growing groups such as organized labor, immigrants, and blacks. Writing of the 1974 election, Everett Carll Ladd, Jr., asked, "Can anyone seriously describe a contest in which Democrats secured the support of two-thirds of young college-trained, professional and managerial white voters as a 'New Deal type' election?"[39] Maybe not, if one looked strictly at class/income/education relationships. But in another sense 1974 was quite traditional, with one more group (this time, an in group) entering the Democratic coalition.

The massive departure of "young high status whites,"[40] an over-whelmingly Republican constituency in the thirties, for the Democratic party looked grim for GOP prospects; but in a way, oddly enough, it also threatened the Democrats. Critical among the interests of these young people were updated versions of the quality of life issues which leading liberals had talked about a good deal in the fifties. Some called for a "new politics" which would elevate cultural concerns to preeminence. What could a Detroit assembly line worker find here to vote for? Not much. Cultural politics was largely a politics for haves. Abortion, land-use planning, drugs, and the like were crucial questions, but not bread-and-butter issues, and they proved brutally divisive. Rather than dividing old-line Democratic conservatives against liberals, they pitted social liberals against bread-and-butter liberals. Exponents of the "old politics" in the New Deal-Fair Deal-Great Society tradition confronted "new politics" types with their suspicion of conventional liberal economic wisdom, big government, labor, economic growth, personalistic politics, and the bourgeois social orthodoxies.[41] Many blue-collar whites, ethnics, and Catholics joined southern whites in falling away from the party.[42]

During the Eisenhower-to-Ford period the character of the Democratic party changed more than the GOP. One source of change originated in the last hurrah of the old urban machines. The bosses may not all have run efficient city governments, but they were efficient at rounding up votes. The New Deal reflected the legend of the machine at the national level: politics for the sheer love of it, a politics that was *political*. By the Kennedy era, though, the machine tradition had all but disappeared.[43]

In some ways, too, while the Democratic party broadened, it also weakened, like a heart patient who starts gaining excess weight. The absorption of new groups has greatly increased the cosmopolitanism of the Democratic party in this century, and eventually it produced a majority electoral coalition which covered a far wider gamut than the relatively homogeneous GOP. But all this carried problems. The Democrats' gaggle of interest groups and sections did not necessarily entertain any broad or particularly noble vision of the country's future; nor were these groups necessarily tolerant of one another or of dissent in general. And the Democratic heterogeneity has split the party open from time to time, especially in the twenties and the late sixties, making it appear unreliable or disreputable. The arrival of new groups in the coalition has meant, too, that the party has had to accommodate growing numbers of exceedingly complex demands——that, in time, it could become choked by them. Complexity in itself can diffuse political energy and will, draining off focus, creating entropy. In the seventies and eighties, the era of single-issue politics, that bad dream was coming true.

Coalitions play a crucial role in sustaining a party of reform in America, but by their very nature they tend eventually to dissolve. The history of reform has shown the importance of proceeding in a direction which mobilizes support that will more or less compensate for the backing lost each time a new issue or set of issues is attacked. Beginning in the mid-1960s, balancing new adherents against defectors, the Democratic party wound up gaining fewer voters than it lost. The defectors included many conservatives and substantial numbers of moderates.[44] After 1960, too, disillusionment rose in the political system itself. Loyalty to party sagged among the electorate, and the parties lost strength as organizations.[45] Indifference has risen toward both major parties. The public is not so much disenchanted with or negative toward the parties, it seems, as simply neutral toward them——despite a lingering sense that the Democrats are still the party of the working masses, the GOP the party of business and the comfortable.[46]

Historically, the Democratic party has functioned as the party of outs wanting in, people who have had to alter the status quo in order to get in. Along with various things but more than any other, getting in has meant entry into the middle class. The Democrats depend upon the middle class for votes; they also depend on it as a mobility target for their own coalition of out groups.[47] To the extent that it confronts the status quo as a vehicle for social mobility, the party serves as a party of the left. But the realities of middle-class voting and aspirations keep it comfortably to the center. Again, the arrival of traditionally Republican constituents in the Democratic electorate (the college educated, professionals, the upper middle class) has made it all the more difficult for the party to find a role, and has, indeed, helped precipitate the most recent Democratic identity crises and inertia. Long a party of the North and the South, now it must function, too, as a party of both the poor and the comfortable.

Between the early 1960s and the early 1970s, a polarizing process occurred within both parties: the Republicans passed through an upward-then-downward cycle of conservatism peaking in 1964, while the Democratic party experienced an internal shift to the left peaking in 1968.[48] Such polarizations between——and within——the two parties have typified reform eras.   Yet over the long haul, the GOP grew more and more conservative in the sixties and seventies.   The term "liberal Republican" became almost self-contradictory.   In his Second Inaugural Address (1973), Richard Nixon spoke for the party at large when he ringingly declared (with his typical sleight of tongue), "let each of us remember that America was built not by government, but by people—not by welfare, but by work—not by shirking responsibility, but by seeking responsibility."   Then, Kennedyesque: "In our own lives, let each of us ask—not just what will government do for me, but what can I do for myself?"[49]

Perhaps the GOP's most typical leader in the years between Hoover and Reagan was Gerald Ford.   Ford came into office on the fast-departing heels of the most unethical President in American history. Had it not produced such a lackluster record since TR, the GOP might have been forgiven for Nixon.   But Jerry Ford epitomized the GOP, and this goes far to explain why the party's course had seemed so bleak since TR left office.

For all the drubbing American liberalism has taken because of its blurred, kaleidoscopic means and ends, in truth American conservatism has proceeded about as untheoretically and pragmatically.[50]   Through most of the twentieth century, as Irving Howe has put it, "Europe had conservative ideology, but America had only conservative politicians."[51] Stated differently, conservative theorizing[52] has occurred, but it has not built any overarching framework of conservative theory.   In the lexicon of twentieth century American politics, "to be conservative," in the words of Michael Oakeshott, "is to prefer the familiar to the unknown, to prefer the tried to the untried, fact to mystery, the actual to the possible, the limited to the unbounded, the near to the distant, the sufficient to the superabundant, the convenient to the perfect, present laughter to utopian bliss."   If the liberal has espoused egalitarianism, broadly understood, the conservative's sense of equality has hemmed itself in with qualifications.   As James Burnham describes the conservative, "he not only accepts but approves the hierarchical structure of society, with a large variety and range of stations and conditions."[53]   The values of collectivity and security which underlie the welfare state are new liberal values; the conservative still speaks in the classic liberal idiom of individual initiative, free enterprise, and market economics.

One might say that the cardinal operational quality of twentieth century American conservatism has simply been that where government is concerned, conservatives are cheap.   But not even this applies to the whole century.   The postwar arms race caught conservatives in a trap. They might oppose big government, but they had to support a gigantic military establishment against Communism.   The Cold War proved cruel to conservatives.   Ronald Reagan's doubling of the national debt in his first term as taxes fell but defense outlays shot up merely underlined the point. The Cold War had compromised conservatism by forcing it to invest the state with stupendous standing power to wage war.

In a society which worships newness, even conservatism has iron-ically claimed to be new——the 1920s "new era," the "new conservatism" of the fifties, "neoconservatism" in the seventies and eighties. Nixon's New Majority symptomatically abandoned the optimistic tone of the Great Society in favor of a mere political formula. Since TR, three Republican regimes have emerged which could be described as at least vaguely reformist as opposed to standpat or plainly reactionary: those of Nixon himself, William Howard Taft, and (by intent at least) Hoover. Oddly, each ended catastrophically. This has hardly reinforced the reform tradition in the party. The influence of the northeastern Republican moderates and liberals——who inherited what legacy of TR remained to the GOP after the Democrats had ushered in the welfare state——became heavily dissipated in the forties and fifties in their devotion to foreign policy. Over subsequent decades, their influence has steadily waned.

During the sixties, especially, Republican conservatives lavished the same frustration on the party's liberal wing (which no longer came from the West and Middle West, as in the Progressive Era, but now heavily from the Northeast) that they vented more broadly on the so-called Eastern Establishment headquartered in the Boston-New York-Washington axis. The fact that the Establishment had become so identifiably liberal suggested how much things had changed since the thirties. In any case, suspicion of the Northeast went far back in GOP history. The party's 1964 presidential nominee, Barry Goldwater, produced the most original solution when he remarked, "sometimes I think this country would be better off if we could just saw off the Eastern Seaboard and let it float out to sea."[54]

The Republican party, as Goldwater's comments about the evils of the East suggest, had descended into the role which the Democrats once played, of an un-cosmopolitan, fringe-based opposition: a provincial party. Take Gerald Ford. Ford hails from Grand Rapids, Michigan, which lies not so very far from Middletown or Zenith. Ford is Babbitt. So was Harding. So was Coolidge. So was Hoover. So was Ike. So is Goldwater, and certainly Reagan. And, in his own way, so is Richard Nixon of Yorba Linda and Whittier, California. Symptomatically, when Gerald Ford retired from the presidency, he chose to live near Palm Springs, a haven for Babbitts who have made it; Main Street in the sun. Ford also symbolized the reasons why it has seemed so difficult in recent decades to pin down just what the GOP stands for. "I am," he used to say, "a moderate in domestic affairs, an internationalist in foreign affairs and a conservative in fiscal policy."[55] In Congress Ford voted on 4,000 pieces of legislation without ever authoring any.[56]

Much of what has passed for conservative dialogue shows familiar signs of improvisation, like scattered shots from behind trees along the line of a great retreat. "Goaded on by opposing theories," wrote Karl Mannheim, "conservative mentality discovers its *idea* only *ex post facto*."[57] In one of their great twentieth century achievements, welfare state liberals managed during the thirties to expropriate reality from the conservatives. A cliché holds that it takes liberals to bring about reform and conservatives to make it work.   Pragmatism, loosely the philosophical underpinning of so much of twentieth century reform, justifies social change based upon its practicality. Conservatives have wound up arguing with liberals about what is pragmatic.

Surely American conservatism has had a positive side. It has stood for certain things——the market, the customary moralities, individual responsibility, and so on. But the fact that liberalism had triumphed produced a kind of siege mentality in the postwar right, which, combined with its role as the opposition, gave conservatism a predominantly negative, often cranky tenor.   The things it favored commonly got phrased inversely, in terms of what it generally opposed: centralized, interventionist government; Communism and socialism; moral relativism; a weak national defense; and the decline of traditional religion and individual responsibility.   Most conservatives took fright at Supreme Court decisions that seemed to coddle criminals or endorse pornography or undercut organized religion.   A good deal of the frenzy and churlishness on the far right resembled earlier peculiarities of the far left——a lunatic fringe must raise a storm and seem outrageous in order to get any hearing at all.   This, I think, accounts for much of what Hofstadter called "the paranoid style in American politics,"[58] a style suited to an opposition with no audience. Having lost its grip on the present status quo, conservatism had no choice but to preach reaction, a return to a prior status quo in which it did command the agenda.

Perhaps the most important single strand that has unified conservatives has been anticommunism, and this, too, helps explain the negativism of a right conjoined by what it opposes.   Foreign policy has been a bigger obsession for the right than for the left in part because the left has had innovative priorities to worry about at home.   But anticommunism (as the name suggests) has been so distinctly a counterrevolutionary ideology that for this reason alone negativism would have hovered over the conservative mind since 1917.

By the mid-1970s, the remnants of the GOP looked like protruding bones and concave flesh. While half again as many people identified themselves as conservatives as called themselves liberals, affiliation with the GOP kept on sagging, reaching a forty-year low at 20 percent (1940: 43 percent).[59] Even fewer belonged among the under-thirty generation. It was not that the party had failed to win the presidency: during the three decades since the end of World War II, Republicans had occupied the Executive Mansion half the time. Rather, the GOP resembled a gangrene patient expiring from the feet up. Its Eleventh Commandment symbolized its weakness. A healthy party would not need to dictate that its members "speak no ill" of one another. The GOP split between right-wing ideologues, some of whom set cause ahead of party, and moderates/liberals who wanted to broaden the base by bringing in blue-collar workers, blacks, and the young (shades of Teddy Roosevelt). The GOP chafed in the knowledge that the so-called Establishment, whose darling it once was, had now heavily defected. The burgeoning intelligentsia, the media, to a degree even big business, had edged at least part way toward the Democratic party. The party of the elite could no longer count on the elites. It seemed that the Democratic reform tradition had reached its zenith of influence and power.

NOTES

R. G. Tugwell, "The New Deal: The Progressive Tradition," *Western Political Quarterly* 3 (September 1950): 395-96 (Wilson quote); Hartz, *Liberal Tradition*, p. 57.

[1]A useful introduction is Silbey, *Electoral Behavior*, passim.

[2]This paragraph draws heavily upon Schlesinger, "Tides," pp. 79, 81.

[3]*Politics: Who Gets What, When, How* (Cleveland: World Publishing Co., Meridian Books, 1958).

[4]See Samuel Lubell, *The Future of American Politics*, 3d ed., rev. (New York: Harper & Row, 1965), ch. 10, and especially pp. 191-93.

[5]R. Hal Williams, "'Dry Bones and Dead Language': The Democratic Party," in *The Gilded Age*, ed. H. Wayne Morgan, rev. ed. (Syracuse, N.Y.: Syracuse University Press, 1970), p. 141.

[6]*Letters and Addresses of Grover Cleveland*, ed. Albert Ellery Bergh (New York: Unit Book Publishing Co., 1909), p. 349.

[7]*The American Commonwealth*, rev. ed., 2 vols. (New York: Macmillan Co., 1923), 2:21.

[8]The following discussion of the Democratic party in the Bryan-Wilson era draws very heavily upon Broesamle, "The Democrats," pp. 83-113. Quotations and certain other references are separately cited.

[9]Schattschneider, *Semisovereign People*, p. 85.

[10]Donald Bruce Johnson and Kirk H. Porter, eds., *National Party Platforms: 1840-1972*, 5th ed. (Urbana: University of Illinois Press, 1975), pp. 97, 99.

[11]Meanwhile, though, Illinois Governor John Peter Altgeld provided something of a foretaste of the twentieth century northern, urban, liberal Democrat.

[12]"Ideology and Political Culture," p. 548. This paragraph also draws on Richard Jensen, "Party Coalitions and the Search for Modern Values: 1820-1970," in *Emerging Coalitions in American Politics*, ed. Seymour Martin Lipset (San Francisco: Institute for Contemporary Studies, 1978), pp. 24-27.

[13]*The Letters of Theodore Roosevelt*, ed. Elting E. Morison, vol. 7: *The Days of Armageddon: 1909-1914* (Cambridge, Mass.: Harvard University Press, 1954), p. 597.

[14]Only to be overridden the second time.

[15]See Buenker, *Urban Liberalism*, pp. 222-23. For a comparison of urban progressivism with the New Deal, see ibid., pp. 230ff.

[16]Lewis L. Gould, *Reform and Regulation: American Politics, 1900-1916*, Critical Episodes in American Politics series (New York: John Wiley & Sons, 1978), pp. 174-75.

[17]"Progressive Reform," p. 133.

[18]Lawrence W. Levine, *Defender of the Faith: William Jennings Bryan; The Last Decade, 1915-1925* (New York: Oxford University Press, 1968), pp. 80-81. Original in caps.

[19]On the insurgents, see especially James Holt, *Congressional Insurgents and the Party System: 1909-1916*, Harvard Historical Monographs, no. 60 (Cambridge, Mass.: Harvard University Press, 1967), p. 10.

[20]"Progressive Reform," p. 134.

[21]Broesamle, "The Democrats," p. 111.

[22]Gould, *Reform and Regulation*, p. 178.

[23]Ibid., pp. 178-79.

[24]Samuel P. Hays, "Political Parties and the Community-Society Continuum," in *The American Party Systems: Stages of Political Development*, ed. William Nisbet Chambers and Walter Dean Burnham (New York: Oxford University Press, 1968), pp. 159-60.

[25]"The Republicans under Roosevelt and Taft," in Gould, *Progressive Era*, p. 82.

[26]Ibid., pp. 55, 82; Gould, *Reform and Regulation*, p. 178; Allan J. Lichtman, *Prejudice and the Old Politics: The Presidential Election of 1928* (Chapel Hill: University of North Carolina Press, 1979), p. 244.

[27]Bartlett's *Familiar Quotations*, 14th ed., p. 911.

[28]Robert F. Himmelberg, *The Origins of the National Recovery Administration: Business, Government, and the Trade Association Issue, 1921-1933* (New York: Fordham University Press, 1976), p. 44.

[29]Henry Fairlie, *The Parties: Republicans and Democrats in This Century* (New York: St. Martin's Press, 1978), p. 146.

[30]David Burner, *The Politics of Provincialism: The Democratic Party in Transition, 1918-1932* (New York: Alfred A. Knopf, 1968), p. 181.

[31]Lichtman, *Prejudice*, pp. 227, 231. In this book, Lichtman also offers a critique of critical election theory.

[32]The Democrats of the 1880s had opposed prohibition and other coercive regulations; but just as the party was drawn away from economic libertarianism, it was also drawn away from social libertarianism.

[33]The terms are Lippmann's. *Men of Destiny*, p. 32.

[34]*Semisovereign People*, p. 86.

[35]Richard Jensen, "The Last Party System: Decay of Consensus, 1932-1980," in Paul Kleppner et al., *The Evolution of American Electoral Systems* (Westport, Conn.: Greenwood Press, 1981), pp. 221-22.

[36]Ibid., pp. 213-14. Over the two decades of the forties and the fifties, the Republican party shrank from 43 to 28 percent of the population. The Democrats hovered around 50 percent throughout that period. Ibid., p. 221.

[37]See Hamby, *Liberalism and Its Challengers*, p. 341.

[38]*Changing American Voter*, pp. 241-42.

[39]"Liberalism Upside Down," p. 582.

[40]Ibid., p. 586.

[41]I. A. Lewis and William Schneider, "Handicapping Democrats' Merry-Go-Round," *Los Angeles Times*, 12 November 1978.

[42]See Everett Carll Ladd, Jr., and Charles D. Hadley, *Transformations of the American Party System: Political Coalitions from the New Deal to the 1970s* (New York: W. W. Norton & Co., 1975), pp. 230-31; and William Schneider, "Half a Realignment," *New Republic*, 3 December 1984, pp. 21-22.

[43]On this point, see the astute observations in Fairlie, *The Parties*, pp. 161-63.

[44]Schneider, "Half a Realignment," pp. 21-22.

[45]Jensen, "Last Party System," p. 219.

[46]Martin P. Wattenberg, *The Decline of American Political Parties: 1952-1980* (Cambridge, Mass.: Harvard University Press, 1984), pp. 30, 37, 50, 57, 66, 126, and passim. On the endurance of the parties, however, see Xandra Kayden and Eddie Mahe, Jr., *The Party Goes On: The Persistence of the Two-Party System in the United States* (New York: Basic Books, 1985).

[47]See Thomas Byrne Edsall, *The New Politics of Inequality* (New York: W. W. Norton & Co., 1984), pp. 31-32, 63.

[48]Nie, *Changing American Voter*, pp. 196-97, 203.

[49]*Los Angeles Times*, 21 January 1973.

[50]See Kevin P. Phillips, *Post-conservative America: People, Politics and Ideology in a Time of Crisis* (New York: Random House, 1982), p. 41.

[51]*A Margin of Hope: An Intellectual Autobiography* (San Diego: Harcourt Brace Jovanovich, 1982), p. 225. See also Lionel Trilling, *The*

Liberal Imagination: Essays on Literature and Society (New York: Viking Press, 1950; reprint, London: Secker and Warburg, 1955), p. ix.

[52]On which see Nash, *Conservative Intellectual Movement.*

[53]Oakeshott and Burnham quotes from James Burnham, *Suicide of the West: An Essay on the Meaning and Destiny of Liberalism* (New Rochelle, N.Y.: Arlington House, 1964), pp. 182-83.

[54]*Chicago Tribune*, 30 September 1961, quoted in Arthur Frommer, ed., *Goldwater from A to Z: A Critical Handbook* (New York: Frommer/Pasmantier Publishing Corp., 1964), p. 45.

[55]Jerald F. terHorst, *Gerald Ford and the Future of the Presidency* (New York: The Third Press, 1974), p. 67.

[56]According to Nicholas von Hoffman, "Just Plain Jerry," *New York Review of Books*, 19 September 1974, p. 17.

[57]*Ideology and Utopia*, p. 207. Italics in original.

[58]*The Paranoid Style in American Politics and Other Essays* (New York: Alfred A. Knopf, 1965).

[59]"Is America Turning Right?" *Newsweek*, 7 November 1977, p. 35; Jensen, "Last Party System," p. 221.

6

THE FORTUITOUS
PRESIDENCY

My view was that every executive officer, and above all every executive officer in high position, was a steward of the people bound actively and affirmatively to do all he could for the people, and not to content himself with the negative merit of keeping his talents undamaged in a napkin. . . . I did not usurp power, but I did greatly broaden the use of executive power.

Theodore Roosevelt

Lincoln, Franklin Roosevelt once remarked, "was a sad man because he couldn't get it all at once. And nobody can." Every President must endure a gap between what he would like and what is possible.

John F. Kennedy

When scholars focus excessively upon parties, structures, processes, and trends, a critical element—the individual—may easily get lost. Two of the crucial roles of party require it to provide the machinery with which individuals may bring about change, and to produce the leaders who can do it.

We need not revel in hero-worship to recognize that individuals have had an extraordinary impact on American reform. The most important of these people have been Presidents. A President may propose legislation or veto it; these powers alone make the Executive office the main locus of governmental change. Our major reform movements in this century have invariably corresponded with strong presidencies——together with ripe conditions socially, economically, and intellectually, and a Congress in the mood for change.

The study of the presidency has become a major growth industry, and I do not intend to recapitulate the literature here. (Much of it, indeed, is summarized in the quotations with which this brief chapter begins.) What I do want to do is look especially at the peculiar *fragility* of the reform presidency. We will examine certain other aspects of the Executive role in this and the chapter which follows.

Beginning with TR, the modern pattern of government found form.[1] The President identified the problems the nation faced, established priorities, and proposed a concrete legislative program to address them. Congress then acted on it. The "congressional government" about which Wilson had complained[2] was over. By the end of the Wilson era, the President had grown supreme in Washington, and from now on worriers would decry presidential government. With the modern presidency established, American reform had taken a crucial step.

The struggles of Jimmy Carter should remind us that an effective presidency requires a powerful working relationship with one's party and Congress, consistent control over one's own cabinet, and, in a more general sense, influence over the government at large. Influence lies at the heart of it: "His influence," Richard E. Neustadt writes, "becomes the mark of [presidential] leadership."[3]

Leadership involves "a symbiotic relationship" between the leader and the led, as James MacGregor Burns reminds us.

> "One-man leadership" is a contradiction in terms. Leaders, in responding to their own motives, appeal to the motive bases of potential followers. As followers respond, a symbiotic relationship develops that binds leader and follower together into a social and political collectivity.[4]

Organization must accompany the exercise of power by any such collectivity; but once organized, the power flows through individuals who assume the role of leaders.[5] These leaders dramatize[6] great issues of their day. Effective Presidents must identify the imperatives of a given period and make these their administrations' overriding priorities. "Modern Presidents," writes Doris Kearns, "have the ability to command the nation's attention. They are the only public leaders with the ability to select issues for public discussion, and establish the terms of that discussion."[7] The reform President also becomes a therapist.[8] On one hand, the Executive deals with problems which have caused people great anguish; on the other hand, these dealings lower the level of national anxiety.

The President, then, serves as a combined power-wielder, party leader, dramatist, therapist——and educator. Often the role of President-as-educator gets forced upon a Chief Executive by a mass movement which first must teach the President. Presidential candidates may educate as well. Bryan, for instance, that Don Quixote of politics, raised issue after issue even as he lost time after time. So did Hubert Humphrey. The candidate or President works, too, as a sales person: a marketer of causes, solutions, lines of policy. Charisma is the essence of Executive salesmanship. American reform in this century has rested centrally upon strong Presidents who were also charismatic leaders: the Roosevelts, Kennedy, and, in their own ways, Wilson, Truman, and even Johnson——whose charisma confined itself to the legislative chamber or the Executive bathroom and never transmitted effectively to the country at large.

The case of Johnson points to the inadequacy of mere effectiveness with Congress. An individual is required who can personify reform, galvanizing it through the weight of personal appeal as a teacher, dramatist, and actor. All this, as Alonzo L. Hamby points out, vests liberalism with a certain "fragility." Speaking of TR, Wilson, and FDR, Hamby notes that "each for a time was the living representation of the new liberalism; each also demonstrated the fragility of a political faith so dependent upon charisma."[9] The liberal embodiment in an individual gives liberalism a vulnerability which conservatism, of the GOP sort at any rate, has not shared (at least until Reagan). TR became erratic, Wilson broke down, FDR and the Kennedys died. Hamby remarks that FDR "threatened to undermine the liberal movement in a more subtle way. In a very real sense, he *was* liberalism; there was no separate, organized liberal movement with an identity which transcended Roosevelt's personality and political appeal."[10] "The progressive army, such as it is," said Edgar Kemler in typically militant prose, "has depended largely on the cult of hero-worship for Franklin D. Roosevelt."[11] "After Roosevelt's death in 1945," writes Robert S. McElvaine, "liberals drifted for years, awaiting a new leader of his style and stature. They thought that they could accomplish little without such a dashing champion."[12] FDR's successes placed an ironic burden on the presidency and on liberal reform, the next-to-impossible task of measuring up to this record——the virtually inevitable failure to succeed.[13]

"I think it may be true," wrote Machiavelli, "that fortune is the ruler of half our actions, but that she allows the other half or thereabouts to be governed by us."[14] Once an epoch passes, it freezes in time like stopped film; its events, in retrospect, turn into foregone conclusions. *Of course* Theodore Roosevelt became the first reform President of the century. *Of course* Woodrow Wilson led us into World War I. *Of course* the New Deal happened. In truth, a profound role in shaping the course of twentieth century reform has been played by chance——by the fortuitous.

It always figures into who becomes President. Theodore Roosevelt, His Accidency, took office only by the chance event that Leon Czolgosz decided to assassinate William McKinley and succeeded. TR, who entered politics at a time when it had ceased to be considered a gentleman's business, was an aberration anyway, assertive like the parvenu and averse to the conventional marketplace amoralities. In the presidency he staked out a basic role as educator. He proved extraordinarily good at it. As we have seen, he chose to designate the big issues of his era and, having done that, to lay out solutions, get them adopted, and administer them.[15] His solutions were limited, but powerfully charged symbolically.[16]

The same role came more or less naturally to Woodrow Wilson, who went into politics after a remarkable career in scholarship, teaching, and university administration. In his own way Wilson was an aberration, too, superior by far to the rest of his party's leadership. When the 1912 Democratic national convention gathered, Wilson trailed at second place on the initial ballot. Not until the forty-sixth ballot did he finally get the nomination——no inevitability here. During the course of the campaign, a fanatic shot Theodore Roosevelt in Milwaukee——the fortuitous again. ("Stand back. Don't hurt the man," Roosevelt cried. Then, with the bullet lodged in him, he proceeded to deliver a speech for nearly an hour.)[17] Had TR not run and split his party, Wilson might not have won. Wilson won again in 1916, but never did he have the support of a majority of the voters. Nothing inevitable here, either.

Without FDR, the case for liberal reform would seem far less persuasive today than it does. Yet, as much of a fixture in our memories as the New Deal has become, it, too, reflects in large degree the fortuitous. For one thing, a bomb had come fairly close to killing Roosevelt in 1919.[18] The Depression, together with Hoover's performance, laid such firm groundwork for a reform regime that the New Deal naturally seemed like a triumphal march. But like Wilson, Roosevelt——who in retrospect was far preferable to anyone else in the Democratic field——very nearly failed of nomination. FDR got the nod on the fourth ballot. Had one more been taken, the nomination might well have gone instead to another man, Newton D. Baker, who later developed deep reservations about New Deal liberalism.[19]

Once elected, in mid-February 1933, Roosevelt nearly died in Miami at the hand of an assassin. This out-of-work bricklayer missed Roosevelt, mortally wounded the mayor of Chicago, and shot four others. Had Roosevelt died, the new President would have been Vice-President-elect John Nance Garner, an unlikely candidate to put through anything as ambitious as the New Deal. In 1932 Garner had expressed the deathless opinion that "the great trouble today is that we have too many laws."[20] In 1936 Garner voted only reluctantly for Roosevelt, even though the two happened to be running together for a second term.[21] They did not run together again.

What Raymond Moley called Roosevelt's "militant tenderness"[22] perfectly suited itself to the Depression era. FDR was luckier than TR or Wilson because the thirties offered more opportunities to a President than had the Progressive Era. As Moley wrote, "many of the New Deal measures, even those that have failed, have had an important educational value, for they have shown what will not work."[23] Even after the New Deal ended, Roosevelt still offered liberals what Wilson had once given the Democratic party: cohesion, enthusiasm, liveliness, and a sense of identity. "In the Progressive era," wrote Richard Hofstadter, "national reform leadership was divided among Theodore Roosevelt, Wilson, Bryan, and La Follette. In the age of the New Deal it was monopolized by one man, whose passing left American liberalism demoralized and all but helpless."[24]

Roosevelt's was an impossible performance to follow and, particularly at first, Truman struck liberals as a clumsy man with a nest of conservative advisers. But Lyndon Johnson later remarked of him, "Harry Truman used to say that 13 or 14 million Americans had their interests represented in Washington, but that the rest of the people had to depend on the President of the United States."[25] Time and again, Truman's legislative proposals got beaten back. Truman had reason to know when he predicted of Eisenhower: "He'll sit here and he'll say, 'Do this! Do that!' *And nothing will happen.* Poor Ike——it won't be a bit like the Army. He'll find it very frustrating." And: "I sit here all day trying to persuade people to do the things they ought to have sense enough to do without my persuading them. . . . That's all the powers of the President amount to."[26] Just the same, the proposals got made, the ideas aired——the people educated (or sold). And once out, the ideas would not go away; Truman identified a location where others would build. When Johnson signed Medicare into law, he did it at Independence, Missouri, in the presence of Harry Truman.

Like Truman, TR, and FDR, Kennedy found himself stymied by a conservative Congress. Kennedy moved with caution. So had TR and Truman, but with major national goals in view. Though TR and Truman lavished attention on foreign affairs, they balanced this with heed to the necessities at home. TR and Truman seized the opportunity to educate. On the record, I find it hard not to agree with Bruce Miroff's harsh judgment of Kennedy:

> His mastery of facts and his underlying adherence to conventional values were vital sources of strength to John

Kennedy in his role as politician——but they placed an equally crucial limitation upon him as a political leader. He was knowledgeable and incisive when it came to existing political realities——but almost completely devoid of fresh ideas. Kennedy had nothing new to teach to the American public.[27]

But what if the too-brief record had continued? Chance intervened again, before it could take final shape. Certainly Kennedy echoed TR and Truman as a man who, however cautiously, prepared the way for bigger things to come. Like TR, he made reform (however vague in substance) seem at once glamorous, masculine, and fashionable. In the end, he lacked his predecessors' good fortune. TR and Truman came to the presidency when McKinley and FDR died. Each then survived assassination attempts. John F. Kennedy did not.

And so Lyndon Johnson became another in the line of, so to speak, accidental Chief Executives. As a man to set national priorities, Johnson——for all his grievous shortcomings——would prove far Kennedy's superior, and he was a far abler legislator. Yet like Kennedy, Johnson failed to qualify as a great teacher. Johnson aspired to be; Kennedy, not aspiring very high, had little to impart.

During the decade of the sixties, assassinations decimated the leadership of reform liberalism in this country, as both Kennedys and King (surely the decade's greatest teacher) were slaughtered. Before very long they were joined in death by others: Johnson, Hubert Humphrey, Henry Jackson, Walter Reuther. American reform was practically decapitated. It has not fully recovered to this day.

I have not meant in these pages to overstress the role of leaders, even Presidents. As James Willard Hurst has emphasized, during this century legislation has typically evolved through pressure and legislative channels over a span of years, with the President becoming involved during the final phases.[28] Still, the tie between reform and the powers and impulses of this one individual has increased dramatically since the turn of the century. The phenomenon of the strong President centralizing power in Washington and in the office of the Executive and identifying new things for the federal government to do, together with fresh approaches with which to do them, has epitomized the process of reform.[29]

The essential liberal-reform rationale for the powerful presidency has had the simplicity of an equation. Enormous, ever-growing concentrations of private power, particularly corporate power, pose a fundamental danger to the public interest unless held accountable to some broader authority. The only possible authority——the one counter to corporate weight——is Washington. It represents the public at large. It can advance the general welfare. The primary "steward of the people" is the President. To balance private power, government has to become more powerful; as private power grows, runs the logic, so must public power, especially the President's. The President, indeed, has become government personally epitomized, so that expectations fall not on Washington alone, but on this human embodiment of Washington.[30] But, given the rationale, how has all this governmental and presidential leverage been applied? To that question we turn in the next chapter.

NOTES

Roosevelt, *Autobiography*, p. 357; John F. Kennedy, foreword to Theodore C. Sorensen, *Decision-Making in the White House: The Olive Branch or the Arrows* (New York: Columbia University Press, 1964), p. xii.

[1]Although some of its lineaments had begun to appear earlier. See, for example, Lewis L. Gould, "William McKinley and the Expansion of Presidential Power," *Ohio History* 87 (Winter 1978): 5-20.

[2]*Congressional Government: A Study in American Politics*, 4th ed. (Boston: Houghton Mifflin Co., 1887).

[3]*Presidential Power: The Politics of Leadership* (New York: New American Library, Mentor, 1964), p. 16.

[4]*Leadership*, p. 452.

[5]See Adolf A. Berle, *Power* (New York: Harcourt, Brace & World, 1969), passim.

[6]The term is borrowed from Cooper, *The Warrior and the Priest*, p. xi.

[7]*Lyndon Johnson*, p. 247.

[8]As Richard Hofstadter saw in Theodore Roosevelt. *The American Political Tradition and the Men Who Made It* (New York: Random House, Vintage Books, 1948), p. 231.

[9]*Beyond the New Deal*, p. xvi.

[10]Ibid., p. xvii. Italics in original.

[11]*Deflation*, p. 125. William E. Leuchtenburg has thoughtfully pursued this theme of hero-worship for Roosevelt. See *In the Shadow of FDR: From Harry Truman to Ronald Reagan* (Ithaca, N.Y.: Cornell University Press, 1983), passim.

[12]*Great Depression*, p. 327.

[13]On this whole theme of the FDR legacy, see Leuchtenburg, *Shadow of FDR*.

[14]*The Prince and The Discourses* (New York: Random House, Modern Library, 1950), p. 91.

[15]John Morton Blum, *The Progressive Presidents: Roosevelt, Wilson, Roosevelt, Johnson* (New York: W. W. Norton & Co., 1980), pp. 27-28.

[16]See Hofstadter, *American Political Tradition*, ch. 9.

[17]William Henry Harbaugh, *Power and Responsibility: The Life and Times of Theodore Roosevelt* (New York: Farrar, Straus & Cudahy, 1961), pp. 448-49.

[18]Frank Freidel, *Franklin D. Roosevelt: The Ordeal* (Boston: Little, Brown & Co., 1954), p. 29.

[19]On the closeness of the Roosevelt nomination, see Elliot A. Rosen, *Hoover, Roosevelt, and the Brains Trust: From Depression to New Deal* (New York: Columbia University Press, 1977), ch. 10.

[20]Morton Borden and Otis L. Graham, Jr., *Speculations on American History* (Lexington, Mass.:   D. C. Heath & Co., 1977), p. 127.   Borden and Graham, too, pursue this matter of the fortuitous.

[21]Ibid., p. 128.

[22]*After Seven Years* (New York: Harper & Bros., 1939), p. 391.

[23]Ibid., p. 399.

[24]*American Political Tradition*, p. 315.

[25]Fairlie, *The Parties*, p. 176.   Johnson added: "That is how I felt about the 35 million American poor.   They had no voice and no champion.   Whatever the cost, I was determined to represent them."

[26]Neustadt, *Presidential Power*, p. 22.   Italics in original.

[27]*Pragmatic Illusions: The Presidential Politics of John F. Kennedy* (New York: David McKay Co., 1976), p. 7.

[28]*Law and Social Order in the United States* (Ithaca, N.Y.:   Cornell University Press, 1977), pp. 148-49.

[29]Writes Steven Kesselman: "Henry George and Edward Bellamy needed and expected to create mass movements.   The New Dealers would regard mass movements as an imposition upon their professional competency." *Modernization*, p. 194.

[30]See Theodore J. Lowi, *The Personal President: Power Invested, Promise Unfulfilled* (Ithaca, N.Y.:   Cornell University Press, 1985), p. 96 and passim.

7

THE NATURE OF THE REFORM REGIME

It will be seen that they [the great princes] owed nothing to fortune but the opportunity which gave them matter to be shaped into what form they thought fit; and without that opportunity their powers would have been wasted, and without their powers the opportunity would have come in vain.

Machiavelli

No man is justified in doing evil on the ground of expediency. He is bound to do all the good possible. Yet he must consider the question of expediency, in order that he may do all the good possible, for otherwise he will do none.

Theodore Roosevelt

Have a revolution, all right, but don't say anything about it until you are entrenched in office.

Lyndon Johnson

One cannot talk meaningfully about reform in this society without speaking of government. Along with war and Cold War, drives for reform have played the dominant part in producing a more active state; so that twentieth century reform and the rise of centralized, powerful government have occurred roughly in parallel. Reform regimes have pursued their aims from generation to generation through essentially similar techniques and under similar restraints. And when a generation of leaders passes from the scene, fresh governmental institutions always remain as its permanent legacy.

During the intervals between reform eras, the notion that the individual owes anything to society at large tends to fall out of fashion, but the reverse holds true in reform years——a condition which liberal governments find useful and even try to induce. In all of our reform episodes, the idea of disinterested public service has returned to style. A TR, an FDR, or a Kennedy inspires the young.   Influxes of intellectuals challenge decrepit bureaucracies. People set out to help the poor. Reform movements require at least some spirit of self-sacrifice and generosity. They also require focus. One of the chief roles of the reform administration is to create that focus.

Over time, the main locations of governmental decision making have worked their way higher and higher; in the countryside, from the township to the county; in cities, from the ward to the city as a whole; and nationally, from the states to Washington. At the turn of the century, a number of states operated as experimental laboratories for reform (a phrase which TR applied to Wisconsin). The federal-state system offered the possibility of each state working out its particular problems in ways which served its individual needs. Bryce spoke of federalism permitting "experiments in legislation and administration which could not be safely made in a large centralized country."[1] While new ideas bubbled forth in books and magazines, state after state tried out fresh approaches. One of the problems with state action, however, has been that it has also offered a fertile field for reaction. Some of the state and city progressive "reforms" hardly stand as monuments to popular democracy. In the South, for instance, racist laws masqueraded as reforms. Washington did not really emerge as *the* reform center until the thirties. Yet the process of federal intervention supplanting state action appeared early on, notably in the Interstate Commerce Act (1887) and the Sherman Antitrust Act (1890).

Within the federal government, as the initiative has passed more and more to the President, presidential intervention has followed a course best referred to as *opportunism*. Once the reform process gets into motion, a TR, Wilson, FDR, or Johnson will pick the right moment and dive like a hawk. *Webster's* defines opportunism quite simply as "the art, policy, or practice of taking advantage of opportunities or circumstances, esp. with little regard for principles or ultimate consequences." The term almost always bears this negative, amoral connotation.[2]   Theodore Roosevelt provided a more useful definition: "In the proper sense opportunism should merely mean doing the best possible with actual conditions as they exist."[3]

> In internal affairs I cannot say that I entered the
> Presidency with any deliberately planned and far-reaching
> scheme of social betterment. I had, however, certain strong
> convictions; and I was on the lookout for every opportunity of
> realizing those convictions.[4]

We might label this the higher opportunism. A President must gauge
when some issue has migrated into the circle of the national anxieties.
This presents the chance for opportunism——to seize the issue as one's
own, in short, to *lead.* "He could watch with enormous patience as a
situation developed," Eleanor Roosevelt wrote of her husband, "and
would wait for exactly the right moment to act."[5] "I am like a cat," FDR
remarked. "I make a quick stroke and then I relax."[6]

But as Peter J. Ognibene has put it, "if the nonideological American
system requires politicians to be opportunistic and pragmatic, to be
successful they must not seem so."[7] While pursuing an opportunistic
course, a President must not appear an opportunist. "Make ideological
consistency or purity the test for nominating candidates and there is the
losing slate."[8]

Lest this sound too much like a prescription for politicians in
general, not just for reformers, at this point we should distinguish again
between liberals and conservatives. Most conservative political thought
in this century, as we have noted, has been pretty bland. A great deal
of liberal thought and rhetoric has been, or at least seemed, just as
sterile. When we look at the campaign speeches of, say, Woodrow
Wilson in 1912 or FDR in 1932, we realize that the listener could have
derived only inklings of what was actually coming. True enough, plans
had not fully taken shape yet; but by hearing, for example, what FDR
had to say in 1932, one would hardly jump to the conclusion that any
drastic departure lay in the offing. In fact, one could not firmly conclude
all that much of anything. Wilson and FDR ran as centrists. The
system favors candidates like this. It murders the McGoverns and
Goldwaters. And if anything, Reagan notwithstanding, this calculus has
become even firmer in recent decades.

Throughout this century, government has involved itself
(opportunistically) in patterns of "promotionalism" leading to the creation
of many new institutions. In the process, government has also promoted
government. This is neither uniquely American nor at all new: the
tradition of government promotionalism goes back beyond Hamilton and
Clay. But the nature of promotionalism has passed through considerable
evolution. For the most part, the progressives developed *policies*, many
fitting together loosely if at all. The New Deal, on the other hand,
produced *programs*, and that has been the main pattern since.
Throughout this evolution, opportunism has generally taken a reactive

form, responding to initiatives already under way outside the Executive Office. This has worked better for liberals than for conservatives, because the liberals have pushed *for* something, and opportunism manifestly thrives on the search for opportunities to act. Along with shelving its negative connotations, we should add to our definition of political opportunism its usual tendency to operate for rather than against, in the positive better than in the negative.

Reform involves a great deal of strategy and trading and manipulation, in short, political behavior. A reformer will sometimes do best when screening ultimate aims. Samuel P. Huntington has noted that

> in theory two broad strategies are open to the reformer who desires to bring about a number of significant changes in social-economic structure and political institutions. One strategy would lead him to make known all his goals at an early time and to press for as many of them as he could in the hope of obtaining as much as possible. The alternative strategy is the foot-in-the-door approach of concealing his aims, separating the reforms from each other, and pushing for only one change at a time. The former is a comprehensive, "root," or blitzkrieg approach; the latter is an incremental, "branch," or Fabian approach.[9]

In each of the reform movements we have examined, the President began by taking a class-unity tack. The interests of all groups supposedly having been considered, the ensuing reforms ostensibly served everyone, or nearly everyone. After skimming off the top of the agenda, each regime then plunged deeper into the territory of straight-out special interest legislation. Partly because of uncertainty in the administrations themselves, they never made it clear just where the nation would emerge. At times they could see far enough through the brush to spot something ahead. As often, they cut through thickets one by one, obstacles leading them to veer first one way, then another.

Even with the most precise aims, anyone who had tried for very long to substitute a broad-front strategy for this infiltrating would have failed quite simply because opponents could mount the maximum of resistance all along the line. While reformers often fall under criticism for moving rather aimlessly, one step at a time, as they get buffeted or pushed along this way and that, one cannot easily see how they can proceed in any other way given our pattern of government. The function of piecemeal reform, which forges ahead on narrow fronts, has been to ease the process of getting things done, even if at the expense of ultimate clarity of goals and coherence of programs. In effect, the leading American reformers have usually tried to follow Admiral Halsey's famous dictum on war: "Hit hard, hit fast, hit often." Huntington carries the military analogy still further, pointing out that

> a Fabian strategy of isolating one set of issues from another . . . tends to minimize the opposition which the reformer confronts at any one time. Similar considerations lead the reformer to employ blitzkrieg tactics in handling each individual issue or set of issues. Then the problem is to enact and to implement legislation embodying a specific reform policy. Celerity and surprise——those two ancient principles of war——here become tactical necessities. . . . [The leader needs] to put through his reforms before the opposition can mobilize its supporters, expand the number of participants and the amount of power in the system, and thus block the changes.[10]

American reform, then, comes to life in a climate of opportunism. Together with the legislative and other political reasons for quick, opportunistic bursts, others exist: a prevailing atmosphere of discontent, the demands of groups that stand to benefit and want action at once, and the emphasis of the press on fast, visible results. Off year congressional elections almost never benefit the party in power, which adds to the pressure to move quickly, before a new President faces the first one.

But some unfortunate consequences occur when legislative processes get hurried. In the first place, programs emerge full-blown where pilots should be tried first. The pilot may appear unaffordable because the opportunity to drive through the full program will pass.

In the second place, the legislation that does pass tends to fuzz essential differences, often at the expense of the ultimate program. Examples of this abound, among them the Federal Trade Commission Act, the National Industrial Recovery Act, and Medicare. Their sense of direction might sometimes have become clearer had reformers been able to rely on the prescriptions of economists, at least of liberal ones; but economists have legendary disagreements, or so it often seems, about almost everything. A liberal tendency exists in any case to pass opaque legislation, the partial rather than the complete reform, and to assume that eventually administrative processes will give it shape. (Failing that, half-steps will at least muffle the hue and cry for full solutions.) Ultimately, after the battle leaves Congress, it goes right on inside the bureaucracy, the courts, or both.

One perennial hallmark of liberalism has been experimentation, which has sometimes, as FDR eloquently put it, taken bold and persistent forms. The New Nationalism, the New Freedom, the New Deal, and the Great Society all ran experimental risks. The pace of change in this century has demanded experimentation. Yet it has also made some of the experiments which succeeded obsolete merely because they survived into new times. And one of reform's legacies has been engorged, self-protective bureaucracies which frequently limit further possibilities for experimentation. Although these bureaucracies serve legitimate purposes, their very existence commonly creates inertia, resistance, and inefficiency.

Inefficiency inheres in the process of reform in any case. The basic conservatism of this country virtually guarantees that change will be inefficient. The lunges through which reform occurs produce sloppy legislation and then a backlash against reform. After twenty or thirty years, the process repeats itself. And besides their inefficiency, some reforms simply fail outright. Experiments often do, after all, fail.

Take, for instance, the Noble Experiment, prohibition. Whether it was liberal or conservative always remained unclear. The people who tried to bring the state into a formerly private domain, the choice of whether to drink and if so how much, were the drys. Both wets and drys insistently cast themselves as underdogs.[11] Confronted by the mandate of a constitutional amendment, Congress handled a substantially symbolic crusade[12] with a symbolic solution. The law was the law, but the government provided cynically light funding for enforcing it.[13] Americans have displayed a notorious tendency to shove through this ordinance or that in order to bring a halt to things they do not like, or to slow down things they feel ambivalent about, without any real consideration of implementation or the broader impact of the legislation itself. Will Rogers joked that Mississippians would keep on voting for prohibition as long as they could stagger to the polls.[14]

The New Deal provides the outstanding example of opportunism and experimentalism in reform. As FDR prescribed, "take a method and try it. If it fails, admit it frankly and try another. But above all try something." Many old progressives criticized this approach. Conservatives grumbled that it turned the public into guinea pigs. But by designating programs as experiments, the New Dealers gained two benefits: they furnished, in the words of James Holt, "both a justification for the novelty and diversity of their programs and a useful alibi for any setbacks that occurred."[15]

"I have never known a man so receptive to the new and unorthodox" as FDR, wrote Raymond Moley. "He would launch an idea as an experiment, but, once it had been launched, he would not subject it to the pragmatic test. It became, in his mind, an expression of settled conviction, an indispensable element in a great, unified plan."[16] The problem with the experimental approach in public life——"admit it frankly and try another"——is political: the political price of admitting failure runs too high. And once programs get settled in, it becomes difficult if not impossible to empty them down the drain like test tubes. Political reform resembles marriage——it is astonishing how quickly commitments get entered into which one cannot easily or painlessly undo.

Perhaps Lyndon Johnson provides the best example of the pitfalls of the twentieth century President as experimental promoter. The climate for opportunism was warmed by the situation he stepped into during the early to mid-sixties: the growing awareness of poverty, the emergent or ripe black, woman, ecology, and consumer movements, diminished stress between the superpowers, and the jolt of Kennedy's murder. Johnson, as George E. Reedy has put it, gained leverage with Congress because he "looked like a savior after the traumatic shock of the assassination."[17]   For a moment, the nation's attention turned inward. The Great Society passed through a window between the death of Kennedy and the emergence of Vietnam. In this period a healthy economy and abundance appeared assured.[18]

Believing that his backing resembled "a Western river, broad but not deep,"[19] Johnson realized he must act rapidly. He had little time. "He was just waiting until it silted up on him."[20] "I knew from the start," he said, "that the '64 election had given me a loophole rather than a mandate and that I had to move quickly before my support disappeared." Adds Doris Kearns:

> In this recognition, Johnson was correct. A study of public opinion in 1964 suggested that the consensus behind the Great Society merely signified an acceptance of the individual programs Johnson had sponsored——Medicare, education, voting rights; it did not represent a shift in underlying philosophy. On the contrary, the majority of Americans still resisted the idea of federal intervention.[21]

The need to act while this "consensus" survived defined Johnson's strategy——more or less, a blitzkrieg. The 89th Congress (1965) harbored the biggest Democratic majorities since the New Deal, better than two-to-one in each house, with a heavy new crop of liberals. Johnson had a strict order of battle for pushing his programs through: first the big bills with prime prospects for approval, then a second rank of measures, and finally a third with the poorest chances.[22] No matter that he confronted complex, shifting problems, or that even the "experts" knew too little about them. "He shaped the effort to enact his legislative program," Kearns writes, "not with an eye to the needs of the next generation, but in response to the sensed urgencies of the moment. Every technique reflected the importance being given to movement and speed."[23] In truth, he had no option. The evanescence of his power dictated a "politics of haste." Like his mentor FDR, he saw his opportunity and seized it.[24] The years 1964-66 passed quickly, ended by a war.   The frantic pace as well as the upshot of these two years practically parodied a twentieth century reform era.

And *of course* a good deal of the legislation which resulted turned out sloppy, ill-conceived, and wasteful. "Pass the bill now, worry about its effects and implementation later—this was the White House strategy," notes Kearns. "For now, the legislative architects must be guided by the need to design each program in the manner best calculated to attract support as to make it politically easier for reluctant Congressmen to join with Johnson."[25] In getting bills passed lay the key to the whole thing. Johnson later remarked that he wished the people had viewed the poverty problem the way they saw the moon program, "where they accepted mistakes and failures as a part of the scientific process.   I wish they had let us experiment." But once the time came frankly to admit a failure here or there, the game would be up—so, at least, Johnson thought.[26] As a result, full-bore programs debuted which were actually experiments.

In at least one significant respect Johnson's administration proved an exception to a pattern which harks back at least as far as Jefferson's time. One of the curious ironies of early nineteenth century politics saw Jeffersonianism revise itself in power, moving toward policies which seemed to contravene Thomas Jefferson's earlier beliefs. We can find analogies in every twentieth century reform administration, including Wilson's professedly Jeffersonian tenure.   The outsider will behave differently as insider.   "Second acts" characterized in one degree or another progressivism as a whole, the progressive administrations themselves, and the New Deal, but not the Great Society—that is, unless one thinks of Kennedy-Johnson as a single administration.

So while a political platform offers a reasonably good litmus test of where a party stands, or thinks it stands, at a given time, a platform does not necessarily indicate where the party will go if it wins.   Liberal Presidents tend to move left of the platform they ran on, educating and leading their parties along the way much as they do the public. As if anticipating this, many such Presidents have already taken a step or two to the left earlier in their lives.   The pattern generally involves a Democratic Executive shifting left to deal with the initial agenda, and subsequently moving further left, usually in some disorder and confusion. Referring to first and second "stage[s]" of policymaking, Eric F. Goldman described the general process this way in writing of the Wilson and FDR administrations:

> Both began by taking care of unfinished business and putting through legislation toward which public opinion had long been moving and which was wanted, or at least accepted, by a broad

cross section.   Then the Presidents moved to face new problems in new ways, and in doing this they "could no longer depend on a consensus.   While maintaining as much general support as possible, they had to build special rapport with the most dynamic element in the society——the one particularly influential by virtue of rapidly growing numbers, general drive and role in determining national attitudes."[27]

Seymour Martin Lipset writes that "in most stable democracies there is an inherent drive to the left.   Over time, the left parties win support for measures which increase the relative power and security of the lower strata."[28]   While their client groups pushed administrations to the left, during the 1960s and 1970s this "pressure of the rising entitlements" (in Daniel Bell's phrase) drove up outlays, drove up taxes, and drove up inflation, all of which led to mounting public unhappiness.[29]   Yet this, too, is typical.   An administration's second stage legislation will likely prove more divisive than its original acts from consensus.   As reform movements trend left, they alienate some of their early supporters.   They seem to go too far or too fast.   They also upset business.   At length, should the reform drive run any farther, most voters will probably become upset.

One of the central problems facing reform regimes involves the difficulty of administering their new programs.   Woodrow Wilson, for example, set up plenty of boards but showed scant talent for staffing them.   The FTC proved mediocre, and the Federal Reserve Board turned into a veritable hotbed of strife.[30]   FDR built conflict right into the administrative apparatus of the New Deal, a style of administration which produced ambiguous results.   Harry Truman pursued Wilson's course in following liberal words with conservative appointments.   Some of Truman's hirings and firings shocked liberals.   Yet all this is a very common pattern.   Liberal Presidents often follow up "drastic" legislation with weak administration, funding, or enforcement.

Nor will any reform regime squarely confront all the questions which need attention, or give them the attention they deserve.   Quite the contrary.   To get reelected, politicians must generally do what they said they would do during the campaign——they must deliver, or, at a minimum, try to deliver or seem to deliver.   In this trying and seeming, we find the key to many of the merely symbolic solutions to problems, as well as the pseudo-solutions, which run through the history of American reform.   Wilson had to pass some sort of business legislation, even if he could not realistically solve the trust problem.   Otherwise the opposition would have hung the issue around his neck.   Even at its least complicated levels, politics involves high trading in this sort of symbolism.   Classic variations among the symbolic approaches include tokens, appointments, token appointments, and study commissions. There are also the strategies of delay; selective response (which targets notorious or dramatic or publicized cases for attention but not all cases); and other methods or combinations of techniques.[31]

These approaches share the attraction that they can be used to blunt or co-opt protest through a limited, perhaps very restricted, response. The original demand can then be turned around: "Look at all we have done for you! Why aren't you satisfied?" An effective response to that question may come hard. Tokenism may have drawn down anxiety or the sense of oppression even though it amounts to merely a placebo. At times——some regulatory legislation offers an example——an alarmed public receives symbolic reassurance at the very same moment that particular interest groups receive benefits to the contrary.

One of the broad areas where these kinds of non-reforms or partial reforms have made themselves notable, or notorious, is race. A principal struggle new groups face involves establishing their legitimacy. Since outs who want to move in have the least resources for doing so, the problem proves doubly difficult. The first sign that an ethnic or racial group will eventually become a client of Washington appears when it begins to receive appointments.[32]   Today, as in the past, the race question crisscrosses economic polarizations. The politics of race has combined some of the worst aspects of the reform process with some of the best. It makes an enlightening case study.

Lamentably, most twentieth century reform has either embodied one degree or another of racism, or has failed to mount a frontal attack against racism, or both. After the early 1890s the GOP dropped blacks as a cause while retaining them where possible as a constituency.[33] Not until the 1940s, following the conversion of masses of blacks away from the GOP, did the Democratic party come to advocate civil rights. In between lay a half-century of slack in which neither party spoke in any meaningful way for black Americans. The GOP found it could afford not to, and the Democrats, with their critical white southern constituency, thought they could not afford to. For the GOP, the ultimate loss of the black vote was fully deserved yet utterly unnecessary; just as the party could live without black voters, it could also have done things for them. In effect, it took them for granted and tossed them aside——one of the most galling of the party's historic mistakes.

At first the Democrats took an even worse approach. As the nation's most socially conservative region——and as a section which has exercised dramatically disproportionate influence in Congress——the South has shaped Democratic politics in certain reactionary and certain liberal ways. The race issue has perennially undermined or corrupted reform in the South. During the Progressive Era, southern progressives moved for black disfranchisement and segregation. Blacks, the logic ran, divided whites among themselves, smothering the prospects for reform; so isolating blacks seemed a precondition for positive social change! Segregation and disfranchisement became integral to progressivism in the South; indeed, reformers regarded "cancellation" of the race issue in this fashion as the foundation for progressivism. In this sense, reform became reaction: the hole from which blacks would have to struggle now ran even deeper.[34]

The influx of southerners into the presidency and the cabinet in 1913, together with southern prominence in Congress, produced a degree of sectional nepotism which in itself promised no good. But rather than just being illiberal on race, the Wilson Administration turned coldly reactionary. In 1912 the Wilsonites had gone after the black vote, practically an unprecedented strategy for the party. One of the black leaders who backed Wilson was W.E.B. DuBois.[35] But once in Washington, Wilson fell under great pressure from southerners to segregate and to fire blacks; and the administration wound up doing both.

All this stemmed from a political decision. Wilson was a racist but not a dedicated hatemonger. Yet the South provided his——and the party's——most important constituency. Without southern support in Congress, Wilson could not push through the New Freedom. The price for the New Freedom was the blacks. The upshot: a surge of discrimination, segregation, and dismissals. "I will never," the President declared, "appoint any colored man to office in the South because that would be a social blunder of the worst kind."[36]

In order for the Democratic party to free itself from its late nineteenth century conservatism, it first had to give the South a stake in reform. In order to accomplish that, it had to make reform seem safe. The southern establishment had found itself on the receiving end of the last great (Republican) reform crusade in America, capped by the Civil War. The South desired things from Washington, but wanted its caste system left alone. This is precisely what Wilson had to offer. He defused the race issue. So it should come as no surprise that the administration which represented the height of progressivism also turned into the most racist regime of the twentieth century. Meantime, even the Progressive party, so farsighted in other issues of social justice, took no such role with race. "Roosevelt and his followers," writes John Allen Gable, "had a blind spot in regard to race."[37]

During the post-World War I era, the KKK exerted a significant influence on the Democratic party. Among others, Hugo Black and Harry Truman both belonged.[38] Then came the New Deal. Like Wilson, Franklin Roosevelt confronted the veto power of the congressional South. Put simply by Harvard Sitkoff, "Roosevelt believed that party unity necessitated placating Democrats from Dixie on all issues of race." For decades this had amounted to "the first rule of national Democratic politics." Of all problems pending as of 1933, civil rights seemed the most important one to dodge.[39] Most blacks still lacked the franchise, but the white South did vote and did have influence. Throughout the New Deal era, southern Democrats held onto the majority of leadership posts in Congress, including committee chairs. Nor had race yet risen very high on the agenda of white liberals. Tragically——but realistically——Roosevelt had little choice but substantially to set aside the race issue, even had he wished to pursue it.[40]

Despite symbolic gestures, he showed few signs of wishing to pursue it. Not once in his twelve years did a civil rights bill see enactment. Black leaders desperately wanted federal anti-lynching legislation, which split Democrats North against South. "But I've got to get legislation passed by Congress to save America," Roosevelt explained. "The Southerners by reason of the seniority rule in Congress are chairman or occupy strategic places on most of the Senate and House committees. If I come out for the anti-lynching bill now, they will block every bill I ask Congress to pass to keep America from collapsing. I just can't take that risk." "First things come first," he said, "and I can't alienate certain votes I need for measures that are more important at the moment by pushing any measures that would entail a fight."[41] This "realism" about confronting racism head-on extended to the local administration of numerous New Deal programs.

The most one can say in its favor is that on race the New Deal ultimately produced a mixed record. Many of its programs did benefit blacks. "For almost the first time in the history of the nation," wrote Gunnar Myrdal, "the state has done something substantial in a social way without excluding the Negro."[42] The New Deal also strengthened reformers who would challenge the South's racial system and improved their chances of succeeding. And it set off the beginnings of the massive conversion of blacks from the GOP to the Democratic party.

The ambiguity in Roosevelt's policies continued during the war. Limited steps were taken toward employment opportunity through the new Fair Employment Practices Committee, but only in response to pressure from blacks. As John Morton Blum has put it, Roosevelt

> would have done more, perhaps, had he thought conditions permitted it, but he needed Southern support in Congress and he feared the effect on the war effort of agitation and counteragitation. The Negroes would simply have to wait.[43]

Though the southern veto held up, times had changed through the thirties and forties. If the priority of the race issue remained low, the race question had edged at least into the penumbra of liberal attention, and blacks had made a few gains. Still, something else had always seemed more important——first the Depression, then the war. In 1936 FDR could have both southern whites and blacks, and get them cheap. But by 1948 Harry Truman had to make an expensive choice. Truman advanced a moderate civil rights policy, and in 1948 Dixiecrats bolted the party. Under Strom Thurmond, they swept the Deep South. Civil rights in the Truman era, while a brave new departure, also reflected calculated political expediency. Though Truman initiated the desegregation of the armed forces, most of his civil rights proposals had no prospect of going anywhere. They were gestures calculated to symbolize, to educate, and to garner political advantage. Adlai Stevenson, unfortunately, represented something of a throwback on the race issue. It was simply not his cause.[44] Stevenson wanted the Solid South, but Eisenhower broke it.

The Kennedy era arrived and liberals still hesitated. Kennedy was painfully slow to come to terms, or help the nation come to terms, with race as a profound moral issue. His other domestic programs, as well as his foreign policy initiatives, could best proceed if he soft-pedaled civil rights. "If we go into a long fight in Congress," he told Martin Luther King, Jr., "it will bottleneck everything else and still get no [civil rights] bill."[45] Moving out front on the issue would upset southerners in Congress whose backing he needed for the New Frontier. To appease them, outright racists received federal judicial appointments in the South.[46] Hence, too, the rest of the circumspect Kennedy approach: blacks would gain from the President's executive actions; meanwhile, the party would preserve its unity by not pushing ahead with civil rights legislation. And the nation would get the New Frontier.[47]

Throughout the century race had strung a tightrope which Democratic Presidents must walk. They had temporized and appeased the South, either willingly or reluctantly, knowing they must as long as other priorities came higher than racial justice. But then, through politics and mass protest, blacks and their white supporters closed off the option. They insisted that Washington begin to take them *seriously*. Since the race question became the primary moral issue before the nation, the old expedient tradeoffs would no longer work. Traditional "pragmatic" liberalism, manipulating the situation from Washington as though blacks represented just one more interest group, no longer worked either. Civil rights could no longer be contained, nor the race issue confined simply to civil rights. Straddling and symbolic tactics——verbal support, black appointments, intervention in a few notorious civil rights cases and the like——got swamped by mass, morally outraged upheaval, an upwelling movement from below for social change. The issue came down to a question of morality and mass power. Events spread out of control from any one place, including the Executive Mansion.

By the time Kennedy died, civil rights had finally become a central federal priority, and a major bill pended in Congress. It would become the first of the Johnson civil rights acts. Like a good many other southerners, Johnson had a past to live down on the issue. Yet he sympathized with the plight of blacks, and he was a master legislator. He became the great civil rights President of the twentieth century.

As had happened many times before, opportunism and expediency served a high cause. In the postwar era, race had probably become the most distinctly polarizing question in U.S. politics.[48] Its time, as an issue, had finally come. The pressure generated within the Democratic party by racial liberals had grown. Where once the Solid South had provided the party's most consistent and important base of support, by the mid-seventies blacks comprised the most predictably loyal backers the party had. "When their interests are directly at stake," Ken Bode has written, "blacks have demonstrated themselves to be the most cohesive voting bloc in American politics."[49] The South no longer played anything like the role in the Democratic party that it had in the Wilson era, even though it retained considerable power in Congress. The voting rights legislation of the Johnson era meant that even more than before black votes could be used partially to offset white defections.

And whites did defect. Ultimately, the Democratic party did pay the price for embracing civil rights which had caused so many of its leaders in earlier years to shrink from the issue. That price was nothing less than the end of the one-party, Solid South.[50] In exchange, liberal reform achieved its greatest triumph of the 1960s, the downfall of legally sanctioned racial discrimination.

The mad-dog southern sheriff and the racist governor provided the black movement of the fifties and sixties with tangible targets and moral authority.   By the mid-1960s it had become clear that, however inadequate the concessions they had received, blacks had finally gotten a foot part way in government's door alongside workers, farmers, and business. What wore down the black struggle was not Bull Connor or George Wallace, but the next bastions it encountered, management and bureaucracy.[51] These obstacles stood at a distance, half-hidden, complex, defying a focused assault like China absorbing some foreign army. The pall of black poverty endured as well. And the problem of poverty, like that of race, reveals important aspects of the nature of reform regimes.

"There is," as Arthur M. Schlesinger pointed out, "a tender-hearted as well as a tough-minded streak in the national character." One surely encounters both in the confrontations over civil rights. And in the struggle for other highly controversial reforms the two strains have had to be blended in correct proportions for success.[52] America has a reform tradition partly because of ideas and sentiments, among them the Judeo-Christian, Puritan, and Enlightenment traditions. Organized religion, for instance, served the civil rights cause in the sixties with particular distinction. But the United States also has a history of reform because of hard facts. Some of these have been very hard indeed. One of them is poverty.

John Adams observed that

> the poor man . . . feels himself out of the sight of others, groping in the dark. Mankind takes no notice of him. He rambles and wanders unheeded. In the midst of a crowd, at church, in the market . . . he is in as much obscurity as he would be in a garret or a cellar. He is not disapproved, censured, or reproached; he is only not seen.[53]

Perhaps this is the most important point about poverty in America; it has been ignored, thus politically invisible. The poor share this quality of invisibility, if little else, with the rich.[54] The invisibility of poverty runs its own episodic pattern. At the outset of reform eras, while radicals are rediscovering the oppressive ruling elite or that capitalism is a breeder of war, liberals rediscover poverty. They legislate at it. Then poverty gets lost again. The phenomenon has occurred three times in this century, during the Progressive Era, the Great Depression, and the 1960s. Always it produced shock. Early in 1963 Dwight Macdonald wrote, "in the last year we seem to have suddenly awakened, rubbing our eyes like Rip van Winkle, to the fact that mass poverty persists."[55]

Not at all accidentally, the three "discoveries" run precisely parallel to our three reform waves. The best single index of any given period's reform potential is its attitude toward poverty. Sometimes the discoveries have taken a personal turn. Theodore Roosevelt discovered poverty when Samuel Gompers showed him the living conditions of New York cigarmakers. Kennedy was jolted by the poverty he found in West Virginia during the 1960 primary campaign. These encounters personify a general rediscovery at the national level. Poverty, typically denied or written off as a dead or doomed phenomenon in conservative eras, becomes a national issue in liberal ones.

Americans' attitude toward poverty has traditionally bound pessimism together with optimism. The un-poor have taken a negative attitude toward the poor, blaming their situation on a supposed lack of character or industry——which is one reason why our welfare programs have often contained punitive barbs.[56] Yet we have felt optimistic about the prospects for elevating the poor. Robert H. Bremner observed in the mid-fifties that by contrast to the peoples of less fortunate lands, who have accepted poverty as inevitable, Americans have tended to regard it as an abnormal condition. Our belief that want is unnatural and unnecessary originated in a hopeful view of human nature. It has been strengthened by our faith in the unlimited resources of the New World and, especially in more recent years, by pride in the productive achievements of the American economic system.[57]

Two different sorts of optimism concerning poverty have actually clashed with one another at least since the turn of the century, yet have shared a fundamental assumption. On one hand lies the congenially optimistic idea that economic growth (perhaps aided by relatively minor governmental or welfare capitalist participation) will eliminate poverty. As Herbert Hoover put it in 1928:

We in America today are nearer to the final triumph over poverty than ever before in the history of any land. . . . We shall soon with the help of God be in sight of the day when poverty will be banished from this nation.[58]

The other sort of optimism, especially prominent in the sixties, wants economic abundance to underwrite the *governmentally* sponsored abolition of poverty. Both types of optimism have flourished in flush times and grounded their optimism on growth; but they have halted at different points.

America has created a particularly insidious variety of easily denied poverty, a poverty which today includes television sets and automobiles. Those disinclined to confront it may simply respond, "They're not poor. Look! They have a car and a TV." Will Rogers called the phenomenon going "to the poor-house in an automobile."[59] Even the Joads had a Hudson. Technology and mass production have ironically blurred class distinctions, making them harder to see. And, in a nation of relative affluence, the definition of poverty changes. As Michael Kammen has put it, "we breed expectations among the less privileged but fail to fulfill them, thereby creating social tensions and personal frustrations."[60] Poverty always remains a relative thing. The American poor are poor compared to other Americans; but by and large they do not have to endure the poverty of Bangladesh or Ethiopia, or for that matter America 100 years ago. The threshold of poverty has risen.

Many among the less privileged are minorities, and many, children or the aged. Because poverty so often seems a problem of others——the urban immigrant working class and tenant farmers of the early twentieth century, say, or ghetto blacks today——it is all the more easily dismissed since the poor seem so "different" (read inferior). Poverty helps to spawn racism and xenophobia, which in turn reinforce poverty.

Still, as poverty has diminished in this country, and overall it has,[61] its presence has become, to some, even less acceptable. (Tocqueville held that "the desire of equality always becomes more insatiable in proportion as equality is the more complete.")[62] As soon as the economy produced enough abundance potentially to eradicate poverty the cry went up to do it.[63] The relationship between affluence and antipoverty came fully into its own in the sixties.

Because the poor have never properly or permanently organized, though, antipoverty campaigns have depended heavily on current fashion or individual presidential whim. James T. Patterson observes that "the major 'discoveries' of poverty in America . . . occurred either in times of great depression, as in the 1930s, or in boom times that generated great confidence about the future——times like the progressive era or the early 1960s."[64] The deepest encounter came with 1929, which declassed a good many normally middle-class people. As we have seen, Roosevelt had no political choice but to respond. Even at that, as William E. Leuchtenburg has written, resistance soon developed:

> In the early years of the depression, the nation was united by a common experience. People felt genuine compassion for the victims of hard times. By Roosevelt's second term, as it seemed that the country might never wholly recover, the burden of the unemployed had become too exhausting a moral and economic weight to carry. Those who held jobs or drew income from other sources could hardly help but feel that the depression had been a Judgment which divided the saved from the unsaved. Increasingly, the jobless seemed not merely worthless mendicants but a menacing *Lumpenproletariat*. America, Harry Hopkins wrote in 1937, had become "bored with the poor, the unemployed and the insecure."[65]

The poor usually have had relatively little political leverage, and "the circumstances that lead to mass defiance by the lower class are extremely difficult to predict."[66] Perhaps the greatest burden carried by the poor in this country is that, unlike labor or agriculture or business, until the sixties they remained basically unorganized and largely quiet. Without organization, they could wield little political clout. They had little economic clout. And anything they received would likely be done *for* them, even if out of anxiety about what the poor might do to upset things. In any case, reform involving the poor has always tended to hit the easiest targets, the best-off among the worst-off, and not the hardest-core.

In time, poor people go out of fashion and become invisible again. They do so because they come to seem unsalvageable, or unregenerate, or ungrateful, or (notably in the sixties and seventies) undeserving. Or we assume that the private sector will take care of the poverty problem. The poor wear out their welcome as a national priority. They become *uninteresting*. They must go.

Several important books have influenced the discovery/rediscovery of poverty in America, among them Jacob Riis's *How the Other Half Lives* (1890) and Robert Hunter's *Poverty* (1904) for the Progressive Era, and Michael Harrington's *The Other America* (1962) for the Kennedy-Johnson years. Another work of the early sixties, Betty Friedan's *The Feminine Mystique*, heralded the revival of feminism and the emergence of yet another claimant group: women. The woman movement provides us with a final case study of reform processes in action.

A sense of antagonism, a them-versus-us dimension, has always been one of the essentials of group identity leading to political gains. Agriculture developed it, as did labor, and business, in its way, simply embodies it.

One of the drags on feminism has always been the ambivalent uncertainty of the movement. If any status quo has endeared itself to Americans, males and many females alike, it is the sexual status quo. For most people, the question (when asked at all) seems generally to have been, *How much* can we alter conventionality without breaking down the fabric of society, ruining morals, or degrading the national character and identity? And for most, the answer has been, Not all that much. Feminism has tended in general to gravitate toward moderate channels concerned primarily with equal pay and other conditions of work.

During the twentieth century, feminism has found itself either on the fringe of reform movements or else practically excluded. Working in behalf of others, great masses of women have participated in these movements. Yet the cause of women themselves has been sadly peripheral. Marginality became substantially the pattern of the thirties. In the Progressive Era and the sixties, women got their principal gains late, as reform faded out. This was true of national child labor legislation (1916) and prohibition (1919), two causes dear to many feminists, and of the vote (1920). During the sixties, women arrived on the scene behind blacks and even the poor.

One reason for this lateness lies in the reform process itself. Reform tends to move quickest when it confronts a crisis. Workers and farmers purposely created crises in the thirties, blacks and Mexican Americans in the sixties. Behind most of these crises lay threats. Women have had less success in generating the kinds of encounters which bring things to a quick boil.

Another reason why the woman movement has failed to catch on more effectively in politics has involved an enduring tendency for power brokers to downplay its importance. For the most part, men have run reform movements, a fact which helps to explain these movements' lack of interest in causes viewed as benefiting only women. Many of the gains of the Progressive Era were conceived paternalistically. Women as members of the "weaker" sex required legislation providing special benefits in the workplace to themselves and their children. Suffragists tailored their arguments to the Victorian mode. The vote was not demanded alone as a natural right, but to purify politics, give old-stock whites greater numbers at the polls, and protect the family. Victorianism had placed the woman on a pedestal, and now society's better half received the right to mop and wax the political system.

Writing of women, Carl N. Degler has pointed out that "the most successful of American reforms have always been those of an impromptu and practical nature."[67] One of the primary impulses toward female equality in the twentieth century occurred at a time when ideological feminism rested on a back hook in the closet. "The war," William H. Chafe has said of World War II, "made possible what no amount of feminist agitation could achieve: it propelled women into a new and wider sphere of activity." Millions of women went to work——gainfully, that is, for women had of course always worked. And "once having entered the job market, most women decided to remain. Their activity outside the home expanded rather than contracted with the passage of time, and by 1950 the wife who worked had become a permanent feature of American life."[68] All this generated a good deal of rationalizing. Women took employment to help win the war, and after the war, to help, say, improve their families' standard of living. Then came the sixties, when rooting out discrimination and injustice suited the national mood. In the past, despite their limitations, reform eras had been the only periods that had proved especially hospitable to ideological feminism. The same held true again. But alongside feminism, un-ideological inflation began to play its own role in nudging women into the labor pool.

Sixties feminism passed several steps beyond the earlier movement. Beyond the old cause of birth control, for instance, newer options appeared for non-parenthood and abortion. The newer feminism moved from protective legislation for children to day care centers; from prohibition as a means of personal protection against male oppression to rape laws and wife abuse shelters; from the chance for a job to equal pay and affirmative action.

Much of this, for all the good it represented, generated opposition among women themselves. During the seventies, the woman movement fragmented, with little consensus over what the most important issues were and with various groups emerging around different questions and approaches.[69] These divisions symptomized two old shortcomings in the woman movement: women held only a toehold in politics; and they did not vote as a bloc, nor, until the gender gap recently appeared, even vote differently from men. Women have tended to divide along class lines, with relatively separate sets of goals. In this sense the differences of class and skill which have traditionally kept workers apart have had an analogue among women. Even had women been more united, the whole socializing process, with its emphasis on submissive femininity, would have discouraged the development of hardball power strategies. Society has trained women to fight for men; to be nurturing; to succor both men and children; and to help the helpless, often as unpaid volunteers. The woman cause has shown what can happen when the best intentions are unmatched by commensurate power and selfishness. Again, once women do at last find their way onto the reform bandwagon pursuing their own interests, they tend to arrive late, after the greatest energies and resources have already been spent and reform has started to ebb.

And there has been co-optation. During the seventies, career women headed into the capitalist workplace, no longer content to have a vicarious stake through husbands and insisting on a personal piece of the action. In the self-co-opting tradition of American social movements, the organization man got transformed into the organization person. It was progress of a sort, to be sure, but not of a sort that answered the best prayers of radical feminism.

One of the chief institutions on which feminists have relied in recent decades, together with blacks, the poor, and others who have wanted to advance social causes, has been the court system. In theory, at least, changes in public opinion echo in the courts. Popularly elected Presidents appoint philosophically compatible types to the bench. The Supreme Court "follows the election returns" in various ways and degrees. But if general opinion changes do affect the courts, they often move them (as the Framers intended) glacially. Because its members hold appointive office, the Supreme Court can thwart a reform drive— or else help it to survive when its own momentum falters.

The progressives, with largely modest goals, encountered courts so conservative that they provided Gilded Age philosophies with a very long afterlife. Progressives tried to outflank the courts through other, potentially more liberal, branches of government. FDR struggled with the same thing when the Supreme Court began striking down New Deal legislation in the mid-thirties. "The Court of 1935," writes Arthur M. Schlesinger, Jr., "had been created basically by Warren G. Harding. Though only two of his justices were still alive in 1935 . . . his nominee as Chief Justice, William Howard Taft, had done most to give this Court its distinctive character."[70] At the cost of his congressional majority and much of his public support, Roosevelt succeeded in bringing off a judicial transformation. Substantially because of it, the New Deal had spent itself by 1939; but a new, liberal constitutional era emerged from the Court fight, and the old strategy-mapping of Theodore and Franklin Roosevelt for ways of getting around the courts or breaking down judicial power gave way to a new impulse to work through the courts by using judicial leverage for advancing reform. The Roosevelt Court, and then the Warren Court, provided a liberal echo much as earlier courts had done for conservatism. The Warren Court accomplished much of the "legislating" of the 1950s while Congress and the White House relaxed.

Yet reform by the Supreme Court since the fifties has proved a blunt instrument precisely because of its unpolitical bent. The judicial system does not innovate in the political fashion which the rest of our constitutional system employs. Courts' potential indifference to public opinion in itself can prove enormously costly to reform by generating public backlash. In recent years, advocates of myriad causes, many of which lie uneasily on the public stomach, have turned to the courts precisely as a way around popular and legislative-presidential opposition or inertia. Often they have won, and fresh bureaucracies have been thrown up to enforce court orders. Blame for all this falls almost automatically on the Democratic party, the great umbrella for unpopular claimant groups in our society.[71] The Brown, Gideon, Miranda, and Roe decisions, while dramatic and important, had the cast of a judicial dictate, inevitably angering vast numbers of people. This added to the malaise generated by other reforms originated by the White House and Congress. In mauling liberal causes, the Supreme Court used to come under attack from the left; more recently the onslaught against it has originated on the right. Activist courts since World War II have cut public confidence in the legal system significantly; in the Supreme Court astonishingly; and in the legitimacy of governmental coercion generally.[72]

Our examination of the twentieth century reform regime and three of its beneficiary groups, women, blacks, and the poor, leads us toward some afterthoughts about the nature of reform in this society. In the first stages of a reform era the easy issues and the problems around which consensus already exists are confronted and managed. Then more difficult questions, together with newer issues just emerging (and often involving groups just moving toward political visibility) are either treated or set aside. This stage tends toward more disorderliness than the first. Finally, with the agenda still changing, reform loses its energy. Loose ends remain which, though usually controversial initially, often move onto the primary agenda of the next reform era. To alter metaphors, a spillover effect occurs, much of the generated force of one reform epoch going unfelt until the next one comes on.

A considerable part of this spillover effect has been, so to speak, unintentional.   Reformers usually start more things going than they originally intend.   Once the early part of a reform agenda begins to be met, groups on the bottom of the agenda (or not on it at all) raise their own demands.   Things now become less predictable.   Reformers with modest goals discover that they have unintentionally precipitated more governmentalism than they want or more reform than they desire. By the next reform era, though, the controversy surrounding the new demands has often dissipated and they have aged into priorities.

Numerous causes have linked one reform epoch to another, among them business regulation, conservation-ecology to a degree, and the rights of minorities and women.   Yet I would venture that the key linkage is the concern for social welfare and social justice.

In his study of the relationship between progressivism and the New Deal, Otis L. Graham, Jr., finds that along with the clergy, academics, and women, another type of progressive (sometimes overlapping with these) responded positively to the New Deal or went left of it.   These were people who tended to live in a big city, notably New York, and had involved themselves in social work of one kind or another.[73]   During the thirties some observers exulted or complained that the government was sliding into the hands of social workers.[74]   Yet the city at its squalid worst demonstrated the need for reform, and such individuals as settlement workers had seen the squalor at first hand.   Common among these reformers was a strong ethical-theological bent which flared in response to the poverty they encountered in urban America.[75]

The difference between this sort of reformer and others, from progressivism to the present, lies in the evidence through which they have perceived reality.   For a person of strong ethical inclinations— particularly, I suspect, one whose ethics derive from a powerful moral socialization within the family—what goes on in Harlem is neither abstract nor ignorable.   If this individual is an academic, a cleric, or a volunteer, he or she will likely operate at some distance from the laissez-faire counter-socialization of the business culture.   If the reformer feels guilt over personal comfort, as a Judeo-Christian upbringing may produce, then the personal strain which poverty and degradation will impose runs even deeper.   Reform acquires a certain urgency which emphasizes results over inhibitions.   For such individuals, the duty of redress will virtually always fall on government.   To this sort of progressive, the New Deal would seem no threat.

Among the many links binding one reform era to another, then, the primary human link seems comprised of people who respond strongly to the tugs of a social conscience and perhaps to guilt.   They are strongly inclined toward uplifting the lowliest.   This inclination may also involve trying to alter the moral behavior of the poor, as it often did early in the century. Reliance on the state, in any case, always remains central. "The test of our progress," said Franklin D. Roosevelt in 1937, "is not whether we add more to the abundance of those who have much; it is whether we provide enough for those who have too little."[76]

NOTES

Machiavelli, *The Prince*, pp. 20-21; Roosevelt, "Latitude and Longitude," pp. 44-45, 56-57; Leuchtenburg, *Shadow of FDR*, p. 133 (Johnson quote).

[1]Quoted in Schlesinger, *American as Reformer*, p. 22.

[2]It also occupies a special place in the radical left's dictionary of pejoratives. Note, too, the use of the term in Thurman W. Arnold, *The Folklore of Capitalism* (New Haven: Yale University Press, 1937), pp. 220-21; and Hofstadter, *American Political Tradition*, ch. 12. See also Daniel Joseph Singal, "Beyond Consensus: Richard Hofstadter and American Historiography," *American Historical Review* 89 (October 1984): 983.

[3]"Latitude and Longitude," p. 45.

[4]*Autobiography*, p. 385.

[5]Schlesinger, Jr., *Coming of the New Deal*, p. 529.

[6]Burns, *Leadership*, p. 281.

[7]"Reconsideration: Men and Politics" [retrospective on Hofstadter's *American Political Tradition*], *New Republic*, 29 December 1973, p. 24. Italics in original.

[8]Last quote in paragraph only, ibid., p. 25.

[9]The thoughts which follow draw heavily upon a conceptual framework applied to modernizing countries by Samuel P. Huntington, *Political Order in Changing Societies* (New Haven: Yale University Press, 1968), ch. 6. Quoted matter is from p. 346.

[10]Ibid., p. 352.

[11]These points are well illustrated by Paul A. Carter, "Prohibition and Democracy: The Noble Experiment Reassessed," *Wisconsin Magazine of History* 56 (Spring 1973): 189-201.

[12]Joseph R. Gusfield, *Symbolic Crusade: Status Politics and the American Temperance Movement* (Urbana: University of Illinois Press, 1963).

[13]See Norman H. Clark, *Deliver Us from Evil: An Interpretation of American Prohibition* (New York: W. W. Norton & Co., 1976), pp. 160ff.

[14]Andrew Sinclair, *Prohibition: The Era of Excess* (Boston: Little, Brown & Co., Atlantic Monthly Press, 1962), p. 31.

[15]"The New Deal and the American Anti-statist Tradition," in Braeman, *New Deal*, 1:29.

[16]*After Seven Years*, p. 365.

[17]*The Twilight of the Presidency* (New York: New American Library, Mentor, 1971), p. 85.

[18]Kearns, *Lyndon Johnson*, p. 211.

[19]Goldman, *Tragedy*, pp. 335-36.

[20]Walter Rostow, quoted in "The Presidency: Can Anyone Do the Job?" *Newsweek*, 26 January 1981, p. 36.

[21]*Lyndon Johnson*, p. 291.

[22]Goldman, *Tragedy*, pp. 282, 284.

[23]Kearns, *Lyndon Johnson*, p. 217.

[24]Ibid.

[25]Ibid., p. 218.

[26]Ibid., p. 291.

[27]*Tragedy*, pp. 488-89. Quoted portion from memo, Goldman to Lyndon Johnson, n.d. (1966?). Goldman served LBJ as Special Consultant. I am aware, of course, of the two New Deals debate and the question as to whether the later New Deal was or was not more liberal than the earlier.

[28]*Political Man*, p. 299.

[29]*The Cultural Contradictions of Capitalism* (New York: Basic Books, 1976), p. 235.

[30]On this latter, see John J. Broesamle, "The Struggle for Control of the Federal Reserve System, 1914-1917," *Mid-America* 52 (October 1970): 280-97.

[31]On such techniques, see Michael Lipsky, "Protest as a Political Resource," in Zaltman, *Creating Social Change*, pp. 298-301.

[32]During the Progressive Era, and even more in the New Deal, it was Jews. In 1906 TR appointed the first Jew to the cabinet. A decade later, Louis D. Brandeis became the first on the Supreme Court. Bernard Baruch headed the War Industries Board. Opponents attacked the New Deal as the Jew Deal.

[33]Stanley P. Hirshson, *Farewell to the Bloody Shirt: Northern Republicans and the Southern Negro, 1877-1893* (Bloomington: Indiana University Press, 1962), pp. 233, 236, 255, and passim.

[34]Thomas K. McCraw, "The Progressive Legacy," in Gould, *Progressive Era*, p. 194. Progressivism did, however, have a (marginally) more encouraging side for blacks. On this and on the various rationales for disfranchisement, see Dewey W. Grantham, *Southern Progressivism: The Reconciliation of Progress and Tradition*, Twentieth-Century America Series (Knoxville: University of Tennessee Press, 1983), pp. xx, 112-13.

[35]Broesamle, *McAdoo*, p. 158.

[36]Ibid., p. 159. For a more extensive account of Wilsonian segregation, see Joel Williamson, *The Crucible of Race: Black-White Relations in the American South since Emancipation* (New York: Oxford University Press, 1984), ch. 12.

[37]*The Bull Moose Years: Theodore Roosevelt and the Progressive Party*, National University Publications, Series in American Studies (Port Washington, N.Y.: Kennikat Press, 1978), p. 74.

[38]David M. Chalmers, *Hooded Americanism: The First Century of the Ku Klux Klan, 1865-1965* (Garden City, N.Y.: Doubleday & Co., 1965), pp. 80, 136.

[39]*A New Deal for Blacks: The Emergence of Civil Rights as a National Issue*, vol. 1: *The Depression Decade* (New York: Oxford University Press, 1978), p. 42.

[40]Re these very controversial points, see ibid., p. 45; and Nancy J. Weiss, *Farewell to the Party of Lincoln: Black Politics in the Age of FDR* (Princeton: Princeton University Press, 1983), pp. 39-40, 112-13, 241-46.

[41]Sitkoff, *New Deal for Blacks*, 1:44, 46, 136-38.

[42]*An American Dilemma: The Negro Problem and Modern Democracy* (New York: Harper & Bros., 1944), p. 74.

[43]*V Was for Victory: Politics and American Culture During World War II* (New York: Harcourt Brace Jovanovich, 1976), p. 12.

[44]See also p. 440.

[45]Arthur M. Schlesinger, Jr., *A Thousand Days: John F. Kennedy in the White House* (Boston: Houghton Mifflin Co., 1965), p. 931.

[46]Burner, *Torch Is Passed*, p. 166; Miroff, *Pragmatic Illusions*, pp. 240-41.

[47]Foley, *New Senate*, p. 42.

[48]Nie, *Changing American Voter*, p. 104.

[49]"Black Democrats at the Tower of Babel," *New Republic*, 27 December 1975, pp. 10-11.

[50]Alexander P. Lamis, *The Two-Party South* (New York: Oxford University Press, 1984), p. 4 and passim.

[51]See Marshall Frady, "Black Power Now," *New York Review of Books*, 29 May 1980, p. 15.

[52]*American as Reformer*, p. 49.

[53]Herbert G. Gutman, *The Black Family in Slavery and Freedom, 1750-1925* (New York: Pantheon Books, 1976), p. [viii]. Italics deleted.

[54]This last point is made by Paul Fussell, "A Dirge for Social Climbers," *New Republic*, 19 July 1980, p. 19.

[55]"Our Invisible Poor," *New Yorker*, 19 January 1963, p. 84.

[56]See Katz, *Poverty and Policy*, pp. 239-41.

[57]*From the Depths: The Discovery of Poverty in the United States* (New York: New York University Press, 1956), p. xi.

[58]Hofstadter, *American Political Tradition*, p. 295.

[59]Michael Kammen, *People of Paradox: An Inquiry Concerning the Origins of American Civilization* (New York: Alfred A. Knopf, 1972), p. 275.

[60]Ibid., p. 277.

[61]See Patterson, *Struggle Against Poverty*, pp. 13, 160-61.

[62]Quoted in Robert A. Nisbet, "The New Equalitarians," *Columbia Forum*, Winter 1975, p. 8.

[63]Bremner, *From the Depths*, pp. 128-29; Patterson, *Struggle Against Poverty*, p. 113.

[64]*Struggle Against Poverty*, p. 209.

[65]*Roosevelt and the New Deal*, pp. 273-74.

[66]Frances Fox Piven and Richard A. Cloward, *Poor People's Movements: Why They Succeed, How They Fail* (New York: Pantheon Books, 1977), p. 26.

[67]"Revolution Without Ideology: The Changing Place of Women in America," in *The Woman in America*, ed. Robert Jay Lifton (Boston: Beacon Press, 1967), pp. 204-5.

[68]William Henry Chafe, *The American Woman: Her Changing Social, Economic, and Political Roles, 1920-1970* (New York: Oxford University Press, 1974), p. 195. For an intriguing comparison of the post-World War II movements of blacks on one hand, and women on the other, see Chafe's *Women and Equality: Changing Patterns in American Culture* (New York: Oxford University Press, 1978), pp. 99ff.

[69]See Sara Evans, *Personal Politics: The Roots of Women's Liberation in the Civil Rights Movement and the New Left* (New York: Alfred A. Knopf, 1979), p. 225.

[70]*Politics of Upheaval*, pp. 454-55.

[71]Christopher Lasch, "Liberalism in Retreat," in MacLean, *Liberalism Reconsidered*, p. 112.

[72]Morris Janowitz, *The Last Half-Century: Societal Change and Politics in America* (Chicago: University of Chicago Press, 1978), pp. 369, 383.

[73]*Encore*, pp. 167-70.

[74]Kesselman, *Modernization*, p. 259.

[75]Graham, *Encore*, pp. 144-46, 167.

[76]Roosevelt, *Public Papers*, 1937 volume: *The Constitution Prevails* (New York: Macmillan Co., 1941), p. 5. Sar A. Levitan and Robert Taggart have pointed to an apparently cyclic pattern in "social welfare change." *Promise*, p. 19. On social welfare and politics, see also John R. Petrocik, *Party Coalitions: Realignment and the Decline of the New Deal Party System* (Chicago: University of Chicago Press, 1981), p. 136; Graham, *Encore*, pp. 39-40, 181; and Barbara Deckard Sinclair, "The Policy Consequences of Party Realignment——Social Welfare Legislation in the House of Representatives, 1933-1954," *American Journal of Political Science* 22 (February 1978): 83-105.

II

RESISTANCE

In Part I we explored the surge phase of reform; yet every reform era has encountered resistance which in time has destroyed its momentum. Part II deals with resistance. Often difficulties emerge from within the movement itself: chapter 8 discusses the problem of blurred focus earlier raised in our examination of progressivism. Blurred vision derives in particular from ambivalence among reformers themselves, an ambivalence which emerges in large part from the nature of the U.S. economic system. It is impossible to divorce reform in America from the underlying constraints placed on it by the capitalist economy.

Chapter 9 explores the ambiguous relationship that has developed between American reform and a business culture dominated in this century by large corporations. Despite a great deal of anti-business rhetoric, mainstream reformers have always had to return to the fact that their success heavily depends upon the health of the capitalist order. This awareness has put enormous limits on endeavors to regulate business behavior. Ambivalence has simply pervaded antitrust and regulatory policies, a theme discussed at length. Finally, chapter 9 looks at the conundrum of labor——its perennial junior partnership in the political economy.

This exploration of the dilemmas of the American labor movement opens up a far broader subject taken up in chapter 10. The causes of what I have termed mass inertia have spurred scholarly debate for decades and are the subject of a good deal of work among a variety of disciplines today. The core question is: Why throughout the urban-industrial era have the American people thought and acted so very conservatively, especially in comparison to the people of other nations? Why no socialism? Why no mass radicalism? Why, in other words, has the United States been so different?

8

BLURRED VISION

> I am a man who believes with all fervor and intensity in
> moderate progress. Too often men who believe in
> moderation believe in it only moderately and tepidly and
> leave fervor to the extremists of the two sides——the extremists
> of reaction and the extremists of progress.
>
> Theodore Roosevelt

In 1903 the Women's Trade Union League (WTUL) appeared, aimed at helping organize working women into unions. Initially, the league concentrated on just that, organizing; but by the time it had lived out a decade, the WTUL began to focus instead on labor legislation and education. The league had always been shared between two groups, one oriented toward unionism per se, the other toward education, investigation, and reform bills. The one side emphasized action from below; the other, amelioration from above. Some among the latter group were wealthy patrons whose presence in the league made the unionists feel uneasy.

The second group eventually won out. Reform and uplift came to take priority over organization. Margaret Dreier Robins, the league's president (1907-22), patron, and leading policymaker, declared, "the League believed that the first need of these [working] girls was the awakening of their imagination and sense of beauty," since "the dullness and monotony of factory life had starved them of the very essentials of a young girl's life."[1] So along with everything else, there were concerts, literature classes, and poetry readings.

The continuing struggle between its uplifters and its organizers sapped the WTUL. By 1925 unions were furnishing just 3 percent of contributions to the league, with its patrons and sympathizers giving more than 90 percent. The league tried to unionize southern textile workers, but the drive concentrated less on unionization per se than on attempting to enlist the support of non-textile workers. The WTUL never did merge its split personalities. The AFL kept it at a distance. In 1926 the league jettisoned its school for organizers. Contact with women workers faded. By the thirties, despite some real accomplishments in the past, about all that remained of the WTUL was its shadow, a sad thing indeed. The WTUL was the only national organization at least supposedly devoted to unionizing working women.

The story of the WTUL illustrates the difficulty which reformers have commonly faced in maintaining direction; in retaining a clear vision of what they want and how to get it; in keeping their eyes on the ball.[2] Given the right climate, reform has flourished when its leaders have set a limited number of achievable priorities. Excessive focus, true enough, may pose hazards, as in the case of the Populists and free silver or women and the vote. (A glut of issues all at once impels people to want to focus on just one or two.) But inadequate focus has posed the greater problem. Sometimes objectives cannot even be defined precisely or stated clearly. There are always many demands on reformers and a wide range of approaches toward change. Some of these approaches take years to work out and years more to implement, while the basic problems themselves alter in the meantime. Focus comes hard.

Among departments of the federal government, too, the clear, comprehensive definition of objectives has been a spectacular exception to the rule——with important consequences for reform since government so often serves as its vehicle. Part of the reason for governmental confusion, no doubt, grows out of the difficulty of achieving sustained definition. Public moods shift, the economy shifts, parties shift, administrations shift, plans get scaled up or scaled down. But directly or indirectly, lack of definition generates public hostility toward government. It helps to explain why federal agencies so often have trouble justifying what they do and defending themselves from attack. When inter-reform eras set in, these agencies often seem to turn limp (the Defense Department excepted). Their very listlessness gives credence to the suspicion not only that they have no objectives but that they do nothing useful and thus are wasteful, expendable, or both. The situation literally resembles the absence of a sense of direction or an outmoded set of aims found in stagnant industries or senile philanthropies. "Unless the business sets demanding and exciting goals," notes a board chair of AT&T, "it runs a heavy risk of losing vitality."[3] So, too, with government. Nor do the problems of mixed goals, ambiguity, and ambivalence stop with bureaucracies. As Michael Kammen has written:

> The Congress, perhaps more than any other political
> institution, is a repository of American ambivalence. The
> founders created a bicameral body so that it would expressly
> embrace contradictions. The House was dedicated to the
> proposition of majority rule, and the Senate to the sacredness
> of minority rights.[4]

Thus government's very constitutional structure guarantees a confusion
of goals.

And thus the problem of blurred focus. As we have seen, part of
the trouble with progressivism, for instance, was its pervasive confusion
of purpose. Blurred focus became one of the cardinal characteristics of
the period. Being "progressive" on any one of a number of issues, or in
any one of a variety of ways, identified a person as a progressive in the
broadest sense of the term. The upshot was an exceedingly ambiguous
movement reflecting an equally ambiguous following.

In the center-dominated politics of this country, politicians tend not
to address first principles or dig to the root of issues. Real clarity can
be politically punishing. In progressivism, the wide gap between rhetoric
and reality betokened a lapse between analysis (sometimes radical,
sometimes brilliant) and prescription (often muddled but politic).
Wilson, for example, had his finger on some very fundamental problems.
He also had a positive genius for frequently saying practically nothing,
but saying it with exquisite flair. We can see one crucial difference
between the Wilsonians and the New Dealers precisely here. While the
Wilsonians indulged in "class legislation," a logical outgrowth of their
analysis, they denied that they were doing it. They carried on a politics
of illusion, blurred by design as well as by ambivalence and confusion.
This much had been worked out by the thirties: that while plenty of
confusion inhered in the New Deal, and some ambivalence, too, the New
Dealers positively thrived on class legislation and advertised the fact.

But the New Deal did not resolve the country's ancient ambivalence
toward the power of government. And for all its tone of self-assurance,
one of the dominant themes in twentieth century American liberalism
both before and since the New Deal has remained ambivalence——toward
the corporate order, the benefits that workers should receive, the nature
of the welfare state, and much more. Ambivalence endures as a feature
not just of liberalism, but of center politics in general. Who could be
more ambivalent, for instance, than the Republicans under Eisenhower
in their attitude toward the immediate New Deal past? Only people on
the extremes feel dead sure.

One thing that has helped liberals to escape from the harsher
implications of their ambivalence, and particularly its implications in
terms of income distribution, has been an expanding economy. Since

World War II, liberal programs have risen or fallen on "growth dividends." Indeed, the Kennedy-Johnson stress on a fiscal dividend had been foreshadowed half a century before by the Wilsonian quest for export markets that would boom production, muting social conflict at home. (The New Freedom's main proposal for underwriting the country's prosperity lay in what Wilson called a "conquest of the markets of the world" by U.S. business. Everyone would benefit, and without redistributing income.)[5] All this implies that the success of liberal regimes has depended heavily upon a healthy, expanding private sector. This dependence has involved these administrations, whatever their rhetoric, in continuous endeavors to help business flourish. And it is crucial to accounting for the blurred vision of American reform.

NOTES

Roosevelt, *Letters*, 7:532.
[1]Chafe, *American Woman*, p. 73. This account of the WTUL draws heavily on Chafe, especially pp. 69-76.
[2]My use of this cliché in such a context is not original. Though I hesitate to employ it, this Americanism strikes me as too suitable to avoid.
[3]Charles H. Granger, "The Hierarchy of Objectives," in Zaltman, *Creating Social Change*, p. 534.
[4]*People of Paradox*, p. 280.
[5]Broesamle, "The Democrats," p. 108.

9

GOVERNMENT, LIBERALS, AND THE BUSINESS CULTURE

I hope we shall crush in its birth the aristocracy of our monied corporations which dare already to challenge our government to a trial of strength, and bid defiance to the laws of our country.

Thomas Jefferson, 1816

Although the outlook for the future is bright, it must not be taken for granted that the corporations will submit passively to legislation that seriously affects their own interests. Corporations have a habit of bending before the storm of public opinion to keep from breaking. Men have long realized that one of the most effective ways to block real reform is to support mock reform and that "honorable surrender" often offers an excellent opportunity to enter and study the defenses of the enemy.

Benjamin Parke De Witt, 1915

Federal economic regulation has failed.

Mark Green (an associate of Ralph Nader), 1977

Under all administrations, whether liberal or conservative, the responsibility for broad economic policy includes stabilizing and encouraging the expansion of corporate capitalism. Theodore Roosevelt preached that the country must learn to accept big business. Woodrow Wilson presided over the creation of the industrial-military complex.

And Franklin D. Roosevelt's first administration saw cooperation between government and business reach an apogee.

True enough, twentieth century liberalism has regarded business and the profit motive with a certain suspicious unease. Reform administrations have often employed state power to discipline business——and to the extent that it has become disciplined, they have largely done it. Yet over the past two decades or so, the investigations of a number of historians have disclosed that business has played a far larger role in generating and directing reform than most scholars had previously imagined. Amid growing talk of "corporate liberalism," a corresponding disgruntlement with the reform tradition has appeared. Is a "reform" really a reform, it is asked, when it attracts the backing of corporate or banking interests aiming to improve their operations or to undergird the political economy of capitalism?

Scholars on the left have generated a good deal of this literature of exposure, and much of what they say is true.[1] As we examine the history of some reform measures, it is like breaking open a wall and seeing mice scurry across the dusty boards. Far from standing en bloc against government intervention in the economy, at various junctures and for various reasons certain business interests have positively encouraged it. Among other things, they have wanted to limit competition and create a stable environment in which to operate. Nor has every corporate executive pulled and tugged against social justice legislation. "Yielding," many have known, might co-opt the left and help to stabilize the system. The federal government has also intervened in the economy in order to stimulate business and economic growth. During the nineteenth century, for instance, it underwrote transportation, notably the rail lines, and an agricultural system organized around the family farm. It set tariff rates so as to spur growth and protect it. Today, countless firms and workers rely on government for contracts and jobs.

On nearly all important questions historians disagree, not least on the matter of business intervention in politics under a guise of reform. The nature of business involvement, and its results, seem to present an even more ambiguous record than most of the rest of the reform tradition. As Ellis W. Hawley has written:

> One of the central problems of twentieth-century America has revolved about the difficulty of reconciling a modern industrial order, necessarily based upon a high degree of collective organization, with democratic postulates, competitive ideals, and liberal individualistic traditions inherited from the nineteenth century. This industrial order has created in America a vision of material abundance, a dream of abolishing poverty and achieving economic security for all; and the great

majority of Americans have not been willing to destroy it lest that dream be lost. Yet at the same time it has involved, probably necessarily, a concentration of economic power, a development of monopolistic arrangements, and a loss of individual freedom and initiative, all of which run counter to inherited traditions and ideals. Americans, moreover, have never really decided what to do about this industrial order. Periodically they have debated the merits of "regulated competition" and "regulated monopoly," of trustbusting and economic planning; and periodically have embarked upon reform programs that would remake the economic system. Yet the resulting reforms have been inconsistent and contradictory. Policies that would promote competition have been interspersed with those that would limit or destroy it. And American economists as a whole have never reached any real consensus in regard to the origins and nature of monopoly, its effects, or the methods of dealing with it.[2]

One underlying form of consensus does endure, however: the capitalist spirit lies at the heart of this country's system of values. In the broadest sense, this is a business culture, and Mr. Coolidge's famous dictum about the business of America being business remains accurate. C. Wright Mills argued that "the dominance and the near sacrosanct character of the business system have meant that when things go wrong in the political economy, blame is displaced from the businessman to the politician."[3]

Americans have linked their conception of big business with their images of rising living standards and an economy of abundance——even as they remain suspicious of big business for its various travesties and harbor a nostalgic regard for petty capitalism. We have wanted at one and the same time to avoid centralized control and power, to preserve democracy and opportunity, and yet to reap the benefits we associate with size.[4] By limiting the possibilities, this ambivalent adherence to capitalist norms automatically induces a dramatic constriction in the mainstream of reform (though not radical) thought.

Substantially because the health of the corporate-capitalist economy is central to the shaping of reform, one of the fundamental weaknesses of reform throughout this century has involved its failure to focus adequately upon the problems posed by the corporation and to develop solutions which range beyond the merely symbolic. Reformers have not even agreed on what the problems are, still less on responses to them.

The pervasive capitalist ethos also saturates the party system. While the GOP is basically a business party, rather than countering it as a labor party pure and simple, the Democrats represent both labor and business. This sprawling across the center provides one way of beating the GOP. But it means that vis-à-vis labor, the Democratic party automatically becomes half-compromised. None of this for a moment implies that business does better under Republican than Democratic administrations. It doesn't. Despite all the invective that liberals have hurled against the GOP's trickle-down theory, for example, the fact is that both parties have espoused trickle-down. Capitalism mandates it and indeed, trickle-down has quite a remarkable bipartisan appeal. The Democrats' juicy tax incentives in the sixties made spectacular use of it, with the wealthy getting their usual prime cut. As the party of the "left," the Democrats, unlike the GOP, bear a special onus of reassuring the business community; of *demonstrating* how capitalistic their party really is. In short, roughly speaking, business stands astride three-quarters of the two-party system.

All this reflects itself in the presidency. One might not naturally expect either of the two major parties to nominate a steelworker or a teamster for the office, but one might expect the Democrats to put forward someone distantly connected with union affairs now and again. Not so. As Dave Beck, onetime Teamsters president, deathlessly put it: "Unions are big business. Why should truck drivers and bottle washers be allowed to make big decisions affecting union policy? Would any corporation allow it?"[5] From Woodrow Wilson, the university president, to Franklin Roosevelt, the onetime trade association president, to Harry Truman, the haberdasher, to John Kennedy, the moneyed playboy, to Lyndon Johnson, the Texas millionaire, to Jimmy Carter, the peanut baron, Democratic Chief Executives have been comfortably removed from the assembly line. Henry Wallace, the "pinko" candidate of 1948, had appeared in a previous incarnation as Secretary of *Commerce*.

Then too, there is the matter of structure. With what realm of the private sector does government have the most in common? Clearly, with business. This is especially true of the military. The state, like business, means management, control, and power. Today, government is the biggest employer of workers in the country. The structural affinities of business and government become clearest in wartime, when individuals from the private sector get recruited to join federal officials in public management. Labor, in both sectors, gets managed.

Of the three major private sector economic interest groups, business, agriculture, and labor, two, agriculture and business, are essentially managerial. In either segment, labor constitutes a dependent party which bargains but by and large does not share control. Business and labor offer competing models of how to improve the general welfare. Labor's is redistributionist; business's, expansionist.

During the Gilded Age, the prospect of expanding productivity enjoyed very high priority. Laissez-faire promised to fan the national output, and its proponents advocated restricting government as one way of doing that. It soon enough became apparent, however, that business interests agreed neither over laissez-faire nor among themselves. This has been typical of business. When we bore into the politics of any era in this century, we find business internally split. It divides along interest lines: some farmers and shippers against certain railroads, for example. It divides along internal lines: some railroads against other railroads. It divides over specific policies: some railroads want state regulation, some want federal, some want no regulation at all. (Meanwhile, farmers and shippers split over just how, or whether, to do the regulating.) Business divides according to size: some country bankers want one thing, some city bankers another. Big firms take on little firms. Industries with tidy profit margins line up against industries with shaky ones.

These kinds of splits and others make it clear that business does not march in lockstep. Internal divisions have had the same impact upon this interest group as they exercise on any other, cutting its ability to get what it wants. Splits among business interests allow government executives, legislatures, and regulatory commissions to pursue more independent policies.

It would be easy, too, to view conservative administrations as following a more uniformly pro-business line than they really have. Rifts in the business community itself have made it difficult to satisfy everyone at once. And philosophical uncertainties and ambivalences have existed among conservatives as well. For all his support of business association, for example, Herbert Hoover was more interested in pursuing antitrust than, on the whole, the Coolidge Administration was.

But liberal administrations have shown even less consistency than have their conservative counterparts. When dealing with business, reform Presidents have always tended toward indecision. Partly this reflects a general societal ambivalence. As Jonathan R. T. Hughes has observed, turn-of-the-century "Americans wanted both; they wanted the efficiency and stability of big business and the freedom and flexibility of competition."[6] At the end of the 1970s, an examination of public opinion concluded that

> for over four decades, Americans have been ambivalent in their attitudes toward regulation. A majority has always said they opposed greater regulation, but over the years——as more and more regulation has been enacted——a majority has also voiced approval of existing regulation and indicated that it did not want to roll back the tide.[7]

A good deal of the ambivalence toward interfering very drastically with American capitalism has come from a fear of killing the goose that laid the golden egg, or even risking cutting her rate of production by making her nervous.   In this age of government-amended capitalism, business still carries the basic responsibility for making the economy go. In a capitalistic society, government's ability to provide services and to grow rides on the success of the market economy.   This includes the volume of tax revenues on which governmental activity is based.   The health of the economy, together with the health of the party in power, defense programs, and the welfare state itself all rest squarely on a flourishing capitalism.   Politicians of whatever stripe will listen to business advice.   They *have* to listen.   Their rivalries aside, the public and private sectors intermesh.   Government, in its own interest, will seek to sustain a flourishing private sector because it depends on it, and likewise because the private side insists upon it.   Meantime big government and the welfare state undergird capitalism by helping to maintain demand and to moderate economic cycles.

The two sectors interact in such a way, and with so much mutual dependence, that it becomes almost misleading to speak of "public" and "private" sectors at all.   Robert L. Heilbroner has described the system as one "in which capital calls the tune by which the state normally dances but takes for granted that the state will provide the theater within which the performance takes place."[8]   In theory and practice, the Kennedy Administration, for instance, veritably epitomized corporate liberalism.   Government revenues, and "thus our success," Kennedy told a business audience, "are dependent upon your profits and your success——and . . . far from being natural enemies, Government and business are necessary allies."[9]   The rhetoric was effusive, but the formula, timeless.   Theodore Roosevelt stated it this way:

> Our aim is to promote prosperity, and then see to its proper division. We do not believe that any good comes to any one by a policy which means destruction of prosperity; for in such cases it is not possible to divide it because of the very obvious fact that there is nothing to divide. . . . But it is obvious that unless the business is prosperous the wage-workers employed therein will be badly paid and the consumers badly served. Therefore not merely as a matter of justice to the businessman, but from the standpoint of the self-interest of the wage-worker and the consumer, we desire that business shall prosper; but it should be so supervised as to make prosperity also take the shape of good wages to the wage-worker and reasonable prices to the consumer, while investors and business rivals are insured just treatment, and the farmer, the man who tills the soil, is protected as sedulously as the wage-worker himself.[10]

For all its internal divisions, business has known better what it wants from the state than the state has of business. When it comes to regulating business, government policy has wavered. Reformers' attention to politics typically undulates, and at some point wanes. But business has a concrete economic stake in the political process every day.[11] And business will pour out campaign money to defeat incumbents or candidates who threaten its interests, compelling the makers of policy to think twice.

Robert Lekachman called another method by which business has maintained its leverage "the business confidence racket."[12] The way this interesting folk ritual works is summarized in a 1977 headline: "Stocks Soar as Blumenthal Plays Down Tax Reforms." Beneath this: "Dow Gains for Second Day After Statement That Carter Will Seek Levy Cuts but No Major Revisions." What had the administration done to provide this "psychological uplift"? Treasury Secretary W. Michael Blumenthal had informed Congress that the administration planned to "propose a 'relatively simple' tax measure, with reductions for individuals and business but no complicated tax reform provisions." Blumenthal also "reaffirmed President Carter's support of the monetary policies of Federal Reserve Board Chairman Arthur F. Burns," and talked about keeping inflation down. Presto: "The stock market devoured this good news and spurted ahead."[13]

A broader scenario, applicable to many situations, would run this way. Business or large elements thereof concludes that the (Wilson, Roosevelt, Carter, whatever) administration has put it under excessive stress. Some of the irritants may be "purely imaginary," but the key to the whole thing amounts to a "question of psychology."[14] Unless business people feel "confident," how can they expand production and employment? At issue is not what *is* happening to business, but what business *thinks* is happening to it——business psychology does not ground itself wholly or necessarily on fact. And in general, business health on one hand, and government regulation and pressure on the other, have always appeared to represent opposite poles.

Business will call for a breathing spell, and when one comes stock prices likely will rise. Denied a breather, business may bluster. The threat of a strike of capital does not merely mean layoffs, production slowdowns, or refusal to invest. It even extends to the local level, where business can undercut its opposition by playing off localities against one another.

The underlying rationale for the business confidence game is that in order for business to prosper, its practitioners must be willing to take risks so as to make profits. Investment must flow. When uncertainty prevails, investment will not flow, risks will not get taken, and that will affect production, which in turn will depress employment. Business wants a sense of where Washington is heading, and it wants governmental encouragement. More arcane than mere spending or tax policy or antitrust, all this has to do as well with soothing rhetoric, comfortable bromides, and generally un-threatening demeanor. Business has an exquisite sensitivity to mere words.

The decade of the thirties provides us with a classic instance of the business confidence game in action. Before FDR arrived, the game had already rendered Hoover an even more cautious Executive than he might otherwise have been. In trying to revive business confidence, Hoover became a sort of stiff Pollyanna and drained what remained of his reputation in a series of roseate pronouncements. The crisis, he announced in March 1930, would end in sixty days. He was off, of course, by about ten years. As Theodore Rosenof has observed, "the confidence thesis was the vital economic ingredient in American conservatism during the thirties."[15]

Perhaps the central vulnerability of the New Deal was that so much of its success, most notably reviving the economy, depended on restoring a healthy hue to capitalism. FDR never resolved the old Wilsonian uncertainty about what to do to check the threat posed by big business. His original approach rested fundamentally on restoring business confidence and prosperity. One rationale behind allowing business to dominate the National Recovery Administration (NRA) planning apparatus was that business provided, after all, the fount of recovery.[16] The New Dealers spent and spent, so they argued, to spread purchasing power. In reply, conservatives hurled back the confidence thesis: confidence-would-produce-investment-would-produce-recovery. The New Deal was undermining confidence and braking revival.[17] In the fall of 1934, *Time* remarked that "private fulminations and public carpings against the New Deal have become almost a routine of the business day."[18] Two years later the Democratic party collected the names of prominent business people who wanted FDR reelected. The list added up to all of twenty-five persons.[19] Conservatives' prescriptions for curing the economic disease ran along lines which, from era to era, have taken a fairly conventional direction. Simply put, government's experimentation and anti-business rhetoric must stop, and government should devote itself to stimulating confidence. "Evidently nothing . . . discouraged" FDR "more than his futile efforts to get ideas from business leaders," writes Arthur M. Schlesinger, Jr. "To every problem they offered a single answer——the restoration of 'confidence' through balancing the budget, halting reform, and reducing government regulation."[20] Scrap a good deal of the New Deal; cut government power; change the tax laws.

How should Washington respond to such demands? Edgar Kemler pinpointed part of the problem the administration faced in searching for an answer. "Progressives are never sure they have penetrated enemy territory, except by the outcry in the Tory press. And even there the powers of Wall Street are so sensitive and the structure of business confidence so fragile that it is difficult to know whether a scratch or a mortal wound has been inflicted."[21] Business yells more sharply than it hurts. When it does, its cry penetrates all the cracks and crevices of American ambivalence. As a general matter, in the face of any powerful counterforce, ambivalence usually stimulates retreat if not flight.

William E. Leuchtenburg has observed that "the New Dealers were never able to develop an adequate reform ideology to challenge the business rhetoricians."[22] Neither have any other reformers. A sharp-edged ideological response to business has proved difficult to produce or sustain in a major political party vying for power in a country given over to capitalism. Again, government itself must depend both economically and politically on a privately run corporate economy, and must, therefore, collaborate with it. Furthermore, as Theodore Rosenof has pointed out, "modern liberals have tended to share the conservatives' dogmatic assumption that 'too much' government economic intervention of itself led to totalitarianism, differing only as to where to draw the abysmal line."[23] The New Dealers, like liberals before as well as since, tied capitalism and democracy together inextricably. In the absence of an adequate New Deal counter-ideology, late in the thirties the older traditions of individualism and anti-statism provided conservatives with a desperately needed advantage.

Historically, conservative and business sensitivity has often taken ironic twists. During the Wilson Administration, for instance, conservatives castigated Treasury policy to stimulate the U.S. merchant marine, branding it socialistic. Yet the policy was aimed precisely at advancing the private economy, in this case exports. It has required remarkably little to get oneself branded an anti-business radical in this society. Conservatives lambasted the New Deal for cutting enterprise and liberty by expanding the state: if only the New Deal would stop smothering confidence and energy by cementing them beneath socialism, spending, and bureaucracy, then prosperity could take root and flower, and freedom could survive.[24] More recently, some historians have viewed such New Deal expedients as government expansion, social insurance, work relief, and deficit spending as means of co-opting the left and shoring up the capitalist system. The overwhelming majority of corporate executives at the time, however, viewed things differently, and there was much talk of immorality, taxes, shackles on the private sector, bureaucracy, political corruption, and waste.[25]

The New Deal eventually countered this onslaught with one of its own. Unpleasantries were exchanged about a "strike of capital" and business "sabotage," and there was an antitrust crusade.[26] But as a more typical pattern, economic slumps usually tempt reformers to placate business.[27] The panic of 1907 braked TR's drive to get the corporations in harness.[28] The same thing happened in the Wilson Administration. "The chief cause of the ebbing of the reform impulse," writes Arthur S. Link, "was the insidious depression that began during the fall of 1913 and mounted in severity during the late winter and spring of 1914." The GOP blamed the slump on the administration's tariff and antitrust policies.

> In the spring of 1914 the President embarked upon a campaign calculated to win the friendship of businessmen and bankers and to ease the tension that had existed between the administration and the business community. The accommodation of the antitrust program to the desires of the business world was the first step, along with Wilson's repeated expressions of confidence in and friendship for businessmen. Next the President began to welcome bankers and business leaders to the White House. In the palmy days of 1913 he had not wanted their advice.[29]

"I have not been inviting businessmen to see me," Wilson remarked, "I have been welcoming them."[30] He "clarified" his earlier sentiments concerning big business and issued optimistic economic prognoses. "Wilson," Link continues, "climaxed his little campaign to win the friendship of the business classes by turning over control of the Federal Reserve Board, in effect, to their representatives, as if he were trying to prove the sincerity of his recent professions."[31] For good measure, he threw in the FTC.

Setting a liberal agenda founded on growth in the post-World War II era has automatically required playing the business confidence game, thus automatically compromising the possibilities for change.[32] "The problem is," remarked John F. Kennedy, "that the business community no longer has any confidence in itself. Whenever I say anything that upsets them, businessmen just die. I have to spend my time and energy trying to prop them up."[33] Yet business has continued to find more comfort in the GOP than among the Democrats, even when an Eisenhower gives it three recessions and a Kennedy cuts tax levies and hands it a tax credit. "The only forms of reassurance that serve," John Kenneth Galbraith mordantly observed in 1978, "are lower taxes and general inaction, and these are required and expected no matter who wins elections." It all seems slightly bizarre. "Three Presidents in the last half century have enjoyed supreme business confidence——Herbert Hoover, Richard Nixon and Gerald Ford. Under Hoover and Ford we had the worst depressions of those 50 years, and under Nixon and Ford we had the worst inflation in our entire history."[34]

One of the ways in which reform administrations try to mute their differences with business we will call the unity approach. The unity approach is based upon the general proposition that a reform will produce less resistance if it has been endorsed in advance by groups which have already reached a consensus. If the advocates can empathize with their antagonists and as much as possible pull the reform's sting, so much the better.[35] Even if reconciliation proves impossible, reformers can pretend that it has already occurred, and proceed to act as though the wished-for had actually taken shape in reality.

This reform-as-consensus was well illustrated when progressivism got under way at the turn of the century. One side of progressivism insistently denied that anybody had interests different from anybody else. Toward the end of the era, this pretense came under considerable strain. But even the New Deal began with an emphasis on neighborly unity, cooperation, and stability. Rugged individualism seemed a threadbare coat. The New Dealers emphasized that interest groups must learn to cooperate for the benefit of all.

As early as the New Deal's first winter, though, the honeymoon of interest groups began to plunge toward its quick and acrimonious end. "Cooperative action came to mean governmental action," writes James Holt, and with this "the idea that the New Deal was inaugurating an entirely new set of social values was bound to wither." The right began lambasting the New Deal. Democrats responded with fusillades of progressive anti-privilege rhetoric. Early in 1936 Roosevelt himself joined in with a broad-front rhetorical onslaught against the "economic autocrats." Adds Holt:

> In the early days, New Dealers had often compared the economic crisis to a wartime situation, especially the war of 1917-18. By 1936, they found a more congenial analogy in Andrew Jackson's war on the Bank of the United States. Having failed to unite the country, they now embraced divisiveness. Instead of summoning a united people to battle against a common enemy, New Dealers were now calling the common people to war against an enemy within.

As questions of social justice and economic autocracy replaced the unity approach, "conflict and the coercive power of the state" intruded, too, though neither the new approach nor the old implied any ideology of massive structural transformation.[36]

In a way the quest for unity in the Kennedy-Johnson era proved far simpler than in the thirties, because the economy no longer stagnated. Growth, so it seemed, provided a way of underwriting reform and other priorities without income redistribution, tax hikes, or tax reform. All this had been foreshadowed by Leon Keyserling, who chaired Truman's Council of Economic Advisers. Dismissing the New Deal's pessimism about capitalism, Keyserling had envisioned an endlessly growing economy which would provide more for everybody, including the poor. The point, Keyserling believed, was to focus liberal energies on expansion, not on redistribution. Government would involve itself deeply, to be sure, but Keyserling included a thread of voluntarism which had wound through the early New Deal until the unity approach had ended. "Voluntary cooperation," Keyserling called it.[37] Keyserling's techniques, then, included intergroup cooperation, not strife; economic expansion rather than redistribution; and, through these, the eclipse of poverty. All this conformed nicely to the cautious spirit of postwar liberalism.[38]

As we have seen, a liberal regime, however cautious, will make business nervous. Responding to a 1962 poll of 30,000 business people, 86 percent opined that the Kennedy Administration was anti-business; 52 percent found it "strongly anti-business."[39] A celebrated confrontation Kennedy had with the steel industry prompted his famous remark: "My father always told me that all businessmen were sons of bitches, but I never believed it till now."[40] Sons of bitches or not, the fact remained that the administration posed no threat to American capitalism. Growth lay at the heart of its economic policy. In order to get the economy moving again, the corporations must have the mood and strength to pull. All this went well beyond domestic policy, for which Kennedy designated growth the cardinal priority. Growth was also critical to America's competition with the Soviets.[41]

These priorities, together with the power of the corporations, dictated a unity approach. The approach echoed Keyserling: more for everyone, with no significant redistribution of income or power. "Our primary challenge," Kennedy announced to the U.S. Chamber of Commerce, "is not how to divide the economic pie, but how to enlarge it." Kennedy told a business conference early in 1961:

> We know that your success and ours are intertwined——that you have facts and knowledge that we need. Whatever past differences may have existed, we seek more than an attitude of truce, more than a treaty——we seek the spirit of a full-fledged alliance.

Growth, revenue, profits, confidence——each of these things intermeshed with the others.[42]

But although the administration sought its full-fledged alliance, business continued to balk. Reminiscent of the Progressive Era, attitudes toward the administration differed, with most of business chary and its more cosmopolitan elements less so. On the whole, though, business missed Ike. When stock prices dropped in May 1962, business blamed Washington for wrecking confidence. Like Woodrow Wilson, Kennedy tried to appease the business community with verbal assurances: "The fact of the matter," he said, "is that most of the problems, or at least many of them, that we now face are technical problems, are administrative problems. They are very sophisticated judgments which do not lend themselves to the great sort of 'passionate movements' which have stirred this country so often in the past." Again: "The central domestic problems of our time . . . relate not to basic clashes of philosophy or ideology but to ways and means of reaching common goals——to research for sophisticated solutions to complex and obstinate issues."[43] Following much of the social thought of the fifties, Kennedy opted for a reliance on expertise that would have done managerial progressivism proud. Enough, he said in effect, of the New Deal.

And, in the spirit of Wilson, Kennedy did give business concrete benefits, notably tax and foreign trade benefits. Since expanded trade seemed crucial to a healthier economy, greater domestic prosperity, and Cold War foreign policy, the "centerpiece" legislative initiative for 1962 became a Trade Expansion Act. Bruce Miroff has suggested that in his desire to spur the economy, Kennedy boosted business simply as a byproduct, "but the two ends could not be separated."

> Corporate executives may not have had Kennedy's ear, but the functional result was not so different than if they had. Economic doctrine and political calculation were enough to make him respond more often to business desires than to those of the economic constituencies that actually supported him.[44]

Johnson, while carrying on the Kennedy program for the economy, was able to maintain a comparatively warm partnership with business. The Great Society, most significantly, did not assume the anti-business coloration of earlier reform eras. Along with Johnson's social benevolence went the other basics of sixties liberalism: economic growth, tax cut stimuli, bigger pie, blurred lines of class and interest. Johnson maintained a deep devotion to the unity approach; his consensus positively embraced business. The warmth radiated in both directions. Johnson tried to give something to everyone, and while it lasted, the Johnson consensus cloaked itself in un-partisanship and interest-group tradeoffs.[45] The Kennedy-Johnson era witnessed the longest-sustained economic expansion in peacetime yet recorded in this country. For the majority of people, the proverbial pie did expand. Corporate profits, in particular, showed extraordinary gains. That the already well-off and the corporations benefited most from the harvest of higher profits and lower taxes does not deny that nearly everyone came away with something from liberal growth policy.

Antitrust and Regulation

> Concentration and cooperation in industry in order to secure efficiency are a world-wide movement. The United States cannot resist it.

> Charles R. Van Hise, 1912

> What I am interested in is getting the hand of government on all of them [corporations]——this is what I want.

> Theodore Roosevelt, 1912

Despite Johnson's fixation with consensus, during the sixties business in general and big business in particular fell under a cloud of scrutiny and disapproval.[1] This always happens in reform eras: society at large rediscovers that corporations dominate government, build unsafe products, pollute.   Typically, though not always, popular regard for government and business runs inversely. Respect for business falls, then rises. Regard for government rises, then falls. When public confidence in business takes a downslide and anxieties concerning business behavior mount, a fresh emphasis in Washington on regulation or prosecution rarely arrives far behind. In the name of the broader public interest, liberal reform has endeavored to strip some of the jagged edges off of capitalism, notably those which have threatened social stability and the survival of the economic system itself.

A good deal of the American reform tradition grew out of the entrepreneurial spirit, and that side of reform has concentrated on opening the doors to business opportunity. When the doors palpably began to close around the turn of the century, Theodore Roosevelt performed the trick of rationalizing this constriction, along with big organization in general, in his New Nationalism. Roosevelt offered a way of resolving the ambivalence between admiration of and anger toward bigness and tycoons. By implication, the scrambling entrepreneur would give way to the management bureaucrat. Big business would grow bigger and bigger——under federal regulation.

But not all people felt convinced. Wilson, for one, was not yet ready for the age of corporate gigantism or the business bureaucrat to dawn. Yet he did not know what to do about it. Economic life to him was a matter not just of ledger books or power, but of morals, national character, and, not least, of symbols. The Jeffersonian-Jacksonian side of Wilson inclined him to look backward, while the material forces of the country obliterated the past——thus much of the opacity in Wilsonian reform. In 1912 Wilson had a good deal to say about oligarchy and the possible demise of American democracy. Much of what he said still sounds fresh today. Wilson played to a suspicion of authority that had characterized his party's past and which has ingrained itself in the national temper among liberals and conservatives alike. This suspicion toward authority cut both ways: against business *or* government.[2] Likewise, Wilson's critique cut both ways, against political "bossism" and against monopoly.

Once corporate power had achieved stupendous heights, though, the nation——or large elements of it——grudgingly accepted the growing power of government to offset it. In the nature of things, as with other varieties of reform, this eventually meant the federal government. There was simply nowhere else to go, even if federal power might easily be compromised by the corporations themselves. And the regulation of business in this country has a long tradition, going all the way back to the colonial era.[3] But ambivalence toward the business order has characterized the entire run of twentieth century reform. Not surprisingly, when it came down to legislating, the nation's ambivalence about industrial gigantism got written into law. As Hofstadter observed:

> The Progressive discussion of the so-called trust or monopoly question is . . . filled with all that uneasiness and inconsistency which we may expect to see when men find themselves enmeshed in institutions and practices that seem to be working to considerable effect but that violate their inherited precepts and their moral preferences. When a social problem is, in its largest aspects, insoluble, as this one was, and when the feelings aroused over it are as urgent as the feelings of the Progressive generation, what usually happens is that men are driven to find a purely ceremonial solution.[4]

The problem was that many Americans found a lot to like about gigantism. They respected success and the size it bred, along with the efficiency which size seemed to signify. They associated big business with economic growth and rising living standards.[5] And in any case, a strong streak of conservatism about the proprieties of private property would have kept antitrust or regulation from going too far, particularly if either social stability or prosperity had begun to seem threatened. Whatever "solution" the nation arrived at to limit business abuses had to follow TR's 1905 dictum "to work out methods of controlling the big corporations without paralyzing the energies of the business community."[6]

In a capitalist system, indubitably.   What would serve as the main indicator of whether or not business energies began lapsing toward paralysis?   In a capitalist system, business itself.   With its exquisitely sensitive nervous system, if it started to hurt, business would instantly scream.

As David M. Chalmers has pointed out, "antitrust has remained a possible means to economic well-being which the American government and people have never been quite willing either comprehensively to use or completely to abandon."[7]   This has guaranteed that the forays against business would turn out less literal than rhetorical.   Along with the rhetoric has gone a very great deal of naïveté, together with an equal but predictable measure of inconsistency.   Since in the public and the political minds the trust problem has remained ill-defined, not much could be done about it, realistically, except to handle it as a symbolic issue with symbolic "solutions."   From the first, antitrust in America has existed in a sort of symbol-charged never-never land.   Thurman Arnold, in his famous examination of the antitrust laws as "symbol[s]" and "moral gesture[s]," argued that they actually retarded effective regulation.   As with the political machine, no replacement for big business existed, and onslaughts against it largely sputtered out.[8]   In retrospect, so long as the nation could claim to remain a democracy with a free enterprise economy sustaining significant surviving levels of competition, reformers would have found the common denominator which conjoined their goals.   For the rest, size could get written off as progress.[9]

And if, after passage of the antitrust and regulatory laws had dampened public anger and concern, the new federal commissions came under control of pro-business conservatives, business might actually gain.   The thorn would be pulled, the public pacified——and the commissions put to use in the interest of business itself.   This pattern took shape early.   The 1887 Act to Regulate Commerce mandated——but did not provide any definition for——"just and reasonable" rates.   The Interstate Commerce Commission (ICC), whose powers were also vague, started out circumspectly, and even then the federal courts undercut it.   As the new century opened, the ICC found itself in an abject state.   Meanwhile, the courts also undermined the Sherman Antitrust Act, which had been shaky enough to begin with.   There was a general tendency to identify recently rejuvenated prosperity with the corporations, and to fear damaging them.

But this was the time, if ever a time existed, to confront the trust issue.   The century's first big wave of business consolidation ran from 1895 to 1904.[10]   TR proceeded to distinguish between "good" and "bad" corporations and rather arbitrarily to litigate against some of the most obnoxious.   The ICC was revived.   Railroads and the food industry came under meaningful regulation.   Wilson's administration attempted to get a tighter definition of the Sherman Act's ban on "conspiracy in restraint of trade," but left this idea in the lurch part way through its legislative passage in favor of a regulative approach through the Federal Trade Commission. The new FTC made a meek debut. Meantime, with politicians arguing over what position government ought to take, the great consolidation wave swept on by.

The FTC and Clayton measures enacted a good deal of Wilson's (and the nation's) ambivalence toward big business into law. At the same time, though, these acts helped to resolve the Democratic party's ambivalence toward centralization, in this case in favor of federal authority. Again ambivalently, as we have noted, Wilson proceeded to appoint more than enough conservatives with a strong business orientation to prove, if proof had ever been needed, that he had hardly set out to wreck big business. Business received large concessions from the Wilson Administration.

The progressives, Robert H. Wiebe has observed, created "no more than a framework" for business regulation with the expectation that "the right men in the right offices" could carry things from there.[11] But where to go? The primary brake on effective regulatory commissions has not been this administration or that, nor the judiciary, but instead, public uncertainty over what, if anything, to do about business concentration and unfair competitive practices. Winds blow hither and yon as the public mood changes and as commissioners come and go.[12] During the twenties GOP Presidents packed the already weak FTC with conservatives. The Supreme Court battered the FTC into a smoking hulk. Meanwhile, another surge of business consolidations swept through. Government seemed to exist only as business's helpmate, stimulating the trend. Business consolidation had gone on so long that the old progressive sense of ambivalent anxiety had significantly drained away through familiarity. Business developed into a sort of secular religion. As a social group, like the medieval clergy, it had no peer. "Machinery," Henry Ford proclaimed, "is the new Messiah."[13]

Then came 1929. Not only did the Depression shatter confidence in the leadership of American business; it generated a great deal of sentiment for chastising big business. What to do about consolidation now? The old dispute was still going on when the New Deal opened. Over time, the question generated a considerable measure of presidential uncertainty.[14] The New Deal never produced a well-defined answer, which kept it comfortably within the wandering tradition of twentieth century business reform. Like other important things, the issue of size fell behind recovery in order of priority. We have seen that New Deal "policy" wrote a veritable textbook on inconsistency, embracing elements of business planning, antitrust, regulation, and here and there a dab of socialism. Business opportunists got plenty of openings from the New

Deal, in the context of the economic collapse and all of this uncertainty and fluidity. While, in time, the New Deal did turn to antitrust, it did so only following the NRA experiment, which had brought in the federal government as a full partner for cartelization.[15] The cardinal issue remained recovery, and the administration's approach emphasized pricing practices over size per se.

Critically important, the New Deal's analysis of the problem, like the progressives', proved far more sweeping than the solutions. As Theodore Rosenof has emphasized, "the central tradition——and the most crucial influence of tradition" operating on the country's political leadership——

> lay in certain overall American assumptions about the economy:
> that private enterprise was somehow more virtuous than public
> enterprise, that central planning and dictatorship somehow
> followed in logical and inevitable sequence, that free enterprise
> and political liberty were somehow intertwined and inseparable.

The New Dealers fell within this tradition and then disagreed with conservatives (who did as well) "as to where to draw the line."[16] All of this put severe limits on what the New Dealers would ultimately prove willing to do. The administration had to make obeisance to differing traditions; it probably had to proceed inconsistently. The ultimate upshot "was an economy characterized by private controls, partial planning, compensatory governmental spending, and occasional gestures toward the competitive ideal."[17]

On the whole, then, neither antitrust nor other governmental policy has carefully defined or consistently upheld measures affecting business concentration. Antitrust enforcement itself, as James Willard Hurst has put it, has in general "tended to put aside the concentration issue and to content itself with seeking to establish administrative control of the operations of oligopolistic markets." While "balance of power" in the political and social realms had been an important consideration in earlier laws, after the late thirties efficiency seemed the most important antitrust concern.[18]

Beyond the gross confusion which has accompanied the development of governmental policy toward business, business has shown a genius for weakening policy after the fact and bending it to fit its own interests. This has been true since the moment regulation began. Even if they do not start out that way, regulatory bodies frequently turn into allies and defenders of the interests they supposedly govern. The regulated regulate their regulators. Onetime FCC Commissioner Nicholas Johnson remarked that "the only way to keep regulators upright is to lean on them from all sides."[19]

Antitrust survives, of course.   So does the ideal of government regulating business.   But one might say that antitrust has marched at least halfway into the oblivion which welcomed prohibition. Antimonopoly-antitrust, so important a part of the nineteenth century legacy, no longer takes the central place in public debate which it held during the Progressive Era.   The problem posed by the corporation, and the deep structural issues revolving around it, have lost their salience in American reform.   TR and Wilson addressed these issues; Kennedy and Johnson   ignored   them.   Huge,   abstract,   modern   multinational corporations make rather opaque targets.   The whole meaning of the competitive "ideal" changes when it turns from Smith-versus-Jones to Nissan-versus-Ford.   And, as a creator of competition, antitrust has proved a massive disappointment.   "At best the laws break one very large firm into two or three large firms after a very lengthy and costly legal battle," writes Lester C. Thurow, "and the industry becomes slightly less oligopolistic."[20]   It is not that antitrust or regulation have become totally obsolete; but since the New Deal, they have ceased to maintain a prime position on reform's agenda.   Of all the principal themes in the twentieth century reform tradition, this one wound up the most ambiguously.

Which resulted, largely, from ambivalence.   But if Americans (and liberals) have shown ambivalence toward big business, business has also shown ambivalence toward the welfare state.   In the forties, Joseph Schumpeter brutally chided

> the very characteristic manner in which particular capitalist interests and the bourgeoisie as a whole behave when facing direct attack.   They talk and plead——or hire people to do it for them; they snatch at every chance of compromise; they are ever ready to give in; they never put up a fight under the flag of their own ideals and interests——in this country there was no real resistance anywhere against the imposition of crushing financial burdens during the last decade or against labor legislation incompatible with the effective management of industry. . . . The only explanation for the meekness we observe is that the bourgeois order no longer makes any sense to the bourgeoisie itself and that, when all is said and nothing is done, it does not really care.[21]

Considering the anguished cries of the thirties against the New Deal, one might have thought these words a bit premature.   But during the forties, for a variety of reasons (among them the wartime "partnership" with Washington), business substantially acclimated itself to the New Deal.   Government became even more massively involved in the economy as an arms purchaser, and, correlating in one degree or another, as an underwriter of scientific research and education. "A mixture of properly limited 'welfare statism' with 'responsible' labor unions, pressure-group 'planning,' and devices to maintain 'workable' competition," the majority of corporate leaders concluded (in the words of Ellis W. Hawley), "did make for a stable environment in which corporate organizations could prosper and grow." The accommodation was mutual——to the degree that things had ever been otherwise in Washington.[22]   Along with finding protection in the liberal order, big business adjusted itself to this order because established business respects and feels most comfortable with the status quo. Within certain bounds, that means whatever the status quo happens to be at the time.

Once little was expected of business in the way of "social responsibility." But the antitrust laws helped to legitimate the great corporations in the public mind,[23] and very early in the century, the new PR began cleaning up the image of the snarling captain of industry. Today, a good deal is expected: corporations should supposedly behave responsibly like other good "citizens," or at least make obeisance to that expectation (since, like every other canon relating to government and business, this one remains a little vague). Business schools have become a key mechanism for the upward mobility of disadvantaged individuals who get co-opted in their passage toward success. The decline of the nakedly authoritarian employer in favor of more subtle, manipulative approaches has had a similar impact. At the end of a reform era, we always like to assume that legislation has tamed business abuses. Business people assure us that they have been tamed and that they now understand their civic duties. A new general anxiety sets in, this time over government regulation going too far.

All this presents the would-be trustbuster with a vague target, a seemingly humane and public-spirited corporate order, coated in a honey glaze of public relations. A hard target——"the public be damned" ——would serve far better. And the increasing opacity of the corporation has left politicians, by comparison, more exposed than ever before, because they are so excruciatingly visible.

When things went wrong in the sixties and seventies, politicians made wonderfully easy targets. Like their progressive forebears, Americans now feared the demise of their way of life——for example, the disappearance of cheap energy. They lashed out at government just as they lashed out at the corporations (especially big oil companies) which they held responsible. Beset by Ralph Naderesque muckraking, the stench of corporate involvement in the Vietnam War and the Nixon scandals, and other factors, business suffered in the public image much as government did. In lambasting the regulatory bureaucracy, Nader inadvertently reinforced people's growing grudge toward government.[24]

While mass confidence in government leadership was falling in the decade after the mid-sixties, confidence in big business leadership plummeted as well.[25]

In the end, the public, it appears, complains about regulation at the same time that it insists on regulation in order to keep business in line. "The people of the United States," declared Theodore Roosevelt, "have but one instrument which they can effectively use against the colossal combinations of business——and that instrument is the government of the United States."[26]   While the old struggle over size no longer generates the passions it used to, more recent years, notably 1965-72, saw the restrictions on business proliferate.   Though not new in concept, we might call this neoregulation.   It includes programs involving equal opportunity, occupational safety and health, environmental protection, consumer rights, consumer product safety, nondiscrimination, and energy use.   It involves relatively new agencies, for example, the Equal Employment Opportunity Commission, the Consumer Product Safety Commission, the Environmental Protection Agency, the National Highway Transportation Safety Board, and the Occupational Safety and Health Administration.   The activities of these agencies have caused a good deal of unhappiness in the business community. As Steven Kelman pointed out in 1978, while "most of the regulatory agencies established before the last decade were set up to regulate prices and conditions of entry in various industries," neoregulation is "intended to regulate non-market behavior by business firms," generally "acts that injure third parties."[27]   Rather than overseeing particular industries, neoregulation tends to affect many at once.   And a good deal of the business antagonism neoregulation has generated, apart from billowing complaints about costs, forms, and red tape, arises precisely from its success.[28]

The Conundrum of Labor

Working women today have not the faintest inkling of what the conditions were before the terrific increase in trade-union organization, nor do they begin to realize what their predecessors went through in order to change those conditions.

Rose Schneiderman, 1967

Like business, labor has a concrete financial interest in politics. Yet labor and management in America are not equal, nor do they relate to one another as equals. Vested with superior power and prestige, management has by and large defined the context of the relationship.

Labor has generally restrained the breadth of its demands. For decades, unions viewed with suspicion federal intervention in their relationship with management. When labor finally did join capital at government's table, it made a predictable but unpleasant discovery. The order of seating was arranged so that as the dishes got passed, business always received its helping first. Once in a while a plate of relishes or olives got handed across the table or the wrong way around, but this was a breach of etiquette and rarely done.   When it did occur, business invariably commented on the bad manners of the new guests.

Labor's junior partnership reflects the realities of leverage and power. Throughout the early twentieth century, reformers embraced the idea of legislating for workers, but remained chary of unionism and its consequences. This concern most clearly characterized the progressives, who feared rifts along class lines and who also worried about the potentially coercive leverage of organized labor. If unions gained power, it seemed, the class battle would become permanently fixed. And the subject of unions brought up a number of other facts which many progressives were loath to acknowledge, having to do with institutional size, organization, the decline of individualism, and threats to the ethic of work and merit.

In other words, the middle-class progressive attitude toward labor was *paternalistic*. This too grew out of realities of power.   Even reformist middle-class employers had no reason to feel enthusiastic over the unionization of their employees, still less over the emergence of an organized proletariat suddenly dining at government's table. But as with so many other things, the progressives felt ambivalent toward unionization; some of them, indeed, were unionists.

All this historians have known for a long time, and running through much of the historical literature one encounters a latent assumption that the New Deal resolved the ambivalence, the power anxieties, and the problem of paternalism in labor's favor. True enough, as Everett Carll Ladd, Jr., and Charles D. Hadley have written, "the New Deal era stands as the political high-water mark of the urban, white working class." "This," they add, "was the heroic age of American labor."[1] Yet FDR's first impulse was precisely the middle-class progressive impulse: to help labor without necessarily helping unions.[2] Much of what ensued benefited labor inadvertently and because of the aggressive interloping of men like John L. Lewis and Robert Wagner. As Ellis W. Hawley has pointed out:

> Union leaders did not win a share of the corporation's power
> over production, pricing, and resource allocation. For the most
> part, they did not even reach for it; and, as a result, their rise
> did not bring much redistribution, much restructuring of

business itself, or much of an increase in consumer purchasing power.[3]

When World War II arrived, the junior nature of labor's partnership became starkly clear. The war brought to maturity the military-industrial complex, and what Samuel Lubell has labeled "the military-industrial job complex." "It represents a sizable voting constituency," Lubell observes, "directly responsive to the president's manipulations, which can generally be counted on to support the government's foreign and defense policies."[4] Massive employment in defense industries gave a large segment of labor a big stake (when it came to a choice) in weapons expenditures as against antipoverty or other social outlays. Today, civilian and defense expenditures compete directly, so that heavy spending on the military helps to guarantee the status quo at home. A faltering economy, reduced commitment to reform, antitax outbreaks, and the rapidly inflating costs of defense all conspired to aggravate the situation in the seventies. This paled in comparison to the way in which Reagan pitted defense against social outlays in the eighties.

Since the New Deal, the unity approach has simply assumed that labor, having nowhere else to go, subscribes to the liberal consensus. The trick, so it appears, lies in persuading business to join. This helps to explain why business has gotten such extraordinary concessions out of the unity gambit. Meanwhile, over the past several decades the proportion of the working population wearing blue collars, as well as the percentage belonging to unions, has steadily declined. Unlike business, a ubiquitous force, the influence of organized labor varies widely from state to state, region to region. The involvement of some unions in crime and corruption has tarnished unionism's image. And union members have grown more conservative, so that as liberal material, workers are an uneven catch.

The pivotal decade was the 1950s. Like the twenties, the fifties produced stagnation in the labor movement. Liberal intellectuals made the unpleasant discovery that while labor remained more or less reliable on the great mundane questions——wages, security, working conditions——it could show itself quite cold to liberal ideals concerning civil liberties and other "soft" issues. If anything, the perennial cultural rift between intellectuals and blue-collar workers widened. Most intellectuals did not number themselves among the more fervent devotees of bowling leagues or stock car racing. The new priorities of prosperity produced curious consequences for labor. Questioned about how he intended to vote in 1972, as reported by Lubell, a carpenter in Tampa responded: "I'm sixty years old and have been a union man all my life. The Republicans have never been for labor." But "a few questions later, he disclosed that he owned two apartment houses and his strongest economic concern was the taxes paid on this property; also that he had already decided to vote for Nixon against 'any Democrat other than Wallace.'"[5]

Stewart Alsop remarked that "the fire has gone out in labor's belly."[6] The labor movement had not simply turned to paste. Probably more than anything else (since both major parties are to one degree or another parties of business), the adherence of unions to the Democratic party has made it different from the GOP. Labor participation has remained crucial to any liberal coalition. In the sixties and seventies, the AFL-CIO continued to push for antipoverty measures, tax reform, Medicare, civil rights and voting rights, housing, truth-in-lending, occupational safety and health, and consumer protection. Yet the American labor movement inched along with little if any real ideology, still less one of class struggle—a movement in the cautious spirit of Gompers and now George Meany; of middle-classized labor.

The conundrum of labor, its junior partnership, suggests a good deal more than the difficulties of labor alone. The relative conservatism of the U.S. labor movement has reflected patterns of caution that imbue society as a whole, and which explain why it has been so very difficult for American reform to define its goals and keep them in focus. A people who think of themselves as dynamic, Americans have demonstrated an abiding hesitancy where innovations in social policy are concerned. To this broader conservatism, the conservatism of the masses, we now turn. We will also probe more deeply into the conservatism of American labor.

NOTES

Lawrence Goodwyn, *The Populist Moment: A Short History of the Agrarian Revolt in America* (New York: Oxford University Press, 1978), p. [xxix] (Jefferson quote); De Witt, *Progressive Movement*, p. 114; Mark Green, "Consumer Agency: Pro," *New Republic*, 18 June 1977, p. 14.

[1] Among the important works (not all from the left) are Robert H. Wiebe, *Businessmen and Reform: A Study of the Progressive Movement* (Cambridge, Mass.: Harvard University Press, 1962); Gabriel Kolko, *The Triumph of Conservatism: A Reinterpretation of American History, 1900-1916* (New York: Macmillan Co., Free Press, 1963); Weinstein, *Corporate Ideal*; Mansel G. Blackford, *The Politics of Business in California, 1890-1920* (Columbus: Ohio State University Press, 1977); *Business History Review* 52 (Autumn 1978), the entire issue devoted to the subject of "corporate liberalism"; R. Jeffrey Lustig, *Corporate Liberalism: The Origins of Modern American Political Theory, 1890-1920* (Berkeley: University of California Press, 1982); and Martin J. Sklar's fine recent study, *The Corporate Reconstruction of American Capitalism, 1890-1916:*

The Market, the Law, and Politics (Cambridge, England: Cambridge University Press, 1988).

[2]*Monopoly*, p. vii.

[3]*White Collar: The American Middle Classes* (New York: Oxford University Press, 1956), p. 344.

[4]See Hawley, *Monopoly*, pp. 472ff.

[5]Bert Cochran, *Labor and Communism: The Conflict that Shaped American Unions* (Princeton: Princeton University Press, 1977), p. 339.

[6]*Governmental Habit*, p. 122.

[7]Michael Pertschuk, *Revolt Against Regulation: The Rise and Pause of the Consumer Movement* (Berkeley: University of California Press, 1982), p. 49.

[8]*The Nature and Logic of Capitalism* (New York: W. W. Norton & Co., 1985), p. 105.   My thinking has also been influenced by pp. 89-90, 95, 104-6.

[9]Matusow, *Unraveling of America*, p. 33.

[10]"Confession of Faith," pp. 323-24.

[11]Corresponding, it should be added, is the concrete economic stake of labor.

[12]"The Business Confidence Racket," *New Republic*, 14 January 1978, pp. 10-12.

[13]*Los Angeles Times*, 12 November 1977.

[14]Moley, *After Seven Years*, p. 292.   My thoughts on this whole subject have been influenced by pp. 292, 318, 331, 370-72, and passim.

[15]*Dogma*, p. 35.

[16]Otis L. Graham, Jr., *Toward a Planned Society: From Roosevelt to Nixon* (New York: Oxford University Press, 1977), p. 30.

[17]Rosenof, *Dogma*, p. 35.

[18]"Business and Finance," 24 September 1934, p. 57.

[19]Kim McQuaid, "Corporate Liberalism in the American Business Community, 1920-1940," *Business History Review* 52 (Autumn 1978): 363-64.

[20]*Coming of the New Deal*, p. 501.

[21]*Deflation*, p. 168.

[22]*Roosevelt and the New Deal*, p. 273.

[23]*Dogma*, pp. 8, 10-13.

[24]Holt, "Anti-statist Tradition," p. 27.

[25]Ellis W. Hawley, "The New Deal and Business," in Braeman, *New Deal*, 1:65.

[26]Moley, *After Seven Years*, p. 372.

[27]An exception was 1937.   Roosevelt set off the extraordinary depression-within-the-Depression that began in September of that year by, in effect, acceding to business demands; then he turned left once more.   See Romasco, *Politics of Recovery*, pp. 225-26, 234.

[28]Blum, *Progressive Presidents*, pp. 44-45; De Witt, *Progressive Movement*, p. 51. See also Nell Irvin Painter, *Standing at Armageddon: The United States, 1877-1919* (New York: W. W. Norton & Co., 1987), pp. 212-15.

[29]*Woodrow Wilson and the Progressive Era, 1910-1917*, New American Nation Series (New York: Harper & Bros., 1954), pp. 75-76.

[30]Gould, *Reform and Regulation*, p. 157.

[31]*Wilson and the Progressive Era*, p. 76.

[32]See, on this point, Alan Wolfe, *America's Impasse: The Rise and Fall of the Politics of Growth* (Boston: South End Press, 1982).

[33]Schlesinger, Jr., *A Thousand Days*, pp. 639-40.

[34]"The Trouble with Economists," *New Republic*, 14 January 1978, pp. 17, 21.

[35]See Goodwin Watson, "Resistance to Change," in Zaltman, *Creating Social Change*, p. 617.

[36]"Anti-statist Tradition," pp. 35-42.

[37]Hamby, *Beyond the New Deal*, p. 301.

[38]For a clear statement of the liberal switch from redistribution to economic growth, see John Kenneth Galbraith, *The Affluent Society*, 3d ed., rev. (Boston: Houghton Mifflin Co., 1976), pp. 79-81.

[39]Lipset, *Political Man*, p. xxxiii.

[40]William E. Leuchtenburg, *A Troubled Feast: American Society since 1945*, updated ed. (Boston: Little, Brown & Co., 1983), p. 133.

[41]Miroff, *Pragmatic Illusions*, pp. 168-69.

[42]Ibid., pp. 172, 194.

[43]Ibid., pp. 172, 181-82, 197.

[44]Ibid., pp. 190, 201-2. See also Jim F. Heath, *John F. Kennedy and the Business Community* (Chicago: University of Chicago Press, 1969).

[45]Foley, *New Senate*, pp. 52, 54-55.

Antitrust and Regulation

Charles R. Van Hise, *Concentration and Control: A Solution of the Trust Problem in the United States* (New York: Macmillan Co., 1912; reprint, New York: Arno Press, 1973), pp. 277-78; Sklar, *Corporate Reconstruction of American Capitalism*, p. 356 (Roosevelt quote).

[1]As of the mid-1960s, although public confidence in business's ability to turn out goods continued unchallenged and unabated, the reputation of business, its "perceived legitimacy," fell. Pertschuk, *Revolt Against Regulation*, pp. 13-14; quotation from James Q. Wilson.

[2]Hofstadter, *Age of Reform*, pp. 226-27.

[3]See Hughes, *Governmental Habit*, especially ch. 2.

[4]*Age of Reform*, pp. 230-31, 243.

[5]See especially Hurst, *Law and Social Order*, p. 260.

[6]Arthur A. Ekirch, Jr., *The Decline of American Liberalism* (New York: Atheneum, 1967), p. 173.

[7]*Neither Socialism nor Monopoly: Theodore Roosevelt and the Decision to Regulate the Railroads*, America's Alternatives Series (Philadelphia: J. B. Lippincott Co., 1976), p. 10.

[8]Arnold, *Folklore*, pp. 209, 217, 220.

[9]On all this, see Hofstadter, *Age of Reform*, pp. 242-43.

[10]See Naomi R. Lamoreaux, *The Great Merger Movement in American Business, 1895-1904* (Cambridge, England: Cambridge University Press, 1985).

[11]*Businessmen and Reform*, p. 4.

[12]McCraw, "Progressive Legacy," p. 198.

[13]William E. Leuchtenburg, *The Perils of Prosperity, 1914-32*, Chicago History of American Civilization (Chicago: University of Chicago Press, 1958), pp. 187-89.

[14]Especially revealing are Hawley, *Monopoly*; and Wilson D. Miscamble, "Thurman Arnold Goes to Washington: A Look at Antitrust Policy in the Later New Deal," *Business History Review* 56 (Spring 1982): 1-15.

[15]Miscamble, "Thurman Arnold," passim.

[16]*Dogma*, pp. 10-11.

[17]Hawley, *Monopoly*, pp. 15-16, 475-76, 490.

[18]*Law and Social Order*, pp. 265-66.

[19]Green, "Consumer Agency: Pro," p. 15.   What is quoted here is Green's paraphrase of Johnson's quip.   There is no uniform pattern to the history or behavior of regulatory agencies.   See Thomas K. McCraw, *Prophets of Regulation: Charles Francis Adams; Louis D. Brandeis; James M. Landis; Alfred E. Kahn* (Cambridge, Mass.:   Harvard University Press, Belknap Press, 1984), p. 301.

[20]*The Zero-sum Society: Distribution and the Possibilities for Economic Change* (New York: Penguin Books, 1981), pp. 126-27.

[21]Joseph A. Schumpeter, *Capitalism, Socialism and Democracy*, 3d ed. (New York: Harper Torchbooks, 1962), p. 161.

[22]"New Deal and Business," p. 74.

[23]McCraw, *Prophets of Regulation*, p. 145.

[24]Pertschuk, *Revolt Against Regulation*, p. 64.

[25]Edsall, *New Politics of Inequality*, pp. 112-13.

[26]Gable, *Bull Moose Years*, p. 125.

[27]"Regulation that Works," *New Republic*, 25 November 1978, pp. 16-17.

[28]For a good brief description of the many functions which regulation can perform, see McCraw, *Prophets of Regulation*, pp. 300-301.   On neoregulation itself, see David Vogel, "The 'New' Social

Regulation in Historical and Comparative Perspective," in *Regulation in Perspective: Historical Essays*, ed. Thomas K. McCraw (Boston: Division of Research, Graduate School of Business Administration, Harvard University; Cambridge, Mass.: Harvard University Press, 1981), pp. 155-85. See also Kim McQuaid, *Big Business and Presidential Power: From FDR to Reagan* (New York: William Morrow & Co., 1982).

The Conundrum of Labor

Rose Schneiderman and Lucy Goldthwaite, *All for One* (New York: Paul S. Eriksson, 1967), p. 260.

[1]*Transformations*, pp. 191-92.

[2]The Wagner Act, Labor Secretary Frances Perkins wrote, "did not particularly appeal to [Roosevelt] . . . when it was described to him." "He always regarded the Social Security Act as the cornerstone of his administration and, I think, took greater satisfaction from it than from anything else he achieved on the domestic front." Both Perkins and the President leaned toward the social welfare approach, at least at first, in preference to hammering out new relationships between management and labor. Likewise, Lyndon Johnson wanted to bestow gifts on people, but gifts specifically chosen by him to meet their needs. He wanted to be trusted to do this, and wanted thanks for it. Frances Perkins, *The Roosevelt I Knew* (New York: Harper & Row, 1964), pp. 239, 301; Milton Derber, "The New Deal and Labor," in Braeman, *New Deal*, p. 111; Kearns, *Lyndon Johnson*, p. 54.

[3]"New Deal and Business," p. 70.

[4]*The Future While It Happened* (New York: W. W. Norton & Co., 1973), p. 103.

[5]Ibid., p. 71.

[6]Ladd, *Transformations*, p. 194.

10

MASS INERTIA

It is to be noted . . . that the institutions of to-day——the present accepted scheme of life——do not entirely fit the situation of to-day. At the same time, men's present habits of thought tend to persist indefinitely, except as circumstances enforce a change. These institutions which have so been handed down, these habits of thought, points of view, mental attitudes and aptitudes, or what not, are therefore themselves a conservative factor. This is the factor of social inertia, psychological inertia, conservatism.

Thorstein Veblen

It must be considered that there is nothing more difficult to carry out, nor more doubtful of success, nor more dangerous to handle, than to initiate a new order of things. For the reformer has enemies in all those who profit by the old order, and only lukewarm defenders in all those who would profit by the new order. . . . On every opportunity for attacking the reformer, his opponents do so with the zeal of partisans, the others only defend him half-heartedly, so that between them he runs great danger.

Machiavelli

Common sense is not so common.

Voltaire

We might define a reform era as a period in which the majority or a strong minority of the public translates its needs into idealism, the better to pursue its needs. The definition is not complete, of course, nor do I mean to imply that a one-to-one relationship exists between public opinion and the ultimate formation of policy; far from it. But given the proposition that at least some significant relationship exists (a fairly comfortable assumption), we arrive at two perplexing questions. Why have we had so few reform movements? And why have they failed to cut any deeper? We have already posed these questions and have gone at them from a number of different directions.

But one fundamental approach remains——to investigate the mind of the general public. Here inertia[1] assumes its most intractable form. It is simply very difficult to get great masses of people to do anything in particular, especially at one time.

We can better understand the inertia problem if we slightly clarify the nature of the public. In truth, no such thing as *the* public exists. In a free society people cannot be organized uniformly, which helps keep the society free. But it also leaves the widest latitude available for the drag of human inertia.

Lincoln's aphorism is probably the most familiar observation by an American on the nature of public opinion: "It is true that you may fool all the people some of the time; you can even fool some of the people all the time; but you can't fool all of the people all the time." Looked at carefully, instead of the usual way as a sort of singsong, Lincoln's seemingly ringing affirmation becomes less ringing. "All the people some of the time" was Nazi Germany.

Public opinion has had far less depressing consequences in this country, of course. Rather than worshipping the state, we have done the opposite. Ironically, the very openness of democratic government has itself produced public disillusionment, cynicism, and withdrawal. Politicians inevitably do things they shouldn't do. Lincoln himself could behave like a rascal. Democratic government demands certain degrees of compromise and hypocrisy. But because these things tend to get publicized, and look like a kind of visible scum floating across the surface of political life, the public will always remain mistrustful of democratic government. A free press and open investigations breed skepticism like a lab culture. A measure of suspicion is a healthy thing, and sometimes intense mistrust is healthy, too; but at other times public suspicion simply functions as one more leaden mass holding down constructive change.

In wide realms of social and business reform, the would-be reformer enters regions of deep public ambivalence where pressures continuously push toward the status quo. The issues themselves often seem to lie beyond the comprehension of the mass public except in largely personal terms: not welfare policy per se, for instance, but food stamp spenders at the supermarket, or the welfare chiseler down the block. These personalized perceptions often push individuals to the right: *my* taxes, competition for *my* job. Many liberals, as a result, have shown considerable ambivalence toward the people and their general reliability. This, in turn, makes twentieth century liberalism a respecter of expertise, including the expertise of the corporate managerial elite. And middle-class liberals maintain sufficient suspicion toward labor that the socialist notion of worker-dominated production also remains suspect.

If we ponder reform in these personal terms, it will tell us something about ourselves as consumers of the political product. Years ago, Abraham H. Maslow suggested that there exists a hierarchy of human needs, with each prepotent over the one just below. The lower needs never get erased, but once fulfilled tend to relinquish priority to the higher ones. This is the hierarchy:[2]

PHYSICAL

1. *Physiological*—the fundamentals of survival, including hunger and thirst.

2. *Safety*—concern over physical survival, ordinary prudence, which might be overlooked in striving to satisfy hunger or thirst.

SOCIAL

3. *Belongingness and love*—striving to be accepted by intimate members of one's family and to be an important person to them. This striving could also include others to whom the person feels close.

4. *Esteem and status*—striving to achieve a high standing relative to others, including desire for mastery, reputation, and prestige.

SELF

5. *Self-actualization*—a desire to know, understand, systematize, organize, and construct a system of values.

We can grasp one thing immediately from this, that different social classes and groups have arrived at different stages of priorities. Some

Americans today are still struggling at level 1, while others "struggle" at level 5. And time makes the whole scheme dynamic. A good many Fitzgeraldesque characters who basked on levels 3, 4, or 5 at the beginning of 1929 had slid to level 1 by the end of the year. Ordinary prudence, item 2 tells us, might at least temporarily be overlooked——say, to vote for the Communists or even the Democrats in 1932.[3]

Whatever measure of accuracy we ascribe to the Maslow hierarchy, clearly people's needs do vary from individual to individual, group to group, and time to time. The basic concept of the hierarchy is what concerns us here. Someone reduced from level 2 to level 1 has a different set of priorities from a déclassé from 5 to 4. They may both want government to do something, but disagree entirely on what it should do because, since their personal needs are so very different, they cannot join on priorities.

This helps us understand why the unity approach amounts to more than it seems to at first. The unity tactic characterizes the initial period of a reform wave. Consensus implies doing the things which most people agree on doing——addressing the widest-shared, highest priorities. In this period reform most clearly responds to the hierarchy of needs; reform implies a recognition of those needs, hence a recognition of groups which share them. This explains why phase one is generally easier than later periods for masses of people to identify with. The later phases usually venture beyond broad recognition and adjustment, into the realm of legislating for specific, often narrow interest groups, whose needs may not match those of most of the public.

In any case, at this point we can safely say that to the long list of obstacles to reform which we have already encountered, we must add the resistance of the mass public. American political behavior has shown itself far more conservative than the nation's "activist creed" might suggest.[4] The rest of the book could be given over to an examination of popular reluctance. Instead, we will simply take a brief look at some of the ways in which popular attitudes and biases throw up barriers against change, and some of the reasons why these attitudes exist. Out of perhaps hundreds of factors, we will mention only dozens. We will not per se ask Werner Sombart's famous question, "Why is there no Socialism in the United States?"[5] We will not speak of "false consciousness." We will emphasize factors politically relevant to this particular constitutional system, as well as some of their social origins. Our concern will mostly lie with mainstream political change.

Historians have faulted many progressives for their naïveté. Yet about what were they most naive? About "the People." Although this century has chastened us——we no longer expect quite so much of the initiative, referendum, and recall, for instance——we remain, I believe, naive about the people.

The Gallups show a remarkably persistent conservatism among Americans on questions of individual morality, civil liberties, and the political economy. Early Gallup polls, for instance, suggest that the New Deal, with all its moderation in retrospect, operated in many crucial ways to the left of public opinion as a whole at the time.[6] Abundant evidence from polls also suggests that liberal Presidents have moved broadly in accord with or at most somewhat ahead of public opinion, without ever taking drastic flight from it. Criticism of presidential policies should incorporate an understanding of the public which, along with educating, Chief Executives have had to please.

In any society, change usually takes place slowly, so that reformers nearly always find life difficult. Resistance confronts them from every direction. Perhaps their role demands as much as the revolutionary's. The revolutionary tries to polarize and rigidify. But the reformer wants to adjust social realities through political agility and maneuver.[7] In this society the moderates have borne power, while the extreme left and the extreme right have for the most part enjoyed freedom of attack without the responsibilities imposed by power. These responsibilities ——demonstrating political skill, maintaining a balance between goals and demands——together resemble a juggling act taking place in the midst of a tug of war. No wonder so many reforms have been shallow or patronizing, or that reform movements have been episodic.

Goodwin Watson has observed that "all of the forces which contribute to stability in personality or in social systems can be perceived as resisting change." These forces interact.[8] Inertia amounts to far more than mere stinginess or simple obstructionist politics. It is engraved on our psyche and our society in patterns which help to prevent us from going mad. This psychological-sociological conservatism characterizes not just Americans, but the entire human race. As Veblen put it:

> The revulsion felt by good people at any proposed departure from the accepted methods of life is a familiar fact of everyday experience. . . . The aversion to change is in large part an aversion to the bother of making the readjustment which any given change will necessitate; and this solidarity of the system of institutions of any given culture or of any given people strengthens the instinctive resistance offered to any change in men's habits of thought, even in matters which, taken by themselves, are of minor importance.
>
> A consequence of this increased reluctance, due to the solidarity of human institutions, is that any innovation calls for

a greater expenditure of nervous energy in making the necessary readjustment than would otherwise be the case. It is not only that a change in established habits of thought is distasteful. The process of readjustment of the accepted theory of life involves a degree of mental effort——a more or less protracted and laborious effort to find and to keep one's bearings under the altered circumstances.[9]

Most people accept numerous social norms without seriously questioning them. The very process of childhood socialization exerts a conservative influence. The family helps to undergird the status quo by imparting conventional values to its offspring (though the young may in turn rebel against them). We learn about things as they are from the moment we become aware, long before we have developed any significant capacity for criticizing what exists around us. At the same time we get taught from infancy on that this is the way things are, we also learn that this is the way they ought to be. Here are the norms; here is what we should think of them. As to much of what we dislike, the socialization process simply teaches us toleration: we do *not* criticize Uncle George for his bad table manners, or Old Mr. Grindle who in seventy years on this planet has failed to learn about deodorants.

People are most suggestible in childhood; afterward, suggestibility ebbs. As one grows older, views become more set. By common (though by no means universal) consent, people typically become increasingly conservative or at least more rigid with age. "Adolescence," Walter Weyl remarked in a classic essay on "tired radicals," "is the true day for revolt. . . . But one cannot forever remain adolescent and long before a man's arteries begin to harden, he sees things more as his father and grandfather saw them."[10]   Belief systems tend to remain remarkably strong even in the face of severe personal adversity. Unless proposals appear unthreatening or else conform to previously held views, we will likely resist them. True enough, beliefs can change, but the tendency persists to adhere to them. Besides their inherent attributes, good or bad, they give us peace because we have gotten used to them. They are, after all, *our* beliefs.

So a society's preexisting values become deeply internalized in its members. "If an individual's temperament, education, expression, or cognizance of certain events does affect his acceptance of current norms," wrote Hadley Cantril, "it is likely to be in a relatively mild rather than in a drastic way. The individual does not usually want to overthrow most of the culture. He wants rather to modify it, to amplify the meanings of some old concepts, to adjust a few traditional standards to modern conditions." A person will tend to address distinct individual norms instead of broad structural ones: cracking down on welfare cheaters, for example, not unhinging the entire social welfare system——still less the capitalist system.[11]

If the need for one's personal identity to maintain a certain basic consistency over time impels one toward the status quo, the same kind of continuity inheres in society at large. When reformers struggle with anti-reformers over some pattern of change, they really battle one another over society's image of itself. Like any individual, a social organism will recoil at a sudden, wrenching shift. The whole structure of life, in a primitive society or a modern one, bases itself upon some significant degree of continuity——the expectation that things will remain essentially the same.[12] The need for personal predictability parlays into a need for social predictability. Hence an orientation toward the present and the concrete will provide a political organization with an advantage because this stance reflects, in turn, an orientation toward the familiar.

Historically our national dispensation has emphasized the practical. Liberals get criticized when they airily waft theories of how life ought to be, because we Americans have traditionally taken such an interest in the plumbing of the thing as opposed to its architecture. Reformers always encounter resistance to modernizing an ancient and for the most part comfortable house, an anxiety that the architect may botch the plans and make the place more unlivable than before. One can earn a good deal of applause by resolutely standing up for things as they are. For, who knows? Starting down the reform road may generate too much momentum, a pleasant ride through the country ultimately leading to a sickening crash.[13]

Politically speaking, a great many people——the majority most of the time——are either timid or indolent or both. They go along with the group. They wear their torpor with all of the comfort of a warm, shabby old coat. Politically, they somnambulate. Ordinary habit and the everyday routines of existence influence them toward conservatism.[14] And some people are perennially "busy." Matters of state seem far-off concerns to them. Nor do those who do get involved necessarily remain politically activated. Engaged one year, they may become apathetic the next. Their degree of involvement and attention will vary from time to time. True enough, democracy should be fashioned so as to fit the people, not the other way around. But the fact remains that in this century, anyway, the people have shown themselves, by most standards any democratic optimist might impose, a disappointment.

Individuals will not, for instance, necessarily back a reformist party even when they are oppressed. Quite frequently, those most in need simply do not vote. People who shun political involvement entirely include (in James MacGregor Burns's terms) the apathetic, the alienated, and the anomic.[15] Nonvoting can reflect contentment with affairs as they stand. Perhaps nonvoting among some people simply suggests that they would rather do other things, although the franchise represents a pretty minimal investment of time and energy. Or, depending upon the person, it could be that political indifference reflects realism, an accurate acknowledgment of one's own powerlessness. Or it may symbolize alienation. To the list of self-disfranchised individuals we must add those shut out of the system by others, for historical example, blacks by the KKK.

Whatever the cause, nonvoting has functioned as one of the conservative influences in this country. It has driven the center of political gravity to the right.[16] Low turnout has typically accompanied other lows: low socio-economic status, income, education, skill, and occupational status. Turnout has also correlated inversely with age; and women have traditionally (though not recently) voted in low proportions compared to men. To the extent that the "highs" maintain greater rates of participation, conservatism has an edge. Relatively high turnout has accompanied elevated income, education, and age, and has characterized whites, men, jobholders, people who belong to organizations, property owners, and business and other relatively skilled groups. In 1982 people with family incomes over $35,000 voted at more than twice the rate of those with incomes under $5,000.[17] Voting disparities reflecting income and class have grown dramatically over the past generation.[18] "Unlike other Western industrial nations," writes Kevin P. Phillips, "the United States has a huge 'missing' low-income electorate."[19]

To what exact degree all this affects the outcome of elections remains in dispute. But clearly "the combination of a low vote and a relative lack of organization among the lower-status groups," as Lipset writes, "means that they will suffer from neglect by the politicians who will be receptive to the wishes of the more privileged, participating, and organized strata."[20] Clearly, too, the Democrats have suffered over the years as the electorate has grown more affluent.

Change generally brings pain, at least to a few. Freud argued that what people want from life is "happiness," which includes "an absence of pain and unpleasure" on one hand and "the experiencing of strong feelings of pleasure" on the other. Hence "the pleasure principle": on the "positive" side, "gaining pleasure"; on the "negative . . . avoiding unpleasure."[21] But all reform costs. Some of it costs a lot. It isn't just a question of who gets what, when, and how, but also of who loses what, when, and how. People dislike losing anything.

A society, much like an individual, naturally tries to avoid pain. Sometimes this impels masses of people to accept easy panaceas. (We have seen that panaceas have been common "solutions," for example, to problems involving corporations.) Most societies, again like most individuals, incline toward pleasure. We will call all this the pleasure principle of politics. The absence of pain is entirely fundamental. Political change often causes pain, or the anticipation of it. We risk pain to establish a welfare state or some equivalent device, in order to provide a hedge against greater pain and unhappiness and to relieve some of our fear of living. But we do not by this opt against the positive goal of gaining pleasure. We conceive of the welfare state in primarily *negative* terms; thus we imagine that the welfare state should go no further than to aid us in averting unpleasure and help produce the *conditions* for pleasure. We will turn on the welfare state if its demands interfere excessively with our positive pursuit of gratification. And social concerns bringing pain will eventually get consigned to the attic, as they did in the twenties, the fifties, or the seventies.

Since World War II, three factors in particular have militated against the preeminence of reform issues: the rise of foreign policy preoccupations and the threat of war; the relative health of the economy; and the relative prosperity enjoyed by most people. Each will attract our close attention further along, but the last calls for some general observations here. In his study of human happiness, Jonathan L. Freedman writes that

> once some minimal income is attained, the amount of money you have matters little in terms of bringing happiness. Above the poverty level, the relationship between income and happiness is remarkably small. The effect of income within our country shows up almost entirely at the very bottom of the income scale. The very poor and the poor say that they are less happy than everyone else.

But even among these unfortunates,

> a high percentage seem to find life pretty good: in most studies, considerably more than half of the low income groups still describe themselves as either very happy or moderately happy, while fewer than 5 percent say they are very unhappy. These figures vary only a little from study to study. In other words, within our society, even those with the lowest incomes seem to find considerable happiness in life and few of them are miserable.[22]

It seems to take very little, financially speaking, to make most people happy. Well-off or relatively so, the American worker in decent employment no longer lives on the margin, no longer has to concentrate just on subsistence.[23]   And to the extent——the very significant extent——that economic setbacks fuel the reform impulse in this society, reform movements cannibalize themselves. If they succeed, they cancel or moderate the conditions that aggravate their own constituencies. The supporters, in turn, may veer to the right. The welfare state itself has undercut its own expansion by fostering better working conditions which undermine the potential of radicalism, and, more broadly, by sponsoring an expansion of the middle class, which does the same.

The American economy has performed well through most of the postwar era.   Inflation and unemployment have existed along with environmental blight and other problems, but material goods have veritably spouted from the system.   Affluence, while not so widely distributed as we should like, nonetheless *is* widely distributed.   The public behaves quite conservatively toward matters of fundamental economic reform. Having something, people fear losing that. Americans do not expect to keep up with the Rockefellers. They do want to keep up with the Joneses. If they cared more about the Rockefellers, they would probably grow a lot angrier. Americans possess, I believe, an extraordinary sense that life is fair, or at least fair enough.

Since social change invariably brings a measure of suffering, the question becomes: Who shall bear the burden? Who will suffer? Who will pay? The Democratic party, so the story goes, tells you what you ought to do, and the Republicans tell you how much doing it will cost. Plenty of people always stand around holding tally sheets. Offsetting factors, such as a rapidly expanding economy, may partially mitigate the suffering. If the economy is stagnant, though, giving to Paul means taking from Peter, and Peter will likely complain that he is being robbed.

We should not express surprise at the ambivalence toward government felt by those who pay it thousands of dollars each year in taxes.   Most people do not view taxes as an important personal investment; instead, they see taxes as an income cut.[24] It is a cut which interferes with their own ability to consume.

Hostility to taxation, the genesis of the Revolution, belongs to the national legend.   Resistance to taxes can coexist with demands for increased public services; but the obvious way of reducing taxes is to cut these services. The cutting impulse can direct itself toward government as a whole, or toward specific beneficiaries of government; not against payments for me, but against benefits for welfare mothers subsidized by my taxes. By 1972, for example——as Samuel Lubell has pointed out——the racial connotations of the term "law and order" four years before had given way to the racial connotations of "welfare." The idea of kicking welfare recipients off the rolls usually meant ejecting blacks. ("The government keeps giving them things," but "whites have to work for what they get.")   Welfare for whites, on the other hand, usually drew support.[25]

Much of what reform confronts, such as welfare, seems unpleasant or arcane. Few people by choice want to deal with, even talk about, poverty. Part of this may represent a pattern of denial——what poverty?——but it also reflects the fact that so many other pleasant things exist to dwell on. As we have noted, social change very often produces a great deal of pain or unhappiness, and it virtually always generates some. So there will always be pressure to avoid it, or once started, to get it over with. If a reform fails to manifest clear-cut, demonstrable benefits, it will arouse resistance. We can fully gauge the importance of this truism with reference to an indeterminate, gut issue such as busing to achieve school integration.

Any administration, including a liberal one, will alienate some of its backers over time simply by making choices as to which of two or more conflicting interest groups it will support on issues such as this. And wholly apart from its immediate costs, reform has a tendency to produce new problems, which get blamed in turn on reform. So the minute that government begins to respond to the demands of a particular group, it stimulates opposition to that group and to further concessions. The group's enemies become embittered. Public opinion begins to move toward the view that enough has been granted. Attitudes start to harden against further change.

The psychological, sociological, and political considerations we have examined begin to tell us why reform takes place gradually and incrementally. Our politics is a politics of incrementalism, in which the possibilities of change must always contend against the potential relative safety of doing nothing. We tend to innovate by fits and starts, by what we might call dramatic increments. Smaller increments occur in between. We hint at all this in the words which we use to describe our reform programs. Whether Square Deal, New Deal, or Fair Deal, each implies that the cards are being dealt again, but the game remains the same.

Much of the game of reform seems impossibly dull and occurs behind the scenes or on the fringe of public awareness: in city planning commissions, for example, or the tax-writing committees of Congress. And it takes place over long spans of time, which further compounds the difficulty of bringing the weight of broad public opinion to bear on the issues such bodies address. It is harder, in other words, to mobilize the public behind a *process* than against a *problem*. And pressure from this direction and that further blurs vision, making it harder yet to identify the proper road, or, once found, to stay on it.

Then there is the matter of who actually does the deciding——which, in turn, very heavily reflects the class structure of this society. That we have drawn our political leadership from the economically secure upper and upper middle classes profoundly conditions the kinds of political change which occur. Not at all surprisingly, leaders have tended by and large to reflect and represent the interests of these same classes.[26] (When FDR didn't, he got labeled a traitor to his class.)

Patricians, notably the Roosevelts, have spearheaded the twentieth century reform presidency. No President has ever come from any particularly exotic ethnic or religious group. Few have even had urban origins. (John Kennedy combined, in a limited way, all these qualities. Not an Al Smith, instead he reflected what the northeastern Irish became once they left the fish market for the Ivy League.) As Edward Pessen has written, "most of the Presidents were born to families at or near the top of the American social and economic order."[27] Certainly none of them has ever fallen outside the mainstream of capitalist values. Since the Civil War, only a third have been Democrats. Of those, fewer than half rank as major reformers.[28]

Richard Hofstadter wrote that "one of the primary tests of the mood of a society at any given time is whether its comfortable people tend to identify, psychologically, with the power and achievements of the very successful or with the needs and sufferings of the underprivileged."[29] Progressivism led the comfortable to peer beneath them; so did the New Deal and the sixties. But this is always a relative thing. The American middle class looks downward sometimes, but upward all the time, so that even its downcast eyes suggest compromise.

The same applies to government. We do not enjoy terribly representative representative bodies. If Presidents do not get pulled out of a crowd on the street, neither do judges, cabinet members, or lawmakers. Pessen has observed that "the significant political fact about the men who have typically held public office over the course of American history is not that they were well off but that they behaved politically as though they were."[30] Workers add up to only a tiny fragment among the membership of U.S. representative bodies. The poor and downtrodden have remained quite spectacularly absent. People who do serve come disproportionately from among the well-to-do, and for various reasons, including self-interest, they have acted just as Pessen suggests. Perhaps a quarter to a third of U.S. senators in 1900 had backgrounds in business. They became known as the millionaires' club. Most senators of the 1890s (57 percent) were lawyers, and attorneys turned up in extraordinary proportions in other legislative seats at both the state and federal levels. In one Progressive Era Congress, lawyers comprised over 80 percent of the Democrats and almost 70 percent of the Republicans.[31] Most of the Presidents have come from backgrounds in law. We tend to think of attorneys as professionals and to forget that, broadly speaking, they also run businesses, just as physicians or dentists do. Grounded on precedent and tradition, the law——their seat of training and practice——in and of itself produces inertia.

In terms of education and professional status, then, the political mainstream is clearly unrepresentative of the American mainstream. So, too, with sources of political funding. American politics has depended enormously on the large contribution. To expect most persons in government consistently to act without reference to their own backers' interests would of course be utterly unrealistic.

To a significant degree, though, the Democratic party has succeeded in combining elite leadership with a working-class base. Seymour Martin Lipset argues that this powerful theme of "Tory radicalism" has reduced sectional and class stresses. The patricians, by their prominent participation in politics, tie the disinherited to the system through reform, but also bind in conservatives who oppose reform; temper the nature and pace of change; and smudge class distinctions between the parties.[32]

Naturally, we cannot expect people to know everything about government or governing; even perceiving where their self-interest lies is so difficult that many commonly fail at it. Poor southern whites who have refused to unite with poor southern blacks provide a classic instance. The woman movement, too, has positively invited divisiveness. Never did men try to rebel as a sex. Because they have held power to begin with, men's insurgencies have originated around ideological polarities or interest-group demands. Feminists could not possibly try to speak for half the population without inviting attacks from within their intended bloc over just where women's interests truly reside. In recent decades, indeed, the task of determining one's own interest has become increasingly hard.[33]

Political scientists tell us that the masses are no fools. There is even evidence that people's "political reasoning" has improved to some degree.[34] But anyone who has engaged in, say, retail sales, or who has gone door to door in a political campaign, will have learned not to feel overly sanguine yet. Perhaps 60 million American adults are illiterate or semiliterate.[35] A 1977 Gallup poll disclosed that after four years of the energy crisis, only half the respondents knew that the United States had to import oil in order to fulfill its energy requirements.[36] No, it would not do to suggest that the voting public has become politically sophisticated. It has not. And one can make a strong argument that the recent growth in "independence" among voters suggests that they are *less* sophisticated than before about how a political system actually ought to operate.

Over the course of this century, liberals have trimmed their optimism about human nature. Progress, whether of society or of individuals, has seemed less certain. World War I played a role in this; so did World War II, with its hideous displays of human depravity. The drive for the welfare state was compatible with these lowered expectations. The welfare state is, after all, in its way an acknowledgment of individual and societal frailty. It provides a medium for accommodating people's political isolation through collective, interest-group politics; a buffer for the debilities of age, unemployment, and economic dislocation; a measure of compulsion; in sum, a method of dealing with the realities of human need as well as the realities of human nature. Perhaps Americans' traditionally exaggerated notions about human perfectibility help to explain why the development of our own welfare state has lagged behind the more pessimistic Europeans'.

For many reasons, in any case, social change in the United States must often be gone about in strikingly cautious ways. "The surprising thing about the progressive movement in America," Walter Mondale has remarked, "is how conservative it is. This nation is a conservative nation. By most standards in most democratic societies, I'm conservative. We're for free enterprise, we're for limited government, we're for the human development strategies."[37] Reformers must not subject traditional values and attitudes to assault if these beliefs remain (or seem to remain) viable. Changes in values will often lag far behind changing realities. The New Dealers, for instance, continued to affirm old and cherished attitudes even as they presided over great transformations.

Either subtly or quite directly, the primary animating factor in American politics has been class. Yet Americans do not like to talk about class, still less about class struggle. Various reasons account for this, among them resistance to the concept that real stratification does pervade society, and, no doubt, the sometime feeling that growth can provide more for everyone without taking away from the haves. The class consciousness which survived feudalism in Europe did not prevail in the United States. As David M. Potter observed:

America not only practiced a full measure of mobility and social equality [?] but also developed a creed of equality and articulated a myth to accompany the creed.

The myth of equality held that equality exists not merely as a potentiality in the nature of man but as a working actuality in the operation of American society—that advantages or handicaps are not really decisive and that every man is the architect of his own destiny. It asserted the existence in the

United States of a classless society, where no one is better than anyone else and merit is the only recognized ground of distinction.   Despite their patent implausibility, these ideas received and still retain a most tenacious hold.   Americans are notoriously unresponsive to the concept of class warfare, and American workers, while fully alert to the protection of their economic interests, have never accepted identity as members of a working class in the way in which workers in England and other countries have.

No such thing as a genuinely classless society of complete equality exists, but significant mobility creates an *image* of classlessness.   "America," Potter wrote, "has apparently had in the past more than enough mobility to sustain the illusion."[38]

While Europeans have tended to think of redistributing wealth as a matter of taking from one group in order to give to another, a sort of broad-scale Robin Hoodism, Americans have inclined toward the giving without the taking.   Rather than seeing wealth as a more or less static resource, as Potter put it, "the American mind, by contrast, often assumes implicitly that the volume of wealth is dynamic, that much potential wealth still remains to be converted; and that diverse groups——for instance, capital and labor——can take more wealth out of the environment by working together than they can take out of one another by class warfare."[39]   "In particular," added Arthur M. Okun, "people show surprisingly little resentment toward the extremely wealthy.   While they express some concern about inequalities of opportunity and discriminatory treatment, most view those aspects as flaws rather than fundamental defects of the system."[40]   No President, including those who have lamented inequality of opportunity, ever overtly acknowledged an intention to reduce inequality of income.[41]

Americans cherish the ideal of equality of opportunity, but not of result.   Hence they will tolerate a wide range of social inequality and resist redistribution.[42]   The rationale behind unequal income distribution in a capitalist democracy such as ours lies in the economic efficiencies supposedly produced by financial rewards which channel behavior in certain useful ways.   Okun referred to "the double standard" of such a democracy, "professing and pursuing an egalitarian political and social system and simultaneously generating gaping disparities in economic well-being."   The catch, Okun argued, is that "pursuit of efficiency necessarily creates inequalities.   And hence society faces a tradeoff between equality and efficiency."   Inequality takes the familiar forms——income, wealth, status, and power.[43]

Broad-scale inequality is one of those subjects that have come up comparatively rarely in ordinary discussion during the quieter periods of our past. Yet "in the United States," write Sidney Verba and Gary R. Orren,

> equality is a recurring theme. It has flared into a fervent moral issue at crucial stages of American history: the Revolutionary and Jacksonian periods, the Civil War, the populist and progressive eras, the New Deal, and the 1960s and 1980s. In each era, the legitimacy of American society is challenged by some set of people unhappy with the degree of equality. . . . In the moments of egalitarian ascendancy, libertarians are on the defensive. In the moments of retrenchment, egalitarians cling to previous gains. And in either period the enemy is likely to be the "special interests" that have too much power. In egalitarian times, these are the moneyed interests. In times of retrenchment, these are labor or big government and its beneficiaries.
>
> The periods of fervor in American politics——the moments of creedal passion, in Samuel Huntington's words——have usually been outbursts of egalitarianism.[44]

Despite all this, the weak identification with class in this country compared to other industrial democracies has injured the left, and by virtue of that, reform, and has set limits on what equality means. Whenever a depression or labor strife sets in, the idea that workers and their employers enjoy a mutual harmony of interests partially breaks down. Yet classes do not see themselves in fundamental opposition to one another. The dominant American labor unions have been relatively conservative, relatively distant from politics, and, through most of our history, relatively weak. A good many theories attempt to explain the weakness of working-class politics, among them that little class consciousness exists among American workers, the individualistic American dream, the early decision by union chiefs not to align their organizations with one party, and divisions on the left. Traditional explanations also include workers' relative affluence and mobility; a pervasive egalitarianism; the very domination of the political system by two parties; long-established political rights and traditions, including broad suffrage; and the widespread sense that government resides exclusively in the hands of the governed. These explanations have recently come under considerable scholarly scrutiny, but it will not serve us to rehash that debate here; we will simply examine facets of it.

Reflecting its weak class identification, in contrast to Western Europe the United States has not produced a powerful working class movement. The major parties have never found themselves genuinely threatened in their domination of the political system by a labor party.

That there has never been an authentic mass working class political party in America or a great socialist following makes this country unique among advanced capitalist nations. Distinctly working-class perspectives have trouble getting stated, or achieving any credibility once they are. Our non-working-class self-image[45] functions like an enormous magnet, pulling the Democratic party and all but extremists toward the middle-to-upper-class core of politics.

In order to understand this, we must again touch on the ideology of union leadership. As head of the AFL Gompers found himself attacked by the left as an apologist for the capitalist system. He wanted neither an independent labor party, nor, in particular, did he take an interest in great theoretical systems or plans for the overthrow of capitalism. What Gompers did want was the fulfillment of intermediate demands such as better wages and shorter hours. From the start, unionism on the dominant AFL model meant a striving toward respectability; meant conceding the broad policy decisions to management; meant business unionism and embracing the values of corporate capitalism. So around the turn of the century, the big question for labor was not "How long will it take to overthrow the capitalist system?" but "How much accommodation can we squeeze out of it?" This remained true despite widespread anticapitalist impulses; it remained true despite the emergence of the Industrial Workers of the World (IWW), which did call for worker seizure of the means of production.

Deep divisions have traditionally plagued the American labor movement, including a conflict between skilled and unskilled workers. The Knights of Labor tried to bring all workers together in the late nineteenth century. The AFL took a different, more conservative tack by concentrating on skilled labor. Skilled-versus-unskilled: labor has its own internal class structure.[46] Racial and ethnic rifts have also cut across the labor force. Immigrants brought over old ethnic hatreds with them on the ship and learned new passions after they arrived. This proved an employer's dream. Workforces could be mixed among antipathetic groups with different cultures and languages, reducing the possibility of their uniting on anything. Likewise, skilled jobs could be withheld from the new immigrants, splitting labor further along old stock-new stock and income axes.[47]

Jerome Karabel takes all this an important step further:

> If class consciousness grows not only out of common experiences of exploitation at the work place but also out of common experiences of association in the community——as the more subtle of the Marxist historians have argued——then its relative weakness among immigrant workers is understandable.

The immigrants were often clustered together in tightly knit ethnic neighborhoods and their experiences there tended to reinforce their identity, as, say, Italians, Irish, or Poles, rather than their consciousness of themselves as members of the working class.

"The split between the worker as laborer and the worker as community resident" may, as Karabel points out, explain why a proletariat that could behave militantly on the job failed to broaden its claims. Workers interrelated with the political system through their communities, and so the clash between workers and their employers isolated itself in the factories. The political system was heavily oriented toward the local and thus the ethnic. Urban machines acculturated workers into existing political arrangements, not toward socialism. The "Americanization" of immigrants involved inducting them into the world of private property and free enterprise, and it exacted a toll on people unwilling so to acculturate.[48]

In the end, labor became one more interest group, clashing with other interest groups——with farmers, for instance, whom many liberals have considered labor's natural allies. Sometimes they have allied. But workers are landless. Farmers' long days have given them little reason to appreciate labor's drive to cut hours, while workers have proved less than eager to pay higher prices for farm products in order to drive up farm income. Most basically, farmers are business people; and while a tradition of aspiration to that status has existed among the working class, the nature of the toil itself essentially differs.

Trotsky eventually came to wonder about the radical potential of the proletariat. More recently others on the left have again bleakly raised the question, among them C. Wright Mills, Herbert Marcuse, and the New Left. Elsewhere organized labor has typically formed the backbone of socialist power; in the United States, it has become the rib cage of capitalism. Generally desiring no workers' party, for the most part it has simply wanted more, as Gompers put it. A public opinion poll released in 1939, after a decade of depression, showed that 88 percent of the public identified itself as middle-class, with just 6 percent each affiliating with the upper and lower classes.[49] Limited even then, class consciousness has considerably eroded, so that since the thirties, Americans have thought less in class terms and class has become less closely related to actual political views.[50] Throughout the post-World War II era, Americans have shown a growing tendency to regard themselves not as working-class but as belonging to the middle or upper strata. The public appears to feel that obstacles to social mobility have lessened since the war, and that the importance of social class per se is diminishing. A widespread sense has emerged that the upper and middle classes have somehow converged.[51]

Meanwhile, the poor divide. Their positions on issues are not identical, as liberals often have learned. Poor people have traditionally faced the problems of residing out on the fringe of politics: hard to make contact with; often uninformed; typically though certainly not always submissive; isolated by their own difficulty in communicating with the privileged world because of illiteracy, under-literacy, and verbal nonconformity; short of self-confidence; in brief, shut off, and by virtue of that, shut out. Because they are so often under-educated if literate at all, those at the bottom have tended to read less than others. Thus they become especially vulnerable to the drivel and middle-to-upper-class biases of television.[52] The disadvantaged have shown low levels of involvement in political organizations. They have tended to know less about what goes on in the political realm. They have voted in relatively low proportions.

When it becomes bitter enough, poverty may wreck even the hope of mobility and the possibility of effective mobilization. "The abjectly poor, and all those persons whose energies are entirely absorbed by the struggle for daily sustenance," said Veblen,

> are conservative because they cannot afford the effort of taking thought for the day after to-morrow; just as the highly prosperous are conservative because they have small occasion to be discontented with the situation as it stands to-day.

Hence, "a considerable degree of privation among the body of the people is a serious obstacle to any innovation."[53]

Backward areas, for all their socio-economic deprivation, can generate quite conservative voting patterns. Traditionalism——the complex of obligations, loyalties, and class structure of such a region——can mix with terror or other means of intimidation to repress political dissent. Sometimes, too, reformers inadvertently stir the anger of groups which were formerly politically passive, for example, by stoking lower-income white backlash against aspiring blacks. All this tends to polarize politics along unproductive axes and undercut change.

Such things reflect themselves in how Americans respond to polls. Since 1936, when national surveys on this question began, most Americans have identified themselves as political conservatives, not liberals. The percentage calling themselves conservatives grew from 53 in 1936 to 59 in 1974. In 1936, 63 percent of Democrats regarded themselves as liberal, 37 percent, conservative; by 1974 the percentage stood exactly fifty-fifty.[54] At about this time, a lower-class 28-year-old female survey respondent expressed herself this way on the subject of equal income distribution: "It's communism——everybody is the same and they all share. I wouldn't want it. If I work harder than somebody else, why should I share or . . . why shouldn't I be able to . . . live better?"[55] This appears to be a pretty standard perspective.

Though sensitive to gradations in social position,[56] then, Americans have shared a widespread tendency to think of themselves not as a society of classes but as a society of interrelated producers involved in a larger, joint enterprise. We have conceived of class, if at all, in exceedingly fuzzy ways, and with a bias toward the idea that nearly everybody somehow belongs to the middle class (if such a thing as class actually exists).[57] The United States has a property-owning and relatively conservative "middle-class" working class, because blue-collar workers *think* of themselves as middle-class. Radical thought in Europe, Potter wrote,

> is prone to demand that the man of property be stripped of his carriage and his fine clothes; but American radical thought is likely to insist, instead, that the ordinary man is entitled to mass-produced copies, indistinguishable from the originals. Few Americans feel entirely at ease with the slogan "Soak the rich," but the phrase "Deal me in" springs spontaneously and joyously to American lips.[58]

Deal me in——with a New Deal, or at least a Square Deal.

Louis Hartz called "the master assumption of American political thought . . . the reality of atomistic social freedom."[59] Capitalism almost seems a part of our individual genetic makeup. As Arthur Mann has pointed out, "the United States is the only major country in the world where socialists have failed to generate a movement of genuine size."[60] This nation equates freedom with capitalism as one and the same thing. We have held private property to be sacred, or close to it. The great American dream of fame and fortune takes root in the individual search for reward. We pursue opportunity competitively. We have tended to expect that our virtue in the pursuit will yield its own rewards; yet failure also strikes us as an individual phenomenon.

In 1972 George McGovern proposed a high inheritance tax on large estates. He got a cold response from blue-collar America. "They must think they're going to win a lottery," he remarked.[61] (One remembers the various gold rushes in U.S. history, or lunkheads pulling slot machine levers in Las Vegas.) Today, as Daniel Yankelovich puts it, "many Americans favor leveling *up* under certain conditions but are unalterably opposed to leveling *down*."[62] For all their egalitarian rhetoric (which increases dramatically in reform eras), even liberal Americans tolerate extraordinary disparities in income, so long, at least, as its possessors have acquired their pile playing by the rules.[63] We elevate the ideal of success, but define it in a personal, individualistic sense. Americans tend to regard equality in terms not of egalitarian results, but of equal opportunity. By traditionally emphasizing equality of opportunity, our reform movements have simply remained in touch with the public temper. Schemes for income redistribution do not excite most among the working class; they expect to move up in the world, not through government or even labor union action, but by themselves. So the American, as Potter put it, "has traditionally expected to find a gamut ranging from rags to riches, from tramps to millionaires."[64]

Faith in the American dream of opportunity has defused class tension and deflected guilt and anger inward instead of outward. In a society of plenty, anyone with the requisite character can succeed. Those who do not can blame themselves. People want a shot at winning; but when they lose, the emphasis on individualism——on individual responsibility——directs their anger less along explicitly political channels than inward as depression.[65] An old and powerful attitude holds that the deserving can fend for themselves, and that the remainder deserve to suffer. Meantime the winners can enjoy their gains. There is a huge lure of "jackpot prizes," and enough people do make it big——with their winnings sufficiently well publicized——to keep others' hopes aloft.[66]

This is the rags to riches motif. Rags to riches——jumping from the bottom of the economic ladder to the top——is largely a myth.[67] The usual trend around the turn of the century appears to have involved slowly pushing generation by generation one rung at a time up the economic-class ladder. Some working-class families acquired property: they bought into the capitalist system, even if only to the tune of a few hundred dollars.[68] And what makes one more conservative than property ownership, or even the prospect of it? No sooner do people today move into the suburbs than they begin to worry about potential threats to their property value brought on by the people moving in next door. A job, too, may tend to make its possessor more conservative, especially when the job seems threatened. All this reflects the negative, even punitive, side of the business confidence argument: if not prosperity, there will be collapse and unemployment.

At the outset of the century, the novels of Horatio Alger and similar literature bolstered the myth of rags to riches, with titles like *Luck and Pluck* and *Sink or Swim*. The rags to riches motif was inculcated from childhood up. The key lay in what people *thought* they could achieve. Algerism, with its notions of *individual* responsibility, provided a potent antidote to Marx's blaming the economic *system*. Among the able, industrious, or unscrupulous of the working class, many have escaped into a higher class. Not only have many poor experienced upward mobility from generation to generation, but they have expected that this will continue in the future: if we fail to make it, our children will. Algerism held (and holds) out the promise of continued escape. "Americans," David A. Shannon observes, "have generally believed it easier and more desirable to rise *from* their class rather than *with* their class."[69] And again, although the statistical probabilities have militated overwhelmingly against it, a handful of those in business who have made it big have borne out the Alger myth. They have come up off the bottom.

The traditional American emphasis on individualistic free enterprise competition, in combination with a very restricted role for government, presupposes individual success and failure. It is utterly grounded on producing both winners and losers. Picking losers up off the pavement has a far weaker place in the American system of values than does producing them in the first place. So long as the economy continues to expand——another underlying presupposition——people can theoretically pick themselves up.

Ironically, mobility either up or down the social scale has been associated with conservative voting behavior.[70] Certainly the prospect of upward mobility reduces the inclination to back either the political left or labor unions. This has supplied a principal explanation for the distinction between the far-left inclinations of many among the European proletariat, and American labor's relative satisfaction with reformism.

Other forms of mobility have existed, too——not just from one class to another, but from one section of the country to another, or from one industry to another, or from one neighborhood to another, or (with extraordinary frequency), from the United States back to Europe decades ago. The remarkable geographic mobility of the working class surely has undercut the chances of organizing it. When people move, they bleed off the collective identity underlying collective action. "All migration," Alfred Marshall argued, "tends to foster isolated action and individualistic aims: separated from old associates, each one is apt to care mainly for his own interests."[71] And in the insular suburban environments so typically the end points of post-World War II migration, opposition to social programs will likely grow even greater. The needy may have disappeared from view. Or the local examples of welfare and food stamp recipients may seem relatively well-off. Levittown is no Harlem. Not surprisingly, as people have bought into the suburbs, they have frequently tended to go Republican.

Through most of this century, the ways in which the economy operates have undercut the left just as has mobility. Employment has remained high, or relatively so; and the nature of the economy has fostered a consumerism which emphasizes keeping up with the Joneses

instead of trying to cooperate with them. The United States is one of
the world's most materialistic societies, and materialism implies a
commitment to things as opposed to people: *my* new house, *my* new
car; my new house or car as opposed to (I hope) the "inferior" models
that other people own.   "We look at our fellows projectively," writes
Kathleen Nott, "estimating their lot as better or worse than our own;
but with calculation, seldom empathy."[72]   The material success this
country has produced, together with its competitive distribution, has
worked against sharp political-economic-class confrontations.   Some
people have gotten far more out of the race than others, but by and
large the gains seem fairly acquired, and, in any case, being down at one
point does not mean one will not bounce back at another. Rising living
standards dampen questions of how to divide the pie, and until recently
living standards have risen rather consistently through most of this
century.[73]

The other side of our individualism has always been conformity, and
at its worst, the tyranny of the majority. Dissent has gotten controlled
and hushed up in all sorts of ways, ranging from ostracism to red scares
to crushing strikes to murder. Reform has borne a close relationship to
violence.
    Violence can put a spotlight on social injustice, and can ultimately
help lead to reform when enough resources exist with which to produce
change.[74] A violent revolution opened American national history. The
Civil War——preceded by a good deal of violence over the slavery
question——was both the most violent episode in our history and the
prerequisite for our greatest reform, ending slavery.   As Robert H.
Walker has noted, "although violence is a consistent part of the reform
scene, passive resistance is also recurrent and, although less common,
may be a superior long-term agent for constructive change."[75] In fact,
the history of American reform has seen a kind of balancing act between
violence and nonviolence as strategies of protest.
    Eventually, though, recurrent violence grows stale, tending to
undermine conciliatory governmental responsiveness.[76] And the great
risk with violence as a strategy is the risk of public backlash and general
repression. When the left goes violent, or seems to, as it did after
World War I or in the late sixties, it simply invites Palmer raids, Kent
State, and law and order crackdowns of all kinds. This nation has
traditionally shown a hair-trigger attitude toward leftist disorder.
    And there has been plenty of disorder. We have the worst record
of labor-management violence in the world. Perhaps this should simply
be expected in a society of enormous violence generally; violence finds

its way into industrial relations just as into all sorts of other relationships.

Yet industrial violence has also powerfully reflected class hostility in a society that has widely denied the existence of class. These flash points have clearly revealed the underlying structures of power. Other outlets for class antagonism have been racism and nativism. A society can deny it has a class structure, while channeling the frustrations which that (hidden) structure creates through class-based outrage manifesting itself as xenophobia and ethnic antagonism.[77]

Behind a willingness to use force on dissidents, popular attitudes toward various groups among the needy, different, and deviant vary. The elderly, for example, are favored over the poor. I suspect that this amounts to a matter of values——the poor appear "losers." It also stems from self-interest. Payments to the elderly amount to payments to our parents or to ourselves a few years down the road——after we have withdrawn from competition in the capitalist milieu. And if we have become needy by then, we can explain this by our departure. The poor seem inferior; the aged, merely aged.

As for the young, education, with its quiet compulsions, has generally leaned toward the status quo. Elementary and secondary public education (and even more, parochial education) has not been in the business of unhinging the socio-economic system. We have thought of higher education, on the other hand, as a liberalizing influence. Yet it has also compounded social distance, the layer of contempt which the educated perennially tend to hold for the uneducated (in this case, the *less* educated majority). To the extent that it has liberalized large populations, higher education has probably been most important in elevating their social and cultural tastes——or, in the minds of many less well educated, making them more degenerate, thus further aggravating the sense of social distance.

Like education, religion has had an ambiguous impact on reform. On one hand it seems to serve as a conservative influence, because it helps people adjust to things as they are. While cleansing the tycoon's conscience on Sunday morning, churches have often reminded the oppressed that their greatest concern should lie in the hereafter, not the here and now. In this sense, by producing an adjustment to social conditions, religion undercuts the impulse to change these conditions. It serves as one more diversion.

Yet on the social gospel side, religion has clearly encouraged reform. As we have seen, the reform conscience has often been driven by it. The humanitarian crusades of the Progressive Era, for instance, were propelled by guilty consciences, notably Protestant consciences upset by the plight of the poor. Whether the social gospel or anti-nuclear war activism, church agitation can lend an issue a cosmic tone of moral imperativeness. It ushers the Protestant sense of mission into politics, if often with a certain vagueness. Like the courts since the thirties, ministers, priests, and rabbis help provide reform with an afterlife and with continuity through bleak times. But one reason for the frequent mushiness of religion in reform is that clerics generally preach in generalities; the specifics remain opaque. Religion-driven reform also has a weakness, as we have seen, for red herrings and naïveté. And whenever a reform era takes on a religious, even millennial hue (a danger particularly acute when clerics get heavily involved), the risk of ultimate disillusionment runs even deeper. Finally, some denominations have assumed an explicitly reactionary political posture.[78] Still, the impulse to "do good," often religion-motivated, remains omnipresent in this nation. Even during the fifties, at a time when the American poor had receded to near-invisibility, a great deal of interest existed in helping the impoverished abroad through individual and federal aid.

Whenever the domestic or foreign oppressed and disinherited receive help from above, though, by strict definition they are patronized. In this society, when a high degree of contentment and economic satisfaction exists, any antipoverty effort will take on the attributes of charity for the submerged portion of the population. Welfare becomes "handouts," i.e., hand-downs. If the dispossessed could help themselves, after all, they would not remain dispossessed. Walter Mondale opined in 1978 that liberalism's principal problem involved difficulty articulating its aims: "I don't think we do a very good job, and we leave doubts and suspicions about whether we're going to take money from working people and give it away to people who are lazy. We haven't been using our best arguments."[79] But the difficulty goes beyond mere explanations. Along with help from certain interest groups, American reform campaigns have typically received financial support from wealthy angels, organizations, and fund-raisers. The patron-client relationship inheres in the political scheme of things. In a way, it lumps patronized candidates right alongside the patronized poor.

Whether poor or not, "people," Leonard W. Doob has written, "are likely to accept a proposed change when it is introduced by people whom they consider *important and competent* and who have *adequately consulted* them or their respected leaders."[80] High status will likely bear weight, but, of course, it also carries inertia. "The institution of a leisure class," wrote Veblen,

> hinders cultural development immediately (1) by the inertia proper to the class itself, (2) through its prescriptive example of conspicuous waste and of conservatism, and (3) indirectly

through that system of unequal distribution of wealth and sustenance on which the institution itself rests.

To this is to be added that the leisure class has also a material interest in leaving things as they are.[81]

If anything, the rich have become more difficult targets to hit than in Veblen's time. Haloed by omnipresent, well-publicized philanthropy, wealth has become "democratized," so to speak, hence less odious. Philanthropy aside, except in the post-Civil War era, most of the really wealthy have traditionally maintained a low profile.[82] Lower visibility makes them softer targets. The bureaucratization of corporate life has robbed critics of flesh and blood villains like Gould or Frick or Rockefeller. Reform itself has created the benign image of regulated business. The public has more or less accommodated itself to the giant corporation, anonymously managed.[83] Meantime, distracting competitors for popular attention have emerged, some of them wealthy (rock stars, movie stars) but not Men of Wealth. We envy the rich and famous. We imitate them.

Distractions do undercut social change, sometimes directly, sometimes obliquely. Distractions range from spending a turn-of-the-century Sunday afternoon at Coney Island to devoting oneself to the consumption of professional football today. More basically: Marx's perception that economic relationships provide the foundation and everything else the superstructure of life is, for all its bluntness, a fairly subtle assessment. Even if they tended to agree with Marx——and they don't——Americans would have difficulty concentrating their attention on that basic fact and rearranging all their other priorities accordingly. A gaggle of other issues, ideas, distractions, and diversions cries for our attention. It is simply easier, more enjoyable, and socially more comfortable to personify, particularize, and simplify——to discuss the latest murder, for example——than to talk about class structure. It sounds more American, less foreign, and especially, less Soviet.

The fundamental ways in which we communicate reinforce inertia.[84] News can be censored, of course, which has happened in the United States. But things generally occur more subtly than that.

Life is far too complex for any individual fully to comprehend it. We need shorthand guides to understanding——convenient simplifications. "The world that we have to deal with politically is out of reach, out of sight, out of mind," wrote Walter Lippmann. "It has to be explored, reported, and imagined." But the avenues for misreporting and for inadequate or inaccurate perception have conspicuous breadth and carry heavy traffic. Lippmann expressed a special concern about the deformed "pictures" of reality purveyed to modern mass society by modern mass communications.[85] Lippmann's "point," as C. Wright Mills put it,

> was that the citizen was unable to know what was going on politically, to think about it straight, or to act upon it intelligently. There was a great gap between individual men, on the one hand, and events and decisions of power, on the other; this gap was filled by the media of communication, which, in their necessity to compress the volume of communication into shorthand slogans, created a pseudo-environment of stereotypes that stood for the unseen political world and to which the citizen reacted.[86]

We tend, as humans, to try to grasp events by way of personalities, symbols, and the like; we simplify and distort. The media help us do it.

Television may furnish our best current index of the general level of public intelligence; in 1974 it provided the favorite pastime for 46 percent of the population.[87] The TV set in the average American home is on over six hours per day. Only sleep and work consume more of people's time.[88] True, many adults watch TV simply to relax, escape, and be entertained, and much of television gears itself to a common denominator which includes children and adolescents. But saying this defends the medium more than it deserves. In recent years, network TV, at least, has gotten notably worse, significantly more infantile. We like to complain that television talks down to people, but in truth TV has found their common denominator—and then further debased it. If today's television by and large reflects the popular culture, then popular *culture* is a contradiction in terms. No wonder the vulgarity and sterility of mass entertainment put intellectuals under stress and strain, feed their alienation, exile them to PBS, and beckon their anti-populist sneers. If we visualize the TV mentality as at least roughly analogous to the public's political mentality, the result becomes genuinely unsettling.

Television and the other media focus upon individuals as against social currents, and a good deal of this bias orients itself toward stories of success. People identify with—many want to *be*—superstars.[89] Decades ago C. Wright Mills contended that "this generous romanticism of success, resting upon an easy identification with those who succeed, undoubtedly lessens the psychological pressure of economic inequality, which otherwise might find collective outlet in political action aimed at the social ideal of more equality of wealth and power."[90] To a degree, TV has become the new Horatio Alger. It puts us all in direct and continuous one-way contact with wealthy people who seem just like us (or just as we would wish to be). Who would want to expropriate Bill Cosby or Mary Tyler Moore?

Television, radio, and newspapers do cover the "news." In fact, TV and the other media have partially usurped the communications role that parties once filled. TV has become the main source of news. Television reportage can also dramatize injustice and arouse a healthy sense of outrage, as it did with the army-McCarthy hearings, southern racism, Vietnam, and Watergate. But it has been estimated that public affairs comprises under 5 percent of the total content of the mass media;[91] and the priorities of most media news do not merit the name. Robberies get lumped with nuclear testing, sports with foreign policy, and virtually nobody talks about the fundamental structure of the political economy. Everything translates into "entertainment": the big questions, when covered at all, typically get personalized into human interest stories; nearly everything becomes oversimplified. One can find major exceptions (notably PBS). But considering the average news broadcast or the average newspaper, most of the news isn't news. It is trivia.

As Mills put it: "The truth is, as the media are now organized, they expropriate our vision." "The whole marketing animus is put behind prevailing clichés."[92] Media content gets mediated, so to speak, by the sponsors which underwrite the programs. Along with their products, they market Mills's clichés. The underprivileged have notoriously little access to the media, the comfortable and powerful, broad access. Their disproportionate influence on communication channels enables the affluent persuasively to masquerade as the masses.

Through this century, the protest tradition has become increasingly direct and less abstract. A long and close association has existed between the print media and the exposé (Nast's cartoons, *Uncle Tom's Cabin*, *The Jungle*, *Unsafe at Any Speed*). The muckrakers were professional journalists and intellectuals, their work highly "processed," their medium the written word. During the thirties muckraking in the grand tradition failed to revive. The protests of workers and farmers reached the public through newspapers and mass magazines as before, but now as well through the more direct media, radio and newsreels. These depended less on written symbols and appealed to a nonreading audience. In the 1960s the outbursts of demonstrators, blacks, women, and others entered the living room directly on television. As political communication, this represented the rawest method yet. Even less processed and symbolic, these messages could be understood by a moron. By the sixties, the muckraking tradition had not only become institutionalized as Naderism; it had also been institutionalized by TV, which provided packaged outrage in regular time slots on national networks, for example, the capsulized Sunday anger of "60 Minutes."

Muckraking or otherwise, the journalistic approach to problems carries its own marketing mechanisms, including the big scoop, human interest, sensation, controversy, and a bias toward the understandable

—all this commonly at the expense of underlying currents and genuine complexities. The growth of adversary journalism—neomuckraking—may have altered all this; it has not altered it enough. At one time, by and large the media blasted the Democrats. Today, leading journalists, at least, have become rather liberal. Yet today, too, the media lambast all politicians and politics itself, deepening the general malaise about public life and authority.[93]

Underlying these surface misgivings, the constitutional-political setup itself constantly thwarts political change. As James L. Sundquist has written, "the United States is unique among the world's democracies in the extent to which the institutional system is weighted on the side of restraint regardless of the mandate of the people." "Of all major democratic governments in the world . . . the United States government is the one that gives to minorities in the legislative process the most devices by which to obstruct and thwart majorities." Time and again, attempts at reform have gotten cut off by these entrenched minorities. We live under a constitutional arrangement predicated upon weak government and the separation of powers. The federal system dictates that reformers must pursue many of their national goals through often-indifferent or hostile state and local governments and a complex network of courts.[94] When reformers have assaulted the labyrinthine system of checks and balances (climaxing in Roosevelt's Court fight), they have typically created even more friction to slow things up.

The two-party system has undergirded inertia. Two-party politics pulls both major parties toward the middle by compelling them to fight for the center. The President must then govern from there. As contrasted with Western Europe, the American political system lacks strong parties. Ours are decentralized and ideologically inconsistent. We give very short shrift to third parties. Outside the protective shell of party, the lone citizen feels more vulnerable and to a degree *is* more vulnerable, which doubtless helps to explain the recent proliferation of organized interest groups as the parties have decayed. One of the oldest traditions in American liberalism has been the inclination to work outside of party, or to keep party at arm's length. This independence deprives the liberals who practice it of the leverage which a party can bring to bear. It makes them vulnerable to attacks by other parties. And, widely practiced, it undermines the party system.

The old American suspicion of politics and politicians, exemplified in the dictum that the government which governs least governs best, survives to the present, but in amended form. While Americans may describe themselves as conservative, they have a taste for government, too; and they intend to preserve the basic welfare state. People will naturally resist proposals that put a tax load on their shoulders, and will be most accepting of proposals to help themselves. Social Security and national defense expenditures get backing because they provide a means of *self*-protection. More subtly, support for farm programs has no doubt been enhanced by the extraordinary affinity for country life among people who do not dwell in rural surroundings.

Yet along with our perennial fascination with the political game and our support for many programs does run that equally ancient and powerful distrust of politics. American "political culture" has as its "central themes . . . opposition to power and suspicion of government," writes Barbara Kellerman.[95] Even our radicalism (except for the Marxist version of the thirties) has shown about as much inclination toward individualism as American society at large, which helps to account for its common shallowness. Americans seem almost allergic to being led. Our hostility toward constituted power and governmental authority mixes with ambivalent attitudes toward the leadership which carries that authority. We lack any certainty as to how the public sector ought to be run, and energetic leadership makes us wary, puts us on our guard.[96] Heavy ambivalence marked Americans' attitude toward government in the nineteenth century, so that while they wanted its help they still distrusted it;[97] much the same remains true today. Thomas Gordon has observed that

> it seems to be a universal response of human beings at any age to feel deeply resentful and angry toward someone on whom they are, to a greater or lesser degree, dependent for providing gratification of their needs. Most people don't respond favorably to those who hold power to dispense or withhold rewards. They resent the fact that someone else controls the means for satisfying their needs. They wish they themselves were in control.[98]

People do not want to run the risk of depending on someone else, or to have to conform to some pattern of behavior demanded in exchange for these rewards.[99] Along with benevolence, government also signifies the draft, taxes, jury duty, intrusive social workers, and traffic tickets. Great numbers of immigrants have come here to escape the state——state-supported religion, bureaucracy, the military, persecution, and much more that they have not wanted to see re-created in the United States.

Because Americans, traditionally marked by economic individualism and anti-statism, tend to perceive Washington as something not of but apart from them, they often resist solutions handed down from Washington as things imposed on them. They will prefer that, whatever the project, it be their project, at least partly planned and run by themselves instead of by the "feds." They want to harmonize it with the nation's strong traditions of self-reliance, minimal government, philanthropy, and voluntary associations. They want help and autonomy at the same time.[100]

Our national reluctance to call on government flows in part from the inefficiency of our constitutional arrangements. These——the division of powers, the federal-state order——virtually guarantee slippage and sloppiness once many welfare state programs become established. A system purposely designed to yield change reluctantly also turns out to implement it inefficiently. All this contrasts dramatically with other countries where governmental arrangements work more smoothly. The sheer size, sectionalism, and complexity of the United States bleed reform.

Americans regard themselves as practical people who want results. We want more government services than we did decades ago, effectively delivered.[101] Unfortunately, though a great deal has been spent on them, the usefulness of many social programs has remained unclear. This makes such programs extremely vulnerable to attack, very hard to defend. We rage at governmental, as opposed to private sector waste, in part because we wrongly suppose that the one kind involves *our* money, *our* taxes, but that the other does not. (Incompetent managers do not throw away their own funds.)[102] And governmental waste is often much more visible than the private variety, Edsels excepted.

The public has shown a clear preference for centrist candidates, or for candidates it views as centrist, depending on where the center lies at any particular time. We have traditionally regarded leftist ideological systems with suspicion. William Dean Howells remarked that socialism "smells to the average American of petroleum, suggests the red flag, and all manner of sexual novelties, and an abusive tone about God and religion."[103] Once turn-of-the-century Socialists, Howells's contemporaries, took office in this city or that, they tended to behave more or less like other reform regimes in other cities——in other words, not like Socialists, but like centrists.

The Great Depression displays the ways in which many of the political and social considerations we have discussed, taken together, can brake even the fastest-running political movement. Other words besides "radical" characterize the thirties, such words as guilt, fear, exhaustion, resignation, timidity, physical debilitation, hopelessness, and confusion. A very standard individual response to unemployment involved losing trust in other people and drawing away from society. The Depression, as John A. Garraty has pointed out, seemed so vast that mere humans could not deal with it.[104] The massive fear it generated in turn produced not some great, unified, focused political drive by the unemployed, but mainly inertia.[105]   Like victims of a public flogging, those the Depression struck often became so beaten down that they could not respond.   People showed a tendency more appropriate to better times, to try to hold onto what little they still possessed.   The worse off one was, the more likely to be apathetic.[106]   "Insecurity," Garraty emphasizes,

> caused the unemployed to be fearful and dependent. Fear and dependence eroded their confidence and destroyed hope. Lack of confidence and hopelessness undermined their expectations. Typically, when workers lost their jobs they had not suffered enough to become rebels. By the time they had suffered they had lost the capacity for militant protest.[107]

A striking tendency developed among the unemployed to blame not the existing socio-economic structure but themselves: "It was my fault that I lost the job; I shouldn't have said what I did!" or, "I ought to have stayed on in school."[108]   A majority of Americans viewed the Depression as a personal rather than a class phenomenon.   To them as individuals belonged the responsibility for their joblessness.[109]   In one sample, "only about one in five wanted to change the economic system; the majority blamed themselves only."[110]   As Garraty puts it,

> when workers lost their jobs their response, perhaps after a brief period of waiting for something to turn up, was to search feverishly for a new one.   Then they became discouraged, sometimes emotionally disorganized.   Finally, after months of continuous idleness, most either sank into apathy or adjusted to their condition, leading extremely circumscribed lives in apparent calm.[111]

Then too, most people were *not* unemployed; and the interests of jobholders and the jobless tended to diverge.   Workers who still had jobs saw prices fall so far that their living standards actually suffered scant erosion.[112]   According to the results of the first Gallup poll (September 1935), 60 percent of the public regarded government outlays for relief and recovery as "too great," with only 9 percent responding "too little."[113]

Along with the anger and withdrawal it spawned, the Depression also tended to bond people together in some degree.   Privately mounted drives did aid the downtrodden; and I suspect that however short it may fall, a Community Chest or United Way campaign will generate a pacifying impulse far out of proportion to its actual benefits.   At all events, the middle class remained basically conservative during the

Depression, while the working class kept well clear of revolutionary upsurge.[114]

Measured against the crushing impact of the collapse, the astounding thing about the Old Left is how little influence it wielded. Proletarian literature went unread by the proletariat. One leftist writer complained that "the overwhelming majority" of the working class "hardly reads anything apart from the local Sunday and daily newspapers and an occasional copy of Liberty, True Romances, Wild West Tales or Screen Romances."[115] "Historically," writes John P. Diggins,

> what was remarkable about the public during the Depression
> was not the extent of its protest and sense of conflict but the
> extent of its patience and sense of contrition.
>   The extent of this psychic wound indicates how much
> America's working classes had absorbed the values of capitalist
> individualism.[116]

Inertia carried remarkable weight, too, at the local level. In Boston, for example, the Depression apparently deepened ethnic identities and antipathies, further fragmenting the city. As for the New Deal, groups in Boston damned its programs if they got injured by them, no matter how beneficial the effects on people elsewhere in the country. When a program helped one group or another, it found a welcome. This parochial pattern of happiness-unhappiness, sorting programs out one by one, produced an unfavorable environment for broad-brush national economic planning. "Signs were few that a comprehensive ideological change had occurred toward social and political innovation," writes Charles H. Trout. Along with the suspicion of Washington, a tendency existed to tamper with or dilute the programs which Washington sent down.[117]

"For those who would argue that the New Deal brought drastic change," Trout continues, "the Boston story would give little comfort—not so much because of the nature of the New Deal, but because of recurrent obstacles at the national level. Boston during the Great Depression was, on balance, a city which feasted on the cake of custom." The big questions associated with the New Deal took second place in municipal elections to the usual litany of personalities, taxes, and corruption.   "The idea of a national or even a municipal communality of interest was seldom grasped."   The factionalized Democratic party kept clear of ideological questions, and anyone hunting for possibilities to the left of it had to bend over and squint. Trout's conclusion: "Through most of the Depression Bostonians . . . lagged behind the New Deal."[118]

By way of Boston fifty years ago, we have concluded our long foray through a nether world which might be called the realm of fragmented consciousness.   If the experience thus far in the twentieth century provides any guide for the future, the dicta for any reform presidential candidate——rather perverse dicta, unfortunately——would run:

If you can avoid it, do not tell the public what you intend to do except in generalities.   Pundits will grumble at the banality of political discourse, but at the first hint of some upsetting or radical new proposal they will attack like wolves.   One runs the risks of verbally blundering and of turning off one's own constituents.   Our political campaigns are so banal mainly because the public, those very constituents, are at most times so timid.   The best advice is caution.   Cleave to the center.

If you feel you must inform the public what you intend to do, particularly in order to establish a mandate for doing it, try to avoid explaining *how*.   The details are usually boring, damaging, or both.   Never, ever, say too much.[119]

Finally, while flexibility may be crucial to success in the presidency, avoid an image of *excessive* flexibility.   People will read it as opportunism.   Be opportunistic, but be subtle about it.

Issue blurring in a campaign may leave the candidate identityless.   This may suit a person who expects to win anyway.   In view of the public's conservatism, the danger in taking the opposite, quite specific route is that while some voters will be attracted, others will recoil.   The candidate's image may become frozen at the wrong time in some awkward posture.   A candidate may get typecast as a fool or a lunatic.

All of which serves to remind us that American politics has operated as a politics of continuity, adjustment, compromise, and expediency.   The two-party system embraces the principle of broad, diverse coalitions.   Political appeals are geared toward similarly broad common denominators.   Though the Democratic party has functioned like a huge amoeba ingesting causes, it has not heavily emphasized ideology or organization along class lines.   Opacity gets built into politics, together with a substantial measure of bland and meaningless rhetoric matching bland and meaningless goals.

NOTES

Thorstein Veblen, *The Theory of the Leisure Class: An Economic Study of Institutions* (New York: Modern Library, [1934?]), p. 191; Machiavelli, *The Prince*, pp. 21-22; Bartlett's *Familiar Quotations*, 14th ed., p. 417 (Voltaire quote).

[1]Not by any means an original use of the term.   Along with Veblen, Schlesinger, Sr., and others have employed it in similar fashion.

[2]Taken from Philip Kotler, *Marketing Management: Analysis, Planning, and Control*, 2d ed. (Englewood Cliffs, N.J.: Prentice-Hall, 1972), p. 100.

[3]See also pp. 303, 435.

[4]Kammen, *People of Paradox*, p. 253.

[5]*Why Is There No Socialism in the United States?* (1906; reprint, White Plains, N.Y.: International Arts & Sciences Press, 1976). As Aileen S. Kraditor has shown, the way we have generally gone about answering Sombart's question raises certain severe problems. It "illustrates the *post hoc ergo propter hoc* fallacy: the American working class is not radical; certain characteristics prevail among the American working class; ergo, those characteristics, whatever they are, account for its nonradicalism." The Sombartian approach presupposes that the normal, logical, predictable thing for workers to be——but for all the obstacles which historians and others have identified that stop them——is socialists. That their behavior has conflicted with this destiny, at least down to the present, reflects "false consciousness."

But what if socialist ideology is not the universal "norm for workers in advanced capitalist countries"? What if the turn-of-the-century American worker had a great many central personal priorities, among them community, religion, and family? What if the worker did not share the radical organizer's perception of the entire capitalist society as a "system," of which these things which the worker held terribly dear merely represented the superstructure?

Let us say that socialism is not normative for the working class. Does this mean that the obstacles which scholars have identified as barriers to *radical* change do not impede *political change more generally*? Clearly not. For example, whether or not turn-of-the-century workers would have shared sharper socialist leanings in the absence of a strong individualist ethos pervading the society may be moot; but the fact that individualism threw up obstacles to *all* broad political change emanating from the left, including even so moderate a movement as progressivism, lies beyond dispute. Our focus, then, will center not on barriers to socialism, but on obstacles to every sort of left-leaning political transformation. It will acknowledge, too, that where working-class attitudes are concerned, despite years of debate, our knowledge remains relatively rudimentary.

Throughout the first two paragraphs above I rely heavily on Kraditor, *The Radical Persuasion, 1890-1917: Aspects of the Intellectual History and the Historiography of Three American Radical Organizations* (Baton Rouge: Louisiana State University Press, 1981), pp. 37-44, 54, and 320-21, from which the quotations are taken, and passim. See also Seymour Martin Lipset, "Why No Socialism in the United States?" in Seweryn Bialer and Sophia Sluzar, gen. eds., *Radicalism in the Contempo-*

rary Age, 3 vols. (Boulder, Colo.: Westview Press, 1977), vol. 1: *Sources of Contemporary Radicalism*, pp. 30-149; and Sean Wilentz, *Chants Democratic: New York City and the Rise of the American Working Class, 1788-1850* (New York: Oxford University Press, 1984), especially pp. 15-16.

[6]Wesley T. Wooley, "Profiles of a Conservative America: The Gallup Poll, 1935-1975," *Midwest Quarterly* 21 (Spring 1980): 307 and passim.

[7]Huntington, *Political Order*, pp. 344-46.

[8]"Resistance to Change," in Zaltman, *Creating Social Change*, p. 610. Watson's article is exceedingly rich and suggestive, and I can only refer the reader to it.

[9]*Leisure Class*, pp. 202-3.

[10]*Tired Radicals and Other Papers* (New York: B. W. Huebsch, 1921), p. 11.

[11]*Psychology of Social Movements*, pp. 13-14, 42, 53 (example mine).

[12]See Abraham Zaleznik and David Moment, "Change," in Zaltman, *Creating Social Change*, p. 41.

[13]Schlesinger, *American as Reformer*, p. 66.

[14]See Cantril, *Psychology of Social Movements*, p. 15; and Flacks, *Making History*, passim.

[15]*Leadership*, pp. 135-36.

[16]Or at least so it has in the past. The present impact of nonvoting, though, is disputable. It has been argued, for instance, that if everyone eligible voted, the political spectrum might move somewhat leftward on welfare state issues, but somewhat rightward on social issues. For an important examination of the whole voting/nonvoting question, see Paul Kleppner, *Who Voted? The Dynamics of Electoral Turnout, 1870-1980*, American Political Parties and Elections series (New York: Praeger, 1982). See also Michael E. McGerr, *The Decline of Popular Politics: The American North, 1865-1928* (New York: Oxford University Press, 1986); and Frances Fox Piven and Richard A. Cloward, *Why Americans Don't Vote* (New York: Pantheon Books, 1988).

[17]*Los Angeles Times*, 11, 13 December 1983.

[18]Except in 1982. See Edsall, *New Politics of Inequality*, p. 191.

[19]*Post-conservative America*, p. 100; Walter Dean Burnham, *The Current Crisis in American Politics* (New York: Oxford University Press, 1982), pp. 290-91.

[20]*Political Man*, p. 227.

[21]*The Standard Edition of the Complete Psychological Works of Sigmund Freud*, ed. James Strachey and Anna Freud, vol. 21: *The Future of an Illusion; Civilization and Its Discontents; and Other Works* (London: Hogarth Press, Institute of Psycho-analysis, 1961), pp. 76, 83 (from *Civilization and Its Discontents*).

[22]Jonathan L. Freedman, *Happy People: What Happiness Is, Who Has It, and Why* (New York: Harcourt Brace Jovanovich, 1978), pp. 136-37.

[23]But see also p. 452.

[24]Bell, *Cultural Contradictions*, p. 247.

[25]*The Future While It Happened*, p. 90.

[26]For a stimulating discussion of all this, see Edward Pessen, "Social Structure and Politics in American History," *American Historical Review* 87 (December 1982): 1290-1325.

[27]One might hasten to add, though, that a fair number were not.

[28]Edward Pessen, *The Log Cabin Myth: The Social Backgrounds of the Presidents* (New Haven: Yale University Press, 1984), pp. 170-71, 175. See also Philip H. Burch, Jr., *Elites in American History*, 3 vols. (New York: Holmes & Meier, 1980-81).

[29]*Age of Reform*, p. 241.

[30]"Who Rules America? Power and Politics in the Democratic Era, 1825-1975," *Prologue* 9 (Spring 1977): 22.

[31]These figures come from Keller, *Affairs of State*, p. 305; Allen, "Progressive Reform," p. 139; and G. William Domhoff, *The Powers that Be: Processes of Ruling-Class Domination in America* (New York: Random House, Vintage Books, 1979), p. 159.

[32]*Political Man*, pp. 321-22.

[33]See Janowitz, *Last Half-Century*, p. 547.

[34]See Nie, *Changing American Voter*, p. 116. But see also Wattenberg, *Decline of American Political Parties*, p. 115. A classic statement is V. O. Key, Jr., and Milton C. Cummings, Jr., *The Responsible Electorate: Rationality in Presidential Voting, 1936-1960* (Cambridge, Mass.: Harvard University Press, Belknap Press, 1966).

[35]Joseph S. Murphy, review of *Illiterate America*, by Jonathan Kozol, in *New York Times Book Review*, 14 April 1985, p. 36.

[36]*Los Angeles Times*, 2 June 1977.

[37]Ibid., 5 September 1978.

[38]*People of Plenty: Economic Abundance and the American Character* (Chicago: University of Chicago Press, 1954), pp. 97, 99, 121. A useful cautionary note on Potter's thesis of plenty is sounded in David Hackett Fischer, *Historians' Fallacies: Toward a Logic of Historical Thought* (New York: Harper & Row, 1970), p. 172. See also Jerome Karabel, "The Reasons Why," *New York Review of Books*, 8 February 1979, p. 23.

[39]*People of Plenty*, p. 118. Much recent scholarship disagrees in one degree or another with some of my bleak conclusions about labor history. See, for example, Leon Fink, "The New Labor History and the Powers of Historical Pessimism: Consensus, Hegemony, and the Case of the Knights of Labor," *Journal of American History* 75 (June 1988): 115-36.

[40]*Equality and Efficiency: The Big Tradeoff* (Washington, D.C.: Brookings Institution, 1975), p. 34.

[41]Robert J. Lampman, "Growth, Prosperity, and Inequality since 1947," *Wilson Quarterly* 1 (Autumn 1977): 155.

[42]Sidney Verba and Gary R. Orren, *Equality in America: The View from the Top* (Cambridge, Mass.: Harvard University Press, 1985), p. 50.

[43]*Equality and Efficiency*, pp. 1, 51.

[44]*Equality in America*, p. 246.

[45]For strong exception to this and to my general line of argument about class, see Reeve Vanneman and Lynn Weber Cannon, *The American Perception of Class* (Philadelphia: Temple University Press, 1987).

[46]See especially Peter R. Shergold, *Working-Class Life: The "American Standard" in Comparative Perspective, 1899-1913* (Pittsburgh: University of Pittsburgh Press, 1982).

[47]For a useful critique of the contention that ethnic division, geographic mobility, and the absence of a powerful socialist or labor party retarded the movement toward governmentally sponsored social programs, see Patterson, *Struggle Against Poverty*, pp. 30-31.

[48]"The Reasons Why," pp. 25-27. See also John Gaventa, *Power and Powerlessness: Quiescence and Rebellion in an Appalachian Valley* (Urbana: University of Illinois Press, 1980); and, on a cautionary note, Richard Oestreicher, "Urban Working-Class Political Behavior and Theories of American Electoral Politics, 1870-1940," *Journal of American History* 74 (March 1988): 1257-86.

[49]Cantril, *Psychology of Social Movements*, p. 42.

[50]Schlozman, *Injury to Insult*, pp. 223, 347.

[51]Richard P. Coleman and Lee Rainwater, *Social Standing in America: New Dimensions of Class* (New York: Basic Books, 1978), pp. 294-96. See also Stuart M. Blumin, "The Hypothesis of Middle-Class Formation in Nineteenth-Century America: A Critique and Some Proposals," *American Historical Review* 90 (April 1985): 299-338.

[52]Nor is this new. On the role of radio and other media in reinforcing the status quo in the thirties, see Richard H. Pells, *Radical Visions and American Dreams: Culture and Social Thought in the Depression Years* (New York: Harper & Row, 1973), especially pp. 267-68.

[53]*Leisure Class*, p. 204.

[54]Janowitz, *Last Half-Century*, pp. 121, 150-51. One must, however, take into account the changing meaning of such terms as "liberalism" and "conservatism."

[55]Okun, *Equality and Efficiency*, p. 34.

[56]Daniel Yankelovich, *New Rules: Searching for Self-Fulfillment in*

a World Turned Upside Down (New York: Random House, 1981), pp. 139-42.

[57]Pessen, "Social Structure and Politics," p. 1293. People's social identities often get mixed up or conflict with one another, some pulling them left, others pulling them right. (The case of the low-paid, high-status college professor serves as a classic, perennial example.) As a whole, these mix-ups probably favor the right. Vertical and horizontal mobility may also produce political disengagement. People climbing the occupational ladder frequently unburden themselves of old friends, neighborhoods, and voting patterns along the way. On these considerations, see Lipset, *Political Man*, pp. 217-19, 240-41.

[58]*People of Plenty*, pp. 118-19.

[59]*Liberal Tradition*, p. 62. "The values of capitalism and democracy are the principal components of the American political culture," write Herbert McClosky and John Zaller. *American Ethos*, p. 12.

[60]"Socialism: Lost Cause in American History," *Criterion* (Divinity School, University of Chicago), 19 (Autumn 1980): 11.

[61]Hodgson, *America in Our Time*, pp. 426, 488.

[62]*New Rules*, p. 140. Italics in the original. "The limits to redistribution are the limits of American beliefs about equality," write Verba and Orren. "Those limits are in large measure defined by the more affluent classes." *Equality in America*, p. 51.

[63]Sidney Verba and Gary R. Orren, "The Meaning of Equality in America," *Political Science Quarterly* 100 (Fall 1985): 369-87.

[64]Quoted in Hodgson, *America in Our Time*, pp. 86-87. See also pp. 488-89.

[65]Though now, in this age of heightened expectations of the government and the welfare state "safety net," probably less. See p. 415. Another response: violent rage.

[66]Okun, *Equality and Efficiency*, pp. 48-49.

[67]For cautionary points on social mobility and its effects, see Stephan Thernstrom, *The Other Bostonians: Poverty and Progress in the American Metropolis, 1880-1970* (Cambridge, Mass.: Harvard University Press, 1973), pp. 258-59. On the realities, see pp. 249-50. See also Seymour Martin Lipset and Reinhard Bendix, *Social Mobility in Industrial Society* (Berkeley: University of California Press, 1964); and Shergold, *Working-Class Life*.

[68]Health plans and pension funds——"private welfare"——have brought workers into the system in even more ways. Janowitz, *Last Half-Century*, pp. 146-48.

[69]*Socialist Party*, p. 266. Italics in the original.

[70]Lipset, *Political Man*, p. 272.

[71]Quoted in Keller, *Affairs of State*, p. 286.

[72]*The Good Want Power: An Essay in the Psychological Possibilities of Liberalism* (New York: Basic Books, 1977), p. 23.

[73]Not that financial well-being *necessarily* undercuts the left. See, e.g., Irving Howe, *Socialism and America* (San Diego: Harcourt Brace Jovanovich, 1985), p. 121. As evidence that working-class "affluence" does not in itself explain the comparative conservatism of U.S. labor, examples exist of socialist tides running in other countries amid relative comfort; and plenty of well-paid workers have been good, upstanding socialists.

Various conditions in the modern world, economic and otherwise, may in fact have dampened and deflected "moral outrage" generally. So Barrington Moore, Jr., has argued, listing as causes mass production and markets, government-directed economies in socialist societies, the emergence of mammoth bureaucracies, and a growth in sheer numbers of people (smothering the impact of the impulses of any one). "On Moral Outrage," *New York Review of Books*, 1 June 1978, p. 35. Eighty years ago, Edward Alsworth Ross suggested something similar. See *Sin and Society: An Analysis of Latter-Day Iniquity* (Boston: Houghton Mifflin Co., 1907).

[74]Button, *Black Violence*, pp. 174-79.

[75]*Reform in America*, pp. 74, 177.

[76]Button, *Black Violence*, p. 175.

[77]I would not argue, however, that class is the *only* basis for ethnic hostility.

[78]Lipset, *Political Man*, p. 23. It has been hypothesized that religion, notably of the sect variety, has provided an escape valve for extremist politics.

[79]*Los Angeles Times*, 5 September 1978.

[80]"Psychological Aspects of Planned Developmental Change," in Zaltman, *Creating Social Change*, p. 69. Italics in the original.

[81]*Leisure Class*, pp. 199-200, 205-6.

[82]See Ferdinand Lundberg, "The Ranks of the Visible Super-Rich Are Thinning," *Los Angeles Times*, 11 February 1979.

[83]See Galambos, *Public Image of Big Business*, pp. 261-62.

[84]See Schlesinger, *American as Reformer*, p. 10.

[85]Walter Lippmann, *Public Opinion* (1922; reprint, New York: Macmillan, 1961), pp. 25, 29, and passim.

[86]*White Collar*, p. 325.

[87]Janowitz, *Last Half-Century*, p. 337.

[88]Joel Swerdlow, "A Question of Impact," *Wilson Quarterly* 5 (Winter 1981): 86.

[89]See Freedman, *Happy People*, p. 211.

[90]*White Collar*, p. 337.

[91]Janowitz, *Last Half-Century*, p. 353.

[92]*White Collar*, pp. 333, 335. The recent explosion of cable systems has created a forest of alternatives to network pap. Rather than appealing to some dull middling level of taste, cable pitches to all levels, from the most exalted to the most jejune. It remains to be seen whether the gains in cable news or Mozart will offset a further debasement of the popular taste in cable porn and rock videos. For a trenchant statement on the current implications of TV, see Neil Postman, *Amusing Ourselves to Death: Public Discourse in the Age of Show Business* (New York: Viking, 1985).

[93]"Journalists vs. Businessmen," *Wilson Quarterly* 7 (New Year's, 1983): 23-24; Huntington, *American Politics*, p. 218; Edsall, *New Politics of Inequality*, pp. 95-96, 105-6, which also suggests broader damage done to the left by TV.

[94]*Politics and Policy*, pp. 9, 510, 536.

[95]*The Political Presidency: Practice of Leadership* (New York: Oxford University Press, 1984), p. 7.

[96]Ibid., pp. 3-4, 11, 31.

[97]See, for example, Irving Howe, *Politics and the Novel* (New York: Horizon Press, Meridian Books, 1957), p. 159; and Richard L. McCormick, "The Party Period and Public Policy: An Exploratory Hypothesis," *Journal of American History* 66 (September 1979): 291, 294.

[98]*P.E.T.: Parent Effectiveness Training; The Tested New Way to Raise Responsible Children* (New York: New American Library, Plume, 1975), p. 177. Italics deleted.

[99]Ibid.

[100]"The modal structure of public opinion," writes Paul Kleppner, "continues to support particularized government intervention, while simultaneously displaying hostility to 'big government' and considerable ambivalence toward redistributive economic policies. It tends as well to be atomized, because individuals fail to connect distinguishable issue domains." *Who Voted?* p. 160.

[101]Lowi, *Personal President*, pp. 95-96.

[102]Thurow, *Zero-Sum Society*, p. 132.

[103]Hartz, *Liberal Tradition*, p. 243.

[104]Garraty, "Radicalism," pp. 102-3.

[105]John A. Garraty, *Unemployment in History: Economic Thought and Public Policy* (New York: Harper & Row, 1978), pp. 182, 186.

[106]Garraty, "Radicalism," p. 103.

[107]*Unemployment in History*, p. 187.

[108]Watson, "Resistance to Change," p. 614.

[109]Diggins, *American Left*, p. 108.

[110]Watson, "Resistance to Change," p. 614. This tendency toward self-reproach is evaporating quickly and appears minuscule today. See Garraty, *Unemployment in History*, pp. 251-52; and Frances Fox Piven and

Richard A. Cloward, *The New Class War: Reagan's Attack on the Welfare State and Its Consequences* (New York: Pantheon Books, 1982), p. 136.

[111]Garraty, *Unemployment in History*, pp. 177-78.

[112]See ibid., pp. 188-89, 262; and Garraty, "Radicalism," pp. 109-10.

[113]George H. Gallup, *The Gallup Poll: Public Opinion 1935-1971*, vol. 1: *1935-1948* (New York: Random House, 1972), p. 1.

[114]For other reasons why the jobless did not rebel in the thirties, see Garraty, *Unemployment in History*, p. 182; and E. Wight Bakke's classic *Citizens Without Work: A Study of the Effects of Unemployment upon the Workers' Social Relations and Practices* (New Haven: Yale University Press, 1940; reprint, n.p.: Archon Books, 1969). On the present, weak correlation between unemployment or other forms of personal economic trauma and political activity, see Verba, *Equality in America*, p. 249.

[115]Feuer, *Ideology*, pp. 160-61.

[116]*American Left*, p. 108.

[117]*Boston, the Great Depression, and the New Deal* (New York: Oxford University Press, 1977), pp. 257-58, 311-15, 321.

[118]Ibid., pp. 316-17, 321-22.

[119]See Peter Gruenstein, "The Best Advice for Winning the Presidency: Shhhhh . . . ," *Los Angeles Times*, 23 March 1976; and Page, *Choices and Echoes*, ch. 6, aptly titled "The Art of Ambiguity."

III

REACTION

One of the central arguments of this book holds that while reform eras emerge in something other than predictable, cyclic ways, their demise assumes a strikingly consistent pattern from era to era.

Chapter 11 details the types of foreign policy distractions which have ripped reformers away from their domestic moorings. In particular, chapter 11 stresses the single greatest destroyer of reform: war. One of the reasons war has proved so destructive is that the behavior of the government changes in wartime. The welfare state, concerned at least ostensibly with broad questions of social justice, becomes a police state devoted to punishing forms of dissent which had earlier animated reform——but which are now classed as subversion (chapter 12).

War has always stimulated the U.S. economy; and while prosperity in itself does not undercut reform, the bursts of prosperity which have followed our wars, each of them accompanied by inflation, have always operated at cross-purposes to reform. The theme is explored in chapter 13.

The next chapter looks at the changing moods of a postreform era, a time when reformers and their concerns drop out of fashion. Those whom reform has sought to benefit are relegated to the back shelf of American politics, while cynicism mounts about them and about people more generally——themes examined in chapter 15.

In the following two chapters I take up a constant in reform's undoing: disaffection. The two key groups in question are intellectuals (chapter 16) and the young (chapter 17). Often radical, youth and intellectuals have animated mainstream reform as well. But both groups tend to fall away as reform fades.

Meantime, the tendency of some intellectuals and young toward outbursts of libertinism has typically upset large numbers of people holding conventional bourgeois values.   Libertinism throws up a competing set of (typically narcissistic) priorities.   And libertinism summons a mass of political red herrings which can produce great resistance to change in general among elements of the mass public. Opportunists in their own right, conservatives use the new "social issue" to try to slow down further political change (chapter 18).

Reformers in this century have relied fundamentally on government to transform their priorities into programs.   As a reform movement declines, the state in general, and the presidency in particular, fall under broad, acute suspicion. Whipped by conservatives, this growing suspicion of government makes it extremely difficult to employ the state toward further change (chapter 19).   Their sense of direction lost, many reformers, aping the public at large, sink into a sense of resigned, exhausted, sour apathy (chapter 20).   Some are finished with great commitments for the rest of their lives. For years to come, reform is finished too.

11

DISTANT DISTRACTIONS

The Foreign Policy Escape Hatch

No triumph of peace is quite so great as the supreme triumphs of war.

Theodore Roosevelt

Earlier I defined reform in such a way as to eliminate any necessary connection with foreign affairs. Yet if reform is best thought of as a domestic pattern, this does not deny the existence of recurrent tendencies in relations with other countries. We have seen that liberal predispositions in foreign policy have often tended to distract liberals from reform, and that in this way liberalism may actually undermine reform. I do not wish to imply for a moment that these values and perspectives——activism, internationalism, and the like——are in themselves wrong; they comprise a vital part of the Western tradition. But when they take such precedence that domestic issues become secondary, or when their advocacy makes domestic reform vulnerable, then they can become very damaging indeed.

We can say much the same of liberal antimilitarism, which sometimes has carried over into pacifism. Rampant militarization does offend most liberals. So does flag-waving, at least with both hands, and excessive throwing around of the national weight. Liberal consciences respond to starvation and unhappiness abroad but tend to recoil at war. It is one thing to hope and to plan for a world without war; quite another to face charges of weakness, cowardice, or even treason for such hopes from political critics at home. When all is said and done, most liberals——aside from the Truman and Kennedy types——do not wave the flag very convincingly. This, too, can make liberals vulnerable.

Beyond its destructiveness and inhumanity, a strong liberal theme holds that war is simply irrational. This, again, has been a tendency: it has not utterly precluded "just" wars or military interventions, especially where fertile fields have awaited the sowing of American (liberal) democratic ideals and institutions. Usually the optimism on this score has exaggerated itself; germination has failed, or the seedlings withered.

Finally, liberals have opposed war because they know what it does to reform. War——hot or cold——diverts revenue. It also diverts attention. And it generally palls the political and social climate for broad innovation at home. "War," wrote Richard Hofstadter, "has always been the Nemesis of the liberal tradition in America."[1]

In essence the presidency has always involved carrying on a juggling act between domestic and foreign policy. But each of the three major reform administrations of this century has eventually become fixated not just with foreign affairs, but with winning a war. The theme of peace keynoted Wilson's 1916 campaign, Wilson labeling the GOP "the war party." The campaign's most memorable slogan was "He kept us out of war." The President declared, "I am not expecting this country to get into war."[2] During the 1940 campaign, FDR told one of his audiences: "And while I am talking to you mothers and fathers, I give you one more assurance. I have said this before, but I shall say it again and again and again: Your boys are not going to be sent into any foreign wars."[3] And Lyndon Johnson in October 1964: "We are not about to send American boys nine to ten thousand miles away from home to do what Asian boys ought to be doing for themselves."[4] The foreign policy fixations have not ended when the wars did. For Wilson, after the defeat of Germany it was permanent peace and the League; for New Deal legatee Truman, the whole atmosphere of the early Cold War, then Korea.

Each of the Presidents in question began his administration avowedly or in effect as a domestic policy specialist with a strong domestic orientation. Contrasted with Roosevelt or Johnson, Wilson represents only an exaggerated case. "It would be an irony of fate," he told a friend not long before taking office, "if my administration had to deal with foreign problems, for all my preparation has been in domestic matters."[5] Wilson's New Freedom called for the expansion of markets abroad, true enough, but supposedly as a lever for lifting the domestic economy. Foreign affairs per se went almost completely ignored by both Wilson and Roosevelt in 1912. Yet Wilson's administration, like the others, ended up awash in foreign troubles. Meanwhile, by late 1914 most of TR's own legendary energy focused on the war and preparedness. The New Nationalism as a philosophy took on a distinctly militarized cast.[6] Preparedness drove Roosevelt back toward the GOP. Wrote William Allen White, "He won back many of his old enemies, the big businessmen who, now saw eye to eye with him and applauded as the

Colonel raged at Wilson."[7]

If Wilson and Theodore Roosevelt provide classic instances of reformers' distraction by foreign policy and war, the great case study remains Lyndon Johnson. One of Johnson's aides said (before his boss's presidency got very far along), "He wishes the rest of the world would go away and we could get ahead with the real needs of Americans." "Lyndon Johnson," Eric F. Goldman wrote, "entered the White House not only little concerned with the outer world but leery of it." At least at first, Johnson intended to focus primarily on domestic policy. In 1965 Mrs. Johnson ominously remarked: "I just hope that foreign problems do not keep mounting. They do not represent Lyndon's kind of Presidency."[8]

"LBJ was great in domestic affairs," commented Averell Harriman. "It was fantastic what he did. If it hadn't been for . . . Vietnam he'd have been the greatest President ever."[9] In later years Johnson would claim to have seen what would happen to his Great Society if America plunged into Indochina, and certainly Vietnam did hit his domestic momentum like a hard foot on the brake. Yet ultimately Johnson believed he *had* to escalate. As Johnson looked back, he stared into a mirror: "I knew from the start," he said of early 1965 some five years later,

> that I was bound to be crucified either way I moved. If I left the woman I really loved——the Great Society——in order to get involved with that bitch of a war on the other side of the world, then I would lose everything at home. All my programs. All my hopes to feed the hungry and shelter the homeless. All my dreams to provide education and medical care to the browns and the blacks and the lame and the poor. But if I left that war and let the Communists take over South Vietnam, then I would be seen as a coward and my nation would be seen as an appeaser and we would both find it impossible to accomplish anything for anybody anywhere on the entire globe.
>
> Oh, I could see it coming all right. History provided too many cases where the sound of the bugle put an immediate end to the hopes and dreams of the best reformers: the Spanish-American War drowned the populist spirit; World War I ended Woodrow Wilson's New Freedom; World War II brought the New Deal to a close.

But, if Johnson's retrospection deserves any credence, he believed his administration faced ruin if he failed to act in Vietnam. Johnson's explanation for his actions, as related by Doris Kearns, involved a strange stew of machismo, dubious historical analogies, personal, political, and geopolitical anxieties, and weird dreams. The Great Society, as Kearns puts it, was to have been "his monument, his passport to historical immortality." Still (quoting Johnson), while "losing the Great Society was a terrible thought, . . . [it was] not so terrible as the thought of being responsible for America's losing a war to the Communists. Nothing could possibly be worse than that."[10]

The most striking thing about this sorry tale is the degree to which its ending was foreseen—its strictly domestic ending, that is. We can glimpse the distorting impact of Johnson's decision on ideology in the candidacy of Eugene McCarthy. In 1968 this man—who had strikingly conservative impulses—could come off as a left-liberal or some sort of radical solely on the question of Vietnam. Foreign policy and red herring issues can indeed produce some curious "liberal" heroes. Vietnam: J. William Fulbright. Watergate: Sam Ervin. By the 1970s, the term "Cold War liberalism" had broken into its component parts, as it should have long before. "Come Home, America," urged a George McGovern campaign slogan. Such individuals as Hubert Humphrey and Henry Jackson, who continued trying to carry cold warriorism on one shoulder and domestic liberalism on the other, were identified by virtue of their foreign policy (but not their domestic liberal) positions as conservative Democrats.[11]

The impulse of reform administrations to chart their course toward foreign seas, then ultimately sail into the shoals of war, has often attracted comment. Any explanation must partly take account of the coincidental, the accidental, and the unlucky—the fact, for example, that FDR and Hitler took power within weeks of one another. But more is involved than this, I believe, and we can see it if we visualize foreign affairs as a source of relief from domestic imbroglios: as a kind of escape hatch.

An administration's foreign policy can cost it support, including the backing of reformers; yet the remarkable thing about the foreign sphere in contrast with the domestic is the freedom of maneuver which Presidents have enjoyed, particularly during the Cold War years and prior to Vietnam. The Constitution is biased toward the freer exercise of presidential power abroad. Congress plays a weaker hand than at home. So do the various interest groups. Aaron Wildavsky's study of the fate of presidential proposals in Congress, 1948-64, discloses that "Presidents prevail about 70 percent of the time in defense and foreign policy, compared with 40 percent in the domestic sphere."[12] For a Chief Executive, perhaps buffeted and damaged for years by competitors for power domestically, bursting out into foreign affairs resembles a successful cavalry charge through massed infantry. To a liberal (or conservative) Chief Executive with a yen for greatness, the lure must seem tremendous—especially since foreign achievements have increasingly provided the main measure of greatness, and especially after domestic policymaking has bogged down.

Thus the attractions to a President of the foreign policy escape hatch:

1. It produces comparatively scant domestic resistance, possibly none at all. Foreign policy offers far more room for maneuver than do domestic problems, entangled as they are in a web of interest-group, congressional, and other complications, and virtually always divisive. Foreign policy has often attracted less media criticism and friction than domestic. It has appeared easier to deal with.

2. In part because foreign policy is by its very nature more opaque than domestic, fewer concrete goals are attached, fewer yet expected to be met. Accountability limits itself both by this and by secrecy. Vagueness serves as a shield.

3. Hence the risks seem more limited than in domestic affairs; and though the rewards may also be more limited, they come cheaper.

4. An Executive stands to gain significant recognition and ego gratification, not merely among the small fraction of humans who are Americans but across the planet. Foreign policy promises one immortality as an international statesman.

5. There is an aura of sophistication and glory attached, particularly so in the decades since the United States became a superpower. International questions offer excitement, glamor, even regal acclaim, and a spurt of popularity. In short, they seem more presidential.

6. Temporarily, anyway, foreign policy can unify the public behind the President in a sort of political "quick fix." Even to a "domestic" President——especially an activist, or one whose programs have grown shaky, or who has gotten bound up in political difficulties——the foreign policy escape hatch becomes tempting.[13]

7. For a conservative administration with limited appeal at home on economic issues, foreign policy diversions can prove a political godsend.

But for domestic reform, major diversions into events abroad have more often than not turned out disastrously. As Dennis H. Wrong has noted, "foreign-policy choices——war and peace, military spending, 'entangling alliances'——have more than any other issues created the splits and factionalism for which the Left has always been so notorious."[14] Given the events that have distracted and sundered their party over the past two decades, Democrats should need no reminding of this. Complicating things all the more for the Democratic party, its ethnic heterogeneity has frequently projected into foreign policy, and its foreign policy has often upset these same ethnic constituencies. Historically the Irish issue, and more recently the Middle East, have provided extremely favorable habitats for breeding foreign policy red herrings which distract from priorities at home. The very diversity of Democratic ethnic support makes it far more vulnerable than the GOP to this particular kind of fission.

John Kennedy remarked in 1961 that "when Franklin [Roosevelt] had this job, it was a cinch. He didn't have all these world problems. He had only to cope with poverty in the United States, but look what I've got."[15] It is no accident that the *relatively* isolationist 1930s also became our most productive era for domestic legislation. During the Progressive Era, Americans' attention remained primarily on themselves and their own concerns; the same held true in the thirties. The fact that foreign distractions and defense outlays did not compete against social programs helps explain the New Deal's great success. A strong corps of outright isolationists flourished among reformers in those years. Whatever the justice of their attitudes in terms of international relations, there was eminent justice to reform. It *should* be conceived and carried out independent of foreign concerns. But it cannot, at least not anymore. The Cold War and the nuclear era catapulted foreign policy from relative marginality into a position of perennial, bipartisan preeminence.

War

The Spanish War finished us. . . . The blare of the bugle drowned the voice of the Reformer.

Tom Watson, 1910

Every reform we have won will be lost if we go into this war.

Woodrow Wilson, 1914

This discussion of foreign policy may have led the reader to anticipate that I intend to tie in reform with war. The theme, familiar enough, is summarized in the old saw, "Democrats get you into wars, Republicans get you out." Some have surmised that American liberalism carries within it a tendency toward war, supposedly because of liberalism's missionary inclinations, energy of leadership, governmentalism, desire for national unity, and economic assertiveness. None of these characteristics in and of itself *necessarily* demonstrates a truly dangerous foreign policy, one by its very nature warmongering or even inclined toward war. Yet on three occasions in this century reform eras have ended in war. The nature of war is such that it speeds up and focuses the film of change——it allows us to see with greater clarity and in greater rapidity processes already, more obscurely, at work in peacetime. Here, we will examine the two world wars and Vietnam.

At the outset, we must reflect on war in two ways. On one hand, it provides the ultimate digression from serious business at home, including reform. But on the other hand, war can in itself *be* a variety of reform——eradicating slavery, for example, or eradicating Nazism. And it can lay the groundwork for reform——for instance, by making a managed economy necessary. Yet in each of its major twentieth century wars this country has singlemindedly spent vast energies upon things of little or no domestic consequence. True enough, war does bring to a zenith the centralizing tendencies of reform periods, notably the power of the President. (Richard Henry Dana, Jr., observed after meeting General Grant, "How war, how all great crises bring us to the one-man power!")[1] And considerable social reform theoretically could occur in wartime; World War I held out this hope, with talk of "industrial democracy" and the expectation that permanent adjustments in American society could emerge from wartime expedients. What followed World War I, however, was a severe reaction; to the degree that the war experience provided any precedents at all, it furnished them to the New Deal fifteen years later. World War II was similar. Unlike Britain, which made major commitments to social reform during the conflict, the American record was substantially barren.

The very nature of war has favored conservatism in this country, undercutting reform. Ironically, after a reform era has carried negation to the point of exhaustion, war, of all things, looks peculiarly like affirmation. It shifts national priorities squarely to foreign policy and military strategy. It enables conservatives to grab the flag and wave it, to seize the high ground by becoming war's loudest champions. It forces a shotgun marriage between reformers and reactionaries. War brings a craving for wholeness, for oneness, for unity of classes, groups, and parties epitomized in Wilson's declaration that for the duration, "politics is adjourned,"[2] or, more bleakly, in the Americanization-anti-radical campaigns of World War I. Superpatriots can conveniently label anything which seems unpleasant as unpatriotic and un-American. Wars tend to alter agendas by rendering the naysaying which necessarily goes into reform unfashionable. Outright muckraking becomes positively hazardous. Armageddon makes reform seem mundane, boring. It engenders a scale of disaster and upheaval which leaves the population reeling afterwards and yearning to relax. Reformers' proposals to root out corruption and sin have the same chilling effect after a big war as Moses's arrival with the law at the end of an old Hollywood biblical orgy. Prewar optimism turns to hardness.

In contrast to the tortuous incrementalism of reform, the very totality of war——Americans versus Germans, the clash of great armies,

the clarity of victory or defeat——may almost come as a relief. Edgar
Kemler caught this when he wrote of 1917-18:   "Along with the
debasement of the progressive ethic there was the diversion of
progressive aims towards nationalism. . . . How could progressive aims
compete with a massacre?" "Again," Kemler asked,

> what satisfaction has the progressive in a final victory? It is
> true that politicians offer their followers a "more abundant
> life," with more food, work, better housing and living
> conditions. Yet an economy is a most intangible thing to
> manipulate, and when a reform program has been completed
> on the statute books, who can say that it will really bring
> recovery and widespread bounties, and if it does, who can say
> that the politicians really planned it that way? Yet everybody
> knows that a nation has triumphed when its armies have
> entered an enemy capital!
>
> [Comparing progressivism to nationalism] is almost like a
> debating match trying to draw its audience from a football
> game. Which draws the greatest [sic] crowds and evokes the
> loudest [sic] cheers? For which are banners made and
> flaunted? And which rewards its heroes with the most
> glamorous women?[3]

Harold Stearns wrote of the Great War:

> Here was something we understood——*doing* something. No
> more unpleasant spiritual introspections! No more self-
> depreciations! No more uneasy conscience to tell us that
> perhaps there was something radically wrong in the whole tone
> of our national life! Here was something to summon from us
> our best traditional efforts of achievement and accomplishment.
> Better still, it seemed plausible to wrap our activity in the
> midst of a vague, yet genuine idealism. Thus the cycle was
> complete; we disliked self-analysis, the war gave us our chance
> to return whole-heartedly to action; yet we also disliked to
> think that we were not also serving some inner, noble purpose
> in this activity, the war gave us our chance for idealism.[4]

War is the ultimate red herring: its clamors shout down anything
which gets in its way, anything which competes for attention or
resources. It wrenches national agendas and priorities. It splits
reformers themselves. Some intellectuals assume the new role of
justifying the war. The symbiotic relationship between radicals and
liberals turns to anger when the liberals support a war and radicals

demur. Only the galvanic experience of Pearl Harbor, the popular front, and the enormity of the stakes prevented this from happening in World War II. War helped shatter reform and reformist presidential coalitions in both 1917-18 and Vietnam, mortally wounding radicalism in the first case and splitting generations apart in the second. Each time liberals themselves divided and began attacking one another, arguing among other things over which group seemed the more "pragmatic," the more "realistic." World War I began to corrode American reform from the moment it broke out in 1914. After the war, many liberals denounced the conflict they had formerly supported and turned on Wilson for betraying liberalism. In time, Vietnam, too, saw many of its hawks turn into doves.

Anomalous for its very lack of ambiguity, World War II generated a comparatively slight degree of reaction. America's most effective major military endeavor of the twentieth century, it was a war for survival against a European government of unambiguous evil. In the military sense, this cancer operation was totally successful. Yet in its diversion of priorities, it closely resembled 1917-18 and Vietnam. Referring to German fascism, Kemler wrote that "we, in this country, can no longer afford the luxury of improving our institutions."[5]

The striking quality of this remark, of course, is Kemler's perception of reform as a luxury, and one incompatible with war. Coming early in the struggle, his comment foreshadowed an inclination to sell off reform cheap. Just as the Americans, unlike the British, tended to give military strategy priority over diplomatic strategy, their singleness of purpose diverted them from the British experience in planned domestic change.

World War II provides us with a case study of the way in which reform loses its confrontation with Mars. On one hand, the war did stimulate a third Roosevelt term. It afforded a chance to consolidate the New Deal and produced an opportunity for government to redistribute income (the last significant downward redistribution to date).[6] On the other hand, no fresh reform momentum developed. From the moment it broke out and well before the United States entered, the war distracted Roosevelt, causing him to exchange foreign for domestic priorities. It led him to soft-pedal reform in order to build national unity and bipartisan political support on these issues.[7] At a press conference in December 1943, Roosevelt drew the same line which Kemler had drawn earlier, in effect pulling a curtain between the fight at home and the fight abroad: "Dr. New Deal," who had attended the patient since 1933, had turned the case over to "Dr. Win-the-War."[8] "Why," David Brody has asked, did Roosevelt and Harry Hopkins fail to share Eleanor Roosevelt's perception of the connection between war and reform? The nature of the New Deal itself must serve as the starting point. Lacking a comprehensive blueprint for change, lacking even any clear vision of the new society, the New Deal was essentially *reactive* in character; the Great Depression had given it direction and momentum. The outbreak of war in Europe rapidly deprived the New Deal of the crucial stimulus for action. As unemployment shrank during 1940-41 and virtually disappeared by 1943, as farmer purchasing power zoomed by 1943 to almost double the level of 1939, as industrial production rose to record heights by 1943, the urgency vital to Roosevelt's brand of reformism departed. Indeed, the crisis mode of thinking that had shaped the New Deal now worked counter to reform; war posed the great emergency now, and Roosevelt, temperamentally inclined as he was to deal with the immediate and the concrete, would not turn his attention from the war effort.[9]

Unlike Wilson, Roosevelt would not "elevate wartime emotions into a domestic crusade."[10] Public support was inadequate to make it worthwhile. Nor, because of overwhelming national unity, did Roosevelt have to make such reform promises as Wilson had in order to build enthusiasm for the struggle. Why fight a losing political battle now? Reform would continue, but after the war.[11] The New Deal approach had always involved interest-group accommodation; that much, at least, would continue during wartime.

In Congress, by 1943-44 an obstructionist coalition of conservative southern Democrats and conservative northern Republicans had come fully into its own.[12] Roosevelt did not wish to throw himself against them. This was realistic. So, perhaps, was his willingness to trade congressional support for foreign and military proposals in exchange for domestic programs.[13] From 1939 on, the conservatives had cut him off except for questions related to international affairs and war, the southerners and some eastern Republicans breaking away on these matters. In the foreign sphere, Roosevelt could secure bipartisan backing; the congressional onslaught had domestic targets.

At all events, the compromise of domestic policy in the interest of support for foreign and defense priorities had begun even before the United States entered the war.[14] "Aware of the uncertainty of effective support on Capitol Hill," John Morton Blum has written, "Roosevelt accepted" assaults and setbacks on the domestic front

as if by default. He was preoccupied by the war and prepared to subordinate other issues to his quest for victory. Disinclined therefore to engage in causes he considered peripheral, divisive, and probably futile, he ordinarily gave only rhetorical attention to questions of social or economic justice, including those that the progressive minority within his own party were eager to advance.[15]

A split between the Executive and Congress has characterized the later phases of every reform era. In this case, while Roosevelt concentrated on the Axis, Congress skewered the New Deal. With conservative power reasserting itself on the Hill, the conservative Republicans and southern Democrats went after New Deal agencies like lions after Christians, not just in order to consume the New Deal, but to cut presidential power vis-à-vis Congress. Devoured were the WPA, the Civilian Conservation Corps, the National Youth Administration, the Farm Security Administration, and the National Resources Planning Board. In many ways, large and small, Congress undid the work of the 1930s. Presidential resistance was weak. At times Roosevelt even joined the attack. New Dealers (social workers, attorneys, economists) lost their jobs; in came a wave of business executives, to placate and enlist the support of the business community.[16] Without that support, vital in a capitalist system, the United States might lose the war. Like other reform Presidents in wartime, Roosevelt had set his priorities. The war must come first, as big wars inevitably do.

Still, some prospect of reform survived where it could be tied in with prosecution of the war and with the public's postwar aspirations (the G.I. Bill). A war-related drive for social justice could get started in the private sector (the Fair Employment Practices Committee). Reform could put in an appearance without the label (millions of women entering the work force, child care). Between 1939 and 1944 some income-leveling did occur. Despite the collapse of a number of its most famous garrisons, the New Deal was arguably more securely entrenched at war's end than at the beginning. And a measure of direction emerged for the postwar era in such areas as economic rights, housing, health, and education. Yet ultimately, as Robert S. McElvaine writes, "just as World War I had killed the Progressive Era's spirit of sacrifice, the second war stretched beyond their limits the capacities of most Americans for selflessness."[17]

Flushed with victory, the United States came out of World War II supreme, with a strong sense of hope for the future of the planet. But by 1950 the Cold War was on, the Soviets had the Bomb, Mao had taken control of China, and just as after World War I, a mean, divisive, and destructive debate had broken out at home over why things had gone wrong.

Korea had an impact on Harry Truman's flickering Fair Deal similar to World War II and the New Deal.   Once again the President and Congress found their attention diverted by a foreign emergency. The war had already injured reform before the Chinese intervened late in 1950. What sparks remained, Mao doused. Conservatism swelled in Congress. Forced to choose between a good chance of saving his foreign policy coalition and a very poor chance of creating a reform majority, Truman chose as Roosevelt had.   Truman's strategy called for unifying his party behind the war by placating the southern Democrats.   Once more a liberal President found himself depending on southern antagonists for "bipartisan" foreign policy support.   He still backed the Fair Deal, Truman explained to a press conference, but "first things come first, and our defense programs must have top priority."[18] Even Hubert Humphrey and Paul Douglas got behind domestic spending reductions. The reform impulse would remain, as it had with Roosevelt, but, once again, largely reduced in magnitude to hopeful prognostications.   The Cold War numbed reform until the 1960s by shifting attention abroad, keeping the country on a psychic war footing with an emphasis on patriotism and national unity, and diverting funds to the military. In short, the politics of the Cold War muted conflict at home, and sometimes repressed it outright, in favor of conflict abroad.

Having watched war overtake the New Deal, Lyndon Johnson had no interest in seeing priorities similarly skewed against his Great Society. Nevertheless, Vietnam forced an end to the politics of something for everyone. It compelled Johnson to rethink priorities; and his military commitment ultimately dictated what the priorities would be. Vietnam was a far smaller conflict than World War II, of course, and unlike FDR, Johnson persisted for a time in the notion that he could have guns with butter. This meant that the Vietnam involvement had to succeed quickly and that the economy had to remain healthy. When both the war and the economy began to go badly, Johnson's consensus started to fall apart. As the magnitude of the conflict became apparent, just as Johnson had feared, Congress increasingly balked at the Great Society. The resistance proved all the more effective because so much of it came from conservatives who sustained him on Vietnam and thus held a position from which they could demand domestic tradeoffs. Meantime, Johnson's support eroded among the reformer-doves, who delivered incendiary speeches in Congress and participated in demonstrations around the country.

Johnson found the war an immense distraction of attention and time. "At the very moment when new and imaginative thinking was essential," Kearns writes,

Johnson's mind was elsewhere. Many times, Johnson later recalled, he consciously and deliberately decided not to think another thought about Vietnam. Nonetheless, discussions that started on poverty or education invariably ended up on Vietnam. If Johnson was unhappy thinking about Vietnam, he was even less happy not thinking about it. Away from [key advisers], . . . separated from his maps and his targets, he felt anxious. He found himself unwilling, and soon unable, to break loose from what had become an obsession.[19]

The war became the sun in Johnson's universe; domestic policy simply revolved around it.[20] "After the middle of 1965," writes Godfrey Hodgson,

> the Vietnam War meant that resources——tax revenue and the attention of the President and his men——were scarcer for programs aimed at helping the poor and blacks. At the same time, such programs became less popular——with the President, with elected politicians, and with the public.[21]

Eric F. Goldman concluded the tale: "By the Summer and Fall of 1966 the domestic reformer of the Great Society days had become a war chief, finding more and more congeniality with conservatives, even avoiding the phrase 'Great Society' in his speeches."[22]

While Johnson escalated in 1965, he tried to anesthetize the public like a patient entering surgery. It would neither see the knife nor feel the pain. One method was to shun fresh taxation. In not going to Congress for higher taxes for 1966, Johnson snared himself into a forced choice between guns and butter. He chose guns, but along with them, issuing from the decision (or nondecision) on taxes, he got inflation. Although Great Society expenditures did continue to grow, the President engaged in heavy trading between these programs on one hand, and war and inflation on the other. Meanwhile his relations with Congress slid, and when Johnson finally did decide to go after fresh tax revenues, the price exacted on the Hill came right out of the Great Society. The 1966 congressional elections went badly. Johnson's grip on Congress loosened steadily. The administration which prosecuted the Vietnam war had no further claim to make on the fund of idealism which has always accompanied social reform.

If Congress's spoiling role provides a common theme from war to war, so does the return of big business to the halls of government. Of course this overstates the case——business influence never really departs. The resurgence is in relative influence. Here again, the record is unmistakable. Not only does war lead reformers to associate with congressional conservatives; they must also deal with conservative business interests.   Prior to the first and second world wars, the administration in power found itself to some degree at odds with business.   But total wars seem to make industrial size imperative, antitrust subversive, and oligopoly virtuous.   The strain of war turns peacetime standards upside down.   War makes a fetish of first things first——productivity, efficiency, and the application of business techniques to government, together with the recruiting of business personnel to apply them.   In order to prosecute the world wars, a rapprochement between government and business became necessary.   Both stood to expand.   Both stood to gain status.   The money-changers received engraved invitations to return to the temple.   As they returned, they were cleansed, their credibility restored.

This kind of thing requires that a new spirit of unity and accommodation supersede the old stormy atmosphere of disunity.   World War I brought the following comment from the *Saturday Evening Post*: "War, with its demand for a common purpose and a common sacrifice, makes this a good time to discard popular prejudices against Wall Street as merely stupid and demagogic."[23]   Remarked Wilson: "If war comes, we shall have to get the cooperation of the big businessmen and, as a result, they will dominate the nation for 20 years after the war comes to an end."[24]   As the dollar-a-year types return, so does a refreshed emphasis on that great conservative bromide, "national unity."   A spirit of partisanship is crucial to a reform era, though the partisanship may take a more or less muted cast.   Bipartisanship can prove deadly.   Yet bipartisanship comes to appear imperative during a war.   The purchase price for accommodation amounts to the medium of antagonism in which reform usually thrives, and once begun, the process becomes extremely difficult to reverse.

Again we can take the New Deal as a case study.   In its later period, hostility toward business had increasingly provided a New Deal mainstay.   But hesitancy over alarming business is a constant in government, liberal or conservative, and it becomes even more of a concern during a war.   The plans for winning World War II kept the business mind at ease.   Donald Nelson of Sears, Roebuck, chair of the War Production Board, put it this way: "What we did was to establish a set of rules under which the game could be played the way industry said it had to play it."[25]

War gives industry a chance to polish up its tarnished prestige——in this case the tarnish of 1929——because war demands productivity and because business supplies government with management expertise.   Basic rifts of interest and direction must be smoothed over, at least for the duration, much as World War II papered over U.S.-Soviet differences. Demands of the armed forces, both necessary in themselves and specifically conservative in an ideological sense, must be indulged. These demands bear a close relationship to the health, thus the productivity, of the military's big business allies. So, axiomatically: to fight a total war, Roosevelt wanted industry's wholehearted backing, which seemed critical to him; business feared more reform; this fear constrained the President's sense of the wartime reform possibilities.[26]

No wonder big business felt unthreatened by Washington's extraordinary economic power during World War II. Roosevelt, who had recently been denouncing business for "price-rigging, unfair competition . . . and monopolistic practices . . . that flow from undue concentration of economic power," warmed dramatically to big business with the war——a suspension of tone rather than a complete abandonment of purpose, but a suspension nonetheless. The men Roosevelt had attacked as "economic royalists" ("they are unanimous in their hatred for me——and I welcome their hatred") got grudging invitations from the administration to take over critical posts.[27] And within the mobilization process itself, business either sat next to the throne or else sat on it. As in World War I, the World War II mobilization-diplomatic hierarchy read like a Who's Who of American industry, finance, and law: Henry L. Stimson, William Knudsen, Robert P. Patterson, Charles E. Wilson, James Forrestal, John J. McCloy, Harvey Bundy, Robert A. Lovett, Edward Stettinius, Jr., Nelson Rockefeller, William L. Clayton.

Business's alliance with the military culminated in the maturity of the military-industrial complex. The War and Navy departments maintained an especially close affinity for *big* business, which had the bulk of resources quickly at hand. Risk was eliminated. "If you are going to . . . go to war . . . in a capitalist country," Stimson declared, "you have to let business make money out of the process or business won't work." The big companies became the big beneficiaries of federal contracting. In 1940, 100 companies produced 30 percent of the nation's manufacturing output, and some 175,000 companies the remaining 70 percent; by 1943 the ratio had reversed while production doubled. Sentimental attempts to preserve small business in the face of this onslaught proved largely futile.[28]

Meantime, echoing 1917-18, Dr. Win-the-War insisted on suspending Dr. New Deal's vigorous antitrust therapy. War recasts big business as "efficient" and "patriotic," antitrust, the opposite. Once again, the administration chose to wage but "one war at a time," as antitruster Thurman Arnold put it, and Roosevelt "was content to declare a truce in the fight against monopoly. He was to have his foreign war; monopoly was to give him patriotic support——on its own terms."[29] The suspension of prosecutions did not, in the end, become so total as all this suggests, but it still contrasted remarkably with conditions at the close of the New Deal.

Because free enterprise has acquitted itself well in wartime, its reputation has been correspondingly enhanced. Capitalism reconfirms itself through prodigies of production. Corporate size reconfirms itself as well. In World War II, business gained the best of all possible worlds: predominance in mobilization, together with the bulk of the applause for the spurt of wartime productivity and revived prosperity. All this carried on into the Cold War era, with its lavish focus on new technology and productivity.[30] Dear to liberals, the economic growth-expanding pie totem served business interests after World War II in the same way that the drive for war production had earlier. As Galbraith puts it, "the prestige which the businessman derives from production was reinforced by the nearly full weight of American liberal comment."[31]

Meantime, business antagonism toward the New Deal, once so very bitter, yielded to reconciliation as business learned to live with trade unionism and other changes. The accommodation went both ways. Business and government together could glimpse a future built not on confrontation, but on prosperity and consumer spending. Soak-the-rich and regulatory tax schemes gave way to tax incentives. Washington began to be seen as a needed instrument of prosperity. Many business leaders succumbed to Keynes. The adversary style so fundamental to the earlier reform mood and impulse, and specifically liberalism's suspicion of big business, substantially ebbed during the war.[32] Cleavages between left and right melted together, so that while the confrontational school continued to persuade some, the postwar style became considerably softer. Having played so vital a part in defeating Hitlerism and presiding over a revived economy, the dollar-a-year types could even claim to have broken the New Deal's monopoly on idealism, service, and virtue. For better or worse, an age had ended.

What of the workers and farmers while all this went on? As in the case of relations between government and business, for these groups, too, war has had a tendency to smooth over inherent difficulties—poverty, structural unemployment, and so on. This leads us once again back to 1917. For farmers, World War I produced price supports. For workers, besides full employment, the federal labor program brought significant help, including protection by the administrative boards of the rights to organization and collective bargaining. Government boards and trade associations operated "a voluntary cartelization of the American economy on an industry-by-industry basis."[33] In exchange for the right to organize, AFL unions gave up the right to strike. Union membership jumped; hours dropped; working conditions improved; and with government attempting to ensure workers a living wage, real income rose despite spectacular inflation. Following the war this experiment in federal intervention and control was junked, but the precedents remained.

By the time of World War II, the New Deal had already established machinery through which farmers and workers could press their demands, and these groups ignored the wartime potential for reform in part because of this.[34] Through the war, income for both groups jumped. In some ways, big agriculture and big labor came out of the conflict stronger than when it began. During World War I, AFL membership had leaped from some 2 million (1916) to 3.25 million (1920). From 1941 to 1945 total union membership increased once more, from 10.5 million to 14.75 million, again with full employment. Weekly earnings rose ahead of profits, and tax policies working in tandem produced a noteworthy downward redistribution of income, the only such occurrence since 1919.[35]

World War II may not have represented Nirvana for workers, but by contrast with the thirties they had a right to think it did. The Crash had made reform and employment almost synonymous. When jobs appeared with the war this in itself (together with the preexisting New Deal machinery for advancing labor interests) helped to undercut reform, success in effect canceling further success. When John L. Lewis pushed too hard for more, he and his miners intensified an already deepening public hostility toward the labor movement and triggered a reaction in the Smith-Connally Anti-Strike Act.

The power of labor within the government-business-military combine actually sagged over the course of the war, and the New Deal era's tilt toward labor ended. True, most workers' real incomes went up, for some quite remarkably. Overall, earnings in manufacturing saw a 27 percent hike after discounting for inflation. But starting in 1943, there were also rising outbreaks of unauthorized strikes in key industries. On behalf of the government, the CIO got stuck trying to enforce discipline on its balky members.[36] Labor found itself denied any but an exceedingly junior partnership in the councils of war, while "more and more manipulation and threats," as Paul A. C. Koistinen writes, "had to be employed to keep the nation's work force in line."[37]

Yet in general war has tended to reinforce conservatism, not militance, in the American labor movement. Through federal intervention, World War I had provided examples and precedents for countering the structural weakness of labor and agriculture in the economy. These organization-collective bargaining and price support policies became permanent in the New Deal. "The second war experience," David Brody points out, "acted wholly to reinforce the adherence of both agriculture and labor to the existing framework."[38] The attachment of these groups to things as they were increased over the span of years between World War II and Vietnam. With the continuing concentration of farming, agriculture increasingly became agribusiness. For labor, the Vietnam escalation, like other military conflicts, produced jobs in its opening phase. The economic dislocations that led to stagnation came only later. And in May 1970, the nation was treated to the spectacle of hardhats battling hirsute war protesters in the streets of New York.

On the whole, we can say that war bears an ambiguous relationship to reform. It may produce reform directly, or lead to it indirectly. In every case since the Civil War, reformers have seen the conflict's end as the opportunity to renew their reform drive. And each time a reaction has set in which has stifled or twisted the reform impulse. In itself, war may advance reform, but eventually it maims it. World War I undermined confidence in the uses of government for noble goals, casting a pall over the possibilities of positive change and over democracy itself. Both world wars raised doubts about the rationality of the masses. Vietnam curdled reform in similar ways. World War II and the Cold War produced a big, permanent, voracious, and very public interest group in the military. Now the garrison state vies with the welfare state; it is enormously competitive with all other interest groups for resources because of its unique claim and its alliance with the private sector. War stretches the individual's attention and idealism farther than they are accustomed to reaching, to international spheres normally of little concern. No wonder that on the rebound many people's interest springs backward into a narrower-than-normal realm. Idealism simply goes slack.

Our discussion of foreign policy, war, and strained idealism leads us to an examination of yet another phenomenon which, while it can emerge in peacetime, has erupted with particular severity during wars. We will call it the liberal hubris. We will look at it briefly in its peacetime manifestations, then examine it with considerable care in the setting of war.

The Liberal Hubris

When Roosevelt reached the summit of his power, he took on the gods of Olympus and got rolled back, and he never reached those heights again.

Lyndon Johnson on FDR

He had gone a long way, from the dust of the hill country to the loneliest peak of American political power and opportunity. And then, like Roosevelt before him, he . . . reached too far, believed too much, scaled the heights, only——in the blindness of his pride——to stumble and fall.

Tom Wicker on Lyndon Johnson

The liberal hubris[1] combines three tendencies—overestimating one's own strength, overestimating public tolerance for change, and pushing too hard. Not the same sort of hubris as the negative, self-protective variety exhibited by, say, a Richard Nixon, the liberal hubris is a distinct phenomenon. Conservative regimes have not displayed it, at least before Reagan, because their nature and philosophy have more generally been typified by caution.

But liberals and liberal administrations do suffer hubris—not just a willingness to gamble, but something more. For Wilson, there was World War I and Versailles; for FDR, the Court fight; for Johnson, Vietnam. Each time, whether domestic or foreign, the crisis bored into reform like termites into a house. Nor are Presidents the only victims of the liberal hubris. In the 1910s, thirties, and sixties, newly powerful groups mobilized behind change. But some of these groups always experienced their own form of hubris, whether by the mistakes of their leadership or as victims of their own collective impulses. In the thirties and forties, for instance, it was sit-down strikes, in the sixties, black nationalism and radical violence. Each time, public attitudes chilled.[2]

The problem of hubris ties into the problem of selling a political program which, we earlier saw, resembles any other kind of marketing. Overselling[3] always looms as the cardinal temptation. One thinks of such terms as New Freedom or New Frontier. If a reform drive produces a third or half of what its supporters want, it does well. But people are led to anticipate more—to expect everything, a Great Society. They don't get it. What they do get has often become pretty badly watered down. Measures cannot possibly live up to expectations. Old problems persist. Fresh ones emerge. A credibility gap develops. Yet often—often enough to say generally—reforms have had to be oversold in order to sell at all. The overselling, wholly aside from the inherent merits of any reform in itself, leads almost inevitably to disappointment and disillusionment. A classic example of the phenomenon comes from the woman movement. Woman suffrage had enormously inflated expectations surrounding it, visions of a panacea.

This kind of overselling occurred so commonly in the Progressive Era that time and again people found they had bought products which—however well they worked—did not function as well as reformers had led them to expect. Neither the Clayton Act nor the Federal Trade Commission Act, for example, met what the general thrust of the New Freedom had implied, a genuine resolution of the trust problem; nor did the Federal Reserve Act exactly bring down the Money Power. Along with tending to claim that their reforms and proposals for reform would carry further than they actually did, neither Theodore Roosevelt nor Woodrow Wilson provided a clear definition of where, exactly, reform ought to stop.

We have good reason to suspect that just as many progressives eventually recoiled from the New Deal in the thirties, many had earlier begun to recoil from the big government and social justice sides of Wilsonism by 1916-17. Wilson's apparent personal reluctance to do some of the things he ultimately wound up doing mattered little in terms of what the public actually saw.   Taft, for example, thought he saw an administration which had begun surrendering to organized labor.[4]

However severe the disappointments produced by overselling may become in peacetime, they appear mild when compared to the aftereffects of overselling a war.   One of the first places we should lay the blame for this is on the promises made by leaders and the expectations they have raised.   Not one of our twentieth century wars—not World War I, Vietnam, even World War II—could possibly fulfill the expectations it created. Wars elevate goals to extremes, often ultimately generating a sense of revulsion against the very ideas and ends for which the wars are fought.   This leaves a mark of defeat even in victory. The preeminent example of the phenomenon in this century is World War I. It makes a useful case study.

Woodrow Wilson tied domestic reform to a foreign crusade whose results were difficult for people to perceive as enhancing their personal interests. Wilson led the nation into this particularly vile struggle and then attempted to turn the conflict into a theological event. Ultimately he asked Americans to reform the entire planet, to bring progressive democracy to the world. It was simply too much.

True enough, it would have been difficult in 1917 to galvanize a reluctant public behind the opaque cause of neutral rights and international law. Rather than focusing on the realistic concerns behind intervention, Wilson, like other war leaders, had to transform the nature of the conflict in order to make the sacrifices seem worth more than the actual reasons for which the nation went to war.   Ultimately Wilson interlocked the war with progressivism in such a way that total war became the climax of reform. As a strategy of mass mobilization, this made sense. As Richard Hofstadter observed, our involvement in the struggle "put an end to the Progressive movement. And yet the wartime frenzy of idealism and self-sacrifice marked the apotheosis as well as the liquidation of the Progressive spirit."[5]

So the struggle became a war to break militarism, uplift Europe, make the world safe for liberalism and democracy, a war to end all wars leading to a peace among equals and without victory. The Committee on Public Information labeled the conflict "a Crusade not merely to re-win the tomb of Christ, but to bring back to earth the rule of right, the peace, goodwill to men and gentleness he taught."[6] Good Lord! *Of course* disillusionment and cynicism set in afterward. The goals and ideals had run not only beyond immediate reality, but beyond any possibility of reality. Young men were asked to make the supreme sacrifice for aims so elevated that they could not outlive the war. Had these men died in a lost cause, then military defeat could have explained away the failed ideals. Ironically, the disillusionment materialized because the Allies won. No millennium appeared. A feeling of betrayal set in, of having gotten gulled; a feeling that the lives and treasure had been spent for nothing.

Wilson's crusade continued in his battle for the League of Nations. Peace negotiations, as Hofstadter pointed out, even "repeated with ironic variations the themes of American domestic Progressivism": the unselfish innocent against the interests, the reformer against the bosses, "the spokesman of the small man, the voiceless and unrepresented masses, flinging his well-meaning program for the reform of the world into the teeth of a tradition of calculating diplomacy and an ageless history of division and cynicism and strife."[7] "Talking to Wilson is something like talking to Jesus Christ!" grumbled Clemenceau.[8] "God gave us his Ten Commandments, and we broke them. Wilson gave us his Fourteen Points—we shall see."[9] Compromise Wilson dismissed as "dishonorable."[10] His failure to bring a liberal, humane peace represented progressivism's greatest, most bitter, most obvious defeat.

American idealism would not, could not, reach far enough, especially in the unfamiliar direction of Europe and an unregenerate planet. War liberals wanted the conflict to yield a perfect result.[11] Their expectations had no prospect whatever of fulfillment. Overused, overstrained, progressivism sheared apart piece by piece—the sense of responsibility for others, idealism and the rhetoric of idealism, muckraking, morality, altruism—they flew off in all directions. By pushing the progressive zeal for self-sacrifice to its utter peak in war, Wilsonian rhetoric vented off the moral and guilt-driven imperatives that had moved progressivism to begin with, and vented them, of all places, abroad. Ironically, the progressive conscience found its most fervent realization, its final expiation, squandered in the bloody trenches of Western Europe.[12]

Guilt remained after the war, but not of a sort which would serve reform. Instead, this sense of guilt grew out of remorse for our having entered the conflict at all. The public's disenchanted isolationism welled. Many liberals pinned the demise of their hopes on sham and betrayal, with Wilson the biggest culprit. In time, liberals learned to blame themselves—their own illusions, overoptimism, and inflated aims. "Undoubtedly," Stuart I. Rochester has written, "the liberals' most grievous error was their gross overestimation of the human character." Ultimately, "not Wilson, but humanity had failed them. This was the heavy revelation that completed their reckoning and crowned their disillusionment."[13] Wilson and Wilsonism had turned into a standing threat, or, seen another way, a caricature of the progressive impulse. He had placed enormous personal prestige on the line, together with the prestige of his office and the credibility of his presidency, and he had failed.   Wilson became transformed into a sort of leper-priest, contaminated along with his ideals yet still insisting on his holiness. It was a tragedy for the man and the nation.

If the Wilson episode provides the leading instance of the twentieth century liberal hubris, this is simply because it represents the only case of outright presidential messianism. Plenty of other examples of hubris exist, with similar consequences.

The liberal hubris returned after a fashion with FDR. Normally a master politician, his temporary loss of touch appeared most disastrously in the Court fight. The courts had always provided twentieth century reformers with one of their choice targets. The provocation to attack the Supreme Court certainly existed now——Roosevelt passed his initial term without a single Court appointment, making him the first President since Monroe with such poor luck; and the Court began undoing the New Deal. But, as onetime New Dealer Raymond Moley complained, the packing plan which the administration developed represented FDR at his worst:

> There was the snatching at a half-baked scheme which commended itself chiefly because of its disingenuousness. There was the essential carelessness of its preparation. There was the arbitrary secrecy before its launching. There was the indifference to the fact that it was an unjustifiable means to an end.   There was the conviction that he epitomized the progressive will, that his New Deal represented the Ultima Thule of progressive reform.   There was the assurance of unquestioned mastery.   There was the incredibly stubborn refusal to yield when he still might have escaped absolute defeat.   There was the ruthless way in which he lashed supporters, . . . insisting that they serve him beyond their power to serve with conviction or effectiveness.   Finally, in defeat, there were the supreme confidence that "the people are with me" and the bitter determination to exterminate politically all who had committed the treason of disagreement.[14]

Too harsh, perhaps; yet most of Moley's description of Roosevelt's presidential hubris would also apply to Wilson or to Lyndon Johnson. With five appointments in his second term, Roosevelt finally got his new

Court. His power had become so thoroughly diminished, though, that he generated few fresh measures to send to the Hill.

In 1938 Roosevelt attempted a congressional purge. In this country the word "purge" signals weakness, not strength, and is a virtual synonym for political failure. Conservatives would actually end up gaining seats. The purge was followed by failing attempts at administrative reform, which split liberals and led to charges of dictatorship.

Fortunately, World War II produced a thinner atmosphere for disillusionment than World War I had. Roosevelt was not the evangelist Wilson had tried to be. In a particularly hard-bitten decade, the New Deal prided itself on its "realism." Hitler and Mussolini were evil men. Japan's attack on Pearl Harbor made the causes of war exquisitely tangible to the mass public. A tough-minded reform administration grounded heavily on the selfish interests of millions of people could stand up better to a tough-minded war.

But the liberalism of the 1960s produced yet another variety of hubris, a complete assurance, even to the point of complacency, that liberals could solve the nation's along with many of the world's problems.[15] This came to ashes in Vietnam. It may be that the efficient prosecution of a war, at least a war involving Americans, requires great goals. Sometimes, as in 1941-45, wars absolutely have to be won; the goals take shape easily. The very totality of total war implies the potential totality of utter defeat. Deep, demonstrable evil in one's enemy makes a drastic contrast with the seemingly selfless sanctity of one's own war aims.

But none of these considerations applied convincingly to Vietnam. As in World War I, a President (or Presidents) tried to whip a skeptical public into supporting a foreign conflict. This time, the steed turned balkier and balkier while the war was being fought. Johnson's hubris reached a truly magnificent scale: he committed over half a million men to an undeclared war on another continent, attempted to hide the depth of his overseas entanglement from members of his own administration as well as from Congress and the public, and tried to keep his domestic programs flourishing despite the war. In contrast with the inflated expectations of the Wilson era, which envisioned a transformation of world affairs, Johnson's war goals merely aimed at preserving the status quo in Indochina. Yet, here again, the costs of the conflict summoned justifications which to all appearances at the time became increasingly unbelievable: the war was not merely fought to sustain an alliance system or conserve U.S. credibility, but to prevent dominoes from falling in rows (Cambodia? Thailand? India? Japan?).

From 1964 to 1968, as Vietnam poisoned life at home, Johnson's rating of popular support plunged thirty-six points. A nation may want a war leader when it finds itself at war; but Johnson could hardly pose as a leader like Wilson or Roosevelt, because this conflict was small compared to theirs, undeclared, and (on the American side) far from total. Johnson supplied only a half-war. Unlike Wilson, the failed Messiah, Johnson was a failed technician. His image became that of a scheming wheeler-dealer. A nation in domestic crisis will hunt for a leader who can bring resolution and consensus, but Johnson and his policies had become an inextricable part of the crisis itself. So Johnson became a target. Like Wilson and Roosevelt, he paid a monstrous price in credibility and leverage.

Each of these administrations had passed through an early period favored by a paucity of disasters. The disasters arrived later, but when they did arrive, they were big, led to an outburst of recriminations,[16] and devastated reform. The crises came during second terms, in FDR's and Johnson's case after landslide reelections of the sort which can easily mislead an incumbent. Nothing threatens a Chief Executive's sense of proportion more surely than a new mandate. The parallel between Johnson and Wilson is especially compelling. Twice in this century, high-flying rhetoric, plus impossibly elevated expectations, plus the failure of those expectations, plus the ensuing reaction and disgust in the public mind, have proved utterly lethal to reform.

Afterword: The Cold War

Foreign policy matters, as we have seen, diminish or fog disputes at home. In light of that, we can now also see that the Russian Revolution has proved a longstanding disaster for American reform, distracting it, often profoundly, since 1917. The United States has fought brutal wars with Germany, Japan, and other countries, but over time Russia has proved the greatest source of foreign grief for domestic reformers. Only when the Soviet issue has been more or less set aside, along with other foreign distractions, have we witnessed bursts of reform. The very fact that the nature of American foreign policy since the forties (and to a considerable degree before) has been predominantly anticommunist —which is to say, "conservative" in the world context—may have spilled into the overall pattern of U.S. domestic politics, tinging it, too, in more conservative hues. To what degree has America's conservative role abroad, even its counterrevolutionary rhetoric, stunted liberalism and radicalism at home? At certain times, we can say, considerably. Especially since World War II, it has proved a quite persistent virus.

In earlier chapters we observed how American reform has tested boundaries, often probing just how far change might go. In domestic policy, utopianism had pretty much been worked out of the picture by 1900, but it affected foreign policy far longer, indeed as late as World

War II. Then Cold War liberalism, in many respects a sort of dour anti-utopianism, descended. A very early indicator of just how distracting *that* would become was Henry Wallace's splinter candidacy of 1948, which took issue with the Truman Administration quite specifically over foreign affairs. The Democrats concluded from McCarthyism that they must never again expose their foreign policy to charges of "softness on Communism."

Always rather inchoate, liberal foreign policy inclinations became partly homogenized into the Cold War consensus and bipartisan policymaking ethic of the 1950s. Debates with conservatives went on, but over style and tactics, not grand designs. The liberal disdain for pinched nationalism—manifested in liberal support for the UN, for example—aroused enough wrath from the far right that the depth of genuine consensus in these years often got obscured. We can partly explain the absence of a domestic focus during the fifties by the fact that the society was mobilized for war. The threat seemed so clear that the "home front" unified against it. Foreign affairs came first, with domestic issues falling well behind. In other words, a situation prevailed which was in important ways analogous to the world wars. As Clinton Rossiter put it, "a nation that considers itself a success and finds itself under attack has little use for progressive reform and none at all for radical ferment."[1] The Cold War, like hot wars, seemed to put a premium on liberals' and conservatives' willingness to work together with some measure of harmony.

For two postwar reform Presidents, Truman and Kennedy, both cold warriors, foreign affairs had a clear priority over domestic from the moment they took office. The militance of Kennedy's Inaugural Address—an eloquent speech on foreign policy—has often attracted comment. In Kennedy's first State of the Union Address, he dismissed domestic issues by saying that "all these problems pale when placed beside those which confront us around the world."[2] No remarks could better illustrate the distracting role which foreign policy has played since World War II. At home, things blurred: especially at first, the President did not appear to know which questions required his attention, or in what sequence, or how to come to grips with them.[3] He tended to proceed dispassionately from adjustment to adjustment. Kennedy liberalism ("technocratic liberalism")[4] assimilated much of its antiseptic, bloodless nature from the Cold War, reflected particularly in demands for fresh military technology and hardware. "He's imprisoned by Berlin," one of his cabinet members observed in 1961.[5] Liberal anticommunism and the linkup between liberalism and the Cold War escape hatch reached an apogee with Vietnam, "the liberals' war."[6] Liberal ideals—parliamentary democracy and land reform in South Vietnam—intertwined oddly with free-fire zones and napalm.

Meanwhile, the country had gone through its first postwar aperture of domestic policy preeminence between 1962 or 1963 and the Vietnam imbroglio. Ironically, an artifact of the Cold War, Sputnik, even helped to stir the beginnings of the sense of policy activism which would characterize the mid-sixties, by making the self-centered complacency of the prior decade seem a threat to national security.[7] Yet the very fact that this small window was so important symbolized the desperation of reform in the Cold War era. The next such window would come with Reagan, and would look out on a very different scene indeed.

NOTES

The Foreign Policy Escape Hatch

Frederick W. Marks III, *Velvet on Iron: The Diplomacy of Theodore Roosevelt* (Lincoln: University of Nebraska Press, 1979), p. 133 (Roosevelt quote).

[1]*Age of Reform*, p. 270.

[2]Link, *Wilson and the Progressive Era*, p. 243; Goldman, *Tragedy*, p. 411.

[3]Goldman, *Tragedy*, p. 411.

[4]Louis Filler, *Vanguards and Followers: Youth in the American Tradition* (Chicago: Nelson-Hall, 1978), p. 173.

[5]Cooper, *The Warrior and the Priest*, p. 221.

[6]Gable, *Bull Moose Years*, pp. 240-41.

[7]*The Autobiography of William Allen White* (New York: Macmillan Co., 1946), p. 513.

[8]Goldman, *Tragedy*, pp. 25, 378-79.

[9]Kearns, *Lyndon Johnson*, p. 251.

[10]Ibid., pp. 251-53, 259-60.

[11]Hamby, *Liberalism and Its Challengers*, p. 345.

[12]"The Two Presidencies," in *The Presidency*, ed. Aaron Wildavsky (Boston: Little, Brown & Co., 1969), p. 231.

[13]Kennedy and Johnson, for instance, knew they could immediately drive up their Gallups ten points by taking a strict public stand against "Communist aggression." And a President can generate popular appeal the fastest by succeeding at a military escapade abroad. Hodgson, *America in Our Time*, p. 46.

[14]In "What Is a Liberal—Who Is a Conservative? A Symposium," *Commentary*, September 1976, p. 113.

[15]Leuchtenburg, *Shadow of FDR*, p. 110.

War

C. Vann Woodward, *Tom Watson: Agrarian Rebel* (New York: Macmillan Co., 1938), p. 334 (Watson quote); Ray Stannard Baker, *American Chronicle: The Autobiography of Ray Stannard Baker* (New York: Charles Scribner's Sons, 1945), p. 301 (Wilson quote). "War means autocracy," Wilson added. "The people we have unhorsed will inevitably come into the control of the country, for we shall be dependent upon the steel, oil and financial magnates. They will run the nation."

[1]Keller, *Affairs of State*, p. 17.

[2]Wilson's declaration did not materialize as fact. See especially Seward W. Livermore, *Politics Is Adjourned: Woodrow Wilson and the War Congress, 1916-1918* (Middletown, Conn.: Wesleyan University Press, 1966).

[3]*Deflation*, pp. 168, 171.

[4]*Liberalism in America: Its Origin, Its Temporary Collapse, Its Future* (New York: Boni & Liveright, 1919), p. 62.

[5]*Deflation*, p. 30.

[6]Lasch, "Liberalism in Retreat," pp. 105-6.

[7]Richard N. Chapman, *Contours of Public Policy, 1939-1945*, Modern American History series (New York: Garland Publishing, 1981), pp. 60-61.

[8]Richard Polenberg, *War and Society: The United States, 1941-1945*, Critical Periods of History series (Philadelphia: J. B. Lippincott Co., 1972), p. 73.

[9]"The New Deal and World War II," in Braeman, *New Deal*, 1:271.

[10]Ibid.

[11]Blum, *V Was for Victory*, p. 13; Chapman, *Contours of Public Policy*, p. 270.

[12]Chapman, *Contours of Public Policy*, p. 54.

[13]But on this matter of a tradeoff, see also McElvaine, *Great Depression*, p. 310.

[14]Brody, "The New Deal and World War II," pp. 273-75.

[15]*V Was for Victory*, p. 222.

[16]Chapman, *Contours of Public Policy*, p. 268.

[17]*Great Depression*, p. 322.

[18]Hamby, *Beyond the New Deal*, p. 442.

[19]*Lyndon Johnson*, p. 299.

[20]Goldman, *Tragedy*, p. 498.

[21]*America in Our Time*, p. 272.

[22]*Tragedy*, p. 499.

[23]Greene, *America's Heroes*, p. 299.

[24]Goldman, *Rendezvous* (1958), pp. 247-48; Arno J. Mayer, *Political Origins of the New Diplomacy, 1917-1918* (New Haven: Yale University Press, 1959; reprint, New York: Howard Fertig, 1969), p. 12.

[25]Brody, "The New Deal and World War II," p. 289.

[26]On these latter points, see ibid., p. 272.

[27]Blum, *V Was for Victory*, pp. 117-19.

[28]Ibid., pp. 122-25, 130.

[29]Ibid., pp. 134-35.

[30]Mary Sperling McAuliffe, *Crisis on the Left: Cold War Politics and American Liberals, 1947-1954* (Amherst: University of Massachusetts Press, 1978), p. 2; Wiebe, *Businessmen and Reform*, p. 223.

[31]*Affluent Society*, p. 138.

[32]Blum, *V Was for Victory*, p. 327.

[33]McQuaid, "Corporate Liberalism," p. 344.

[34]Brody, "The New Deal and World War II," p. 278.

[35]On this latter point, see Blum, *V Was for Victory*, p. 141.

[36]Nelson Lichtenstein, *Labor's War at Home: The CIO in World War II* (Cambridge, England: Cambridge University Press, 1982), pp. 83, 109, 111, 113, 201. See also Paul A. C. Koistinen, *The Hammer and the Sword*, American Military Experience series (New York: Arno Press, 1979).

[37]*Military-Industrial Complex*, p. 89 and ch. 4, passim; Harold G. Vatter, *The U.S. Economy in World War II*, Columbia Studies in Business, Government, and Society (New York: Columbia University Press, 1985), p. 149.

[38]"The New Deal and World War II," p. 281.

The Liberal Hubris

Leuchtenburg, *Shadow of FDR*, pp. 148, 150 (Johnson, Wicker quotes).

[1]Others have used the term "hubris" to describe presidential behavior, but not, to my knowledge, in the distinct sense intended in this chapter. Kevin Phillips has come close, though, by quite accurately portraying the risk of hubris during second presidential terms of whatever ideological hue. See "A History of Hubris Living at the White House," *Los Angeles Times*, 14 December 1986. The Iran-Contra mess suggests that activist administrations in general are hubris-prone. Unlike Reagan's, such administrations have typically been liberal ones. I would not object to a broader term than liberal hubris. Perhaps "activist hubris" would do. In light of Reagan's claims of ignorance concerning his own foreign policy imbroglio, it should be added that the liberal hubris has originated in knowing behavior.

²Newly empowered groups, I am persuaded, will likely go overboard regardless of their ideological predispositions. Conservative fundamentalists, for instance, beautifully exemplified the phenomenon during the 1980s.

³The idea of overselling has been set forth by a number of scholars in various political contexts, though not, so far as I am aware, quite so sweepingly with respect to domestic affairs as I have developed it here.

⁴See pp. 53, 123-24.

⁵*Age of Reform*, p. 273. See also Barry D. Karl, *The Uneasy State: The United States from 1915 to 1945* (Chicago: University of Chicago Press, 1983), p. 47.

⁶Leuchtenburg, *Perils of Prosperity*, p. 46.

⁷*Age of Reform*, pp. 276, 278.

⁸Thomas A. Bailey, *A Diplomatic History of the American People*, 7th ed. (New York: Appleton-Century-Crofts, 1964), p. 608.

⁹William Allen White, *Woodrow Wilson: The Man, His Times, and His Task* (Boston: Houghton Mifflin Co., 1924), p. 384.

¹⁰Gene Smith, *When the Cheering Stopped: The Last Years of Woodrow Wilson* (New York: William Morrow & Co., 1964), p. 120.

¹¹Stuart I. Rochester contends that

> because liberals——both young and old——construed the war in the context of social reconstruction or spiritual conversion rather than primarily as a military encounter, the measure of success and satisfaction during the war was social and spiritual progress rather than the conventional yardstick of military victories. Thus it was possible that as the war progressed quite satisfactorily on the battlefield, liberals could express deepening disappointment at the failures at home and in the Allied councils. No matter how well the war went militarily, if the crusade for a liberal peace and a new world order foundered, then their efforts were for naught——and, by their own exacting standards, actually criminal.

American Liberal Disillusionment in the Wake of World War I (University Park: Pennsylvania State University Press, 1977), pp. 52-53. See also pp. 39ff.; and Kennedy, *Over Here*, p. 246.

¹²McElvaine, *Great Depression*, pp. 10, 12.

¹³*American Liberal Disillusionment*, pp. 90-97.

¹⁴*After Seven Years*, pp. 362-63.

[15]See Hodgson, *America in Our Time*, pp. 75, 162, 463.
[16]Among which one might well include the debate over Yalta.

Afterword: The Cold War

[1]*Conservatism in America: The Thankless Persuasion*, 2d ed., rev. (New York: Random House, Vintage Books, 1962), p. 163.
[2]Miroff, *Pragmatic Illusions*, pp. 42-43.
[3]Graham, *Planned Society*, pp. 127-29.
[4]Burner, *Torch Is Passed*, p. 10.
[5]Ibid., pp. 159, 189.
[6]Stephen E. Ambrose, *Rise to Globalism: American Foreign Policy, 1938-1980*, Pelican History of the United States, vol. 8, 2d ed., rev. (New York: Penguin Books, 1980), p. 277. Just as the perpetual demand for weaponry in hot wars like Vietnam and throughout the Cold War has elevated the role of the state, the perpetual frustrations of U.S. foreign policy since World War II, despite its tactical successes, have no doubt put a perennial drag on public confidence in government. Nothing, not even public unease over the Korean War, did so as much as Vietnam.
[7]See Matusow, *Unraveling of America*, pp. 8-9.

12

THE WELFARE STATE
AS POLICE STATE

The actions taken during World War I affecting civil liberties
were unprecedented. For the first time a national policy of
deliberate and massive mind control was adopted.

Paul L. Murphy

The war . . . changed an abiding faith in the state into
questionings of it.

Frederic C. Howe on World War I

. . . that bloodless Moloch, the State.

Harold Stearns after World War I

Modern total war has had a dual impact on the American civilian
population. The demands it puts on the economy pleasantly affect the
immediate economic fortunes of business, workers, and farmers. On the
other hand, total war places an absolutely tremendous emphasis on one
hundred percent Americanism and blind conformity. It encourages such
impulses as antiforeignism and extreme anticommunism to seep to the
surface. In wartime, the number of life's nuisances multiplies. War
brings with it bureaucracy and more bureaucracy, controls and more
controls, taxes and more taxes, demands upon demands for sacrifice,
patience, centralization,[1] planning, and the immersion of self. War may
be perceived—and may be portrayed by hostile politicians—as
epitomizing the same aggravating regimentation generated by the mildly
collectivizing peacetime reform waves which have preceded it. Yet in a

society such as our own, organized for the narrow pursuit of self-interest, government will be goaded toward extremes in trying to mobilize millions of people behind a cohesive mass effort. And the severe collectivization of modern total war virtually guarantees an individualistic reaction afterward.[2]

Sorokin summarized the response of societies to major crises this way:

> When a given organized group faces a grave emergency menacing its existence or its basic values, the governmental control over it tends to become more rigid and severe and tends to expand to embrace many social relationships of its members hitherto free from such control. As the emergency passes and conditions become more nearly normal, the governmental controls tend to relax.[3]

In this century wartime regimentation has taken many forms: planned shortages, rationing, price and wage controls, higher taxes for some and taxes for the first time for others, and intricate schemes of regulation and allocation. World War I set the pattern. For the first time, Washington took broad-scale charge of the economy. The War Industries Board coordinated production, and government agencies directed all the other important segments of the economy. There was a Railroad Administration, a National War Labor Board, a Fuel Administration, an Emergency Fleet Corporation, a War Trade Board, and a Selective Service Act. The war brought death to over 100,000 Americans. It brought an end to conditions valued by millions, among them isolation and peace itself. It threatened and accelerated the decay of yet other values by stimulating cosmopolitanism——"how you gonna keep 'em down on the farm, after they've seen Paree?"——and by undermining decentralization, voluntarism, and competition. Despite prewar preparations, some of these changes came so abruptly and so completely that it seemed as though Wilson had ripped the blankets off a sleeping child. However much they want to win their wars, Americans naturally resent the price they pay. They resent mobilization, controls, and pervasive planning. And they resent promotion taken to its epitome: buy, buy, buy war bonds; save, save, save food.

If regimentation simply stopped with buying and saving, it would already have had a corrosive impact on reform. But war also imposes a fierce order of conformity on attitudes and speech. Most dangerously, it offers a chance to "get" people who are unpopular in peacetime: Socialists, the IWW, Japanese Americans, radical college students. A good deal of domestic violence has accompanied our twentieth century wars. Even in peace and especially in war, civil liberties has not been a very popular cause in America.[4] Regimented conformity has run roughly an inverse relationship to the degree of public unity behind each war. It reached its most extreme level in World War I, which most people probably opposed our entering. Henry F. May has observed that

> the earliest and most consistent supporters of the Allies were the beleaguered defenders of nineteenth-century tradition, and particularly the professional custodians of culture. Conversely, those who were doubtful about the sanctity of the Allied cause were often those who had been involved, before the war, in some kind of intellectual revolt.[5]

As a result of the war, David M. Kennedy has written,

> many reformers would be destroyed. Some would be driven further left. The majority, who with fear and trembling decided to take their stand with Wilson, began almost immediately to feel the withering effect of war on the liberal spirit.[6]

With some notable exceptions, and unlike their European counterparts, by an enormous majority American Socialists opposed the war before America went in. Their opposition continued after U.S. entry. They left themselves cruelly exposed to charges of anti-patriotism, not just from conservatives but from progressives and even bolting Socialists. Together with Wobblies, other radicals, and conscientious objectors, the antiwar Socialists became particular targets for prowar zealots and government suppression. To the delight of private interests outside of government which had fought the left before the war, now, in one more assumption of responsibility, the federal government determined to do it for them. Ironically, fatefully, the administration mounted a domestic war against radicalism. In cannibalizing one another, reformers and radicals displayed a perfectly ravenous appetite. Suppressed and attacked by the administration during the war, the radical and progressive left and the pacifists, who might have backed Wilson even during the conflict and certainly afterward, got muzzled. The bleak civil liberties record of the Wilson Administration and of the President personally helped sow disillusionment among progressives toward both the war and Wilson.[7] Amos Pinchot bitterly remarked of the President, "he puts his enemies in office and his friends in jail."[8] Meanwhile, the right, still free to speak and to dissent from Wilsonism at home and abroad, set off the postwar stampede toward reaction. In 1919 the administration came out with a plan for the universal peacetime conscription of young American males.[9] Meantime opponents of the war remained behind lock and key, Debs among them. A campaign for a general amnesty failed. American socialism has never recovered from the domestic consequences of World War I and the Russian Revolution.

U.S. entry into the war in April 1917 had followed right after Wilson's peace campaign of the previous November; many among the public at large had had no clear grasp of U.S. war aims. Irish Americans understandably had no love for a war fought in alliance with England. German-American antagonism requires no explaining. In light of this, the motives for the excesses of the Creel Committee, the espionage and sedition legislation of 1917 and 1918, and private vigilantism become at least intelligible. The furor could not have dissipated during the short period of U.S. involvement in the war. It spilled over into peacetime. Racial tensions mounted, for instance, and in the last six months of 1919, race riots erupted in about twenty U.S. cities; 120 people lost their lives. The war and the peace, the hue and cry for immigration restriction, and drives for "Americanizing" the "hyphenates" heated up ethnic tensions generally.[10] Many Americans clearly appear to have been unwilling to relinquish the psychological rewards which war had brought: identity with the nation state, security, national unity in place of the disunity reflected in and aggravated by reform, relief from domestic complexities so long fought over, and a foreign target for lingering reform impulses.[11]

Stanley Coben has suggested that millions of Americans may stand in a state of permanent readiness for the kind of purge brought on by World War I. The country had experienced a great wrenching by the war and the urbanization and industrialization which had preceded it. Patterned with old values and shielding out the future, the hysteria resembled a curtain which people pulled in front of their eyes.[12] Following the Armistice, bolshevism and domestic aliens simply replaced Germany as the antagonists. Attacking this proposed reform or that as pro-Soviet could kill it. More generally, the enemies at home remained the same after the war as they had been before and during it: the "un-American" people who fell outside the center or the center-right or the Victorian consensus on political propriety, interclass relationships, sexual and moral standards, religion, ethnicity, and race; the radical and intellectual and urban cynics and naysayers. The great sociocultural split of the 1920s, in significant (though by no means exclusive) measure, grew out of the hysteria and one hundred percent Americanism of the war.[13]

Some progressives had hoped for fresh reform gains from World War I. Their hopes did not go completely unrewarded. With policies they had advocated for years being adopted as war measures, for instance, social workers found themselves summoned to administer new governmental social programs. The war seemed a great unifier behind inspiring causes both at home and abroad. Yet among reformers, a new caution set in about the place of government in American life and about assertive political leadership generally. Progressives had commonly viewed government all along with hesitation, and now, it seemed, even less of a consensus existed over the state than before.[14]

The association between the welfare state and the police state did not end with World War I, nor the checkered relationship between liberals and civil liberties. During the New Deal, CCC camps were built to house young men out of work. During World War II, Japanese-American internees found themselves stuffed into some of these same camps.[15] Apart from the tragic incarceration of the Japanese Americans, repression during World War II came nowhere near the severity of World War I. In a high-unity war, it did not need to. The real reaction came afterward, through McCarthyism, a subject of discussion for another chapter.[16]

A far closer welfare state-warfare state-police state conjunction emerged out of Vietnam. The public had no clear grasp of war aims. Escalation followed on the heels of Johnson's peace campaign of 1964. As with World War I, or for that matter World War II, so again liberal rhetoric was projected onto a foreign war, tying domestic reform in with a conflict which many Americans considered utterly mad. Though mobilization did not begin to approach the totality of the world wars, the conflict produced a major intrusion into the lives of ordinary Americans in its demands for national sacrifice and patience, and later in its indirect offshoot, the Nixon system of economic controls. Government promotionalism returned, with all of Johnson's gross hucksterism and Nixon's pseudo-pieties. The conspiracy theory now was the domino theory, linked to quickly outmoding ideas of a planetary Communist plot. This time war did not bring as compensations the cherished unity of 1941-45; this time the nation split wide open. Since the government did not impose censorship, administration propagandists had to contest TV with the dissenters. The FBI and CIA infiltrated and subverted the New Left as if carrying out covert operations in some hostile foreign country. The CIA titled one of its enterprises Operation Chaos.[17] Police cracked skulls across the country. Intolerance mounted to the point of the slaughter at Kent State, and Nixon, of all people, being asked in the 1968 campaign to "bring us together again."[18] Families split. Universities split. Generations split, the defenders of the old Cold War realism testing their definition of truth against the new avatars of antiwar. Droves of dissenters fled the country. Reformers and radicals cannibalized one another.

War kills young men, and if the war seems unnecessary or unjust or is lost, this becomes unforgivable. Vietnam was the biggest single vial of poison poured into the nation's bloodstream in this century. The doubts about leadership and morality which ate up American politics in the late sixties and seventies grew right out of it. Television brought this particularly horrible conflict right into the American living room in vivid color. In comparison to the two world wars, each heavily filtered both by censorship and by propaganda, Vietnam, a relatively limited conflict, *seemed* huge because of the fantastic media coverage it received. Not only was the war vile. It also involved a draft which selected some (notably the poor) but not others (notably college students). The guilt over not getting taken compounded the guilt over national complicity in an "immoral" war. But going to Vietnam meant possible death for nothing. The war elevated the police state image to a kind of apogee. Along with everything else, Vietnam featured the appearance of authority trying to thwart new moral styles, especially drug use, which functioned, however inadequately, as protest vehicles against and as escapes from the war. More than any other one factor, the Vietnam conflict alienated the young. And on top of all the rest, the United States proceeded to lose it.

NOTES

Paul L. Murphy, *World War I and the Origin of Civil Liberties in the United States* (New York: W. W. Norton & Co., 1979), p. 248; Frederic C. Howe, *The Confessions of a Reformer* (New York: Charles Scribner's Sons, 1925; reprint, Chicago: Quadrangle Paperbacks, 1967), pp. 279, 282, 317; Stearns, *Liberalism in America*, p. 4.

[1]Though this and the other qualities I mention can easily be overstated. Regarding centralization in World War II, for instance, see Philip J. Funigiello, *The Challenge to Urban Liberalism: Federal-City Relations During World War II*, Twentieth-Century America Series (Knoxville: University of Tennessee Press, 1978), p. 250.

[2]On this point, see Borden, *Speculations*, p. 108.

[3]*Society, Culture, and Personality*, p. 466. Italics deleted.

[4]See Wooley, "Conservative America," pp. 309ff.

[5]*End of American Innocence*, p. 363.

[6]*Over Here*, p. 36.

[7]See ibid., pp. 87-89; Cooper, *The Warrior and the Priest*, p. 262; Murphy, *Origin of Civil Liberties*, pp. 249, 269-70; and on the Socialists, James Weinstein, *The Decline of Socialism in America, 1912-1925* (New York: Random House, Vintage Books, 1969), ch. 3 and passim.

[8]Stearns, *Liberalism in America*, p. 128.

[9]Ekirch, *Decline*, p. 224.

[10]Ellis W. Hawley, *The Great War and the Search for a Modern Order: A History of the American People and Their Institutions, 1917-1933* (New York: St. Martin's Press, 1979), p. 50.

[11]Burl Noggle, *Into the Twenties: The United States from Armistice to Normalcy* (Urbana: University of Illinois Press, 1974), p. 100;

Leuchtenburg, *Perils of Prosperity*, pp. 45-46.

[12]"A Study in Nativism: The American Red Scare of 1919-20," *Political Science Quarterly* 79 (March 1964): 52-75.

[13]See Hawley, *Great War*, pp. 52, 71.

[14]LeRoy Ashby, *The Spearless Leader: Senator Borah and the Progressive Movement in the 1920's* (Urbana: University of Illinois Press, 1972), pp. 12-13.

[15]Michi Weglyn, *Years of Infamy: The Untold Story of America's Concentration Camps* (New York: William Morrow & Co., 1976), pp. 125-26, 150-51.

[16]See especially pp. 379-80, 384-85.

[17]Chafe, *Unfinished Journey*, pp. 412-13.

[18]Leuchtenburg, *Troubled Feast*, p. 211. Original capitalized.

13

FORTUNES OF WAR

I tell you, it's damned discouraging trying to be a reformer in the wealthiest land in the world.

Fiorello La Guardia

WAR IS PEACE.

George Orwell, *1984*

In America, ironically, war has often undercut reform by generating prosperity. The two world wars created a rosy economic glow against which, despite postwar dislocations, reform paled for years afterward. I would not argue that prosperity in and of itself dulls reform. Reform may *emerge* in an optimistic economic atmosphere. Yet the economic expansions that have *followed* wars have helped to destroy reform in at least two fundamental ways——by redirecting reformist groups and individuals toward pursuing their narrow self-interest, and by creating the general sense that GNP growth per se will generate the results which reform has failed to produce.

In order to understand all this, we must examine more closely the connection between broad economic patterns and reform itself. Reform movements emerge from crises, whether depressions or not, which invariably include an economic dimension. A depression compels attention to economic issues and to fundamental questions of concrete material interest. "In periods of general social dislocation," Arthur M. Schlesinger wrote of depressions, "injustices long endured become intolerable."[1] While a reform movement may develop in better times, it will not likely have quite the same issue discipline as in bleak ones, and may involve a panoply of matters which——given the bigger perspective——have relatively little significance.

In general, political issues which have not centered on economic and class relationships have worked to conservative advantage. Many such issues exist, of course, including ones as fundamental as the image of the candidates themselves. But some types of noneconomic questions are especially significant, among them Protestant, middle-class moral concerns, corruption, civil liberties, foreign policy, and national defense. "To the extent, therefore, that the conservative parties can make elections revolve around noneconomic issues," Lipset writes, "they can reduce the pressure for reform and increase their chances of electoral victory."[2]

By dulling the cutting edge of the economic issues, prosperity, too, in and of itself damages reform. In examining why, we will begin with four propositions.

1. Any unfavorable swing in the national economy——depression, inflation, whatever——will intensify the confrontation between social classes and interest groups.

2. Any significant change in the economic fortunes of important groups, or of the nation as a whole, in which major economic interests become threatened or compromised, will produce a potentially fertile environment for reform.

3. Outright depression may prove particularly stimulating. Any severe economic slowdown——the thirties, even the 1970s and early 1980s——generates battles over who should get what.

4. Depression forces people to concentrate even more than they ordinarily would on their own economic well-being——in other words, it makes them financially self-centered. This self-centeredness will lead to demands on the state.

A highly stable prosperity does not necessarily preclude reform. It may throw the condition of the downtrodden into relief and stimulate demands from above and below that conditions change. In the 1960s, it helped free students to rebel and underlay the widespread early optimism that reform would alter things for the better. The Great Society depended on prosperity. And prosperity will undergird the credibility of any administration, including liberal ones, to whatever degree the government can take credit for it. To the extent that prosperity yields higher employment and bigger paychecks, it furthers the social ends of reform by other means and with far less dissension than a reform movement typically creates.

Overall in this country, though, prosperity has tended to chill public receptivity to change. Quick economic growth may induce people to turn toward private concerns and the main chance.[3] And prosperity produces the widespread delusion that everybody is doing all right, or else soon will. Prosperity typically masks poverty, making it less visible; and good times make it easy to write off poverty as something prosperity itself will end in any case. In prosperous years the working class, having become better off, loses the charm it had possessed as a deprived group. By endorsing reliance on the private sector to smooth out any surviving inequities in distribution, prosperity becomes a surrogate for reform. Now people want to open all the doors to personal consumption.

The classic twentieth century example of how all this works comes from the 1920s. Following World War I, U.S. productive capacity soared. Coolidge prosperity was honeycombed with rot, but for the moment the economy promised cash in everyone's wallet or purse, the elimination of poverty, and an end to class antagonism. The twenties was the birth-decade of the consumer society of perpetual abundance, with living standards perennially on the rise. So it seemed then, anyway.

The very existence of such an environment generates overstatements about its supposed beneficence. From accounts of the decade one might easily conclude that everyone was actively speculating in securities (in 1929 fewer than a million were).[4] For workers, true enough, things did improve: real income rose and hours dropped. Yet on the eve of the Depression, over 40 percent of the American population fell below the poverty line.[5]

To say that prosperity alone explains the conservative resurgence of the twenties would place far too much weight upon prosperity. Progressivism had also coincided with a generally healthy economy. But unquestionably prosperity did mix with other factors to undercut the progressive movement. "During the last four years," wrote Walter Lippmann in 1927,

> the actual prosperity of the people, combined with the greater enlightenment of the industrial leaders, has removed from politics all serious economic causes of agitation. There has been no pressing reason for an alignment of 'haves' and of 'have nots.'
>
> . . . .
>
> . . . from about 1922 on almost everybody has had the feeling that he had a lot of money in his pocket, and would soon have

more. It was this feeling which robbed progressive idealism of
its urgency, and made it appear abstract and unimportant.

Lippmann entitled his essay "The Causes of Political Indifference Today."[6]

    For the moment, business upstaged government. The business
person, the organization man, replaced the politician as America's
lionized type.[7] "The more or less unconscious and unplanned activities
of business men," wrote Lippmann, "are for once more novel, more
daring, and in a sense more revolutionary, than the theories of the
progressives."[8] Lincoln Steffens slipped out of character and proved an
awful seer when he wrote: "Big business in America is producing what
the Socialists held up as their goal; food, shelter and clothing for all.
You will see it during the Hoover administration."[9] If enlightened
business leadership could point the country toward the promised land,
then election of a man like Coolidge ("the business of America is
business") made perfectly good sense.

    Something else is involved here, rather intangible but deserving
close attention. Bursts of prosperity always unleash material, along with
psychological, hedonism.[10] In the 1920s and since, the public's surging
consumption and its approval of the status quo have run hand in hand.

    Not only did business during the twenties provide Americans with
new ways to buy, like the installment plan, and new places to do it, like
chain stores. The economy poured forth new or nearly new products in
astonishing abundance. Bread and circuses in this decade meant
automobiles, movies, radios, phones, electric refrigerators, vacuum
cleaners, and washing machines. After World War II it all happened
again, with bigger, flashier cars, television sets, garbage disposals,
dishwashers, and the rest. New products have appeared continually
throughout the century, but one thinks of the twenties and the
forties/fifties——the postwar eras——for their peculiar fecundity in technical
wizardry. The very appearance of these products stimulated materialism
because people wanted to own them. The innovations produced
enormous new distractions of time: one listened to radio, went to the
movies, watched television. One shopped for everything one could
afford, and then some; one shopped for the sake of shopping. And the
new products did uplift what we conventionally think of as the standard
of living. Things could be had, done, and used which had never been
available before. In time the pace of profusion would generate its own
ironic "crisis." What next? The garbage disposal could get invented only
once; what could engineers come up with for an encore?

    Despite interruptions by the Depression and World War II, the
materializing of American life had already gone a long way by the 1950s.
To a considerable degree, in the fifties the environment of causes was

co-opted again by the environment of things. Instead of the widely predicted postwar depression, a boom occurred. Real wages jumped; unemployment stayed down. Between 1947 and 1973, the real median income of American families practically doubled.[11] And of course people wanted to spend. During the first forty-five years of the century, a full-blown consumer economy had existed only for a scant decade, in the twenties, but that decade had exposed the possibilities. The country had passed through a depression into a war in which demand built up behind controls like water behind a dam. Before the conflict ended, industry had already begun tantalizing potential consumers with the new goods and gadgets which would flow with reconversion. When the economy did not go under at the end of the war, consumers and business wanted government to get out of the way. Opportunity beckoned. Skilled workers and white-collar people (there were more and more of them) moved to Levittown, bought cars and dishwashers, and developed an even deeper stake in consumer capitalism, the affluent society, and the status quo. Since high living standards meant the widespread ownership of houses, cars, and TV sets, regardless of the fact that incomes widely varied, disparities in wealth were significantly camouflaged. Class boundaries, and class hostilities, faded—and with them much of the New Deal basis for partisanship. It seemed that economic equality, or at least real economic equity, had arrived or else would.

Post-World War II prosperity, then, trimmed the welfare state's momentum. It rendered the hazards of economic insecurity less a collective, shared, societal experience than during the Depression, and more a matter of individual misfortune.[12] One could even see all this happening well before the war ended. Writing of the 1942 elections, which produced a Republican surge, Hadley Cantril observed that substantial "numbers of the poor who for a decade had seen a very direct connection between a Democratic victory and their daily lives were now making enough money to feel temporarily secure and to indulge in political indifference."[13] Groups came to compete with one another, divide, then compete again, over who would get what share of continuing government-distributed largesse. And because steady economic growth made the dispensation of gains relatively painless to government, the kind of political mobilization characteristic of thirties welfare statism diminished. Ideology could, hence, "end." With the welfare state established, indeed, the end of ideology made a certain sense—unless one assumed that not just tinkering but a great deal more building needed to be done. And this had to be demonstrated. The fiscal dividend, the ease of it all, meant that debate, and the pro-welfare state political muscle behind it, relaxed, lost tone. Benefits got shuffled out piecemeal,

in response to groups' demands for "fairness" and "justice."[14] Meanwhile,
prosperity underwrote a decade or so of national self-congratulations.

Along with the prosperity factor, we must look for a moment specifically at prices. Any significant shift in the price cycle will likely have
some impact on reform. The downward-trending prices of the period
after the Civil War helped bring on agrarian unrest. Prosperity returned
at the end of the nineties, reaching a good many in the grieving rural
regions. Prices rose. If, after the disaster of 1896, Populism needed a
coup de grace, inflation (which farmers had lobbied so hard for) fired the
finishing shot. This upward push after 1897 fanned progressive reform.
The whole Progressive Era was a period of rising prices; in the decade
and a half after 1897, the cost of living went up 40 percent.[15] The
inflation of the time must have seemed especially shocking because the
nation had previously experienced several decades of declining price
levels. By 1919 the cost of living had rocketed 77 percent over the 1914
mark, and in 1920 it reached 102 percent.[16]

During the Progressive Era, the thirties, and again in the 1960s,
consumer unrest welled up. Each period saw the emergence of a politics
oriented in part toward consumer issues. Usually, inflation has had a
role in loosing consumerism. Inflation in the 1970s spurred suspicion of
corporations and a good deal of outright hostility toward them; likewise,
during the progressive period it helped to generate the antitrust surge.
Finally, to the extent that it encourages free spending, inflation
undermines economic and social (as distinct from political)
conservatism.[17]

But in the long run, inflation typically deadens reform, and during
this century heavy inflation has always paralleled reform's demise.
Postwar demobilizations have been consistently accompanied by inflation
and by confused economic policies engineered from Washington. Each
tests not just the immediate competence but also the fundamental image
of government and the governing party. Once prices start moving up,
certain groups begin losing ground, at least relative to others. Inflation
sets classes against one another in a struggle over governmental budgets.
In trying to make inflation the country's number one priority,
conservatives emphasize its damaging impact on the middle class.
Inflation preempts the primacy of other issues. It can simply dominate
the public's priorities, shouldering others aside. It can increase support
for reactionary cuts in social programs, shifting the emphasis of politics
from high employment and social progress to price restraint. It "justifies"
cutting back these programs by making them appear unaffordable.
Inflation in the sixties and seventies, for example, threw damaging doubts
on a good many of the economic underpinnings of recent American
liberalism, including its Keynesian base and its penchant for business
regulation and social welfare spending. During this century, every time

the GOP has taken the presidency away from the Democrats, a war-linked inflation has been running (1920, 1952, 1968, and less directly, even 1980 with the economic aftereffects of Vietnam).

Americans have worried about inflation at whatever level it existed, from 1 percent to the astronomical heights of the seventies. Inflation and declining productivity have served, much as war does, to give business a rationale for gloves-off capitalism, tax benefits, and deregulation. Inflation can contribute to unemployment, which may conceivably give reform a slight push; yet inflation faces people with a choice inimical to traditional liberal goals. They can have inflation, or they can have unemployment. They cannot have both, and a majority will likely lean toward unemployment.[18] Finally, the "liberal wars" always leave a legacy of higher, and sometimes remarkably higher, taxes, reinforcing conservative mutterings about tax-and-spend, tax-and-spend. Cutting wartime tax burdens, then, becomes a key political priority. As John Kenneth Galbraith has put it:

> With inflation the costs of government go up and so do taxes. When taxes, property taxes in particular, are relatively stable, they are much less noticed. When they are going up, they are greatly visible and much resented. This resentment is then transmuted into an attack on all public services. And the inability to control inflation conveys a further impression, not unjustified, of government inadequacy or incompetence.[19]

Abundance generated by prosperity has provided a glue which has bound together the seemingly contradictory American ideals of individualism and equality. The very old concept of the expanding economy has meant that no one's success need come at the cost of someone else. Ultimate outcomes get played down, except for the success stories. "Prosperity," as William Schneider has written, "undermines the moral justification for a redistributive policy." With a healthy economy, the society as a whole seems healthy; so the fault for failure rests with the person who is failing. Aid to the losers takes on the attributes of charity. Redistribution becomes difficult if not impossible. How can we morally justify redistribution if the system as a whole is working?[20] Business derives a great deal of its prestige from the high standard of living which, for many, capitalism has produced. Prosperity puts a fresh shine on its prestige. Meanwhile, in such decades as the 1920s and the 1980s, prosperity serves neatly to mask the upward redistribution of income.

NOTES

Arthur Mann, *La Guardia: A Fighter Against His Times, 1882-1933*
(Philadelphia: J. B. Lippincott Co., 1959), p. 285 (La Guardia quote);
George Orwell, *1984* (New York: New American Library, Signet, 1949),
p. 7.

[1]*American as Reformer*, p. 19. Yet a short-term downward business
cycle may help kill off a reform drive.

[2]*Political Man*, pp. 264, 299-300, 318.

[3]See Hirschman, *Shifting Involvements*, p. 15.

[4]John Kenneth Galbraith, *The Great Crash: 1929* (Boston:
Houghton Mifflin Co., 1961), pp. 82-83.

[5]Maurice Leven, Harold G. Moulton, and Clark Warburton,
America's Capacity to Consume (Washington, D.C.:   Brookings
Institution, 1934), p. 87.

[6]*Men of Destiny*, pp. 24-25.

[7]See, for example, Greene, *America's Heroes*, pp. 232, 287.

[8]*Men of Destiny*, p. 26.

[9]Leuchtenburg, *Perils of Prosperity*, p. 202.

[10]See Clecak, *Ideal Self*, p. 111.

[11]Ladd, *Transformations*, p. xix.

[12]Hugh Heclo, "Toward a New Welfare State?" in *The Development
of Welfare States in Europe and America*, ed. Peter Flora and Arnold J.
Heidenheimer (New Brunswick, N.J.: Transaction Books, 1981), pp. 395-
96.

[13]Chapman, *Contours of Public Policy*, p. 198.

[14]Heclo, "New Welfare State," pp. 396-98.

[15]Abrams, *Burdens of Progress*, p. 59.

[16]Robert H. Ferrell, *Woodrow Wilson and World War I, 1917-1921*,
New American Nation Series (New York: Harper & Row, 1985), p. 193.

[17]On this last point, see David S. Broder's perceptive "Inflation:
The Bone in Our Political Throat," *Los Angeles Times*, 25 October 1978.
As an example of the relationship between inflation and progressivism,
see David Graham Phillips, *The Treason of the Senate* (1906; reprint,
Chicago: Quadrangle Books, 1964), p. 91.

[18]See Schlozman, *Injury to Insult*, p. 345.

[19]"The Conservative Onslaught," *New York Review of Books*, 22
January 1981, p. 34. On the general tendency of prosperity to slow the
drive for federal social welfare programs, see Berkowitz, *Creating the
Welfare State*, p. 118.

[20]The quotation and the basic perspectives which follow come from
William Schneider, "What the Democrats Must Do," *New Republic*, 11
March 1985, p. 17. See also Domhoff, *The Powers that Be*, especially p.
8.

14

MOODS CHANGE

From 1968 on, public interest in the national political drama was beginning to wane. By the middle of the 1970s, it was fading as fast as a tropical sunset. People were yearly more and more interested in social, as opposed to political, questions, and in personal and private, as opposed to public and political, solutions.

Godfrey Hodgson

For a reform era to emerge in this society, whether in prosperous or in bleak times, the public as a whole must more or less welcome change. Yet there comes a point when every fad dies, and so it is with reform. As we have seen, reform is only partly attributable to the ebb and flow of fashion, but to this degree, it responds to the cyclic nature of style. If a conservative phase lasts too long, people weary of it; if a liberal one, they tire of *it*. They grow sick of moralists, moralism, and moralizing. Perfectionism slips out of style, supplanted by pessimism. Selfishness returns to fashion, competitiveness to favor. Reformers begin to look foolish, or dangerous; their sermonizing sounds silly, or threatening; they become subjects of derision, or denunciation. In this materialistic society——a society which remains materialistic whatever the state of its economy or its public mood——making a reformer look "square" and reform appear foolish always becomes easy toward the end of a reform phase. As fads change, reformers start to suffer the embarrassed self-doubt of the out-of-date.

After World War I, for instance, the progressive coalitions dispersed. Some people went right, others left——becoming conservatives or radicals. Some differed little from their prewar selves and carried on as before.

Some disappeared into private existences in Europe or their own backyards. Some soured; some didn't. "The more courageous liberals have begun to align themselves with the parties which draw their strength from the labouring class," wrote William Bullitt in 1920, "while the less courageous are lapsing into an impotent faction scarcely distinguishable from the conservatives."[1]

"No one," William Allen White complained as progressivism collapsed, "pays attention to us anymore."[2] A number of progressives assimilated this new reality rather slowly. In 1920, with Warren Harding calling for a return to normalcy, the ailing Woodrow Wilson reacted incredulously when Navy Secretary Josephus Daniels suggested that Democratic candidate James M. Cox stood no chance of getting elected. "Do you mean it is possible that the American people would elect Harding?" Wilson responded. "It is not only possible," Daniels replied, "but they are going to do it." "Daniels," Wilson shot back, "you haven't enough faith in the people!" "You need not worry," Wilson told his cabinet. "The American people will not turn Cox down and elect Harding. A great moral issue is involved. The people can and will see it."[3]

They didn't. That same day Harding scored one of the greatest landslides of the century, burying Cox 16 million to 9 million. As Burl Noggle has put it, the Republicans in convention had "haggled for days between a jingoist general and a competent governor and finally chose a senator of marginal distinction. No one else of notable record, charisma, or talent offered his services to the nation in 1920 except Eugene V. Debs, and he was in the Atlanta penitentiary."[4] Not a Democrat alive, progressive or otherwise, could have beaten Warren Harding in 1920. "What a God-damned world this is!" White exclaimed that December. "If anyone had told me ten years ago that our country would be what it is today . . . I should have questioned his reason."[5]

The classic problem for reform is staying power, a problem which Tammany ward boss George Washington Plunkitt immortalized when he remarked of urban reform movements, "they were mornin' glories —looked lovely in the mornin' and withered up in a short time, while the regular machines went on flourishin' forever, like fine old oaks."[6] In time a quavering note of uncertainty always resonates among reformers. Assuredness fades off into disorientation and disillusionment. Thermidor arrives.

These things do not all take place at once, nor in an identical sequence every time. Events often mask their emergence. Each reform era, for example, has left an afterbirth campaign which has taken aspects of the earlier movement to an epitome. Such was the La Follette campaign of 1924, the Wallace crusade of 1948, or the McGovern and even the successful Carter races of 1972 and 1976. In their own way, however, such campaigns are additional symptoms of demise.

Nor do individual movements often completely die out. Neither political radicalism nor feminism, for example, has ever been totally extinguished in this century. Such movements often adopt more constrained alternative strategies to tide them over until a better day returns.[7]

Meanwhile, though, reformers whose willpower does endure pass through the political wilderness. Often they come upon it unexpectedly, as public moods change.

When a conservative trend begins running, the values of practically everyone will shift right to some degree at least—even the values of many who do not consciously want to grow more conservative. A sense of helplessness or indifference replaces a sense of responsibility. A tendency exists, I think, to anticipate future public behavior and adjust one's own to it. Even the lifestyles of opinion leaders and trendsetters provide clues to the future. One who wants to emulate them steers his or her behavior in that direction. Marriage is out, everyone is swinging; so, despite the fact that I am pretty uncertain about swinging, I'm going to swing. This also works in the negative: everyone is swinging, swinging is a mortal sin, hence fundamentalists must wage a holy war for marriage. Either way, social and political debate stretches well past reality, coming indeed to parody reality. Liberals wind up espousing capitalism with only a little less exuberance than conservatives.

Much of this derives from subtle changes in the national mood during the later stages of reform: anxiety over inflation; grumbling over wartime rationing and shortages, taxes, bureaucracy, and the sense of "they're-doing-it-to-me"; the failure of one's circumstances, however comfortable, to catch up with one's aspirations, which always run ahead. People turn chilly toward change, toward beneficence. They become harder. As Irving Howe has written:

> By its very nature the welfare state cannot long maintain an equilibrium. It is always subject to serious inner conflicts. It becomes vulnerable to the attacks of newly enfranchised or empowered groups, as well as the counterattacks of traditional ruling elites which turn against it as soon as they have been brought to new confidence by its ministrations.[8]

Lyndon Johnson's unity approach, for example, sagged when the Great Society—originally grounded on a projected federal revenue surplus—revealed itself as redistributive: fewer jobs for whites, more for blacks; more welfare for the poor, less income for the nonpoor;[9] and more outlays for defense industries.

Too, as the reformer defines it, reality often has an inherent unpleasantness. Hallowed institutions are rotting. The country is ill. Times are grim. People can tolerate this sort of reality for only so long.

A common tendency exists to forget or repress how bad things recently were. This began to happen even before the Depression had passed. "Our present gains," FDR declared in 1937,

> were won under the pressure of more than ordinary circumstance. Advance became imperative under the goad of fear and suffering. The times were on the side of progress.
>
> To hold to progress today, however, is more difficult. Dulled conscience, irresponsibility, and ruthless self-interest already reappear. Such symptoms of prosperity may become portents of disaster! Prosperity already tests the persistence of our progressive purpose.[10]

Then came the war, which, as James T. Patterson has put it, "provided a heaven-sent opportunity for Americans to soften the class divisions that had sharpened in the Depression years."[11]

As conditions improve, people congratulate themselves on their current success just as they had blamed themselves for their earlier poverty. In all periods, it seems, government aid, whether the federally funded highway, the state-supported university, the mortgage assistance, or the public service job, easily gets forgotten or taken for granted or ignored. Then the question asked of Washington, or Albany, or Sacramento, becomes. "What have you done for me lately?" Or, "How have you picked my pocket lately?" Or, "I may have needed the CCC in the thirties, but that was different. Why should I pay out my hard-earned tax money now so that ghetto kids can go to work for the government? Today, it's different." (Or, "they" are different.)

Together with the return to individualism and materialism, postreform phases reflect what Arthur M. Schlesinger called a "moral slump" or "moral letdown."[12] As commentators have often noted, this appears in particular to be an aftereffect of war. We can adduce a variety of reasons for the slump. For one thing, a wartime boom suddenly multiplies the opportunities for sin. Psychologists have, for instance, documented a strong connection between violence and sex. Aspects of war are exceedingly erotic: perhaps no other mass human activity besides sex itself contains so many Freudian metaphors (guns, soaring aircraft, missiles, even the very premise of war itself, conquest and submission). The sensually charged wartime atmosphere is laden with erotic opportunities, which of themselves help to undercut conventional sexual norms. The soldier in Paris no longer falls under the watchful eye of Mrs. Grundy peeking from behind her lace curtains.

Emotions release themselves in wartime which can be hard to contain after hostilities have ceased. The violent passions aroused by World War I poured into succeeding years like adrenalin into a bloodstream. One ironic legacy of the antiwar movement of the sixties and seventies was the killer Weathermen. Socially sanctioned total violence has a liberating impact from the more civilized, mundane behavior of normal times.

A final observation on morality has to do with demography. Apart from raw numbers, we know remarkably little about the impact of war on populations. The paucity of scholarly research is ironic in this century of total war. But speculation suggests at least the following. Ample reason exists to suspect that modern warfare kills disproportionate numbers of young men with high self-esteem and high motivation. An ancient cliché attests to the truth that the good die first. The effect may not be so extreme as to support, say, the old supposition that the slaughter of the elites and the middle classes from 1914 to 1918 produced a leadership vacuum in Europe between the world wars. But did, for example, the deaths of more than 20,000 young Englishmen in one day on the Somme have no impact whatever on postwar Britain?

The significance of all this for the United States in the twentieth century remains open to debate. Compared to other nations, America has experienced relatively "light" losses. But the Civil War generated staggering losses, roughly as many as in all our twentieth century wars combined. Among a total population of around 32 million, some 600,000 died of all causes. This extraordinary fact raises extraordinary questions. Did it leave a genetic legacy? (As a consequence of the war, a huge cohort of children was not born.) What was the impact on feminine roles and feminism as a result of the shortfall in married or marriageable young males? What was the impact on the broader attitude and behavior structures of the late nineteenth century? (Can we attribute a part of the legendary atmosphere of political misbehavior after the Civil War, the boodling and cynicism, to wartime deaths?)

Whatever the case, war leads to a moral slump. So do other factors. Americans tend to be both distrustful of the existing order and idealistic. The two moods continually coexist, but they undulate in relative importance. Most people can pursue high ideals only so long. Like war, reform may and likely will interfere with their ordinary routines. The agitating reformer at length becomes a nuisance.[13] Together with materialism and moral change, the end of reform witnesses a decline in idealism. Though a reform movement can scarcely proceed without it, this magic commodity has a way of curdling. It might be far better if we could change things realistically and incrementally from year to year, with a minimum of gush, but in this country that appears to be impossible.

The decline may not set in at once; at first a lingering halo of idealism may remain. Aspirations for a better world and for progress at home received wide expression after World War I. It took months for the disillusionment and reaction to set in. As Burl Noggle has emphasized:

> A common mood at war's end was that of hope, of eagerness, over the future. Not war but the war's aftermath produced the weariness and apathy associated with normalcy. Warren G. Harding's presidency and the Twenties of legend were, in considerable measure, products of reconstruction, coming into view in 1921 but not in 1918.[14]

Yet by 1918 the charges had already been laid and lit. On the defensive intellectually and in the face of new onslaughts over such matters as race and sex, most of the cultural establishment had meshed its value system with the Allied cause. When the explosion came, timber and plaster got stripped away, the foundation cracked, and many of the certainties of the Victorian order collapsed. Nineteenth century Americans had perceived history as progress; this comfortable assumption halfway caved in. An awareness of human wickedness and a feel for the irrational replaced the confidence in human dignity and decency which had been shot away in the trenches. The expectations of a coming age of Christian brotherhood, an element deeply rooted in the social gospel, became vastly less tenable. Much of the previous levity disappeared, along with hope and the sense of the basic morality of life. The idealism of the Victorian age rested in rubble. Seven decades later, most of the rubble remains. The war spelled, as Henry F. May has put it, "the end."

> This was the end of American innocence. Innocence, the absence of guilt and doubt and the complexity that goes with them, had been the common characteristic of the older culture and its custodians, of most of the progressives, most of the relativists and social scientists, and of the young leaders of the prewar Rebellion.[15]

Idealism in demise often produces its opposite. In the sixties, the idealism of the King phase of the civil rights movement gave way to the anti-idealism of ghetto riots. The anti-Vietnam movement left behind it the sybaritic "me" generation. Evidence that the public mood had changed by the seventies abounded. In comedy, for instance, the iconoclastic style of Lenny Bruce, Mort Sahl, and Dick Gregory had yielded to the antics of Steve Martin, a well-groomed WASP from Orange County by way of Disneyland, given to wearing bunny ears and spitting water on the floor. Martin reminded his older fans of the unthreatening fifties humor of Red Skelton and Jerry Lewis. "Steve is exactly right for the current atmosphere," remarked another comedian. "We are burned out on relevance and anger. He offers a special form of escape and there is no hostility in his act."[16] Once flared off, idealism can leave behind a crusty residue of cynicism. The *National Lampoon*, which at the outset of the seventies had satirized the Establishment, by the end of the decade was going after blacks, women, and homosexuals. The magazine, writes Arthur Lubow,

> was built on the fault line that separates the hip from the straight. It was unstable ground. In the early years of the 1970s, the hip people were left-wing, countercultural and pop. The straights were conservative, pompous and boorish. But as the decade wore on, the politics shifted and the sides reshuffled. The hip people became those clever enough to make a bundle of money and spend it on the right clothes, the right food, the right drugs and the right discos. The straights were everybody else.[17]

Priorities change. Working our way up the Maslow hierarchy, we eventually run out of creature needs. We enter the realm of desires. These desires can prove far more difficult to meet. The whole picture takes on a generational aspect: the Depression generation did a pretty good job of meeting its creature demands after the war, but that generation produced a new one whose desires, often inchoate and vaguely articulated, ran beyond the political or any other possibilities. Once the economy started to sag under the weight of stagflation and productivity losses, though, the old creature demands returned in force. The society worked its way back down the hierarchy. From desires it returned to needs.

In June 1978, the people of California employed the initiative process—a vestige from 1911 of the progressives' faith in the popular intelligence—to pass (two to one) a crude measure appropriately numbered Proposition 13. Thirteen was designed to slash burdensome property taxes by more than half. Lowering taxes became one very popular way of combatting inflation and governmental inefficiency, even though no consensus existed for drastically chopping back the welfare state. It was a conservative approach, to be sure, but the governor and legislature had fallen behind on the issue, the state had a huge surplus, and liberals offered less convincing alternatives.[18]

Though the tax revolt of the late seventies had a brief and limited life, Proposition 13 revealed what can happen to reform when public attitudes take certain vectors. The deadliest combination of all may be a situation in which people are relatively well off, but feel mistrustful of "politicians" and anxious about inflation, high taxes, and a stagnant standard of living. While the left has pushed to expand the role (and costs) of government, the right has had great success in institutionalizing a trickle-down tax system which operates in the interests of business. The distributed benefits of taxation, including its loopholes, so the story goes, will seep down to everyone, including the poor. The end result has had the middle class paying taxes to the hilt. By caving in to pressure to slash taxes inequitably rather than making them fairer, California's liberal politicians educated people, as politicians should do—but educated them in reverse, to accept the sort of distortions which Proposition 13 guaranteed.

By 1978 the country had moved a long way from 1968. The anger of the Vietnam era drained like an abscess. As Mary McGrory had put it earlier, "hating has gone out of style."[19] The mass majority, Joseph Kraft pointed out, had become greedy, "the most discomforting feature of the present time."[20] Having made enduring changes in society, the minority movements of the sixties declined. The student movement had earlier dissipated its energies across a gamut of causes; now students became depoliticized, and, in the face of the recessions of the seventies, returned to their previous interests in grades and money. Women did rather well in the job market, but feminists less well with the outcome of the battle over the Equal Rights Amendment. Economic concerns, along with Watergate, had supplanted the cultural and social issues of 1964-72.[21] Reactionary "populist" eruptions broke out. Looking back over the past decade, Kraft observed in 1978 that

> the tactics devised to foster minority aspirations are now being used by the majority to protect its taste for easy living. The violence has gone out of national politics, but so has the idealism. We are left with the sour realization that when minorities go on a spree, they inevitably license the appetites of the majority.[22]

Overall, people showed a deep ambivalence toward government. They had become fed up with much that had happened. Yet despite the loss of faith, polls in the late seventies disclosed that most people wanted to spend more public monies on such things as education, medical care, the environment, and on the unemployed and elderly, though not on blacks or on welfare programs. Once again, self-interest prevailed. People desired education or medical care for themselves at the same time that they wanted lower taxes and less interference in their lives by Washington. "What looks like a trend toward conservatism," speculated *Newsweek*, "might actually be a matter of selective social consciousness

——the view that the government has given too much welfare to the minority poor, not enough to the middle class caught in an unaccustomed economic squeeze."23

Like the perseverance of reformers, the concern or outrage of the public at large which fuels reform ultimately runs low. Everything which discourages the reformers also discourages their mass following. Sooner or later, a cry for normalcy will arise. The eras of reaction which ensue seem to combine a rather predictable chemistry of disillusionment, cynicism, unfocused discontent, and sour nihilism. Partly as a result of changing fashions, new reformers fail to materialize, and many old ones fall away. Others go halfway, or all the way, toward joining their former antagonists.

The American reform tradition has carried within it many assets which also function as liabilities. One of these, often commented upon, has been guilt. Progressivism, for instance, in many respects represented a wringing-out of conscience, self-blame, and collective guilt. The problem with guilt serving as a motive force in reform, I believe, is that once the sin becomes expiated, the motive force plays out. And expiation may have as much to do with personal witnessing, too-simple answers, or mere symbolic behavior as it has with any truly effective form of action.

When a reform fad comes on it allows atonement to occur in an environment of mass enthusiasm. But when the fad ends the cleansing is, or more likely *seems*, accomplished. This actually may bear only a slight relationship to what really needs doing. I do not mean to imply that guilt necessarily serves as a weak inducement, but I would suggest that one can rather painlessly work it off. In the case of poverty, for example, perhaps the fewer poor Americans exist, the more intolerable poverty comes to seem; but a war on poverty can burn away the guilt which more favored individuals *feel* toward poverty without ever solving the problem. Poverty gets symbolically witnessed against, not eradicated. Furthermore, personal sensations of guilt, once they burn off, may leave their respondents relieved but listless. It feels good to have the responsibility off one's shoulders——and good to be able to forget it. The way guilt is managed offers us a key to much of the shallowness of progressivism, for instance, and also to the emphatic nature of its demise. The disintegrative stage of a social or political movement yields such confessional autobiographies and other writings as Frederic C. Howe's *The Confessions of a Reformer* (1925) or Jerry Rubin's *Growing (Up) at Thirty-Seven* (1976). Occasionally these become so contrite that they belong to a genre which we might label guilt chic.

Burned-out reformers may turn to a variety of interests and pursuits, from narrowly intellectual activities to religions of various sorts. This turning to the inner world or the otherworld implies either that problems once considered solvable no longer seem so; or that their solving is not worth the cost; or that salvation lies not in society but in personal thought, experience, or revelation.   When the great reform bubble burst in 1896, for example, the crisis of the nineties dispersed or dispatched its reformers in interesting and generally permanent ways. The process ran what would become a familiar gamut in the new century. People dramatically constricted their perspectives, pursuing various forms of escapism (inner pondering, spiritualism), simply selling out, following experiments in cooperative communities, or chasing red herrings, especially foreign policy red herrings and the Spanish-American War.

One sign of a reform breakup specifically involves a resurgence of religion.   Every reaction phase——the twenties, the fifties, the seventies——has witnessed a reaffirmation of conventional religiosity. Between 1940 and 1955, for instance, the proportion of Americans who were church members jumped from under 50 percent to 60 percent.[24] Original sin was big in certain conservative circles.   An upsurge of outspoken religiosity may also take the form of the Elmer Gantryism which followed World War I, or the often-vulgar born-again Christianity of the 1980s.   Just as spiritualism and the occult provide some ex-reformers with socially harmless diversions, the new, orthodox or unorthodox religiosity, often politically reactionary, may actively work to pinch off the reform impulse. Related changes characterize the public mood as reaction sets in.   In the face of (to many) frightening social transformations, the twenties, fifties, and seventies saw a reemphasis on traditional family structures and values. And an upwelling of educational fundamentalism occurred: back to basics, the three Rs, curbs on the autonomy of teachers.

Different people fall away from reform in differing ways and degrees.   Graham has found that among a sample of dropouts from progressivism, writers made themselves especially conspicuous along with lawyers and politicians.

> These concentrations . . . suggest that a controlling factor was a change in the temper of the constituency for which a man served. Reform enlisted some men because of, and only after, the general outcry against public evils. These were the men who dropped out first, and most irrevocably, when the public changed its tastes. They were often the sort of people one is surprised to find among the reform element in the first place, and for them the sensational critical effort of progressive campaigns was not only in the long run distasteful, but had never been exactly what they had wished to do.

Graham concludes that

> apparently it was chiefly those whose reformism had both
> intellectual and occupational roots—clergymen, academics, or
> social workers whose agitation sprang from a combination of
> ideas and a steady association with those whom laissez-faire
> had condemned to poverty—only these, with few exceptions,
> did not retreat from reform.

One might label the bolters soft reformers, and the stickers—those
willing to struggle on, risking interclass hostility and big, intrusive
government—the hard reformers. Yet it had to do with more than
philosophy, temperament, or proximity to the poor. It also had to do
with money. As Graham has observed, "progressivism, when it infected
the businessman or the lawyer who had the potential for a lucrative
career, tended to have a short life."[25] This reminds us once again of the
materialism which pervades a postreform era, and suggests as well that
those in need have become a diminished priority for many onetime
reformers. Not only have moods changed. Attitudes toward entire
groups of people have altered also.

NOTES

Godfrey Hodgson, *All Things to All Men: The False Promise of the
Modern American Presidency* (New York: Simon & Schuster, 1980), pp.
205-6.

[1]Rochester, *American Liberal Disillusionment*, pp. 107-10, 119, 134-35.

[2]Robert Sherman La Forte, *Leaders of Reform: Progressive
Republicans in Kansas, 1900-1916* (Lawrence: University Press of Kansas,
1974), p. 260.

[3]Smith, *When the Cheering Stopped*, pp. 167, 169.

[4]*Into the Twenties*, p. 199.

[5]White to Ray Stannard Baker, 8 December 1920, in *Selected Letters
of William Allen White, 1899-1943*, ed. Walter Johnson (New York: Henry
Holt & Co., 1947), p. 213.

[6]William L. Riordon, *Plunkitt of Tammany Hall: A Series of Very
Plain Talks on Very Practical Politics, Delivered by Ex-Senator George
Washington Plunkitt, the Tammany Philosopher, from His Rostrum—the
New York County Court House Bootblack Stand* (1905; reprint, New York:
E. P. Dutton & Co., 1963), p. 17.

[7]See, for example, Leila J. Rupp and Verta Taylor, *Survival in the
Doldrums: The American Women's Rights Movement, 1945 to the 1960s*
(New York: Oxford University Press, 1987).

[8]"The Right Menace," *New Republic*, 9 September 1978, pp. 13-14.

[9]Kearns, *Lyndon Johnson*, pp. 298-99.

[10]*Public Papers* (1937), p. 4.

[11]*Struggle Against Poverty*, p. 84.

[12]*American as Reformer*, pp. 18, 23.

[13]On these latter points, see Brinton, *Anatomy of Revolution*, p. 203.

[14]*Into the Twenties*, p. 111.

[15]*End of American Innocence*, pp. 354-55, 361, 391-93. May stresses that all this climaxed a process already under way. This paragraph also draws upon Kemler, *Deflation*, p. 172, and Leuchtenburg, *Perils of Prosperity*, pp. 142-43.

[16]"Comedy's New Face," *Newsweek*, 3 April 1978, pp. 61-62.

[17]"Screw You Humor," *New Republic*, 21 October 1978, p. 19. For an examination of the theme of humor in relation to social transformation, see Joseph Boskin, *Humor and Social Change in Twentieth-Century America* (Boston: Trustees of the Public Library of the City of Boston, 1979).

[18]On Proposition 13, see especially Robert Kuttner, *Revolt of the Haves: Tax Rebellions and Hard Times* (New York: Simon & Schuster, 1980), and David O. Sears and Jack Citrin, *Tax Revolt: Something for Nothing in California* (Cambridge, Mass.: Harvard University Press, 1982). It is worth noting that only about 40 percent of California's adult population voted on 13 at all.

[19]Thousand Oaks (Calif.) *News Chronicle*, 23 February 1976.

[20]"The Vanishing Violence——and Idealism," *Los Angeles Times*, 16 June 1978.

[21]Ladd, "Liberalism Upside Down," p. 580.

[22]"Vanishing Violence."

[23]"Is America Turning Right?" pp. 34-35.

[24]Nash, *Conservative Intellectual Movement*, p. 58.

[25]*Encore*, pp. 153, 160-61.

15

DEMYTHOLOGIZING
THE BENEFICIARIES

> I learned my lesson about human nature and discovered that
> practically the only difference between the poor classes and
> the rich classes was that one had money and the other had
> not.
>
> I have only lost my faith in man, not my pity for him. That
> is stronger than ever.

Fremont Older, 1926

One of the eternal themes in the reformers' eventual disillusionment
arises from their recurring discovery that people are weak, both in the
mass and even within their claimant groups. This typically comes as a
shock; it has helped lead many reformers to turn away in disenchantment or disgust. Yet at the outset reformers have always shown an
inclination to idealize both the masses and reform's specific beneficiaries.
"The power which is at once spring and regulator in all efforts of
reform," wrote Emerson, "is the conviction that there is an infinite
worthiness in man, which will appear at the call of worth, and that all
particular reforms are the removing of some impediment."[1]

This sort of idealizing, or mythologizing, serves two purposes. It
sustains the morale of the reformers themselves, and, through
propaganda, it bolsters the willingness of society at large to accept their
changes. If it is poor, probably the most effective way in which to
portray a beneficiary group is to represent it as if it were within the
penumbra of the middle class. Thus the impoverished become middle-
class in all important respects except income, which they undeservedly

lack. Or blacks share the essential elements that characterize the white middle class except for color and often income. Anything which alters this middle-class image will damage a reform movement by providing a rationale for inaction or resistance on the part of the middle class which comprises a large majority of the electorate.

Reformers have often oversold a rosy image of humanity. But faith in the mass public—in "the people" and their rationality—comes and goes. It came, for instance, during the Progressive Era. A good deal of disillusionment eventually developed over the very limited, mixed results of such popular democracy reforms as the initiative, referendum, recall, or even woman suffrage. Yet during the Progressive Era many reformers positively romanticized the masses, attributing to them a secret, hidden, overriding, commonsense wisdom. America was insufficiently democratic, these Jeffersonians insisted.   The proper cure was more democracy. Progressivism depended enormously on publicity and education, and on appealing to the better side of human nature. This presupposed—utterly depended on—a reasoning, sensible, responsive mass public operating as citizens in a democratic milieu. But World War I blasted progressives' faith in enlightened social change grounded on publicity, education, and rational, educated public opinion. "Publicity" or propaganda had been put to the most effective service in the cause of war, and masses of people had gone berserk. Writes David M. Kennedy:

> Even less tenable in the aftermath of wartime hysteria was the presumption that the public at large was rational and decent. Increasingly, that benign appraisal of human nature succumbed to a more cynical assessment, and the idea of "the people," good and educable, gave way to a concept of "the masses," brutish and volatile. Publicity, in which the prewar progressives had placed so much political hope, became in the postwar decade little more than an adjunct to the new economy of consumerism, as the fledgling industry of advertising adopted the propagandists' techniques of mass communication and persuasion.

. . . .

> [There arose] a substantial nagging fear of the people among modern liberals, a fear sharply at odds with traditional liberal purposes and one that threatened mortally to divide the liberal spirit against itself. One of the casualties of the war for the American mind thus seemed to have been the progressive soul, and the spiritual bloodletting very nearly drained the last reserves of utopianism from American social thought. . . . The

war had killed something precious and perhaps irretrievable in the hearts of thinking men and women.[2]

The liberal image of the public varies over time. Idealization of the people typifies a reform wave in full tide; de-idealizing takes place as reform wanes. During the thirties, liberals again identified with the mass public, seeing "the people's" struggle with "the interests" as central to the decade's dynamics. But in the fifties, the masses were widely portrayed by liberal intellectuals as "enemies of civil liberties and threats to the stability of the political system."[3] Whatever Christian faith in human perfectibility remained in the wake of World War II now had to survive Reinhold Niebuhr, with all his emphasis on human sinfulness. Pluralism and consensus became cults. A fear of mass behavior with its potential for disastrous irrationality spawned a deep suspicion of ideology itself. While a good many liberal intellectuals were expressing disdain for "mass society" and "populism," a number of conservatives ironically chose to identify with the masses.[4] Liberals and conservatives alike embrace the public when the public embraces them.

The specific beneficiaries of reform probably have to be mythologized in order for any significant change to occur at all. Unfortunately, the public's receptivity to proposals for change has little to do with the beneficiaries' actual needs. Rather, it relates to *perceived* need, together with *perceived* deservingness, and the perceiving is done by the middle and upper classes. Take, for example, the 1960s. While, as two scholars have argued, the Great Society-era "redistribution was mainly from the affluent to the poor," and while the federal government never intended that the middle class pay for uplifting the poor,[5] the poverty question became impregnated with middle-class symbols——the idea that the poor got more than they deserved, or that they got more than they really did, or that only they got anything. Dwindling real income growth doubtless reinforced these illusions. Disillusionment with the beneficiaries, on the part of the mass public and often on the part of reformers themselves, will almost inevitably follow reform. This is particularly so if the beneficiaries have a strong mind and will of their own and fail to stay within the confines of the image carefully molded for them.

In time a claimant group runs out of moral capital, even overdrawing its account. This does not mean that it does not need more, or that it should not have more, only that it will not likely get more. In 1975, for example, the antipoverty agency of the Roman Catholic Church suggested that the United States still had 40 million poor people, 65 percent more than the 24.3 million indicated by government estimates for 1974.[6] Measured either way, the figure was enormous. But——and California's Proposition 13 provided one indication of this——the public seemed anything but eager for government to embark on new programs or expand on old ones aimed at eliminating poverty. The middle class is a standing beneficiary of the welfare state through Social Security, Medicare, unemployment compensation, and so on. The "welfare crisis" of the late sixties and seventies amounted substantially to the fact that many of these same, good middle-class folk resented putting out a few more percentage points of GNP in order to ameliorate conditions for the bona fide poor.[7]

The public sees minorities like the poor the way it wants to, in such fashion as comports with its interests and prejudices, or with its sense of fairness, justice, and humanitarianism. One suspects that at some points a single, notorious, well-publicized case of welfare chiseling could offset the impact of an entire government report justifying higher welfare benefits. The ghetto riots of the mid-to-late sixties caused special damage in precisely this way. As we have seen, violence, or the potential for violence, can spur reform by publicizing crisis. Violence may even occasionally resolve the crisis (the Revolution; the Civil War). Yet while "the novelty of the technique" may serve reform up to a point, eventually violence tends to become a cliché and ceases to arouse the same response, or else shoots completely beyond government's willingness to respond. Violence may spur the cry for order, allow reform to pose as order-bringer, and lure conservatives into backing order-through-reform.[8] But violence also contains immense potential for reactionary backlash, and so its role in reform is in fact ambiguous.

The early civil rights movement, for example, emphasized respectability and nonviolence, giving it leverage through the media and with those in power. But the urban riots transformed the movement into a political liability. They demonstrated to middle-class whites that not all blacks resembled Martin Luther King, Jr. Riot after riot, summer after summer: all the earlier optimism began to look misplaced, even foolish. In 1964, 34 percent of the public felt that blacks were attempting to push too fast. By 1966 this 34 percent had become 85 percent. Backlash cost the Democrats in that election year. Many whites indicated to interviewers that their respect for blacks had dropped. To these whites, the point of hubris had been reached——blacks had over-stepped themselves and wanted too much. Blacks and whites disagreed fundamentally over what the riots signified. Many whites believed the rioters had Communist support.[9] Meanwhile, the inflation-ridden economy placed the old New Deal coalition under extreme strain, with blacks and blue-collar whites battling one another for the same jobs. Part of the problem of the late sixties and seventies was that onetime questions of class had now become issues of race, thus even more divisive than before.[10]

All this points to another instance where reform's beneficiaries have lost their appeal. Perhaps the most traumatic experience through which liberalism has passed since the thirties has involved the debunking of the supposed virtues and deservingness of the working class. This central fact has robbed liberalism of much of its purpose and impetus, if not its very direction.

In relatively conservative eras, public suspicion toward organized labor expands, which, together with anti-union drives by management, makes a bleak climate for union-backed reforms. After World War I, for example, unions came under fire as kicking up the cost of living and undermining productivity. The differences between moderate unions and radical ones got blurred. Unions in general were attacked as subversive and corrupt. By the late thirties, fear welled again both of unions——which made up the left's greatest constituency——and of labor radicalism. These anxieties multiplied following World War II, when, as after World War I, a rash of strikes broke out. In the sixties, many among the New Left learned a great deal about the cultural and social gap between themselves and the proletariat which they had often mythologized. Was the American working class prepared to strike off its chains and raise the banner of class revolution? Hardly. A great many workers displayed a remarkable propensity for voting against the radicals, liberals, and minorities who offended them, and for supporting candidates who in turn would back business once elected. Among these were Richard Nixon and George Wallace. More than most, union members supported the Vietnam war.[11] On the left, a bitter disillusionment set in.

Michael Novak has remarked that intellectuals and liberals "empathize more with nearly any group in the United States than the lower-middle-class white or the ethnic voters."[12] Watching Archie Bunker each week, otherwise impeccable liberals began to do what conservatives had always done: laugh at the foibles of the working class. Meanwhile, Spiro Agnew's attacks on the intellectuals and the political antics of George Wallace got a warm response among blue-collar ethnics. Bunker's beer-guzzling bigotry and movies like *Joe* symbolized the end of the line for the sentimentalized working class.

Emerson was right. The sense of human worthiness is the——or at least a——spring and regulator in reform movements. Conservatives have always grumbled that reformers look at the masses through rose-colored glasses, and certainly reformers of whatever stripe have tended toward an optimistic view of the people, their rationality, and their educability. When this becomes shaken, as it was by the world wars and the indirect consequences of Vietnam, much of the motive force for reform gets lost. What does liberal reform amount to without the sense that human beings are good to begin with?

Yet in this century, reformers and social critics have repeatedly confronted the disappointment of mass inertia and mass cantankerousness. "If we accept the Greek's definition of the idiot as a privatized man," complained C. Wright Mills in 1951, "then we must conclude that the U.S. citizenry is now largely composed of idiots."[13] Carl Becker, I think, captured in his wry way the long-term truth of things when he wrote: "Although humane lovers of the masses, we [liberals] are, on the other hand, highly differentiated individuals who prize our liberties, including the liberty of not belonging to the masses whom we love."[14]

In the twenties William Feather, a business commentator, observed that "there is no doubt that the American business man is the foremost hero of the American people today." He added this revealing note on the nature of the success which was prized: "The John D. Rockefeller who gives away millions is not a hero, but the Rockefeller who made a billion dollars out of oil is a hero. The Carnegie who made steel and millions of dollars was a hero, but the Carnegie who gave medals to heroes and built libraries was just a sweet old lady."[15] As Feather implied, the public reputations of the deprived and the elites alternate as if on a teeter-totter, and his observations fit the 1980s nearly as well as they did the 1920s. During a reform period, wealth, even the idea of wealth, becomes less fashionable. When the era ends, we return to normal and the dollar olympics revives. It becomes significantly less fashionable to be poor, minority, or working-class——or, for that matter, to proclaim the virtues of democracy.

NOTES

"Where Are the Pre-war Radicals?" p. 561 (Older quote).
[1]"Man the Reformer," p. 83.
[2]*Over Here*, pp. 90, 92.
[3]McAuliffe, *Crisis on the Left*, p. 70.
[4]Nash, *Conservative Intellectual Movement*, p. 129.
[5]Levitan, *Promise*, p. 251.
[6]*Los Angeles Times*, 22 December 1975.
[7]See George F. Will, "*The Welfare State*: Reform Means Only Tinkering," *Los Angeles Times*, 25 May 1977.
[8]Huntington, *Political Order*, pp. 358-60.
[9]Kearns, *Lyndon Johnson*, pp. 304, 308.
[10]See Robert J. Donovan, "Why Are Americans Rushing to the Right?" *Los Angeles Times*, 26 December 1975 (citing Walter Dean Burnham).
[11]Heath, *Disillusionment*, p. 293.

[12]Buenker, *Urban Liberalism*, p. 213.

[13]*White Collar*, p. 328.

[14]*Everyman*, p. 98.

[15]James Warren Prothro, *The Dollar Decade: Business Ideas in the 1920's* (Baton Rouge: Louisiana State University Press, 1954), p. 44.

16

THE DEMISE
AND DEPARTURE
OF THE INTELLECTUALS

> Whatever the intellectual is too certain of, if he is healthily playful, he begins to find unsatisfactory. The meaning of his intellectual life lies not in the possession of truth but in the quest for new uncertainties.
>
> Richard Hofstadter

> Racing nervously from decade to decade and from doctrine to doctrine, fearful of "falling behind," clutching the latest news from Paris, American intellectuals seem capable of almost anything except the ultimate grace of a career devoted to some large principle or value, modulated by experience and thought, but firm in purpose. Creatures of short breath, they bend and turn.
>
> Irving Howe

We come now to a key theme in reform's undoing: the departure of the intellectuals, and with them the intellectual underpinnings and élan of reform. Actually, we are not talking about *the* intellectuals at all, but only about certain individuals. And as the terms "demise" and "departure" suggest, we are not discussing a single process, but in fact two different kinds of process, one substantially voluntary, the other involuntary.[1]

For all the conservatives among them, intellectuals have played so important a part in reform throughout this century that we can hardly contemplate a reform drive without them. Made famous by the New Deal, the brain trust idea actually goes back at least to the Progressive

Era.[2]   The role of the intellectual in government has undergone a
dramatic change since the days of FDR. Intellectuals and academics have
become permanently ubiquitous in Washington, their emergence running
parallel to the growth of executive power and becoming particularly
notable in reform administrations. So important are they that even the
shape of their heads has attracted attention, being variously described as
egg-like or pointed.[3]

In examining the relationship of the intellectual to reform we must
draw a distinction between different types of intellectuals.   The
government service intellectual, for instance, often belongs to the
technical intelligentsia, an expert in farming or guided missile design or
internal medicine.[4] Brain trust types tend to be social scientists. They
will occupy us here. And we will take a similar or greater interest in
ideological literary radicals and bohemian philosophers who influence
social change without ever getting close to government service at all.

Many nontechnical intellectuals are, by virtue of being intellectuals,
perennially marginal, alienated from society and critical of it.[5]
Dissatisfied with the present, intellectuals——especially younger ones——
measure the real against the ideal. "Nothing," Stephen Spender has
commented, "is clearer to a later generation than the naivety of an earlier
one, just as nothing is clearer to the earlier one than the naivety of the
later."[6]   Lewis S. Feuer has contended that

> young intellectuals in generational revolt find in some version
> of the ideological myth a charter and dramatization of their
> emotions, aims, and actions.   Since each generation of
> intellectuals tends to reject its predecessors' doctrines, a law of
> intellectual fashion arises,——the alternation of philosophical
> tenets.[7]

Despite the standing alienation of many intellectuals, over this
century the fundamental direction for intellectuals interested in reform
has taken them from the outside in——from assaulting privilege or
corruption or whatever on the outside, like Joshua blowing trumpets at
the walls, to a more or less post-New Deal phenomenon of being
swallowed up like Jonah in the belly of the bureaucracy.[8]   One can
overstate this: TR and La Follette had their inside intellectuals and
experts, just as Johnson had his. But the fundamental change has moved
the intelligentsia from outgroup to ingroup, no matter whether they
actually enter government or instead reside in such places as the
universities or the media.   Since intellectuals by trade question the
conventional orthodoxies, this arrival, together with their sheer
proliferation, has brought with it almost an embarrassment of critical
riches.   Yet by making them insiders, it has also tended to compromise

their classic ability as outsiders to function as social or policy critics.

In the decline phase of each of our reform movements, some intellectuals—often key intellectuals—have abandoned reform. Such people may take a number of avenues. They may, for example, renounce the old approaches and proceed to de-ideologize an intellectual field, or claim to. They may attempt "to spiritualize the present," much as a resurgence of religiosity or myths would do. Or they may drop radical or reform politics in favor of sheer disillusionment itself.[9] We will focus for a moment on this last.

Often intellectuals by their very nature as gadflies, critics, and challengers take an adversary posture vis-à-vis government. At all times some of them have associated government with the bourgeoisie and its "repressive" values. At key points—after each world war and following Vietnam—the state as a whole or various elements of government have gotten involved in suppressing dissent from the intellectual left. In each case liberal administrations have implicated themselves to one degree or another. During World War I and the McCarthy years, various intellectuals were discredited. In the Vietnam era, many intellectuals who remained in government were attacked by other intellectuals on the outside. And the importance of all this lies in the fact that at the end of each reform period some intellectuals who had served as trendsetters, eyes for society in general or for some reform administration in particular, either left the movement or found themselves forced out. These intellectuals have then sometimes adopted the confessional vogue, writing guiltily of their years on the left.

Throughout the century, certain idealistic radical intellectuals have wanted to become comrades of the proletariat but then have become disillusioned in the role. Among the elites, no group has matched the intellectuals in their regard for society's less privileged.[10] Both here and in Europe, workers and intellectuals have traditionally been identified as natural components of the left. Yet the alliance between workers and intellectuals tends to be uneasy, forced, and artificial.[11] Workers do not typically base their behavior on elaborate mental schematics. One reason for the artificiality of the link in this country may also have to do with the lesser role which theory has played in American social reform as against the European. On the basic material level, leftist intellectualism and labor's perceived self-interest have not always converged. The conservative, "practical" tone of the American labor movement, its aspiration to middle-class status for the working class, has galled a good many intellectuals who have agitated for something more exalted.

The intellectuals' identification with the outs sometimes stems from guilt. Reason exists to believe that intellectuals also identify with the left and with the underprivileged in part because they identify *themselves* as underprivileged.[12] Some intellectuals have found themselves caught between their sensations of guilt over their favored position vis-à-vis the proletariat, and resentment over having less than their wealthier "inferiors" in the upper classes. The problem with guilt-as-motivation is that the efforts taken in response to it need not necessarily be effective. Primarily, they serve to help the individual assuage the guilt. An intellectual can identify with the poor by wearing shabby clothing and living in a dump without actually doing a single thing to help the poor.

All this offers one explanation for the ultimate departure of so many of the intellectuals. Their affinity for the downtrodden probably reflects the psychic and group needs of the intellectuals more than it does the needs of workers or the poor. While intellectuals may serve as instruments for these classes, performing rhetorical and analytical functions normally associated with their calling, the alliance as an alliance of types proves awkward. The intellectual sentimentalizes blue-collar workers or the poor and damns the middle class. The proletariat, to the contrary, wants to *be* middle class. Much that the intellectuals have tried to tell the working class has either offended it or seemed irrelevant to it. In the realm of values——culture, sex, race, nationalism, religion, and so on——divergences have frequently come to resemble chasms. The oppressed have shown a disappointing obstinacy in sticking to the Church, voting for the machine, or backing Joe McCarthy. Labor leaders will pound the bargaining table over wages, fringe benefits and working conditions——pale stuff in the life of the mind. The working class refuses to behave with consistency the way many dissident intellectuals have wanted it to behave. The potential for profound disaffection exists on both sides.[13]

Time and again, the disillusionment of the intellectuals has recurred in American life. In the wake of the antislavery movement and the Civil War, emerging postwar organization politics led to disenchantment. The war had satisfied the abolitionist cause, at least to the extent of ending slavery as a formal institution. Then new, "unsavory" types moved into politics. The Henry Adamses and E. L. Godkins found themselves left out on the chilly doorstep of power. "Most intellectuals," Morton Keller has written, "assumed that scientific laws governed politics, the economy, and society——laws that an educated elite was best able to interpret." Now, complained scientist Simon Newcomb, men governed "who are not only ignorant of social laws, but incapable of exact reasoning of any kind whatever." Ralph Waldo Emerson grumbled that "the country is governed in bar-rooms and in the mind of bar-rooms. The low can best win the low, and each aspirant for power vies with his rival which can stoop lowest."[14] Oliver Wendell Holmes, Jr., a fervent abolitionist in the prewar era, later remarked, "I had my belly full of isms when young." He warned Harold Laski: "The only thing I am competent to say from the experience of my youth is that I fear your getting into the frame of mind that I saw in the Abolitionists (and shared)——the martyr spirit." "[I]n my day I was a pretty convinced abolitionist. . . . How coolly one looks on that question now but when I was a sophomore . . ." Returning from the Civil War, Holmes's new causes had become his studies and his career.[15]

World War I presents us with *the* great model of intellectual disaffection. Through governmental service, the war lofted numerous intellectuals to an influence unimaginable in peacetime. (Wrote Harold Stearns, "President Wilson not only silenced his critics by putting the outspoken ones in jail but by putting many others in the government.")[16] Some of these intellectuals had embraced the war like a new mistress. They expected it to bring social direction and cohesion and a more powerful state.[17] Randolph Bourne mordantly labeled the phenomenon "war-liberalism." "The intellectuals," he said,

> have identified themselves with the least democratic forces in American life. They have assumed the leadership for war of those very classes whom the American democracy has been immemorially fighting. Only in a world where irony was dead could an intellectual class enter war at the head of such illiberal cohorts in the avowed cause of world-liberalism and world-democracy. No one is left to point out the undemocratic nature of this war-liberalism. In a time of faith, skepticism is the most intolerable of all insults.[18]

The expectations of Bourne's war liberals——their grandly inflated expectations of what America could wring from World War I——provide a classic instance of the liberal hubris.[19]

Like soldiers pulling out of trench lines in the dead of night, the left-intellectuals' silhouettes later pierced the gloom as they trudged to the right. As Henry F. May has written:

> Through the war and its outcome, through the cycle of hope, hatred and disillusion, the credo which Wilson embodied was discredited and torn apart. The principles of moralism, progress, and culture, already linked disastrously to snobbery, racial pride, and prudery, were linked now to the Wilsonian version of the Allied cause. Inevitably, the country was to turn against both. The war brought about the victory of our intellectual rebellion, and in so doing, changed its nature.[20]

Christopher Lasch adds, "The radicals and bohemians of the twenties claimed to have lost their illusions about the world, but if their own earlier testimony is to be believed, they had never had any illusions to begin with——not, at any rate, the particular illusions they later claimed to have lost." Lasch draws a very helpful distinction between types of progressivism: "If . . . progressivism meant social control, if it meant the scientific approach to politics, if it referred, more broadly still, to the 'pragmatic' habit of mind, then the new radicals were progressives; and they did not cease to be progressives even after they had repudiated 'progressivism.'" But these same radicals had stood against progressivism as uplift or as "puritanism" all along, and from this angle little changed after the war. The snare derives partly from the ambiguity in the word "progressivism." A tendency existed among some intellectuals to despise *political* progressivism, which they linked with middle-class culture. The process of moving from illusionment or un-illusionment before the war, to disillusionment in the twenties, Lasch suggests, reflects the importance which disillusionment per se had attained in the metabolism of radical circles.[21]

This said, the exalted sense of hope which so many intellectuals brought to the war strikes the jaundiced late twentieth century mind as bizarre. It speaks ill of their sense of reality and possibility. Liberals of conscience and sensitivity had fallen in behind the conflict, often with a passion which concealed their previous pacifism. "Admission of failure or blunder," Stuart I. Rochester writes, "thus required a particularly agonizing and labored confession." [22] Ultimately, the war and the peace left a good many intellectuals feeling guilty and ashamed. The process of disillusionment sledded many into depths of lugubriousness from heights they should never have scaled in the first place. Perhaps the key lies here: that, as Arthur Frank Wertheim has found of New York's "Little Renaissance," while most of its writers and artists never backed Roosevelt or Wilson or their kind of progressivism——while most, indeed, were socialists——they shared in the spirit of idealism and progress.[23] In any case, the war's aftermath saw a great many once-flourishing ideas sprawled on the field, among them political progressivism, the idealism which might have provided a medium for reform's revival, the confidence and faith in progress so important to progressivism, and the old, happy optimism.[24]

Perhaps the type of disillusionment we are discussing is a kind of luxury, unique to intellectuals by virtue of their shared peculiarity: they think. Total war hits intellectuals precisely where they live, in the realm of free speech and the free exchange of ideas, because total war suspends these things. To a poor person, who thinks little of big issues and whose thoughts run day-to-day at that, disillusionment has to do with such matters as failed friendships or products that taste bad. Flights of fancy concerning, say, a League of Nations, have a distinctly middle-class aura to them, suggesting as they do rewards expected in the future as a consequence of present renunciation and suffering.

Finally, the retreat toward disillusionment begins and ends for different individuals at different places. In the case of World War I, the literature has focused rather heavily on the disillusionment of literary and other radicals who left eloquent records of their suffering. In their now-legendary sense of isolation from the rest of American society, twenties intellectuals began to exalt failure. As if hunting wild boar, they hunted despair. But while they debunked the successes of the Babbitts, most found their isolation delicious as they savored their own feelings of superiority.[25]

These kinds of conversions have varying consequences. Very important, from the immediate standpoint of reform, was the breakup of the circle around the *New Republic*. The old causes, political-cultural nationalism and progressive reform, were abandoned by Herbert Croly and the others. Walter Weyl, his confidence in humanity ebbing, grew tired of idealistic reform. Walter Lippmann, the onetime socialist, later came out against the New Deal's limited state planning. Before the war, the writings of the progressive intellectuals had provided the country both with penetrating, often brilliant insights into the nature of the twentieth century, and with optimistic, enthusiastic plans for change. The war and the peace left them (as Weyl put it) "tired radicals." In the face of reaction at home and abroad, they now felt uncertain about the changeability of the social order and powerless. How could the old reform ideas retain validity if society was more inert, people less disinterested and rational, and progress more uncertain, than had seemed true before the war? An expanded faith in the intellectuals' own superiority countered their humbled faith in the people.

For many intellectuals, the Progressive Era had raised an opportunity to change both culture and politics, art and society. But while the assault on the bourgeois, the narrow, and the Philistine continued, the direct political critique substantially dissipated in the twenties. Concerns shriveled from the broad public to the individual self, and often from the politically radical to the personally bohemian. Intellectuals rebelled against the middle class and the dull in general. Debunking superseded muckraking. But regrettably, political progressivism fell into the same debunked category as political conservatism. Both were orthodox, both bourgeois—and in any case, the state seemed a threat. Numerous intellectuals of the twenties fought for greater sexual freedom, against legislation to regulate behavior, against prohibition, and against censorship. They wanted toleration, and for some if not most, reform became opprobrious because it suggested control. Writers focused on the individual; society as a whole got lost. H. L. Mencken sniffed at democracy as he did at all the other once-safe values of the "booboisie." "It was characteristic of the Jazz Age," F. Scott Fitzgerald observed, "that it had no interest in politics at all."[26]

Yet things did not remain entirely so. The execution of Sacco and Vanzetti in 1927 and the struggle which preceded it became a tocsin for the thirties. The twenties' fascination with individuals gave way during the Depression to a fascination with systems. "All in all," wrote Dixon Wecter of the Depression era,

> literary folk discovered closer affinity with the Muckrakers of the century's early years than with the debunkers of the 1920's, whose behavioristic psychology had tended to return man to his animal origins and laugh at his consequent discomfiture.

The H. L. Mencken school fell out of fashion. The masses Mencken had pilloried and which the twenties had ignored became fashionable once again. While Jeffersonian interpretations flourished in historical writing, "social significance" found its way into movies, art, music, and literature.[27]

From the far left, though, liberal reform looked as foolish and futile in the New Deal era as it had from the anti-ideologists' vantage point in the twenties. The decade of the Great Depression was also the decade of Marx, of historical determinism and ideological dialectics. As usual, the public proved unpromisingly inert, and ultimately, disillusionment became the Marxist intellectuals' lot. While the labor movement surged, it moved within conventional bounds; no great proletarian uprising occurred. International events ultimately played a significant part in eroding the unity of the left as well as in undercutting a good deal of its optimism. The 1939 Nazi-Soviet nonaggression pact sent American Communists swarming out of the party. For many intellectuals, Stalin suddenly assumed something of the egregious image which Wilson had had twenty years before. Meanwhile, most non-Marxist intellectuals had followed Roosevelt into the New Deal coalition. Many had joined the administration.

In the twenty years after 1936, a massive tide swept numerous Marxists along toward more comfortable and conservative shores. To the extent that fascism and Stalinism repelled American intellectuals and curdled their optimism, idealism, and faith in human nature—to the extent that the Enlightenment died at Auschwitz—foreign entanglement exerted its disorienting influence once again. If Marxism had provided the dominant mode of rebellion in the thirties, Western ideologies were probably most heavily influenced in the postwar generation by existentialism. Some former left-ideologues swung over to the right; Whittaker Chambers of *Time* and the *National Review* personified the phenomenon. But most by middle age had likely become "de-ideologized,"[28] skeptical of all creeds of the left or the right.   Mary Sperling McAuliffe has written:

> Those liberal intellectuals who generally endorsed the foreign policies of the Truman administration, and who supported the purging of Communists from American life, sought to redefine American liberalism in response to the demands and pressures of an increasingly powerful domestic conservative movement as well as the dangers of the Cold War world.   In the process they abandoned many traditional liberal tenets—the belief in progress, in man's goodness, in popular democracy, and in world peace—replacing them with a chastened and, in their view, "realistic" philosophy which stressed man's sinfulness, the seeming inevitability of conflict among nations, and the dangers of democratic rule.   The new liberals identified not with the left, as had been the case in the 1930s, but with the center; they identified not with the people, but with an elite.   Unlike the liberals of the thirties, who had criticized the social order, the new liberals stressed the beneficence of American political and economic institutions.[29]

Something else had happened, too: by the 1950s, the intellectuals had become integrated into society as a favored social group, what some later called a new class.   Their influence throughout American life magnified enormously.   "On matters of substantive public policy," writes Alonzo L. Hamby, "the intelligentsia and its following tended to identify with the liberal tradition.   Geographically mobile, independent-minded, and scornful of intense partisan attachments, they constituted a large new free-floating, quasi-alienated segment of American political society with few traditional institutional reference points."[30]   During the fifties and sixties, liberalism reflected all this in its emphasis on style, power, wealth, and the media, and in its elitism.[31]   Among liberal intellectuals, the progress which had taken place under Roosevelt and Truman turned into a realm to be defended, not an empire to expand.[32]

However important this new Establishment status was in shaping the ideology of the intellectual community, another factor, I think, served equally.   The intellectuals of the fifties reacted to a fundamentally inauspicious era for reform.   Like the Supreme Court, they responded to the election returns.   Following World War II, it became fashionable to agree that an "end of ideology" had occurred.[33]   Particularly after the arrival of Eisenhower, the political system was both homogenized and anesthetized.   Big domestic issues did remain, but they were temporarily buried in shallow graves.   It took a bit of time for the stench to waft up through the cracks in the soil.   The economy generally functioned well;

society appeared stable. After one decade of depression and half a decade devoted to total war, quietude suited the public mood. Tensions relaxed. The lines separating liberalism and conservatism blurred. Stridency and masochism passed out of fashion.

Among the intellectuals, optimism faded. Some left politics. Some turned right. Some found religion. A remarkable redirection of emphasis occurred, from Marx and utopianism and society toward Freud and the inner self.[34] A good deal of guilt surrounded much of this, a sort of collective confession of past infections with Marxism or popular frontism and "the sin of romantic delusion."[35] The life of the mind found fascination not in the old passionate certainties, but now with ambiguity, irony, complication, and paradox. Taken up with the notion of American exceptionalism, the new style held moralizing, passionate politics in suspicion. "American intellectuals as a group," Seymour Martin Lipset wrote at the outset of the sixties, "seem to have shifted toward the center, although most of them probably remain to the left of that imaginary line; and a significant minority have become conservative in their thinking." Among other factors, Lipset attributed this trend to prosperity and "to the rise of Communism as the main threat to freedom"; and he pointed out that many liberal or leftist intellectuals had given up politics in favor of their own intellectual pursuits.[36] Robert Booth Fowler has noted that "the mood that dominated American political thought in the years after World War II was *skepticism*." Most postwar intellectuals, he writes,

> were skeptical . . . of any proposals for radical social change and earnest hopes that one or another utopia might be achieved . . . [and] of the rational capacities of citizens in political life and what they considered to be the unfortunate tendency of many past intellectuals to worship the goal of ever-expanding democratic participation.

Postwar skepticism involved debunking ideology as well as absolutes and utopias. This aversion to ideology reflected a reaction against Nazism and Communism, essentially *foreign* ideologies with pretenses to absolute truth.[37]

And the implication? A strong vote essentially for America as it was. The end of ideology, in other words, proved highly ideological. Characterized by "realism" and caution, loath to take chances, the new, tepid liberalism oriented itself toward safety, security, and social stability.[38] There was a feeling that the nation's basic difficulties had either seen resolution or were headed that way; an assumption, too, that Americans operated on a firm groundwork of consensus. Human nature and behavior, including political behavior, fell under suspicion.

Optimistic notions of solidarity with the workers faded. This reflected, not a profound pessimism or a complete jettisoning of hope for some incremental progress, but rather, a chastened balance. "Toughminded realism" and "pragmatism" came into vogue.[39] All this added up, though, to a liberalism so defensive, cautious, and centrist—so *conservative*, indeed—that it posed little if any real threat to the status quo.[40]

One could find throughout a new emphasis on, for want of a better term, "Americanism." The sunny image of Russian Communism had gone black with Stalinism and the demise of the popular front. The Cold War was on, Cold War liberalism, in. The signs of the new national focus sprang up all around: in the pluralist school of social scientists, for example, or the consensus school of historians. As McAuliffe has observed, "fundamental to pluralist thought in all its postwar manifestations—realism, consensus, and the Vital Center—was a loss of optimism, a dwindling assumption of progress, and a declining conviction of the fundamental goodness of mankind."[41] Pluralism substituted interest-group complexity for what was—from the standpoint of reform—a healthier class dichotomy, with all the clarity of them-against-us. The earlier politics of class had treated labor as something more than just another interest group. This was true regardless of the accuracy or inaccuracy of the class interpretation. Among other things, intellectuals on the left now gave religion and intuition a fresh hearing. The loss of innocence theme returned: evil acknowledged, fate considerably given way to.[42] Mass movements, the great hope of the thirties, fell under suspicion as they had done in the twenties. Many now linked big, interventionist government with totalitarianism.[43] The literary intellectuals came home, literary critics finding new levels of meaning in Melville, Hawthorne, Whitman, Henry James, and T. S. Eliot. Social gospel theology felt the chill un-millennial cautions of Niebuhr, who spoke of human un-perfectibility and about the boundaries of reform.[44] From discipline to discipline, so it went.

As if the chagrin of the radicals and fellow travelers returning from the far left were not enough, McCarthyism soured things further yet. When, as during the two great red scares, the intellectuals are reminded of how little most people care about either their perspectives or the Bill of Rights, it comes as a terribly disillusioning experience. And now, conservatives, or people who called themselves conservatives, were being listened to. No wonder elitism revived, or that, as in the twenties, intellectuals debunked mass society and the grossness of the popular tastes.

Pessimism mingled oddly with upbeat complacency. Such terms as "end of ideology," "pluralism," and "consensus" suggested a faith in the ability of interest groups more or less to balance one another off in a New Deal-amended capitalism.

The Kennedy Administration embodied or paid tribute to so many intellectual styles and values current in the fifties and early sixties that its appeal to the intellectual community comes as no surprise. To whatever degree status anxieties among the intelligentsia help to explain their leftist reflexes, I suspect that the recognition of intellectuals by reform regimes offsets some of these anxieties and directs thought toward the political center. The prominence of intellectuals or quasi-intellectuals like Stevenson or Kennedy also makes politics seem more legitimate and appealing. Their style numbs doubt. So recently hounded by the McCarthyites, the intellectuals' independence now became jeopardized by government's warm embrace. Suddenly they found that they really *had* arrived. Recruited to Washington, the best and the brightest found their way to power and prestige——just in time for Vietnam.

In the sixties, the intellectuals' impulse to take their ease with the nation as it was quickly faded. As Godfrey Hodgson puts it:

> One by one, each of the main components of the Roosevelt coalition began to flake away. The intellectuals were not important to that coalition in terms of numbers; they were vital to it because their ideas were the cement that held it together. In the late 1960s, some came to the conclusion that liberal policies had failed, and wanted to proceed more cautiously. Some thought they had never been fairly tried, and wanted to go faster. Both groups were impatient with the steady plod along the via media of traditional Democratic policy. Many who had once been firm liberals were deeply troubled or outright shocked by the war. Many more lost the robust optimism that had powered the old liberal creed and adopted more or less radical critiques of society.[45]

Genuine radicalism arrived again, together with its plastic imitation, radical chic. The decade produced its own crop of left-intellectuals. It also enhanced the reputations of leftist scholars like C. Wright Mills and William Appleman Williams who had continued to write through the long drought of the fifties.

For all their alliterative viciousness, Spiro Agnew's attacks on the intelligentsia did hit home. The intellectuals who played such a strong role in shaping liberal opinion did occupy a different sphere from the day-to-day realities of the Bunkers whom many of them ridiculed. These intellectuals did show significant tolerance, on the whole, toward student radicalism, drug use, the sexual revolution, even toward the criminal. They did tend toward delight with the offbeat, the nonconformist. They did tend to sneer at Main Street materialism and the commercial ethic.

And, to the very considerable degree that they set the tone of liberal ideology in the sixties and seventies, they did draw it away from main line American conventions.[46]

Caught between two constituencies in the sixties——the students and the broader public——the universities, administrators and faculty alike, attempted to appease both. As convenient and fairly pliable whipping boys, the universities could give student radicals part of what they wanted but not all, simply because, in and of themselves, they could not end the Vietnam war, racism, or sexism, or clean up the environment. So they traded what they had the power to trade. The students got certain indulgences——representation on this or that committee or governing board; curricular concessions (general education, widely demolished, was a favorite); and conciliation (exemplified by the determination of faculty on some campuses to interpose themselves between the students and the police).

As the sixties faded into the seventies, disillusionment returned. Some liberal intellectuals lambasted past liberal programs, notably Johnson's. Others confessed that they hadn't sufficient knowledge to have sustained these programs in the first place. Many chanted their contrition over Vietnam. In an interview, Patricia Roberts Harris, a cabinet member in the Carter Administration, caught the tone and temper of much that was happening by the late seventies. Behind the new fashion——talk of lowering expectations and such——Harris found liberal intellectuals abandoning earlier fights against poverty, urban decay, and racism in what she termed a "grand cop-out." Harris saw the fad syndrome operating here, together with a "new boredom" among liberal reformers. (Regrettably, following as it did on the New Nationalism, the New Freedom, the New Deal, and the New Frontier, the New Boredom seemed a suitable catchword for Carter's brand of liberalism.) Addressing problems of the cities, the blacks, and the poor, Harris observed of reformers:

> They're really bored, I think, with it all. And it seems rather too difficult to stay on the problem in a realistic sense. . . . [They] feel that somehow because the problem does not solve itself in two splendid years of demonstration that it does not merit continued activity. I think that there is considerably less activity, considerably less thoughtfulness on the part of the intellectual community, the liberal reformist community, if you like, that used to think very carefully about ways in which we could move forward in dealing with the next level of the deprived.

Harris also touched on the matter of hubris, in this case minority hubris:

> I think that it is boredom because one doesn't have a sense of
> people being grateful for the lord and lady of the manor having
> made their gesture. And so one turns to areas of greater
> personal satisfaction.

Attitude

> is at the crux of the problem; it's the grand cop-out. It's an
> attitude that says we will avoid dealing with the problem by
> saying that it is not there. . . . It's a very good way to avoid
> dealing with problems, to say that the problem doesn't exist, or
> that the person with the problem created his own problem.

"Do you think," she was asked, that "there's been a major shift in the
thinking of intellectuals, and when did it happen?"

> When black people began competing with intellectuals for jobs.
> I mean as long as black people were only competing for jobs
> on the assembly line, and as long as black people were only
> sending their children to newly integrated Southern schools, no
> problem. But when the integration question began to reach
> those who were the developers of new theories, right where
> they lived——in the schools of their children and in their own
> faculties——they began to rethink the whole issue.[47]

As part of this sorry picture, a collection of intellectuals and
others——onetime liberals, most of them, and many if not most still
Democrats——had emerged, known as the neoconservatives. Considering
the intellectual vacuousness or otherworldliness of preceding postwar
conservatisms, they mounted an unusually sophisticated critique of
contemporary American liberalism and radicalism. Unhappy with the
results of the Great Society and with some of the often-unintended
consequences of liberal reform; upset by student insurgency and the
counterculture; fearful of the assault on the meritocracy and on standards
which affirmative action seemed to portend; and alarmed by the anti-
Semitism of some black radicals, many of the neoconservatives had also
become chastened or disillusioned by their own (liberal) government
service. They criticized what they saw as reform's flawed assumptions
and byproducts: excessive government interventionism, a bloated
bureaucracy, larded budgets, waste, inflation, redistribution, a warped tax
system, sentimentalism, and the assurance that Washington knows best.
Neoconservatives spoke now of individual initiative, self-help, market

efficiencies, and the assorted virtues of business, order, gradualism, standards, and traditional, stable social values and institutions.   The neoconservatives scarcely found themselves in full agreement on the issues, but they shared concerns about Washington and the nature and direction of modernization which symptomized the uncertainties, or, more harshly, the loss of nerve, of the 1970s.[48]

This sketch of intellectual reaction in the twentieth century has not pretended to speak to the attitudes of all intellectuals or all academics, but rather has identified key groups as they relate to political processes and the political mood at given times.   Intellectuals have certainly influenced these moods.   The fads and fashions of the intellectual community have also reflected or exaggerated fashions in society at large. There is good reason to believe that certain groups of intellectuals—humanists and social scientists in particular—have gotten rolled around by these currents more than others.   I have no idea how fluid attitudes have been among the technical intelligentsia in general over this century, but I strongly suspect that their views change far less from decade to decade than do those of, say, philosophers or anthropologists.

This the dual intellectual cultures do have in common, though: a general comfort and sense of place which has grown increasingly secure as the century has worn on.   Two results have ensued.   On one hand, government service contracts and such have given many intellectuals a deeper stake in the system as it is.   Yet on the other hand and to the contrary, the lack of a direct stake in the system through firsthand participation in market economics has left intellectuals personally free to criticize as far as their courage will carry them.   Finally, their criticism has had a volatile character because the intelligentsia does react sharply to fads.   Intellectuals resemble other people in this way: odd though they may seem to outsiders, they want to belong to their own group. Their peer culture produces its own peer causes and ideologies.   When the reform-radical fads end, they are replaced by disillusionment and a sense of rejection—the new fads.[49]

Fads probably have greater difficulty than they might entrenching themselves as enduring causes in this society because most of its intellectuals are fairly comfortable.   Just as they maintain no direct stake in the market economy, they have no direct stake in welfare benefits or food stamp allowances.   Ideological avenues remain wide open because the personal consequences are so slight.   Intellectuals can afford to follow red herrings, become hedonists, or fall into ideological vacuousness.   If, in time, social analyses based on class slip out of fashion, no matter.   Politically, intellectuals truly enjoy the best of all possible worlds.

NOTES

Richard Hofstadter, *Anti-intellectualism in American Life* (New York: Alfred A. Knopf, 1963), pp. 30, 413; Howe, *A Margin of Hope*, p. 341.

[1]For an examination in a single life of many of the patterns which I shall take up as collective behavior, see David W. Levy, *Herbert Croly of "The New Republic": The Life and Thought of an American Progressive* (Princeton: Princeton University Press, 1985), especially ch. 9.

[2]Or even to the Constitutional Convention. See Paul B. Cook, *Academicians in Government from Roosevelt to Roosevelt*, Modern American History series (New York: Garland Publishing, 1982), especially pp. 8, 62.

[3]Richard Hofstadter found "cyclical fluctuations" in "regard for intellectuals," as well as alternations in the intellectuals' relationship to the public. See *Anti-intellectualism*, pp. 6, 214.

[4]On this distinction between the technical intelligentsia and the broader range of intellectuals which interests us here, see Hofstadter, *Anti-intellectualism*, pp. 24-29; and Alvin W. Gouldner, *The Future of Intellectuals and the Rise of the New Class: A Frame of Reference, Theses, Conjectures, Arguments, and an Historical Perspective on the Role of Intellectuals and Intelligentsia in the International Class Contest of the Modern Era* (New York: Seabury Press, Continuum, 1979), pp. 48 and passim, as well as Gouldner's cautions about the political radicalism and nonradicalism of the intellectuals, p. 49.

[5]On the alienation of American intellectuals, see Hofstadter, *Anti-intellectualism*, ch. 15.

[6]Diggins, *American Left*, p. 155.

[7]*Ideology*, p. xiii.

[8]An analogy shared with me by my graduate student Stephen C. Neale, together with his valuable thoughts on intellectuals and reform in general.

[9]See Mannheim, *Ideology and Utopia*, pp. 233-34. The quotation is from p. 233.

[10]Hofstadter, *Anti-intellectualism*, p. 29. See also Alvin W. Gouldner, *Against Fragmentation: The Origins of Marxism and the Sociology of Intellectuals* (New York: Oxford University Press, 1985).

[11]Wrote Schumpeter:

> Labor never craved intellectual leadership but intellectuals invaded labor politics. They had an important contribution to make: they verbalized the movement, supplied theories and slogans for it——class war is an excellent example——made it conscious of itself and in

doing so changed its meaning. In solving this
task from their own standpoint, they naturally
radicalized it, eventually imparting a
revolutionary bias to the most bourgeois trade-
union practices, a bias most of the non-
intellectual leaders at first greatly resented.
But there was another reason for this.
Listening to the intellectual, the workman is
almost invariably conscious of an impassable
gulf if not of downright distrust. In order to
get hold of him and to compete with non-
intellectual leaders, the intellectual is driven to
courses entirely unnecessary for the latter who
can afford to frown.

Capitalism, Socialism and Democracy, pp. 153-54.

Contrasting the European and American experiences, Stanley M.
Elkins adds:

In Europe, the intellectual institutionally
connected——with church, labor movement, or
the like——is seen to act, in a crisis, along
specified lines. He produces explanations for
the followers of the institution, and his
formulations, as a matter of course, give the
institution a central place in the solution of
the crisis. Certain things are thus expected of
the intellectual; his role has specifications.
The intellectual without connections,
chronically the case in America, finds himself
in a fundamentally different position. Society
normally asks little or nothing of him; a
reform situation, on the other hand, seems to
present him with a role. Yet even here the
only pressures exerted on him involve the
maintenance of a steady stream of new and
exciting ideas; his only measurement of effect
must be that of audience appeal; his principal
question must continue to be, How many are
listening? The pressures he does not feel are
the concrete demands of an institution as such;
he feels no direct responsibility for a clientele;
he has, in short, no vested interest. The result

for the intellectual is a situation of no limits. His reform thinking will tend to be erratic, emotional, compulsive, and abstract.

It is in such a setting that guilt——always a necessary element in any reform movement anywhere——comes to assume a unique and disproportionate role in American reform activity. A gnawing sense of responsibility for the ills of society at large appears to be experienced most readily in this country by groups relatively sheltered, by groups without connections and without clear and legitimate functions (a prime example being furnished by the Transcendentalists), and by people who have seen older and honored standards transformed, modified, or thrown aside.

Reforming energy, or a sense of social responsibility, could be designated in terms other than "guilt." But the conditions of American society have made such energy peculiarly a personal, an individual, phenomenon. It is the absence of clear channels for the harnessing of these drives that has made it so. Contrasted with the civilizations of Europe, our Protestant culture with its strong secular inclinations has been conspicuous for its lack of institutions, religious or secular, among whose functions has been the absorption and transformation of guilt. Guilt must be borne as an individual burden to a degree not to be observed elsewhere. Guilt in a structured situation has formalized outlets, limits within which it may be expressed constructively and with effect. Otherwise, it has no such channels. It will thus accumulate, like static electricity; it becomes aggressive, unstable, hard to control, often destructive. Guilt may at this point be transformed into implacable moral aggression: hatred of both the sinner and the sin.

Slavery, pp. 160-61.
[12]See Lipset, *Political Man,* pp. 346-47.

[13]Irving Howe has written:

> A radical movement forms a fraternity proclaiming that all brothers and sisters are equal, but the intellectual, no matter how sincere his egalitarian convictions, has to claim that he knows some things better than other people. The intellectual deals with ideas, those mysterious values radical groups also claim as their own. Yet insofar as they aspire to a collective "line," these groups can never be quite comfortable with free-lance writers and thinkers who work as individuals. As a result, the intellectual in politics must always be in an uncomfortable position, suspect as much as admired, often wanted but seldom embraced. He irritates the activists. He seems arrogant and elitist, he holds himself above the petty tasks of organization, he focuses upon complications of analysis when the "burning need" is action. . . .
>
> The activists are at least as ambivalent toward the intellectuals as the intellectuals toward them. The activists shift between an excessive respect for intellectuals and an irritable hostility; they want some intellectuals in the ranks, but as a decorative auxiliary, to be used or brushed aside as convenient. Between genuine workers and genuine intellectuals there sometimes starts up an odd, amused sort of friendliness, each side at ease in its distance from the other; but intellectuals and semi-intellectuals rub each other raw.

A Margin of Hope, p. 84.

[14]*Affairs of State*, pp. 270-71.

[15]Feuer, *Ideology*, p. 80.

[16]*Liberalism in America*, pp. 109-10.

[17]See Rochester, *American Liberal Disillusionment*, especially pp. 39ff.; and Kennedy, *Over Here*, p. 246.

[18]*War and the Intellectuals: Essays by Randolph S. Bourne, 1915-1919*, ed. Carl Resek (New York: Harper Torchbooks, 1964), p. 5.

[19]See Rochester, *American Liberal Disillusionment*, p. 46.

[20]*End of American Innocence*, p. 355.

[21]*New Radicalism in America*, pp. 253-55.

[22]*American Liberal Disillusionment*, p. 59.

[23]*The New York Little Renaissance: Iconoclasm, Modernism, and Nationalism in American Culture, 1908-1917* (New York: New York University Press, 1976), p. 244.   See also May, *End of American Innocence*, p. 393.

[24]May, *End of American Innocence*, pp. 394-97.

[25]See Leuchtenburg, *Perils of Prosperity*, pp. 142, 146-47.

[26]*The Crack-up*, ed. Edmund Wilson (New York: New Directions, 1956), p. 14.

[27]Dixon Wecter, *The Age of the Great Depression: 1929-1941* (New York: Macmillan Co., 1948), pp. 252-53, 295.

[28]Feuer's term, *Ideology*, p. 90.

[29]*Crisis on the Left*, p. 63.

[30]*Liberalism and Its Challengers*, p. 8.

[31]Lasch, *New Radicalism in America*, p. 316.

[32]Graham, *Planned Society*, p. 93.

[33]See on this tortuous subject Chaim I. Waxman, ed., *The End of Ideology Debate* (New York: Funk & Wagnalls, 1968), as well as Nathan Liebowitz, *Daniel Bell and the Agony of Modern Liberalism* (Westport, Conn.: Greenwood Press, 1985).

[34]Carl E. Schorske, *Fin-de-Siècle Vienna: Politics and Culture* (New York: Alfred A. Knopf, 1980), pp. xxiii-xxiv.   The course of intellectuals and youth who were Communists in the thirties is ably treated in Harvey Klehr, *The Heyday of American Communism: The Depression Decade* (New York: Basic Books, 1984), chs. 4, 16, 18.   See also William L. O'Neill, *A Better World: The Great Schism. Stalinism and the American Intellectuals* (New York: Simon & Schuster, 1982).

[35]Matusow, *Unraveling of America*, p. 4.

[36]*Political Man*, pp. 368-69.

[37]*Believing Skeptics: American Political Intellectuals, 1945-1964* (Westport, Conn.: Greenwood Press, 1978), pp. 3, 5, 40, 55. "Skepticism" italicized in original.

[38]McAuliffe, *Crisis on the Left*, pp. 146-47.

[39]Fowler, *Believing Skeptics*, pp. 48-50, 58-59, 62-63, 121, 141, 149. Arthur M. Schlesinger, Jr., sees liberal optimism turning more pessimistic

between the "First" and "Second" New Deals, much in the manner associated with the post-World War II era. See *Politics of Upheaval*, pp. 397-98.

[40]See Arblaster, *Western Liberalism*, pp. 331-32.

[41]*Crisis on the Left*, p. 73.

[42]Latter points, ibid.

[43]Theodore Rosenof, *Patterns of Political Economy in America: The Failure to Develop a Democratic Left Synthesis, 1933-1950*, Modern American History Series (New York: Garland Publishing, 1983), p. 234.

[44]Concerning the influence of Niebuhr and the new pessimism about humankind, see Arthur M. Schlesinger, Jr., *The Vital Center: The Politics of Freedom* (Boston: Houghton Mifflin Co., 1962), pp. xxii-xxiii, 169-70. For a useful examination of the legacy of patterns of thought in the fifties to the youth and intellectual outbreaks of the sixties, see Richard H. Pells, *The Liberal Mind in a Conservative Age: American Intellectuals in the 1940s and 1950s* (New York: Harper & Row, 1985), pp. 401-9.

[45]*All Things*, p. 173.

[46]Hamby, *Liberalism and Its Challengers*, pp. 327, 346-47.

[47]*Los Angeles Times*, 24 May 1978.

[48]Perhaps the most searching study of neoconservatism is Peter Steinfels's fascinating *The Neoconservatives: The Men Who Are Changing America's Politics* (New York: Simon & Schuster, 1979), on which I have relied heavily.   See also Irving Kristol, "Looking Back on Neo-conservatism: Notes and Reflections," *American Spectator*, November 1977, pp. 6-7.

[49]See Feuer, *Ideology*, pp. 56, 75-77, 86-87.

17

THE DISAFFECTION AND DEPARTURE OF THE YOUNG

If the country submissively pours month after month its wealth of life and resources into the work of annihilation, . . . bitterness will spread out like a stain over the younger American generation. If the enterprise goes on endlessly, the work, so blithely undertaken for the defence of democracy, will have crushed out the only genuinely precious thing in a nation, the hope and ardent idealism of its youth.

Randolph Bourne, 1917

Here was a new generation . . . dedicated more than the last to the fear of poverty and the worship of success; grown up to find all Gods dead, all wars fought, all faiths in man shaken.

F. Scott Fitzgerald, 1920

One generation abandons the enterprises of another like stranded vessels.

Thoreau

Just as many intellectuals depart when reform runs down, so do many of the young. Because this country has a very limited standing left, every insurgent generation must produce its own new one. The processes of involvement and withdrawal are exceedingly complicated for youth, partly due to the complexities of adolescence and early adulthood, and partly because of the esteem in which American society at large has come to hold being young.

During the twentieth century, America has become a "filiarchy" (in Gilman M. Ostrander's term), a nation taking its youth as an exaggerated model or authority.[1] The age-old antagonism between youth and maturity——traditionally between optimism and outrage on one hand, and restraint and resignation on the other——has assumed a fascinating twist. An unprecedented segregation of the generations has set in during this century; yet the worship of youth has led generations of no-longer-young Americans to try to cross back over the line separating them from their juniors, and to imitate them. The youth movements and rebellions of the early twentieth century, and even in a way of the sixties, titillated that very bourgeois America against which the rebellions erupted. Many among the middle-aged middle class have wanted to copy youth itself, with all its aura and style.[2] This means that the importance of what youth think or do——which might otherwise be contained, or absorbed, as it once was by such institutions as the family and the church——magnifies through imitation.

Youth first became "a recognized class in society" during the Progressive Era. In the twenties a chasmic generation gap opened up. Yet so attractive was the other side of the chasm that many among the older and supposedly wiser ventured across with ropes and ladders, rendering the doings of youth less and less distinctly youthful doings. "A children's party taken over by the elders," Fitzgerald called the Jazz Age.[3] Younger Generations have been emerging ever since. But while college youth have repeatedly rebelled against their parents socially, "ideological revolt against the politics of the parents," as Ostrander has emphasized, "has always been a minority movement." Although political radicalism did erupt in the thirties, by and large even that generation chose security over rebellion. If past behavior provides a guide, in general those young will revolt who already feel economically secure.[4]

We will rarely encounter youth in the mainstream of politics. During one generation, they may show indifference toward politics; in the next, many may turn up in large numbers on the left. At the end of a reform era, youth will be found in the van of those retreating from old causes. Their social behavior may help to conceal this fact; yet their social behavior symptomizes as well their fading idealism, waning seriousness, and growing political apathy. Such was the case in the twenties, in the forties and fifties, and again in the seventies.

I do not propose to examine the culture of youth from the perspective of every subculture within it. Little will be said here of teenage factory workers in the twenties, of the duck-tailed and motorcycled storm troopers of the fifties, or of those who backed George Wallace in 1968. Instead, we will focus on political and social trendsetters on the left, which is to say people who are mostly white, middle-class, urban, college educated, and affiliated with student movements.[5]   This bias will, regrettably, reflect biases built into social and political trendsetting itself. The core group consists of a very sensitive age cohort which both shapes and manifests changes in the society at large, and which carries considerable influence. This influence is central to our understanding of radicalism in America. Exploring it will require that we follow some leads established in our earlier examination of radicalism (chapter 4), relating them specifically to youth.

Before proceeding, we must take a look at the nature of adolescence and post-adolescence in this society. Coming of age is no easy thing. The key years for our purposes are those between seventeen or eighteen and twenty-two or twenty-three: the college years and, in developmental terms, what Daniel J. Levinson and his colleagues have called "the Early Adult Transition." Levinson lists two important transformations which must be accomplished in this transition: a termination of adolescence, and a preliminary entry into the realm of adulthood——"to explore its possibilities, to imagine oneself as a participant in it, to make and test some tentative choices before fully entering it." One leaves the world of adolescence, where adults serve "as authorities, teachers, helpers and enemies but not as peers"; yet one remains an adolescent as well as a "novice adult."[6]

Kenneth Keniston has contended that "youth is a *psychological* stage,"[7] and that "millions of young people today are neither psychological adolescents nor sociological adults; they fall into a psychological no man's land, a stage of life that lacks any clear definition."[8] Suspended between adolescence and adulthood, they do not fully belong to the realm of the child or that of the grown-up. Biological and instinctual powers have reached or approached their peak.   The period characterizes itself by stress——inner conflicts, external pressures, and struggling to find one's place in society.   Even when achieved, Levinson emphasizes, the adult identity of the twenties remains a "preliminary" identity.

> As compared with later eras, . . . early adulthood is
> distinguished by its fullness of energy, capability and potential,
> as well as external pressure. In it, personal drives and societal
> requirements are powerfully intermeshed, at times reinforcing
> each other and at times in stark contradiction.[9]

A generation of youth reflects an identifiable set of attitudes and styles characterizing young trend-leaders and their followers over a particular span of time. The emergence of a generation of youth bears only a tangential relationship to biological generations. The vicissitudes of societal experience during their adolescence, together with their reaction, form the character of a generation as we use the term, and generations so shaped may pass in quick succession (even as collegiate "generations" do, every four or five years). Between 1949 and 1963, for instance, no fewer than four generations took some sort of form: the silent, the conservative, the basically apolitical beat, followed at last by the highly politicized New Left.[10] Generational experiences vary from era to era. The youth of the fifties, for instance, had no memory of the Depression. This distinction of subjective experience creates barriers against understanding between the generations, and helps to explain why lefts must constantly be re-created.

While not every generation of youth produces great public outbreaks of dissent, each generation passes through a relatively favorable phase for doing so. This phase involves minimal job, family, and community ties and obligations, and maximum internal pressures; taken together, these nurture "movement" as against "stasis."[11] Separation from one's past is taking place, including separation from one's family. College exposes the young to new, "alien" ideas, both social and political. A truly decent idealism may surface, an outrage at social injustice. Commonly, severe conflicts with parents break out; less extreme reactions range from alienation or indifference to a simple establishment of physical or social distance.[12] "Perhaps the central conscious issue during youth," writes Keniston, "is the *tension between self and society*." Ambivalence becomes a basic characteristic—"*pervasive ambivalence* toward both self and society is the rule: the question of how the two can be made more congruent is often experienced as a central problem of youth." One upshot of this may be activism; another, withdrawal. Temporary roles and identities grow out of this transitional age, and commonly these have a tentative, experimental quality. Here again, the aim of change may be strictly personal and internal, or may direct itself at the wider society. The potential for fanaticism on one hand, or for self-immersion on the other, crests in youth.[13]

Inevitably, the volatile character of this precarious age transition shows up in reform movements, both when young people join and as they leave. No group in society has proved so fad-prone as the young. The faddish nature of youth movements helps account for the striking dissimilarities between them from one generation to another—the presence, for example, of a widely acknowledged generation gap in the sixties and its absence in the thirties, or the way in which outbursts of bohemianism alternate with eras of relative (though never absolute) social conformity. Over the course of the century, the primary question about youth has been whether the bandwagon would carry the young toward political action or away from it. The choice of routes depends quite heavily on what is taking place in the broader society. If a massive depression has come on, or if blacks have reacted against flagrant discrimination, or if the United States has gotten mired down in a Vietnam War, activism has erupted.

Youth will rebel against the very things which many of their liberal or radical elders also deplore. Indeed, youth will hold these elders to the standards of justice and decency in which the older generation professes to believe. (The rhetoric-reality gap exposed by youthful probings can be profound.) This is not to imply that the young will lack their own corps of concerns. They may also accentuate issues which seem of but minor moment to older people. Yet the fundamental questions that animate the young in any given generation will tend to be the issues which drive the society as a whole to the left. What distinguishes youth is not so much the substance of their grievances as their remarkable energy and the unique manner in which they express them.

Young people can rebel politically, or they can rebel culturally, or they can combine the two. In the sixties, as we have seen, students explored several routes at once: New Left activist commitment, hippieism, and the pop left inspired by the writings of Joseph Heller and Ken Kesey and embodied in the Yippies. While the youth outbursts of the pre-World War I and Vietnam eras combined social with political radicalism, that of the thirties largely confined itself to the political variety. John R. Howard has labeled these different approaches the "political" and the "expressive-affective."[14] The personal, individual expressive-affective side of youthful rebelliousness gives it much of its immediacy and strength——yet also much of its weakness, because it provides an avenue for escape into a purely private domain. Political and cultural rebellion exist in constant tension with one another.

The youth movements we are discussing have consistently emerged out of the same class against which the radicals have rebelled: the middle class. Walking into the Greenwich Village of 1914, for example, one would have found young intellectual radicals——enthusiasts of the poor and the recently immigrated——who themselves had been born into the comfortable upper middle class. Or peer in the door of a settlement house and, attending the downtrodden, one would have found young graduates of the same Ivy League universities as the Villageites.[15] For the most part, the young settlement workers were idealists trying to come to grips with the travails of an urban-industrial society. Yet, Allen F. Davis tells us, their own alienation and anxiety were also involved, along with the sense of guilt so commonly associated with social reform.[16] In saying this one runs the risk of suggesting that a person has to feel guilty or show other signs of disturbance in order to get involved in reform. Much more important than guilt or anxiety or alienation, Davis argues, "was recognition of the authentic need for settlements."[17] Still, the guilt did exist, and the Greenwich Village types (some of whom had done settlement work too) also experienced it when they thought of the underclass around them.

As Romantics, the Greenwich Villagers wanted radically to reshape society, not just politically in terms of social justice, but, as we have noted, for individual freedom and equality between the sexes. Conventional morality they denounced. Bourgeois conformity and materialism they spurned. The culturally, intellectually, and politically avant-garde they welcomed; now, they thought, the political and artistic spheres were one. Yet politics operated at cross-purposes with art. Ideas and causes contradicted one another or got thrown together into a brackish stew. Precious little had anything to do with helping the downtrodden. To the degree that the rebels' outbursts took an inward, self-gratifying turn, this tended to dull whatever political edge they had. And in the Village, it was easy to shift back and forth between the bohemian and the modishly respectable.[18]

"With the onset of war in Europe and the demise of international socialism," Robert E. Humphrey has written, "it became increasingly more difficult to anticipate a revolution. Accordingly, Villagers turned inward, focusing on group activities and each other." This does not surprise us. Their main interests all along had been individual freedom, new literature and art, feminism, freer sexuality, and fun. "Ignoring social realities and the power of institutions, Villagers advanced cultural and sexual solutions to political and economic problems." Unwilling to dig day to day in the rocky clay of institutional change, despising progressivism, they took up utopian liberation instead. From the start they had chiefly cultivated their inner selves; now they focused inward even more.[19] As Louis Filler has written, "the youth movement, born in an atmosphere of freedom and hope, ended in an era of repression. It was to reappear in post-War years as irreverent, disdainful of tradition, and impatient with reform."[20]

Without actually creating the social revolt of the twenties, Greenwich Village influenced the decade through its artists, writers, and fashions. Business, in turn, picked up these influences in order to push products. Madison Avenue has a remarkable flair for trivializing reform into commercials. It turns passion into pap. Much as in the sixties, the twenties foreshadowed the combined impact which bohemians and capitalists could wield in changing the national tastes and mores. In the Village, as in the nation, after political radicalism burned away, cultural innovation survived; "talk about revolution" as Malcolm Cowley remarked, "gave way to talk about psychoanalysis."[21]

Culturally, the bohemian Greenwich Village outpouring in many ways resembled similar deviations of the late sixties——in its faith in the young, for example, and the potential which youth supposedly had for salvaging the world; in its crusade for new freedoms and against old taboos and repressions; in the notion of living for the moment; in the belief in maximum individual liberty artistically and otherwise, down to neopagan modes of expression; in feminism; and in escapism even through exile. One thing did distinguish the sixties outburst from previous youth upsurge, though, and that was the sheer size of it. Far more young people passed through bohemianism than ever had before. "The great political rebellion of the sixties was rooted in cultural alienation," writes Godfrey Hodgson. "And its specific character can be traced back to the ideas of a tiny *avant-garde*." Rebellion became democratized.[22] But mere numbers did not resolve some very essential weaknesses.

The problem with the sixties counterculture was that, as an expressive-affective phenomenon heavily preoccupied with matters of taste and style, so much of it operated on the periphery of social problems. (In this sense it ironically resembled a great deal of fifties liberalism.) Fragile bonds——no coherent or unified ideology——loosely held the New Left together. Though the inward and outward, cultural and political sides of sixties radicalism never proceeded completely separately, many of the attributes of the counterculture bore only a marginal relationship to its politics. Because they were emphasized, and because they drew so much anger from outside, the social goals obscured the purely political ones. Sometimes social aims themselves turned political. As an upshot of all this, the range of American politics widened, in that far more issues got discussed; but at the same time, because there were simply too many issues to deal with, the focus of politics blurred. Meantime, what Howard calls the "plastic hippies" dispensed or consumed the strictly "pop" side of counter-existence: "a pop phenomenon, part of pop culture, a successor to the hula hoop and blue suede shoes," and very, very lucrative for their purveyors.[23] As with Greenwich Village four decades earlier, products trivialized causes.

Even so broad a youth movement as this in the end proved remarkably fragile and transitory. Increasingly becoming *the* focus of anger and action, when the war wound down, the Movement declined with it. Genuinely ideological, dedicated, disciplined radical cadres would have outlived Vietnam. The slaughter at Kent State would have spurred them on. We have tended to visualize young people of the late sixties as the last "committed" generation before the great turning off-and-inward of the seventies. But most young people were not radicals. And much of the behavior of the actual radicals represented in varied forms the past or emergent self-centeredness of the turned-off fifties and seventies.

In saying all this I run the risk of seeming too cynical about what happened in the sixties. I do not mean to deny the fundamental importance of moral questions to the young radicals or the legitimacy of their moral concerns. *Of course* Vietnam or racism or environmental destruction should have been protested.[24]

My point, quite simply, is that very few Jane Addamses come along. The kind of creative, activist dissent which stretches over the span of a lifetime, and which, for that matter, does not require that one be an outright radical, occurs but rarely. The sixties radicals who remained actively committed in the 1980s were no doubt vastly exceeded in number by radicals who had become stockbrokers, middle management executives, realtors, and the like. The support of youth for any social cause is volatile, particularly if the cause appears external to the interests of youth as a group. In most cases, the impulse that puts a young middle-class white in the slums to work with lower-class immigrants or blacks will run out. When it ends, the young man or woman will leave——in part because the guilt burns off or burns thin, and in part because the angst of adolescence and the early adult transition lessens simply in that these *are* transitions. And the leave-taking, multiplied by thousands or millions, will mean that the fad has changed. Youth culture will have passed on to the next fad.

If anything, modern society's obsession with the present has stimulated even more of an obsession among the young. The fads seem to run in shorter and shorter bursts. Though cutting off from the past appears essential to contemporary rebellion, youth merely shows a difference in degree but not in kind from the larger society. The tendency to move from progressivism to anti-progressivism, from saving-the-ghettoism to ignoring-the-ghettoism, exhibits changing reactions within the revolving kaleidoscope of fad. The generation gap has become a cultural fixture. What changes——repeatedly——is *how* one rebels, and against what.[25]

Christopher Lasch has written of Malcolm Cowley and Cowley's peers who approached maturity at the end of the Great War:

> Even at seventeen, Cowley and his friends were self-consciously "disillusioned and weary." Each of their successive enthusiasms quickly became passé; enthusiasm itself was passé; and having already lost sight of what it was they were rebelling against, having in fact no pressing need to rebel at all (since they were the children of indulgent parents), they found themselves reduced to going through the motions of what had become at once a ritual and a game, according to which one took whatever position was least expected and abandoned it as soon as others adopted it as their own. . . . However frivolous the amusement, and however frivolously Cowley later chose to write about it, it was nevertheless a response to the inescapable question that had begun to confront each successive generation

of dissenters: when rebellion becomes orthodox, against what does one rebel?

Rebellion has become the orthodox pattern for youth in the twentieth century. One rebels for the sake of rebelling.[26]

Much as the youth culture shows a sort of natural volatility, it is singular in the type of achievement it seeks and the kinds of gains it tends to score. These achievements, most of them, are *negative*.[27] Largely, I suspect, this is because so much in the early adult transition is negative: the breaking away, the anxiety of searching for a self midway between selves. "We felt," wrote Cowley, "that society in general was terribly secure, unexciting, middle class, a vast reflection of the families from which we came."[28] Of course!——rebellion against society amounted to rebellion against the family, and vice versa.

What should we list among the major achievements of youth movements in twentieth century America? *Debunking* organized religion. *Undermining* authority. *Eroding* Victorian morality and traditional values. The *counter*culture. *Exposing* the weaknesses of technocratic, incremental liberalism with its arid resistance to morally impassioned causes. Aiding the victimized——or, stated another way, *fighting* racism and discrimination against minorities, youth, women, and others. Helping to *end* the war in Vietnam. Participation in *dumping* Lyndon Johnson. Creating the climate for *terminating* the draft. Struggling to *stop* environmental degradation. Some of these have represented real accomplishments, and have involved building as well as tearing down. They have humanized the entire society. But the overriding thrust has been negative. Reacting to some of the negativisms of youth——the inversion of conventional middle-class adult tastes through different clothing, personal slovenliness, and fecklessness-by-design——Midge Decter sourly adds: "Not for nothing did you call the collective products of your search for group style and group meaning by the name of 'the counterculture.' For it was a search that utterly depended on, and was positively defined by, that which it opposed. . . . In overcoming us, it seems, has lain your major, perhaps your only, possibility for tasting the joys of triumph."[29]

We can find nothing unique to the sixties here. Youth movements have traditionally demonstrated hostility toward much or most of American society. The anti-Victorians of the teens and twenties reviled the Anglo-American nineteenth century. Young or old, the Marxists of the thirties reviled the capitalist system.[30] The rebels of the sixties perceived all sorts of things in reverse from the "silent majority's" consensus: optimism/pessimism; economic growth/no growth; technology/"natural" lifestyles; marriage/nonmarriage; children/childlessness; interracial accommodation/black power; hawkishness/dovishness; New Deal governmentalism/antigovernment decentralization; patriotism/anti-patriotism; America as good/America as evil.

If a person grows up in a slum, the middle class and the suburbs can look terribly inviting. One may dedicate one's life to a quest for these things. But to the individual whose first eighteen or twenty years are spent with them, Penrod and Ozzie and Harriet and Lawrence Welk and Norman Rockwell can seem absolutely suffocating. As in Cowley's youth, to the sixties young the middle class appeared boring. Liberal incrementalism was boring. Things seemed too dull and too complex at the same time. In rebellion, one must both reduce ideas to their essentials and stimulate opposition. Youth has a particular gift for combining the two.

So the young lash out against middle-class hypocrisy and politics. No reform movement has ever lived up to its billing, and youth take reluctantly to any gaps between promise and performance. This society has promised abundance, yet condoned poverty; held minorities and women back at the same time that it proclaimed equality of opportunity; purveyed sex through the media, but said "wait!"; placed a ladder (a career ladder, an education ladder, a status ladder) in front of youth, and advised them to climb it quickly in their teens and twenties, at a time when instinctual distractions peak. It is upon the most promising young people that the greatest demands in this juggling act fall. No wonder youth rebel——even if no great political issues exist to arouse them. No wonder that the most promising among them so often rebel first.

The counterculture has remained endemic among the middle-class young, social rebellions erupting over and over again around the same issues. Because the 1950s was a neo-Victorian period, for example, the generation of the sixties had to refight old battles of the teens and twenties. Both revolts erupted against the older, comfortable, secure, middle-class lifestyle which had been such a grand goal of the dominant culture in the nineteenth and early twentieth centuries, and the Depression and war-ridden thirties and forties.

In their rebellion——whether muted or part of a generational outburst——the young seek like the intellectuals to identify and ally themselves with groups or classes that share their oppression. As Feuer observes, "every student movement . . . has a populist ingredient. A student movement always looks for some lowly oppressed class with which it can psychologically identify itself."[31] During the early twentieth century it was the workers, the poor, the immigrants, and the ethnics; in the sixties, blacks and browns, then women and gays. As usual, the sixties Movement recruited itself, for the most part, from the middle class. This meant that to whatever degree it tried to speak for the downtrodden, it represented them by proxy. This identification of youthful protestors with the problems of *others* made them especially vulnerable to co-optation and the temptation to drop out of political activity. Many developed a new loathing for the square and repressive hardhats, rednecks, and Bunkers. Films such as *Easy Rider* and *Joe* symbolized their loathing. Uneasily, youth juggled populism with elitism. One of the few groups left reminiscent of the thirties crusades was migrant workers, particularly Mexican Americans. Many among the young befriended their cause.

One reason for the estrangement between young radicals and organized labor inhered in changing attitudes toward economic growth. After World War II, blue-collar workers, many of them newly affluent, demonstrated a remarkable propensity to consume, even when they might well have felt satiated; "more" had always been the great cause of organized labor. Young emigrés from the middle class might choose to live in dingy communes, protest Vietnam, and drive small, fuel-conserving cars; plumbers and machinists picked suburbia, instructed college students to Love It or Leave It (the United States), and drove overpowered pickups and motorhomes. From Wilson to Galbraith, economic expansion had held a crucial place in liberal theory. Labor wanted none of zero growth. Workers and students skirmished across the environmental barricades.

The counterculture held big government and all other large institutions in suspicion; in this sense it was unconsciously Brandeisian. The New Left lambasted bureaucracy and lauded participatory democracy. In a way, it wanted to return to the preindustrial era, or at least the pre-New Deal era. In calling attention to big government as dangerous and self-serving, New Leftists lumped it with business. While the general legacy of this anti-institutionalism was partly good for reform——stimulating the emergence of consumer watchdog groups, environmental organizations, and so on——it also undercut reform because it tended to blur the distinctions between all big institutions at the expense of government.

The history of politicized youth suggests that they will view two-party politics and "mere" bread-and-butter issues as a bore or a threat, and will swing more deeply left, more deeply right, or more deeply into apathy than will the public at large. All of these characteristics carry on from decade to decade; what changes is the proportion of youth in the various states of attitude. But none of this should surprise us. As an outgroup, the young either opt out or else affiliate with other outgroups. They seem particularly given to movements or individuals who promise simple or sweeping or uncostly solutions to national problems, including those of the young. Discovering that life has unpleasant complexities, that few choices can be made without cost——these things come with maturity. And then the vigor which accompanies false clarity begins to wane. This is why youth on occasion make such fine shock troops.

The young will incline toward a social movement that mixes artistic and spiritual liberation with its politics. Bohemianism of one kind or another will front the movement like a pane of colored glass, tinting the image of observers and observed alike. The stereotypical male college student who in 1972 campaigned door-to-door for McGovern wearing sandals and a beard represented his subculture to the broader culture. The person who opened the door saw the young campaigner as a personification of the values of George McGovern. The student may have felt that spending his time in this way was a highly moral act. But he would likely have the door slammed in his face if its owner wore a blue collar to work. The hardhat would impulsively dismiss the student as, among other things, immoral.

Yet the New Morality never represented No Morality. At the very same time that they have seemed to challenge most of society's fundamental moral precepts, youth movements have often claimed they operated on a higher plane than society at large. However much contempt they have shown for conventional bourgeois values, they have at least been moral on their own terms. One can argue that each of them has been touched by the spirit of transcendentalism, however little of Emerson or Thoreau their leaders may have read. Varieties of religious experience, idealism, and mysticism also ebb and flow through them, making youth movements more various and colorful (as well as even more unintelligible to the public).[32] No doubt the tension between the other world and this world creates a pull toward and yet a pull away from political action in the minds of many of the young. But their inclination to disdain traditional Methodism or Catholicism, like their disdain for traditional Republicanism, may prove costly to the left where culture intersects with politics. A cross on the chest of our hirsute McGovernite might at least have kept the door open, or ajar.

The affinity between the left and "deviant" lifestyles also grows in part from the left's contempt for property and authority. To a conservative, marriage, for example, may signify one more form of property ownership clothed in the sanctity of contract. An authoritarian conservative male will relish his role as head of the family. A radical will react to marriage with particular suspicion if marriage is perceived as just one more symbol of property and authority——as wed*lock*.

In the realm of the symbolic, remarkably small things serve to separate even persons with similar economic interests. The classic example in this country is skin color. Another, during the late sixties and early seventies, was male hairstyles. People actually got *angry* over hair. Before the Civil War, beards had symbolized the left. Then the beard moved "right":[33] post-Civil War Americans saw the heavy beard as a symbol of masculinity and reliable adherence to the Victorian virtues. During the 1960s a beard suggested precisely the opposite. Now the symbolism of men's hairstyles ran like this:

Long unkempt hair (particularly with a beard in a similar state) = radical

Shorter hair, sideburns reaching down as far as the earlobes, perhaps a moustache = liberal

Still shorter hair, especially if carefully shaved around the neck and ears, no sideburns, no moustache = conservative

A similar pattern appeared in clothing styles. The sixties demonstrator commonly looked like Christ in Levis. Wide ties, broad lapels, flared trousers, and bright colors went with medium-length hair, sideburns, and trimmed moustaches. Narrow ties, narrow lapels, conservative colors, and conservative hair matched conservative men. And in music: to the average, middle-aged, middle-class ear, acid rock had all the charm of, say, Schoenberg.

Symbols change; times change. The fundamental personal qualities that most fraternities and sororities value never entirely disappear among the student population, and as activism, unrest, and nihilism recede, these qualities reassert themselves. One might summarize them as personableness without abrasiveness; an emphasis on group success within the value structure of the campus polity (for example, through college governance or sports) rather than through the national polity; and a de-emphasis on personal depth in favor of the superficial traits of the social mixer. Other-directedness (in David Riesman's term), always abundant on campus, fully returns to fashion. Individualism of the sort oriented toward causes and commitments becomes an eccentricity. The new prevailing mood might be described as upbeat cynicism. To the degree that radicalism continues through a decade like the 1920s or the 1950s, it takes more a cultural form than a political one.[34]

The archetype of this conservative peer culture emerged in the 1920s. "Never before," writes Paula S. Fass, "had so many youths been so insulated in a world so completely dominated by other youths and sheltered from adult example." Campuses in the twenties became levers of a sort for social change, but the change had to do with "sexuality and style" rather than with the economic system, class conflict, or the other, bigger structural issues which had engaged the progressives. "The peer culture thus socialized the young to stability and change; it anchored attitudes in basic social structures and directed values toward personal liberties and rapid changes in cultural tastes and styles."[35] In periods of reaction, students make their peace with the Chamber of Commerce and prepare to join it.

The atmosphere need not be quite so anti-academic and fraternity-oriented as in the twenties to act with similar corrosiveness on matters of political significance. During conservative eras, young people still raise hell——while conforming. In the early seventies male business majors might live with their girl friends rather than simply petting with them as in the twenties, but the suits and vests they donned upon graduation looked remarkably similar to their grandfathers'. "On the whole," Fass writes of the twenties,

> the young were politically apathetic. Little interested in political or economic issues, they neither pressed for change nor partook actively in political discussions. [Uplift drew snickers or sneers.] Nevertheless, in the context of the period, they were an intensely political generation.

What stirred their ardor was neither economics nor politics——here they were conservative——but individual freedom. And this explains the paradox of their political nonpolitics: they could object to repressive "reforms" like prohibition and look political or even liberal doing it. "They were thus able in their beliefs and actions to separate political conservatism from cultural liberalism, and to become businessmen and jazz hounds, Republicans and flappers."[36]

In the familiar mold of youth, the pallid goals of the twenties stressed the negative. Thus the issue that came closest to breaking the political somnolence on campus was compulsory ROTC. Other generations of youth seethed over questions of war and peace. The ROTC issue, instead, focused on freedom of choice. Fass again: "Youth were not self-consciously political because they acquiesced in most of the policies embraced by the nation." Posing no challenge to the country's fundamental institutions, not even to marriage, students developed the better part of what political consciousness they had by braking movements against personal freedom and modernity. A student at UCLA remarked in 1926 that "the only subjects that are getting any attention from the 'political minded' are Prohibition, Birth Control and the Bible Issue, none of which are [sic] in the least related [a telling overstatement] to politics or political wisdom."[37] Permissive in matters private and individual, students were conservative, like the decade, in matters political and economic. At the same time, they discounted such issues in general. To a remarkable degree, they reflected the mass political anesthetization and relative political issuelessness of the 1920s. For all their sexual expressiveness, they did not get involved in an ideological-generational upheaval, but only in a cultural outburst.[38]

As in so many other realms, the twenties left a paradigm for the future. One had to wait for the fifties for a college generation which shared such apathy. If anything, the youth of the fifties plunged even deeper into aimlessness. The devastation of the far left and the rightward shift of liberalism weakened resistance to a national conservative swing among all age groups. True, to some degree one could preview what the sixties would bring—in the coffee houses, among the beats, in the poetry of Lawrence Ferlinghetti, in rock music, in the recordings of Tom Lehrer, and in the pages of *Mad* magazine. Some elements of student radicalism bridged the 1950s.[39] Generally, though, the decade produced as close to a politically comatose younger generation as the century has seen. No one could doubt in the twenties that it was a decade of at least social transition. The fifties gave the false sense that the transition had been completed. Students lived in isolation and often anomie, suspended without community between the social camaraderie which had gone before and the political camaraderie which would arrive in the sixties. Indeed, the fifties amounted to a decade of suspension, neither politically activist nor socially especially adventurous. "The investigator attempting to describe the political flavor of contemporary American campuses," observed one study as late as 1960,

> is immediately and forcefully struck by two themes. The first is what seems to be a remarkable absence of any intense or consuming political beliefs, interests or convictions on the part of the college students. The second is extreme political and economic conservatism.[40]

In the early seventies, as the Movement expired, it began to dawn on observers that student activism had fallen off again. Talk could be heard on all sides comparing the oncoming generation to its fifties counterpart. The potential had always existed for decay. As Godfrey Hodgson has observed:

> Both the heavily committed political radicals and those who took seriously the search for a private salvation were tiny minorities surrounded by the half-serious multitudes of their occasional followers. While an inner minority plunged deeper and deeper into alienation from society either through commitment to political extremism or through withdrawal to the north woods of Oregon or to some Oregon of the mind, for the majority the counter culture soon degenerated into a complex of fashions and attitudes. . . . By the end of the decade, for a majority the counter culture had degenerated into

> a mere youth cult. Its values were often no longer determined
> by the aspiration to build a freer society so much as by an
> Oedipal hostility to the older generation.[41]

Sixties political radicalism had always furnished a therapeutic sense of direction for some among the otherwise directionless.[42] In the seventies, escape and comfort edged aside confrontation. The familiar correlation between political apathy and social innovation——sex, drugs——remained. (During the twenties, after all, the flapper had coexisted with Coolidge politics. Even the Eisenhower era had produced a Presley, a Dean, and other rebels without causes.)   A survey disclosed that fewer college students identified themselves as "left" or "liberal" by 1975 than had in 1969 (35 versus 44 percent).   Attitudes toward busing and capital punishment had moved significantly to the right——but more students favored legalizing marijuana than before.[43] Peter Frampton and Olivia Newton-John became the reigning king and queen of mellowed popular music.

Prosperity had significantly underwritten the Movement; sixties America thought it could take affluence and security for granted. The seventies brought an end to this. There was a recession from 1969 to 1972. Stagflation implied that automatic income and automatic jobs no longer existed, if they ever had. The New Left had practically ignored economics, which dated it after the downturn began. Once young people had to begin thinking about the economy again, they also had to contemplate their economic self-interest. Affluence no longer seemed so contemptible under threat. As the job market tightened up, grades and degrees became more important.   In education, including higher education, it was back to basics——accounting instead of anthropology. Shorter, tidier hair greeted corporate recruiters.

During the thirties, the New Deal had co-opted radicalism; Nixon's so-called Vietnamization, along with his China trip, détente, the draft lottery, and the volunteer army operated toward co-opting it again. Not content with that, the Nixonians pummeled the New Left with verbiage as well as such less reputable methods as the misuse of undercover agents who infiltrated it, inciting political cannibalism and even violence from within.[44] Nixon's fancy political footwork made him a hard figure for the left successfully to attack. As the Movement dissolved, some of its adherents opted for the more vacant varieties of Marxism-Leninism, or else for equally unsuitable ideologies of Third World revolution. They fired polemical barrages at one another in sterile echoes of the 1930s. Though a number found a route into the seventies for continued political activity, the Movement per se had come apart in factional mitosis, revolutionary theory, terrorist practice, and countercultural escapism.   Some envisioned an emerging, left-trending coalition comprised of excluded minorities, labor, intellectuals, and professionals, but this never took hold.[45]

Perhaps the simple act of pushing reforms too long and too hard produces these effects. Like any other fad, reform wears out. But clearly, too, the left's own stridency undermines it. In each era when liberalism has been strong, the radical left has shown strength as well. Its publicity and demonstrations have aided liberal causes. But its moralistic shrillness and carping in time tangle up the reform environment and generate a violent backlash.[46] The campus radicalism of the sixties did just this: it moved so far left that it lost whatever touch it had had with the masses. It relinquished its hold on the public mind. It would have given little comfort to the students who got attacked by construction workers in New York to know that previous lefts had made the same mistake. Carried along by their own rhetoric and ideologies, radicals dissolve into sectarian bickering or irrelevant verbalizing or violence.

The 1960s demonstrated that when a reform movement ebbs, the left will find itself holding the rear positions, a suicide operation. Sometimes the radicals grow more radical and go on shooting away. Often they surrender, or even switch sides. A left-leaning political maverick who mainly wants to influence the system can go on for years getting defeated, making small gains here and there, and accepting it all. But the genuinely ideological radical, unlike the maverick, often turns bitter after leaping for transforming power and missing it. Embitterment seems virtually inevitable because the ring, for the radical left, almost always remains out of reach.

Some veterans of the New Left underwent a change of heart, or at least of tactics. Huey Newton announced in 1972 that the Black Panthers had thrown over their desire to smash the system in favor of rendering it "more relevant and kind."[47] Fellow Panther Bobby Seale ran for mayor of Oakland the following year. Tom Hayden kept up the fight, but through political channels and wearing a suit and tie. Perhaps the saga of Jerry Rubin became the most famous of all: "In five years, from 1971 to 1975, I directly experienced est, gestalt therapy, bioenergetics, rolfing, massage, jogging, health foods, tai chi, Esalen, hypnotism, modern dance, meditation, Silva Mind Control, Arica, acupuncture, sex therapy, Reichian therapy, and More House——a smorgasbord course in New Consciousness."[48] So it went.[49]

While youths' old impulse to accommodate themselves to the political and economic system reasserted itself yet again, much of the cultural radicalism stirred by the sixties endured.[50] One might say that society at large co-opted it; the "counter" became reconciled with the "culture." The step from hippiedom in the sixties to est, consciousness raising, and health food in the seventies was short. Predictably, then, the cultural sixties long outlived the political sixties. The cultural twenties had done the same. The countercultural conventions that (more or less) became American conventions during the subsequent Me Decade included feminism, suspicion of officialdom and established institutions, emphasis on personally chosen lifestyles, changes in the family and in attitudes toward it, the new morality in sex, and the drug culture. Some of these trends would have emerged or were emerging anyway; yet even if they predated the sixties, each received a distinctive twist and emphasis from the rebellion of youth. Other trends developed as well, some important, some merely symptomatic, among them swearing, bralessness, the reappearance of hair on the male face, health food, unisex fashions, blue jeans and other casual styles of clothing, meditation, biofeedback, some lingering communes, new patterns of humor, and free clinics. And the afterlife of the counterculture could still be seen years later in the antinuclear movement, environmentalism, and the consumer movement, as well as in the new watchdog role which Congress assumed for itself in foreign and domestic affairs. Important though many of these were, most of them seemed tame compared to the hard social and political realities which radicals had once confronted and to the solutions they had once offered.

The Movement had never equated entirely, or perhaps even principally, with helping other people. What Peter Clecak terms "the search for personal authenticity and fulfillment" grew in importance as time passed.[51] This helps us understand why the cultural legacy of the sixties for society as a whole was more important than its distinctly political legacy. The cultural realm involved a confrontation with power only obliquely, and the power structure could yield a good deal here anyway. Cracking through political barriers by way of political confrontation engendered far more resistance.

If anything more cultural than political in its critique, the Movement called for revolution in a hostile setting. It merely generated a revolt. No wonder the New Left had trouble finding older allies. Its very shallowness helps explain the suddenness of its decline. Insufficiently and improperly grounded ideologically, yet emotionally charged, it tended to float away from reality. Nor, as it turned out, could an impassioned crusade in behalf of this society's victims burn for long on the quickly evaporating fuel of moral outrage.[52]

NOTES

Bourne, *War and the Intellectuals*, p. 21; F. Scott Fitzgerald, *This Side of Paradise* (1920; reprint, New York: Charles Scribner's Sons, 1960), p. 282; Henry David Thoreau, *Walden* (New York: Doric Books,

1950?), p. 10. See also John Strachey, *The Strangled Cry and Other Unparliamentary Papers* (New York: William Sloane Associates, 1962), pp. 185-86. My distinction in chapters 16 and 17 between intellectuals and youth may seem artificial. The youth we will discuss are by and large budding intellectuals of one sort or another, in that they are students. Hence Richard Flacks's term, "intellectual youth," seems apt. Yet enough differences remain between this younger incipient intelligentsia and the established intellectuals to require that we examine them separately. Richard Flacks, *Youth and Social Change* (Chicago: Rand McNally, Markham, 1971), p. 53.

[1]*American Civilization in the First Machine Age: 1890-1940* (New York: Harper & Row, 1970), p. 2 and passim. I am indebted to Joseph Morris for pointing out that today the worship of youth in this society may well be on the decline. With the U.S. population aging, youth represent a smaller fraction of society than formerly. And proportionately fewer yet come from the white middle-class mainstream, the traditional opinion leaders. We may, in short, have seen filiarchy pass its peak.

[2]See Filler, *Vanguards and Followers*, p. 191.

[3]*The Crack-up*, p. 15.

[4]Ostrander, *First Machine Age*, pp. 20, 22, 24-25.

[5]I take this term from Feuer, who, however, does not see particularly great generational disequilibrium breaking out in the first thirty years of this century. I do, in the broader sense of what occurred in Greenwich Village, as well as in the cultural rebelliousness of the twenties. But to collectivize such things as a "movement" of one sort or another would strain the term, as Feuer would doubtless agree. See Feuer, *Conflict of Generations*, pp. 20, 341-44, 351.

[6]Daniel J. Levinson et al., *The Seasons of a Man's Life* (New York: Alfred A. Knopf, 1978), pp. 20, 22, 51, 72-74.

[7]*Youth and Dissent*, p. 17. Italics in original.

[8]Ibid., p. 3. Italics deleted.

[9]*Seasons*, pp. 22-23.

[10]Feuer, *Conflict of Generations*, p. 373.

[11]Keniston, *Youth and Dissent*, p. 10. Italics deleted.

[12]Levinson, *Seasons*, p. 74.

[13]Keniston, *Youth and Dissent*, pp. 8-10, 18, 150. Italics in original. This discussion of the general background of youth movements should not be understood as foreclosing specific explanations of specific movements. Youthful rebellion in the sixties, for example, has been interpreted as an outgrowth of the tightening organizational constrictions of modern society; of the sudden jump in the numbers of young (and attendant competition to get a leg up in society); of the declining status associated with the college degree; and of other factors. See Bell,

Cultural Contradictions, pp. 189-90. For a particularly bleak view of the motivations of the student left of the 1960s, see Stanley Rothman and S. Robert Lichter, *Roots of Radicalism: Jews, Christians, and the New Left* (New York: Oxford University Press, 1982).

[14]*The Cutting Edge: Social Movements and Social Change in America* (Philadelphia: J. B. Lippincott Co., 1974), pp. 171-72. Italics deleted. Howard is writing here specifically of the sixties and seventies. Compare Keniston's terms, "political activism and cultural alienation." *Youth and Dissent*, p. 150.

[15]May, *End of American Innocence*, p. 304; Allen F. Davis, *Spearheads for Reform: The Social Settlements and the Progressive Movement, 1890-1914* (New York: Oxford University Press, 1970), p. 33.

[16]Davis, *Spearheads for Reform*, pp. 38-39.

[17]Ibid., p. 39.

[18]Humphrey, *Children of Fantasy*, pp. 7-10, 20. Humphrey elaborates: "Villagers hoped to build a sanctuary for rebels and to revolutionize society; they wanted to live freely and to influence public policies. Village rebels thought that they could isolate themselves from society and yet have an impact on it. They assumed that there was a positive relationship between self-development and social reform, and they infused personal gestures with political meaning. Their first priority was an unstructured existence in Greenwich Village. They wanted to establish an open community based on social and sexual equality that could serve as a model for the rest of society. But expectations exceeded opportunities and capabilities.

"Villagers acclaimed private acts of rebellion as significant attacks on conventional values." Ibid., p. 237.

[19]Ibid., pp. 22-23, 34-35, 50.

[20]*Vanguards and Followers*, p. 64.

[21]*Exile's Return: A Literary Odyssey of the 1920s* (New York: Viking Press, Compass Books, 1956), pp. 64, 67.

[22]*America in Our Time*, p. 310.

[23]*Cutting Edge*, pp. 191-92.

[24]Ironically, the highest rate of opposition to the Vietnam War was among people over age 64. Timothy M. James, "The Trade," *Wilson Quarterly* 9 (New Year's 1985): 122.

[25]Christopher Lasch has argued along similar lines. See *New Radicalism in America*, pp. 70-71.

[26]Ibid., pp. 71-73.

[27]See also Christopher Bone, *The Disinherited Children: A Study of the New Left and the Generation Gap* (New York: Schenkman Publishing Co., John Wiley & Sons, 1977), part 2. For a discussion of the negative side of *liberalism*, by contrast, see Doudna, *Concerned about the Planet*, pp. 9-10.

[28]*Exile's Return*, pp. 18-19.

[29]*Liberal Parents, Radical Children* (New York: Coward, McCann & Geoghegan, 1975), p. 35.

[30]I treat the quite important student movement of that decade in another context. See p. 367.

[31]*Conflict of Generations*, p. 20.

[32]During the fifties, for instance, organized religion made something of a comeback on campus. In the sixties, organized religion became one of many targets for the young. Religion had replaced ideology, only to see itself replaced in turn. Feuer, *Conflict of Generations*, p. 376.

In the seventies and eighties, religion staged another recovery on campus as ideology waned.

[33]See Feuer, *Ideology*, pp. 86-87. On the symbolism of male facial hair in general, see Alison Lurie, *The Language of Clothes* (New York: Random House, 1981), passim.

[34]This paragraph has been heavily influenced by Paula S. Fass, *The Damned and the Beautiful: American Youth in the 1920's* (New York: Oxford University Press, 1977), pp. 156-57, 245; and Bell, *Cultural Contradictions*, pp. 42, 45.

[35]*The Damned and the Beautiful*, pp. 246-47.

[36]Ibid., pp. 278, 328-29. See also Filler, *Vanguards and Followers*, pp. 64-67.

[37]Fass, *The Damned and the Beautiful*, pp. 262, 346, 355-56.

[38]See ibid., pp. 326, 354-57.

[39]See Maurice Isserman, *If I Had a Hammer . . . : The Death of the Old Left and the Birth of the New Left* (New York: Basic Books, 1987).

[40]Rose K. Goldsen et al., *What College Students Think* (Princeton: D. Van Nostrand Co., 1960), p. 97.

[41]*America in Our Time*, p. 350.

[42]Christopher Lasch, *The Culture of Narcissism: American Life in an Age of Diminishing Expectations* (New York: W. W. Norton & Co., 1978), p. 7.

[43]Thousand Oaks (Calif.) *News Chronicle*, 9 March 1977.

[44]William H. Chafe, *The Unfinished Journey: America since World War II* (New York: Oxford University Press, 1986), p. 413.

[45]See Clecak, *Ideal Self*, especially pp. 52, 55.

[46]Long ago, Theodore Roosevelt noted the impact of the "professional impracticables" on reform: "Some decent men, following their lead, withdraw themselves from the active work of life, whether social, philanthropic, or political, and by the amount they thus withdraw from the side of the forces of good they strengthen the forces of evil, as, of course, it makes no difference whether we lessen the numerator or increase the denominator. Other decent men are so alienated by such conduct that in their turn they abandon all effort to fight for reform,

believing reformers to be either hypocrites or fools."   "Latitude and Longitude," pp. 51-52.

[47]Unger, *The Movement*, p. 202.

[48]*Growing (Up) at Thirty-Seven* (New York: M. Evans & Co., 1976), p. 20.

[49]A good many New Leftists lowered their goals and went into such enterprises as food cooperatives, tenants' unions, and the like, a phenomenon which Michael Walzer has aptly termed "the New Left in pastoral retreat." *Radical Principles: Reflections of an Unreconstructed Democrat* (New York: Basic Books, 1980), pp. 176-77. But emphasis on the defection of sixties radicals easily lends itself to overstatement. See, for example, Tom Hayden, "America and the Populist Impulse: The New Left's Legacy," *Los Angeles Times*, 17 September 1978; and Richard Flacks's quite positive assessment in *Making History*, pp. 167-68.

[50]See Robert C. Toth, "'60s Movement Seeps into U.S. Life-Style," *Los Angeles Times*, 3 September 1978; and William G. McLoughlin, *Revivals, Awakenings, and Reform: An Essay on Religion and Social Change in America, 1607-1977*, Chicago History of American Religion (Chicago: University of Chicago Press, 1978), p. 212.

[51]*Ideal Self*, pp. 123, 221.

[52]See Matusow, *Unraveling of America*, pp. 309, 321, 343.

18

BACKLASH

Liberalism and Libertinism

Like a prairie-fire, the blaze of revolution was sweeping over every American institution of law and order a year ago. It was eating its way into the homes of the American workman, its sharp tongues of revolutionary heat were licking the altars of the churches, leaping into the belfry of the school bell, crawling into the sacred corners of American homes, seeking to replace marriage vows with libertine laws, burning up the foundations of society.

> A. Mitchell Palmer, ca. 1919

Young men and women who a few years before would have been championing radical economic or political doctrines were championing the new morality and talking about it everywhere and thinking of it incessantly.

> Frederick Lewis Allen on the 1920s

You know the young comrade X. He is a splendid lad, and highly gifted. For all that, I am afraid that he will never amount to anything. He has one love affair after another. This is not good for the political struggle and for the revolution.

> Lenin

The backsliding of the intellectuals and young in the decline phase of a reform era interconnects with another process which accelerates the left's demise. At the risk of subsuming too much under one word, I shall call this the rise of libertinism. Self-indulgence, self-centeredness, narcissism, "me-ism"——these terms help describe the phenomenon. So do the words hedonism and sybaritism; but both phenomena have always characterized this society, especially since the twenties, and in common usage suggest too many things: automobile tail fins, jewelry-encrusted fingers, conspicuous consumption of all kinds. We will employ the word libertinism, then, for it will suggest the precise connection I wish to identify between politics on one hand, and licentiousness——involving such things as sex, drugs, alcohol, and escapism——on the other.

By its very nature, the right stresses the traditional values: authority, private property, family, and religion. To the degree (a very significant degree) that the left has questioned or attacked these values, it has generated its own opposition. The problem is that the person who is prone to question anything may likely question everything. "In the history of the world," Emerson observed in 1841,

> the doctrine of Reform had never such scope as at the present hour. Lutherans, Hernhutters, Jesuits, Monks, Quakers, Knox, Wesley, Swedenborg, Bentham, in their accusations of society, all respected something——church or state, literature or history, domestic usages, the market town, the dinner table, coined money. But now all these and all things else hear the trumpet, and must rush to judgment——Christianity, the laws, commerce, schools, the farm, the laboratory; and not a kingdom, town, statute, rite, calling, man, or woman, but is threatened by the new spirit.[1]

It would not do to argue that political radicalism necessarily and always cohabits with cultural radicalism; that, for example, an individual may not at the same time be a socialist and a sexual prude. (One sees the phenomenon on a mass basis, for instance, in Mao's China.) But where the tendency to speak out against cultural norms does exist, it usually arises somewhere on the left. Thus libertinism is a hazard to political liberalism precisely because it competes with and threatens liberalism's priorities. Ironically, though, the hazard derives from exactly the same liberal rationalism and skepticism which nourish both political liberalism and social nonconformity. All of this likewise suggests a problem for conservatives: that while the United States is basically politically conservative, it has given itself over more freely to economic and social change. Hunting for points of social consistency and cohesion on which to ground a conservative tradition resembles a search for surviving structures amid the swirling eddies of a flood. This is especially so with sex.

While this society has enjoyed technological and constitutional sophistication for a very long time, it has had to overcome the most naive attitudes toward sexuality. Sex has been called America's last frontier.[2] Complex reasons lie behind America's historic sex-negativism, having to do, among other things, with Judeo-Christianity and the prudery of the rising bourgeoisie. But Daniel Bell suggests an important transformation when he argues that

> the cultural, if not moral, justification of capitalism has become hedonism, the idea of pleasure as a way of life. And in the liberal ethos that now prevails, the model for a cultural image has become the modernist impulse, with its ideological rationale of the impulse quest as a mode of conduct. It is this which is the cultural contradiction of capitalism. It is this which has resulted in the double bind of modernity.[3]

Capitalism, Bell argues, wrecked the Protestant ethic "through mass production and mass consumption . . . by zealously promoting a hedonistic way of life. . . . The rising standards of living and the relaxation of morals became ends in themselves as the definition of personal freedom."[4]

Clearly a relationship exists between affluence and economic growth on one hand, and hedonism on the other. In itself, rising affluence helps to fuel libertinism generally.[5] This holds true both over the long haul and during those periods (the Gilded Age, the twenties, the fifties) when prosperity and affluence have boomed. As abundance became more democratized, so did the kinds of "loose" behavior which often had traditionally accompanied it among the favored classes. Social rebellion of the sort that once belonged to small groups has expanded into freewheeling sex, widespread use of drugs, and so on. On the great social and cultural questions, more or less unlike the economic ones, business has not taken any single, unified stand. Much of what it has done has conspicuously encouraged social "deviance."[6] Business aside, conservatives have traditionally argued that a permissive society, one without absolutes, is both hollow and tyranny-prone. Ironically, the liberty and individualism which they cherish help to stimulate the permissiveness they deplore.

Some of the shackles of sexual conservatism have been worn through by a steady process of filing which has gone on throughout the century. Others have yielded to a very sharp saw applied twice, just before and during the 1920s, and in the 1960s. But it would overstate things to say that this country has even yet achieved sexual maturity.

Inverting Victorianism, many Americans tackled sexual activity after the sixties with such exhausting industriousness that the Protestant ethic seemed to be working in reverse.

The generations of the twenties and the sixties claimed to have rediscovered sex (despite considerable biological evidence to the contrary). In the twenties and the late sixties to early seventies, sex became a national obsession.[7] Suggestively, these two so-called sexual revolutions followed the ebb of reform movements. One corollary of a waning interest in reform politics, and politics in general, has apparently been a rising interest in and/or focus on sex. In the 1920s, and again in the 1970s, we abandoned political liberalism but embraced social libertinism: sex, alcohol, drugs.

Why? Historians of civilization have often commented upon the tendency of a generation bent on conquest or other great tasks to yield in turn to an age of sensuousness. At the level of the individual, too, there appears to be a conflict between the pursuit of animal pleasures and of great causes. Libertinism is a distraction, an escape. Like other forms of self-indulgence, it may provide a release from a prior state of overwrought purposefulness.

Our reform eras have been times of such purposefulness. They have also been periods when everything has gotten questioned. And while "everything" pertained mainly to matters of economics, class, and politics (narrowly construed) in the thirties, the questioning delved far more widely in the progressive period and the Kennedy-Johnson era.

The eruption of major wars at the end of each of these periods complicated things further yet, at great cost to constructive idealism. A depression or a total war generates immense pressures to conform, for the sake of personal survival in the case of the former and for personal and national survival in the latter. When wars end, conformist tension relaxes. Boredom sets in. The question becomes, what next? Lacking a societal answer to that, society being exhausted by this time, the tendency is to turn inward and ask the question of oneself—what may *I* do for excitement? Libertines cultivate an overriding sense of the Me in the Now. The tense is Now, and they want to be indulged in the Now.

We have identified three factors, then, which link politics directly or indirectly to libertinism: a widespread questioning of all conventionalities; the desire to escape from purposefulness; and the extinguishing or dampening of idealism. Sexual adventurism appears to tie into several other phenomena which have also followed our reform eras and wars. One is prosperity, which underwrites all the champagne, motel rooms, and divorces. Another is disillusionment with the various forms of authority which enforce conventional moral codes, and most particularly with government. Yet another factor has involved women's growing financial independence, characteristic of urban women in the twenties (despite the decline of organized feminism) and likewise in the seventies. Together, all these factors suggest that periods of political reform tend to set loose social upheavals. To the extent that the thirties proved an exception, this is attributable to the rather narrower, economic focus which the Depression compelled, and the fact that World War II did not produce anything like the reaction which had erupted against World War I or which burst out over Vietnam.

Radicalism provides a special window into libertinism because it so often exaggerates it. "Most American radicals," David Popenoe wrote in 1977,

> feel that the answers to America's problems lie not only in radical political change, but also *radical cultural change.* Political socialism is not enough; most American radicals tend to side with the counterculture (if they are not in fact themselves members of the counterculture) in its antipathy toward "law and order," "familism," "middle-class morality," instinctual repression, restraints on behavioral freedom, and so on. They seek a more pleasure-oriented, do-your-own-thing value pattern and life style.[8]

This cultural antipathy toward the bourgeoisie costs the left political support; it even splits the left itself. Yet it is a very old tradition. To follow the tradition we must first take another, closer look at the Lyrical Left.

The early twentieth century American left emphasized feeling and passion as much as reason. We have seen that the Lyricals intermingled social with political revolt——against Victorianism, against capitalism. As Henry F. May has observed:

> Moralistic progressivism, like the whole nineteenth-century culture on which it rested, was a fundamentally unstable compound. It called for questioning ideas and institutions, yet it rested itself on values that must not be questioned. Inevitably, a few dissenters began to push through this limitation.[9]

Ordinary politics did not amount to enough. Education, childhood, and especially sex became *political* questions.[10] Greenwich Village in the teens produced a fusion of "art and activism" which "celebrated everything and anything that was new."[11] Anything which made up the genteel tradition came under attack: its confidence in the supposedly enduring truths it had found, its literature, its manners, its prudery, its tastes. Steeped in the likes of Freud, Nietzsche, Bergson, and D. H.

Lawrence, many radicals substituted a "new morality" of joyous and carefree sensuousness. To hell, they said, with responsibility. Their new politics combined activism, culture, art, and sex.

Village rebels regarded sexual rebellion as a political statement. Largely uninterested in hard political commitment and discipline, many flaunted their personal behavior as a political act; some let their quest for social change stop there. Their world lived on symbols, not power; on gestures, not systems.[12]   So Greenwich Village became a complex amalgam of Freud and Marx, free love and exotic dance. It sneered at the hypocritical-moralistic bourgeois cant of the older generation and embraced those who did not belong to the great Anglo-Saxon club. But it did not produce a program. It had no ism; it had isms. The sex and the art on one hand, the politics on the other, could easily be disassembled. A coal miner complained that the "radical bourgeois" had more interest in free love than in the "stomach ideals" of the working class: "They can steal over into the capitalist camp at any time——we can't. They can retire from the firing line——we can't."[13] Precisely this happened in the twenties.[14]   As Malcolm Cowley wrote, by 1919

> a curious phenomenon was to be observed. The New York bohemians, the Greenwich Villagers, came from exactly the same social class as the readers of the *Saturday Evening Post*. Their political opinions were vague and by no means dangerous to Ford Motors or General Electric: the war had destroyed their belief in political action. They were trying to get ahead, and the proletariat be damned. Their economic standards were those of the small American businessman.[15]

The young women of the twenties require our special attention. The previous generation's feminists had particular reasons for disappointment with them. Measured by what feminist leaders had expected, the twenties should have turned out a boom decade for women's rights, but it didn't. Young women, including young college women, proved largely indifferent to the onetime crusade.   The privatized flapper represented a varied kind of emancipation from the causes and careerism so many feminists cherished, and the flapper, not the militant careerist, embodied the spirit of the decade. On the campuses a new moral code, driven by the quest for individual freedom, emerged. With the young as its cutting edge, sexual liberty provided a new kind of female emancipation, more exciting than older struggles, which now seemed largely past.   Feminists lambasted the sexual revolution and the shallowness of youth. In reply, sexual freedomites dismissed feminism. To the degree that political insurgency and sexual insurgency each reflected a reaction against Victorianism, both could loosely be identified as feminist. But the sexual revolution achieved little toward redistributing power or redefining roles in America.

During the thirties—the nature of the economic crisis virtually dictated this—social hedonism took second place to political activism. The sexual innovations of previous years were consolidated, but flaming youth pretty much ceased to flame. "The young people of the early nineteen-thirties presumably knew just as much about life as those of the early and middle twenties," wrote Frederick Lewis Allen, "but they were less conspicuously and self-consciously intent upon showing the world what advanced young devils they were."[16] The great peacocking over sex and alcohol appeared to diminish. A fundamental concern now was finding a job. According to contemporary spectators, college students became more serious. Intellectual and cultural concerns received more attention, academicians more respect.[17] As interest in politics rose, student radicalism flowered. But "among those in whose blood the fires of rebellion burned," Dixon Wecter observed, "economic rather than sexual heterodoxy came to be flaunted as the red badge of courage."[18] Students did move left in the thirties—the decade produced "the first nationally organized student movement in America," along with great Communist influence—but most never by any means became radicals. And the main focus of campus activism was actually war, together with that old perennial, ROTC.[19]

The youth tide began running next when the beats broke the placid waters of the fifties. As the bohemian atmosphere revived, Greenwich Village returned to the map, along with San Francisco's North Beach and Los Angeles's Venice. But the beats—in their anti-middle-classism, Zen Buddhism, Hindu mysticism, emotional and artistic avant-gardism, marijuana, hard drugs, and sexuality—cultivated themselves, not the outer world. They were alienated, all right, but not overtly political.

When the New Left dropped social activism into this stew, it added a note of ambiguity and ambivalence. The New Left, as I have emphasized, embodied the same tense duality as the Lyrical Left—the same leanings toward social justice pulling against leanings toward self. As the left became a movement, it carried forward the beats' suspicion of the bourgeois world. Uneasy with the rational, young leftists felt much more comfortable with their subjective selves. If middle-class liberals wanted to make everyone below them middle-class, New Leftists countered that both they themselves and the poor suffered oppression; that through social action lay possibilities of fulfillment in their own lives and a transformation of the system. If America was affluent, affluence did not add up to enough. Life must have something more than its conventional, obvious meaning, something less flaccid and dull.

How would the revolution occur? Would Consciousness III tame society without politics or violence? Few thought so in the late sixties.

By the early seventies, though, with the road to political change strewn with more and more tacks, increasing numbers of counterculture types took hope in spontaneous change through altered mass attitudes. Once again, in the face of political bankruptcy, people set hopes on the pale chances of a revolution touched off by example.

The road between hippiedom and radical activism remained an open one. Individuals passed in both directions, toward politics or toward withdrawal into themselves.   Young people often were alternately politicized and depoliticized. (These alternations rather mimicked the longer cycles of activism and withdrawal which we have been tracing across society at large.) Splits occurred which reflected the schizoid inner-outer nature of the New Left. Too narrow a focus on drugs or eroticism drained energy. Drugs became a red herring, "a way of saying . . . 'My pleasure is more important than your misery.'"[20] If a revolution was coming through activism, then clearly a bacchanal was self-defeating. Yet if, on the other hand, change occurred spontaneously, by altered consciousness, then the revolution could proceed *through* internalization and by example.   In the event, some youth internalized; some externalized; some did both; still others flipped back and forth between the two.

Kenneth Keniston emphasized at the time that "it is important constantly to underline the enormous vulnerability of the counterculture to seduction, encapsulation, and co-optation by the very culture it nominally opposes."[21] This is what happened, though the co-optation ran both ways: the majority culture ingested some of the counterculture, and the counterculture got swallowed. Ultimately, Christopher Lasch has observed, as the New Left broke up, "cultural and political radicalism, briefly joined in a period of rising political hopes, split apart, the political radicals increasingly absorbed in their ideological pronouncements, the cultural radicals denouncing all politics as a snare and a delusion."[22]

Among the legacies of the sixties that most visibly endured a decade later was the new sexuality. When young people had leaned against the social and governmental bulwark against sex, they had tumbled through a barrier constructed of tissue paper. A good deal of softening up had weakened Victorianism over a long span of time, from the behavior of the Lyrical Left to the twenties to *Playboy*. Millions of Americans had gone overseas in two world wars, which had themselves provided spectacular opportunities for sin. Reminiscent of the twenties, during the sixties and seventies the middle class flocked to see *Hair* and buy *Penthouse* or *Hustler*. Options exploded: swinging, open marriage, gay bath houses, the disco culture. The whole image of sexuality changed. "Shacking up" became living together. "Queer" became gay. Adultery became swinging.

During each era, outsiders thought they saw collapse and chaos, where in fact far less went on than they imagined and more restraints endured or emerged than they thought. Concluding his fascinating study entitled *Sexual Behavior in the 1970s*, for example, Morton Hunt found

> the results of our survey contradicting what both the evangelists and the Cassandras of sexual liberation have been saying about what has been happening of late. We find ourselves validating the more balanced (but little heeded) appraisals made by many behavioral scientists . . . to the effect that there has been no chaotic and anarchic dissolution of standards, but, rather, a major shift toward a nonpuritanical, hedonistic, and highly organized set of attitudes and behaviors that remain integrated with some of our most important social values and with the institutions of courtship, love, marriage and the family.[23]

This was not what one heard at the time, however. The amount of actual change brought on by the sexual revolution of the twenties and the sixties is easily and commonly exaggerated. In May 1978, for instance, *Newsweek* ran a "special report" called "Saving the Family," whose title made the institution sound like some endangered species.[24] Television and the print media trumpeted Sexual Revolution and concentrated so heavily on what still remained statistically deviant behavior that millions of Americans must doubtless have come to the glum conclusion that they were missing out.

College life, in particular, was widely associated with hedonism: not just political radicalism, but the sexual revolution, drugs, irreligiosity, offbeat clothing, and the generation gap. Any such transformations, particularly changes involving marriage, motherhood, or the family, set off the extremely sensitive nerve endings which surround these critical institutions. In both the twenties and the sixties, the indications of social change were everywhere. Gutter expressions found their way into common discourse in both decades, notably in the patois of the young. One subparticle of the New Left called itself Up Against the Wall, Motherfuckers. The hip "damns" and "shits" in personal conversation felt as alienating to the older and the square as they seemed cognitively lubricating in more "advanced" circles. One source of middle-class disillusionment in the sixties, I suspect, amounted simply to the fact that with all of the idealism which parents of the forties and fifties had devoted to child rearing they had produced so many rebels. No wonder average people recoiled when some radicals began taking on not just private property but the conventional family and even rationality and objectivity as ideals.

Assessments of moral change at any given time tend to assume that a previous status quo has begun giving way to its *opposite*. The use of words like "collapse" and "decadence" suggests a revolution, e.g., the Sexual Revolution, rather than more moderate and slower evolution, or if one prefers, devolution.   True to the spirit of moral panic, for instance, early in the 1920s the *Ladies' Home Journal* opened a "crusade" against "Unspeakable Jazz"——"of as great importance to-day to the moral well-being of the United States as the prohibition crusade was in the worst days of the saloon."[25] When a political/sociocultural phase burns off, its most easily identified remnant will likely be the sociocultural. What retains the greatest visibility is not politics, but the apolitical or antipolitical element: the social transformation, a legacy both deviant and self-indulgent, more emotional than rational.

These patterns suggest the broader relationship which links political with sensual trends.   By concentrating on the topmost levels of government, we might easily lose sight of this relationship. Such liberal luminaries as Bryan, Wilson, and Truman may have been social conservatives; but in general, it is the more affluent liberals along with the radicals who respond most actively to change on the cultural, not just the political, level.

Several things stand out, for example, in the two sexual "revolutions" we have examined: their self-consciousness, their drivenness, and their brave sense of invention. Fought again and again, the struggle for sexual freedom has shown the ratchet effect, the tendency to lunge forward, then slip part way back. As in the 1930s, during the seventies the excitement of sexual revolution——the sense that an older world was being turned on its head——gradually ebbed. The revolution did not turn out so revolutionary as the media or the imagination at first supposed.[26] The almost frenzied preoccupation with sex died down as the newer moral code became stabilized. Sexual excitement remained as always, of course, but excitement *about* sex dimmed. Romance and glamor peeked out again from behind the tree of forbidden fruit. During both decades, a certain nostalgia even set in for Victorianism.[27]   In such times of consolidation, sexual innovations spread up and down the age scale, but they cease to attract the same notoriety or anxiety. There seems to be a return to longer, more stable, more conventional personal relationships. There is no longer a Great National Sexual Problem.

Suspicion, Disgust, and the Social Issue

Alice began to feel very uneasy: to be sure, she had not as yet had any dispute with the Queen, but she knew that it might happen any minute, "and then," thought she, "what would become of me? They're dreadfully fond of beheading people here: the great wonder is, that there's any one left alive!"

Lewis Carroll, *Alice's Adventures in Wonderland*

Not only do turns toward libertinism in America alter the social agenda. They also alter the political agenda. They twist the axis of political confrontation. Rather than debating issues of class or economics, we argue over "permissiveness," the death penalty, school prayer, or abortion. One might almost call this a Gresham's Law of politics.

Glancing at our history, we see periods when national debate has focused on the really crucial problems with which politics must deal. At other times, blood has flowed over matters which defied solution by politicians of whatever caliber. It has proved very difficult in America to fix and hold public and governmental focus on the truly big questions. Repeatedly there emerges a stubborn insistence on tilting somewhere out on the periphery with marginal issues or non-issues. These are the questions which fail to deserve the attention they receive, or against which any political motion will be flung ineffectively, or even toward which political action is altogether inappropriate.

At times new issues arise which do legitimately alter the political agenda. In a medium-sized California community in 1974, for example, a George Wallaceite and a liberal Democrat could be seen working together to collect signatures on petitions opposing the construction of a regional shopping center which threatened to overwhelm the town. The ecology movement intruded into politics by disrupting older priorities and producing new coalitions. Still, there was no doubting the importance of the environmental issue or its propriety for political debate.

Yet one key indicator of the decline of a reform wave is the return to relatively low priority issues. This combines with negative reference group[1] voting—casting ballots against "*them.*" All this occurred in the twenties, and again in the forties and late sixties. It is not a matter of great new questions cutting across coalitions formed around older great questions. Rather, new, divisive issues of relatively little importance seize the spotlight.

A great many so-called liberal-conservative struggles have had very little to do with any sort of real social progress. Some of these might loosely be termed holding actions of one sort or another—for instance, the red scares or prohibition. Occasionally some particularly upsetting incident involving, say, the death penalty (Sacco-Vanzetti with its broader implications) may serve as a focus for social and political mobilization.

But in general, distractions remain distractions. A case like Caryl Chessman's 1960 execution in California will summon liberals to the barricades quicker than will the plight of a thousand more deserving poor. In a scheme of priorities solidly oriented toward the quality of life most people lead, even Watergate would take a lower place than it did. Great battles have been fought over these issues; yet the illusion of progress they have sometimes left behind reflected in reality little more than a return to the previous status quo, however much energy got burned away getting there.

These issues are red herrings.[2] Reform has gotten undercut continually by the tendency of the public, as well as of both liberals and radicals, to run off chasing such issues as if they were the real thing. Since most voters (even most liberal voters in recent decades) do not require additional social justice legislation to protect their most immediate interests, it does not viscerally concern them whether the great moral question in politics is Communism, Watergate, or mass starvation. The public may vote on the issues, but these may or may not be the "right" issues for the time. And the public may perceive them rationally or irrationally: people can render an informed judgment on an irrelevancy, or cast an ill-considered ballot on some critical problem. Half the game involves establishing a framework in which people can make decent decisions about things which genuinely matter.

It does not take many points of disillusionment with liberal reform to create a general disillusionment in lots of minds. Unhappiness over a violent convention in Chicago, or over busing, or over the failures of an administration like Carter's, or over any number of other things can turn many people to the right. Along with benefiting at certain times from the effects of economic phenomena (taking credit for prosperity, denouncing the Democrats for inflation, or, as in 1980, blaming them for unemployment), since World War II Republican success in presidential races has rested quite markedly on what have been termed "cultural, regional, racial and patriotic factors."[3] The GOP will typically emphasize non-class questions. If people "buy" these, the left will be undermined; the reverse, and the right will weaken.[4] Toward the end of a reform era the politics of culture begins to flourish, and for reasons easy to understand.

A character in Oscar Wilde's *The Picture of Dorian Gray* declares: "A new Hedonism——that is what our century wants."[5] Clearly, a great many Americans have not wanted that at all.[6] Unhappy with the direction which reform and its offshoots have taken, they will fight back. But at first their causes may appear hopeless.

In the case of each of this century's lefts, while political reality has proved hard to change, the cultural realities remain relatively soft. When lefts cease to be radical, they cease sounding radical politically; their cultural deviance tends to continue, the under-boring carried on along cultural veins. For this they arouse widespread enthusiasm and seem to own the future. One reason why society as a whole moves culturally "leftward" is that every new generation coming up will treat present values as a starting point for its own rebellion.[7] It will denounce them as the status quo, as repressive, as Victorian. From one generation to the next, this form of the ratchet effect acts powerfully upon the whole society.

The social side of youthful and leftist rebelliousness can severely undermine political reform, though, and for two reasons. It draws off energy; and it supplies opponents with dual targets to aim at——political innovation *together with social innovation*. Because the two become linked in the public mind, tending to become more so in the heat of change, smearing one amounts to smearing the other. The left-orientation of American intellectuals and their preference (in recent decades, anyway) for the Democratic party also help to explain why the Democrats run into trouble over the social issue. Intellectuals thrive on undermining old shrines, values, and traditions; they live to question. Taken far enough, questioning begs for reaction.

For all their espousal of a role for government, liberals have tended toward libertarianism in private morality, while conservatives (except, perhaps, for the libertarians among them) have inclined toward just the opposite. The phenomenon has deep historic roots which we have examined. It became especially obvious in the 1960s, 1970s, and 1980s. Nixon wrapped himself politically in the cloak of family. The Reagan Administration made big play of its opposition to abortion and its support for marriage and monogamy. Reform became extremely vulnerable to charges that liberalism equals libertinism. During this century reformers have also been environmentalists in the sense that they often interpret individual failings in broad social terms. Rather than blaming individuals alone for their shortcomings, liberals cast the responsibility for turning people into addicts or murderers on poverty or discrimination. The supposed tie-in between liberalism and "permissiveness" has, especially in recent years, badly damaged liberalism. So, too, has the link between liberal reform and the growth of the welfare system in a society where welfare and its clients carry a heavy stigma. And in a multiracial society which has harbored considerable racism, government benefits will always seem to the majority to accrue excessively to minorities, undercutting the majority's enthusiasm for the welfare state.

In the face of all this, upheavals of conservative religiosity have repeatedly erupted in response to surges of cultural change. The cultural uprisings coincide with reform eras; the fundamentalist impulses accompany reactive eras. This pattern typified the twenties, and the seventies and eighties. The same sort of thing occurred in the fifties, with the trend running less toward the rube sects than toward conventional denominations with more respectable practices.   The greatest outbreaks of social change have clearly stimulated the most conservative and exotic responses. People try to offset the chaos and uncertainty of change with some degree of assuredness. Not accidentally, in such eras some of the most popular preachers rank among the country's notable reactionaries. They cry for a nostalgic reversion to the norms of less threatening times.   All this reinforces the general atmosphere of reactionism, red-baiting, flag-waving, and machismo.

Red herring issues emerged spectacularly in the 1920s. Progressivism had started to show signs of souring before World War I, in the rise of prohibitionism, for example, or in certain forms of anti-immigrationism. During the 1920s, red herrings multiplied in the context of postwar disillusionment and fears of "Europeanization" and foreign subversion, cosmopolitanism and relativism, urbanism and immigration and Catholicism. In the face of this, the country produced a brand of "political fundamentalism" (in William E. Leuchtenburg's phrase)[8] aimed at returning to the old ways. Great political battles erupted over the underlying question of whether or not the nation really wanted to join the twentieth century—almost as though the country had not already proceeded two decades through it. Thus Americans argued about Al Smith's Catholicism, the Ku Klux Klan, the demon rum, John T. Scopes, New York City, or the ethnic attractiveness of restricting immigration. These questions cut through progressivism like a tornado, tearing apart past coalitions of workers and farmers and burying more important social and economic issues in debris.

At its outset, the storm stirred up the century's first great red scare. In such scares, all manner of change gets lumped together into one overarching radical threat. Since, traditionally, liberalism has oriented itself toward protecting civil liberties and the rights of political minorities and dissidents, including radicals, liberals' tolerance makes them especially fair game. Red scares always undercut reformers as well because, however mildly, reformers are deviant types: they argue that things are wrong with a system which the witch-hunter insists is perfect.

Their traditional moderation aside, liberals themselves have often shown an astonishing inclination to junk civil liberties and go on witch hunts of their own. Wilson's Attorney General, A. Mitchell Palmer, amassed an awful reputation which compounded the bad wartime civil liberties record of the administration as a whole. The undermining of individual freedom did not end when the war did, but went right on with fresh repressive measures to put down the far left. Radicalism did flare up after the war; a postwar surge of strikes, race riots, bombings and bomb scares, and the class tensions they revealed, poured gasoline on the embers of hysteria. Labor militancy made unions seem a part of the red menace. In 1919 a fifth of the work force, more than 4 million people, involved themselves in 2,600 strikes.[9] Over a third of a million steelworkers went out. In Boston, the police force struck. The strikes shocked the country. The middle class was put off when a general strike hit Seattle, underlining the apparent danger of social upheaval. And opponents began pointing their fingers toward an outbreak of radicalism when the strikes hit steel and coal. A great cry went up from the public to bring peace back to the workplace. Labor's 1919 outburst also jarred a good many progressives, who, averse to a politics of class or interest, proceeded to side with the right. The NAM and other employers' groups backed Palmerism, which gave them a club to use on the labor movement. Patriotic though Gompers had been during the war, the AFL got hammered as bolshevik. A big open-shop campaign broke out. In the end, organized labor suffered enormous losses, including the departure of a million and a half union members.[10] After backing La Follette in 1924, the AFL cautiously retreated toward conservative politics and behavior.

Palmer's personal role in all this was symptomatic. In the past he had represented much of the best in Wilsonian progressivism, including its emergent bias toward labor. Now Palmer seemed to epitomize the welfare state-turned-police state. He began stabbing labor with injunctions. And although he emerged fleetingly in the garb of a public hero, resistance to the Attorney General developed within the administration itself (notably in the Department of Labor). Yet the administration's wartime repression and propaganda had done a good deal to kindle the hysteria that fueled Palmerism in the first place. Palmer's wolf-crying eventually grew so erratic that he left even the public behind. Progressivism had thrived upon imputations of conspiracy. But now conspiracy theories veered off in such absurd directions that the public had a chance to observe the progressive cast of mind at its most frantic. A reaction virtually had to set in. As 1920 faded, so did the scare. But it had happened under Wilson, a fact not lost on Warren Harding in his campaign that fall. "The Red Scare," notes William E. Leuchtenburg, "left a bitter heritage of suspicion of aliens, distrust of organized labor, hostility to reformers, and insistence on political conformity, which created a smothering atmosphere for reform efforts in the 1920's."[11] The scare left liberals trying to cling to civil liberties like a life raft, something the Klan would keep them doing later in the decade.

Despite its poisonous legacy, the red scare ended fairly quickly. Prohibition, however, lasted far longer, providing the best example of what Richard Hofstadter called the "political absolutism" of the era.[12] To the degree that the twenties generated a burning national issue, that issue was prohibition. Complex motives lay behind it, and it will not do simply to dismiss the movement as the clodhoppers' last hurrah. Many Americans perceived prohibition as a reform. Many, indeed, saw it as the most important question on the reform agenda, as the most significant issue before the nation. Prohibition evoked images of Protestantism-versus-Catholicism, urbanism-versus-ruralism, and the legacy of an old producer society coming into conflict with a new bourgeois consumer society. Then as now drinking in itself produced major social problems, which attracted support for the movement.

Historians have since debated whether prohibition was or was not a reform. But legitimate reform or mawkish reform or no reform at all, the point remains that the alcohol issue did not deserve a place as the centerpiece of domestic political debate in the 1920s. During the Progressive Era it had resided where it belonged, on the periphery of things; later, the New Deal quickly disposed of it. In part, political warfare erupted around prohibition during the twenties simply because its proponents had finally succeeded in slipping it into the Constitution, disrupting the lifestyles of millions. The issue pulled many reformers to the right. It drove other liberals into an awkward alliance with certain conservatives to blot it out. La Follette, whose priorities remained saner than most, trimmed on the issue; for anyone with a sense of survival as well as priority, this was probably the best thing to do. "Damn the liquor question, anyway," Hiram Johnson grumbled.[13]

Prohibition became one of the key points of contention in the Democrats' great struggle at Madison Square Garden in 1924, a national convention which reflected every significant sociocultural division of the time. In 1912 the Democrats had quite appropriately argued about the proper role of government in this society and about regulating or breaking up corporations. In 1924 they split apart in complete futility over religion, ethnicity, and city-versus-country. The two major candidates, each with credible progressive credentials——William Gibbs McAdoo of the West and South, and New York's Al Smith——canceled each other out. John W. Davis——nominated after 103 ballots——was one of America's foremost corporation lawyers. His vice-presidential candidate was William Jennings Bryan's brother!

The social issue died down in the thirties, mainly, no doubt, because that decade placed such unique primacy on economic issues. The intellectuals of the Old Left did not put the repressiveness of the nuclear family or the small town very high on their agenda. Little room remained in the proletarian-revolutionary Old Left for the sensuousness of the Lyricals; the dogmatic *New Masses* tried to divorce bohemianism from radicalism. But if sexual rebellion had become old news, the prohibition question showed remarkable staying power. Delegates to both parties' 1932 national conventions demonstrated far greater anguish over prohibition than over unemployment. This was three years into the Depression. John Dewey grew perturbed: "Here we are in the midst of the greatest crisis since the Civil War and the only thing the two national parties seem to want to debate is booze."[14]

Suspicion and disgust welled again late in the Thirties, notably as a result of the Court fight. Roosevelt *thought* workers and farmers were upset by the Supreme Court's decisions against the New Deal. But to the public, attacking the Court was like attacking the Constitution. Few Americans actually connected overhauling the Supreme Court with concrete, immediate benefits for themselves.[15] Roosevelt's public standing became tarnished. So did confidence in his leadership. The New Deal's bipartisan backing slipped. The struggle wasted the edge which the 1936 victory had provided, split the Democratic party, and upset liberal Republicans. It alienated and divided other reformers. It siphoned off a good deal of FDR's middle-class support. It injured Roosevelt's relationship with Congress. And it played a major role in producing the congressional conservative coalition which would tie up liberal programs in decades to come.[16]

Repeating 1919, the 1937 sit-down strike wave spurred considerable fear. Most people believed—incorrectly—that revolutionism lurked behind the strikes. Two out of three Americans wanted sit-downs outlawed and wanted force used against the unions involved. Roosevelt was accused of complicity. Especially in the South, in rural regions, and among the middle class, labor outbreaks undermined the administration, as many who had felt warm toward organized labor turned chilly.[17]

In preference to just weakening administration proposals, Congress, shifting right, began to kill them. It tried to regain some of its power vis-à-vis the President, whose new leverage it resented. The overwhelming Democratic majorities on the Hill, and the wide margins by which many Democrats had been elected, ironically provided a fertile environment for in-party splits and maverick behavior. The proposals Roosevelt sent to Congress were controversial, divisive sectionally and otherwise. They encouraged the hurling of charges that the President was trying to act like a dictator.[18]

As congressional resistance mounted, the House Committee on Un-American Activities made its appearance in 1938 and promptly took on the New Deal. Substantially because of widespread popular backing for the committee, which extended right across the class spectrum and included Democrats as well as Republicans, Roosevelt attempted for the most part to steer clear of a confrontation with it.

Meanwhile a surge of nativism erupted. "In the two years before the outbreak of World War II in September 1939," Richard Polenberg writes, nativist sentiment appears to have increased sharply. This affected the New Deal because in the minds of some people the Roosevelt administration was playing into the hands of the very groups that seemed to pose the gravest danger——Communists, Jews, and labor agitators. Charges that the president had surrounded himself with alien advisers and had embraced an alien ideology were by no means new; what was new was the frequency with which they were voiced and the degree of public acceptance they received. Unlike Roosevelt's first term, when such assertions found a hearing mainly among the very rich, after 1937 they won a wide audience among the middle classes and among immigrants, particularly Irish-Catholics and Germans.

As in the past, nativist fears were associated with working-class militancy.[19]

All these crosscurrents damaged reform. A generation before, similar ones——an upsurge of nativism, fear of radicals, anxiety about the working class——had helped to kill progressivism. The Democrats suffered remarkable losses to the GOP in 1938. Among the reasons were xenophobia, a sharp economic recession, and allegations that liberal Democrats were tied in with Communism and labor militancy. As a result of the casualties among northern and western Democrats, the new Congress saw a resurgence of southern power, which further undercut the New Deal.[20]

"The New Deal declined after 1937," Polenberg has noted, "because most Americans did not want to extend it much further."[21] "For God sakes," a covey of congressmen pressed FDR, "don't send us any more controversial legislation."[22] Not only Congress balked. Opinion polls taken in 1938 and 1939 showed that between two-thirds and three-quarters of the public wanted the administration to move right. The recession of 1937-38 largely resulted from Washington's drive at balancing the budget by slashing outlays, but business snorted that low confidence in the administration was at fault. The solution: cut spending, cut taxes, stop reform. Even among Democrats and the poor, a larger number wanted Washington to be more conservative than more liberal.[23]

The administration did pull back. "I am sick and tired of having a lot of long-haired people around here who want a billion dollars for schools, a billion dollars for public health," Roosevelt remarked testily in July 1939. "Just because a boy wants to go to college is no reason we should finance it."[24] Europe stood on the brink of war. The President's focus shifted even more heavily to defense and foreign policy, where the primary legislative priorities now lay. These priorities called for treating the southerners in Congress and the business interests outside with bosomy indulgence. New Deal agencies legitimated what they were doing as defense measures. Ongoing New Deal programs got bent to help court Congress.[25] Slipping support among the public, increasing congressional resistance, and the new prominence of foreign policy and defense undid reform.

Many of the crosscurrents that undercut the New Deal have remained quite powerful since. Welfare state and economic questions have continued to pull workers and others toward the Democratic party. But the complex of cultural and social questions has inspired defections to the GOP, especially when these matters move to the fore.[26] Red herring "issues" produce their best results politically after a reform movement has peaked. This had held for the twenties and late thirties, and continued after World War II. Liberalism, although passing through a creative phase, had reached the end of an era. More than anything else, prosperity and the Cold War dominated politics in the fifties. Each of these produced disorientation: the Cold War reversed the thirties' priorities as between domestic and foreign policy, and prosperity undercut domestic priorities further yet. "Liberalism," James A. Nuechterlein observes, "seemed for a time largely defensive and uncertain."[27] And a bill came due for a good deal of previous sloppiness in employing the word "liberal" so loosely as to suggest (for those who had political reasons to suggest it) that liberals, Communists, and Socialists all slept together, that only shades of difference divided them, and that in becoming a liberal one had simply taken the first step toward becoming a Communist.[28] Liberalism was distracted once again by a battle over civil liberties.

One of the startling ironies of the liberal record through most of this century, as we have seen, has been the impulse liberal administrations have shown to abuse civil liberties. War brings this abuse on; and had conservatives held power in 1917-18 or 1941-45, the same thing might have occurred. Whatever the case, the Wilson story was abysmal. Despite an otherwise excellent civil liberties record, the Roosevelt Administration incarcerated Japanese Americans in concentration camps. Precedents were not overly encouraging, then, when the second big red scare hit in the late forties and early fifties. "Conservatives," Alonzo L. Hamby has written,

> quickly perceived that anti-Communism was a powerful political issue; especially after the rise of Senator Joe McCarthy, it served as an effective bludgeon against the Fair Deal and the liberal movement. Conceiving of politics as a rational exercise, neither the Truman administration nor the vital center could devise a strategy against McCarthyism. By mid-1950, the

> president and the liberals were unsuccessfully fighting an
> irrational Red scare with little more than a forlorn faith in the
> ultimate reason and libertarianism of the American public.[29]

Liberals fought, and, at important junctures, compromised themselves. Truman himself had helped launch the red scare, indirectly through the rhetoric and policies of Cold War anticommunism, and quite directly by ordering a massive loyalty review of federal employees.   Other civil liberties "proponents" wound up hurling plenty of anticommunist invectives.   Some liberals bitterly split with other liberals over civil liberties;[30] as usual, the issue divided the left.   The Alger Hiss case, together with the response of the many liberals who rushed to back Hiss, at least at first, exposed the sagging flanks of postwar liberalism to ravenous attacks.   The case set a good number of liberals and intellectuals to quarrelling with one another.   And it revealed a streak of "penitential liberalism" among many intellectual ex-radicals, a form of leftist guilt.[31]

The electorate, taken broadly, was markedly un-ideological in the 1950s, and its image of what the two parties stood for blurred. In part this resulted from ignorance and apathy, but it also stemmed from contemporary similarities between the parties over a wide gamut of questions.[32] Together with the "end of ideology," these things made the fifties a fertile environment for the emergence of personality voting and for red herrings. As in any other such period, these conditions naturally favored the right. In 1952 the GOP classically sloganized the political issues of the day in the formula K1C2. The pseudochemicals were Korea, Communism, and Corruption. For all his grace and wit and eloquence, Adlai Stevenson's response to the red-baiting fell somewhat short of a foursquare endorsement of civil liberties.[33] Viewed from the perspective of liberal priorities, the fifties looked pretty grim.

Meanwhile, the red-hunting (along with other problems, including the departure of the intellectuals) sacked the Old Left. Between 1945 and 1958, Communist party membership plunged from between 75,000 and 80,000 to under 3,000.[34] One left-wing bastion which did continue to hold out was the peace movement; but in terms of strictly domestic concerns, its stress on international relations amounted to just one more red herring.

By the late sixties, when mass political disgust re-emerged, conditions had warmed for it once more. Affluence, education, and leisure——ideal preconditions for jettisoning old norms——had reached a peak. Sexual mores changed, patriotism declined, and personal expression and fulfillment achieved a new priority. Attitudes toward marriage and family, and toward work and the relationship between success and material gain, changed too. Deference slackened for structures of authority which had once automatically received respect. The ranks of the affluent, the traditional moral and cultural innovators, had grown far larger, and their attack on older social conventions grew more vehement. Social questions had emerged of importance unrivaled since the twenties, with traditionalists again defending the past against modern inroads. As in the twenties, norms became redefined and roles changed, especially women's roles. During the twenties new technology had seemed to threaten old moralities (the automobile, movies); now the same thing happened again (synthetic drugs, the Pill).

These challenges of the late sixties and early seventies would in a short time generate many changes in society at large which gave every appearance of permanence. Others—fads—flitted across the class structure and among different age groups. Self-fulfillment, self-realization, self-actualization, whatever one wanted to call them, these drives spread from the young and the campuses of the sixties to the broader society, making the seventies the celebrated decade of Me.[35] Many Americans regarded all this as a mammoth threat. There were so many issues that their very number choked the stream of political debate, and their emotional wallop made it easy to convert some of them to red herrings. Evaluating the attitudes of the mass public, one study concludes that "by 1972 we find substantial correlations between domestic and cold-war issues, strong relationships between positions on these issues and attitudes on the civil liberties of dissenters, and a moderate to strong relationship between all these issues and the new social issues."[36]

As in the 1920s, many older Americans challenged tradition and openly aped the young (radical chic). Others quietly welcomed change. But both groups were hard put to keep pace with the scope of the young radicals' critique of everything from the work ethic to conventional mores, standard clothing, etiquette and "proper" behavior, competition, science, and the trained, disciplined mind. Remarkable in the number and variety of ways in which they confronted the Establishment, elements of the New Left went so far as to challenge Western culture itself. This obscured the fact that most students who stood for civil rights or against the war did not belong to the student left, nor were they truly radical.[37] The main difference between an era like the twenties or the fifties on one hand, and the sixties on the other, is that while in the earlier decades the older majority had had to worry merely about turning the tastes of the nation over to the young, in the sixties they feared turning over the whole society.

With social attitudes joining economic attitudes as litmus tests of liberalism, a "liberal" position was identified on the death penalty, abortion, or school prayer just as on Social Security or Medicare. This made the Democratic party extremely vulnerable to massive defections by its own members so long as economic issues did not emerge to override the social ones.[38]   Liberals found themselves accused of indifference toward the family, traditional moral standards, and religion.

Once reform became an avant-garde cultural movement as much as or more than an economic one, a profound rift between liberalism and members of the working class became inevitable. These people, notably the white males among them, stood to lose, or, just as important polit-ically, to perceive themselves as losing financially or symbolically in relative status: losing to affirmative action, women's rights, busing, soft and forgiving courts steeped in environmentalistic jurisprudential theory, the erosion of the conventional nuclear family, "giveaway" programs for the poor a rung or two down (and often of a different race), sexual liberation, abortion, gay rights, and the patronizing ridicule of *All in the Family* and *Archie Bunker's Place*. These people felt abandoned—*were* abandoned—by elitist liberals who talked more and more in terms of a postindustrial society no longer geared to precisely the sorts of jobs that blue-collar voters occupied.[39]   Such voters did remain more liberal on bread-and-butter economic questions—occupational safety and health legislation, labor law reform—than on social ones—the ERA, busing, relaxation of drug laws. In the presidential elections of the 1960s and 1970s, when social issues seemed dominant over issues of class, large numbers of workers switched to the GOP (1968, 1972). Otherwise, blue-collar voters tended to stay with the Democrats (1964, 1976).[40]   One study reported

> a nearly complete inversion of the political cleavage that predominated until the 1960s, which pitted a conservative business-oriented middle class against a reformist working class. The new radicalism brought the concerns of a growing leftist intelligentsia to the center of political discourse. The bread-and-butter issues that had historically divided the working and middle classes were now supplemented by sociocultural "life style" issues that pitted blue-collar and lower-middle-class groups against the college-educated professional and managerial "knowledge elites."

. . . .

The great mass of American voters was always quite hostile to the liberal cosmopolitan stance adopted by the Democratic party in the late 1960s.[41]

As chair of Americans for Democratic Action (ADA) in 1969, Joseph Duffey had warned that "liberalism is becoming the abstract activity of the affluent."[42]

Shrewdly, Wallaceites and Nixonites traded on code words like "silent majority," "welfare," and "law and order" to mask crass appeals to race and class. In 1968 Wallace attracted strong blue-collar support. The racial clash shifted more voters to Nixon in 1972 than any other issue.[43] Nixon, who had served his apprenticeship in the war against the Old Left, brought his dark talents to bear against the New. During the Wilson and Truman administrations, the Attorney Generals had played leading and dubious roles in undercutting radicalism. In the late sixties, Nixon unleashed John Mitchell on the student left and antiwar groups.

Nixon and his minions knew that certain kinds of polarization serve conservative interests very well. By this I do not mean the sorts of polarization which typified, say, 1916 or 1936 and revolved around economics and class. Instead I refer to such years as 1924, 1968, or 1972, in which polarization signified reform's demise. In any politically charged era, the center will erode to some degree as people separate to the left and right. As time passes and the political scene becomes more bland, the flanks wither, and the center expands again.[44] For conservative politicians, the point is to exploit the sort of polarization that runs along sociocultural as opposed to class-economic lines. And this, in turn, demands that they exercise a certain degree of opportunism.

The Opportunism of the Conservatives

Just as Vietnam had become "Johnson's war," so drugs, crime, urban riots, and sexual license were collectively characterized as "Johnson's society."

Michael Foley

As a general proposition, taking a negative stand on an issue will usually get politicians farther than taking a positive one. The system weights itself toward voting no. And in a conservative era, as the fulcrum of politics shifts to the right, it brings the liberals along with it. Conservatives compel liberals to fight it out on the borders of the conservatives' own territory. Liberals who cleave to the left wind up looking like a foolish minority divorced from reality. The whole political system takes a negative turn.

As we have seen, twentieth century American politics has produced no conservative tradition particularly worthy of the name. Along with their general pattern of naysaying, though, and along with occasionally resorting to principle, conservative politicians have shown themselves to be almost as opportunistic in their own way as the liberals. Once reform movements begin to falter, the GOP always cries for normalcy, less government, and lower taxes. The opportunism of the liberals gives way to a conservative variety which is negative and oriented toward red herrings. As Robert Kelley has put it, "when cultural fears predominate, Republicans traditionally benefit."[1] Conservatives do not have to attack the Democratic party frontally; they can denounce instead its constituencies (labor, blacks, gays) or alleged constituencies ("Communists," "socialists," "deviants"). The classic formula involves making social criticism appear un-American and unpatriotic. Red herring politics, the get-on-the-bandwagon politics of negativism, can generate huge political payoffs.

Meanwhile, business interests go to work. Mobil Oil takes out ads attacking state regulation. Big companies hire consultants on union-busting. Political action committees pour money into conservatives' campaigns. The automobile, meat-packing, tobacco, medical, and funeral industries decry federal nosiness and seek to terminate it.

Opportunism plays a constant part in political life. It has to. Herbert Hoover's anti-opportunism injured him terribly after 1929 and disabled the Republican party. When the GOP right later accused the party's less conservative presidential candidates from Landon on of sounding too much like their Democratic counterparts, the right in effect accused the Landons and Willkies and Nixons of opportunism. Of course, the charge was leveled opportunistically.

Conservative opportunism becomes especially tempting during conversions from wartime to peacetime. The economy must readjust. Battles erupt over whether the peace has brought what was fought for, what was promised, and what was possible. Superheated emotions and aggressiveness must find some outlet——and often do in scapegoating and red-baiting. Red herrings give a conservative out-party something around which to unite. Yet in office, conservatives themselves are not completely exempt from getting tarred by their own opportunism. Tremendous tension, for example, developed between the McCarthyites and the Eisenhower Administration. But in general, conservatives with little on their agenda find themselves less vulnerable to red herrings than liberals, who may have ambitious plans which require a good deal of unity and momentum for enactment.

The possibilities for outright conservative demagoguery have received repeated demonstrations, most notoriously by Joe McCarthy. Reformers typically take civil liberties more or less for granted. But when civil liberties come under attack by the right, many reformers will spring to their defense. One of the best ways to throw reform off its intended path is to desecrate the Bill of Rights. In a red scare, people, whether "red" or not, who push for change become the enemy. McCarthyism handed those willing to pick it up (not all conservatives did) a large hammer with which to bludgeon the Truman Administration.

They used it as effectively as a carpenter drives nails. It was a wonderful time to be a conservative politician of a certain unscrupulousness. McCarthyism became the most important factor in American political life. Turmoil and distractions over foreign policy gave it momentum. Korea made things worse; and together with Korea, McCarthyism killed the Fair Deal.

Meantime, many intellectuals carrying the baggage of guilt for their past association with the left found themselves virtually disarmed by the McCarthyite onslaught.   Under attack, some of them proceeded to cannibalize one another.[2] And among the legacies of McCarthyism, Eric F. Goldman identified

> the subtle effect on more than a few liberals, especially among the highly educated, who came out of the drubbing eager to prove that they could be just as hairy-chested, just as "practical," just as ready for the big stick against Communism as any bomb-brandishing politician unencumbered with a Ph.D.[3]

Writes William H. Chafe:

> Because of the anticommunist crusade, domestic dissent was stifled, civil liberties were compromised, and advocates of social reform risked being pilloried as agents of a foreign state. The prospect for change that had given hope to activists, blacks, labor leaders, and women after the war had shrunk before the chill wind of anticommunism. Another moment of possibility had passed.[4]

Nearly everyone came away from McCarthyism dirtied by it. The free and easy attitude which many so-called conservatives displayed toward civil liberties amounted to a betrayal of the very things for which conservatism ought to stand, together with an ugly impulse to label their opponents disloyal. How could people who claimed to speak for the principles of Burke and Hamilton (and not just the Chamber of Commerce) possibly support the junior senator from Wisconsin? McCarthyism prostituted the best values of genuine conservatism in favor of temporary political gain——opportunism in the worst meaning of the term.

The politics of the 1970s displayed two quite different varieties of the conservative opportunism. One saw conservatives move with alacrity to help liberals immolate themselves by transforming sociocultural issues into the predominant political questions of the decade. At this they succeeded. The Democrats suspended bread-and-butter in favor of contentious lifestyle issues, and opened a door for the still-minority conservatives to storm through. The party of rum, Romanism, and rebellion was updated by one California state senator, an Orange County troglodyte, as "the party of grass, gays and godlessness."[5]   As Henry Fairlie wrote, "prohibition, the Klan, fundamentalism, Romanism, immigration: these issues of half a century ago have their counterparts today in drugs, the Equal Rights Amendment, abortion, homosexuality, pornography, and still immigration."[6]   While lower-class voters fell away from politics, the right mobilized precisely around the social changes which embittered some conservatives and stung them to action.   The GOP simply collected the votes.

The other variety of conservative opportunism saw a conservative administration steal liberals' clothing. A past master of McCarthyism, as President, Richard Nixon evinced many of the worst attributes of the red herring tradition.   Nixon's own agonies and misbehavior reflected the misanthropy of postwar conservatism, its suspicion of the Establishment, the courts, and the Kennedy types. Watergate added the coup de grace. Here was another unprincipled betrayal of genuine conservatism. Yet for half a decade, Nixon presided over a continued expansion of the welfare state.

True enough, Nixon did dismiss the domestic dimensions of the presidency as "building outhouses in Peoria."[7] He did remark that "I've always thought this country could run itself domestically without a President; all you need is a competent Cabinet to run the country at home."[8] But between fiscal 1969 and 1974, federal outlays which aided poor people practically doubled.[9] This rise in expenditures was heavily due to the momentum and delayed impact of the Johnson programs, as well as to the effects of recession and unemployment.[10] This said, the Nixon era saw significant gains in a number of realms—among them occupational safety and health, public employment, affirmative action, environmental protection, tax levels on the poor, and unemployment insurance coverage—and major hikes in Social Security and food stamp allotments.[11] All the while Nixonites continued bashing the left for its supposed devotion to hedonism, un-Americanism, governmentalism, and other assorted evils.

In its fundamental, most familiar form, as Nixon's darker impulses suggest, the conservative opportunism has seized upon pseudo-issues not to spur but to arrest movement toward a broadened welfare state. Behind every other tactic, conservatives have employed a persistent strategy toward undercutting the credibility of government itself. To this side of the conservative opportunism we now turn.

NOTES

Liberalism and Libertinism

Schlesinger, Jr., *Vital Center*, pp. 194-95 (Palmer quote); Frederick Lewis Allen, *Only Yesterday: An Informal History of the Nineteen-Twenties* (New York: Harper & Bros., 1931), p. 120; Clara Zetkin, "Lenin on Sexual Love," in *Feminist Frameworks: Alternative Theoretical Accounts of the Relations Between Women and Men*, ed. Alison M. Jaggar and Paula Rothenberg Struhl (New York: McGraw-Hill, 1978), p. 400 (Lenin quote). See also Aldous Huxley, *Brave New World* (New York: Harper & Row, 1969), p. xiii.

[1]"Man the Reformer," p. 70.

[2]David Riesman's observation. Leuchtenburg, *Troubled Feast*, p. 189.

[3]*Cultural Contradictions*, pp. 21-22.

[4]Quoted and analyzed in David Popenoe, "Sweden as a Post-industrial Society," *Social Science* 52 (Winter 1977): 14. Bell has carried forward this argument at some length and in considerable detail. Rather than looking at all of the cultural ramifications of capitalism, our task will be to keep Bell's basic argument in mind as we examine the intersection between liberalism and libertinism.

[5]See Janowitz, *Last Half-Century*, pp. 407, 409-10, 415-16. See also Michael Walzer, "Nervous Liberals," *New York Review of Books*, 11 October 1979, pp. 5 and passim.

[6]Bell, *Cultural Contradictions*, pp. 78-79.

[7]An obsession, yes; but then, in a somewhat different way, the Victorians had been obsessed with sex, too.

[8]"Sweden," p. 212. Italics in the original.

[9]*End of American Innocence*, p. 28.

[10]*Lasch, New Radicalism in America*, p. 90.

[11]Diggins, *American Left*, pp. 33, 75, 78.

[12]Humphrey, *Children of Fantasy*, pp. 237, 242, 252.

[13]Diggins, *American Left*, p. 30.

[14]The moral upheaval of the decade had actually gotten well under way before World War I, in the Village and elsewhere. See, for example, James R. McGovern, "The American Woman's Pre-World War I Freedom in Manners and Morals," *Journal of American History* 55 (September 1968): 315-33.

[15]*Exile's Return*, p. 58.

[16]*Only Yesterday*, p. 350. See also Wecter, *Great Depression*, p. 193.

[17]Joseph F. Kett, *Rites of Passage: Adolescence in America, 1790 to the Present* (New York: Basic Books, 1977), p. 267; Ralph S. Brax, *The*

First Student Movement: Student Activism in the United States During the 1930s (Port Washington, N.Y.: Kennikat Press, 1981), pp. 12-13.

[18]Great Depression, pp. 194-97.

[19]Brax, First Student Movement, pp. 3 (quoted), 57-58, and passim; Feuer, Conflict of Generations, pp. 363, 369.

[20]Unger, The Movement, p. 143.

[21]Youth and Dissent, p. 340. Italics deleted.

[22]World of Nations, p. 130.

[23](Chicago: Playboy Press, 1974), pp. 361-62.

[24]15 May 1978, pp. 63-90.

[25]Fass, The Damned and the Beautiful, p. 22.

[26]On this point, see Hunt, Sexual Behavior, passim.

[27]An interesting sort of nostalgia indeed. The Victorian woman was supposedly sexually repressed. But she arguably looked more overtly sexual than any female who has followed her. The big, protruding bust, the bustle, and the wasp waist accentuated the female form into a steatopygous marvel of improbable anatomy. The more sexually liberated twenties woman, on the other hand, had a straight, flat-chested body and short, bobbed hair. Eras of sexual liberation——the twenties, the sixties ——ironically have women looking more like men (the flapper, unisex fashions, jeans). In the thirties and again in the eighties, clothing styles for women grew more conservative, even frilly and ruffled. In both decades, as Frederick Lewis Allen put it for the thirties, "the red-hot baby had gone out of style." Only Yesterday, p. 348.

We tend of think of women's wear as a gauge of social change, but men's styles may be just as revealing. Regarding hair, for example, see pp. 350-51. For more on the whole subject of fashion, see Lois W. Banner, American Beauty (New York: Alfred A. Knopf, 1983); and Valerie Steele, Fashion and Eroticism: Ideals of Feminine Beauty from the Victorian Era to the Jazz Age (New York: Oxford University Press, 1985).

Suspicion, Disgust, and the Social Issue

[1]After Robert K. Merton, Social Theory and Social Structure, rev. ed. (Glencoe, Ill.: Free Press, 1957), especially pp. 300-301.

[2]The term comes from a Truman press conference. See Robert J. Donovan, Tumultuous Years: The Presidency of Harry S. Truman, 1949-1953 (New York: W. W. Norton & Co., 1982), p. 32. I have opted not to join an old debate over class/interest versus cultural/status politics, sometimes raised in connection with the issues which follow.

[3]American Political Report, 9 August 1985, p. 5.

[4]Lipset, Political Man, p. 326.

[5]*The Picture of Dorian Gray and Selected Stories* (New York: New American Library, Signet, 1983), p. 39.

[6]On the continuing traditionalism of the American public's moral values, see McClosky, *American Ethos*, pp. 52-59.

[7]See Bell, *Cultural Contradictions*, p. 41.

[8]*Perils of Prosperity*, ch. 11.

[9]David Brody, *Workers in Industrial America: Essays on the Twentieth Century Struggle* (New York: Oxford University Press, 1981), p. 45; Ferrell, *World War I*, p. 195.

[10]Brody, *Workers in Industrial America*, p. 45.

[11]*Perils of Prosperity*, p. 81.

[12]*Age of Reform*, p. 280.

[13]Thelen, *La Follette*, pp. 77, 139.

[14]Leuchtenburg, *Roosevelt and the New Deal*, p. 9.

[15]Richard Polenberg, "The Decline of the New Deal, 1937-1940," in Braeman, *New Deal*, 1:249.

[16]In reconstructing the legacy of the Court fight, I have found especially useful William E. Leuchtenburg, "Franklin D. Roosevelt's Supreme Court 'Packing' Plan," in *Essays on the New Deal*, ed. Harold M. Hollingsworth and William F. Holmes (Austin: University of Texas Press, 1969), pp. 109-15.

[17]Polenberg, "Decline of the New Deal," p. 257; Wecter, *Great Depression*, p. 297.

[18]Ibid., pp. 246-47.

[19]Ibid., pp. 256-57.

[20]See James T. Patterson, *Congressional Conservatism and the New Deal: The Growth of the Conservative Coalition in Congress, 1933-1939* (Lexington: University of Kentucky Press for the Organization of American Historians, 1967), pp. 288-91; and David L. Porter, *Congress and the Waning of the New Deal*, National University Publications, Series in Political Science (Port Washington, N.Y.: Kennikat Press, 1980). Roosevelt's attempted congressional purge of anti-New Deal Democrats aroused remarkably weak support from lower-class Democrats, the unemployed, and people on welfare. Polenberg, "Decline of the New Deal," pp. 258-59.

[21]Ibid., p. 255.

[22]Leuchtenburg, *Roosevelt and the New Deal*, p. 272.

[23]Polenberg, "Decline of the New Deal," p. 254.

[24]John Morton Blum, *From the Morgenthau Diaries*, vol. 2: *Years of Urgency, 1938-1941* (Boston: Houghton Mifflin Co., 1965), pp. 41-42.

[25]Polenberg, "Decline of the New Deal," pp. 261-63.

[26]See James Ceaser, "Can Ronald Reagan Revive Republicanism?" *Los Angeles Times*, 20 April 1980.

[27]"Arthur M. Schlesinger, Jr., and the Discontents of Postwar American Liberalism," *Review of Politics* 39 (January 1977): 15.

[28]Arblaster, *Western Liberalism*, p. 315.

[29]*Beyond the New Deal*, p. 379.

[30]Anticommunism will not generally divide Republicans, but it will split Democrats. Liberals in Congress all opposed McCarthy's tactics. Yet the old liberal ambivalence about civil liberties remained; nor did liberals want to face ruination by the red herring of domestic Communism. A group of them in the Senate wound up co-sponsoring a preventive detention measure to derail the notorious McCarran bill, and when the McCarran Internal Security Act of 1950 did pass, liberals divided over it. In 1954 a number of congressional liberals joined in sponsoring the Communist Control bill to outlaw the U.S. Communist party. Hubert Humphrey introduced the measure in the Senate. Adlai Stevenson supported it. So did John Kennedy, who liked and defended McCarthy (a friend of the family). Concerning all of this, see McAuliffe, *Crisis on the Left*, pp. 78-81, 132; and Burner, *Torch Is Passed*, pp. 55-56.

[31]Allen Weinstein, *Perjury: The Hiss-Chambers Case* (New York: Alfred A. Knopf, 1978), pp. 513-16.

[32]Angus Campbell et al., *The American Voter*, abr. ed. (New York: John Wiley & Sons, 1964), pp. 281-82.

[33]Hamby, *Beyond the New Deal*, pp. 497-98.

[34]Unger, *The Movement*, p. 9.

[35]On this point, see especially Yankelovich, *New Rules*, passim.

[36]Norman H. Nie and Kristi Andersen, "Mass Belief Systems Revisited: Political Change and Attitude Structure," *Journal of Politics* 36 (August 1974): 564.

[37]Rothman, *Roots of Radicalism*, pp. 387, 389.

[38]See Burnham, *Current Crisis*, pp. 297-300; and the shrewd contemporary assessment by Richard M. Scammon and Ben J. Wattenberg, *The Real Majority* (New York: Coward-McCann, 1970), especially ch. 3.

[39]My discussion here is inspired in particular by Lasch, "Liberalism in Retreat," pp. 113-15.

[40]Paul Blumberg, *Inequality in an Age of Decline* (New York: Oxford University Press, 1980), pp. 225-26.

[41]Rothman, *Roots of Radicalism*, pp. 393-94. For a suggestive examination of all this as a conflict between "modern" and "postmodern" values, see Jensen, "Last Party System," pp. 227-30.

[42]*Los Angeles Times*, 25 June 1978.

[43]Lubell, *The Future While It Happened*, p. 13.

[44]On this point see Nie, *Changing American Voter*, pp. 142-44.

The Opportunism of the Conservatives

Foley, *New Senate*, p. 61.

[1]"Ideology and Political Culture," p. 553.

[2]Hofstadter, *Anti-intellectualism*, p. 40.

[3]*Rendezvous* (1977), p. x.

[4]*Unfinished Journey*, pp. 109-10.

[5]John Briggs, quoted in "The New Issues," *Newsweek*, 2 October 1978, p. 56.

[6]*The Parties*, p. 121.

[7]Hodgson, *All Things*, p. 105.

[8]Theodore H. White, *The Making of the President 1972* (New York: Atheneum, 1973), p. 353.

[9]Levitan, *Promise*, p. 193.

[10]For evidence that such rises are normal for Republican administrations, see Robert X. Browning, *Politics and Social Welfare Policy in the United States* (Knoxville: University of Tennessee Press, 1986), pp. 156-57 and passim.

[11]There was also the dramatic but ambiguous Family Assistance Plan, which failed.

19

THE PRESIDENT
AND THE STATE
UNDER SUSPICION

Foul deeds will rise, Though all the earth o'erwhelm them, to men's eyes.

Hamlet, Act I, Scene II

My God, this is a hell of a job! I have no trouble with my enemies, I can take care of my enemies all right. But my damn friends, . . . my God-damn friends, . . . they're the ones that keep me walking the floor nights!

Warren G. Harding

The King, the King's to blame.

Hamlet, Act V, Scene II

We have observed that the public's political interest appears to have risen during each reform period, together with confidence in government and the prestige of politics as a career.[1] Then things begin to go wrong. When a reform movement's prognosis turns terminal, politics becomes depleted, discredited. Public confidence weakens in government as a whole, and in the President in particular. And each decline phase has seen a resurgence of congressional power vis-à-vis the Executive.

Disenchantment with government is a fluid thing; it does not just suddenly appear when a President grows hubristic or a war ends. During the reform phase itself, conservatives have already felt alienated. In time they are joined in their disenchantment by the left. Once the reaction sets in, it follows that the right will again get appeased, at least in some degree, and thus grow more contented; but now the left will become increasingly unhappy.

A successful presidential candidate will have run on a bundle of issues. But, having gotten committed, it becomes very hard to change the bundle later on, or even to add to it. To the degree that the original problems get resolved, the candidate's own base is undercut for future elections. And the nature of democracy itself produces more or less continuous disillusionment. Democracy is inefficient, and its inefficiencies are usually public ones. Politicians always seek office by denigrating the accomplishments and foibles of incumbents. Then they become incumbents, and the process repeats. The term "the system" has a way of attaching itself to politics at times when a good many of its practitioners attract unusual suspicion——at the very outset of the century, and in the more recent sixties and seventies. As reform declines, the whole "system" begins to look like a broken-down treadmill. Politics and government get discounted; their apparent trustworthiness and prestige fall. A politics of disillusionment sets in.

In saying this I risk making it all seem mechanical and predictable, like a roller coaster ride. I do not mean to imply that things are ever this simple. Nor do we have the evidence we would like covering the entire century. For the early years, in particular, things remain very impressionistic. Still, what strikes one is the consistency of the evidence, whether journalistic, quantitative, or otherwise. The public becomes offended and "turned off" by such events as World War I, Vietnam, and Watergate. The ensuing reactions run roughly true to form every time.

Though antigovernmental reactions have erupted throughout this century, the one that set in during the sixties focused on distinctly post-New Deal phenomena——the scale and distance of the federal establishment. Michael Pertschuk has written that, as of the mid-1960s, "reaching back to the early nineteenth century is a strong strain of antipathy to the increasing massiveness, remoteness, and concentration of business enterprise, while no comparable antipathy had yet emerged with regard to the size or remoteness of the federal government."[2] All this was changing by decade's end. Congress adopted a spate of measures to curb presidential power, and as the Executive's declined, that of Congress rose. Beyond this internal rearrangement, "the authority of government" as a whole fell, in the words of Samuel P. Huntington, "as people ceased to see it as dedicated to the public interest."[3] Trust in government, and support for governmental power, plunged, particularly among those of low income who had the most to gain from government.[4] More and more of them chose not to vote. All this created terrific headaches for the Democratic party.

In eras of reaction people come to see Presidents as part of the problem, and at times, no doubt, as most of it. A President may personify a set of widely applauded responses to issues, but if the personal image fades or sours, the damage will spread to the once-popular programs as well. Every one of the great liberal Executives we have discussed finally became the Messiah who could not deliver. And so the people backslide, fall into their old ways, damn the Master for promising so much and demanding so much and, ultimately, for costing them so much. We think once more of Wilson in Paris or Johnson and Vietnam, each of them casting seeds to germinate on solid ice. "How is it possible that all these people could be so ungrateful to me after I had given them so much," Johnson asked again and again.[5] What had disappeared? His credibility, the belief that he could deal even with problems like Vietnam or desegregation on which a majority of the populace still agreed with him. People want to personalize. Presidents become lightning rods for anger at individuals or groups over whom they have no control and whom they may indeed oppose. War = strikes = reds = Wilson. War = riots = demonstrators = Johnson.

Once reform movements start to slip past their peak, politics begins to lose its previous sense of seriousness; and as public expectations of politicians dwindle, so does the seriousness with which people view the political process itself. Interest in politics wanes; so does political involvement.[6] In 1977 former Senator John V. Tunney of California, reflecting on his defeat for reelection the previous year, contrasted his style with that of the man who had beaten him, S. I. Hayakawa:

[Hayakawa] is a person who ran his campaign saying that he didn't know anything about government, and in a sense that's a very pessimistic view of life, to hold yourself out as a candidate for high public office, saying that you don't know anything, because what you're really saying is that it doesn't make any difference anyway whether you know anything or don't know anything. . . .

The climate of opinion now in this state, and I think it's becoming true nationally, is one that people want detachment, because they are detached. They don't want to make passionate commitments because they're afraid of getting hurt. They don't like father figures because they were disappointed with Johnson and Nixon. They are uncommitted, particularly in interpersonal relations, but uncommitted to ideologies [too].

They want a politician who is cool, and Hayakawa is cool. He is the ultimate in cool, if you will. Jerry Brown is very cool, too. He's detached.

Tunney described himself as "a passionate person," not the "cool, uncommitted, detached" type that had become so popular. Tunney had fallen victim to the change in fads: "I think that I would have been far better off, not just in a political sense of getting reelected but better off as a person if I'd spent more time in California learning that one of the major things that was on people's minds out here was that they didn't want Washington to do things."[7]

The cool style: keep cool with Coolidge.   In the reaction phase, shrewd politicians may be found practicing an anti-politics which exalts, if anyone, the antihero.   Hence Coolidge, Nixon, Brown, Carter, and Hayakawa; even Eisenhower, the war hero, who pretended to stand above the political stage.   A classic case is Harding.   Capitalizing on public disenchantment with Wilson, Harding rode into office in 1920 astride one of the greatest electoral margins in American history.   He captured the national mood in his famous prescription: "not heroism, but healing, not nostrums but normalcy."   Running mate Coolidge described "the end of a period which has seemed to substitute words for things."[8]   Harding spelled a return to basics, a return, many doubtless hoped, to a simpler time symbolized by simpler people.   If Warren Harding could become President, anyone could become President.

Another man who reflected the vogue of the anti-politician was Henry Ford.   In 1923 *Collier's* came out with the results of a crude poll in which more than one-third of the 260,000 respondents named Ford their pick for President.[9]   If Ford represented the old virtues, the flivver king also bore considerable responsibility for the automotive explosion which was doing so much to undermine them.

In 1926 Walter Lippmann described the decade's other great exemplar of old faiths, Calvin Coolidge.   Noting, like Tunney, that "a widespread distaste of political activity is the controlling mood of public life in this country to-day," Lippmann remarked:

> Mr. Coolidge's genius for inactivity is developed to a very high point. It is far from being an indolent inactivity. It is a grim, determined, alert inactivity which keeps Mr. Coolidge occupied constantly. . . . It is . . . a steady application to the task of neutralizing and thwarting political activity wherever there are signs of life.
>
> . . . The naive statesmen of the pre-Coolidge era imagined that it was desirable to interest the people in their government, that public discussion was a good thing, that indignation at evil was useful. Mr. Coolidge is more sophisticated. He has discovered the value of diverting attention from the government, and with an exquisite subtlety that amounts to genius, he has used dullness and boredom as political devices.

Coolidge fit the national mood. He answered the fears of people who worried about an overly complicated and too powerful federal government. "The people like him, not only because they like the present prosperity, and because at the moment they like political do-nothingism, but because they trust and like the plainness and nearness of Calvin Coolidge himself."[10] William Allen White described the man as "a Puritan in Babylon."[11] To Lippmann, Coolidge offered an un-Puritan age a chance "for vicarious virtue."[12]

With the emergence of a Coolidge or his more recent incarnations, a new issuelessness seeps into politics. Having lost the punch of change, politics appears to the ordinary citizen to devaluate into one more vocation or avocation, simply a struggle between ambitious individuals or grasping parties and interest groups.[13] Meantime, popular writers and scholars set to work debunking the major leaders of the prior reform era: TR, Bryan, Wilson, Kennedy, Johnson, each in turn comes to look flawed or silly.

The period between 1964 and 1972 witnessed a marked increase in distrust of government. "Antipresidentialism" emerged out of the Johnson experience, then peaked with Nixon. Nie and his colleagues speculate that

> a more politically involved public with more coherent political views runs right into the troubles of the late 1960s. The result: a growing disenchantment with government——reflected in the sharp rise in expressions of distrust in the government. The issues of the 1960s, furthermore, do not clearly coincide with party lines; thus the parties offer no meaningful alternatives that might tie citizens more closely to them. Thus the political parties reap the results of the disaffection. Citizens come to look at the parties in more negative terms; they also begin to abandon the parties in growing numbers.[14]

Interest in politics fell.

During the seventies, a fresh awareness emerged of the limitations of government in addressing social problems. The New Deal came in for considerable retrospective blame. Even Arthur M. Schlesinger, Jr., was taking another look at *The Imperial Presidency*. The question, Has the President too much power?, erupted first around Vietnam, that consummate foreign distraction. Watergate, the consummate domestic distraction, spread the infection. Between them, Vietnam and Watergate corroded the myth of the strong but benign President. Stagflation and the energy crisis discredited government further yet.

With welfare state liberals confessing their past statist sins, together with an upsurge of neoconservatism and neomugwumpery, political rhetoric became so fogged that liberals could barely be distinguished from conservatives. Stung by Nixon in the realm of foreign policy and civil liberties, liberals rushed to attack the state as a whole. In the face of Vietnam, Watergate, and anxieties about presidential accountability and the imperial presidency——and in keeping with the general pattern of reform's season of decline——some power tipped toward Congress. As reform gave way to reaction, the charms of expansive government faded.

Paul Starr observed in 1975 that "government in America is sustained by a host of particular interests clamoring for satisfaction; it has little general support or enthusiasm. With no one in decisive control of the state, everyone feels, in one way or another, oppressed by it." "Few sentiments seem more characteristic of political life today than a widespread irritation with the works and scale of government."[15] Late in the sixties, Norman H. Nie and Kristi Andersen point out, "a sense began to emerge among the leadership of the liberal community that big government was merely acting to reinforce existing injustices." By the early seventies, among the mass public, most liberals agreed with conservatives that government had grown too large.[16]

All this stood in drastic contrast to the thirties. Then, one could distinguish liberals from conservatives by their views toward government's size and responsibilities. The population still divided in this classic way as late as 1964: only 25 percent of liberals felt government had become too large, compared to 71 percent of conservatives. By 1968 the cleavage had begun to narrow. And by 1972, 65 percent of liberals agreed that government had grown "too big" as against just 54 percent of conservatives.[17] Conservative reservations, indeed, had receded, very probably because Roosevelt had become Nixon; World War II, Vietnam; aggressive liberalism, aggressive conservatism and repression.[18]

When as many Democrats question big government as did in the 1970s, the signs of disorientation become abundantly clear. One set of poll results released early in 1979 revealed that "only 42% of the voters—— . . . divided equally between Republicans and Democrats——felt government basically was protecting them. The other 58% thought it either was interfering with their lives or they were not sure." Respondents handed government the biggest blame for inflation, and considered labor unions, which came in second, more culpable for inflation than business. Two-thirds would willingly trade a tax cut for cuts in services.[19] Asked to pick "the biggest threat to the country in the future," 14 percent of poll respondents identified "big government" in 1959; in 1978, 47 percent.[20] In 1964, 62 percent agreed that they could generally count on Washington "to do what is right"; by 1980, 23 percent.[21] Signs of irritation abounded. In a way, the alienation of the sixties far left had infected the whole society.

As the *New Republic*, that old flagship of liberal magazines, put it in 1979,

> the age of innocence is over——or it should be. Surely we are no longer inclined to assume the best about our government. It has proven itself too callous with the people's liberties, and too casual with the truth for the nexus of trust between government and citizen to be secure.[22]

Both liberals and conservatives had plenty of reason for cynicism over the tax system; they had also become upset with bureaucracy. Liberals showed more inclination to berate the CIA or the FBI, and conservatives HEW, but no matter. The bureaucracy had become the target, the one group especially reacting against the warfare/national security state, the other against the welfare state. Where government had seemed the great problem-solver in the thirties, now political action became suspect as government took on the image of one more inchoate, fallible, bumbling institution. No wonder campaigning against Washington became the rage. "Get off our backs," demanded Washington's Governor Dan Evans in 1975.[23] He was talking about the other Washington, of course. Evans was a Republican. So was the President.

A leadership burnout, such as afflicted reformers in the twenties or the seventies, confronts conservatives with less of a problem. Typically having fewer and smaller goals, they generally show less need of leadership. Not that issues disappear. They never really disappear. They can still be heard, like footsteps in the fog; but they cannot be seen. Issues, parties, leaders——these mean less and less to the ordinary voter. The phenomenon runs two ways: it both responds to public sentiment and reinforces it. The political system becomes anesthetized.

In saying these things I do not wish to overstate them——to be so sweeping, for example, as to obscure the continuing strength of the woman movement in the seventies. But in focusing too heavily on the remaining activism of certain groups, we would risk missing the mass depoliticizing of the 1920s, the 1950s, and the 1970s. People turn inward. They want to spend their paychecks by themselves, on themselves. The style becomes unpolitical and latently or actively antipolitical. Tunneys get defeated. A Carter finds himself in trouble trying to push through a very modest reform program, and steps back.

Like the mediocre Carter, every single great liberal President in this century has ended his reform drive suffering one rebuff after another at the hands of Congress. The chief difference between them and their less successful liberal counterparts has been progress for a while. A Truman, a Kennedy, or a Carter encounters balking right from the start. Exhausted, distracted, stymied, even a fruitful administration in time will ask Congress for next to nothing.   As the anesthesia seeps in, Washington and, typically, the state capitals begin to drift off.

Now one more irony becomes apparent. Among the public, the myriad of complaints about government keeps on building up. Nothing is better for government than to confront a crisis and meet it. Often the *process* of meeting it becomes more important than the actual results. But stasis in itself causes damage. Either government grows or it faces an accretion of grievances and negativism which lead to inertia and decline.   Unless some sort of unifying domestic or foreign policy initiatives can actively proceed, when the forward phase of a reform period bogs down, the switch into reverse becomes virtually automatic. Then the public carps about drift in Washington.

All of this grows much worse when a big scandal breaks out. This has happened every time a reform movement has started to wane. The curious relationship of scandal to reform and especially reaction will provide a coda for this chapter. (We will not go into the multifold scandals of the Reagan Administration——some of which lie beyond the time span of this book, and all of which remain to be assessed as to their historic importance.)

A Diversion on Scandal

One day in 1923 a White House visitor who had an appointment with the President was mistakenly conducted to the wrong floor. Nearing the Red Room, he heard an angry voice; then he saw Warren G. Harding "throttling a man against the wall" and yelling: "You yellow rat! You double-crossing bastard!" The President's victim was Charles R. Forbes.[1] Harding had met Forbes while vacationing in Hawaii and decided to appoint him head of the Veterans' Bureau. Later Harding learned that in two years Forbes had stolen or squandered a fifth of a billion dollars in veterans' funds.

Scandals always exist in government. Most administrations, liberal or conservative, have experienced at least a low-grade case or two of skulduggery. But Forbes belongs to the tradition of truly grand scandals around the presidency. Since the Civil War, these have revealed a fascinating pattern of recurrence: a major outbreak has occurred every fifty years or so (twice coinciding, sadly, with the nation's centennial celebrations). Since we are so generous in ascribing the gains of reform eras to individuals, I suppose we should be equally scrupulous in crediting the scandals——the Age of Grant, the Era of Harding, the Nixon Epoch.

Here we will focus on the propensity of major scandals to erupt——or come into view——during the decline phase of a reform movement, adding their own heavy weight to the buckling process.   We will be more concerned with effect than with cause.   We will acknowledge that the emergence of a Harding, a weak individual who had a way of making wretched appointments, or a Nixon, who combined the same tendency with truly profound personal flaws, involves some degree of chance.   On the other hand, we will relate their scandals to the social setting in which they broke out: the get rich quick aura of the twenties, or the ideological paranoia of the early seventies.

Truly spectacular national scandals on the scale of the Grant era, Teapot Dome, or Watergate can only erupt at the federal level.   Since the sheer scope of government has increased, and since new technologies have multiplied the means of abuse, the possibility for corruption in the grand manner has grown frighteningly.   In 1974, Harold J. Abramson observed:

> American political history can offer nothing to rival Watergate in sheer scope of corruption.   Moreover . . . the motives behind Watergate are new: this time, the scandal was not incurred for sex or money.   Instead, corruption was engaged in solely to enhance the power of an ideology, and to serve a man who is presumed to represent that ideology.   This is what is unique in American history, and in the history of American political scandal.[2]

Since the Civil war, besides emerging about every fifty years, our more stupendous political scandals have held other characteristics in common.

Each has followed a reform wave: the Civil War era, progressivism, the Kennedy-Johnson decade.

Each has also followed a major war: the Civil War, World War I, Vietnam.

All of these wars produced deep divisions among the people, with social and psychological wounds which healed slowly if at all.

Every outbreak has accompanied apparent alterations in the national mood which created a more hospitable environment for scandal.   The Gilded Age sported legendary corruption in the private sector as well as the public.   The same was true of the twenties, some of whose corporate scandals were only exposed after the Depression stripped off the covers. And the sixties and seventies saw startling increases in many forms of crime.

Each burst of scandal has occurred in rough proximity to an economic crisis or collapse.

Each burst, notably Watergate, has erupted at a time when government already stood in considerable public disfavor.

Every scandalous outbreak began or peaked during the administration of a man who was out of his depth in the presidency. ("I am not fit for this office and should never have been here," Harding exclaimed. "God what a job!")[3]

All the scandals erupted during Republican administrations. (Possibly the GOP is more corruption-prone than the Democratic party; certainly in the past its corruption has involved higher stakes.)[4]

Each of these GOP administrations followed a Democratic administration.

Every outbreak brought down key officials in high places. (There has been a particularly spectacular bag of Attorney Generals.)

In the election which followed each exposé, a Democratic candidate or a Democratic figurehead has borne some onus of scandal. This has made it hard for the Democrats to use scandal as an issue.

The scandals themselves have never permanently altered the balance of political power. Teapot Dome roused headlines shouting "Party Chiefs, Alarmed, Call for Action," and "Fear Effect of Mounting Scandal." A Republican senator commented: "The question is not so much whether the Republican Party will be defeated as whether it will survive."[5] Democrats gloated. But in 1924 Coolidge won a smashing landslide. (Scandal-influenced Democratic successes in 1974 and 1976 quickly evaporated, too.)

Coolidge won a landslide, yet with an extraordinarily low turnout. And here, I think, we begin to get a hint of what scandal has meant to reform in this century. Both of the Republican administrations hit by scandal take office with a promise to clean up the mess in Washington. Each time, the Democrats leave under a cloud, their reform aspirations gone awry, and the country winding up a war. Reform stands discredited; war stands discredited; raw wounds cut across society. The voters hunt for a government which will heal these wounds. But the man put up by the opposition is a fool or a cad or both. The ensuing scandals ruin the careers of many in high places. The public gets treated to the spectacle of seeing its leaders ousted, even paraded off to prison, among them officials previously responsible for enforcing the law. Though no permanent party realignment ensues, enough has occurred to add a new dimension to voters' previous disgust with government and attach this disgust to both parties.

So far I have avoided reference to the late forties and fifties because this period does not, on the surface, conform to the dynamics we have examined. The Truman scandals, however embarrassing, scarcely added up to Teapot Dome or Watergate. Yet KlC2 did link the issues of corruption and Communism. If he was guilty, what more egregious example of corruption in high places could there have been at the time than the case of Alger Hiss? Or, so many argued, than the case of Roosevelt at Yalta?

Seen this way, the scheme we have outlined works for the forties and fifties, though less neatly than for the twenties and seventies. Reform and war (though by no means so divisive a war) appear in a Democratic administration. The reform wave ends acrimoniously; the war spawns bitterness, and a postwar red scare prolongs it. A new Republican President gets elected to clean up the mess in Washington supposedly left by his predecessors.

"Every decade or so," writes Page Smith,

> we must have our national morality play: an enactment on television, with millions of viewers, of our own schizophrenia, our inner dividedness. We wish to be assured that the old values still hold and to demonstrate that some people must be punished.
>
> And when the play is over——the Hiss-Chambers play, the McCarthy play, . . . the Watergate play——why then we feel purged, purified, braced. We have seen the villains get their lumps. The true has triumphed over the false; good over evil; justice over crime. That, we say a little smugly, is the American way.[6]

After the fall of Richard Nixon, the *New Republic's* TRB wrote: "So that brings us at last to Mr. Ford. What a relief. The nation is like a child that has swallowed something nasty, and thrown up, and feels better."[7]

But how much better did the nation really feel? All the vast muckraking which had led to this had certainly undermined public confidence in government, just as muckraking at the turn of the century had undermined confidence in business. Nor was the muckraking any longer at the distance of the printed page. Television now brought political gangsterism directly into the living room. Too much had happened to allow real relief: Johnson and Vietnam, then Nixon and Vietnam, then Nixon and Watergate, and, later, Ford's pardon of Nixon.

Half a century before, the upshot of scandal for government's role had not been especially consequential because the Republican administrations of the twenties did not play a great role anyway. There would be no imperial presidency under Harding, Coolidge, or Hoover. The people may have felt that Harding, for example, actually undergoverned them. And the public responded to the disclosure of the Harding scandals in a stunning way. "The most amazing thing about the exposure of corruption under President Harding," wrote Karl Schriftgiesser, "is how this was turned, not against the Republican Party, but against those who made the disclosures."[8] They found themselves

damned as character assassins and questioners of the American way.
Compared to Gerald Ford, who clumsily pardoned his predecessor,
Coolidge acted like a virtuous Cheshire cat——and unlike Nixon, Harding,
conveniently enough, had died.

Ultimately, concluded the *Outlook and Independent* in 1931, "the Oil
Scandals provided strong and discouraging evidence that corruption in
high places no longer moves the American electorate."[9]   But another,
rather different conclusion might have been drawn from Teapot Dome.
In March 1924, the *New York Times* reported that most visitors to the
Capitol from across the country

> testify that the people back home are disgusted with the
> condition of affairs here in Washington as disclosed by the
> evidence before the Teapot Dome Committee and the mass of
> unofficial accusations and rumor that has accompanied these
> revelations. They feel that official Washington is not merely
> impregnated with corruption, but saturated with it. They have
> little respect for public men generally, classing them all as
> selfish or corrupt politicians. They have lost confidence in the
> integrity of Congress and have a low opinion of the intelligence
> of the people's representatives in the Senate and House. . . .
> At the same time this lack of confidence does not apply to
> President Coolidge.

Coolidge, instead, was "credited with being sincere, honest, and able."[10]

The negativism recorded impressionistically by the *Times* half a
century before reappeared in scientific polls measuring public attitudes
of the 1970s. Scholars have viewed political corruption in various ways,
some of them making corruption seem functional, even vital in certain
settings.   The public at large, however, has generally been less
discriminating. The abuses of the Nixon era provided a perfect excuse
to attack the state on civil liberties grounds, hence indirectly to mobilize
civil liberties against social justice by raising suspicion of government and
all its works. A good many liberals did just this, contributing to the
post-Watergate miasma with their own sourness toward the government.
That they did so more or less inadvertently made no real difference.

All of this, in turn, reinforced the anti-statism always inherent in
American political life. Much of the disenchantment over Watergate, I
suspect, arose from the earlier, widespread supposition that the GOP
was at least a party of clean government. Now, which party (if either)
remained untainted? Neither Teapot Dome nor Watergate made the
Democrats seem more respectable; these scandals merely made the GOP,
hence the whole system, appear seedy.   Scandal erodes respect for
government in general, not just for one or the other political party. A

public which has grown this disgusted will not demonstrate enthusiasm over further growth in the public sector; it will, if anything, endorse cuts. The fact that scandal in each period of outbreak has coincided with recent expansions of the federal establishment makes the tie-in between government and scandal seem even closer. If politicians are knaves, why entrust them with still greater power? If the presidency has become imperial, cut it back. No matter that the positive possibilities of government get lost as negative possibilities are trimmed.

All of this belongs to a hallowed political tradition. There was an active tendency in the later nineteenth century, for instance, to conjoin images of corruption on one hand with centralized, interventionist government on the other. The corrupt and their accusers in effect served the same cause: many "reformers" hunted behind every door and in every attic to find means to contain political power. The continuing corruption gave them energy, and their efforts, legitimacy.

Here, precisely, lies the catch. When Watergate conspirator John Dean asks, How can we "use the available federal machinery to screw our political enemies?,"[11] the reflexive response to that is to reduce the available federal machinery. In the case of a Nixon, this provides satisfaction; the nation throws up and feels better. Then it elects a Carter, cannot understand why Carter fails to get things done, and plunges even deeper into disillusionment until rescued by a Reagan.

Summarizing some of the trends of the 1960s, Nie and his colleagues give us a feeling for the effects of scandal, together with other factors, on the political system:

> The issues that loosened party ties were racial conflict and Vietnam, capped off . . . by Watergate. These issues caused substantial discontent. They led the public to turn against the political parties and against the political process more generally. But they led to no new partisan alignments. Vietnam was not an issue that clearly differentiated one party from another, and the racial issue split the majority party. Watergate had more partisan identification. But its major effect seems to have been a rejection of government and politicians. The result of the new issues is weakened commitment to parties and politics, not reconstituted commitments.[12]

Adds William H. Chafe:

> The Watergate tragedy ultimately worked to the disadvantage of those with a different vision for America by diverting attention from issues of class, race, and inequality, and focusing

all energies instead on the constitutional issue of a president abusing power. By 1974, there were few Americans with the psychic or social space to consider economic and social reform. There was a more pressing issue——the very survival of the American system of government. Paradoxically, Nixon had succeeded——despite himself——in achieving many of his most cherished political goals.[13]

Scandal can have some remarkably distorting effects on the political system. It helped lead to the election of Jimmy Carter, for example, with all his pious homilies on honesty and morality in government. Yet in time, given that Americans always remain suspicious of government, a measure of trust in government begins to revive. In 1966, for instance, the percentage of people who expressed "a 'great deal' of confidence in the executive branch of government" stood at 41. In December 1973, it hit 14. Nine months later, Nixon was out; but Carter managed to drive confidence down as low as 10 percent in 1978. Recovery occurred in the eighties. Whether it happened because Reagan appeared to be doing things properly, or because events seemed to have stopped going so desperately wrong, remained a matter for conjecture.[14]

Though Reagan enjoyed some great successes, the decline of party and party discipline has made it far more difficult to do anything with government. The decline has favored, if anything, an overall drift to the right. More broadly, Americans have traditionally resisted the kind of organization that became especially necessary in the 1930s. The relatively high degree of discipline and regimentation inherent in the New Deal produced an inevitable backlash. So have welfare state bureaucracy and procedures ever since. And so has the income tax. As late as the 1930s, over 95 percent of the American public still remained exempt from paying income tax. Of the remaining 5 percent, most paid quite modestly.[15] All that ended with World War II, and people recognized, if they hadn't before, that social services cost money. "As long as the New Deal was painless," writes Samuel Lubell, "the Republican attacks failed to register. Once the bite of taxes was felt, the Welfare State took on a new aspect."[16]

The New Deal created the pluralist state, ministering to the needs of groups which had the power to compel a response. The vogue of pluralism in the academic community of the fifties added intellectual gloss to established fact. But curiously enough, in the big broker state individualism came to flourish in a peculiar way——not in the form of individual aggrandizement, though plenty of that survived, but now in the form of group aggrandizement. And because government could not possibly satisfy all demands, the broker-welfare state inevitably created widespread disappointment.[17] A political party, too, in this case the

Democrats, can only deliver so much. What it does not deliver will be keenly remembered.

Once government became permanently identified in the postwar era with constant preparedness to murder millions of people systematically and basically indiscriminately, its benign image changed. One of the biggest (yet best-concealed) costs of the Bomb and the Cold War has been that they have cast the benevolence of government under a shadow of extreme doubt. Those who raise the most passionate cries about military mass murder are the liberals, who of course have the largest stake in a powerful government. Providing the most extraordinary example imaginable of government waste, Vietnam gave pause to liberalism in general. In foreign policy and defense, the presidency is now foredoomed to being perennially "imperial," at least by contrast to the decades before World War II. When dealing with domestic policy, postwar Presidents have generally proved far less assertive——and often, indeed, extraordinarily passive.[18]

NOTES

Francis Russell, *The Shadow of Blooming Grove: Warren G. Harding in His Times* (New York: McGraw-Hill, 1968), p. 560 (Harding quote).

[1]See Janowitz, *Last Half-Century*, pp. 112-13.

[2]*Revolt Against Regulation*, p. 14.

[3]*American Politics*, pp. 209-10, 212. Huntington sees this erosion as setting in earlier than I have portrayed it here.

[4]Burnham, *Current Crisis*, pp. 295-97, 301, and passim. Some terminology is his.

[5]Kearns, *Lyndon Johnson*, p. 340.

[6]On these latter points, see Huntington, *American Politics*, p. 215.

[7]*Los Angeles Times*, 29 June 1977.

[8]Leuchtenburg, *Perils of Prosperity*, p. 89.

[9]Keith Sward, *The Legend of Henry Ford* (New York: Rinehart & Co., 1948), p. 126.

[10]*Men of Destiny*, pp. 12-15.

[11]See White's *A Puritan in Babylon: The Story of Calvin Coolidge* (New York: Macmillan Co., 1938; reprint, New York: Capricorn Books, 1965).

[12]*Men of Destiny*, p. 17.

[13]On this sort of thing, see Barber, *Pulse of Politics*, p. 3.

[14]*Changing American Voter*, p. 283.

[15]"Politics Against Government," *New Republic*, 27 December 1975, pp. 19, 21.

[16]"Mass Belief Systems," p. 554.

[17]Nie, *Changing American Voter*, pp. 126-27; Ladd, "Liberalism Upside Down,". p. 593.   All this occurred notwithstanding continued strong disagreements on questions of public policy.

[18]See Nie, *Changing American Voter*, pp. 126-27.

[19]*Los Angeles Times*, 15 January 1979.

[20]Huntington, *American Politics*, p. 216.

[21]"Narrowing the Confidence Gap," *Wilson Quarterly* 7 (Autumn 1983): 10.

[22]"The Truth, after Twenty-six Years," 23 June 1979, p. 8.

[23]*Los Angeles Times*, 10 December 1975.

A Diversion on Scandal

[1]Russell, *Shadow of Blooming Grove*, p. 558.

[2]"Watergate: Death at the Roots," *Columbia Forum* n.s. 3 (Winter 1974): 3.

[3]Arthur M. Schlesinger, Jr., *The Age of Roosevelt: The Crisis of the Old Order, 1919-1933* (Boston: Houghton Mifflin Co., 1957), p. 51.

[4]"Public-action administrations," argues Arthur M. Schlesinger, Jr.,

> tend to attract idealists who, whatever their other defects, do not steal.   The kind of corruption that is invited by government regulation and by the disbursement of government funds tends to rise only at the weary end of public-action administrations. But private-interest administrations are staffed from the start by people who are in there to enrich themselves or their industries.   So corruption becomes rampant in the Harding, Eisenhower, and Reagan administrations.

"The Election and After," p. 36.   See also Schlesinger, Jr., *Cycles*, pp. 40-42.

[5]William E. Leuchtenburg, "Waterdome: Or How Democrats Can Lose in '76," Boston *Globe*, 30 September 1973.

[6]*Los Angeles Times*, 11 June 1973.

[7]"Has Our System Really Been Vindicated?" reprinted in *Los Angeles Times*, 22 August 1974.

[8]*This Was Normalcy: An Account of Party Politics During Twelve Republican Years; 1920-1932* (1948; reprint, New York: Oriole Editions, 1973), p. 148.

[9]"Fall Gives Up," 13 May 1931, p. 37.

[10]10 March 1924.

[11]Abramson, "Watergate," p. 8.

[12]*Changing American Voter*, p. 350; Huntington, *American Politics*, p. 143.

[13]*Unfinished Journey*, p. 429.

[14]*Los Angeles Times*, 8 August 1984.

[15]Mark H. Leff, "Taxing the 'Forgotten Man': The Politics of Social Security Finance in the New Deal," *Journal of American History* 70 (September 1983): 378.

[16]*Future of American Politics*, p. 207.

[17]Irving Howe, Introduction to *Beyond the Welfare State*, ed. Irving Howe (New York: Schocken Books, 1982), pp. 10-11.

[18]On this last point see Hodgson, *All Things*, p. 134.

20

FROM DISORIENTATION
TO APATHY

Disorientation

> Government cannot solve our problems. It can't set the
> goals. It cannot define our vision. Government cannot
> eliminate poverty, or provide a bountiful economy, or reduce
> inflation, or save our cities, or cure illiteracy, or provide
> energy.

Jimmy Carter

No matter how much drive a reform era opens with, its fervor eventually
yields to timidity and drift. The moral claims of oppressed groups
appear fulfilled. Society's obligations, it seems, have been met. Under
attack, its energy depleted, reform becomes disoriented. Its confidence
fades. The phenomenon resembles an airplane which has lost its
instruments as well as its fuel. As the craft drops toward the ground its
pilot hunts uncertainly for some place to land.

Progressivism provides us with an especially notorious case study.
Reform peaked around 1914. Then came the war. La Follette found
himself denounced by Theodore Roosevelt as a "hun";[1] Wilson and
Bryan split over the *Lusitania* and the League; Debs went to prison;
Wilson refused to let him out. Along with the battle among the
reformers went a shift in priorities which the war itself dictated,
symptomized early on by TR's switch in emphasis from strident domestic
reform to a strident foreign policy. In the Progressive party, nationalism
shoved reform off the top rung. For the 1916 Progressive and GOP
nominations Roosevelt pushed——of all people——Henry Cabot Lodge.
Ultimately the Progressive party endorsed Republican nominee Charles

Evans Hughes, produced a platform to match, and disappeared into the limbo of history.

Having won numerous converts in 1916, Wilson alienated them over the peace settlement and repression at home.   Meanwhile, Wilson's postwar domestic policies, or the lack of them, quickly fed reformers' doubts and disillusionment.   The Wilsonian ambivalence toward power (including governmental power) was never fully worked out; and if the war represented an apogee of federal authority——"the first American attempt at economic and social control on anything like a national scale and comprehensive basis"——the denouement of the Wilson Administration saw a resurgence of negativism toward the power of government.[2]

In its last years, the administration became a reverse image of its former self.   As David Burner has pointed out, it lost the crucial capacity of discipline, the ability to order and direct the Democratic party, Congress, or even itself.   Wilson remained abroad for months on end, attending to the peace.   "The Democrats in Congress, without his personal leadership, simply went to pieces," wrote the Secretary of State.[3] Domestic matters took second place to the League down to the time that Wilson suffered physical collapse in late September 1919 and a stroke in early October.   Wilson's disability left a vacuum which some of his cabinet members (notoriously, Palmer) moved at least partially to fill.

The failure of reconstruction at home——partly understandable in terms of the stakes in Paris and the President's strokes, but a failure nevertheless——did much to curdle reform enthusiasm after the war, leaving a sour aftertaste of disillusionment and reaction.   Burl Noggle has pointed to the possibility of a deliberate trade here: "Wilson possibly hoped to buy support for his treaty aims in exchange for minimal reconstruction policy."   The contrast between Wilson's design for restructuring the world on one hand, and for reconstructing the country on the other, was startling.   Large elements even of business wanted more control from Washington than the administration was willing to provide.[4]

But the administration had virtually no plan of reconstruction.   As Noggle emphasizes, the nation,

> bereft of direction and leadership, stumbled for some two years through a trying time of demobilization, reconversion, race riots, and a frantic search for security at home and abroad from presumed enemies of the republic, and in the process surrendered to a state of mind that the war itself had already grossly stimulated, namely, a yearning for the national pieties and the political and economic conservatism personified by the Republican party's presidential nominee in 1920, thereby Harding and the legendary 'normalcy' of the Twenties resulting

from America's engagement in and, more importantly, her disengagement from World War I. . . .

The United States, deeply involved in war in 1918, sought to demobilize after the November Armistice and step by step moved through a series of crises and readjustments that prepared the way for Harding's normalcy. The decade of the Twenties——with its intolerance and chauvinism, its search for psychic security, its falling away from whatever reform zeal the prewar Progressives had displayed, its ambivalence over centralization and rationalization of governmental and economic power, as well as its often exciting and innovative cultural and intellectual achievements——began to take form in the months after the Armistice. Harding, Coolidge, Hoover, and their colleagues in governing the American economy and society of the Twenties were more caretakers than innovators; they took command in March, 1921, of a country already predisposed to move in the direction in which they chose to go. The Twenties had, in large measure, already taken form before Woodrow Wilson rode down Pennsylvania Avenue for the last time as President of the United States and surrendered office to his successor. Wilson himself bore much responsibility for this.[5]

The 1920 cost of living stood 105 percent over that of 1914. In the spring of 1920 a depression hit. By the following winter there were nearly 5 million unemployed. The strike wave had erupted. In 1921, 453,000 farmers saw their farms disappear. The Wilson government, when it did not react with repression, responded with inertia or fumbling.[6] When poor Harding took over he walked into a catastrophe: "From Wilson he received a disintegrating presidency, a confused and rebellious Congress, a foreign policy in chaos, a domestic economy in shambles, a society sundered with hatreds and turmoil."[7] Harding did not produce a leadership vacuum; he inherited one.

Disorientation of this sort emerges, broadly speaking, from the tendency of reform movements to skim off the easier issues, or the easier parts of issues, first. The initial phase of a movement is relatively simple and straightforward. Big problems have built up over a span of time. A rough sense of priorities has emerged on how to deal with them. Issues have become personified as villainous institutions or individuals: the oil trust, John D. Rockefeller, segregated schooling, George Wallace. Often the initial legislative prescriptions seem clear-cut. Legislation passes. This leaves reformers with a sense of satisfaction and accomplishment. It is pleasant to vanquish one's antagonists in legislative chambers. Easy targets, easy invocations, easy villains, and (sometimes) easy solutions——it comes as a relief at any time to find life even the least bit simple, especially to discover it simpler than one had expected. Coinciding with a measure of literal fulfillment there emerges in time an illusion of complete fulfillment.[8] Doubt has not yet crept in.

The warm, enveloping glow of prosperity reaffirms this illusion of fulfillment. Not only does prosperity threaten reform by stealing one of its motive forces. Prosperity sustains the liberals' own overly rosy feelings of accomplishment about the reforms they have recently enacted.

So success, combined with illusions of even greater success, disorients a reform movement. More always remains to do later, but an element of self-congratulation about past accomplishments creeps in. The big reforms from the movement's easy phase, the ones that had always had high priority and around which great support could be mobilized, have been enacted. Once the illusion of fulfillment emerges, unity starts to break down. Many people become generationally satisfied——literally satisfied for the duration of their own lifetimes. Others think they are satisfied. It becomes harder and harder to build new coalitions around fresh priorities.

In the case of progressivism, for example, a great deal of the agenda had seen enactment by 1920. Much that remained was mawkish or divisive. In the conventional wisdom, even poverty appeared cured.[9] The question was, where to go from here? A great deal of the progressive impulse had had to do with order——with fashioning an organic society. When World War I and its aftermath seemed to threaten order, reform took on sinister connotations. The question of where to go next could stimulate two very damaging answers: first, that everything of note had already been accomplished; or else that any more agitation would threaten the organic whole. Each answer discouraged further movement.

An even more perplexing problem has emerged since the New Deal. The basic thrust of reform throughout this century has taken it toward the welfare state; but by the end of the thirties, the welfare state stood substantially erected. As with progressivism, something of an illusion of fulfillment developed late in that decade, a dissipation of the crisis atmosphere. In the words of William E. Leuchtenburg: "The more successful the New Deal was, the more it undid itself. The more prosperous the country became, the more people returned to the only values they knew, those associated with an individualistic, success-oriented society."[10] Roosevelt's Court plan and proposals for administrative reform held out promises which seemed at best opaque, and at worst suggested that FDR lusted for power. The 1937-38 recession also undermined faith in reform. Events in Europe, meanwhile, deepened mistrust of presidential authority in general.[11] By appearance the welfare state looked even bigger and more secure than it was. Now reform lost much of its rationale. The impression surfaced that things were far better, and for far more people, than they really were.

"The more advantages secured," Charlotte Perkins Gilman once observed, "the harder it is to rouse the public to see the need of anything further."[12] The welfare state used to stir great enthusiasm. It was an experiment, after all, and much debated. Create it, though, and it would lose its excitement, its ability to make people think great thoughts and do great things. Since the New Deal, the welfare state, and incremental reform in general, have come to seem prosaic and boring. No longer does the welfare state carry any transcendent vision of a good society. It has clearly shown that perfection lies beyond it.

A rising ambivalence toward the welfare state among liberals themselves has severely compromised the case for expanding it. And the welfare state has long since ceased to excite very many intellectuals. On the whole, people will resent the welfare state when it does not help them, or when they believe they have received less from it than others have. In order for welfare statism to work, it must benefit the great mass of the public. Otherwise it becomes altruism, and particularly in hard times, becomes expendable. The truly untouchable programs are those which benefit huge elements of the middle class.

In an affluent society "people simply expect much more in the performance of government and various other social institutions."[13] They forget or never understand that benefits come from government, everything from welfare to education to freeways. Once suffer this form of amnesia, once take the welfare state for granted——if the implementing generation does not, its children surely will——and what will become glaring will not be its benefits but its costs. A tendency will emerge to perceive taxes as too high and benefits going to other people.[14] And once the welfare state runs into this sort of trouble, it becomes a far easier target for conservatives to strike at.

Likewise some of its supporters. During the 1930s, for instance, labor had seemed heroic. But by the fifties, unlike blacks or the extremely poor, it had become more difficult to identify with labor as an oppressed group. The labor movement no longer seemed to be much of a movement. Content with pluralism and incrementalism, it lay like a warm cat across the belly of the fundamental status quo. It had become, more or less, middle-class.

Once they feel fairly satisfied, interest groups increase the general inertia by supporting the status quo even while demanding adjustments for themselves. In this sense, at least, "all established interest groups," as Theodore J. Lowi puts it, "are conservative."[15] From a society of natural rights, we have developed into a society of natural entitlements. But the more satisfied groups become, the more stasis builds into the system as a whole. Over time, too, a very damaging tendency develops to overburden sound liberal policies and programs——to load Christmas trees with leaden ornaments. Two classic examples are the income tax and Social Security. Such decorations break the branches and make the programs shabby in the public eye.

Nor do liberals have Herbert Hoover or Richard Nixon to kick around any more. Along with other major losses which have dulled the liberal edge, liberals have lost their most prized and useful old enemies.

Individuals make much better targets in power than out, and Democrats have held more power than Republicans over the past six decades. When the Establishment turned liberal (however pallidly), liberalism had to absorb it; the *New York Times* became a whipping boy of Republicans, not Democrats. In a sense, this conversion was one of liberalism's greatest triumphs, but the success proved expensive because the Establishment had ideas of its own. Money, votes, and respectability came in, but so did the burden of carrying a great deal more weight on a fragile ideological frame. By the 1950s, conservatism (like radicalism) had been so thoroughly co-opted by liberalism that this in itself accounted quite considerably for the absence of a more sophisticated conservatism. At the same time that many moderate conservatives moved into the Democratic party, they further diluted what little ideological purity it had once possessed. Conservatives who remained Republicans often spoke stridently. They could afford to do so without running up much cost in offending the GOP's dwindling moderates.

Reform movements feed off clusters of unresolved tensions. As demands are met, more or less, and as those tensions shrink, so does the overall impulse for reform. The earlier stages of these movements come easiest. But it is never possible just to set up a series of priorities, meet them, and go home. With their original agenda more or less finished off, in the later phases reformers tend to scatter from beneath their original umbrella, pursuing separate goals. Meantime the reform drive will have attracted a great many hangers-on——the difficulty with a reform movement is that anyone and any group can join in. Rather than getting finished off at some point or other, the agenda simply changes. As claimant groups multiply, the attention which each and its problems attract tends to dissipate, while the coherence of the earlier framework of priorities has long since disappeared.

So, at the end of one of these reform surges as many questions may remain to be dealt with as before (although the questions themselves will have changed). Not only is there a glut of issues, but the old ones come into competition with new ones. Often internally inconsistent, demands frequently conflict. Original priorities fall into question. Struggles erupt among reformers over how to proceed. Nothing can prove more damaging than a sudden switch of political agendas.[16] The danger in the battle over priorities lies precisely in this switch.

This is why the proponents of a particular cause do better if they can secure priority for it at the very outset of a reform movement. At this point a well agreed-on and orderly agenda can be developed. The battle over whether or not to elevate the status of second-level priorities has not yet erupted; all remains in relative harmony. But once the first-line imperatives have at least partially been met, the proponents of second-class priorities try to push them to the fore, and the movement quickly becomes choked with groups clamoring for recognition of their demands. Many original supporters will grow alarmed or disillusioned. The new demands cannot possibly achieve complete fulfillment. This impossibility will spawn dissatisfaction among the latecomers too. As issues multiply they will begin to cancel one another out.

The woman movement of the sixties and seventies provides an example of the phenomenon, particularly in relation to the far left. Radical feminists challenged the left to a profound ideological reorientation when they claimed that the basic split in society ran not along class lines, but along lines of sex. The New Left, including SDS, was originally sexist, so women got involved in their own movement inside the Movement. Males responded with suspicion, partly because of their own chauvinism, but also because they did not want to see the left fragmented. The fragmentation occurred anyway when separatist radicals split off to form WITCH and the Redstockings. Not only did the Movement fall under attack by women; it was also distracted by gays. All this reflected a classic dilemma for reformers and radicals in general: how to respond to the rise of group after group, each demanding its rights. There is a frenzy of issues, and rather than firing artillery at a few problems, reformers and radicals begin scattering buckshot at many.

In any given national political situation a great deal remains unpredictable, and especially in conditions such as these. Reform seems nearly always to generate unpleasant, unpredicted side effects. To the extent that problems get solved at all, the solutions very rarely satisfy everyone or even anyone, while the process of treating the problems in turn spins off new ones. These unanticipated consequences of a reform wave rank among the most powerful forces which can destroy it. The side effects do not stop at dissipation-through-demands. Unanticipated results also flow like ripples from the reforms that have already been implemented. "As the distance between each good intention and its side effect increases," Bernard James has written, "predictability decreases. By the time good intentions interact in the zone of their fourth- or fifth-order side effects, their consequences are virtually impossible to predict, let alone control."[17] New solutions breed new problems on their way to becoming old solutions.

With all of this goes a dose of elitism which disorients the left even more. On one level this has to do with policy. The environmental movement, for example——so important a part of recent liberalism—— contains a strain of elitism. Elitism also reflects itself in personnel: one can tell a great deal about the ideological state of the nation by looking at the leadership of the Democratic party at any given time. We tend to think of that party in terms of a few great names: Bryan, Wilson, FDR. But it takes on different hues when other, less familiar names are mentioned: John W. Davis, John Raskob, or even, of a slightly different genre, Adlai Stevenson or Eugene McCarthy.

As a reform wave progresses, the reformers find that they have more and more to administer and defend. If an individual reform works, it will often generate its own resistance. Much of the friction acting against a reform movement originates out of the opposition, even rage, which its successes produce. Eventually, though, things settle down. The life pattern of a political movement——and of causes within that movement——may be described as a sort of triad, ranging from an early, developmental stage, to the phase of full-blown campaigning, and on to an institutionalized, bureaucratic mode.[18] Very importantly, no great issue of bureaucracy dogged the progressives or New Dealers because no great bureaucracy yet existed. Never again would liberals enjoy this luxury.

Since the turn of the century, administration has played a growing role in the political system. Given the mammoth demands which proliferating interest groups have placed on government, it was inevitable that bureaucracy should have burgeoned as these were met. A complex, insufficiently understood "organizational sector" has emerged between the public and private sectors, fusing elements of the two, with "managerial and technical elites" entrenching themselves in policymaking decisions. Conflict involving this new sector often defies classic description as liberal or conservative. Frequently, the distinction between private and public virtually disappears.[19]

As we have seen, if all goes well, the initial phases of reform are characterized by the easy phrase and the relatively clear issue; but the later phases grow far more complex, involving commission decisions, court cases, and administrative boards. Welfare, for example, has depoliticized people by pulling some of life's sting, and by muffling the residual pain with bureaucracy. The political now becomes the administrative.[20] The visibility of reform diminishes in these circumstances, and often, too, its political rewards. But the possibilities for confusion and inconsistency multiply inexorably. "When the desirability of a policy is debated," writes Robert H. Bork, "we tend not to weigh in the balance the distortions that will be introduced by the workings of institutions that must interpret and apply the policy."[21] As each reform drive moves into what we may loosely call its bureaucratic phase, conservatives benefit from an opportunity to dig into a second line of defense.

Bureaucratization was one of the fundamental forces shaping American life early in this century, and the growth of big institutions containing big bureaucracies planted at arm's reach from the public has remained a major phenomenon ever since in the private sector as well as government. Part of the problem involves the sheer size of this society; everything from churches to schools to corporations has gotten bigger and more remote. "The chief characteristic of modern culture," wrote Karl Mannheim, "is the tendency to include as much as possible in the realm of the rational and to bring it under administrative control——and, on the other hand, to reduce the 'irrational' element to the vanishing point."[22] In the public sector, reformers have assumed the central responsibility for this.

Which leads us to draw a distinction between two kinds of liberal reform. One we will call *activist* liberalism: the process of campaigning for and pushing through political candidacies and legislative programs. The other, *managerial* liberalism, involves the administration of these programs once they pass.

In practice, the two overlap. A great deal of initiating can occur behind the scenes in a bureaucracy. "When an ideology is institutionalized it becomes, paradoxically, less visible," writes Bork, "——even to those who implement it. The basic ideas are no longer apprehended or controverted, and hence it becomes easier to move further along the lines implied by those ideas."[23] Nor is the low visibility level of a bureaucracy all that different from the level inside, say, a congressional subcommittee. Still, the distinction between activist and managerial reform will remain a useful one if we remember that every activist phase leads into a managerial phase, where legislation gets digested and implemented via the bureaucracy. Institutionalization, including bureaucratization, means that after the momentum fades from a reform movement, its goals retain some permanent hold. Like corporations and the courts, bureaucracies have a grip on immortality. The federal bureaucracy (as well as bureaucracies at every other level of government) should, one might think, provide liberalism with a standing army, constantly in place, prepared to defend old gains. And it often does.

But, like any standing army, a bureaucracy can grow slothful and cowardly. The United States, which prides itself on a genius for governing, has also shown a genius for generating unwieldy, inefficient, and above all, big bureaucracies. This is apparent throughout American life, from the corporate world to the way we wage war to the mammoth bureaucracy of the federal establishment.   As Richard H. Pells has written:

> Liberalism came under attack in the 1960s because it had grown administrative and managerial, because it had confused the role of intelligence with the authority of experts, because it had exchanged its historic trust in social criticism and moral rage for a dependence on technology and specialization.[24]

Perhaps rather than disparaging bureaucracy, indeed, conservatives should applaud it as a quiet ally. The bureaucratization which has accompanied twentieth century liberalism has generated drag and broad public antagonism.

Still, the expansion of the federal bureaucracy has gone on throughout this century.   During World War I, for example, literally thousands of individual agencies coordinated mobilization.   These included such critical institutions as the Chalks and Crayons War Service Committee and the Alimentary Paste War Service Committee. As the federal bureaucracy and the services it provides have expanded, the number of power centers within the bureaucracy——each one answerable to its own interest groups and with its own traditions and ways of doing business——has also multiplied. "Iron triangles" bind together agencies, the congressional committees which underwrite them, and their constituencies. Particularly by contrast with foreign affairs, a President enjoys a low level of control over (or even access to) these sometimes half-hidden fiefdoms. Presidents come and go. The bureaucracy stays.

Franklin D. Roosevelt, who did more to bureaucratize America than any other single individual, cursed the drag inherent in bureaucracy. "The Treasury is so large and far-flung and ingrained in its practices," he complained,

> that I find it is almost impossible to get the action and results I want——even with Henry [Morgenthau] there.   But the Treasury is not to be compared with the State Department. You should go through the experience of trying to get any changes in the thinking, policy, and action of the career diplomats and then you'd know what a real problem was. But the Treasury and the State Department put together are nothing compared with the Na-a-vy.   The admirals are really something to cope with——and I should know.   To change anything in the Na-a-vy is like punching a feather bed. You punch it with your right and you punch it with your left until you are finally exhausted, and then you find the damn bed just as it was before you started punching.[25]

Bureaucratization has had certain characteristic effects on the way political and ideological issues get treated. When charity and humanitarianism evolve into administration, pencils, and forms——when compassion professionalizes and bureaucratizes itself ——it loses much of its appeal, and becomes correspondingly easier to attack.[26] Bureaucracy substitutes administrative decision making for political, so that by its very nature bureaucratization shrivels the grass roots. It renders power less visible and less personal. Alienation becomes virtually inevitable. Whether by government or by business, Americans have always taken offense at decisions rendered without their consultation. "In an impersonalized and more anonymous system of control," wrote C. Wright Mills, "explicit responses are not so possible: anxiety is likely to replace fear; insecurity to replace worry." Mills continued bleakly that "a sort of impersonal manipulation" emerges. "Manipulation feeds upon and is fed by mass indifference."[27] As self-conscious individualists, Americans get particularly upset over the ponderous gyrations of bureaucracy, and thus become responsive to business and other outcries against it. Since those who *feel* manipulated, who feel victimized, have difficulty identifying whom to lash out at, their revolt will likely be generalized against the bureaucracy, the political system, and the politicians. Because of this, and because it usurps the territory of conventional democratic politics, mushrooming administration jeopardizes conventional politics, including activist liberalism.

Much that a bureaucracy does, it does sloppily. The prospects for slipshod administration have blossomed in part because the Presidents who have done the bulk of the legislating——Wilson, FDR, and Johnson ——have functioned far better at driving programs through than at running them once passed. Had the great legislators performed equally well as administrators, then many of the problems which have disoriented reform movements might never have developed at all. Nor have Republican Executives——whose (often-professed) forte should, one might think, be orderly, cost-effective administration——proved as efficient as one would wish in straightening out the tangles.

At one point or another, bureaucracies rigidify. They show a notorious tendency to serve their own needs ahead of their clients'. They commonly grow rule-bound and impersonal. More broadly, Theodore J. Lowi has complained:

Liberal government seems to be flexible only on the first round of a response to political need. It allows for a certain expansion of functions to take place and then militates against any redistribution of those functions as needs change. New needs therefore result in expansions, never in planning.[28]

Liberals such as Woodrow Wilson have resisted the emergence of the organization man. They have seen him and his institutions, the bureaucracies and corporate promotion ladders, as instinctive enemies. The New Left showed the same resistance decades after Wilson, except that by then the organization man had long since won out. Political life in the seventies featured an ongoing struggle between certain elected officials and unelected government bureaucracies. The public was warned by politicians belonging to both parties that the bureaucracies had taken on a life of their own, independent of the electorate. The mugwump-progressive ideal of a bureaucracy beyond politics appeared to have turned into a monster beyond popular control.

Symptomatically, Jimmy Carter, who ran against Washington in 1976, pledged during the campaign to rationalize the federal bureaucracy—a Democrat committing himself to undoing some of the errors of past Democrats. "Carter's triumph," William Appleman Williams has noted,

> actually emphasized the extent to which administrative politics had superseded public politics: the extent to which politics was concerned primarily with managing the existing system more effectively and efficiently rather than with creating a better or a different society.[29]

By this time, the task of managing had grown truly imposing. As of 1978, for example, eighty-seven units of the federal government shared responsibility for regulating business, and 143 million man/woman-hours were absorbed each year just filling out those units' 4,400 different forms.[30] The forms, the sometimes petty or absurd regulations (in which the Johnson Administration had proved notoriously prolific), the untrusting scrutiny (together with the scandalous blowups resulting from inadequate scrutiny), the insensitivity—these things undermined public faith even in programs whose necessity received wide acknowledgment. They also undermined receptiveness to new programs. Bureaucratization had become a drag on legislation. And by making government more distant, the centralization of power in Washington had certainly made government more susceptible to generalized, open-ended attack.

Along with bureaucratic arteriosclerosis, one final consideration comes to our attention as we consider the disorientation of reform—the outmoding of the reformers themselves.[31] The anti-New Dealism of Otis Graham's aging progressives, for example, seemed sadly atavistic. By the seventies, the New Deal approach to the nation's difficulties appeared to many ineffective and outdated in turn. FDR's spending strategy flew in the face of the widespread perception that the nation had overdrawn its resources (high taxes, stunning deficits) and that we had arrived at an era of limits. The rub is that when a new generation of reformers replaces an earlier one, they may have more backward or less focused ideas than their predecessors'. To this, precisely, was the nation treated in the 1970s, when, for the most part, reform just drifted.

The Liberal Cannibalism

Ordered to form a firing squad, liberals instinctively make a circle.

The difference between cannibals and Democrats: cannibals consume only their enemies.

The reason for the historic political success of liberalism, as opposed to radicalism, is that liberalism apparently marks the furthest point to the left around which any kind of political cohesion can occur in this country. Yet reform ranks perennially split, even in the best of times; and as a reform movement starts to die, some of the groups behind it begin to indulge in a fascinating folk ritual. They devour one another. Hard leftists attack less strident leftists, and both lambast liberals, who in turn denounce fellow liberals. This is the cannibalism of the reformers.

The process sets in late in reform regimes and goes beyond merely giving up or complaining. It pits reformers against one another. This may occur through four kinds of reaction: against individual leaders, against prevailing philosophy, against specific programs, or as a collapse of constituent support. Unfortunately, all four tend to operate at once.

On the first, or individual, level, personal battles among the reform leadership became one cause of the progressives' demise. Shortly before the 1920 election, former Interior Secretary Franklin K. Lane wrote, "What a hell of a condition the land is in politically. . . . Wilson is as unpopular as he once was popular."[1] Many liberals, as we have seen, made themselves conspicuous among those who shunned Wilson. Liberals have tended to cannibalize their own Presidents while in office and to canonize them only later. Harry Truman did not have memories even of onetime popularity counting for him. Led by the ADA, anti-Wallaceite liberals yearned to drive Truman out of the 1948 nomination, notwithstanding their positive regard for his programs. They wanted charisma; they wanted Roosevelt; failing that, many of them wanted Eisenhower. Lyndon Johnson encountered the same phenomenon——his *personal* unsatisfactoriness vis-à-vis John Kennedy——long before Vietnam gave liberals better reason for despising him. In the late sixties and early seventies, Democrats reverted to their old impulse to split wide open:

Eugene McCarthyites versus Robert Kennedyites, McGovern liberals versus Humphrey liberals, and so on.

The second type of reform cannibalism involves a reaction against prevailing philosophy. Reformers have often shown a remarkable alacrity in growing disillusioned with the results of their own reforms, even sometimes agreeing at length with their sharpest critics. Or they split over where to go from here. A classic example of this emerges from the woman movement of the early twentieth century. Once suffrage had been achieved, the single great unifying cause behind feminism was lost. Women proceeded to split over varying definitions of equality, attitudes toward sex, and questions of partisan politics. These disagreements parlayed into concrete disputes over policy, notably in the case of the ERA.

After it finally re-emerged in the sixties and seventies, feminism tested liberal attitudes much as it had earlier in the century. One instance (of many) revolved around sexuality. "The case against pornography and the case against toleration of prostitution are central to the fight against rape," wrote Susan Brownmiller in the mid-seventies,

> and if it angers a large part of the liberal population to be so informed, then I would question in turn the political understanding of such liberals and their true concern for the rights of women. Or to put it more gently, a feminist analysis approaches all prior assumptions, including those of the great, unquestioned liberal tradition, with a certain open-minded suspicion, for all prior traditions have worked against the cause of women and no set of values, including that of tolerant liberals, is above review or challenge. After all, the liberal *politik* has had less input from the feminist perspective than from any other modern source; it does not by its own considerable virtue embody a perfection of ideals, it has no special claim on goodness, rather, it is most receptive to those values to which it has been made sensitive by others.

If, she added, "we now find ourselves in philosophic disagreement with the thought processes and priorities of what has been . . . a male liberal tradition, we should not find it surprising."[2]

Reform has always shown a tendency to co-opt or contradict itself. In the early and mid-sixties, for instance, liberals had wanted to solve the poverty problem through economic growth. Then a good many younger liberals began denigrating growth on environmental grounds. Organized labor split with these younger liberals over environmental and other issues, notably development and nuclear energy, for fear that any cutbacks might endanger jobs. Meantime, numerous younger liberals had begun to debunk their fundamental patrimony, the whole problem-solution approach to government.

Disputes over ideology in and of themselves can prove healthy. This holds especially true in the emergent phase of a reform era, or in the latency period between eras. How else, after all, can policy be decided and agreed upon? But in the decline phase, many of these disagreements take on a destructive frenzy, as if generals were haggling over strategy while their troops streamed past in flight. Antagonism between Congress and the President particularly typifies the end of a reform wave. Unless resistance can be maintained against conservative pressure at a time when recent achievements are the things most in need of protection, reform programs get eaten alive.

Of this third kind of cannibalism, programmatic collapse, the classic example comes from the Wilson Administration. "Can anyone," Walter Lippmann asked late in 1919, "name a single reform initiated or carried through since the Armistice?" The administration came up with no progressive domestic program after the war. Most of the reform legislation that did pass was left over from the prewar era, and some very bad legislation went through along with it.[3] The ship floated aimlessly, buffeted by this wind and that.

Another classic case of programmatic destruction comes from the Johnson era. Johnson wanted to have both the Great Society and the Vietnam War without a tax hike or wage and price controls, all of this in the face of rising consumer demand. Prices began edging up in 1965. Prominent members of Congress reacted by calling for budget cuts. Shelving original plans for expansion, the President ordered the Great Society agencies to hold down budget requests. Johnson behaved like a man regretfully murdering his wife so that he could marry a fascinating, dangerous mistress.

In the final form of cannibalism, constituencies and coalitions erode or fall apart. For the Wilson Administration, it was the wheat-growing areas, agricultural interests more generally, eastern urban immigrants, antiwar progressives, independents, and the far West and South.[4] We have already examined the decline of the Roosevelt coalition of 1936; among other things, southern and rural congressional support dropped off as the administration increasingly served the needs of the northern cities. And we have touched on the manner in which Johnson's 1964 majority fell away. The year 1968 truly epitomized every form of liberal cannibalism: the personal—McCarthy versus Johnson versus Robert Kennedy versus Humphrey, Johnson's tepid support of Humphrey; the philosophical and programmatic—liberals versus radicals, liberals versus liberals, disillusionment with the Great Society, uncertainty as to how liberalism should proceed; and the constituent—resulting in Nixon's election. Later, in taking on the powers of the imperial presidency,

Democrats cannibalized their own leadership tradition.

By now it has become clear that I have used the term cannibalism in a broad sense, without extensive reference to the specific reasons why individuals or groups turn against reform.   The liberal who wanted Eisenhower on the ticket instead of Truman in 1948 may not have reacted against reform at all——may, instead, have thought that Truman had; or that because of Truman's apparent fecklessness, the President could never translate his best intentions into policy; or that whatever the case, Truman couldn't win and Eisenhower could. Just as for individuals, the same holds true for philosophy or ideology. The dispute over the ERA has never been just a matter of sentiments and platitudes. The ERA has involved cold questions of law, including the survival of hard-won legislation for women which is already on the books. One may very well favor equal rights and oppose the ERA.

So too in the case of program and constituency: the wheat farmer who chafes at price ceilings and believes the Democratic party is discriminating against wheat producers in favor of southern cotton growers will likely shift toward the Republicans in 1918, even if nine-tenths of the other things the Wilson Administration has done remain appealing.   And a southern Democrat on the House Rules Committee who connives with Republicans to prevent a wages and hours law from reaching the floor in 1937 may well do so out of fear that the measure will ruin the South's competitiveness by hiking wages and ending cheap labor, or out of worry over the measure's potential for equalizing wages between blacks and whites.   This southerner may have been a steady supporter of the New Deal in its earlier years, not out of conviction but out of regional and self-interest.

Politics does find its energy source in self-interest, after all, and reform coalitions take shape as individuals and groups join them for self-interest. This banding together makes the movement move. Reformers operating apart from self-interest lack any glue to hold them together quite equal to the profit motive which ties business conservatives to one another.   This helps to explain the reformers' larger tendency to fly apart. Cannibalism occurs when a reaction begins from *inside*. The precise motivation for each defection or attack is less important than the basic fact that, compounded one upon another, for the movement these act like broken bottles on a highway.

Defensiveness, Exhaustion, and Apathy

The turns from the private to the public life and back again are marked by wildly exaggerated expectations, by total infatuation, and by sudden revulsions.

Albert O. Hirschman

Such is the course from radical thought and action, from intense preoccupation with the affairs of humanity, to self—self-culture, self-indulgence. Those who return to self after wandering through a wilderness of altruism, acquire anew something of the child's fresh relish for simple experiences. They find all sorts of important little busynesses and discover in the small world all the absorbing interests in miniature that they abandoned in the great world . . . . So the tired radical . . . applies his grand passion for Universal Housekeeping to a microscopic farm, and he who aspired to overturn Society (that obese, ponderous and torpid Society that hates to be overturned) ends by fighting in a dull Board of Directors of a village library for the inclusion of certain books. . . . Progress is halted by these tired radicals who do not know that they have ceased to be radicals. They turn into pillars of salt.

Walter Weyl

Had enough?

GOP slogan, 1946 congressional campaign and more recently

A period of political exhaustion, souring,[1] pessimism, despair, and apathy has followed every twentieth century reform era. The polarization needed to get anything done becomes too wearying over time; individuals want to reunite, or to feel they have. They want an end to strife. Reformers may grow discouraged by repeated failure, and quit public endeavors in disillusionment. Or they may succeed, then take disappointment in the results of their victory—which may have veered off into something utterly unforeseen, undesirable, and uncontrollable.[2] A reformer fights and fights for a little change, and then one interest group or another reverses it while the public apathetically sits by. The mass public seems immovable, bovine. Expressing scant appreciation, it positively invites reformers to grow disillusioned.

Yet people do get sick of listening to reformers' endless preaching. Run down, in some cases revolted by politics, and numbed and drained by depression or war, many reformers and their supporters want to grasp from life what they can reach close at hand. They turn inward. Passion ebbs. Idealism fades. Optimism, frustrated, may give way to extreme bitterness—it is difficult to remain realistic without in time growing cynical. Hope turns to disillusionment, discouragement, pessimism, and indifference or despair. The morale of many reformers gives way. The inevitability of progress gets questioned. Moral energy runs thin. Moral exhaustion[3] sets in. Disillusionment leaves behind a residue of lassitude. People become uncertain, resigned, timid. Political conformity revives, and often social conformity along with it. What history of the twenties has missed the complacency of that era? What chronicle of the fifties fails to comment on its political quiescence? Who, in the seventies, remained blind to the hopelessness and apathy which typified so much of that decade?

It may well be that, more than anything else, pulling against the leaden weight of mass inertia wears reformers out. But there is more to it than that.

As we have observed, reformers often idealize their causes. They anticipate unrealistic benefits in order to gather the necessary momentum with which to pursue them. The emergence of a reform movement demands idealism, enthusiasm, and, frankly, oversimplification. Problems, even the worst, must be made to seem solvable in order to induce people to try to solve them at all. So oversimplified arguments appear. More gets promised than can be delivered, much as in any other publicity or advertising campaign. The reformers have not yet had to put their prescriptions into operation, and they tend to inflate public expectations in order to push their proposals through. The progressives expected far more of the direct primary, or the initiative, referendum, and recall, or the short ballot, than these could possibly deliver. Likewise, in the sixties, simple terms like "freedom now" symbolized complex goals impossible of literally immediate fulfillment. Ultimate letdown was virtually inevitable.

Let down or not, people will go out of their comfortable, everyday ways only so long. Even in extending themselves, many find that what they can actually *do* has limits. "The trouble with political life," Albert O. Hirschman observes, "is that it is either too absorbing or too tame." "Participation in public life offers only this unsatisfactory too-much-or-too-little choice and is therefore bound to be disappointing in one way or another."[4] Most individuals do not enjoy being deeply involved politically. They wear down quickly. After so many months or years, they run out of energy. When they do, a reform movement runs short of fresh, willing, available people to carry it forward. As the sense of possibility fades, utopias recede in time's mist. Onetime influential reformers lose influence, though they often continue to echo themselves in tinnily discordant ways (Hubert Humphrey, for instance, and his "politics of joy"). The moral force of reform fades. So does its self-confidence. These give way, as much as anything, to a sour sense of irony and often of nostalgia.[5]

We may most easily relate all this to war: to the first lost generation after World War I, the second lost generation after Vietnam, and to those who passed through the Great Depression and World War II not lost, perhaps, but drained and ultimately silent. People want to relax. Sick of calls for self-sacrifice, they tire of all the strife and tumult; want to hear no more of it; will listen to no more of it.

"Even in a country as deeply marked by Puritanism as the United States," writes Godfrey Hodgson, "it is hard to interest the majority for very long in the proposition that they are miserable sinners."[6] Individuals and societies can stand only so much iconoclasm, muckraking, advocacy for outcasts, and exposure before they reach a saturation point. If merely for reasons of their own mental health, they proceed to rebel against more. People can tolerate the questioning of everything, as in the 1960s, only so long.[7] Sooner or later some agreement has to set in on principles of politics and norms of behavior, or at least there must be a truce. Otherwise everyone becomes drained. Reformers, like radicals, are often arrogant, self-righteous, short on patience. Optimism and idealism on one side, despair and pessimism on the other, represent different, coexisting sides of the reform temperament. The sense of despair, even of nihilism, which so often infects determined reformers —their willingness or eagerness to pronounce the whole society incurably sick; their seemingly unquenchable discontent; their more harebrained ideas—distances them more and more from the mass public. Most Americans, even most reformers, cannot dwell endlessly in demoralization and despair. They do not want Jimmy Carter telling them that the nation suffers from malaise.

Americans want to feel inspired after a period of self-depreciation; and however much they may suspect leadership, at length they want it too. The leadership, the inspiration, may come from the center-left or the center-right. Many will listen to a Reagan if his rhetoric sounds optimistic enough. But not a Carter in 1980; not a Mondale in 1984. Abrasive reform leadership especially irritates people. They want national harmoniousness and reconciliation. They want one sense of direction, not many. And they want a sense of humor to go with it.[8] The reformers have exhausted the public (and themselves); war has done the same; the media have overexposed government, along with causes in general; advertisers have trivialized high aims into commercial clichés. The inclination—the natural inclination—is now to retreat from public affairs. Party positions blur and partway converge; the former ideological polarities and commitments shed much of their persuasiveness. Depleted Executive leadership contributes to the blurring focus, encouraging people to wander off into their own projects for change, to cleave to their own groups, or to drop out altogether. Politics loses some of its urgent seriousness. As for "uplift," it may pose an outright danger to reform if, as happened in the twenties, it starts to look foolish. Issues begin collecting dust on the shelf.

In discussing these patterns of decline I do not mean to imply that they work equally on everyone. Sometimes we are talking about the mass public; sometimes about significant individuals, groups, or blocs, and about tendencies in specific periods. We are dealing with apathy and exhaustion relative to levels of commitment and involvement which characterize periods of reform.

During such an era the reformers have expropriated reality. Yet their very publicizing of the political process in a time of great change probably creates friction against further change, as the people get reminded of the convolutions and gritty unpleasantries with which politics operates even in the best of circumstances. Reformers often seem deviant types, quite unlike the mass of people;[9] their "inside scoop" version of reality seems sordid, depressing stuff. In time they become objects of suspicion, distrust, or hostility. Yet the reformist exposés go on inexorably, and as Theodore Roosevelt complained, so broadly as to produce "the searing of the public conscience. There results a general attitude either of cynical belief in and indifference to public corruption or else of a distrustful inability to discriminate between the good and the bad."[10] People become revolted, exhausted, cynical. Indeed, cynicism and pessimism become fashionable. Intellectuals enter a confessional phase. Debunking the reform era just passed becomes a fad.

Reform in retrospect virtually always appears "impure" because it almost invariably embodies compromise. It can prove especially deadly to translate a political issue into a moral one, because compromise thereafter looks immoral. A classic instance of this involved the trap Wilson set for himself with the peace settlement, where anything short of perfection resembled defeat. The ideal—the perfect idea—turns practical in enactment, hence hard, mundane, shriveled, even dull. We almost never achieve a "pure" reform. This wears down the reform spirit and mandate. Why put oneself or a whole society under stress for some very likely watered-down compromise?

Along with this tendency of reform eras to leave a sour aftertaste, within the surviving reform tradition something different from the original main emphasis often emerges to prominence, embittering reformers still more or at least giving them pause. In the fifties, for instance, labor "reform" to many liberals came to mean halting labor racketeering. By the seventies the civil rights struggle, which had opened over the right to sit on a bus, had turned into the more problematic battle over busing school children. In the eighties, some feminists left others far behind by demanding the censorship of pornography.

In time, for all these reasons, many reformers tire of public affairs. They begin to neglect or abandon them. Their confidence ebbs. They grow timid. They withdraw from reform. They return to the realm of personal interests and the concerns that largely occupy most people. For many participants in politics, involvement absorbs only a brief phase of their entire lives. Others take holidays from the struggle. Some radicals discover at length that they have moved so far ahead of the public at large that the people must have a chance to catch up. A Coolidge, an Eisenhower, or a Reagan says that all is well, and while the exhausted liberal may not believe that, the respite of a conservative interval comes as a relief. No more crusading, at least for a while——thank god.

This slack time produces a sense of release. "For myself," Charlotte Perkins Gilman commented in the middle of the twenties, "there is a definite relief in being free from the work demanded by the various 'causes' now won or temporarily in abeyance, and able at last to write and lecture on my own lines of social philosophy."[11] While the liberal (or ex-liberal) can always take comfort in the back yard or the village library, the committed radical can sometimes find corresponding comfort in the triumph of radical values somewhere else, usually abroad. Quitting is a form of indulgence, of self-indulgence. In order to give up, one must feel that one can afford to give up. The party hack, like the lifelong ideologue, never quits. Neither does the business person with an interest involved. The Democrats used to have a rough equivalent in their political machines and southern courthouse rings, but these belong to another age.

I do not mean to suggest that exhaustion in itself comprises a luxury or even a matter of choice. People do tire, become disillusioned, experience ennui. In 1914 William Allen White had this to say about a meeting of Progressive party leaders:

> First of all, I was struck by the big fact that everyone was spiritually weary. We were sapped dry. . . . For two or three, and in some cases for four years——since 1910——we have been living upon our emotions. . . . We need emotional rest. We need complete change.[12]

For the volunteer in particular, with no professional or pecuniary intentions to fulfill from it, politics can be a very wearying, disillusioning experience. Doing good for others wears one out. Reforming political amateurs tend to make mistakes, lots of them; and the frustration of this discourages a continued or repeated experience. They will likely expect too much going in, and feel amazement at the limits of their gains. Involvement in public affairs often comes at a high cost in time, money, and energy. It commonly absorbs far more of all three than the political novice had anticipated. And involvement may prove far less pleasant than expected.   The novice may grow disgusted by gritty political realities.[13] All this helps to explain the enormous rate of turnover among political volunteers[14] from campaign to campaign.   For the radical, too, so often imbued with soaring, even utopian hopes, confronting the messy facts of American politics drains the spirit and saps the will.[15]

For the conservative or liberal professional politician it is all very different. It is not a matter of waging this or that completely absorbing crusade. Politics amounts to the essentially routine business of pursuing self-interest along with (or without) the public interest. No wonder the professionals' endurance holds up; politics is their job.

At length many of the part-time, nonprofessional reformers will turn back to making money, or will disappear into writing, or will seek a security blanket in religion, or will find some other means of escape into their own psychic gardens.   An exhausted reformer will tend to temporize; stall; accept the given as the inevitable; become complacent; disappear.   Problems remain at the end of every reform age, but in giving up, large numbers of erstwhile activists cease to address them any longer.   This surrender actually represents a form of cynicism.   It comprises a significant part of the general cynicism which follows reform eras.

Reform involvement often loads a heavy personal strain on individual reformers by setting them at odds with their own class or social group and with their self-interest generally.   Frederic Howe reflected later on aspects of his involvement in municipal progressivism this way:

> On the one side were men of property and influence; on the other the politicians, immigrants, workers, and persons of small means. . . . And I was not on the side where I would have chosen to be. The struggle brought me into conflict with friends, clients, my class. I preferred to be with them, I liked wealth and the things that went with wealth; I enjoyed dining out, dances, the lighter things of life. I suffered from the gibes of men with whom I had once been intimate, and fancied slights which did not in fact occur.

"I [still] believe in reform," he wrote in 1925, "but prefer the reform that is taking place within myself."[16]

"Public spirit is at best a fragile thing when it comes into competition with the urgent demands of our private lives for money, for power, and for pleasure. So it has not been difficult for Mr. Coolidge to persuade the country that it need not take a vivid interest in public affairs." Walter Lippmann made this observation at a time when the old progressives had by and large returned to their "private lives."[17] "It is a rare autobiography from one of these reformers," writes Otis L. Graham, Jr., "that reveals a restless search for other and more effective measures of social reconstruction in the postwar years because it was a rare career line which forced such a search."[18] "One of the striking characteristics of the era of Coolidge Prosperity," wrote Frederick Lewis Allen,

> was the unparalleled rapidity and unanimity with which millions of men and women turned their attention, their talk, and their emotional interest upon a series of tremendous trifles——a heavyweight boxing-match, a murder trial, a new automobile model, a transatlantic flight.
>
> Most of the *causes célèbres* which thus stirred the country from end to end were quite unimportant from the traditional point of view of the historian.[19]

The tendency of many reformers to view things in blacks and whites probably also helps to trigger their disillusionment and withdrawal. Having difficulty with shades of gray, they become disoriented in the gray landscape of a postreform era. Related difficulties emerge from the act of marketing. Typically, as we have noted, reformers oversimplify: this solution will *solve* that problem. Oversimplification comprises an essential aspect of marketing, obliterating for the moment all possible shades of gray. The temptation to oversimplify grows all the greater in order to make enormously complex problems seem solvable (to one's self and the public) and generate the will to attack them. Hopes soar. But ultimately it becomes clear that the issues are more convoluted than "advertised." This undercuts reformers' credibility. When the reactionary tide sweeps in, oversimplification yields to overcomplexity; conservatives make the nature of the problems which the nation confronts appear so complex that nothing can be done about them at all, or at best, very little. Overcomplexity in turn produces inertia.

Yet, again, the decision to withdraw from reform, and to stay out, represents an act of cynicism. It reinforces the generally jaundiced atmosphere which follows a reform era. And this is true no matter how much agony or reluctance or ambivalence or despair enter into the decision to pull out. What remains behind after a general withdrawal of the kind that followed World War I or the sixties is an assortment of "liberal" interest groups, each pushing for advantage without any significant amount of broad public support. The support does not exist because rather than belonging to a blanket movement imbued with some degree of élan, the individual groups stand isolated.   Without a movement they remain defensive, since, rather than entering in as part of a sweep for the general interest, they expose themselves as representing only their own interest. Lacking the zeal of a committed lay backing, and without a broad aura of idealism behind them, labor unions and farmers' organizations, civil rights groups and women's groups, all come to look remarkably similar to the Chamber of Commerce. Chic terms like "end of ideology" and "postindustrial society" imply that their problems have either been surmounted or transcended. This is usually nonsense. Remaining poverty and oppression have simply moved underground again.

What Edgar Kemler called the "obsolescence" of the reformers also enters into the liberal defensiveness and exhaustion.[20] If, for example, Bryan and much of what he stood for looked half-fossilized by 1900, by 1924-25 he resembled solid rock. "The average progressive," Kemler wrote, "has an alarming rate of obsolescence. After about ten years of service he is washed up." Again, rather uncharitably:

> If we were less sentimental about our public men we would retire them as soon as they showed signs of decay. But they refuse to retire at the end of one historical era. They insist on surviving into the next. They demand audience on grounds of their past eminence and cry down the men who have succeeded them. Hence we have to contend not only with the living, but also with the living dead.[21]

Generally the activists in one generation of reformers wind up only on the fringe of the next, if they find any place at all.

Generation—that is the key word here.[22] The appeal of generation tugs not just at radicals but at liberals, too. Incumbent generations of reformers give inspiration to their successors—TR and Wilson to FDR, FDR to Johnson. Such politicians as the two Roosevelts and the Kennedys have often quite explicitly emphasized the new risks faced, and the responsibilities assumed, by the young-to-early-middle-aged. They have made generation a campaign theme and a theme for reform. At 42 and 43 respectively, TR and John Kennedy were the youngest men ever to assume the presidency. FDR declared: "This generation of Americans has a rendezvous with destiny." And Kennedy: "Let the word go forth from this time and place, to friend and foe alike, that the torch has been passed to a new generation of Americans, born in this century." The generational appeal helps to legitimate politics for the young. "John Kennedy activated my generation politically," Gary Hart has remarked.

Most people my age weren't interested in politics, because that's what guys who smoked cigars did; it was unsavory. Anyone in grad school interested in politics was considered an oddball. Kennedy legitimized politics, even before there was a cause. He created the cause. Now public service was an honorable thing.[23]

But as a yet fresher generation arrives on the scene, old, fervent passions melt into memory. Old ideological commitments become new Establishment ideologies. One reason why reform can never seem to accomplish enough takes us back to Maslow's hierarchy. Once a generation's set of needs becomes more or less fulfilled, the following generation produces a new, "higher" set of demands, insisting that these be fulfilled too. For one generation, jobs and security reign; for the next, ecology and spiritual satisfaction. The hierarchy works both ways; during the seventies and eighties, in a soft economy, some of the issues of the thirties had a partial comeback. But in general, a generation's more or less fixed issue-orientation is what, more than anything else, makes it obsolesce.

Unfortunately, obsolete liberals or radicals have often become not just passive cynics, but committed negativists. One thinks of the later careers of Al Smith, Burton Wheeler, Hiram Johnson, and Oswald Garrison Villard (once known as the Dean of American Liberals). Various explanations have been advanced to account for the obsolescence of reformers. It has been said that their original program from an earlier era may quite simply have become accomplished fact; that they outlive their own time and environment; that one can tolerate the personal pressures experienced in pushing for change only so long; that the emergence of new reform leadership stirs resentment; that switching to the right can earn one certain rewards; and that in its evolution reform has left many reformers behind by casting off comfortable old principles and notions about moral regeneration and Uplift.

No doubt the mix varies from person to person. We are concerned here with symptoms and effects. The symptoms abound in the decline phase, as reformers become more chary of reform. Sometimes this occurs subtly, as when liberals after World War II amended their optimistic view of humankind with a dose of Reinhold Niebuhr. In the decline phase, a corrosive awareness of human and societal complexity, even depravity, re-emerges. The time has returned for a Niebuhr or a Mencken. Ultimately the cult of disenchantment, failure, and discouragement becomes a sort of liberal fad. Debunking Wilsonism or Johnsonism, the accomplishments of progressivism or the Great Society turns into a rite of self-depreciation.

All this became profoundly apparent in the 1960s. Negativism provided the medium in which much of sixties liberalism emerged; and this persistent strategy and tone of negation surely aged that movement more quickly than necessary. The sheer proliferation of social criticism, good and bad, left, right, and center, had a numbing effect. Much of it amounted, as Peter Clecak puts it, to "demystification without understanding."[24] Beyond question, negativism helped sour the public mood. I am sure that this played a crucial part, too, in driving concerns inward to the personal realm, where one could light a candle against the unrelieved bleakness outside. Negation underlay the sense of detachment in the following decade, and the feeling that knowledge remained inadequate for addressing social problems.

Some ex-New Deal liberals, among them Daniel Patrick Moynihan, Nathan Glazer, and Norman Podhoretz, took fright over the failures and difficulties of reform in the Johnson era and began to emphasize the "limits of politics." In contrast to this group——but not in very great contrast——during the seventies we encounter the so-called New Liberals, such as California Governor Jerry Brown or Colorado Governor Richard D. Lamm. The New Liberalism marked something of a return to the negative, symbolic politics and political iconology of the Grover Cleveland Democracy. Like Cleveland, the New Liberals dealt in austere symbols: Brown lived in an underfurnished bachelor pad and got around in a Plymouth. This new variation on the mugwump tradition, like the original, emphasized fiscal austerity and soundness. The New Deal approach, New Liberals insisted, had obsolesced in these pinched times. They scattered their shots at big subdivisions, big cars, and big government almost as if they were talking about equivalent things. They tended to run for office as outsiders, as anti-politicians even when they had been politicians for years. They tended toward a rhetorical chariness of giving political favors or making political deals. They were cold toward welfare, but warm toward administrative efficiency.

Brown, in particular, attracts our attention. He has been called, not without reason, "the finest political sleight-of-hand artist of his generation." J. D. Lorenz, a Brown appointee until the Governor fired him, contended that

> Jerry Brown is the representative American figure of the 1970s. I think he has succeeded in symbolizing the doubt, the detachment, and the escapism of the period as profoundly as Martin Luther King embodied the commitment, the involvement, and the passion of the 1960s.

Brown "was the 'me first' politician for a 'me first' decade."[25]

Brown elevated the politics of manipulating symbols to a high art at a time when more conventional politicians, who tried actually to confront the mass of big issues, got avalanched beneath them. He displayed remarkable agility in coming down on both sides of controversial questions, reversing himself stunningly, for example, on Proposition 13.[26] Fiscally tightfisted, Brown rejected the New Deal's approach to government, trading it for what Marshall Frady has called "hip conservatism"[27]——either that, or a "liberalism" completely at drift, or whimsically unfocused, or political theatre of the absurd. Like Jimmy Carter, Brown seemed personally just a bit strange. "At the least," wrote Frady, "Brown hardly proceeds from the liberal humanitarian-rationalist ethic——a rejoicing in man and all his grand dimensions of possibility."[28] At the least, indeed. Brown sidestepped serious issues like a ballet dancer, skipped around poverty, for example, in pirouettes. "Jerry," Lorenz observes,

> was the totally democratic man. Like the proverbial weathervane, he turned in whichever direction the winds blew him. For as he himself said to me one day long before we were to reach a parting of ways: "Popularity is the only currency of the realm around here."[29]

In spirit, at least, we might call Brown a neo-Wilsonian, though the comparison does not do justice to all sides of Wilson. Woodrow Wilson and a good many others of his generation protested paternalism. Today's liberal appreciates this aspect of progressive thought far more than did the New Dealers. Just as the Democratic urban machines at the turn of the century recognized the anti-political, Democratic good government reformers as enemies, New Dealish liberals instinctively recognized New Liberals like Brown as apostates. "There are two things I like about Jerry Brown," cracked one union official: "his face."[30] The Governor of California engaged in a new form of Brownian motion: a kind of stylized aimlessness which blended whimsy, churlishness, irritability, and inanition into a species of "reform" epitomized by the following exchange between Brown and the executive director of the California Teachers Association. Brown: "I am going to starve the schools financially until I get some educational reforms." Director: "What reforms? What do you want?" Brown: "I don't know yet."[31] Brown reminded more than one onlooker of his predecessor, Ronald Reagan.

Every reform movement requires the presence of compassionate people, even spiritual figures, advocates of change who offer a central human presence. More than anyone else, Theodore Roosevelt provided this presence during the Progressive Era, and FDR, the father figure incarnate, in the New Deal. Following the death of John Kennedy, the absence of such a person in the sixties doubtless caused grave damage. Neither Robert Kennedy nor Hubert Humphrey, nor, certainly, Lyndon Johnson, nor even Martin Luther King, Jr., quite fit the role—though King and Kennedy came close. Jerry Brown, on the other hand, turned reform into an opaque glass eye.

Guilt Revisited: Some Final Speculations

> I am not one of those guilt-ridden, screwed-up, neurotic liberals.

> Saul Alinsky

One side of the liberal defensiveness which Brown reflected harks back to the mugwump tradition: liberal guilt. Freud noted that

> as long as things go well with a man, his conscience is lenient and lets the ego do all sorts of things; but when misfortune befalls him, he searches his soul, acknowledges his sinfulness, heightens the demands of his conscience, imposes abstinences on himself and punishes himself with penances. Whole peoples have behaved in this way, and still do.[1]

I suspect that something such as this was at work in the thirties, producing guilt symptoms we have already described among the down-and-out, and also helping to bring on the partial retreat from the brave new moral world of the 1920s. Whatever the case, and Watergate aside, the confessional mode appears much more characteristic of liberals than of conservatives. "For the most part," Kemler wrote, "Mugwumpery has been the last stand of scoundrels. When a party can think of no institutional changes with which to meet our problems it resorts to the moralities."[2]

We have already associated Judeo-Christian/Calvinist guilt with the ascendant side of a reform movement, reasoning that guilt prods some people into becoming reformers as a means of managing their consciences. The act of "witnessing" is shared by the guilt-ridden liberal as well as by the dynamiting radical, who bears witness in a more exotic way. But guilt, unalloyed by other motivations, generally produces a negative and very shallow form of involvement. Stanley M. Elkins has asked

> what might happen when people to whom daily aggression is not a perennial problem, people who have no knowledge of the

traditional mechanisms whereby such aggression is habitually controlled, are then brought face to face with concrete instances of violence, cruelty, lust, and injustice. The individual whose culture does not contain formalized arrangements for the handling of such matters feels himself personally involved. He pictures direct retribution; this being impossible, he is oppressed by the accumulation of guilt without means of outlet. Having no experience with limited ways of coming to terms with exploitation, being pressed by cumulative and undischarged guilt, he makes an emotional demand for a total solution. Destroy the evil, he cries; root it up, wipe it out.

Such, then, are some of the considerations which make guilt a primary thing to watch in American reform movements. The easing of guilt is always a most important hidden function of such movements, and with this as a disproportionate element in their maintenance, we have a test for movements that seem to disintegrate without accomplishing anything; guilt may have been absorbed and discharged in ways which make unnecessary a literal attainment of the objective.[3]

Among the "soft" or "conscience" participants in a reform campaign, winning will often seem less important than it does to the political professionals. A large part of conscience liberals' involvement has to do with the witnessing itself——with participating wholly apart from winning or losing. As Arnold S. Kaufman put it:

A dramatic flare-up involves a major commitment for a *limited period*. Thus conscience can be appeased at little cost in time and effort. This is both spiritually uplifting and comfortable if one has ambitions that pull in other directions.[4]

In politics, guilt and witnessing eventually run thin. A more dependable driver, whether for the Chamber of Commerce or the political machine, remains money. The pecuniary motive significantly explains their staying power.

As to the further association of guilt with the down-side of reform, we must be more hesitant and tentative. Still, let us proceed with a line of reasoning: a reform wave helps to undo itself by engendering *fresh* guilt in its proponents, who suffer guilt *as a consequence* of their reform efforts. Many reformers seem to run down the country with every breath of criticism of whatever domain——politics, beliefs, traditions, or institutions.[5] But the conservative will never let the reformer forget that he or she is being "anti-American," and eventually the weight of all this piles up. It induces guilt——not in all reformers, but in many. A part of the later liberal guilt may also stem from the failure of recent reforms to bring the promised change. Personal loss of interest in reform may stimulate yet more guilt. And if the crisis of guilt has not set in beforehand, it certainly does after the nation plunges off into war, when muckraking gets classed with sedition.

In September 1946, Harry Truman cashiered Henry Wallace as Secretary of Commerce. A decade and a half later, Wallace told Truman at a dinner honoring the former President, "I'm glad you fired me when you did." Once so given to jousting against the Cold War, Wallace had by this time become something of a cold warrior himself.[6] The sheepishness so often displayed by ex-reformers reflects, I believe, a distinct tinge of guilt and remorse. This country rears us all with the flag: reformers must live with the psychic as well as the political costs of running down some great institutions. In time——especially in wartime——patria exerts its pull. Once pricked, the sense of social guilt may sometimes give way to a sense of self-loathing.

However useful the concept of personal remorse may be, it becomes far more helpful if we think of it in a double sense. On one hand, there is the personal side which we have just discussed——the drag of status quo patriotism against which every reformer must work. On the other hand, we encounter *functional* guilt——acts which, politically, *resemble* signs of contrition. These include, for example, Woodrow Wilson's notorious appointments to the Federal Trade Commission; the Truman loyalty program; the Kennedy investigations into labor racketeering in the 1950s; and Jimmy Carter's forays against the federal bureaucracy. Whether guilt-spawned or not, each of these cases casts an image of liberals finally coming to terms with their own or their party's or their predecessors' past sins.

The confessional mode has prevailed most clearly of all during our postwar red scares. Many liberals, early on, became apologists for the Soviet Union, and a great deal of liberal energy has been expended in living down the popular front phase of American reform. In their ambivalence over the red menace——and over its implications as a political issue——the liberals have often worn their guilt around their necks.

The guilt and the genteel, mugwump tradition endure as perennial elements in American reform. During the twenties, and again in the fifties and seventies, political caution led to ideological prudishness. Through the 1920s, for many reformers issues of individual liberty and personal conformity won priority over economic problems. In Adlai Stevenson three decades later, liberal politics shifted its emphasis to the upper middle class and its concerns. The so-called new politics of the late sixties and seventies reflected these same concerns. It placed cultural above raw economic issues, and in so doing made antagonists of white blue-collar masses. Vital Centrism, with its concern for "the quality of life," had returned with a vengeance.[7] Once having created the welfare state, influential liberals, so it seemed, could not wait to move "beyond" it.

A reform party on the defensive will start to think defensively. It will lose self-confidence and begin to think small. As this occurs, various negative themes work their way into view. The mix changes from period to period, but its elements remain familiar: neomugwumpery, protectiveness, obsolescence, irritability, genteel pretensions and perspectives, political prudery, and, so it seems, a strong measure of guilt.

As for government per se, the lunging pattern of American reform virtually dictates defensiveness in Washington once the reform tide recedes. Government's size—the fact that Washington is the world's biggest conglomerate—expands the possibility of failure, and certainly expands the exposure which failure receives. A number of blunders will already have been committed and brought to light. The bureaucracy will have shown signs of hardening arteries. If a dynamic new administration moves in, the pulse may quicken a bit; reaffirming old goals or setting new ones can stir the blood. But the inherent defensiveness of government will mount, fed by the growth of government itself and the ever-greater fund of resources it seeks to protect.

A sense of disappointment seems inevitable about it all. Reformers can never do enough for the groups they try to help. The resources simply do not exist. Doubt seeps in that problems can be solved at all. Ultimately voters arrive on the scene for whom the old issues and battles lack saliency. These new voters in time replace the older ones who could recall past struggles, and take whatever gains have occurred as their due.

NOTES

Disorientation

Leuchtenburg, *Shadow of FDR*, pp. 199-200 (Carter quote).
[1]Leuchtenburg, *Perils of Prosperity*, p. 121.
[2]Graham, *Planned Society*, pp. 9, 12-13.
[3]Burner, *Politics of Provincialism*, pp. 50, 54.
[4]*Into the Twenties*, p. 51.
[5]Ibid., pp. vii-viii.
[6]Ibid., pp. 200-203.
[7]Robert K. Murray, *The Harding Era: Warren G. Harding and His Administration* (Minneapolis: University of Minnesota Press, 1969), p. 91.
[8]After Wiebe, *Search*, ch. 8: "The Illusion of Fulfillment."

⁹Bremner, *From the Depths*, p. 260; Arthur S. Link, "What Happened to the Progressive Movement in the 1920's?" *American Historical Review* 64 (July 1959): 841.

¹⁰*Roosevelt and the New Deal*, p. 273.

¹¹Polenberg, "Decline of the New Deal," p. 255.

¹²"Where Are the Pre-war Radicals?" p. 564.

¹³Ladd, *Transformations*, p. 209.

¹⁴See Alan Wolfe, "The Death of Social Democracy," *New Republic*, 25 February 1985, p. 22.

¹⁵*End of Liberalism*, pp. 66-67. Italics deleted.

¹⁶See Schattschneider, *Semisovereign People*, p. 74.

¹⁷*The Death of Progress* (New York: Alfred A. Knopf, 1973), p. 32.

¹⁸See, e.g., Smelser, *Collective Behavior*, pp. 298-99; and, more generally, the observations of Trilling, *Liberal Imagination*, pp. xiii-xv.

¹⁹Ellis W. Hawley, "The Discovery and Study of a 'Corporate Liberalism,'" *Business History Review* 52 (Autumn 1978): 310-11.

²⁰J. M. Cameron, "Take Me to Your Leader," *New York Review of Books*, 23 October 1980, p. 44.

²¹*The Antitrust Paradox: A Policy at War with Itself* (New York: Basic Books, 1978), p. 417.

²²*Ideology and Utopia*, p. 101.

²³*Antitrust Paradox*, p. 423.

²⁴*Liberal Mind*, p. 403.

²⁵Neustadt, *Presidential Power*, p. 50.

²⁶For an examination of this theme, see Glenn Tinder, "Defending the Welfare State," *New Republic*, 10 March 1979, pp. 22-23.

²⁷*White Collar*, p. 349.

²⁸*End of Liberalism*, pp. 101-2. On bureaucracy as potentially dynamic and congruent with change, however, see Burns, *Leadership*, pp. 300-302.

²⁹*Americans in a Changing World: A History of the United States in the Twentieth Century* (New York: Harper & Row, 1978), p. 469. Italics deleted.

³⁰"The Regulation Mess," *Newsweek*, 12 June 1978, p. 86.

³¹The classic on the subject is Graham, *Encore*.

The Liberal Cannibalism

¹*The Letters of Franklin K. Lane: Personal and Political*, ed. Anne Wintermute Lane and Louise Herrick Wall (Boston: Houghton Mifflin Co., 1922), p. 359.

²*Against Our Will*, pp. 390-91.

³Burner, *Politics of Provincialism*, pp. 50, 54.

[4]Ibid., pp. 33-40, 70-73; Kennedy, *Over Here*, pp. 243-45; Arthur S. Link and William B. Catton, *American Epoch: A History of the United States since the 1890's*, vol. 1: *1897-1920*, 3d ed. (New York: Alfred A. Knopf, 1967), p. 246.

Defensiveness, Exhaustion, and Apathy

Hirschman, *Shifting Involvements*, p. 102; Weyl, *Tired Radicals*, pp. 12-13.

[1]I borrow the term, as others have, from Hofstadter, *Age of Reform*, pp. 19-20, though I employ it in a rather different and perhaps somewhat broader sense than did Hofstadter.

[2]See Hirschman, *Shifting Involvements*, pp. 93, 100.

[3]The term is from Huntington, *American Politics*, p. 216.

[4]*Shifting Involvements*, pp. 103, 119-20. Italics deleted.

[5]On nostalgia generally, see Clecak, *Ideal Self*, ch. 7.

[6]*America in Our Time*, p. 367.

[7]Writes Charles R. Morris:

> Much of the history of political ideas may be read as the alternative waxing and waning of faith in reason and faith in tradition. Conservatives characteristically overweight the value of stability against the creative possibilities of stress and change; liberals make the opposite error. Prolonged stability can cause a society to calcify. An insistence on articulated rationality generates the examination of first principles that leads to healthy change. But the social bonds can be stretched only so far without breaking. During times of great stress, leaders need an intuitive grasp of social limits and a sense of justice that balances individual rights against the community's need for cohesion and consensus.

A Time of Passion: America 1960-1980 (New York: Harper & Row, 1984), p. 208.

[8]See, e.g., Barber, *Pulse of Politics*, pp. 4, 22.

[9]See, e.g., Graham, *Encore*, pp. 151ff.

[10]Huntington, *American Politics*, p. 104.

[11]"Where Are the Pre-war Radicals?" p. 564. For a suggestive dichotomy between "radicals by environment" and "radicals by temperament" which helps to explain the disappearance of some on the left, see Weyl, *Tired Radicals*, p. 10.

[12]Greene, *America's Heroes*, p. 286.

[13]See Hirschman, *Shifting Involvements*, pp. 96-97, 100.

[14]Voluntary reform organizations of all sorts go back to the roots of American history. See Arthur Schlesinger, Jr., "The End of an Era?" *Wall Street Journal*, 20 November 1980.

[15]Howe, *A Margin of Hope*, pp. 326-27.

[16]*Confessions of a Reformer*, pp. 115, 343.

[17]*Men of Destiny*, p. 21.

[18]*Encore*, p. 63. Regarding privatization generally, see Blumberg, *Inequality*, passim; and Richard Sennett, *The Fall of Public Man* (New York: Alfred A. Knopf, 1977).

[19]*Only Yesterday*, p. 186.

[20]*Deflation*, pp. 72ff.

[21]Ibid., p. 73.

[22]"It is only once in a generation," Woodrow Wilson told FDR, "that a people can be lifted above material things." And: "That is why conservative government is in the saddle two-thirds of the time." Schlesinger, Jr., *Cycles*, p. 31.

[23]Sidney Blumenthal, "Hart's Big Chill," *New Republic*, 23 January 1984, p. 18. Blumenthal's observations on generational politics have significantly aided me in crystallizing my own.

[24]*Ideal Self*, pp. 309-11.

[25]*Jerry Brown: The Man on the White Horse* (Boston: Houghton Mifflin Co., 1978), pp. xi-xii, 231. The reader may object that, in view of Lorenz's relationship with Brown, all this represents bitter afterthoughts. To the contrary, I think that Lorenz has pegged Brown perfectly. For an attempt at a more "balanced" assessment than Lorenz or I provide, however, see Gary G. Hamilton and Nicole Woolsey Biggart, *Governor Reagan, Governor Brown: A Sociology of Executive Power* (New York: Columbia University Press, 1984), including pp. 113-15 on Brown's relationship with Lorenz. The authors emphasize that Brown "took symbols seriously," and point among other things to Brown's record on the environment, toughness on criminals, and high rate of appointments of women and minorities; but they criticize him sharply as an administrator who, "by fighting the system," ultimately "paralyzed government." Pp. 202-3, 213-14.

[26]Charles Krauthammer, "Brownian Motion," *New Republic*, 1 & 8 August 1981, p. 10.

[27]"Jerry for President?" *New York Review of Books*, 28 September 1978, p. 28.

[28]Ibid., pp. 27, 30.

[29]*Jerry Brown*, p. 246.

[30]Ken Bode, "Dumpsters Convention," *New Republic*, 7 & 14 July 1979, p. 13.

[31]Roger Morris, "Proteus Californias," *New Republic*, 28 January 1978, p. 20.

Guilt Revisited: Some Final Speculations

Saul Alinsky and Marion K. Sanders, "The Professional Radical, 1970," *Harper's Magazine*, January 1970, p. 41.

[1]*Civilization and Its Discontents*, p. 126. Footnote reference deleted.

[2]*Deflation*, p. 78.

[3]*Slavery*, pp. 163-64. For a searching examination of the relationship between guilt and American reform, see pp. 157-64.

[4]*The Radical Liberal: New Man in American Politics* (New York: Atherton Press, 1968), p. 54.

[5]On these latter points, see Burnham, *Suicide of the West*, p. 278.

[6]Richard J. Walton, *Henry Wallace, Harry Truman, and the Cold War* (New York: Viking Press, 1976), pp. 351-52; Norman D. Markowitz, *The Rise and Fall of the People's Century: Henry A. Wallace and American Liberalism, 1941-1948* (New York: Free Press, 1973), p. 321.

[7]Fairlie, *The Parties*, p. 189.

CONCLUSION: WHAT DOES IT ALL MEAN?

> The people of the United States do not wish to curtail the activities of this Government; they wish, rather, to enlarge them; and with every enlargement, with the mere growth, indeed, of the country itself, there must come, of course, the inevitable increase of expense.
>
> Woodrow Wilson, 1914

> The taxing power of government must be used to provide revenues for legitimate government purposes. It must not be used to regulate the economy or bring about social change.
>
> Ronald Reagan, 1981

Any study of history which treads as close to the present as this one has will likely cause both its reader's and its author's pulse to quicken——the reader's out of anticipation that the author will now somehow shed brilliant light on the present, the author's out of fear of venturing into "instant history" and setting down words which will look foolish or antique just a few years hence. This book has focused on the range of time from the 1890s into the 1980s. As I conclude it, I want, first, to consider conditions in the near-present as a means of illuminating the past (rather than the other way around); and second, to complete our long examination of "cycles" in American political history. Any extensive discussion of the political patterns of the 1980s would require another entire book. Instead, we will brush with them, allude to aspects of them, and tantalize ourselves by seeing how the Reagan era compares with other times. We will stop at mid-decade so as to allow ourselves at least a small margin of perspective.

On the surface of it, many of the phenomena of the early to mid-1980s seem so strange, so ironic or confusing, as to defy us to fit them into any coherent pattern past or present. Let us glance at just a few of them, almost as if we were scanning a menu for the first time.

Ronald Reagan won reelection in 1984 with the loss of one state and the District of Columbia. Extraordinarily ideological for an American presidential candidate, Reagan in 1980, like Roosevelt in 1936, had waged a controversy-prone campaign which played on social and ideological divisions. He often came close to violating the principles of politics I have set down earlier, but not quite. Like FDR, he generated hostility, and like Roosevelt he knew how to turn it to his advantage. As given to experimentalism as FDR or Johnson,[1] between 1980 and 1984 Reagan implemented the greatest change of policy direction since the New Deal. Coming in the wake of Carter, Reagan's first term provided a heartening demonstration at least that a President could still govern. Reagan tore a good many pages from the book of liberal opportunism, using the lessons to serve his own brand of reactionary activism——a far cry from the GOP's penurious, churlish, opposition-oriented opportunism of the past. And now, for a change, it was the GOP which had to contend with the counterweight of mass inertia.

Reagan arrived in Washington at precisely the proper political moment; Jimmy Carter had exemplified the problem of blurred vision with an improbable perfection. Rather than resolving the disorientation, directionlessness, and division of his party, or its lack of consensus over issues since Johnson's time, if anything Carter compounded them. For all his decency, he confirmed the old stereotype of the liberal——or was he a conservative?——as vacillating and ineffective. By the seventies, the New Deal state——once an immensely powerful anti-Establishment symbol——had become the Establishment orthodoxy. In 1976 Carter chose to run against Washington. It was apt politics at first. The public saw government as a Problem, along with status quo, interest-group liberalism; and for reform, anti-Establishment politics has always proved good politics.[2] But, once elected, Carter never really got inside his own (Democratic) establishment. Symptomatically, Carter became the first elected President to lose since Hoover, whom he resembled in important political and personal respects.

After half a century, the New Deal tradition had, inevitably, aged as an agenda for change. Scarcely departing from that tradition, in his 1984 campaign Walter Mondale tried, as it were, to inflate the tires of a 1935 car with a bicycle pump. It was not that the New Deal per se had grown obsolete, though certainly times and the public had changed.   The problem was that New Dealism had ossified into a set of reflex responses which no longer quite matched the patterns of contemporary reality. More than anything else, liberals like Mondale had forgotten the New Deal's lively zest for experiments.   Reagan hadn't.

Except for such strident times as World War I, liberalism in America had traditionally been (as Harold Stearns put it) "good-natured" and "urbane."[3]   But the sixties-seventies liberalism of busing, quotas, and zero growth looked, at least, stale, negative, defensive, reactive, dogmatic, and even resignedly, pessimistically dour.   This brought to mind another side of liberalism, its skepticism——even of liberalism itself.   Its habit of criticism opens reform to carping by its own friends, not always with compensating advantages.   By the seventies there had been too much carping, too little optimism.   At least for a time, the Democrats lost their place as the party of hope, becoming instead the party of a lugubrious status quo.   Reagan simply collected the Democrats' clothes. He called them Doomocrats.   He told Americans they could do whatever they wanted to do, that their society was a good society, and that a sagging economy and a shrinking world role were not inevitable.   He made himself the avatar of optimism.

Meanwhile vehement radicals of the 1960s continued to come in from the cold.   Tom Hayden had become a member of the California legislature.   Eldridge Cleaver became a conservative, born-again Christian. Jerry Rubin operated a "networking salon" where New York business executives could rub professional elbows.   Rennie Davis was a management consultant.   In 1980 Bernardine Dohrn, who had headed the Weathermen, emerged from the underground after a decade in hiding and joined a painfully proper Chicago law firm as a clerk.[4]

While radicals were metamorphosing into liberals or conservatives or something else, hippies were yielding to yuppies, their concerns quite private and oriented toward ornate, competitive patterns of consumption. Yuppies tended to focus on narrow realms where they could exercise some degree of personal leverage.   They became physical fitness buffs and joggers, devotees of haute cuisine and BMWs.   Former radical Jane Fonda taught them how to exercise.

A New Right emerged, different from the more staid, pre-Goldwater conservatism in significant respects (among them its strong southern and western, lower-middle-class cast, its suspicion of elites and cities, a fundamentalist religious grounding, and a determined stand against abortion).[5]

This New Right was often described as "populistic."   Yet the broad left and right disputed possession of the very term "populism."

Whoever owned the word, clearly the great Social Issue of the sixties and seventies had set off a counterassertion of traditional religious, sexual, and family values. There was a renaissance of ancient symbols: the nation, the flag, the home.[6] Reminiscent of nothing so much as the fundamentalist upsurge of the twenties, right-wing political Christianity made a spectacular comeback, utilizing sixties direct action styles of confrontation. TV evangelism boomed. Darwinian evolution suddenly erupted as a burning issue again. Presidential candidates claimed to have been born more than once. Whatever else it added up to, conservative political fundamentalism with all its diatribes against "secular humanism" was a reactive phenomenon. It reacted against such "liberal" initiatives of the 1960s and 1970s as the movements for minority, gay, and women's rights; the ERA and legalized abortion; drives against censorship and prayer in public schools; and sex education. "Liberals" or "secular humanists" mounted the threat; fundamentalists counterattacked.[7] "Liberal" religious denominations meanwhile stagnated.

The social gospel tradition retained strength among the leadership, at least, of such main line denominations as the Methodists, Presbyterians, and Catholics. To them and to Americans more generally, the poor remained far more "visible" than in earlier reactive eras. Not even Ronald Reagan could entirely ignore their presence.

In retrospect, perhaps the biggest single headache for liberalism in the seventies and early eighties was the Supreme Court's 1973 *Roe* decision.[8] By the 1970s, abortion could be viewed as a new form of freedom, or, more uneasily, as a bad idea whose time had come. But despite its origin in the Burger Court, *Roe* inevitably got tagged as one more "liberal" judicial ruling. It caused an explosion in the religiously conservative community, politicized untold numbers of people, and added one more big fish to the school of red herrings already swimming around the eddies of the social issue. Many people believed that abortion amounted to murder, that a holocaust had broken out in the United States. And if it was a holocaust, indeed, it was surely a liberal one.

Predictably, the outspoken cultural radicalism and social tolerance of the sixties which abortion so vividly symbolized fit beautifully into the privatized seventies and eighties. During the sixties easy sex and drugs had had political overtones. Sex and drugs endured as realms of purely personal consumption long after all the political implications had been forgotten.

In the eighties, though, the busy sex scene of the previous decades turned a little wan. "Men in great numbers," wrote Crane Brinton, "can no more devote themselves heroically and permanently to sin than to holiness."[9] Perhaps people had grown tired of sex as a subject of controversy. Like any other fashion, sex can endure as the Great National Issue only so long. Or perhaps swinging had become so conventional that it seemed a bit dull. Perhaps it all had to do with the baby boomers' aging. By the mid-eighties it certainly had to do with

AIDS.   Whatever the case, the new fashions had increasingly become body-building, careerism, and moneymaking—just as self-centered as swinging, but significantly more respectable and bourgeois.   For the yuppie careerist, only so much time remained in the week for doing the singles scene.   During the 1980s commitment made a sort of comeback.[10] Each political party vied with the other to prove itself the more pro-family.

This had disturbing implications for feminism, or at least for radical feminism, but feminists had plenty to worry about besides.   When middle-aged eighties feminists bemoaned the younger generation, they meant younger women who took all the gains of earlier decades for granted and found the feminists themselves tediously passé.   It was the twenties again: feminist sisterhood gave way to yuppie careerism much as suffragism had succumbed to flapperdom.[11]   Symptomatically, the ERA went down to defeat.   Feminism provided a classic example of a movement which generated popular individual causes (such as equal pay for equal work), but many of whose leaders viscerally offended vast multitudes.

By the 1980s, too, the ideological generation gap—so symbolic of radicalism and change in the sixties—had virtually evaporated.   Student conservatism reappeared in full blossom for the first time since the fifties.   ROTC, driven from many campuses during the Vietnam era, revived.   "As many as two-thirds of all voters under 25," *Newsweek* observed from poll results in 1984, "now consider themselves Republicans."[12] Among voters aged 18 to 24, Reagan garnered some 60 percent of the ballots that year.[13]   South Africa became a burning issue for many students, but one which was morally clear-cut and safely foreign.

Meantime, intellectuals moved both ways—some to the left, but most (and certainly the most publicized) to the right into neoconservatism.

Nationalism was making a big comeback.   People called themselves patriots again.   Heroics boomed on the silver screen.   Talk arose of rock 'n' roll's "New Patriotism."[14]

The much-maligned (by conservatives) "liberal" media shifted perceptibly to the right,[15] following the political drift.

Lee Iacocca became a national hero, an eighties version of Henry Ford.   In a limited way,[16] the idol of organization had returned to fashion.   By the late seventies and early eighties, business's political power had rebounded to heights comparable to the twenties.   Glamor and allure surrounded it.   Meantime, with deregulation also fashionable in both the Carter and Reagan White Houses, and antitrust decidedly out of style under Reagan, another mammoth merger wave swept through.

If after 1981 Washington was occupied by the most pro-business administration since the twenties, an administration whose regulatory and tax policies found nostalgic inspiration in the Calvin Coolidge regime, the case of organized labor was the saddest since the early Depression. Once the core of the New Deal coalition, by the 1980s union membership as a percentage of the nonfarm labor force had been slipping for decades; and after the mid-seventies, an absolute decline set in.[17]   In 1980, 23 percent of all employees were still represented by unions——by 1984, just 19.1 percent and falling. Stiffer competition erupting out of deregulation accounted for part of the drop.[18] Traditional labor-intensive smokestack industries stagnated. A permanent if uneasy accommodation between boardroom and union hall which had appeared to emerge out of the FDR and Truman years yielded once again to more primitive precedents. In an echo of the Coolidge era, the seventies and eighties saw labor besieged by the greatest union-busting outbreak in decades. Unions lost most National Labor Relations Board representation elections every year after 1973.[19] Legislative defeats for labor followed one upon another. During the sixties unions had lost their place as the main engine for change from the liberal left; a good many of the initiatives of that decade aroused unions' scorn or apathy. By the eighties, defensiveness had infected the labor movement. Organized labor had fallen into a torpor of bureaucratized inertia. In competition with foreign workers and in prospective competition with an army of industrial robots, its future looked pretty bleak. With overall wage levels stagnating, the gap widened between rich and poor.

As for agriculture, the eighties forged one more link in the chain of epochal crises for the family farm. The decade produced the worst agricultural crisis since the Great Depression. In the midst of this, the agrarian myth resurfaced, proving that it had remained there all along. Motion pictures and country music loudly decried the accelerated demise of the family farm. Long since had agriculture joined the ranks of the organized interest groups; yet the old farmstead, still idealized, remained the nation's heart and soul.

Meanwhile, liberal politicians continued their quest for some word to attach to themselves besides "liberal." Originally seized from classical liberals by welfare state liberals, the word had been stolen again by *cultural* liberals. "Progressive," rediscovered in the seventies, became modish during the eighties. In some ways, this term may have become more descriptive of the center-left late in the twentieth century than was "liberal" as New Dealers had meant it.

Throughout the 1960s and 1970s issues had kept on proliferating, so that by the outset of the eighties their sheer number became enough to cow anyone approaching them in the traditional liberal, problem-solution way. There was enough by now for the political system to choke on.

Things came to such a pass, indeed, that we had animal lib——the designation of "nonhuman animals" as "an oppressed group." (There emerged an Animal Liberation Front, and, inevitably, a Farm Animal Reform Movement [FARM]. Some people became vegetarians. Some began breaking into laboratories to rescue felines and canines.)[20]

Among his many misfortunes, Carter had entered the White House at a time when the broad constituency for reform of almost any sort, even had he known what to do with it, had evaporated. Democrats controlled Congress, most state governorships, and most legislatures. Almost nothing happened. Virtually no focused liberal agenda existed; Johnson had enacted it, and little time had elapsed in which to develop another one. By no accident, the 1970s saw a resurgent good government drive in the Democratic party, a huge emphasis on arid procedural "reform" of the political system as against the previous decade's stress on social equity. This neo-goo-gooism held political attractions in the Watergate era. It had a certain resonance among the already well-off. It had little to do with social justice.[21] "Throughout the 1970s," Thomas Byrne Edsall writes, "there was a pervasive deterioration in the political forces supporting the interests of those on the bottom half of the economic spectrum and a parallel strengthening of the forces supporting the interests of those on the top."[22]

Among many Democrats, "neoliberalism" came into vogue in the eighties, an updated version of the rather bloodless, economic growth-oriented, technocratic liberalism of the Kennedy era. Neoliberalism also resembled progressivism in its trouble with focus and in its rhetorical stress on the general interest as against the interest-group liberalism which had bogged down the party during the Carter-Mondale era. More finicky than New Dealish liberals about augmenting the scope of government to tackle problems, neoliberals showed greater respect for business——and less for labor——than had many of their reformist predecessors. In numerous ways neoliberalism resembled the Democratic party's prissy, genteel, conservative incarnations of the past.

For the first time since TR, or at least since Hoover, during the early eighties, Republicans seemed awash in ideas. Observing that over the preceding decade the primary source of new political ideas had been the right, in 1985 William Schneider asked, "Where are the Democratic intellectuals?"[23] That liberal theories had become so spent doubtless made conservative views (many of which came from disillusioned ex-liberals) look all the more attractive. For a season, at least, the right was aggressively confident, relatively cohesive, and enthusiastic. It had its own corps of intellectuals. It also had plenty of money and political sophistication. It claimed to have vision.

Just as the GOP's natural decade of orientation under Reagan was the 1920s, the Democrats——feeling most at home with domestic crisis——missed their Depression or its functional equivalent. The thirties had been the heroic age of government. Democrats now needed the sort of national jolt which in the past had provided a catalyst, forcing them to fuse loosely arranged ideas together into a cause. The biggest difficulty was not that they had run short of ideas, nor an absence of competent people behind these, so much as that the ideas floated disembodied in space. The situation revealed an absence of what Robert Kuttner termed a "coherent worldview."[24] Early twentieth century reform had had such a worldview. Turn-of-the-century ideas have provided the broad seedbed for all of subsequent twentieth century liberalism. But the crop has long since been harvested, gleaned, and gleaned again. Very publicly and quite self-consciously, during the 1980s Democrats hunted for a role.

Observers debated whether a party realignment (or dealignment) was on, hunting for evidence in every corner. Whatever the answer, the Democratic party found itself in the deepest trouble since the twenties. The GOP had returned as the party of the agenda——if there still was a party of the agenda. It even reclaimed its pre-Depression credentials as the party of prosperity as against Carteresque zero-sum stagnationism. And more: with the Democrats weighed down by their multiple interest-group identities, the Republicans found themselves able to pose in their nineteenth century attire as the nationalist party of the general interest.

On the surface of things, all these twists and turns seem confusing, even baffling. Yet every one of them fits the tenor of a conservative era.[25] Conservatives, of course, get elected. Liberals lose their sense of direction and initiative. Radicals come in out of the cold. Materialism and self-centeredness revive among youth and in society at large. The young become politically more conventional as politics in general moves to the right. A cultural generation gap survives, but the politically ideological one does not. Bourgeois values stage a comeback, if not all the way back. Conservative religiosity erupts to prominence. Past decisions by reformers in power return like ghosts to haunt them. Past beneficiaries lose their mystique. Large numbers of intellectuals bail out of reform. Flag-waving returns to fashion. Much of it is done by the heroes of business, who have also returned to vogue.

What, by contrast, are the earmarks of an age of reform? The twentieth century experience suggests that they are these:

A state of crisis. There must be a need for change, together with a widespread perception of need——a sense of unease, anxiety, or outrage about some identified set of problems and grievances. I stress identified issues, for identifiability is central to——

Broad public support for change. At the very least, there must be tolerant receptivity. Far better is a state of energetic enthusiasm for transforming important dimensions of the social and political order, a season of what Irving Howe has called "good-tempered activism."[26] Reform becomes a fad.

There must, in short, be a genuine *movement* which sweeps people out of their isolated, random (even if vaguely reformist) concerns and brings them together in a collective (even if loose) sense of purpose and direction. There must be political solidarity and cohesiveness.

Cohesiveness aside, nothing prods liberal reform better than a divergent, vocal, well-publicized *radical left* with its own ideas and a capability of applying pressure.

Public, as opposed to strictly private concerns must become uppermost in importance among broad elements of society and within the political system. A surge of moral outrage will color these issues.

Public concerns should focus on the problems of the nation, not the world. This *domestic emphasis* presupposes that, relative to other eras, foreign and defense policy will remain marginal issues. A strong domestic focus has been rare in the Cold War era, confined to brief phases of the Johnson and Reagan administrations. Unfortunately, the internationalization of the U.S. economy means that in the future it will prove even less possible than in the past to disentangle domestic from foreign problems.

Idealism undergirds the enthusiasm and energy which characterize the beginnings of a reform surge, as opposed to the jadedness so typical of the end. It is best for a reform drive to open with a certain naïveté——about the prospects for change, certainly, but also concerning the people themselves. Optimism about the broad public, the beneficiaries, and the odds for success seems critical. Naïveté has always prevailed among young insurgents. One of the major upshots of reformist experiments which have failed, together with changing insights about human nature itself, is that much of the spirit of perfectionism has gradually been squeezed out of American reform. The sense of possibility has shriveled. Realistic though this may be, rose-colored glasses best serve the opening of a reform era. Plenty of opportunity will emerge for disillusionment later. When reformers concede the sinfulness or hopelessness of humankind, they concede a great deal. Reform rests, if not on outright perfectionism, at least on a sunny view of human nature. Once disillusionment creeps in, the question becomes: Why do anything for anybody? Why care at all?

Better to have idealism, then, and *idealism buoyed by the churches* as a prod to the ubiquitous middle-class conscience and spirit of self-sacrifice. *Reform should originate from the moral high ground.* Along with placing its moral imprimatur upon reform, the clerical conscience sustains that guilt-induced anxiety which serves reform so well.

The churches also stress *collaboration between classes and groups*, the "cooperative values" (in Robert S. McElvaine's term) as against an "acquisitive ethic." The acquisitive ethic needs no defenders in the United States. Cooperative values fluctuate, yet surely a heightened sense of concern for others, or at least about others, distinguishes a reform era.[27]

Thus *the poor, the oppressed, and the downtrodden will come into vogue* as a sort of collective issue. Meliorative reform will become popular. Reformers will concentrate their attention down the class ladder. (When their eyes move upward again, the reform era will have ended.)

Reform emerges independently of major shifts in the economy. Unlike the New Deal, progressivism and the Great Society coexisted with prosperous times. Yet in each reform era concern has brewed over *social factors with a patently economic dimension*——if not the Great Depression, then poverty, the dismal economic corollaries of enduring racism, or the enormous implications of corporate consolidation. Economic crises come in various forms, only some of which directly reflect the business cycle. One of the greatest enemies of reform is certainly rampaging inflation. Moderate inflation may run through a reform period without damage. It may even prove helpful. But the uncontrollable variety, which has typified the down-side of every reform era, dramatically escalates the pace of collapse.

Along with collaboration there must be *polarization*, but in forms which lend themselves to constructive change. The progressives and Lyndon Johnson wanted to create reform movements without class tension. It probably cannot be done. Reform erupts out of preexistent polarizations around class, economics, race, or sex. It tends to widen them. Class-based voting rises. On the other hand, red-baiting, nativism, and xenophobia——or extreme or unusual outbreaks of hostility which shock the public (massive strikes, race riots, bombings)——cut into a reform movement like an axe.

Issues should lend themselves to being dramatized. As part of the polarization-dramatization process, a reform movement simply thrives on a *cast of villains* who fiercely and very publicly seek to salvage the status quo. The more arrogant they are, the better.

Beyond the war of symbols come the realities. Mere compassion and goodwill go only so far in the absence of self- or group interest. *Masses of voters must sense that the benefits of what reformers seek will flow to them, personally.* If the legislation which passes produces these benefits, well and good, but in any case, it must hold out promise of doing so.

Edward M. Kennedy has observed that liberals have generally favored "big issues——like civil rights" around which to mass their forces. "It's easy to focus on something like that."[28] If one *defines issues as discrete problems*, which the progressives usually did, then they become *relatively* simple to address: pure food and drug legislation, banking bills, railroad regulation. If one defines issues as whole groups——agriculture, labor, blacks——things become more complex and difficult. To an extent the New Deal did this. Yet the needs of the thirties had an immediacy and concreteness which made them easier to address than those of the sixties and since, when almost every imaginable group has enjoyed some degree of organization.

Reformers would do well to remember Maslow's hierarchy. While some groups exist on a level that requires them to struggle to make ends meet, others, occupying a higher position, search for more inchoate forms of fulfillment. Both sets of groups may support reform, if, somehow, an agenda can be tailored to meet each distinct kind of need. Issues which at first glance appear peripheral to reform may not actually be peripheral at all. They may help to attract the interest of the middle class or the affluent to reform. If it deals only in bread and butter, reform can seem a bore to those who have both. The problem is to raise "higher" issues without having them turn into divisive sociocultural red herrings.

Over time, the Democrats, in particular, have attracted an extraordinary diversity of groups and causes, from the Klan to blacks to gays. Some of these groups have taken special prominence at moments when the country could afford to worry about things besides filling empty bellies. Other groups, especially labor, are the essence of bread and butter. *When reform liberalism has become too closely associated with relatively peripheral, controversial social causes, it has run into trouble*——as a number of spectacularly disastrous Democratic conventions make clear.

Somehow, reformers must walk a very narrow line. On one side lies a "vulgar materialism"[29] which thinks in none but material terms, which forgets the imagination and real questions of values or tries to distill them at the expense of their complexity and nuance. On the other lies a reformism that, in its fascination with cultural and other broad questions, wafts them into some ethereal region where government cannot function. Reformers and radicals have found themselves criticized for their stress on material concerns, and for proposing material answers to questions that more basically involve morals and values. (Neoconservatism, certainly, has answered with a prominent concern with these latter.)[30] The moral legacy is a progressive one. The material legacy most distinctly echoes the New Deal.

A sense of crisis and self-interest can lead to mere aimless flailing in the absence of *focus*. This bears an utterly critical corollary, one which reformers have tended to miss: that not everything can get questioned at once. *Deal first with a limited number of issues around which a broad consensus has formed.* Too much questioning will spawn red herrings right and left, which will quickly damage the general sense of social and political toleration necessary to a reform drive and stir resistance. Points of resistance must remain at a minimum. Reformers would in general do well to keep cultural conflict second to economic ends, if possible. In any case, they should work as hard as they can for as long as they can to keep side-issues from emerging, since the sooner these do, the sooner the movement is likely to die. It is enormously helpful if the public and the political system together maintain their focus on a central, limited set of domestic problems capable of solution. Once conventional social values come under fire, many people will react, and the whole political debate will shift.

Reform can be spurred along by support from the intellectuals. Ideas do have consequences, and a reform movement should open with *an abundance of ideas.* Yet intellectuals do, as we have seen, tend naturally toward iconoclasm. And so their support requires that they, too, put on the rose-colored glasses. As a group they are as responsive as youth to the tides of political fashion, and help to set them.

The question is how to have a *youth movement* which will give reform momentum without stalling things by precipitating a big social issue. The young and the intellectuals always bear a latent antagonism toward middle- and lower-middle-class values. Only sometimes does this flash into overt antagonism. Periods when youths' cultural opposition has remained most muted (the thirties, the early sixties)——but when their more specifically political outrage has been directed toward conventional political channels——have been the ones most conducive to left-oriented change.

One of the advantages a reform movement carries at the outset, and soon loses, is the *relative virginity of the political questions* it seeks to confront. Hope and optimism run high at this stage. *The party of reform must be the party of hope.*

There must exist some significant measure of *confidence that the problems can be solved.* Preferably worked out in preceding years, there should be a coherent, agreed-upon agenda of priorities for practicable change. This, as much as anything, will produce the élan which reformers must have, the shared feeling of certainty of purpose and direction.

Just as important is the emergence of *leaders wanting to solve the problems.* Leadership must exist at many levels, but especially in the presidency. Without even having much direction in itself, presidential vigor can inspire millions——the Kennedy era showed that. The savior role goes especially well with reform, as FDR proved. But this must be proportioned leadership, aware of its limitations, not leadership taking flight toward hubris. During the 1920s, liberal leaders died. In the sixties they were shot down, and reform has yet to recover. It needs heroes. Unfortunately, issues which cut across the normal liberal-conservative spectrum can elevate conservatives into liberal heroes-of-the-moment. We might call them red herring celebrities.

The President should be a strong one, both in his (or her) own right and vis-à-vis Congress. Antagonists who have raised cries that Executive power mounts alongside liberal political change have seen things accurately. The system operates only this way. It operates best when the President and the two-house congressional majority come from the same party (though this offers no guarantees, as Carter demonstrated); and likewise, when Presidents find themselves able to move in an area relatively free of bureaucratic inertia. If these stars are properly aligned and everything else is right, reform measures will pass quite rapidly one after another. Indeed, along with the content of measures, the simple speed of passage of a clustered agenda helps to delineate a reform period.

During such a period, general interest in politics and government tends to mount. So does the "seriousness" of politics. *A reform era is an intensely political era.* Public confidence in government increases. Numbers of un-radical young, in particular, "feel good" about politics. Levels of partisanship usually rise among the electorate. They rise between the parties themselves. The political system falls under closer public scrutiny. Masses of people become ideologized. More get involved in campaigns as volunteers. The public sector takes on a relatively prestigious reputation, a "clean" image untainted by scandal or incompetence. Especially when built upon the credibility restored to government by the prior conservative regime, the state assumes a benign visage. More often than not this contrasts for a time with the relatively weak reputation of the private sector, and the reform regime makes the most of it by staking out its distance from business. Finally, the Chief Executive must bear a positive, patriotic, masculine (or, in the case of the opposite sex, perhaps a feminine) image which in turn attaches to reform. It is critical that a reform President not appear weak or indecisive.

There must be at least one *party of the reform agenda, with reformers in charge of it.* Since the Progressive Era, this has meant the Democrats. Now and again the Democratic party will undergo its identity crises, as it did in the 1890s, the 1920s, or the 1970s-80s. These crises will always be very public ones, and often acrimonious. They will repel broad segments of the population. But on the approach to a reform era, the party of reform must have some basic sense of what it is and what it wants to do. It must convince the public that it can actually govern.

Finally, though the process of political change will inevitably breed friction, it is critical that *the left not cannibalize itself.* This raises again the importance of dealing first with issues around which some agreement has already emerged.

In the end, is reform cyclic? If by cyclic we mean *periodic*, then, as I have suggested, I think the answer is no. Certainly some considerations might lead us toward attributing a life "pulse" to American politics. Yet crisis underlies all reform eras, and one cannot predict with much certainty just when crises will erupt or what form they will take. Without a Great Depression, would the thirties have seen a New Deal (or any other significant sort of reform surge)? Who knows? The nature of the origins of the crises which lead to reform cannot be predicted. And the human factor, not least the matter of leadership, makes mechanistic formulas about reform very hazardous indeed. No, for all the patterns which intrude on them and can accurately be said to have some earmarks of periodicity, I do not think that we can comfortably assign such familiar analogies as the "wave," the "pulse," or the "pendulum" to reform and reaction.

Yet this word "cycle" has more than just a single meaning. One of them suggests periodicity, and we have dismissed that. But if we investigate reform and reaction much as if we were following a *life cycle*, then the term suddenly becomes useful again. Throughout this book we have, after all, been examining the life cycles of three great reform eras. Reform movements may not emerge with cyclic predictability; but once they have appeared, their course, and particularly their decline, do follow a roughly predictable pattern. We can expect that they will take certain broad forms, and expire in certain ways.

Let us say that all the considerations we have listed earlier in this chapter, and which give life to a reform era, tend to emerge together. A good deal of chance goes into each of these, yet a similar pattern has developed at three distinct times in this century. Just when a precipitating crisis will occur may not be predictable, but within limits the overall configuration that will take shape in addressing it does appear to be.

What, then, of the demise of a reform movement such as those we have described? Here, I think, things become most straightforward of all, even if most complex. Let me list, and where necessary briefly explain, the constants that crop up on the down-side of a reform era:

A fading atmosphere of crisis out of which the reform movement originated.

A growing, widespread public discovery that reform measures have been oversold.

Liberal and presidential hubris.

Presidential diversion down the foreign policy escape hatch: a temptation in administrations of all varieties, but especially for an administration with a long domestic agenda which has gotten stymied. And, true enough, foreign policy can legitimately impose itself above domestic.

A change of public attitudes as the reform "fad" fades.   Hope erodes. People are reminded that many reforms require some degree of centralized planning and control (billed by opponents as "regimentation"). Idealism slides. Materialism rises. People turn toward private and away from public pursuits. The prestige of business revives while government's declines. Conservatives seize the initiative. Private sector values return to favor: low taxes, trickle-down and anti-regulation economics, cries for laissez-faire. Demands arise to placate business. Appeals to conscience become less persuasive. A "moral slump" sets in.

The beneficiaries lose their attractiveness.

The far left decays and sours, with specific forms of disillusionment among previously radicalized intellectuals and youth who (usually noisily) pull away.

Disillusionment with the mass public sets in, notably among the young and the intelligentsia.

Political dialogue becomes choked with red herrings, grouped especially around the social issue and the politics of disgust because these are a reflexive source of sustenance for the right.

Quite distracting forms of polarization emerge. A politics of culture supplants a politics of class-economics.

Like the far left, the liberal left becomes disoriented——in part by its own illusions of fulfillment. Compounding the confusion is an ebbing sense of where to go next——a falloff in purpose, confidence, and focus.

Reformers' ideas and rhetoric obsolesce, or at the very least seem to, slipping decisively out of fashion.

Government at large, and the presidency in particular, lose trust and prestige.   Calls mount to turn important responsibilities over to the states.

The electorate depoliticizes and depolarizes to such a degree that issues of reform no longer seem terribly important.

Politics itself declines as a vogue, and along with it the seriousness of politics both as perceived by the public and as practiced by the politicians. Leadership drifts generally, or takes a reactionary turn, or both.

The far left and liberal left cannibalize one another.   The constituencies and coalitions which have sustained them divide.

At length, a period of issuelessness and drift sets in, with the liberals (or whatever they are now calling themselves) characterized by exhaustion, apathy, defensiveness, and political prudery.

Of all the massive forces which we have discussed throughout this book, and which have done tremendous damage to reform in the past, there are only four that I would not necessarily expect to recur as part of the life cycle of a future reform era: presidential hubris; war, whose fatal linkage to reform administrations has been overwhelmingly situational; political scandal; and libertinism. This last exclusion may strike the reader as an especially curious one. All the questioning that makes up a reform era may indeed help to release hedonistic passions, and the re-privatization which follows a reform era may bring them into full flower. Yet in the end, libertine outbreaks seem as closely tied to other circumstances, including the state of the economy, which moves in its own cycles, independent of reform.

Are historians seers? Of course not. Perhaps we shall find that the patterns we have discussed hold only for the past century or so. Yet that is half this country's history as a nation.

Some things have changed. The multiplication of interest groups over the decades, each tugging this way or that, has made reform a far more complex undertaking than it once was. Dealignment has made it more difficult to mobilize powerful party support behind a reform program. And many of the choice portions of the welfare state have seen enactment; just as the first phase of a reform movement skims off the cream of the issues, each successive era of reform does the same.

Yet issues themselves have multiplied inexorably, and a future endures for the reform tradition. The reflexive, motive force of the Democratic party remains identifying problems in order to address them (and then collect the votes). Liberals always have to face the hard question: If additional social services cannot be delivered by the rather pallid American welfare state, then what do reformers have left to offer? Every crisis which has led to the expansion of governmental power has broadened political representation—for women, for labor, for blacks. If reformers run out of groups to aid, where has reform left to go? Questions such as these require a continual rethinking of where the reform tradition actually finds itself in time.

NOTES

Woodrow Wilson, *The Papers of Woodrow Wilson*, ed. Arthur S. Link, vol. 31: *September 6-December 31, 1914* (Princeton: Princeton University Press, 1979), p. 420; presidential address to Congress, February 18, 1981, audiotape in possession of the author (Reagan quote).

[1]Reagan experimented with economic theory in much the way Johnson had experimented with other social sciences. Supply-side economics was every bit as experimental (for all the trickle-down tradition behind it) as anything Johnson had ever done. Reagan even repeated Johnson's mistakes. Where LBJ had "bought" an enormous array of social programs without adequate forethought or planning, Reagan bought defense programs in the same manner. Each had a way of falling for nostrums. But the Reagan strategy went beyond nostrums. By grinding social programs between the upper millstone of bigger defense outlays and the nether millstone of tax cutting and indexing, the Reagan strategy would make it difficult indeed for major growth to occur in the welfare state. With it all, Reaganism contained substantial quotients of improbable reasoning, arrogant opportunism, and flimflammery.

[2]These remarks draw heavily on William Schneider, "Democrats Redefine Themselves in Retreat," *Los Angeles Times*, 7 April 1985.

[3]*Liberalism in America*, p. 30.

[4]In 1985, however, Dohrn's application to practice law in New York was rejected. Some activists did remain involved——in Democratic party politics, community organizing, and the like. A number of them found their way into academe, where an undercurrent of activism continued in motion, if barely. Sources on the fate of sixties radicals are numerous. See, for example, Lawrence Lader, *Power on the Left: American Radical Movements since 1946* (New York: W. W. Norton & Co., 1979), pp. 338-39.

[5]Phillips, *Post-conservative America*, pp. 46-50. For perspective, see David W. Reinhard, *The Republican Right since 1945* (Lexington: University Press of Kentucky, 1983); Jonathan Martin Kolkey, *The New Right, 1960-1968; With Epilogue, 1969-1980* (New York: University Press of America, 1983); and Gillian Peele, *Revival and Reaction: The Right in Contemporary America* (Oxford, England: Clarendon Press, Oxford University Press, 1984).

[6]See especially Richard Sennett, "Power to the People," *New York Review of Books*, 25 September 1980, pp. 24-28.

[7]See comments by William Schneider, *Los Angeles Times*, 15 May 1985; and the survey information in "A Tide of Born-Again Politics," *Newsweek*, 15 September 1980, p. 36.

[8]On this point, see TRB [Michael Kinsley], *New Republic*, 25 February 1985, pp. 4, 42.

[9]*Anatomy of Revolution*, p. 222.

[10]For a summary of these and other trends, see "The Revolution Is Over," *Time*, 9 April 1984, pp. 74-84.

[11]Ellen Goodman, "Feminists Lament the Yuppie Tangent," *Los Angeles Times*, 8 March 1985.

[12]5 November 1984, p. 35.

[13]Walter Dean Burnham, "The 1984 Election and the Future of American Politics," in *Election 84: Landslide Without a Mandate?* ed. Ellis Sandoz and Cecil V. Crabb, Jr. (New York: New American Library, Mentor, 1985), p. 223.

[14]*Los Angeles Times*, 30 June, 29 August 1985.

[15]Fred Barnes, "Media Realignment," *New Republic*, 6 May 1985, pp. 12-16.

[16]For public confidence in business leadership remained exceedingly low overall. "A Change in the Weather," *Time*, 30 March 1987, p. 32; Edsall, *New Politics of Inequality*, pp. 116-17. This paragraph draws on ibid., ch. 3, passim.

[17]Brody, *Workers in Industrial America*, p. 254.

[18]"More Bad News for Big Labor," *Wilson Quarterly* 9 (Summer 1985): 18-19; *Los Angeles Times*, 7 April 1986.

[19]*Los Angeles Times*, 7 April 1986.

[20]Peter Singer, "Ten Years of Animal Liberation," *New York Review of Books*, 17 January 1985, pp. 46-47.

[21]See Edsall, *New Politics of Inequality*, pp. 46-47, 63-64; Murray Kempton, "The Wind that Blew in Reagan" (review of ibid.), *New York Review of Books*, 28 February 1985, pp. 3-4; and more broadly, Alan Ware, *The Breakdown of Democratic Party Organization, 1940-1980* (Oxford, England: Clarendon Press, Oxford University Press, 1985), as well as Byron E. Shafer, *Quiet Revolution: The Struggle for the Democratic Party and the Shaping of Post-reform Politics* (New York: Russell Sage Foundation, 1983).

[22]*New Politics of Inequality*, p. 207.

[23]"Democrats Redefine Themselves."

[24]"What's the Big Idea?" *New Republic*, 18 November 1985, p. 23. I am reminded of Arthur S. Link's somewhat different observation about the fate of reform in the 1920s, that there existed "a substantial paralysis of the progressive mind." "What Happened to the Progressive Movement in the 1920s?" p. 841.

[25]None of this is to argue, of course, that conditions have remained unchanged in American politics since the twenties or the fifties. And it would be easy to overemphasize the depth of reactionism in the seventies and eighties, or to mistake its nature. For a useful cautionary note, see Kenneth Keniston, "The Mood of Americans Today," *New York Times Book Review*, 8 November 1981, pp. 7ff.

[26]*A Margin of Hope*, p. 285.

[27]*Great Depression*, pp. 201-2.

[28]*Los Angeles Times*, 25 June 1978.

[29]Steinfels, *Neoconservatives*, p. 246.

[30]On the foregoing see ibid., p. 292.

BIBLIOGRAPHIC ESSAY

This book is unconventionally eclectic in its choice of sources. I have hunted for insights in fertile but out-of-the-way fields, in works written long ago, and in works now out of favor but containing salient points which could be reclaimed. By use of footnotes, I have tried throughout the book to direct the reader toward additional sources dealing with pivotal issues. The following essay will provide a brief guide to some of the key sources on the twentieth century reform tradition taken as a whole.

Among the writings underlying reform thought in this century, three of the most important appeared within a few years of one another. Cited in their original editions (each has subsequently been reprinted) these are: Herbert Croly, *The Promise of American Life* (New York: Macmillan Co., 1909); Walter E. Weyl, *The New Democracy: An Essay on Certain Political and Economic Tendencies in the United States* (New York: Macmillan Co., 1912); and Walter Lippmann, *Drift and Mastery: An Attempt to Diagnose the Current Unrest* (New York: Mitchell Kennerley, 1914). A superb study of these three men and their influence is Charles Forcey, *The Crossroads of Liberalism: Croly, Weyl, Lippmann, and the Progressive Era, 1900-1925* (New York: Oxford University Press, 1961).

Historians and other scholars have lavished attention on individual eras of reform, but far less attention on the tradition as a whole. There are, however, a number of crucial studies. These include the early writings of Arthur M. Schlesinger, revised and reaffirmed over the past several decades by Arthur M. Schlesinger, Jr. See the following, in particular, by Schlesinger, Sr.: "The Tides of National Politics," in Schlesinger, *Paths to the Present* (New York: Macmillan Co., 1949, pp. 77-92), and *The American as Reformer* (New York: Atheneum, 1968). Among his many works, the most useful introduction to Schlesinger, Jr.'s interpretations is *The Cycles of American History* (Boston: Houghton Mifflin Co., 1986). The best chronological survey of the reform tradition remains Eric F. Goldman's monumental *Rendezvous with Destiny: A History of Modern American Reform* (New York: Alfred A. Knopf, 1958). Not to be missed is Richard Hofstadter's brilliant, ever-controversial *The Age of Reform: From Bryan to F.D.R.* (New York: Alfred A. Knopf, 1956).

There is an abundant literature of works containing penetrating insights into broad aspects of reform.   Among the most important and enduring are Hofstadter's classic *The American Political Tradition and the Men Who Made It* (New York: Random House, Vintage Books, 1948); Theodore Roosevelt, "Latitude and Longitude among Reformers," in Roosevelt, *The Strenuous Life: Essays and Addresses* (New York: Century Co., 1902; reprint, St. Clair Shores, Mich.: Scholarly Press, 1970, pp. 41-62); Harold Stearns, *Liberalism in America: Its Origin, Its Temporary Collapse, Its Future* (New York: Boni & Liveright, 1919); Otis L. Graham, Jr., *An Encore for Reform: The Old Progressives and the New Deal* (New York: Oxford University Press, 1967); Edgar Kemler, *The Deflation of American Ideals: An Ethical Guide for New Dealers* (1941; reprint, Seattle: University of Washington Press, 1967); Raymond Moley, *After Seven Years* (New York: Harper & Bros., 1939); Louis Hartz, *The Liberal Tradition in America: An Interpretation of American Political Thought since the Revolution* (New York: Harvest/Harcourt Brace Jovanovich, 1955); Theodore J. Lowi, *The End of Liberalism: Ideology, Policy, and the Crisis of Public Authority* (New York: W. W. Norton & Co., 1969); Jonathan R. T. Hughes, *The Governmental Habit: Economic Controls from Colonial Times to the Present* (New York: Basic Books, 1977); Lionel Trilling, *The Liberal Imagination: Essays on Literature and Society* (New York: Viking Press, 1950; reprint, London: Secker & Warburg, 1955); Albert O. Hirschman, *Shifting Involvements: Private Interest and Public Action* (Princeton, N.J.:   Princeton University Press, 1982); James T. Patterson, "American Politics: The Bursts of Reform, 1930s-1970s," in Patterson, ed., *Paths to the Present: Interpretive Essays on American History since 1930* (Minneapolis: Burgess Publishing Co., 1975, pp. 57-101); and Carl L. Becker's shrewd little essay, "Liberalism——A Way Station," in Becker, *Everyman His Own Historian: Essays on History and Politics* (New York: Appleton-Century-Crofts, 1935, pp. 91-100). Gerald Zaltman, Philip Kotler, and Ira Kaufman have gathered a remarkable collection of interpretations under the title *Creating Social Change* (New York: Holt, Rinehart & Winston, 1972).

The literature of disillusionment with and pessimism about liberal reform is voluminous. In addition to Graham, *Encore*, and Moley, *After Seven Years*, both cited above, a brief, revealing tour might begin with two telling personal testaments: Frederic C. Howe, *The Confessions of a Reformer* (New York: Charles Scribner's Sons, 1925; reprint, Chicago: Quadrangle Paperbacks, 1967), and Daniel P. Moynihan, *Maximum Feasible Misunderstanding: Community Action in the War on Poverty* (New York: Free Press, Arkville Press, 1969). See also Walter Weyl, "Tired Radicals," in Weyl, *Tired Radicals and Other Papers* (New York: B. W. Huebsch, 1921, pp. 9-15); John Chamberlain, *Farewell to Reform: The Rise, Life and Decay of the Progressive Mind in America* (New York: John Day Co., 1932; reprint, Chicago: Quadrangle Paperbacks, 1965); Arthur A. Ekirch, Jr., *The Decline of Amerian Liberalism* (New York: Atheneum, 1967); and Peter Steinfels, *The Neoconservatives: The Men Who Are Changing America's Politics* (New York: Simon & Schuster, 1979). An extraordinary set of interpretations by reformers and onetime reformers living at the height of a postreform era is "Where Are the Pre-war Radicals?" *Survey*, 1 February 1926, pp. 556-66.

The more recent political-ideological setting of reform liberalism and conservatism is delineated in "What Is a Liberal—Who Is a Conservative? A Symposium," *Commentary*, September 1976, pp. 31-113, which makes an enlightening companion to the *Survey* symposium above. See also Walter Dean Burnham, *The Current Crisis in American Politics* (New York: Oxford University Press, 1982); Thomas Byrne Edsall, *The New Politics of Inequality* (New York: W. W. Norton & Co., 1984); Kevin P. Phillips, *Post-conservative America: People, Politics and Ideology in a Time of Crisis* (New York: Random House, 1982); George H. Nash, *The Conservative Intellectual Movement in America Since 1945* (New York: Basic Books, 1976); Gillian Peele, *Revival and Reaction: The Right in Contemporary America* (Oxford, England: Oxford University Press, Clarendon Press, 1985); Alonzo L. Hamby, *Liberalism and Its Challengers: FDR to Reagan* (New York: Oxford University Press, 1985); Research Institute on International Change, ed., *The Relevance of Liberalism* (Boulder: Westview Press, 1978); and David De Leon, *Everything is Changing: Contemporary U.S. Movements in Historical Perspective* (New York: Praeger, 1988). In his often-insightful *The End of the Conservative Era: Liberalism after Reagan* (New York: Arbor House, 1987), Robert S. McElvaine has hybridized a scholarly monograph with a political tract.

Two recent volumes interpret the course of liberal reform from quite different perspectives. Robert Higgs's *Crisis and Leviathan: Critical Episodes in the Growth of American Government* (New York: Oxford University Press, 1987) laments the "ratchet" effect which has pushed inexorably toward "Bigger Government" (p. 261). From a sympathetic perspective, Robert H. Walker has taken a brave stab at reinterpreting the whole of the U.S. reform tradition in *Reform in America: The Continuing Frontier* (Lexington: University Press of Kentucky, 1985). Readers of these two works will note that I am not in particular agreement with either.

INDEX

Abortion, as political, social
  issue, 450
Act to Regulate Commerce
  (1887), 34, 194
Affluence. *See* Prosperity
The Age of Reform. See
  Hofstadter, Richard
Agnew, Spiro, 313, 328
Agriculture, 34, 35-36, 224, 413;
  in nineteenth century, 36-39;
  and progressivism, 46-47; and
  Wilson Administration, 53,
  123, 124, 413; and World
  War I, 55, 266-67; and New
  Deal, 63-64; and World War
  II, 266-67; in 1980s, 63, 452
Alger, Horatio, 227-28
Altgeld, John Peter, 135 n.11
Ambivalence: and blacks, 39;
  toward business, 39, 183-84,
  192-99 passim; influence on
  progressivism, 39-55 passim,
  177; influence on reform, 39,
  177-78; and woman
  movement, 39
American Federation of Labor
  (AFL-CIO), 176; and
  Democratic party, 123, 202;

model of unionization, 223;
  and Red Scare, 375; and
  social measures, 202; and
  World War I, 267; and World
  War II, 267. *See also*
  Gompers, Samuel; Labor
Americans for Democratic
  Action, 423
America's Heroes. See Greene,
  Theodore P.
Animal liberation, 453
Anticommunism, 134, 390 n.30.
  See also McCarthyism; Red
  Scare
Antitrust and regulation, 205
  n.19; history of, 192-99; in
  Progressive Era, 53; and New
  Deal, 61, 187; and World War
  II, 265; in 1980s, 451;
  neoregulation, 199; parties
  and, 116. *See also* Business;
  Capitalism
Apathy, of reformers, 427-38
  passim
Arnold, Thurman, 61

Backlash (ch. 18), 92, 229,
  449-50. *See also* Social Issue

Baker, Newton D., 142
Baruch, Bernard, 170 n.32
Beats, the, 367
Bellamy, Edward, 48, 146 n.29
Black, Hugo, 157
Black Panthers, 108, 355
Blacks, 156-60, 170 n.34, 284;
    ambivalence and, 39; and
    Democratic party, 129,
    156-60; and intellectuals, 330;
    in Truman era, 65; in 1960s,
    67, 68, 312
Blumenthal, W. Michael, 185
Boston, and Great Depression,
    239
Brandeis, Louis D., 170 n.32
Browder, Earl, 103
Brown, Jerry, 395, 436-38, 444
    n.25
Bryan, William Jennings, 19, 47,
    121, 122, 370, 411; and 1896
    campaign, 119-21;
    characterized, 101, 141, 434;
    and labor (1908), 123; and
    monopoly issue, 117
Bunker, Archie, 313, 382
Bureaucracy: and disorientation,
    418-22; and inertia, 152,
    176-77; and party system, 167;
    and progressivism, 40-41, 42,
    43, 73 n.6, n.7; and World
    War I, 420
Business (ch. 9): and
    progressivism, 40, 47; and
    New Deal, 61, 186-87, 189,
    195-96; and World War I, 55,
    75 n.35, 76 n.44; and World
    War II, 264-66; in 1980s,
    451-52; ambivalence toward,
    39, 183-84, 192-99 passim;
    business confidence game,
    185-88, 227; consensus within,
    183, 185; consolidations, 194,
    195; government dependence

on, 183-84; and party system,
    116, 181-82, 188; and reform
    (ch. 9), 38, 39, 40, 178, 181,
    192-99, 384; reputation of, 33,
    89-90, 192, 195, 198-99, 204
    n.1, 451; split, 183; and war,
    263-64; and welfare state,
    116-17, 197-98. See also
    Antitrust and regulation;
    Capitalism

Cannibalism, liberal, 423-26
Cannon, Joseph, 51
Capitalism (ch. 9): consensus on,
    116, 181, 193-94, 223, 226-27;
    and hedonism, 363. See also
    Antitrust and regulation;
    Business
Carter, Jimmy, 7, 19, 140, 182,
    298, 329, 406, 422, 429, 448,
    453
Central Intelligence Agency, 285
Chambers, Whittaker, 324
Civil liberties. See Liberalism,
    and civil liberties;
    McCarthyism; Red Scare;
    World War II, and civil
    liberties
Civil rights. See Blacks
Civil service movement, 40-41.
    See also Bureaucracy
Civil War, 229, 301
Class, social: and inertia, 220-29,
    241-42 n.5; and leadership,
    217-19; and reform
    movements, 456; and violence,
    230
Clayton Antitrust Act, 53, 195,
    269
Cleaver, Eldridge, 449
Cleveland, Grover, 24 n.23,
    117-18, 119, 120, 121, 436
Clothing, as symbol, 351
Cold War: and conservatism,

132-33; impact on reform, 262, 274-76, 379; and intellectuals, 324-27. *See also* McCarthyism

Columbia University, 106

Communist Control bill, 390 n. 30

Communist party, 103, 110, 380

Confessional vogue. *See* Guilt

The Conflict of Generations. See Feuer, Lewis S.

Conformity, 229, 282-83

Congress: backgrounds of members, 218-19

Congress of Industrial Organizations. *See* American Federation of Labor

Conservatism, 132-34, 225-26, 330-31, 383, 385-86, 416, 791; era of, characteristics, 454; conservative opportunism, 383-86. *See also* Republican party

Constitutional-political system, and inertia, 235, 237

Consumerism, 40, 294

Coolidge, Calvin, 126, 396-97, 402, 404, 413

Corporate liberalism (term), 16

Counterculture, 92, 103, 104, 107. *See also* Left, New

Courts, 166-67, 195. *See also* Roosevelt, Franklin D., and Court fight

Cowley, Malcolm, 346-47

Cox, James M., 298

Croly, Herbert, 17, 18, 323

Cycles (ch. 3), 1-2, 3, 332 n.3, 460-62; in social welfare, 172 n.76

Czolgosz, Leon, 142

Daniels, Josephus, 298

Davis, Edward M., 8

Davis, John W., 376

Davis, Rennie, 449

Dean, John, 405

Debs, Eugene V., 51, 283, 298, 411

Defensiveness, of reformers, 427-38 passim, 441

The Deflation of American Ideals. See Kemler, Edgar

Democratic party (ch. 5), 223, 240, 379, 404, 418, 425-26, 457; in Gilded Age, 117-21, 137 n.32; in Progressive Era, 53, 54, 121, 122-26, 376; and 1916 campaign, 124-26; in 1920s, 126-28, 137 n.32, 376; in 1930s, 128-29, 376-79; in 1940s and 1950s, 137 n.36; in 1960s and since, 129-31, 385-86, 449, 453-54; and blacks, 156-60; and capitalism, business, 181-82; composition of, 219; and foreign policy, 255-56; and labor, 122-23, 124, 199, 202, 382-83; loss of white South, 160; and welfare state, 122

Dependent Pension Act, 34-35

Depressions, recessions: of 1890s, 37, 40; of 1907, 188; of 1913-14, 188; of 1920, 413; of 1929, 56, 59, 163, 195, 237-39, 300; of 1937, 203 n.27, 414; general impact of, 60; impact on reform, 91, 187-88

Disorientation: and progressivism, 411-14, 432-33; and New Deal, 414-15; and bureaucracy, 418-22

Distractions, and inertia, 232

Dixiecrats, 159

Dohrn, Bernardine, 449, 463 n.4

Douglas, Paul, 262

Draft, 105

Drugs, in 1960s, 368
DuBois, W.E.B., 157

Eastman Max, 102, 106
Economy, and reform programs,
    177-78. *See also* Depressions,
    recessions
Education, in inertia, 230
Eisenhower, Dwight D., 89-90,
    129, 188, 384
Employment Act of 1946, 65
An Encore for Reform. See
    Graham, Otis L., Jr.
Environment (ecology), as issue,
    349, 371, 424
Environmentalism (social), 373
Equal Rights Amendment, 424,
    426, 451
Ervin, Sam, 254
Exhaustion, of reformers, 427-38
    passim

Fad ([mood]; ch. 14): in 1920s,
    298, 302; in 1970s, 302-5; and
    intellectuals, 329-31; and New
    Left, 105-6, 108; in politics,
    87-89, 97 n.22; and poverty,
    163-64; in reform's demise,
    430, 435; and youth, 342-43,
    346
Fair Deal: impact of Korean
    War on, 262, 385; impact of
    McCarthyism on, 385. *See
    also* Truman, Harry
Fair Employment Practices
    Committee, 158
Family Assistance Plan, 391 n.11
Farmers. *See* Agriculture
Farmers Alliance movement, 39
Federal Bureau of Investigation,
    285
Federal Reserve Act, Board, 53,
    155, 188, 269
Federal Trade Commission, Act,

53, 151, 155, 188, 195, 269
Feminism. *See* Woman
    movement
Feuer, Lewis S., 85-86
Filene, Peter G., 46
Fonda, Jane, 449
Forbes, Charles R., 400
Forcey, Charles, 84-85
Ford, Gerald, 132, 133, 188, 404
Ford, Henry, 396
Foreign policy (ch. 11):
    attractiveness to Presidents,
    255
Foster, William Z., 103
Freud, Sigmund, 214
Fulbright, J. William, 254
Fulfillment, illusion of, 414-15

Garner, John Nance, 142-43
Generation, as a factor in
    politics, reform, 30, 85-86, 87,
    99, 102, 303, 434-35, 444 n.22;
    and left, 107; and youth,
    341-42
George, Henry, 48, 146 n.29
Gilded Age, 33-36, 117-21,
    182-83, 320-21
Gilman, Charlotte Perkins, 48,
    431
Goldman, Emma, 106
Goldwater, Barry, 133
Gompers, Samuel, 34, 38-39,
    161, 223, 224, 375
Government: ambivalence and
    suspicion toward (ch. 19), 34,
    39, 50, 153, 193, 198-99, 208,
    235-37, 247 n.100, 280 n.6,
    364; and scandal, 404-5
Governmentalism, 43, 50, 89-90
Graham, Otis L., Jr., 30-31
Great Society, 66-69, 191, 299,
    311; impact of Vietnam war
    on, 252, 253-54, 262-63. *See
    also* Johnson, Lyndon

Greene, Theodore P., 88-89
Greenwich Village, left in. *See* Left, Lyrical
Guilt, and reform, 168, 230, 305, 319, 334 n.11, 380, 438-41

Hair, as symbol, 350-51, 354
Hanna, Mark, 121
Harding, Warren G., 126, 166, 298, 302, 396, 400, 402, 403-4, 412-13
Harris, Fred, 7
Harris, Patricia Roberts, 329-30
Hartz, Louis, 9
Hayakawa, S. I., 395
Hayden, Tom, 355, 449
Hirschman, Albert O., 87
Hiss, Alger, 380, 402-3
Hofstadter, Richard, 31-32
Holmes, Oliver Wendell, Jr., 320-21
Hoover, Herbert, 56, 57, 58-59, 77 n.9, 90, 128, 183, 186, 413; and business, 188; and opportunism, 384
House, Edward M., 48-49
House Committee on Un-American Activities, 377
Howe, Frederic, 432
Hubris, liberal, 268-74, 278 n.1, 279 n.2, n.11, 321, 330
Hughes, Charles Evans, 411-12
Humphrey, Hubert, 141, 144, 252, 262, 390 n.30, 425, 429, 438
Huntington, Samuel P., 95-96 n.20

Iacocca, Lee, 451
Idealism, 47-48, 301-2, 364
Ideology, "end of," 325-26, 327
Ideology and the Ideologists. See Feuer, Lewis S.
Income tax, 406; 1894 law, 34;

under Wilson, 67; in 1960s, 67-68. *See also* Taxes
Increments, change by, 217
Individualism, 43, 92, 226, 227, 228, 363
Industrial Workers of the World, 223
Industrialization, 10, 33
Inertia (ch. 10), 60-61, 166-67, 448; and bureaucracy, 152, 176-77; and interest groups, 415-16; and New Deal, 377-79
Inflation, 165, 188, 294-95, 304; and Populism, 37-38, 57; and 1896 campaign, 119-20; in Progressive Era, 40; in 1960s and 1970s, 68, 263
Initiative process, 20
Intellectuals (ch. 16): in Gilded Age, 320-21; and World War I, 321-22, 323; in 1920s, 323-24; in 1930s, 324; postwar status of, 325, 328; in Cold War era, 324-27; in 1960s, 328-29, 382; in 1970s and since, 329-31, 382, 451, 453; and activists, 335 n.13; alienation of, 318; American, contrasted with European, 333-34 n.11; and blacks, 330; and fads, moods, 329-31; and Feuer theory, 85-86; and guilt, 334 n.11, 385; and labor, downtrodden, 201, 319-20, 332-34 n.ll; and liberalism, 17-18; and McCarthyism, 327, 385; and social issue, 373
Interstate Commerce Act, Commission, 34, 194
Issues, type and priority of, 371-72, 379, 381-84, 388 n.2. *See also* Liberal (as a term); Red herring issues; Social issue

Jackson, Henry, 7, 144, 254
Japanese Americans, internment
    of, 285
Jews, 170 n.32
Johnson, Hiram, 435
Johnson, Lyndon, 141, 143, 144,
    182, 206 n.2, 299, 395, 423,
    434, 438, 456, 463 n.1;
    administration of, 17, 66-69,
    153-54, 299, 421, 425, 455;
    and blacks, 160; and business,
    191-92, 197; characterized,
    233, 350 n.2; and foreign
    policy, 15, 276 n.13; and
    Vietnam War, 252, 253-54,
    273-74. See also Great
    Society; Vietnam War

Kemler, Edgar, 30
Kennedy, John F., 90, 141,
    143-144, 182, 188, 390 n.30,
    434, 437-38; administration
    of, 66, 328; and blacks,
    159-60; and business, 189-92,
    197; characterized, 143-44,
    218; and foreign policy, 24
    n.23, 191, 275, 276 n.13; and
    poverty, 161
Kennedy, Robert F., 141, 144,
    434, 438
Keyserling, Leon, 65, 189-90
King, Martin Luther, Jr., 19, 93,
    144, 438
Knights of Labor, 34, 223
Korean War, impact on Fair
    Deal, 262, 385
Ku Klux Klan, 157

Labor, 34, 35-36, 313, 379, 415;
    under Gompers, 34, 223; and
    Populism, 38-39; and
    progressivism, 46-47, 200; and
    Wilson Administration, 53,
    123-24; and World War I, 55,
76 n.44, 266-67; and New
    Deal, 200-201; and World
    War II, 201, 266-67; in 1960s
    and 1970s, 382; in 1980s, 63,
    452; affluence and, 215-16,
    246 n.73; conundrum of,
    199-202; decline of, 201, 452;
    and Democratic party, 122-23,
    124, 199, 202, 382-83; and
    inertia, 222-24, 241-42 n.5;
    and intellectuals, 201, 319-20,
    332-34 n.11; and socialism,
    241-42 n.5; strikes, (1919)
    374-75, 413, (1937) 377; and
    youth, 349. See also
    Depressions, recessions;
    American Federation of
    Labor (AFL-CIO); Knights of
    Labor; Industrial Workers of
    the World
La Follette, Robert, 298, 376,
    411
Laissez-faire, attacked, 35-36
Lamm, Richard D., 436
Landon, Alf, 128
Leadership, background and
    social class of, 217-19
Left (ch. 4): and negativism, 107,
    110; twentieth century role of,
    110-12. See also Left in
    specific eras; Intellectuals;
    Radicalism; Youth
Left, Lyrical, 102, 103, 107, 110,
    322, 343-45, 358 n.18, 365-66.
    See also Youth
Left, New, 103-11 passim,
    344-46, 357-58 n.13, 367-69;
    demise of, 285, 354-56, 360
    n.49, 368-69; as fad, 105-6,
    108; negative achievements of,
    347-48; and women, 417. See
    also Youth
Left, Old, 102-3, 104, 107, 108,
    109, 110, 239, 367, 376, 380.

See also Youth
Lewis, John L., 200, 267
Liberal (as term), xv-xvi, 7-8, 13, 20-22, 69, 130, 381-82, 452
Liberal hubris, 268-74, 278 n.1, 279 n.2, n.11, 321, 330
Liberalism (ch. 1), 449; activist, managerial, 419; and antimilitarism, 251-52; cannibalism in, 423-26; and capitalism, 20; and civil liberties, 374-75, 379-80, 384, 390 n.30; defined, 8-10; and disorientation, 416; experimentation in, 151-52; and foreign policy, 13-17, 24 n.23; public identification with, 225-26; and intellectuals, 17-18; and labor in 1960s, 382; and libertinism, 20-22, 361-70, 373; and patriotism, 251; contrasted with radicalism, 110-12, 211; contrasted with reform, 8, 16, 17, 22; and religion, 18-19, 22; and tolerance, 20-22; transformation of, 11-12, 20; and war, 24-25 n.24; after World War II, 379. *See also* Reform
Libertinism, and liberalism, 20-22, 361-70, 373
Lincoln, Abraham, 208
Lippmann, Walter, 323
Lodge, Henry Cabot, 411
Love and Revolution. See Eastman, Max

Marcuse, Herbert, 224
Marketing. *See* Reform, marketing of, overselling of; World War I, overselling of
Martin, Steve, 302-3
Maslow, Abraham H., hierarchy

of, 209-10, 303, 435
Massess. *See* People
Materialism, 228-29. *See also* Prosperity
McAdoo, William Gibbs, 53, 126-27, 376
McCarran Internal Security Act, 390 n.30
McCarthy, Eugene, 254
McCarthy, Joe. *See* McCarthyism
McCarthyism, 379-80, 384-85; and intellectuals, 327, 385; and liberals, 20, 275, 390 n.30. *See also* Red Scare
McClosky, Herbert, 87
McElvaine, Robert S., 87
McGovern, George, 254, 298-99
McKinley, William, 43, 121, 142, 145 n.1
Meany, George, 202
Media: and inertia, 232-35, 247 n.92; in 1980s, 451
Medicare, 151
Mencken, H. L., 323-24
Military-industrial complex, 179, 201, 265, 268
Mills, C. Wright, 224
Mitchell, John, 383
Mobility, 228, 245 n.57
Mondale, Walter, 429, 448
Mood (ch. 14). *See also* Fad
Moral slump, 300-301
Movement, the. *See* Left, New
Movements, xvi. *See also specific reform movements*
Moynihan, Daniel P., 18
Muckraking, 234-35
Music, as symbol, 351

Nader, Ralph, 198
National Association of Manufacturers, 375
National Industrial Recovery Act, 151

National Lampoon, 303
National Recovery
    Administration, 186, 196
Nazi-Soviet pact, 324
Neoconservatism, 330-31, 457
Neoliberalism, 453
Neoregulation, 199
New Deal, 30, 46, 49, 67, 91,
    146 n.29, 151, 170 n.32, 376,
    406, 457; administration in,
    155; approach to reform,
    30-32, 68-69, 220; and blacks,
    157-59; and business, 61, 189,
    195-96; decline of, 166-67,
    377-79; and disorientation,
    414-15; duration of, 30;
    experimentalism, opportunism
    in, 152-53; and foreign policy,
    256; history and assessment
    of, 55-65; and labor, 200-201;
    philosophy of, 19; contrasted
    to progressivism, 30-32, 42,
    43-44, 46, 59-60, 62, 149, 177;
    public reaction to, 211, 238,
    239; tradition and legacy of,
    448-49; two, 170 n.27; and
    World War II, 259-61. *See
    also* Roosevelt, Franklin D.
New Freedom, 51-52, 123, 151,
    193. *See also* Wilson,
    Woodrow
New Frontier, 159. *See also*
    Kennedy, John F.
New Liberals, 436-38
New Masses, 376
New Nationalism, 50, 122, 151,
    192, 252. *See also* Roosevelt,
    Theodore
New Republic, 51, 323
New Right, 449
Newton, Huey, 355
Niebuhr, Reinhold, 311, 327, 435
Nixon, Richard, 17, 18, 285, 354;
    and business, 188, 313;
characterized, 129, 132; trip to
    China, 106, 354; presidency
    of, 386; and social issue, 373,
    383; and Watergate, 401,
    404-6

Opportunism, 148-50, 151,
    152-53, 160, 169 n.2
Opportunity, equality of, 227
Overselling (reform). *See*
    Reform, marketing of,
    overselling of

Palmer A. Mitchell, 374-75
Party system, 73 n.15; and
    capitalism, 181-82; and inertia,
    235; and realignment, 116;
    third parties, 94 n.9
Pensions, 50-51, 71 n.10
People: idealizing,
    demythologizing of, 210,
    309-11, 313, 324, 327, 435
Perkins, Frances, 206 n.2
Philip Dru: Administrator. See
    House, Edward M.
Pleasure principle of politics,
    214-15
Political-constitutional system,
    and inertia, 235, 237
Politics: in 1920s, 396-97; in
    1960s, 394-95, 397-98; in
    1970s, 395-96, 397-99; and
    culture, 107-8; disillusionment
    with, 131, 393-94. *See also*
    Government, ambivalence and
    suspicion toward; Scandal
Populism, 36-39; contrasted to
    progressivism, 46-47; as term
    in 1980s, 449
Populist party, 36-39
Poverty, 374; at turn of century,
    33; in 1950s, 231; in 1960s
    and 1970s, 311-12; "war on"
    (Johnson), 66-68; in 1980s,

450; and happiness, 215; and inertia, 225, 230-31; and intellectuals, 319-20; as political issue, 161-64
Presidential candidates, dicta for, 240
Progress, idea of, 220
Progressive party (1912), 157, 411-12
Progressive Labor party, 108
Progressivism, 20, 67, 189, 210, 376, 456, 457; ambivalence and, 39-55 passim, 177; approach to reform, 30-32; and bureaucratization, 73 n.6, n.7; decline of, 51, 374-76, 464 n.24; and disorientation, 411-14, 432-33; duration of, 30; and foreign policy, 256; and guilt, 305; history and assessment of, 39-55; and labor, 200; contrasted to New Deal, 30-32, 42, 43-44, 46, 59-60, 62, 149, 177; "organizational revolution" in, 45; and overselling, 269-70; view of people, 357, 310-11; contrasted to Populism, 46-47; undercut by prosperity, 291-92; and segregation, 156-57, 170 n.34; as a term, xvi, 452; transition in, 51, 53-55, 124-25, 257-58, 279 n.11, 282-85; impact of World War I on, 75 n.35, 257-59, 279 n.11, 282-85. See also Roosevelt, Theodore; Wilson, Woodrow; World War I
Prohibition, 152, 375-77
"Promotionalism," 149
Proposition 13 (California), 303-4
Prosperity (ch. 13), 215-16, 228-29, 364, 379, 414. See also Materialism

Race. See Blacks
Radicalism, 226; and individualism, 236; pop, 103, 105; contrasted to reform liberalism, 110, 111-12, 211; twentieth century role of, 110-12. See also Left; Left in specific eras
Rags to riches motif, 227-28
Raskob, John, 127
Ratchet effect, 93, 373
Reagan, Ronald, 17, 201, 406, 429, 448, 450, 451, 455; and Democrats, 449; experimentalism of, 449, 463 n.1; and national debt, 132-33; and social issue, 373
Red herring issues, 22, 372, 388 n.2; in 1920s, 374-76; after World War II, 379-80, 384. See also Issues, type and priority of; Liberal (as a term); Reform, undermined by social change; Social issue
Red scare (post-World War I), 284, 374-75. See also McCarthyism
Reform (ch. 1), 2-3, 5 n.1, 41, 81-82, 116; activist, managerial, 419; administration of programs, 155; administrations, tendency to move left, 150, 154-55; and business (ch. 9), 38, 39, 40, 178, 181, 192-93, 384; characteristics of an age of, 454-60; impact of Cold War on, 262, 274-76, 379; defensiveness, exhaustion, apathy in, 427-38; demise of, 460-62; impact of depressions on, 187-88; and economy, 177-78; experimentalism in, 151-54; and fad, 88-89, 97

n.22; guilt as motivation for, 168; contrasted with liberalism, 8, 16, 17, 22; marketing of, 56-58, 61, 68, 76 n.2, 141 (*see also* Reform, overselling of); moral emphasis of, 74 n.20; obsolescence of reformers, 422-23, 434-35; overselling of, 58, 68, 269-70, 279 n.3, 433 (*see also* Reform, marketing of); phases of, 210, 413-14, 416-17, 418-19, 425; contrasted with radicalism, 110, 111-12, 211; and religion, 18-19 (*see also* Religion); undermined by social change, 90-92 (*see also* Social issue); social justice as link in, 168-69; as term, xv; types, 82, 419; and war, 251-52, 256-68 (*see also* *specific wars*); welfare as key theme of, 168-69; withdrawal from, by reformers, 305-7. *See also* Fad; Liberalism

Regulation, of business. *See* Antitrust and regulation

Religion: in 1980s, 449-50; and civil rights, 160-61; and inertia, 230-31; and liberalism, reform, 18-19, 22; and progressivism, 42, 230; and reform's end, 306, 373-74; and youth, 359 n.32

Republican party (ch. 5), 188, 372, 379, 383-84; in Gilded Age, 117-21; in Progressive Era, 121-22, 124-25; in 1920s, 56, 126, 127-28; in 1930s, 1940s, and 1950s, 128-29, 137 n.36, 376-77, 380; in 1960s and since, 129-35, 372, 448,

453-54; and blacks, 156; and business, 181-82; and scandal, 404, 408 n.4; and welfare state, 122, 386, 391 n.10

Reserve Officers' Training Corps, 352, 367, 451

Reuther, Walter, 144

Robins, Margaret Dreier, 175

Roe v. Wade, 450

Roosevelt, Franklin D., 46, 90, 93, 141-43, 182, 203 n.27, 218, 377-79, 403, 434, 437; and 1932 campaign, 149; administration of (New Deal), 17, 55-65, 154-55; and blacks, 157-59; and bureaucracy, 420, 421; and business, 180, 186, 189, 203 n.27, 265; and Court fight, 166-67, 235, 272-73, 377, 414; and Democratic party, 128, 273, 328, 389 n.20, 425; and foreign affairs, 15; and labor, 200, 206 n.2, 647; and race, 258-260; and World War II, 252, 259-61, 456-457

Roosevelt, Theodore, 17, 18, 45, 47, 140, 141-42, 143, 144, 269, 434, 437; and agriculture, 63; and business, 52, 179, 188, 192, 194; and foreign policy, 17; and poverty, 161; presidency of, 121-22, 140, 142; and Progressive party, New Nationalism (1912), 49-50, 51, 122, 252, 411; and progressivism, 50-51; and race, 157; and Republican party, 121-22; and World War I, 252-53, 411

Rubin, Jerry, 355, 449

Sacco-Vanzetti execution, 324, 371

Scandal, 400-406

Schlesinger, Arthur M., Jr., 3,
  87, 92, 93, 95 n.19, 97 n.21,
  n.22, 97-98 n.31, 98 n.32,
  n.34, 397
Schlesinger, Arthur M., Sr., 3,
  82-84, 94 n.7, 98 n.34
Seale, Bobby, 355
Sex: in 1920s and 1930s, 366-67,
  370; in 1960s and 1970s,
  368-69, 370, 424; in 1980s,
  450-51; and capitalism, 363;
  and Lyrical Left, 365-66;
  sexual revolutions, 91, 363-64,
  366-67, 369, 370, 387 n.14
Sherman Antitrust Act, 34, 194
Smith, Al, 54, 126-27, 376, 435
Smith-Connally Anti-Strike Act,
  267
Social gospel, 19, 450
Social issue, 130, 167, 370-83,
  449-50. See also Issues, type
  and priority of; Liberal (as a
  term); Red herring issues;
  Reform, undermined by social
  change
Social Security Act, 206 n.2
Socialism, 226, 283-84; and
  labor, 241-42 n.5; popular
  suspicion of, 237
Socialist party, 51, 103, 107, 109,
  124, 237, 283-84
Socialization, childhood, 212
Sombart, Werner, 210, 241 n.5
Sorokin, Pitirim A., 87
South: and FDR Administration,
  378-79; shift toward GOP,
  129; and race issue, 156-60;
  and Wilson Administration,
  123-24
Stalin, Joseph, 324
Statism. See Governmentalism
Steffens, Lincoln, 292
Stevenson, Adlai, 159, 380, 390
  n.30, 440

Straight, Willard, 17
Strikes. See Labor
Students for a Democratic
  Society, 105, 108, 110, 417.
  See also Left, New; Youth,
  and New Left
Sundquist, James L., 86, 95 n.15
Supreme Court. See Courts

Taft, William Howard, 166
Taxes, 295, 406; in 1960s, 67-68,
  191-92, 263; and Proposition
  13, 303-4; resistance to, 216.
  See also Income tax
Teapot Dome scandal, 402,
  403-4
Television. See Media
Thomas, Norman, 103
Thurmond, Strom, 159
"The Tides of National Politics."
  See Schlesinger, Arthur M.,
  Sr.
Trade Expansion Act, 191
Trotsky, Leon, 224
Truman, Harry, 141, 143, 144,
  182, 252, 275, 370, 440; in
  1948 campaign, 423, 426;
  administration of, 65, 143,
  144, 155, 402; and blacks, 157,
  159; and Korean War, 262;
  and McCarthyism, 379-80
Tunney, John V., 395-96

Udall, Morris K., 7
Un-American Activities, House
  Committee on, 377
Unions. See American
  Federation of Labor
  (AFL-CIO); Industrial
  Workers of the World; Labor;
  Knights of Labor
Unity approach, 189-92, 201,
  210, 299
Uplift, 42, 59-60, 352, 430

Vietnam War, 358 n.24; and Johnson, Great Society, 252, 253-54, 262-63, 273-74; and the left, 105; and regimentation, 285-86
Villard, Oswald Garrison, 435
Violence, 229-30, 312
Voting, nonvoting, 213-14

Wagner, Robert, 54, 61, 200
Wagner Act, 206 n.2
Walker, Robert H., 95 n.20
Wallace, George, 313, 383
Wallace, Henry, 182, 275, 298, 440
War, 364, 379, 429; business and, 263-64; and moral slump, 300-301; impact on populations, 301; and reform, 251-52, 256-68. *See also specific wars.*
War Industries Board, 282
Watergate scandal, 401, 404-6
Wealth, and inertia, 231-32
Weathermen, 108, 301
Weaver, James B., 37
Welfare, unpopularity of, 216
Welfare state (ch. 12), 2, 5-6 n.1, 22, 216, 220, 231; attitudes toward, 215, 414-15; business and, 197-98; defined, xv-xvi; Theodore Roosevelt and, 50, 122; types of, 116-17; and Wilson era, 124
Weyl, Walter, 323
Wheeler, Burton, 435
Wilson, Woodrow, 45, 141, 142, 143, 182, 269-70, 370, 422, 423, 434, 437; and New Freedom, 1912 campaign, 49, 51-52, 123, 142, 252; and 1916 campaign, 124-26, 252; and 1920 campaign, 298; administration of, 17, 52-55,

75 n.35, 123-24, 154-55, 412-13, 421, 425; and business, 179, 187-88, 192-93, 194-95; and foreign affairs, 15, 24 n.23, 252-53; and foreign markets, 15, 178; and governmentalism, 52-53; and labor, 53, 123-24; and presidency, 140; and progressivism, 51, 123-24; rhetoric of, 177; and segregation, 157; and welfare state, 124; and World War I, 75 n.35, 252, 257, 270-72, 283, 321, 411; and postwar settlement, 412-13, 430
Woman movement, 91; in 1920s, 364-65, 366-67, 424; in 1960s and 1970s, 417; in 1980s, 451; ambivalence and, 39; divisiveness and, 219; in politics, 164-66. *See also* Women
Women: in 1920s, 1970s, 364-65, 366-67; in 1930s, 367; and World War II, 82, 165; of various eras contrasted, 388 n.27; and reform, 164-66. *See also* Woman movement
Women and Economics. See Gilman, Charlotte Perkins
Women's Trade Union League, 175-76
Working class. *See* labor
World War I: and agriculture, 55, 266-67; and bureaucracy, 420; and business, 55, 75 n.35, 76 n.44; and civil liberties, 283-85; and intellectuals, 321-22, 323; and labor, 55, 76 n.44, 266-67; and optimism/idea of progress/ idealism/attitudes toward the people, 220, 302, 310-11, 322;

overselling of, 270-72; impact on progressivism, 75 n.35; and demise of progressivism, 257-58, 270-72, 279 n.ll, 282-85. *See also* Wilson, Woodrow

World War II, 273, 300; and agriculture, 266-67; and business, 264-66, 378-79; and civil liberties, 285; and labor, 201, 266-67; and demise of New Deal, 257, 259-61; and optimism, idea of progress, 220; and women, 82, 165

Yippies, 108

Youth (ch. 17), 458; and Lyrical Left, 343-45; in 1920s, 351-53, 369; in 1930s, 367; in 1950s, 353, 359 n.32, 367; and New Left, 344-46, 357-58 n.13, 359 n.32, 367-69; in 1970s, 353-56, 368-69; in 1980s, 451; defined, 357; and fad, 342-43, 346; and Feuer theory, 85-86; and generation, 341-42; and government, 349; and labor, 349; nature of, 341-43; negative achievements of, 347-48; identification with oppressed, 348-49; radical generation of, 99; worship of, 340, 357 n.1. *See also* Generation; *Left, entries under*

Yuppies, 449

Zaller, John, 87

About the Author

JOHN J. BROESAMLE is Professor of History at California State University, Northridge. He is the author of *William Gibbs McAdoo: A Passion for Change, 1863-1917* as well as articles in anthologies and professional journals.